VISUAL
PERCEPTION

Key Readings in Cognition

The aim of this series is to make available to senior undergraduate and graduate students key articles in each area of cognition in an attractive, user-friendly format. Many professors want to encourage their students to engage directly with research in their fields, yet this can often be daunting for students coming to detailed study of a topic for the first time. Moreover, declining library budgets mean that articles are not always readily available, and course packs can be expensive and time-consuming to produce. **Key Readings in Cognition** aims to address this need by providing comprehensive volumes, each one of which will be edited by a senior and active researcher in the field. Articles will be carefully chosen to illustrate the way the field has developed historically as well as current issues and research directions. Each volume will have a similar structure to include:

* An overview chapter, as well as introductions to sections and articles
* Questions for class discussion
* Annotated bibliographies
* Full author and subject indexes

Titles in Preparation:

The Psychology of Human Memory	*Edited by Henry L. Roediger, III and Kathleen McDermott*
Cognitive Neuroscience	*Edited by Marie Banich and Neal Cohen*
The Psychology of Language	*Edited by Michael Tanenhaus*

VISUAL
PERCEPTION
Essential Readings

Edited by
Steven Yantis
Johns Hopkins University
Baltimore, MD

USA	Publishing Office:	PSYCHOLOGY PRESS
		A member of the Taylor & Francis Group
		325 Chestnut Street
		Philadelphia, PA 19106
		Tel: (215) 625-8900
		Fax: (215) 625-2940
	Distribution Center:	PSYCHOLOGY PRESS
		A member of the Taylor & Francis Group
		7625 Empire Drive
		Florence, KY 41042
		Tel: 1-800-634-7064
		Fax: 1-800-248-4724
UK		PSYCHOLOGY PRESS
		A member of the Taylor & Francis Group
		27 Church Road
		Hove
		E. Sussex, BN3 2FA
		Tel· +44 (0) 1273 207411
		Fax: +44 (0) 1273 205612

VISUAL PERCEPTION: Essential Readings

1 2 3 4 5 6 7 8 9 0

Printed by Sheridan Books - Braun-Brumfield, Ann Arbor, MI, 2001.

A CIP catalog record for this book is available from the British Library.

∞ The paper in this publication meets the requirements of the ANSI Standard Z39.48-1984 (Permanence of Paper)

Vasily Kandinsky, Composition 8, July 1923, Oil on canvas, Solomon R. Guggenheim Museum, New York.

Photograph by David Heald © The Solomon R. Guggenheim Foundation, New York, FN 37.262

Library of Congress Cataloging-in-Publication Data

Visual perception : essential readings / edited by Steven Yantis.
      p. cm. -- (Key readings in cognition)
  Includes bibliographical references and index.
  ISBN 0-86377-597-7 (case : alk. paper) -- ISBN 0-86377-598-5 (paper : alk. paper)
  1. Visual perception. I. Yantis, Steven. II. Series.

QP491 . V577 2000
152.14--dc21

                                        CIP
                                        00-042311

ISBN: 0-86377-597-7 (case)
ISBN: 0-86377-598-5 (paper)

Contents

About the Editor

Steven Yantis is a Professor of Psychology and Cognitive Sciences at The Johns Hopkins University. He received a B.S. in Psychology from the University of Washington in 1978 and a PhD in Experimental Psychology from the University of Michigan in 1985. He is the recipient of the Troland Research Award from the National Academy of Sciences and the Early Career Award from the American Psychological Association. Professor Yantis's research is concerned with the psychological and neural mechanisms of visual attention and perceptual organization.

Acknowledgements

The Authors and Publishers are grateful to the following for permission to reproduce the articles in this book:

Reading 1: H. von Helmholtz (1925). Physiological Optics. (Vol III, §26. Concerning the perceptions in general. pp. 1-36). Translated from the Third German Edition and Edited by J.P.C. Southall. New York: Optical Society of America. (Original work published 1896).

Reading 2: H. B. Barlow, Single units and sensation: A neuron doctrine for perceptual psychology? Perception, 1, 371-394. Copyright © 1972 by Pion Limited, London. Reprinted with permission.

Reading 3: W. P. Tanner, Jr. and J. A. Swets, A decision-making theory of visual detection. Psychological Review, 61, 401-409. Copyright © 1954 by the American Psychological Association. Reprinted with permission.

Reading 4: J. J. Gibson, The ecological approach to visual perception. Chapter 14: The theory of information pickup and its consequences (pp. 238-263). Boston: Houghton Miflin Co., 1979. Reprinted with permission.

Reading 5: D. Marr, Vision. Chapter 1: The philosophy and the approach (pp. 8-38). San Francisco: W. H. Freeman and Co., 1982. Reprinted with permission.

Reading 6: L. M. Hurvich and D. Jameson, An opponent-process theory of color vision. Psychological Review, 64, 384-404. Copyright © 1957 by the American Psychological Association. Reprinted with permission.

Reading 7: D. H. Hubel and T. N. Wiesel, Receptive fields and functional architecture of monkey striate cortex. Journal of Physiology, 195, 215-243. Copyright © 1968 by Cambridge University Press. Reprinted with permission.

Reading 8: C. Blakemore and F. W. Campbell, On the existence of neurones in the human visual system selectively sensitive to the orientation and size of retinal images. Journal of Physiology, 203, 237-260. Copyright © 1969 by Cambridge University Press. Reprinted with permission.

Reading 9: S. Zeki, J. D. G. Watson, C. J. Lueck, K. J. Friston, C. Kennard, & R. S. J. Frackowiak, A direct demonstration of functional specialization in human visual cortex. Journal of Neuroscience, 11, 641-649. Copyright © 1991 by the Society for Neuroscience. Reprinted with permission.

Reading 10: W. T. Newsome, K. H. Britten, & J. A. Movshon, Neuronal correlates of a perceptual decision. Nature, 341, 52-54. Copyright © 1989 by Macmillan Magazines Ltd. Reprinted with permission.

Reading 11: M. Wertheimer, Untersuchungen zur Lehre von der Gestalt, II [Laws of organization in perceptual forms]. Psycholoche Forschung, 4, 301-350. Excerpts translated and reprinted in W. D. Ellis (Ed.), A source book of Gestalt psychology (pp. 71-88). New York: Routledge, 1999. Reprinted with permission.

Reading 12: E. Rubin, Visuaell wahrgenommene Figuren [Figure and Ground]. Copenhagen: Gyldendalske, 1921. [excerpts translated and reprinted in D. C. Beardslee & M. Wertheimer (Eds.), Readings in Perception (pp. 194-203). Princeton, NJ: D. Van Norstrand Co., Inc.].

Reading 13: L. Kaufman and I. Rock, The Moon Illusion. Scientific American, 207, 120-132. Copyright © 1962 by Scientific American, Inc. Reprinted with permission. All rights reserved.

Reading 14: H. Wallach, Brightness constancy and the nature of achromatic colors. Journal of Experimental Psychology, 38, 310-324. Copyright © 1948 by the American Psychological Association. Reprinted with permission.

Reading 15: I. Rock, R. Nijhawan, S. Palmer, & L. Tudor, Grouping based on phenomenal similarity of achromatic color. Perception, 21, 779-789. Copyright © 1992 by Pion Limited, London. Reprinted with permission.

Reading 16: H. Lissauer (1890), Ein Fall von Seelenblindheit nebst einem Beitrag zur Theorie derselben. Archiv für Psychiatrie, 21, 222-270. [translated and reprinted in 1988 as "A case of visual agnosia with a contribution to theory." Cognitive Neuropsychology, 5, 157-192; commentary by T. Shallice & M. Jackson. Lissauer on agnosia. Cognitive Neuropsychology, 5, 153-156. Copyright © 1988 by Taylor and Francis. Reprinted with permission.

Reading 17: M. Mishkin, L. G. Ungerleider, & K. A. Macko, Object vision and spatial vision: Two cortical pathways. Trends in Neurosciences, 6, 414-417. Copyright © 1982 by Elsevier Science. Reprinted with permission.

Reading 18: E. H. Adelson and J. A. Movshon, Phenomenal coherence of moving visual patterns. Nature, 300, 523-525. Copyright © 1982 by Macmillan Magazines, Ltd. Reprinted with permission.

Reading 19: R. N. Shepard and J. Metzler, Mental rotation of three-dimensional objects. Science, 171, 701-703. Copyright © 1971 by the American Association for the Advancement of Science. Reprinted with permission.

Reading 20: I. Biederman, Recognition-by-components: A theory of human image understanding. Computer Vision, Graphics, and Image Processing, 32, 29-73. Copyright © 1985 by Academic Press. Reprinted with permission.

Reading 21: A. M. Treisman and G. Gelade, A feature-integration theory of attention. Cognitive Psychology, 12, 97-136. Copyright ©1980 by Academic Press. Reprinted with permission.

Reading 22: J. Moran and R. Desimone, Selective attention gates visual processing in the extrastriate cortex. Science, 229, 782-784. Copyright © 1985 by American Association for the Advancement of Science. Reprinted with permission.

Reading 23: K. M. O'Craven, B. R. Rosen, K. K. Kwong, A. Treisman, & R. L. Savoy, Voluntary attention modulates fMRI activity in human MT-MST. Neuron, 18, 591-598. Copyright © 1997 by Cell Press. Reprinted with permission.

Reading 24: L. Weiskrantz, E. K. Warrington, M. D. Sanders, & J. Marshall, Visual capacity in the hemianopic field following a restricted occipital ablation. Brain, 97, 709-728. Copyright © 1974 by Oxford University Press. Reprinted with permission.

Reading 25: D. L. Sheinberg and N. K. Logothetis, The role of temporal cortical areas in perceptual organization. Proc. National Academy of Sciences USA, 94, 3408-3413. Copyright © 1997 by The National Academy of Sciences of the USA. Reprinted with permission.

Appendix: From Research Methods in Psychology (with InfoTrac), 6th edition, by D.G. Elmes, B.H. Kantowitz, and H.L. Roediger, III © 1999. Reprinted with permission of Wadsworth, a division of Thomson Learning. Fax 800-730-2215.

Visual Perception:
An Overview

Steven Yantis

Visual perception allows organisms to obtain knowledge of their surroundings by sensing light reflected from surfaces. Its ultimate purpose is to allow one to know what objects are present so as to behave appropriately and in accordance with one's current behavioral goals. Although recognizing objects is subjectively effortless and nearly instantaneous, the steps that it requires are amazingly complex. Understanding visual perception requires an understanding of a diverse and multifaceted body of knowledge, including physics and optics, neuroanatomy and neurophysiology, psychology, and computation.

This volume contains 25 influential chapters and articles from the vision science literature that reflect the theoretical and empirical themes that have dominated research in visual perception over the last century. They are representative of a huge body of work that is truly interdisciplinary. The fertile crosstalk between psychology and neuroscience in particular is made possible by the close correspondence between neural activity on the one hand and certain aspects of perceptual behavior on the other. This means that we can begin to grasp the neural implementation of vision more readily than that of other cognitive functions like memory, language, or planning and decision making where the link between neurophysiology and behavior is less well understood. What makes this interplay particularly exciting right now are technological advances that have brought new scientific tools to bear in the cognitive neuroscience of vision (e.g., technologies that permit us to collect images of brain activity in behaving human observers), so that new discoveries about how the human brain implements vision are now reported routinely in the scientific literature and the press.

In this introductory chapter, I will outline of some of these theoretical and empirical themes and how they have been influenced by the tools that are available to practicing scientists. Of course, in this brief space it is not possible to adequately cover this topic in all its complexity and richness. At the end of this chapter, a list of several other sources that provide deeper treatments is provided.

I started with the assertion that the purpose of vision is object recognition. Of course, one could quibble with this assertion, but it is a good starting point nevertheless. If we wish to understand how the visual system can take as its input a dynamic pattern of light and color at the retina and produce as its output a label that identifies or categorizes an object, we must first break the problem down into a smaller number of slightly more manageable parts. The selected readings have been grouped according to the following questions:

- The problem of *early vision*: How are elementary sensory attributes (e.g., color, motion) encoded?
- The problem of *perceptual constancy*: How are elementary attributes "corrected" for irrelevant viewing conditions?
- The problem of *perceptual organization*: How are sensory attributes conjoined into representations of surfaces and objects?
- The problem of *object recognition*: How are surface representations used to categorize or identify objects?
- The problem of *attention*: How does the observer select relevant objects and ignore irrelevant objects?
- The problem of *visual awareness*: How is consciousness achieved?

All of these problems are under active investigation; none has been solved. Of course, more progress has been made in some areas than others: we know a very great deal (but not everything) about how elementary sensory properties are represented in the visual system; we know very little about awareness. Although object recognition is arguably the most significant of these problems, there is little consensus about how this is achieved. This is not surprising, of course, given its complexity and that it relies to some degree on success in all of the other areas.

The first section in this book is titled *Theoretical Approaches*. The choice of a theoretical orientation is in some sense orthogonal to the substantive issues sketched above. Of course, one's choice of a theoretical approach is utterly crucial in determining research strategies and identifying relevant questions. Indeed, according to certain theoretical traditions, the questions outlined are simply not the important ones. Yet most scientists do not spend much time mulling possible theoretical approaches. In most sciences one main approach tends to be dominant at any given time, and most scientists implicitly accept that approach. In contemporary vision research, the dominant theoretical approach can be traced to Helmholtz's constructivism, which is the view that we construct internal representations of the objects in the visible scene that are most likely to have given rise to the pattern of light currently impinging on our retinas. This requires us to take into account the early sensory data, of course, but it also allows for the influence of past experiences (i.e., memory), expectation about what is likely in the current context, and what aspects of the scene are important given current behavioral goals (i.e., attention). In other words, the representation of objects in a scene is a joint result of both bottom-up information from the eyes, and top-down information from memory and attentional mechanisms. Almost all of the readings in this volume start from this common theoretical platform. (Gibson's idea that perception is in an important sense *direct* constitutes the most notable alternative view, but his ideas have been extremely influential even among adherents of the constructivist perspective.)

Two Principles of Visual Perception

Before turning to the visual themes themselves, there are two central principles that characterize vision and that will help to orient the discussion. The first principle is that of functional specialization. In the section on methodology that concludes this chapter, the evidence for functional specialization emerged in the late 19th century. There are many ways in which functional specialization can be illustrated.

Perhaps the first point at which specialization occurs in vision is at the very earliest point it *could* occur: in the photoreceptors themselves. There are four different types of photoreceptors grouped into two classes: the rods, and three types of cones. In addition to their shapes, there are at least three ways in which the rods and cones differ, and each of these has implications for their functions. First, the rods are poorly suited to represent color information, while the three types of cones are ideally suited for this task (more on this later). Second, the rods are much more sensitive to low levels of illumination, and they are what we must rely on for night vision; the cones are used under ordinary daylight viewing conditions. Third, the rods and cones are distributed throughout the retinal mosaic differently: the cones are packed densely in the center of gaze—the fovea—with no rods; both rods and cones are interspersed outside the fovea with density gradually decreasing into the periphery. The high density of the cones in central vision allows a very fine spatial sampling of the pattern of light in central vision, which in turn allows us to see fine spatial detail there.

Functional specialization does not end with the rods and cones. The optic nerve, a bundle of fibers that carries visual information from the eye to the brain, consists of at least two distinct subpopulations of fibers that project to distinct regions in the brain. M fibers tend to favor information that varies temporally, such as motion or flicker, while P fibers tend to carry information about static properties such as color, orientation, or depth. This functional distinction continues as the information from the eyes makes its way to higher centers in the visual cortex, and it is intimately related to the distinction between the "what" and "where" pathways suggested by Mishkin et al. (Reading 17). As suggested by Zeki et al. (Reading 9), certain areas of cortex contain a predominance of cells that appear to be functionally specialized for a single visual attribute (e.g., area V4 for color, area V5 for motion).

A second principle of visual perception is that of distributed coding of perceptual attributes. There are (roughly speaking) two ways that any given attribute (e.g., color, edge orientation) can be represented in cortical tissue. According to a local coding approach, any given attribute or combination of attributes is represented by a single specialized cell. In the limit, we might arrive at a cell that responds if and only if your grandmother's face appears somewhere in the visual field (a so-called "grandmother cell"). The advantage of this approach is that all one would need to do is monitor the cells that were most active at each location and these would reveal just what combination of features was present there. One major disadvantage of local coding is that it would require an implausibly large number of specialized cells to adequately capture the richness of the visual world.

An alternative approach, and this is the one the visual system tends to use, is that of distributed coding. Here, there exist cells that will respond to a range of feature values to different degrees. For example, a cell might respond best to an edge oriented vertically, and less well (in a graded fashion) as the orientation is displaced from the optimal one. Such a cell could be said to be *tuned* to orientation, and the location and width of the tuning function characterizes its sensory properties. A given edge would tend to drive a population of cells with different preferred orientations. The edge represented by the *pattern* of activity over that population of cells. This is precisely how orientation representation works, and it is also the basis for the trichromatic theory of color vision, where there are only three different types of color-sensitive cells with highly overlapping wavelength preference functions (called spectral sensitivity functions) that can with great precision encode a vast number of different colors by virtue of their relative levels of activity for any given wavelength.

These two foundational and related principles of functional specialization and distributed coding will reappear throughout the readings in this volume.

In the following sections, some of the progress that has been made in each of the areas outlined earlier is reviewed. Palmer (1999) provides a detailed and highly recommended treatment of these and many other problems in vision.

Early Vision

Early vision refers to the part of vision that creates the initial representation of elementary sensory properties such as color, the orientation of edges, motion, and depth. These representations tend to be local and veridical (in the sense that they closely mimic the properties that are present in the retinal image itself). This is not to say that these representations are simple, however.

Before proceeding, it will be useful to define the concept of a *receptive field*. This is often a difficult concept to grasp, but it turns out to be absolutely crucial to any real understanding of how the brain represents sensory information. A receptive field is a property of an individual sensory neuron. The receptive field of a visual neuron is that portion of the retina that, when stimulated, causes a change in the firing rate of the neuron in question. Imagine you are a visual neurophysiologist and you have placed an electrode next to the optic nerve, so you can "listen in" on the activity of a single optic nerve fiber. From time to time you may detect a stray signal from the cell. When you then present a stimulus on the retina (e.g., a small spot of red light, or a moving vertical bar, or even a toilet brush), you may eventually find a location that will cause the cell to increase its firing rate when illuminated. If you repeat this experiment many times and "add up" all the locations that cause the cell to either increase or decrease its firing rate, you will have defined that cell's receptive field. It is, in essence, the portion of the retina that the cell in question monitors. One also must specify the properties of the stimulus that effectively drives the cell, for example its color, direction of motion, and shape. The extent to which any given cell responds to a visual stimulus depends jointly on where on the retina the stimulus appears, and what the stimulus is. As one measures the receptive field properties of cells at higher levels of the visual system, one finds that more and more complex configurations of light are required to drive the cells. In the retina, cells will respond to small circular spots of light in a very specific location; in V1, cells respond best to small bars of light in a particular location and with a particular orientation. In V4, many cells prefer a corner with a particular color and orientation. In the inferotemporal cortex, many cells seems to prefer highly complex and seemingly arbitrary shapes (Tanaka, 1996).

The following is a brief review of what we know about early vision. For present purposes, the discussion will be restricted to orientation, spatial scale or size, depth, color, and motion; these are the sensory properties that have received the most attention. The first three of these are aspects of spatial vision and contribute to representations of surface shape, which is crucial for object identification. As pointed out by Palmer (1999), knowing the *shape* of an object tells you a lot about what the object is, what it is for, even what its color is likely to be, but knowing the *color* or *motion* of an object tells you almost nothing about what the object is or about what its other attributes are likely to be. Color and motion, of course, are themselves of great importance in enriching our visual experience and in helping us deal with the inherently dynamic world in which we live.

Space

The investigation of spatial properties like orientation, depth, and spatial scale began with Hubel and Wiesel's pioneering investigations (Reading 7) in which they discovered (among many other things) that in primary visual cortex, most cells prefer an elongated, oriented, and specifically located region of stimulation to fire optimally. The representation in V1 was not of spots, but of something more useful for representing shape: oriented edges.

It is useful to step back a moment and think about why an explicit representation of oriented edges is so important. The retinal image contains simply a pattern of light and dark distributed in two dimensions (we can ignore color, depth, and motion for now) and sensed by the mosaic of photoreceptors. One can think of this as a 2D array of numbers, each of which corresponds to the brightness of a small location on the retina. The shape, location, and orientation of objects, shadows, and surfaces is not explicitly given in the array of brightness values. In order to recover these properties, some computation must be performed on the array of brightnesses (e.g., taking the difference between adjacent numbers to ask whether the brightnesses there differ, as they would if an edge was present in that location).

That is just the sort of computation that retinal ganglion cells (RGCs) and cortical cells carry out. RGCs specify whether a given location has more (or less) brightness than the surrounding locations in all directions. V1 cells specify whether a given location contains an edge (or part of an edge) with a particular orientation and a particular polarity (e.g., dark to light or vice-versa). It does so by combining the outputs of a set of RGCs that happen to be aligned properly so as to provide a sample of the retina in the corresponding location and orientation. This V1 representation has essentially thrown away the brightnesses in the retinal image. What is left, however, is much more useful: a representation of localized edges. This is useful precisely because a shape is specified by the locations and orientations of its boundaries. The discovery that cortex was in the business of representing oriented edge fragments was therefore a landmark in the effort to understand object recognition.

Scenes contain (at least) two other sorts of elementary spatial information. One of these is information about the size (or spatial scale) of features. The visual system encodes information about spatial scale with cells whose receptive fields vary in size so as to be selective for different spatial frequencies. This turns out to be important because of the following mathematical fact: any spatial pattern can be represented as the sum of an appropriately chosen set of spatial frequency patterns called *gratings*. (This is a nonintuitive idea that is discussed in more detail in the introduction to Reading 8, Blakemore and Campbell, and in the reading itself.) This means that by representing spatial frequencies, the visual system provides some of the building blocks that are likely to be useful for representing shapes and objects.

The last kind of spatial information that is contained in scenes is surface depth and orientation. Because objects are typically three-dimensional, it is often not sufficient to represent simply the shape of the object's outer boundaries (in fact, it is quite difficult to recognize all but the simplest of objects based only on the object's silhouette). Therefore, it is necessary to know something of the location of the surfaces that bound the object and their distances and orientations relative to the viewer. There are many redundant sources of information in the retinal image, including pictoral cues like linear perspective, overlap, or relative size, relative motion cues (objects a different depths will have different motion trajectories as the observer moves in the environment), and, perhaps most importantly, stereoscopic depth cues. *Stereopsis* is the process of combining the two slightly different views of the visual scene that are available at the two eyes (because they view the world from approximately 6 cm apart) to recover information about the relative depth of features in the scene. This requires a process of matching corresponding features in the two eyes (this is the *correspondence problem*) and estimating the extent to which they fall on corresponding or noncorresponding points on the two retinae. By definition, the image feature at the current point of fixation falls on corresponding points in the two eyes (i.e., the two foveas). Any other image feature that falls on corresponding points on the two eyes (that is, points that are equidistant from the foveas in the two eyes) are said to fall on the *horopter*, an imaginary surface that is defined by all points at the same distance from the observer as the current point of fixation. Any image feature that falls on noncorresponding points in the two eyes exhibits *binocular disparity;* whenever binocular disparity is nonzero, the image feature in question is at a depth other than the depth of the current point of fixation (or, equivalently, it is either closer than or further away than the horopter). The magnitude of binocular disparity for any given image feature is proportional to that feature's distance from the horopter.

It is known that stereoscopic depth information (specifically, the magnitude of binocular disparity) is available early in cortex. Thus depth information can in principle be combined with information about orientation and spatial scale to provide a rich representation of the spatial layout of edges and surfaces in the scene.

Color

The first major steps in coming to understand color vision were taken early in the 19th century by Thomas Young, and then, independently in the mid 19th century by Helmholtz. The story of the trichromatic theory of color vision and the debate about the alternative opponent-process theory advocated by Herring is contained in the introduction to Reading 6, Hurvich and Jamison. We now know in detail the spectral sensitivities of the three classes of cones and how the cone responses contribute to our ability to match mixtures of colors to one another. This is a theoretical success story of the first magnitude. We also know, based on the work of Hurvich and Jamison and of neurophysiologists since, that the opponent color system that receives input from the cones subserves judgements about color appearance. These two mechanisms can together account for a wide range of color perception phenomena, including color adaptation (the fact that after looking at a red patch for a few minutes, one sees green when subsequently viewing a white paper); simultaneous color contrast (the fact that a gray patch surrounded by bright red will appear slightly green, or a gray patch surrounded by white will appear darker than the same gray patch surrounded by black); Mach Bands, first described in the 19th century by Ernst Mach (the fact that the apparent brightness of the regions surrounding a black-white edge is nonuniform: the dark side of the edge looks somewhat darker near the edge than do regions farther away, while the light side of the edge looks somewhat lighter near the edge than do regions further away); and many forms of color blindness (which can often be attributed to a genetic defect in which one or more of the three cone classes is missing).

Motion

The first and by far most common kind of motion experience arises when (a) a stationary observer views a moving object or (b) a moving observer views stationary objects (or some combination of these). The simplest case is for a stationary observer with eyes still, looking at a stationary scene containing a single smoothly moving object. For this case, simple models of motion representation such as that suggested by Reichert and discussed in the introduction to Reading 18 (Adelson and Movshon) are suitable. Needless to say, however, this kind of simple motion is extremely rare. If nothing else, people tend to move their eyes about 3 times a second, and this causes abrupt displacements of the visual scene even if it contains no motion at all. Furthermore, people tend to move through their environment, and yet they have no trouble experiencing the stable parts of the scene as such and tracking objects that are moving relative to them (e.g., the problem faced by an outfielder trying to catch a fly ball; see McBeath et al., 1995). These forms of motion require more complex systems for coordinating self-motion and retinal image motion.

There are several additional motion phenomena, some fairly common, others laboratory inventions, all of which require explanation. These include the motion aftereffect (the fact that after viewing a motion stimulus for several minutes—for example, a waterfall—one sees motion in the opposite direction — in this case, upward—when the view is shifted to a static scene), autokinetic motion (the fact that a small stationary spot of light in a completely dark room will appear to move randomly after a short while), and many forms of apparent motion (motion experiences when viewing a sequence of locations that are stimulated in turn but discretely, as in a motion picture).

Perceptual Constancy and Organization

The early sensory representation of a scene is inadequate for object recognition in at least two major respects. First, it contains representations of image properties and not representations of scene properties. Second, the representation is local in scope but any representation of objects necessarily requires a more global perspective to conjoin parts into wholes.

Perceptual Constancy

First is the problem of perceptual constancy, which can be stated as follows: Most retinal measurements of scenic attributes are affected not only by properties of the object in question, but also by irrelevant and transient factors such as the current illumination, the distance between the object and the observer, and the object's orientation relative to the observer. To be useful, vision needs to represent object properties and to discount the irrelevant environmental conditions that are not intrinsic to the objects. In other words, how can we correctly perceive objects despite irrelevant variation in viewing conditions?

To give just one example of this problem, consider color vision for a moment. Information about color is carried by the wavelength of light: the spectrum of colors in a rainbow depicts the portion of electromagnetic radiation with wavelengths from about 400 (blue) to 700 (red) nanometers. The color of a surface depends on the distribution of wavelengths in the light reflected from that surface from a light source such as the sun or a lightbulb. For example, a red apple will tend to reflect long wavelengths of light and absorb short wavelengths of light. So far, so good. We simply need a way to encode different wavelengths, and we can recover the surface color of the apple.

Unfortunately, there is a problem. The spectral composition of the illuminant (e.g., the sun) affects the distribution of light reflected from a surface. A white light such as sunlight has about equal energy at all visible wavelengths, but some sources, such as a flourescent lightbulb, have quite imbalanced spectral distributions. If a red apple is illuminated by a source that does not have much energy in the red portion of the spectrum, the distribution of light that it reflects into the eye will be very different than if it is illuminated by a source, like the sun, with a fairly balanced spectral distribution. This suggests that our perception of the color of various surfaces will depend both on the (desired) surface properties of the object and on the (irrelevant) properties of the illuminant. An apple could appear to change color when we carry it from our yard into the kitchen where it is illuminated by incandescent light.

Similar problems arise in other stimulus domains. Visual information about object size depends on the object's true size and the object's distance from the observer, because the retinal image size of the object varies directly with distance. How can we come to know the relevant property (object size) and discount the irrelevant property (distance)? Visual information about object shape depends on the orientation of the object relative to our line of sight (so that a square will project a parallelogram or a diamond onto the retina depending on its slant and tilt). How can we come to know the relevant property (shape) and discount the irrelevant property (orientation)?

Each of these is a problem in perceptual constancy. We are, in fact, able to correctly know the color, size, and shape of objects despite variation in irrelevant factors such as illumination, distance, and orientation. The question is how this is achieved. It turns out that the visual system has evolved different solutions in each domain, specialized for the particular properties in question. Although it is implied that the mechanisms of perceptual constancy are not part of early vision by placing them in separately labeled sections, most of perceptual constancy is indeed achieved by what most vision scientists would call early vision. Color constancy, for example, begins as early as area V4, and certain aspects of color constancy, its precursors so to speak, arise even earlier (see Zeki, 1993, for a discussion).

Perceptual Organization

The second main problem of the early sensory representation is that it is local in scope. This is a problem because most real scenes contain multiple objects that are arranged in 3D space and that both occlude one another and occlude parts of themselves. To take an extreme example, consider the problem of looking at your garden through the partially open slats of a Venetian blind. Although the tree and foliage in the garden are broken up into horizontal strips by the blind, we are able to attend to and recognize the objects in the garden with little difficulty. Any understanding of this ability requires us to explain how the visible part of a branch in one horizontal strip are correctly conjoined with the corresponding part of the branch in the next horizontal strip, and more puzzlingly how the occluded parts of the branch are "filled in" to produce a representation of a single, coherent, solid branch despite extreme fragmentation in the retinal image.

Many of the Gestalt principles of perceptual organization are discussed in Reading 11 by Wertheimer. These principles characterize how the visual system puts elements in the retinal image together so as to form coherent object representations. These principles include similarity (the texture and color and depth of the branch are similar at all points along it, and furthermore those properties are different for nearby image regions; thus similarity of surface properties is a good clue that those regions all belong to the same object), proximity (the visible parts of a reasonably compact object tend to be in nearby regions of space, so all other things being equal, two image regions will tend to be near one another if they are part of the same object), and common motion (if the branch is blowing in the wind, all its parts will move together, and other non-branch objects, such as the fence behind the branch, will tend not to move with it; thus common motion in two regions is a good clue that they are part of the same object).

The problem of perceptual completion or "filling in" has also been investigated by perceptual psychologists. There are two sides to this problem. One is that of what Michotte et al. (1991) called *amodal completion*. The partly occluded branch behind the blind is experienced as complete and continuous despite the fact that parts of the branch are completely absent from the retinal image. This is called *amodal* completion, because there is no information coming from a sensory modality to support perceptual completion, and in fact there is a sense that one "knows" that the branch is complete without having an explicit *visual experience* of the branch in the occluded regions. Amodal completion depends on two factors: (1) the edges of the occluded objects must be "relatable" such that they could plausibly be considered part of a single common contour (this essentially requires that there are no implausibly large bends in the contour; see Kellman & Shipley, 1991), and (2) the boundary between the occluding surface and the occluded surface must "belong" to the former and not the latter (this essentially requires that the occluding surface be perceived as in front of the occluded surface; see Nakayama et al., 1995).

The other form of perceptual completion is the perception of *illusory contours*, a phenomenon first described by Kanizsa (e.g., 1979). Illusory contours arise most famously in the context of the Kanizsa triangle at right. Here the segmented disks serve as inducers for the illusory shape. The shape is illusory because there is no physical contrast to define the edges of the triangle where the page is white, yet most observers report that they see a dim but clearly discernable edge there. Furthermore, the brightness of the figure is often reported as being greater than the brightness of the background. Clearly the relatability of the boundaries of the segments (i.e., that they are nearly collinear) supports the perceptual conclusion that a curved white triangle is partly occluding three black disks (which, by the way, are perceived as complete disks by virtue of amodal completion!). The visual system "fills in" where the contrast of the perfectly white triangle with the perfectly white

background is zero, and makes it slightly greater than zero. Von der Heydt et al. (1984) have provided evidence about the neural basis of illusory contours in V2.

Object and Spatial Vision

Recognizing objects visually is a difficult problem for the following reason: the data upon which we must base our identification decision is a retinal projection that can vary dramatically depending on our viewpoint relative to the object (not to mention the lighting, where we are looking, whether we or the object are moving, and so forth; we will ignore these complications because we have enough trouble as it is). Even something as simple as a cube can project a nearly infinite variety of retinal images depending on its orientation and its distance from us. So there is a highly underdetermined many-to-one mapping of retinal images onto the object's true shape. Obviously the visual system has found a way to solve this problem with staggering efficiency and accuracy. The question is: how?

There are two major routes one can take in approaching this problem. They can be broadly classified as view-based or part-based models. View-based (also called image-based) models assume that internal representations of whole objects as they would appear to the observer are stored as such in memory. One approach to dealing with the many-to-one problem discussed in the last paragraph is to store in memory, for every object one might wish eventually to recognize, all the possible retinal images that object could produce (or at least the images one is likely to encounter under normal circumstances, which reduces the number of possibilities from infinite to merely unimaginably large). This is the idea behind simple *template matching* accounts of object recognition. There are, of course, many problems with this approach. First, it would require a very large number of stored templates: more than one could plausibly suppose are stored in the brain. New instances of a familiar category (a strange but recognizable chair, for instance) could not be recognized by this mechanism. Finally, there is no evidence for the sort of unguided search through a huge database of templates that would be required by this mechanism. So this simple brute-force account of object recognition will not work.

A more sophisticated version of template matching, however, does have considerable merit. According to this idea, there exist internal representations of objects depicted in one or, more often, several canonical views (that is, views that permit one to represent most of the critical parts of the object from a view that is often encountered in real life). The reason multiple views are necessary is because any one view usually will not contain information about the part of the object facing away from the viewpoint, and of course we know perfectly well what the back of a chair looks like even when we can't see it (or at least we can make a very good guess). When an object is to be recognized, it is first *normalized*, that is, it is transformed so as to match the size, location, and viewpoint that is likely to be stored for that object, and this normalized representation is then compared to stored object representations. This mechanism avoids some of the problems of the simple template matching models by allowing for normalization so that only a small number of views of each object need be stored.

A very different approach to object recognition is offered by feature- or part-based models of object recognition. According to these theories, object representations consist of lists of features (e.g., oriented lines, angles, the presence or absence of symmetry) or parts (e.g., volumetric primitives such as cylinders), together with some specification of the relations among the parts. These accounts deal with the many-to-one problem by virtue of the fact that they are inherently more abstract than view-based theories: they transform the retinal image into a set of symbolic descriptions that do not depend on rotation, size, and so forth. One major subclass of part-based accounts are *structural description theories*. According to these theories (advocated by Marr and Nishihara, 1978, among others), stored object representations consist of 3D models of objects made up of a set of volumetric part primitives such as cylinders, cones, cubes, etc. that are arranged according to the structure of the object itself. The representation is not viewpoint dependent. They are called *descriptions* because they are not depictive (as in the multiple view plus transformation models). They are abstract and consist of a list of the parts together with a description of the structural relations among the parts (e.g., "cone on top of cylinder"). These models completely bypass the problem of too many representations by using fairly abstract representations that are insensitive to such things as absolute size or viewpoint. As long as the parts and their relations can be recognized, a match to a stored representation is possible. Biederman (Reading 20) describes a detailed model of this type, and makes the case for it on both theoretical and empirical grounds.

These alternative accounts of object recognition are fundamentally different in certain respects, and one might think that if one is the "correct" theory, the other must be wrong. However, it is possible, even likely, that both kinds of theories are correct to some extent (in a way analogous to the trichromatic and opponent-process theories of color vision), and that the challenge will be to specify the conditions under which each class of theories best accounts for recognition performance.

Attention and Awareness

To many people, attention and awareness are one in the same. We are aware of that to which we attend. Ever since Helmholtz and James first discussed these concepts, however, they have been treated differently by the scientific community. A look at the history of investigation of the two phenomena reveals a long and continuous line of scientific investigation into attention. In contrast, awareness (and its related term, consciousness), while of sustained interest in psychology for the past century, has until recently been ignored by neuroscience. In the last 10 years, however, that imbalance has changed, and there has been a surge of interest in the neural substrates of visual awareness.

Attention

Attention is a term with a high potential for confusion, because it can mean different things to different people. One often hears the comment at scientific meetings that the term is meaningless because it has too many meanings. Perhaps the most common use of the term, and the meaning intended here, is that of *perceptual selectivity*, described below. Other meanings include *vigilance*, or the ability to focus for extended periods in anticipation of a signal (as when the operator of a power plant monitors for a particular warning light), and *multi-tasking*, or the ability to switch between two overlapping tasks, like driving and carrying on a conversation.

Attention as perceptual selectivity refers to the problem first brought to prominence by William James at the end of the 19th century: we are confronted with far too much sensory information to grasp coherently at one time. We must select what is relevant and ignore what is irrelevant (which will tend to be almost everything). That means that until you started reading this sentence, you were unaware of the pressure of the chair you are sitting on against your skin, but now, with only a shift in attention to that source of sensory input, you are aware of it. Or of the faint sound of a vehicle out the window. And so forth. These kinds of attentional shifts are purely top-down and goal-driven (that is, you presumably set up, at least informally, a perceptual goal to give priority to certain tactile or auditory inputs and to ignore other inputs that might have been of higher priority previously, and this goal serves somehow to modulate the relative strengths of the sensory inputs available to you). Of course, the stimulus itself may well be capable of modifying your attentive state—an unexpectedly loud handclap will capture your attention in a purely stimulus-driven fashion. In both instances, however, the result is that certain sensory inputs are selected and enter awareness, and others are excluded. As implied by the last sentence, the gatekeeping act of selection and its result (to permit sensory information to enter awareness) are distinct; hence attention and awareness are distinct concepts.

But why is there a need for attention? What is the limitation that requires us to select some objects and ignore others? Broadbent (1958), in his seminal book that brought the study of attention into the modern era, suggested simply that people are information channels in the sense that we transmit sensory information into a behavioral response, and information theory states that any information channel must have an upper bound on its capacity. A more concrete answer was suggested by Treisman and Gelade (Reading 21), who were inspired by the finding of functional specialization by neurophysiologists in the 1960s and 70s. They pointed out that if visual objects are represented in terms of separate "feature maps," one for color, another for orientation, and so forth, then at some point there must come a stage of reintegrating the separate features into a unified and coherent representation of the object we actually see. They proposed that the process of feature integration was carried out by attending to one location at a time (and ignoring all other locations), so that only the attended features there were strongly represented at that moment. This constitutes attentional selection, and results in feature integration.

This was a groundbreaking idea, and it inspired a generation of experimental psychologists to explore its consequences. The problem of feature integration came to be called the *binding problem* and it continues to be a subject of considerable interest 20 years later (see Roskies et al., 1999, and the introduction to Reading 21). Many of the details of Feature Integration Theory have been updated as a result of subsequent empirical work, but the basic idea remains nearly intact.

Investigation of attention over the last decade or so has included a great deal of new work on the neural basis of attention inspired by Moran and Desimone (Reading 22), together with advances in understanding how attention is controlled. This latter problem is a major challenge now, and begins to approach the problem of consciousness because it requires one to think about how goals are specified, and how acts of the will are implemented. Descartes proposed that communication between the Soul (where acts of the will originate) and the Body is mediated by the pineal gland. Today this idea is viewed as a quaint anachronism, and other approaches are being considered, including the notion that a working memory store that is probably located in the dorsolateral prefrontal cortex contains representations of goals that can cause feedback signals to sensory regions that in turn can modulate the strength of neural representations there. This remains an active area of investigation that is really just beginning.

Awareness

If attention is perceptual selection, then what is consciousness? Consciousness is generally broken down into smaller problems, some of which will be harder to solve than others. Philosophers (e.g., Chalmers, 1996) have identified the "hard problem" of consciousness: the problem of qualia. How do we experience the redness of red? As Newton said, there is nothing in the light that is what we would call red; there is only a wavelength that happens to have the ability to evoke a pattern of neural response in the three classes of retinal cones. How does that pattern get translated into a subjective experience like red?

Nobody has any idea (some would say this is a fundamentally intractable problem), and so this will be left to the philosophers for now. But the problem of awareness, that is, of how certain kinds of neural activity correspond to something we experience and can report verbally or otherwise, seems more tractable (see Crick and Koch, 1998, for a discussion). The question can be stated as follows: some of the neural activity in the brain correlates well with our visual experience, that is, with what we are seeing at any given moment, and much of the neural activity in the brain is unrelated to what we are seeing. What is the difference between the parts of the brain (cells, layers, areas) that are and are not correlated with visual awareness. What is it about the type of cell (pyramidal?), the neurotransmitters it uses (serotonin? dopamine?), its connectivity pattern, its location in cortex (layer 4?; area V1?), some combination of these, or something else that endows it with the power to cause visual awareness?

This is a new area of investigation; little is known. Investigators have had to be clever to devise experiments that will be revealing in this regard. Sheinberg and Logothetis (Reading 25) is a good recent example.

Methods in Vision Science

I conclude with a discussion of how different methods have contributed to advances in vision science. As in all sciences, theoretical and empirical advances go hand-in-hand with technological developments. The development of the telescope permitted astronomers to see celestial objects previously unimagined. The microscope provided biologists with a tool to investigate cellular phenomena at the foundation of that science. So it is with any science. Visual perception has been no exception.

Psychophysics and Behavior

The first methodological developments in perception research were behavioral. In his 1860 treatise *Elements of Psychophysics,* Fechner described a collection of techniques for measuring with precision the relation between physical stimulus magnitude (e.g., the brightness of a light) and perceptual experience by collecting behavioral responses from observers in perceptual experiments (e.g., stating whether or not a dim flash was seen). These methods have withstood the test of time and continue to be used (in somewhat modified form) to this day (see Readings 6 and 8 for good examples). Psychophysical experiments provide the very bedrock of vision science, for they provide the precise measurements that are needed of the perceptual phenomena that require explanation. The criterion by which the usefulness and value of any psychophysical technique can be judged is whether that technique provides a measurement of experience that is as direct as possible and free of subjectivity and bias. Observers often have implicit theories of how vision works, and if these are permitted to contaminate psychophysical measurements, they are likely to lead to improper inferences. The development of signal detection theory (Reading 3 by Tanner and Swets) was inspired by precisely this concern.

Further developments during the 20th century gave rise to psychophysical methods that allowed for more precise control of the stimulus than those available to Fechner and his contemporaries. For example, the development of the tachistoscope provided a means of presenting one or more visual stimuli of precisely known brightness and duration to an observer. Such a device was essential for investigating temporal phenomena such as visual masking, where two objects are presented in rapid succession and the effect of one on the visibility of the other is measured. Many other devices were invented to serve a huge variety of special purposes in the investigation of visual function.

In the 1960s and 70s, digital computers entered the laboratories of vision scientists and eventually replaced the tachistoscope and other special-purpose devices. The reason is simple: general-purpose computers permit almost infinite flexibility in creating and presenting stimuli, and largely (but not completely) did away with the necessity to invent and build a new apparatus for each new experimental question, greatly accelerating research efforts.

Neuropsychology

All of the developments described in the previous paragraphs contributed to characterizing how variation in the properties of physical stimuli caused changes in visibility or discriminability as measured by behavioral methods. In parallel with these, a multitude of methods to investigate the neural basis of visual perception emerged. The earliest modern approach to brain-behavior relations was the proposal by Franz Joseph Gall that the brain consists of a number of functionally distinct compartments each of which was responsible for a particular kind of behavior (including such faculties as parental love, hope, and destructiveness). He argued that when a given faculty was exercised, the corresponding part of the brain grew larger (just as a muscle, when exercised, grows larger), and that this in turn was reflected in bumps on the skull, which grew to accommodate the brain tissue beneath them. Gall attempted to assign function to different brain areas by correlating personality traits to bumps on the head, a field of investigation known as *phrenology*. Pierre Flourens tested these notions by removing parts of the brains of experimental animals, and he concluded that the brain is not functionally compartmentalized at all, but is instead functionally undifferentiated. According to Flourens, any part of the brain can carry out any function as well as any other.

Although Flourens' conclusion has the distinct merit that it opposes the highly implausible theory of Gall, it was soon shown to be wrong. In 1861, Pierre Paul Broca (1824–1880) reported his observations of a patient who had suffered damage to his left frontal lobe (discovered after autopsy upon the patient's death) that had prevented him from speaking, while sparing most other cognitive functions, including the ability to understand speech. Broca asserted that the frontal lobes contained the faculty of speech production. This idea of functional localization was met with much skepticism at the time (a continued reaction against Gall), but it was corroborated with subsequent observations. For example, in 1876, Carl Wernicke described a patient who had difficulty understanding speech but not in producing it, a pattern complementary to that reported by Broca. Wernicke found that this patient had a lesion in the posterior temporal lobe, now called Wernicke's area. This double dissociation provided strong evidence that the perception and production of speech are carried out by functionally distinct brain regions.

Among the first evidence for functional specialization in vision was reported by the French ophthalmologist Louis Verrey who, in 1888, described his observations of a patient who had suffered a stroke in her left visual cortex. Among other less dramatic effects, the patient lost her ability to see color in the right visual field—all the objects there were seen in shades of gray. Color vision was normal in the left visual field. The acquired loss of color vision due to cortical damage (in this case, stroke) is known as achromatopsia. The existence of this syndrome strongly suggests that there is a local brain region that is necessary for the experience of color. It is important to keep in mind that other parts of the visual system are also necessary for normal color vision (for example, the cone photoreceptors in the retina are certainly necessary for color vision!), but this brain region appears to be specialized for color because damage there does not much affect other visual abilities, such as form or motion perception. Inspired by the findings of the neurologists, Korbinian Brodmann analyzed the anatomy of the human brain around the turn of the century using the method of cytoarchitectonics, which relies on differences in the form and structure of cortical neurons. He identified 52 distinct areas and suggested that these areas may well be functionally distinct as well. Brodmann's classification scheme continues in wide use today.

Functional specialization in the brain is now as close to a fact as anything in science can be. Brain-damaged patients have been described with specific deficits in motion perception, color vision, the perception of faces or objects, and in the ability to attend to specific regions of space, among many other syndromes, suggesting that each of these functions may rely selectively on the damaged region of the brain. Lissauer (Reading 16) provided an insightful early analysis of a patient with cortical damage that caused not blindness, but an inability to recognize objects that could nevertheless be seen, a condition known as visual agnosia. The blindsight patient of Weiskrantz et al. (Reading 24) revealed a surprising dissociation between explicit visual awareness and measured visual performance. Subtle deficits such as these have turned out to be extremely informative in developing accounts of how the normal visual system works.

Neurophysiology

Vision is an emergent property of neural activity in the brain. A complete understanding of visual perception, therefore, will require an understanding of how neurons subserve vision. Of course, there is much to learn by analyzing visual perception through purely behavioral means using the methods of visual psychophysics and cognitive neuropsychology. But despite its almost infinite complexity, the brain is a concrete medium in which visual behavior is implemented and it can therefore provide important clues about the principles of visual perception.

The development of the microscope provided physiologists with a crucial tool that led to the idea, first promoted by Santiago Ramón y Cajal, that the brain consists not of continuous and undifferentiated cellular tissue but of billions of separate nerve cells that communicate with one another at specialized junctions called synapses. Johannes Müller, Hermann von Helmholtz, and others learned that axons carry electrical signals from the cell body to the synaptic gap, which can in turn activate the next cell.

Neurons are exquisitely complex biological devices whose functional properties are a result of a multitude of molecular, chemical, and electrical forces acting in concert. Modern neuroscience is dedicated to uncovering how the interactions among these forces gives rise to patterns of activity in single neurons. However, for purposes of understanding how neural activity produces visual function, one can view a neuron as a device that produces a discrete signal (an action potential that can be measured with a microelectrode) in response to light (in the case of the photoreceptors) or to the release of neurotransmitters at the synapse (in the case of all other neurons). Cellular neurophysiologists place electrodes in or near the axon of a neuron and record action potentials as they occur. The rate with which action potentials are produced by the cell provide a compact measure of the activity of that cell, and this in turn can reveal how that cell participates in any given perceptual act. For example, as suggested by Barlow (Reading 2), one can characterize a cell's function by determining what sorts of visual stimuli cause that cell to fire most effectively. The neurophysiological studies of Hubel and Weisel (Reading 7), Newsome et al. (Reading 10), Moran and Desimone (Reading 22), and Scheinberg and Logothetis (Reading 25) each provides an excellent example of the insights to be gained from single-cell recording combined with carefully designed stimuli and behavioral tasks.

Functional Neuroimaging

Until the 1970s, direct measurements of brain function in behaving organisms was only possible in two ways. First, one could analyze patterns of impaired performance in brain-damaged patients, relying on "experiments of nature" such as a stroke or closed-head injury to reveal what the intact system must be like in order that it could be damaged in such a way as to have produced the observed functional deficit (e.g., damage causing cortical achromatopsia but not affecting the perception of shape or motion suggested that there exists a distinct "color center" in the brain). The main disadvantage here is that true experiments are not an option (one had to seek out patients that happened to have had a stroke in a focal region that happened to correspond to a functional area). Second, one could perform experiments using animals, recording from single cells or producing focal lesions in cats or monkeys. The disadvantages of the single-cell approach is that although single cell responses are an extremely rich source of data, the evidence is quite local so that global cortical circuits are difficult to study without great effort. The difficulty with lesions is that the interpretation of a pattern of impaired performance is not always unambiguous. Furthermore, there are limitations in what tasks monkeys can be trained to do (for example, language tasks are not available). Finally, the anatomy and function of monkey and cat brain differ from those of human brain in both known and unknown ways.

Over the last several decades, neuroscientists perfected the use of the electroencephalogram (or EEG) to measure electrical field potentials at the scalp that are caused by the activity of millions of neurons in cortex several millimeters below the electrode's scalp location. This technique provides a highly detailed record of the timecourse of brain activity, and has been used very effectively (e.g., Hillyard et al., 1996). The data one obtains from this technique are similar in many respects to single cell recording in monkeys, enjoying the same very high temporal resolution of that technique. It has several advantages over single cell recording: it can be carried out in humans, and it provides measurements over the entire surface of the scalp, potentially overcoming the inherently local measurement that emerges from single cell recording. However, the event-related potential suffers from its comparatively low and sometimes uncertain spatial resolution.

Magnetoencephalography (or MEG) has recently emerged as a new technology that may one day replace the EEG. It operates on principles that are analogous to the EEG, but instead of measuring electrical potentials, it measures extremely small magnetic field inhomogeneities produces by the electrical activity of neurons in cortex. This technique arguably has better spatial resolution than EEG, and similar temporal resolution. It also can provide a map of activity throughout the brain. One of its drawbacks is that it is currently a fairly expensive technology that is available at only a few sites. This is perhaps the newest of the brain-imaging technologies and therefore the least is known about it.

Finally, two techniques that have emerged over the last two decades have generated great interest although their full potential as scientific tools to investigate vision has not yet been reached. Both methods are based on changes in blood flow or in the composition of oxygenated or deoxygenated hemoglobin within the brain that is caused by changes in neural activity. In rough outline, when neurons produce action potentials, they require oxygen and other nutrients that are carried by the blood. They signal their need for blood, and this in turn causes changes in blood flow in those regions. Thus both of these methods are indirect, although surprisingly precise, measures of the location of neural activity.

The first method is positron emission tomography or PET, which was used by Zeki et al. (Reading 9). It requires an injection of a radioactively labeled agent (usually oxygen in water) that is carried by the blood to the brain. The PET scanner can detect the location and concentration of the radioactive agent, and thereby pinpoint the region of neural activity. A major advantage of PET over EEG is its improved spatial precision. The disadvantages of PET are the invasive use of a radioactive substance, which is potentially harmful, and the very low temporal resolution (on the order of several minutes).

The second of the two blood-based methods is functional magnetic resonance imaging, or fMRI, used by O'Craven et al. (Reading 23). It exploits the fact that deoxygenated hemoglobin is paramagnetic and can be detected by an appropriately programmed MRI scanner (see Haxby et al., 1998, for a tutorial review). This is relevant because the concentration of deoxygenated hemoglobin changes systematically where there is neural activity. fMRI has better spatial and much better temporal resolution than PET (on the order of a few seconds) and it does not require an invasive injection. It also has better spatial resolution than EEG. However, fMRI has much poorer temporal resolution than EEG or MEG, and it is currently quite expensive to carry out a study. On the other hand, most modern medical centers own MRI scanners for clinical purposes, and so they are often more readily available than MEG scanners.

The techniques for studying vision, ranging from behavior to brain imaging, are complementary rather than competing. Each represents a tradeoff between cost, spatial and temporal resolution, invasiveness, and other factors. Each requires a unique approach to designing experiments, and the range of questions that can be addressed differs markedly across the methods. The only generalization that can be made is that vision science can only benefit from the development of new methods and new technologies that will allow new questions to be addressed and old questions to be re-examined in new ways.

About this Volume

The articles selected for this volume are among the most influential writings on visual perception published in the last 125 years. These 25 articles were selected from an initial list of more than 200 classic articles culled from many sources. In the end, the selection reflects a need to provide reasonably complete coverage of the major themes and methods in visual perception, and a desire to include articles that are accessible by non-experts. Also included are some articles from the last decade to reflect some recent trends in the field (e.g., the use of functional magnetic resonance imaging to measure human brain activity in vision). Obviously many important topics and many influential works have been omitted. It would not be difficult to compile three more volumes of readings of equivalent quality and impact.

Each of the five sections concludes with a set of questions designed to stimulate discussion of the articles contained in that section. In addition, several additional articles are listed that could easily have been included in this volume if only there had been room. These, together with the references following each of the article introductions, constitute a larger set of essential readings in visual perception that readers are urged to seek out on their own.

In order to include as many articles as are included here, it was necessary to reduce the length of some articles through editing. In each case where this was done, the omitted material included experiments that, while they contributed importantly to the theoretical point that was being made, were not essential to the reader's understanding of that point.

I benefitted greatly from the advice of many colleagues during the process of selection. Stephen Palmer provided an exceptionally detailed and scholarly evaluation of an early list of proposed articles for which I am grateful. Richard Abrams, Jim Enns, Bruce Goldstein, Patrick Green, Glyn Humphreys, Eileen Kowler, William Newsome, Harvey Schiffman, and Nick Wade offered valuable feedback and ideas for readings I hadn't considered. My colleagues at Johns Hopkins – Ed Connor, Howard Egeth, Mike McCloskey, Brenda Rapp, and Trish Van Zandt – were helpful and patient in our conversations over the months I was engaged in this project. To all I offer my thanks.

REFERENCES

Broadbent, D. E. (1958). *Perception and communication.* London: Pergamon Press.

Chalmers, D. J.(1996). *The conscious mind: In search of a fundamental theory.* New York: Oxford University Press.

Crick, F., & Koch, C. (1998). Consciousness and neuroscience. *Cerebral Cortex*, 8, 97–107.

Fechner, G. T. (1860). *Elemente des psychophysik.* Leipzig: Breitkopf and Härtel. (Translated by H. E. Adler, *Elements of psychophysics.* New York: Holt, Rinehart, & Winston, 1966)

Haxby, J. V., Courtney, S. M., & Clark, V. P. (1998). Functional magnetic resonance imaging and the study of attention. In R. Parasuraman (Ed.), *The attentive brain* (pp. 123–142). Cambridge, MA: MIT Press.

Hillyard, S.A., Anllo-Vento, L., Clark, V. P., Heinze, H. J., Luck, S. J., & Mangun, G. R. (1996). Neuroimaging approaches to the study of visual attention: A tutorial. In A. F. Kramer, M. G. H. Coles, & G. D. Logan (Eds.). *Converging operations in the study of visual selective attention* (pp. 107–138). Washington, DC: American Psychological Association.

Kanizsa, G. (1979). *Organization in vision: Essays on Gestalt perception.* New York: Praeger.

Kellman, P. J., & Shipley, T. F. (1991). A theory of visual interpolation in object perception. *Cognitive Psychology, 23,* 141–221.

Marr, D., & Nishihara, H. K. (1978). Representation and recognition of the spatial organization of three-dimensional shapes. *Proceedings of the Royal Society of London B, 200,* 269–294.

McBeath, M. K., Shaffer, D. M., & Kaiser, M. K. (1995). How baseball outfielders determine where to run to catch fly balls. *Science 268,* 569–573.

Michotte, A., Thinès, G., & Crabbé, G. (1991). Amodal completion of perceptual structures (E. Miles & T.R. Miles, Trans.). In G. Thinès, A. Costall, & G. Butterworth (Eds.), *Michotte's experimental phenomenology of perception* (pp. 140–167). Hillsdale, NJ: Erlbaum. (Original work published 1964)

Nakayama, K., He., Z. J., & Shimojo, S. (1995). Visual surface representation: A critical link between lower-level and higher-level vision. In S. M. Kosslyn & D. N. Osherson (Eds.), *An invitation to cognitive science. Vol. 2: Visual Cognition* (pp. 1–70). Cambridge, MA: MIT Press.

Roskies, A. L., et al. (1999) The binding problem. *Neuron, 24,* 7–125.

Tanaka, K. (1996). Inferotemporal cortex and object vision. *Annual Review of Neuroscience, 19,* 109–139.

von der Heydt, R., Peterhans, E., & Baumgartner, G. (1984). Illusory contours and cortical neuron responses. *Science, 224,* 1260–1261.

Zeki, S. (1993). *A vision of the brain.* Oxford: Blackwell.

Suggested Readings

The following books provide excellent overviews of vision science from various thematic and methodological perspectives.

Farah, M. J. (2000). *The cognitive neuroscience of vision.* Malden, MA: Blackwell Publishers, Inc.

Gordon, I.E. (1997). *Theories of visual perception* (2nd Ed.). New York: John Wiley & Sons.

Gregory, R. L. (1970). *The intelligent eye.* New York: McGraw-Hill.

Hubel, D. H. (1988). *Eye, brain, and vision.* New York: W. H. Freeman & Co.

Marr, D. (1982). *Vision.* San Francisco: W. H. Freeman & Co.

Palmer, S. E. (1999). *Vision science: Photons to phenomenology.* Cambridge, MA: MIT Press.

Rock, I. (1984). *Perception.* New York: Scientific American Books.

Zeki, S. (1993). *A vision of the brain.* Oxford: Blackwell.

PART 1

Theoretical Perspectives

Introduction to Reading 1

Hermann von Helmholtz (1821–1894) was responsible for half a dozen truly seminal contributions to science, any one of which might have been worthy of a Nobel Prize. This includes the trichromatic theory of color vision (which he discovered independently of Thomas Young; see the introduction to Reading 7 by Hurvich and Jamison for more details), the place theory of pitch perception (which was corroborated a century later by the Nobel Prize–winning work of Georg von Békèsy), and the first measurement of the conduction velocity of a neural signal (about 100 meters/sec). Among his most influential contributions is the monumental *Treatise on Physiological Optics*, in which he analyzes the functioning of the visual system at many levels in exquisite detail.

This selection is taken from Volume III of that work, subtitled *The Perceptions of Vision*. It contains one of Helmholtz's most enduring theoretical contributions: his articulation of the constructivist perspective (what he terms the *empirical theory*) in perception. According to this view, perception is not merely an "internal picture" of the retinal image; instead, it is a joint result of sensory input on the one hand and what the observer knows and expects on the other. Each of these provide evidence about what is actually present in the world, and a form of perceptual thought that Helmholtz called *unconscious inference* gives rise to veridical experiences despite the limitations and distortions of our senses. As Helmholtz puts it, "such objects are always imagined as being present in the field of vision as would have to be there in order to produce the same impression on the nervous mechanism, the eyes being used under ordinary normal conditions" (p. 25).

The alternative to the empirical theory Helmholtz calls the *intuition theory*, according to which perception does not depend at all on experience or expectation, but is wholly innate and stimulus-driven. He argues persuasively at various points in this selection against this position. He notes, for example, that one's ability to navigate about a room in twilight is dramatically improved if one has had previous experience viewing the layout of the room under good illumination. One's memory of the layout, combined with the indistinct impressions of the dimly illuminated furniture, combine to produce an accurate perceptual experience.

A standard example of unconscious inference is its manifestation in size constancy. The problem solved by size constancy is this: the retinal image size of an object depends directly on the distance between it and the observer: the closer the observer, the larger the retinal image size. Indeed, any particular retinal image is consistent with an infinite number of possible size/distance combinations (small/near or large/far). Yet observers routinely make correct judgements about the true size of objects. This fact of size constancy implies that size judgements cannot be based only on the retinal image, but must also take into account the perceived distance to the object (see Reading 14 by Kaufman and Rock for more on size constancy). Helmholtz's explanation for this and many other phenomena is that the observer unconsciously combines the retinal image size with an estimate of the distance to the object, based perhaps on stereoscopic or other depth cues.

Helmholtz discusses some of the ideas behind the notion of unconscious inference (or, as translated here, unconscious conclusion) that were later to have such a significant impact on the field and continue to hold sway today. He uses as an initial example the effects accompanying mechanical stimulation of the retina (e.g., a finger press on the outer edge of the eyeball). The pressure activates a small set of photoreceptors, producing what are called "phosphenes." The perceptual experience is not of an event occurring at the point of stimulation, however, but of light coming from the direction of the bridge of the nose; such a light would, if present, have stimulated the part of the retina that is being mechanically stimulated. The brain "concludes" that there must be light in the scene in a location that would stimulate the active part of the retina.

In addition to laying out the principle of unconscious inference, Helmholtz brings to the argument examples from his own observations of a wide range of perceptual phenomena, anticipating by more than a century some issue of great contemporary interest. These include the "phantom limb" syndrome in which an amputee experiences sensations (often pain) that appear to come from the limb that is no longer there (e.g., Ramachandran, 1993); the perception of biological motion (e.g., Johansson, 1973); and filling in of the blind spot (the location on the retina where the optic nerve leaves the eye and where, therefore, there are no photoreceptors; e.g., Ramachandran, 1993). He dismisses the notion of isomorphic brain representations, and what Dennett (1991) referred to as the "Cartesian theater" a century later: "Now I ask, what similarity can be imagined between the process in the brain that is concomitant with the idea of a table and the table itself? Is the form of the table to be supposed to be outlined by electric currents? . . . such an electrical reproduction of the table in the brain would be simply another bodily object to be perceived, but no idea of the table" (p. 35).

It should be emphasized that in Helmholtz's view, unconscious inference occurs not only when there are several distinct sources of information that must be combined in an algorithmic way (as in the size constancy example); it plays a role in virtually every percept. A distinction is drawn between the sensation, that pure sensory signal that is not affected by experience or expectation, and the perception, which is an "idea" of the objects the scene must contain. Sensations themselves are difficult to experience because they do not serve any useful purpose, other than to provide evidence for perceptual conclusions ("In the ordinary affairs of life the sensations have no other importance for us. Subjective sensations are of interest chiefly for scientific investigations only," p. 27). One must make a deliberate effort to experience sensations themselves.

J. S. Bruner (1957) proposed a theory in this tradition that also explicitly implicates perceptual hypotheses in vision; Bruner's contribution was part of what came to be termed the "New Look" in perception.

For example, when observers viewed briefly-flashed playing cards that occasionally were colored incorrectly (e.g., a black ten of diamonds), they would sometimes report the color as purple, as if their knowledge of the correct color (a perceptual hypothesis of red) was somehow combined with the sensory evidence (black) to yield a sort of perceptual compromise.

Other modern constructivists include Irvin Rock (e.g., 1983) and Richard Gregory (e.g., 1974). The constructivist position is rarely discussed in the contemporary literature, however. This is because it is now part of the set of commonly held foundational assumptions of almost all vision scientists.

REFERENCES

Bruner, J. S. (1957). On perceptual readiness. *Psychological Review, 64*, 123–152.

Dennett, D. (1991). *Consciousness explained.* Boston: Little, Brown.

Gregory, R. (1980). Perceptions as hypotheses. *Philosophical Transactions of the Royal Society of London B, 290*, 181–197.

Johansson (1973). Visual perception of biological motion and a model for its analysis. *Perception & Psychophysics, 14*, 201–211.

Ramachandran, V. S. (1993) Filling the gaps in perception: II. Scotomas and phantom limbs. *Current Directions in Psychological Science, 2*, 56–65.

Rock, I. (1983). *The logic of perception.* Cambridge, MA: MIT Press.

Concerning the Perceptions in General

H. von Helmholtz

The sensations aroused by light in the nervous mechanism of vision enable us to form conceptions as to the existence, form and position of external objects. These ideas are called *visual perceptions*. In this third subdivision of Physiological Optics we must try to analyze the scientific results which we have obtained concerning the conditions which give rise to visual perceptions.

Perceptions of external objects being therefore of the nature of ideas, and ideas themselves being invariably activities of our psychic energy, perceptions also can only be the result of psychic energy. Accordingly, strictly speaking, the theory of perceptions belongs properly in the domain of psychology. This is particularly true with respect to the mode of the mental activities in the case of the perceptions and with respect to the determination of their laws. Yet even here there is a wide field of investigation in both physics and physiology, inasmuch as we have to determine, scientifically as far as possible, what special properties of the physical stimulus and of the physiological stimulation are responsible for the formation of this or that particular idea as to the nature of the external objects perceived. In this part of the subject, therefore, we shall have to investigate the special properties of the retinal images, muscular sensations, etc., that are concerned in the perception of a definite position of the observed object, not only as to its direction but as to its distance; how the perception of the form of a body of three dimensions depends on certain peculiarities of the images; and under what circumstances it will appear single or double as seen by both eyes, etc. Thus, our main

purpose will be simply to investigate the material of sensation whereby we are enabled to form ideas, in those relations that are important for the perceptions obtained from them. This problem can be solved entirely by scientific methods. At the same time, we cannot avoid referring to psychic activities and the laws that govern them, as far as they are concerned with the perception of the senses. But the discovery and description of these psychic activities will not be regarded as an essential part of our present task, because then we might run the risk of losing our hold of established facts and of not adhering steadily to a method founded on clear, well-recognized principals. Thus, for the present at least, I[1] think the psychological domain of the physiology of the senses should be kept separate from pure psychology, whose province really is to establish as far as possible the laws and nature of the processes of the mind.

Still we cannot altogether avoid speaking of the mental processes that are active in the sense-perceptions, if we wish to see clearly the connection between the phenomena and to arrange the facts in their proper relation to one another. And hence, to prevent any misconception of the plan I have in mind, I intend to devote the latter part of this chapter to a discussion of the conclusions which I think can be inferred with respect to these mental processes. And yet we know by experience that people

---

[1]In this volume (contrary to the usage adopted in the two previous volumes of the English translation), the editor has deemed it best to retain the more intimate language of the original text, and let the author speak throughout in the first person. (J.P.C.S.)

very seldom come to any agreement as to abstract questions of this nature. The keenest thinkers, philosophers like Kant for instance, have long ago analysed these relations correctly and demonstrated them, and yet there is no permanent and general agreement about them among educated people. And, therefore, in the subsequent chapters devoted specially to the theory of the visual perceptions, I shall endeavour to avoid all reference to opinions as to mental activity, as involving questions that always have been, and perhaps always will be, subjects of debate between the various metaphysical schools; so as not to distract the reader's attention from those facts about which an agreement may possibly be reached, by wrangling over abstract propositions that are not necessarily involved in the problem before us.

Here I shall merely indicate at the outset certain general characteristics of the mental processes that are active in the sense-perceptions, because they will be constantly encountered in connection with the various subjects to be considered. Without some previous explanation of their general significance and wide range of activity, the reader might be apt in some special case to regard them as paradoxical and incredible.

The general rule determining the ideas of vision that are formed whenever an impression is made on the eye, with or without the aid of optical instruments, is that *such objects are always imagined as being present in the field of vision as would have to be there in order to produce the same impression on the nervous mechanism, the eyes being used under ordinary normal conditions.* To employ an illustration which has been mentioned before, suppose that the eyeball is mechanically stimulated at the outer corner of the eye. Then we imagine that we see an appearance of light in front of us somewhere in the direction of the bridge of the nose. Under ordinary conditions of vision, when our eyes are stimulated by light coming from outside, if the region of the retina in the outer corner of the eye is to be stimulated, the light actually has to enter the eye from the direction of the bridge of the nose. Thus, in accordance with the above rule, in a case of this kind we substitute a luminous object at the place mentioned in the field of view, although as a matter of fact the mechanical stimulus does not act on the eye from in front of the field of view nor from the nasal side of the

eye, but, on the contrary, is exerted on the outer surface of the eyeball and more from behind. The general validity of the above rule will be shown by many other instances that will appear in the following pages.

In the statement of this rule mention is made of the ordinary conditions of vision, when the visual organ is stimulated by light from outside; this outside light, coming from the opaque objects in its path that were the last to be encountered, and having reached the eye along rectilinear paths through an uninterrupted layer of air. This is what is meant here by the normal use of the organ of vision, and the justification for using this term is that this mode of stimulation occurs in such an enormous majority of cases that all other instances where the paths of the rays of light are altered by reflections or refractions, or in which the stimulations are not produced by external light, may be regarded as rare exceptions. This is because the retina in the fundus of the firm eyeball is almost completely protected from the actions of all other stimuli and is not easily accessible to anything but external light. When a person is in the habit of using an optical instrument and has become accustomed to it, for example, if he is used to wearing spectacles, to a certain extent he learns to interpret the visual images under these changed conditions.

Incidentally, the rule given above corresponds to a general characteristic of all sense-perceptions, and not simply to the sense of sight alone. For example, the stimulation of the tactile nerves in the enormous majority of cases is the result of influences that affect the terminal extensions of these nerves in the surface of the skin. It is only under exceptional circumstances that the nerve-stems can be stimulated by more powerful agencies. In accordance with the above rule, therefore, all stimulations of cutaneous nerves, even when they affect the stem or the nerve-centre itself, are perceived as occurring in the corresponding peripheral surface of the skin. The most remarkable and astonishing cases of illusions of this sort are those in which the peripheral area of this particular portion of the skin is actually no longer in existence, as, for example, in case of a person whose leg has been amputated. For a long time after the operation the patient frequently imagines he has vivid sensations in the foot that has been severed. He feels exactly the places that ache on one toe or the other. Of course, in a case of this sort the stimulation can affect only what is left of the stem of the nerve whose fibres formerly terminated in the amputated toes. Usually, it is the end of the nerve in the scar that is stimulated by external pressure or by contraction of the scar tissue. Sometimes at night the sensations in the missing extremity get to be so vivid that the patient has to feel the place to be sure that his limb is actually gone.

Thus it happens, that when the modes of stimulation of the organs of sense are unusual, incorrect ideas of objects are apt to be formed; which used to be described, therefore, as *illusions of the senses*. Obviously, in these cases there is nothing wrong with the activity of the organ of sense and its corresponding nervous mechanism which produces the illusion. Both of them have to act according to the laws that govern their activity once for all. It is rather simply an illusion in the judgment of the material presented to the senses, resulting in a false idea of it.

The psychic activities that lead us to infer that there in front of us at a certain place there is a certain object of a certain character, are generally not conscious activities, but unconscious ones. In their result they are equivalent to a *conclusion*, to the extent that the observed action on our senses enables us to form an idea as to the possible cause of this action; although, as a matter of fact, it is invariably simply the nervous stimulations that are perceived directly, that is, the actions, but never the external objects themselves. But what seems to differentiate them from a conclusion, in the ordinary sense of that word, is that a conclusion is an act of conscious thought. An astronomer, for example, comes to real conscious conclusions of this sort, when he computes the positions of the stars in space, their distances, etc., from the perspective images he has had of them at various times and as they are seen from different parts of the orbit of the earth. His conclusions are based on a conscious knowledge of the laws of optics. In the ordinary acts of vision this knowledge of optics is lacking. Still it may be permissible to speak of the psychic acts of ordinary perception as *unconscious conclusions*, thereby making a distinction of some sort between them and the common so-called conscious conclusions. And while it is true that there has been, and probably always will be, a measure of doubt as to the similarity of the psychic activity in the two cases, there can be no doubt as to the similarity between the results of such unconscious conclusions and those of conscious conclusions.

These unconscious conclusions derived from sensation are equivalent in their consequences to the so-called conclusions to the so-called *conclusions from analogy*. Inasmuch as in an overwhelming majority of cases, whenever the parts of the retina in the outer corner of the eye are stimulated, it has been found to be due to external light coming into the eye from the direction of the bridge of the nose, the inference we make is that it is so in every new case whenever this part of the retina is stimulated; just as we assert that every single individual now living will die, because all previous experience has shown that all men who were formerly alive have died.

But, moreover, just because they are not free acts of conscious thought, these unconscious conclusions from analogy are irresistible, and the effect of them cannot be overcome by a better understanding of the real relations. It may be ever so clear how we get an idea of a luminous phenomenon in the field of vision when pressure is exerted on the eye; and yet we cannot get rid of the conviction that this appearance of light is actually there at the given place in the visual field; and we cannot seem to comprehend that there is a luminous phenomenon at the place where the retina is stimulated. It is the same way in case of all the images that we see in optical instruments.

On the other hand, there are numerous illustrations of fixed and inevitable associations of ideas due to frequent repetition, even when they have no natural connection, but are dependent merely on some conventional arrangement, as, for example, the connection between the written letters of a word and its sound and meaning. Still to many physiologists and psychologists the connection between the sensation and the conception of the object usually appears to be so rigid and obligatory that they are not much disposed to admit that, to a considerable extent at least, it depends on acquired experience, that is, on psychic activity. On the contrary, they have endeavoured to find some mechanical mode of origin for this connection through the agency of imaginary organic structures. With regard to this question, all those experiences are of much significance which show how the judgment of the senses may be modified by experience and by training derived under various circumstances, and may be adapted to the new conditions. Thus, persons may learn in some measure to utilize details of the sensation which otherwise would escape notice and not contribute to obtaining any idea of the object. On the other hand, too, this new habit may acquire such a hold that when the individual in question is back again in the old original normal state, he may be liable to illusions of the senses.

Facts like these show the widespread influence that experience, training and habit have on our perceptions. But how far their influence really does extend, it would perhaps be impossible to say precisely at present. Little enough is definitely known about infants and very young animals, and the interpretation of such observations as have been made on them is extremely doubtful. Besides, no one can say that infants are entirely without experience and practice in tactile sensations and bodily movements. Accordingly, the rule given above has been stated in a form which does not anticipate the decision of this question. It merely expresses what the result is. And so it can be accepted even by those who have entirely different opinions as to the way ideas originate concerning objects in the external world.

Another general characteristic property of our sense-perceptions is, *that we are not in the habit of observing our sensations accurately, except as they are useful in enabling us to recognize external objects. One the contrary, we are wont to disregard all those parts of the sensations that are of no importance so far as external objects are concerned.* Thus in most cases some special assistance and training are needed in order to observe these latter subjective sensations. It might seem that nothing could be easier than to be conscious of one's own sensations; and yet experience shows that for the discovery of subjective sensations some special talent is needed, such as Purkinje manifested in the highest degree; or else it is the result of accident of theoretical speculation. For instance, the phenomena of the blind spot were discovered by Mariotte from theoretical considerations. Similarly, in the domain of hearing, I discovered the existence of those combination tones which I have called summation tones. In the great majority of cases, doubtless it was accident that revealed this or that subjective phenomenon to observers who happened to be particularly interested in such matters. It is only when subjective phenomena are so prominent as to interfere with the perception of things, that they attract everybody's attention. Once the phenomena have been discovered, it is generally easier for others to perceive them also, pro-

vided the proper precautions are taken for observing them, and the attention is concentrated on them. In many cases, however—for example, in the phenomena of the blind spot, or in the separation of the overtones and combination tones from the fundamental tones of musical sounds, etc.—such an intense concentration of attention is required that, even with the help of convenient external appliances, many persons are unable to perform the experiments. Even the after-images of bright objects are not perceived by most persons at first except under particularly favourable external conditions. It takes much more practice to see the fainter kinds of after-images. A common experience, illustrative of this sort of thing, is for a person who has some ocular trouble that impairs his vision to become suddenly aware of the so-called *mouches volantes* in his visual field, although the causes of this phenomenon have been there in the vitreous humor all his life. Yet now he will be firmly persuaded that these corpuscles have developed as the result of his ocular ailment, although the truth simply is that, owing to his ailment, the patient has been paying more attention to visual phenomena. No doubt, also, there are cases where one eye has gradually become blind, and yet the patient has continued to go about for an indefinite time without noticing it, until he happened one day to close the good eye without closing the other, and so noticed the blindness of that eye.[2]

When a person's attention is directed for the first time to the double images in binocular vision, he is usually greatly astonished to think that he had never noticed them before, especially when he reflects that the only objects he has ever seen single were those few that happened at the moment to be about as far from his eyes as the point of fixation. The great majority of objects, comprising all those that were farther or nearer than this point, were all seen double.

Accordingly, the first thing we have to learn is to pay heed to our individual sensations. Ordinarily we do so merely in case of those sensations that enable us to find out about the world around us. In the ordinary affairs of life the sensations have no other importance for us. Subjective sensations are of interest chiefly for scientific investigations only. If they happen to be noticed in the ordinary activ-

---

[2] Nearly everybody has a dominant eye, which governs the other eye; and in which the vision is superior to that in the other eye. But not many persons are aware of the fact. (J.P.C.S.)

ity of the senses, they merely distract the attention. Thus while we may attain an extraordinary degree of delicacy and precision in objective observation, we not only fail to do so in subjective observations, but indeed we acquire the faculty in large measure of overlooking them and of forming our opinions of objects independently of them, even when they are so pronounced that they might easily be noticed.

The most universal sign by which subjective visual phenomena can be identified appears to be by the way they accompany the movement of the eye over the field of view. Thus, the after-images, the *mouches volantes*, the blind spot, and the "luminous dust" of the dark field all participate in the motions of the eye, and coincide successively with the various stationary objects in the visual field. On the other hand, if the same phenomena recur again invariably at the same places in the visual field, they may be regarded as being objective and as being connected with external bodies. This is the case with contrast phenomena produced by after-images.

The same difficulty that we have in observing subjective sensations, that is, sensations aroused by internal causes, occurs also in trying to analyze the compound sensations, invariably excited in the same connection by any simple object, and to resolve them into their separate components. In such cases experience shows us how to recognize a compound aggregate of sensations as being the sign of a simple object. Accustomed to consider the sensation-complex as a connected whole, generally we are not able to perceive the separate parts of it without external help and support. Many illustrations of this kind will be seen in the following pages. For instance the perception of the apparent direction of an object from the eye depends on the combination of those sensations by which we estimate the adjustment of the eye, and on being able to distinguish those parts of the retina where light falls from those parts where it does not fall. The perception of the solid form of an object of three dimensions is the result of the combination of two different perspective views in the two eyes. The gloss of a surface, which is apparently a simple effect, is due to differences of colouring or brightness in the images of it in the two eyes. These facts were ascertained by theory and may be verified by suitable experiments. But usually it is very difficult, if not impossible, to discover them by direct observation and analysis

of the sensations alone. Even with sensations that are much more involved and always associated with frequently recurring complex objects, the oftener the same combination recurs, and the more used we have become to regarding the sensation as the normal sign of the real nature of the object, the more difficult it will be to analyze the sensation by observation alone. By way of illustration, it is a familiar experience that the colours of a landscape come out much more brilliantly and definitely by looking at them with the head on one side or upside down than they do when the head is in the ordinary upright position. In the usual mode of observation all we try to do is to judge correctly the objects as such. We know that at a certain distance green surfaces appear a little different in hue. We get in the habit of overlooking this difference, and learn to identify the altered green of distant meadows and trees with the corresponding colour of nearer objects. In the case of very distant objects like distant ranges of mountains, little of the colour of the body is left to be seen, because it is mainly shrouded in the colour of the illuminated air. This vague blue-grey colour, bordered above by the clear blue of the sky or the red-yellow of the sunset glow, and below by the vivid green of meadows and forests, is very subject to variations by contrast. To us it is the vague and variable colour of distance. The difference in it may, perhaps, be more noticeable sometimes and with some illuminations than at other times. But we do not determine its true nature, because it is not ascribed to any definite object. We are simply aware of its variable nature. But the instant we take an unusual position, and look at the landscape with the head under one arm, let us say, or between the legs, it all appears like a flat picture; partly on account of the strange position of the image in the eye, and partly because, as we shall see presently, the binocular judgment of distance becomes less accurate. It may even happen that with the head upside down the clouds have the correct perspective, whereas the objects on the earth appear like a painting on a vertical surface, as the clouds in the sky usually do. At the same time the colours lose their associations also with near or far objects, and confront us now purely in their own peculiar differences.[3] Then we have no difficulty in recognizing that the vague blue-grey of the far distance may

---

[3] This explanation in given also by O. N. Rood, Silliman's *Journ.*, (2) xxxii. 1861. pp.184, 185.

indeed be a fairly saturated violet, and that the green of the vegetation blends imperceptibly through blue-green and blue into this violet, etc. This whole difference seems to me to be due to the fact that the colours have ceased to be distinctive signs of objects for us, and are considered merely as being different sensations. Consequently, we take in better their peculiar distinctions without being distracted by other considerations.

The connection between the sensations and external objects may interfere very much with the perception of their simplest relations. A good illustration of this is the difficulty about perceiving the double images of binocular vision when they can be regarded as being images of one and the same external object.

In the same way we may have similar experiences with other kinds of sensations. The sensation of the *timbre* of a sound, as I have shown elsewhere,[4] consists of a series of sensations of its partial tones (fundamental and harmonics); but it is exceedingly difficult to analyze the compound sensation of the sound into these elementary components. The tactile sensation of wetness is composed of that of coldness and that of smoothness of surface. Consequently, on inadvertently touching a cold piece of smooth metal, we often get the impression of having touched something wet. Many other illustrations of this sort might be adduced. They all indicate that we are exceedingly well trained in finding out by our sensations the objective nature of the objects around us, but that we are completely unskilled in observing the sensations per se and that the practice of associating them with things outside of us actually prevents us from being distinctly conscious of the pure sensations.

This is true also not merely with respect to qualitative differences of sensation, but it is likewise true with respect to the perception of space-relations. For example, the spectacle of a person in the act of walking is a familiar sight. We think of this motion as a connected whole, possibly taking note of some of its most conspicuous singularities. But it requires minute attention and a special choice of the point of view to distinguish the upward and lateral movements of the body in a person's gait. We have to pick out points or lines of reference in the background with which we can compare the position of his head. But look through an astronomical telescope at a crowd of people in motion far away. Their images are upside down,

but what a curious jerking and swaying of the body is produced by those who are walking about! Then there is no trouble whatever in noticing the peculiar motions of the body and many other singularities of gait; and especially differences between individuals and the reasons for them, simply because this is not the everyday sight to which we are accustomed. On the other hand, when the image is inverted in this way, it is not so easy to tell whether the gait is light or awkward, dignified or graceful, as it was when the image was erect.

Consequently, it may often be rather hard to say how much of our apperceptions (*Anschauungen*) as derived by the sense of sight is due directly to sensation, and how much of them, on the other hand, is due to experience and training. The main point of controversy between various investigators in this territory is connected also with this difficulty. Some are disposed to concede to the influence of experience as much scope as possible, and to derive from it especially all notion of space. This view may be called the *empirical theory* (*empiristische Theorie*). Others, of course, are obliged to admit the influence of experience in the case of certain classes of perceptions; still with respect to certain elementary apperceptions that occur uniformly in the case of all observers, they believe it is necessary to assume a system of innate apperceptions that are not based on experience, especially with respect to space-relations. In contradistinction to the former view, this may perhaps be called the *intuition theory* (*nativistische Theorie*) of the sense-perceptions.

In my opinion the following fundamental principles should be kept in mind in this discussion.

Let us restrict the word *idea* (*Vorstellung*) to mean the image of visual objects as retained in the memory, without being accompanied by any present sense-impressions; and use the term *apperception* (*Anschauung*) to mean a perception (*Wahrnehmung*) when it is accompanied by the sense-impressions in question. The term *immediate perception* (*Perzeption*) may then be employed to denote an apperception of this nature in which there is no element whatever that is not the result of direct sensations, that is, an apperception such

---

[4] Helmholtz, *Die Lehre von den Tonempfundungen*. Braunschweig 1862. (See English translation by A. J. Ellis, entitled *On the sensations of tone as a physiological basis for the theory of music*. 3rd ed. London and New York, 1895.— J.P.C.S.)

as might be derived without any recollection of previous experience. Obviously, therefore, one and the same apperception may be accompanied by the corresponding sensations in very different measure. Thus idea and immediate perception may be combined in the apperception in the most different proportions.[5]

A person in a familiar room which is brightly lighted by the sun gets an apperception that is abundantly accompanied by very vivid sensations. In the same room in the evening twilight he will not be able to recognize any objects except the brighter ones, especially the windows. But whatever he does actually recognize will be so intermingled with his recollections of the furniture that he can still move about in the room with safety and locate articles he is trying to find, even when they are only dimly visible. These images would be utterly insufficient to enable him to recognize the objects without some previous acquaintance with them. Finally, he may be in the same room in complete darkness, and still be able to find his way about in it without making mistakes, by virtue of the visual impressions formerly obtained. Thus, by continually reducing the material that appeals to the senses, the perceptual-image (*Anschauungs-bild*) can ultimately be traced back to the pure memory-image (*Vorstellungsbild*) and may gradually pass into it. In proportion as there is less and less material appeal to the senses, a person's movements will, of course, become more and more uncertain, and his apperception less and less accurate. Still there will be no peculiar abrupt transition, but sensation and memory will continually supplement each other, only in varying degrees.

But even when we look around a room of this sort flooded with sunshine, a little reflection shows us that under these conditions too a large part of our perceptual-image may be due to factors of memory and experience. The fact that we are accustomed to the perspective distortions of pictures of parallelopipeds and to the form of the shadows they cast has much to do with the estimation of the shape and dimensions of the room, as will be seen hereafter. Looking at the room with one eye shut, we think we see it just as distinctly and definitely as with both eyes. And yet we should get exactly the same view in case every point in the room were shifted arbitrarily to a different distance from the eye, provided they all remained on the same lines of sight.

Thus in a case like this we are really consider-ing an extremely multiplex phenomenon of sense; but still we ascribe a perfectly definite explanation to it, and it is by no means easy to realize that the monocular image of such a familiar object necessarily means a much more meagre perception than would be obtained with both eyes. Thus too it is often hard to tell whether or not untrained observers inspecting stereoscopic views really notice the peculiar illusion produced by the instrument.

We see, therefore, how in a case of this kind reminiscences of previous experiences act in conjunction with present sensations to produce a perceptual image (*Anschauungsbild*) which imposes itself on our faculty of perception with overwhelming power, without our being conscious of how much of it is due to memory and how much to present perception.

Still more remarkable is the influence of the comprehension of the sensations in certain cases, especially with dim illumination, in which a visual impression may be misunderstood at first, by not knowing how to attribute the correct depth-dimensions; as when a distant light, for example, is taken for a near one, or *vice versa*. Suddenly it dawns on us what it is, and immediately, under the influence of the correct comprehension, the correct perceptual image also is developed in its full intensity. Then we are unable to revert to the previous imperfect apperception.

This is very common especially with complicated stereoscopic drawings of forms of crystals and other objects which come out in perfect clearness of perception the moment we once succeed in getting the correct impression.

Similar experiences have happened to everybody, proving that the elements in the sense-perceptions that are derived from experience are just as powerful as those that are derived from present sensations. All observers who have thoroughly investigated the theory of the sense-perceptions, even those who were disposed to allow experience as little scope as possible, have always admitted this.

Hence, at all events it must be conceded that,

---

[5]It is very difficult to find the precise English equivalents for these metaphysical terms, which will prove satisfactory to everybody. And it may not be quite possible to restrict the English word "idea," for example, to the definition here given. It is doubtful whether the author himself is scrupulously careful throughout the remainder of this work to distinguish these shades of meaning always exactly. (J.P.C.S.)

even in what appears to the adult as being direct apperception of the senses, possibly a number of single factors may be involved which are really the product of experience; although at the time it is difficult to draw the line between them.

Now in my opinion we are justified by our previous experiences in stating that no indubitable present sensation can be abolished and overcome by an act of the intellect; and no matter how clearly we recognize that it has been produced in some anomalous way, still the illusion does not disappear by comprehending the process. The attention may be diverted from sensations, particularly if they are feeble and habitual; but in noting those relations in the external world, that are associated with these sensations, we are obliged to observe the sensations themselves. Thus we may be unmindful of the temperature-sensation of our skin when it is not very keen, or of the contact-sensations produced by our clothing, as long as we are occupied with entirely different matters. But just as soon as we stop to think whether it is warm or cold, we are not in the position to convert the feeling of warmth into that of coldness; maybe because we know that it is due to strenuous exertion and not to the temperature of the surrounding air. In the same way the apparition of light when pressure is exerted on the eyeball cannot be made to vanish simply by comprehending better the nature of the process, supposing the attention is directed to the field of vision and not, say, to the ear or the skin.

On the other hand, it may also be that we are not in the position to isolate an impression of sensation, because it involves the composite sense-symbol of an external object. However, in this case the correct comprehension of the object shows that the sensation in question has been perceived and used by the consciousness.

My conclusion is, that *nothing in our sense-perceptions can be recognized as sensation which can be overcome in the perceptual image and converted into its opposite by factors that are demonstrably due to experience.*

Whatever, therefore, can be overcome by factors of experience, we must consider as being itself the product of experience and training. By observing this rule, we shall find that it is merely the qualities of the sensation that are to be considered as real, pure sensation; the great majority of space-apperceptions, however, being the product of experience and training.

Still it does not follow that apperceptions, which persist in spite of our better conscious insight and continue as illusions, might not be due to experience and training. Our knowledge of the changes of colour produced in distant objects by the haziness of the atmosphere, of perspective distortions, and of shadow is undoubtedly a matter of experience. And yet in a good landscape picture we shall get the perfect visual impression of the distance and the solid form of the buildings in it, in spite of knowing that it is all depicted on canvas.

Similarly, our knowledge of the composite sound of the vowels is certainly obtained from experience; and yet we get the auditory-impression of the vowel sound by combining the individual tones of tuning forks (as I have demonstrated) and grasp the sound in its entirety, although in this instance we know that it is really compound.

Here we still have to explain how experience counteracts experience, and how illusion can be produced by factors derived from experience, when it might seem as if experience could not teach anything except what was true. In this matter we must remember, as was intimated above, that the sensations are interpreted just as they arise when they are stimulated in the normal way, and when the organ of sense is used normally.

We are not simply passive to the impressions that are urged on us, but we *observe*, that is, we adjust our organs in those conditions that enable them to distinguish the impressions most accurately. Thus, in considering an involved object, we accommodate both eyes as well as we can, and turn them so as to focus steadily the precise point on which our attention is fixed, that is, so as to get an image of it in the fovea of each eye; and then we let our eyes traverse all the noteworthy points of the object one after another. If we are interested in the general shape of the object and are trying to get as good an idea as we can of its relative dimensions, we assume a position such that, without having to turn the head, we can survey the whole surface, enabling us at the same time to view as symmetrically as possible those dimensions we wish to compare. Thus, in looking at an object, as, for example, a building with prominent horizontal and vertical lines, we like to stand opposite to it with the centres of rotation of the two eyes in a horizontal line. This position of the eyes can be controlled at any moment by separating the double images; which in the case mentioned here are in the same horizontal plane.

Unquestionably, our reason for choosing this definite mode of seeing is because in this way we can observe and compare most accurately; and, consequently, in this so-called *normal* use of the eyes we learn best how to compare our sensations with the reality. And so we obtain also the most correct and most accurate perceptions by this method.

But if, from necessity or on purpose, we employ a different mode of looking at objects, that is, if we view them merely indirectly or without focusing both eyes on them, or without surveying them all over, or if we hold the head in some unusual position, then we shall not be able to have as accurate apperceptions as when the eyes are used in the normal fashion. Nor are we so well trained in interpreting what we see under such circumstances as in the other case. Hence there is more scope for interpretation, although, as a rule, we are not clearly aware of this uncertainty in the explanation of our sense-perceptions. When we see an object in front of us, we are obliged to assign it to some definite place in space. We cannot think of it as having some dubious intermediate position between two different places in space. Without any recollections coming to our aid, we are wont to interpret the phenomenon as it would have to be interpreted if we had received the same impression in the normal and most accurate mode of observation. Thus certain illusions enter into the perception, unless we concentrate our eyes on the objects under observation, or when the objects are in the peripheral part of the visual field, or if the head is held to one side, or if we do not focus the object with both eyes at once. Moreover, the agreement between the images on the two retinas is most constant and regular in looking at distant objects. The fact that the horizontal floor usually happens to be in the lower part of the visual field, apparently influences the comparison of the fields of the two eyes in a peculiar manner. Thus, our judgment as to the position of near objects is not entirely correct when we observe them with the look tilted decidedly up or down. The retinal images presented in this way are interpreted just as if they had been obtained by looking straight ahead. We run across many illustrations of this sort. Our training in interpreting immediate perceptions is not equally good in all directions of the eyes, but simply for those directions which enable us to have the most accurate and most consistent perceptions.

We transfer the latter to all cases, as in the instances just cited.

Now it is quite possible that the similarity between a visual impression of this kind and one of the possible impressions obtained by normal observation may not be so overwhelming and striking as to preclude many other comparisons and corresponding interpretations of that impression. In such cases the explanation of the impression varies. Without any change of the retinal images, the same observer may see in front of him various perceptual images in succession, in which case the variation is easy to recognize. Or else one observer may incline more toward one comparison and interpretation, and another toward another. This has been a source of much controversy in physiological optics, because each observer has been disposed to consider the apperception which he obtained by the most careful observation he could make as being the only valid one. But supposing that we have such confidence in the observers as to assume that their observations were careful and unprejudiced, and that they knew how to make them, it would not be proper in such cases to adopt one of the conflicting interpretations of the visual phenomenon as being the only correct one. And yet that is what they are disposed to do who try to derive the origin of perceptual images mainly from innate factors. The truth rather is, that in a case of this sort various perceptual images may be developed; and we should seek rather to discover what circumstances are responsible for the decision one way or the other.

It is true we meet with a difficulty here that does not exist in the other parts of the natural sciences. In many instances we have simply the assertions of individual observers, without being in the position to verify them by our own observation. Many idiosyncrasies are manifested in this region, some of which are doubtless due to the structure of the eyes, others to the habitual way of using the eyes, and others still perhaps to previous impressions and apperceptions. Of course, nobody save the person who has peculiarities of this nature can observe their effects, and nobody else can give an opinion about them. On the other hand, observation in this region is by no means so easy as might be supposed at first. Steady fixation of a point for a long time while observations are being made in indirect vision; controlling the attention; taking the mind away from the ordinary objective interpretation of sense-impression; estimation of difference of colour and of difference of space in the visual field—all these things take much practice. And hence a number of facts in this region cannot be observed at all without having had previous long training in making observations in physiological optics. It cannot be done even by persons who are skilled in making other kinds of observations. Thus, with respect to many matters we have to depend on the observations of a very limited number of individuals, and hence when the results found by somebody else are different, it is much harder in this subject than anywhere else to judge rightly whether secondary influences have not contributed in an observation of this sort. Accordingly, I must apprise the reader in advance that much of the material that is perhaps new in the following chapters may possibly be due to individual peculiarities of my own eyes. Under such circumstances, there was no alternative for me except to observe as carefully as possible the facts as they appeared to my own eyes, and to try to ascertain their connection. Discrepancies that have been found by other observers have been noted. But how widespread this or the other mode of vision may be, is something that has to be left to the future to determine.

Incidentally, the more the visual impressions are unlike the normal ones, the greater will be the variety of interpretation as a rule. This is a natural consequence of the view which I hold, and is an essential characteristic of the activity of psychic influences.

Heretofore practically nothing has been ascertained as to the nature of psychic processes. We have simply an array of facts. Therefore, it is not strange that no real explanation can be given of the origin of sense-perceptions. The *empirical theory* attempts to prove that at least no other forces are necessary for their origin beyond the known faculties of the mind, although these forces themselves may remain entirely unexplained. Now generally it is a useful rule in scientific investigation not to make any new hypothesis so long as known facts seem adequate for the explanation, and the necessity of new assumptions has not been demonstrated. That is why I have thought it incumbent to prefer the empirical view essentially. Still less does the *intuition theory* attempt to give any explanation of the origin of our perceptual images; for it simply plunges right into the midst of the

matter by assuming that certain perceptual images of space would be produced directly by an innate mechanism, provided certain nerve fibres were stimulated. The earlier forms of this theory implied some sort of self-observation of the retina; inasmuch as we were supposed to know by intuition about the form of this membrane and the positions of the separate nerve terminals in it. In its more recent development, especially as formulated by E. Hering, there is an hypothetical subjective visual space, wherein the sensations of the separate nerve fibres are supposed to be registered according to certain intuitive laws. Thus in this theory not only is Kant's assertion adopted, that the general apperception of space is an original form of our imagination, but certain special apperceptions of space are assumed to be intuitive.

The naturalistic view has been called also a special *theory of identity*, because in it the perfect fusion of the impressions on the corresponding places of the two retinas has to be postulated. On the other hand, the *empirical* theory is spoken of as a *theory of projection*,[6] because according to it the perceptual images of objects are projected in space by means of psychic processes. I should like to avoid this term, because both supporters and opponents of this view have often attached undue importance to the idea that this projection must take place parallel to the lines of direction; which was certainly not the correct description of the psychic process. And, even if this construction were admitted as being valid simply with respect to the physiological description of the process, the idea would be incorrect in very many instances.

I am aware that in the present state of knowledge it is impossible to refute the intuition theory. The reasons why I prefer the opposite view are because in my opinion:

1. The intuition theory is an unnecessary hypothesis.
2. Its consequences thus far invariably apply to perceptual images of space which only in the fewest cases are in accordance with reality and with the correct visual images that are undoubtedly present; as will be shown in detail later. The adherents of this theory are, therefore, obliged to make the very questionable assumption, that the *space sensations*, which accord-

---

[6]See remarks in Appendix I as to misunderstandings connected with the term "projection theory."—K.

ing to them are present originally, are continually being improved and overruled by knowledge which we have accumulated by experience. By analogy with all other experiences, however, we should have to expect that the sensations which have been overruled continued to be present in the apperception as a conscious illusion, if nothing else. But this is not the case.

3. It is not clear how the assumption of these original "*space sensations*" can help the explanation of our visual perceptions, when the adherents of this theory ultimately have to assume in by far the great majority of cases that these sensations must be overruled by the better understanding which we get by experience. In that case it would seem to me much easier and simpler to grasp, that all apperceptions of space were obtained simply by experience, instead of supposing that the latter have to contend against intuitive perceptual images that are generally false.

This is by way of justifying my point of view. A choice had to be made simply for the sake of getting at least some sort of superficial order amid the chaos of phenomena; and so I believed I had to adopt the view I have chosen. However, I trust it has not affected the correct observation and description of the facts.

To prevent misunderstandings as to my meaning, and to make it clearer to the natural intelligence of those readers who have never thought much about their sense-perceptions, the following explanations will be added.

Thus far the sensations have been described as being simply *symbols* for the relations in the external world. They have been denied every kind of similarity or equivalence to the things they denote. Here we touch on the much disputed point as to how far our ideas agree in the main with their objects; that is, whether they are true or false, as one might say. Some have asserted that there is such an agreement, and others have denied it. In favour of it, a *pre-established harmony* between nature and mind was assumed. Or it was maintained that there was an *identity* of nature and mind, by regarding nature as the product of the activity of a general mind; the human mind being supposed to be an emanation from it. The *intuition theory* of space-apperceptions is connected with these views to the fact that, by some innate mechanism and a certain pre-established harmony, it admits of the origin of perceptual images that are supposed to correspond with reality, although in a rather imperfect fashion.

Or else the agreement between ideas and their objects was denied, the ideas being explained therefore as illusions. Consequently, it was necessary to deny also the possibility of all knowledge of any objects whatsoever. This was the attitude of certain so-called "sensational" philosophers in England in the eighteenth century. However, it is not my purpose here to undertake an analysis of the opinions of the various philosophical schools on this question. That would be much too extensive a task in this place. I shall confine myself therefore merely to inquiring what I think should be the attitude of an investigator toward these controversies.

Our apperceptions and ideas are *effects* wrought on our nervous system and our consciousness by the objects that are thus apprehended and conceived. Each effect, as to its nature, quite necessarily depends both on the nature of what causes the effect and on that of the person on whom the effect is produced. To expect to obtain an idea which would reproduce the nature of the thing conceived, that is, which would be true in an absolute sense, would mean to expect an effect which would be perfectly independent of the nature of the thing on which the effect was produced; which would be an obvious absurdity. Our human ideas, therefore, and all ideas of any conceivable intelligent creature, must be images of objects whose mode is essentially codependent on the nature of the consciousness which has the idea, and is conditioned also by its idiosyncrasies.

In my opinion, therefore, there can be no possible sense in speaking of any other truth of our ideas except of a *practical* truth. Our ideas of things *cannot* be anything but symbols, natural signs for things which we learn how to use in order to regulate our movements and actions. Having learned correctly how to read those symbols, we are enabled by their help to adjust our actions so as to bring about the desired result; that is, so that the expected new sensations will arise. Not only is there *in reality* no other comparison at all between ideas and things—all the schools are agreed about this—but any other mode of comparison is entirely *unthinkable* and has no sense whatever. This latter consideration is the conclusive thing, and must be grasped in order to escape from the labyrinth of conflicting opinions. To ask whether the idea I have of a table, its form, strength, colour, weight, etc., is true per se, apart from any practical use I can make of this idea, and whether it corresponds with the real thing, or is false and due to an illusion, has just as much sense as to ask whether a certain musical note is red, yellow, or blue. Idea and the thing conceived evidently belong to two entirely different worlds, which no more admit of being compared with each other than colours and musical tones or than the letters of a book and the sound of the word they denote.

Were there any sort of similarity of correspondence between the idea in the head of a person *A* and the thing to which the idea belongs, another intelligent person *B*, conceiving both the thing itself and *A*'s idea of it, according to the same laws, might be able to find some similarity between them or at least to suppose so; because the same sort of thing represented (conceived) in the same way would have to give the same kinds of images (ideas). Now I ask, what similarity can be imagined between the process in the brain that is concomitant with the idea of a table and the table itself? Is the form of the table to be supposed to be outlined by electric currents? And when the person with the idea has the idea that he is walking around the table, must the person then be outlined by electric currents? Perspective projections of the external world in the hemispheres of the brain (as they are supposed to be) are evidently not sufficient for representing the idea of a bodily object. And granted that a keen imagination is not frightened away by these and similar hypotheses, such an electrical reproduction of the table in the brain would be simply another bodily object to be perceived, but no idea of the table. However, it is not simply persons with materialistic opinions who try to refute the proposed statement, but also persons with idealistic views. And for the latter I should think the argument would be still more forcible. What possible similarity can there be between the idea, some modification of the incorporeal mind that has no extension in space, and the body of the table that occupies space? As far as I am aware, the idealistic philosophers have never once investigated even a single hypothesis or imagination in order to show this connection. And by the very nature of this view it is something that cannot be investigated at all.

In the next place as to the *properties* of objects in the external world, a little reflection reveals that all properties attributable to them may be said to be simply *effects* exerted by them either on our senses or on other natural objects. Colour, sound, taste, smell, temperature, smoothness, and firmness are properties of the first sort, and denote effects on our organs of sense. Smoothness and firmness denote the degree of resistance either to the gliding contact or pressure of the hand. But other natural bodies may be employed instead of the hand. And the same thing is true in testing other mechanical properties such as elasticity and weight. Chemical properties are described by certain reactions, that is, by effects exerted by one natural body on others. It is the same way with any other physical property of a body, optical, electrical, or magnetic. In every case we have to do with the mutual relations between various bodies and with the effects depending on the forces that different bodies exert on each other. For all natural forces are such as are exerted by one body on others. When we try to think of mere matter without force, it is void of properties likewise, except as to its different distribution in space and as to its motion. All properties of bodies in nature are manifested therefore simply by being so situated as to interact with other bodies of nature or with our organs of sense. But as such interaction may occur at any time, particularly too as it may be produced by us voluntarily at any moment, and as then we see invariably the peculiar sort of interaction occurring, we attribute to the objects a permanent capacity for such effects which is always ready to become effective. This permanent capacity is a so-called characteristic *property*.

The result is that in point of fact the characteristic *properties* of natural objects, in spite of this name, do not denote something that is peculiar to the individual object by itself, but invariably imply some relation to a second object (including our organs of sense). The kind of effect must, of course, depend always on the peculiarities both of the body producing it and of the body on which it is produced. As to this there is never any doubt even for an instant, provided we have in mind those properties of bodies that are manifested when two bodies belonging to the external world react on each other, as in the case of chemical reactions. But in the case of properties depending on the mutual relations between things and our organs of sense, people have always been disposed to forget that here too we are concerned with the reaction toward a special reagent, namely, our own nervous system; and that colour, smell, and taste, and feeling of warmth or cold are also effects quite essentially depending on the nature of the organ that is affected. Doubtless, the reactions of natural objects to our senses are those that are most frequently and most generally perceived. For both our welfare and convenience they are of the most powerful importance. The reagent by which we have to test them is something we are endowed with by nature, but that does not make any difference in the connection.

Hence there is no sense in asking whether vermilion as we see it, is really red, or whether this is simply an illusion of the senses. The sensation of red is the normal reaction of normally formed eyes to light reflected from vermilion. A person who is red-blind will see vermilion as black or as a dark grey-yellow. This too is the correct reaction for an eye formed in the special way his is. All he has to know is that his eye is simply formed differently from that of other persons. In itself the one sensation is not more correct and not more false than the other, although those who call this substance red are in the large majority. In general, the red colour of vermilion exists merely in so far as there are eyes which are constructed like those of most people. Persons who are red-blind have just as much right to consider that a characteristic property of vermilion is that of being black. As a matter of fact, we should not speak of the light reflected from vermilion as being red, because it is not red except for certain types of eyes. When we speak of the properties of bodies with reference to other bodies in the external world, we do not neglect to name also the body with respect to which the property exists. Thus we say that lead is soluble in nitric acid, but not in sulphuric acid. Were we to say simply that lead is soluble, we should notice at once that the statement is incomplete, and the question would have to be asked immediately, Soluble in what? But when we say that vermilion is red, it is implicitly understood that it is red for our eyes and for other people's eyes supposed to be made like ours. We think this does not need to be mentioned, and so we neglect to do so, and can be misled into thinking that red is a property belonging to vermilion or to the light reflected from it, entirely independently of our organs of sense. The statement that the waves of light reflected from vermilion have a certain length is something different. That is true entirely without reference to the special nature of our eye. Then we are thinking simply of relations that exist between the substance and the various systems of waves in the aether.

The only respect in which there can be a real agreement between our perceptions and the reality is the time-sequence of the events with their various peculiarities. Simultaneity, sequence, the regular recurrence of simultaneity or sequence, may occur likewise in the sensations as well as in the events. The external events, like their perceptions, proceed in time; and so the temporal relations of the latter may be the faithful reproduction of the temporal relations of the former. The sensation of thunder in the ear succeeds the sensation of lightning in the eye, just in the same way as the sound vibrations in the air due to the electrical discharge reach the place where the observer is later than the vibrations of the luminiferous aether. Yet here it certainly should be noted that the time-sequence of the sensations is not quite a faithful reproduction of the time-sequence of the external events, inasmuch as the transmission from the organs of sense to the brain takes time, and in fact a different time for different organs. Moreover, in case of the eye and the ear, the time has to be added that it takes light and sound to reach the organ. Thus at present we see the fixed stars as they were various long periods of years ago.

As to the representation of space-relations, there certainly is something of this sort in the peripheral nerve terminals in the eye and to a certain extent in the tactile skin, but still only in a limited way; for the eye gives only perspective surface-images, and the hand reproduces the objective area on the surface of a body by shaping itself to it as congruently as possible. A direct image of a portion of space of three dimensions is not afforded either by the eye or by the hand. It is only by comparing the images in the two eyes, or by moving the body with respect to the hand, that the idea of solid bodies is obtained. Now since the brain itself has three dimensions, of course, there is still another conceivable possibility, and that is to fancy by what mechanism in the brain itself images of three dimensions can arise from external objects in space. But I cannot see any necessity for such an assumption nor even any probability for it. The idea of a body in space, of a table, for instance, involves a quantity of separate observations. It comprises the whole series of images which this table would present to me in looking at it from different sides and at different distances; besides the whole series of tactile impressions that would be obtained by touching the surface at various places in succession. Such an idea of a single individual body is, therefore, in fact a *conception* (*Begriff*) which grasps and includes an infinite number of single, successive apperceptions, that can all be deduced from it; just as the species "table" includes all individual tables and expresses their common peculiarities. The idea of a single individual table which I carry in my mind is correct and exact, provided I can deduce from it correctly the precise sensations I shall have when my eye and my hand are brought into this or that definite relation with respect to the table. Any other sort of similarity between such an idea and the body about which the idea exists, I do not know how to conceive. One is the mental symbol of the other. The kind of symbol was not chosen by me arbitrarily, but was forced on me by the nature of my organ of sense and of my mind. This is what distinguishes this sign-language of our ideas from the arbitrary phonetic signs and alphabetical characters that we use in speaking and writing. A writing is correct when he who knows how to read it forms correct ideas by it. And so the idea of a thing is correct for him who knows how to determine correctly from it in advance what sense-impressions he will get from the thing when he places himself in definite external relations to it. Incidentally, it does not matter at all what sort of mental symbols we employ, provided they constitute a sufficiently varied and ordered system. Nor does it matter either how the words of a language sound, provided there are enough of them, with sufficient means of denoting their grammatical relations to one another.

On this view of the matter, we must be on our guard against saying that all our ideas of things are consequently *false*, because they are not *equal* to the things themselves, and that hence we are not able to know anything as to the *true nature* of things. That they cannot be equal to things, is in the nature of knowledge. Ideas are merely pictures of things. Every image is the image of a thing merely for him who knows how to read it, and who is enabled by the aid of the image to form an idea of the thing. Every image is similar to its object in one respect, and dissimilar in all others, whether it be a painting, a statue, the musical or dramatic representation of a mental mood, etc. Thus the ideas of the external world are images of the regular sequence of natural events, and if they are formed correctly according to the laws of our thinking, and we are able by our actions to translate them back into reality again, the ideas we have are also the *only true* ones for our mental capacity. All others would be false.

In my opinion, it is a mistake, therefore, to try to find preestablished harmony between the laws of thought and those of nature, an identity between nature and mind, or whatever we may call it. A system of signs may be more or less perfect and convenient. Accordingly, it will be more or less easy to employ, more exact in denoting or more inexact, just as is the case with different languages. But otherwise each system can be adapted to the case more or less well. If there were not a number of similar natural objects in the world, our faculty of forming shades of conception would indeed not be of any use to us. Were there no solid bodies, our geometrical faculties would necessarily remain undeveloped and unused, just as the physical eye would not be of any service to us in a world where there was no light. If in this sense anybody wishes to speak of an adaptation of our laws of mind to the laws of nature, there is no objection to it. Evidently, however, such adaptation does not have to be either perfect or exact. The eye is an extremely useful organ practically, although it cannot see distinctly at all distances, or perceive all sorts of aether vibrations, or concentrate exactly in one point all the rays that issue from a point. Our intellectual faculties are connected with the activities of a material organ, namely the brain, just as the faculty of vision is connected with the eye. Human intelligence is wonderfully effective in the world, and brings it under a strict law of causation. Whether it necessarily must be able to control whatever is in the world or can happen—I can see no guarantee for that.

We must speak now of the manner in which our ideas and perceptions are formed by inductive conclusions. The best analysis of the nature of our conclusions I find in J. S. Mill's Logic. As long as the premise of the conclusion is not an injunction imposed by outside authority for our conduct and belief, but a statement related to reality, which can therefore be only the result of experience, the conclusion, as a matter of fact, does not tell us anything new or something that we did not know already before we made the statement. Thus, for example:

Major: All men are mortal.
Minor: Caius is a man.
Conclusion: Caius is mortal.

The major premise, that all men are mortal, which is a statement of experience, we should scarcely venture to assert without knowing beforehand whether the conclusion is correct, namely, that Caius, who is a man, either is dead or will die. Thus we must be sure of the conclusion before we can state the major premise by which we intend to prove it. That seems to be proceeding in a circle. The real relation evidently is, that, in common with other folks, we have observed heretofore without exception that no person has ever survived beyond a certain age. Observers have learned by experience that Lucius, Flavius and other individuals of their acquaintance, no matter what their names are, have all died; and they have embraced this experience in the general statement, that *all* men die. Inasmuch as this final result occurred regularly in all the instances they observed, they have felt justified in explaining this general law as being valid also for all those cases which might come up for observation hereafter. Thus we preserve in our memory the store of experiences heretofore accumulated on this subject by ourselves and others in the form of the general statement which constitutes the major premise of the above conclusion.

However, the conviction that Caius would die might obviously have been reached directly also without formulating the general statement in our consciousness, by having compared his case with all those which we knew previously. Indeed, this is the more usual and original method of reasoning by induction. Conclusions of this sort are reached without conscious reflection, because in our memory the same sort of thing in cases previously observed unites and reinforces them; as is shown especially in those cases of inductive reasoning where we cannot succeed in deducing from previous experiences a rule with precisely defined limits to its validity and without any exceptions. This is the case in all complicated processes. For instance, from analogy with previous similar cases, we can sometimes predict with tolerable certainty what one of our acquaintances will do, if under certain circumstances he decides to go into business; because we know his character and that he is, let us say, ambitious or timid. We may not be able to say exactly how we have estimated the extent of his ambition or timidity, or why this ambition or timidity of his will be enough to decide that his business will turn out as we expect.

In the case of conclusions properly so-called, which are reached consciously, supposing they are not based on injunctions but on facts of experience, what we do, therefore, is really nothing more than deliberately and carefully to retrace those steps in the inductive generalizations of our experiences which were previously traversed more rapidly and without conscious reflection, either by ourselves or by other observers in whom we have confidence. But although nothing essentially new is added to our previous knowledge by formulating a general principle from our previous experiences, still it is useful in many respects. A definitely stated general principle is much easier to preserve in the memory and to be imparted to others than to have to do this same thing with every individual case as it arises. In formulating it we are led to test accurately every new case that occurs, with reference to the correctness of the generalization. In this way every exception will be impressed on us twice as forcibly. The limits of its validity will be recalled much sooner when we have the principle before us in its general form, instead of having to go over each separate case. By this sort of conscious formulation of inductive reasoning, there is much gain in the convenience and certainty of the process; but nothing essentially new is added that did not exist already in the conclusions which were reached by analogy without reflection. It is by means of these latter that we judge the character of a person from his countenance and movements, or predict what he will do in a given situation from a knowledge of his character.

Now we have exactly the same case in our sense-perceptions. When those nervous mechanisms whose terminals lie on the right-hand portions of the retinas of the two eyes have been stimulated, our usual experience, repeated a million times all through life, has been that a luminous object was over there in front of us on our left. We had to lift the hand toward the left to hide the light or to grasp the luminous object; or we had to move toward the left to get closer to it. Thus while in these cases no particular conscious conclusion may be present, yet the essential and original office of such a conclusion has been performed, and the result of it has been attained; simply, of course, by the unconscious processes of association of ideas going on in the dark background of our memory. Thus too its results are urged on our consciousness, so to speak, as if an external power had constrained us, over which our will has no control.

These inductive conclusions leading to the formation of our sense-perceptions certainly do lack the purifying and scrutinizing work of conscious thinking. Nevertheless, in my opinion, by their peculiar nature they may be classed as *conclusions*, inductive conclusions unconsciously formed.

There is one circumstance quite characteristic of these conclusions which operates against their being admitted in the realm of conscious thinking and against their being formulated in the normal form of logical conclusions. This is that we are not able to specify more closely what has taken place in us when we have experienced a sensation in a definite nerve fibre, and how it differs from corresponding sensations in other nerve fibres. Thus, suppose we have had a sensation of light in certain fibres of the nervous mechanism of vision. All we know is that we have had a sensation of a peculiar sort which is different from all other sensations, and also from all other visual sensations, and that whenever it occurred, we invariably noticed a luminous object on the left. Naturally, without ever having studied physiology, this is all we can say about the sensation, and even for our own imagination we cannot localize or grasp the sensation except by specifying it in terms of the conditions of its occurrence. I have to say, "I see something bright there on my left." That is the only way I can describe the sensation. After we have pursued scientific studies, we begin to learn that we have nerves, that these nerves have been stimulated, and that their terminals in fact lie on the right-hand side of the retina. Then for the first time we are in a position to define this mode of sensation independently of the mode in which it is ordinarily produced.

It is the same way with most sensations. The sensations of taste and smell usually cannot be described even as to their quality except in terms of the bodies responsible for them; although we do have a few rather vague and more general expressions like "sweet," "sour," "bitter" and "sharp."

These judgments, in which our sensations in our ordinary state of consciousness are connected with the existence of an external cause, can never once be elevated to the plane of conscious judgments. The inference that there is a luminous object on my left, because the nerve terminals on the right-hand side of my retina are in a state of stimulation, can only be expressed by one who knows nothing about the inner structure of the eye by saying, "There is something bright over there on my left, because I see it there." And accordingly from the standpoint of everyday experience, the only way of expressing the experience I have when the nerve terminals on the right-hand side of my eyeball are stimulated by exerting pressure there, is by saying, "When I press my eye on the right-hand side, I see a bright glow on the left." There is no other way of describing the sensation and of identifying it with other previous sensations except by designating the place where the corresponding external object appears to be. Hence, therefore, these cases of experience have the peculiarity that the connection between the sensation and an external object can never be expressed without anticipating it already in the designation of the sensation, and without presupposing the very thing we are trying to describe.

Even when we have learned to understand the physiological origin and connection of the illusions of the senses, it is impossible to get rid of the illusion in spite of our better knowledge. This is because inductive reasoning is the result of an unconscious and involuntary activity of the memory; and for this very reason it strikes our consciousness as a foreign and overpowering force of nature. Incidentally, manifold analogies for it are to be found in all other possible modes of *apparition*. We might say that all apparition originates in premature, unmeditated inductions, where from previous cases conclusions are deduced as to new ones, and where the tendency to abide by the false conclusions persists in spite of the better insight into the matter based on conscious deliberation. Every evening apparently before our eyes the sun goes down behind the stationary horizon, although we are well aware that the sun is fixed and the horizon moves. An actor who cleverly portrays an old man is for us an old man there on the stage, so long as we let the immediate impression sway us, and do not forcibly recall that the programme states that the person moving about there is the young actor with whom we are acquainted. We consider him as being angry or in pain according as he shows us one or the other mode of countenance and demeanour. He arouses fright or sympathy in us, we tremble for the moment, which we see approaching, when he will perform or suffer something dreadful; and the deep-seated conviction that all this is only show and play does not hinder our emotions at all, provided the actor does not cease to play his part. On the contrary, a fictitious tale of this sort, which we seem to enter into ourselves, grips and tortures us more than a similar true story would do when we read it in a dry documentary report.

The experiences we have that certain aspects, demeanours and modes of speech are indicative of fierce anger, are generally experiences concerning the external signs of certain emotions and peculiarities of character which the actor can portray for us. But they are not nearly so numerous and regular in recurrence as those experiences by which we have ascertained that certain sensations correspond with certain external objects. And so we need not be surprised if the idea of an object which is ordinarily associated with a sensation does not vanish, even when we know that in this particular instance there is no such object.

Finally, the tests we employ by voluntary movements of the body are of the greatest importance in strengthening our conviction of the correctness of the perceptions of our senses. And thus, as contrasted with purely passive observations, the same sort of firmer conviction arises as is derived by the process of experiment in scientific investigations. The peculiar ultimate basis, which gives convincing power to all our conscious inductions, is the law of causation. If two natural phenomena have frequently been observed to occur together, such as thunder and lightning, they seem to be regularly connected together, and we infer that there must be a common basis for both of them. And if this causal connection has invariably acted heretofore, so that thunder and lightning accompany each other, then in the future too like causes must produce like effects, and the result must be the same in the future. However, so long as we are limited to mere observations of such phenomena as occur by themselves without our help, and without our being able to make experiments so as to vary the complexity of causes, it is difficult to be sure that we have really ascertained all the factors that may have some influence on the result. There must be an enormous variety of cases where the law is obeyed, and the law must define the result with great precision, if we are to be satisfied with a case of mere observation. This is the case with the motions of the planetary system. Of course, we cannot experiment with the planets, but the theory of universal gravitation as propounded by Newton gives such a complete and exact explanation of the comparatively complicated apparent motions of the heavenly bodies, that we no longer hesitate about considering it as being sufficiently proved. And yet there are Reich's experiments on the gravitational attraction of lead balls, Foucault's experiment on the deviation of the plane of vibration of a pendulum in consequence of the earth's rotation, and the experimental determinations of the velocity of light in traversing terrestrial distances as made by Foucault and Fizeau, that are of the utmost value in strengthening our conviction experimentally also.

Probably there is no event of pure observation that has been found to be so unexceptionally correct as the general statement previously used by way of illustration, namely, that all human beings die before they have passed a certain age. In many millions of human beings not a single exception has been found. If one had occurred, we might assume that we should have heard of it. Among those who have died there are individuals who have lived in the most varied climates and on the most various kinds of nourishment, besides having been engaged in the most diverse occupations. Nevertheless, the statement that all men are bound to die, cannot be said to have the same degree of certainty as any law of physics whose consequences have been precisely compared experimentally with experience in manifold modifications. I do not know the causal connection for the death of human beings. I cannot state the causes that inevitably entail old age, in case life has not been terminated sooner by some rougher external injury. I have not been able to verify by experiments that when I allow those causes to operate, old age inevitably occurs, and that it does not occur when I remove those causes of its occurrence. Anyone who tells me that the life of man can be indefinitely prolonged by employing certain means may be treated, of course, with the utmost incredulity, but he cannot be positively contradicted without knowing certainly that individuals have actually lived in the circumstances he describes, and yet have ultimately perished. On the other hand, when I assert that all liquid mercury will expand when it is heated, if it is free to do so, I know that whenever I have observed the two together, not only higher temperature and expansion of mercury were due to the action of an unknown common third cause, as I might have supposed from pure observation alone, but I know by experiment that the heat by itself was enough to cause the expansion of the mercury. At various times I have often heated mercury. I have deliberately selected the moment when I wished the experiment to begin. If therefore the mercury expanded under these circumstances, the expansion must have been dependent on those conditions that I produced in the experiment. Consequently, I know that the heating by itself was a sufficient cause for the expansion, and that no other latent influences were needed to bring about this result. By comparatively few carefully executed experiments we are enabled to establish the causal conditions of an event with more certainty than can be done by a million observations where we have not been able to vary the conditions as we please. For instance, if I had merely seen mercury expand in a thermometer which was inaccessible to me, and in a place where the air was saturated with moisture at all temperatures, I should have to inquire whether mercury expands on account of heat or on account of the moisture. The only way to determine this would be by experiment, and by finding out whether the volume of mercury changes with change of humidity, when the temperature is kept constant, or with change of temperature, when the humidity is kept constant.

The same great importance which experiment has for the certainty of our scientific convictions, it has also for the unconscious inductions of the perceptions of our senses. It is only by voluntarily bringing our organs of sense in various relations to the objects that we learn to be sure as to our judgments of the causes of our sensations. This kind of experimentation begins in earliest youth and continues all through life without interruption.

If the objects had simply been passed in review before our eyes by some foreign force without our being able to do anything about them, probably we should never have found our way about amid such an optical phantasmagoria; any more than mankind could interpret the apparent motions of the planets in the firmament before the laws of perspective vision could be applied to them. But when we notice that we can get various images of a table in front of us simply by changing our position; and that we can sometimes have one view and sometimes another, just as we like at any time, by a suitable change of position; and that the table may vanish from sight, and then be there again at any moment we like, simply by turning the eyes toward it; we get the conviction based on experiment, that our movements are responsible for the different views of the table, and that whether we see it just at this moment or do not see it, still we can see it whenever we like. Thus by our movements we find out that it is the stationary form of

the table in space which is the cause of the changing image in our eyes. We explain the table as having existence independent of our observation, because at *any moment we like*, simply by assuming the proper position with respect to it, we can observe it.

The essential thing in this process is just this principle of experimentation. Spontaneously and by our own power, we vary some of the conditions under which the object has been perceived. We know that the changes thus produced in the way that objects look depend solely on the movements we have executed. Thus we obtain a different series of apperceptions of the same object, by which we can be convinced with experimental certainty that they are simply apperceptions, and that it is the common cause of them all. In fact we see children also experimenting with objects in this way. They turn them constantly round and round, and touch them with the hands and the mouth, doing the same things over and over again day after day with the same objects, until their forms are impressed on them; in other words, until they get the various visual and tactile impressions made by observing and feeling the same object on various sides.

In this sort of experimentation with objects some of the changes in the sense-impressions are found to be due to our own will; whereas others, that is, all that depend on the nature of the object directly before us, are urged upon us by a necessity which we cannot alter as we like, and which we feel most when it arouses disagreeable sensations or pain. Thus we come to recognize something independent of our will and imagination, that is, an external cause of our sensations. This is shown by its persisting independently of our instantaneous perception; because at any moment we like, by suitable manipulations and movements, we can cause to recur each one of the series of sensations that can be produced in us by this external cause. Thus this latter is recognized as an object existing independently of our perception.

The idea and the cause here combine, and it is a question whether we have a right to assume this cause in the original perception of the senses. Here again the difficulty is that we are not able to describe the processes except in the language of metaphysics, whereas the reflection of the consciousness in itself is not yet distinctly contained in the original form of the conscious perception. Natural consciousness, which is entirely absorbed in the interest of observing the external world, and has little inducement to direct its attention to the Ego that appears always the same amid the multicoloured variations of outside objects, is not in the habit of noticing that the *properties* of the objects that are seen and touched are their effects, partly on other natural bodies, but mainly on our senses. Now as our nervous system and our sensation-faculty, as being the constant reagent on which the effect is exerted, is thus left out of account entirely, and as the difference of the effect is regarded as being simply a difference in the object from which it proceeds, the effect can no longer be recognized as an effect (for every effect must be the effect on something else), and so comes to be considered objectively as being a property of the body and merely as belonging to it. And then as soon as we recall that we perceive these properties, our impression, consequently, seems to us to be a pure image of the external state of affairs reflecting only that external condition and depending solely on it.

But if we ponder over the basis of this process, it is obvious that we can never emerge from the world of our sensations to the apperception of an external world, except by inferring from the changing sensation that external objects are the causes of this change. Once the idea of external objects has been formed, we may not be concerned any more as to how we got this idea, especially because the inference appears to be so self-evident that we are not conscious of its being a new result.

Accordingly, the law of causation, by virtue of which we infer the cause from the effect, has to be considered also as being a law of our thinking which is prior to all experience. Generally, we can get no experience from natural objects unless the law of causation is already active in us. Therefore, it cannot be deduced first from experiences which we have had with natural objects.

This statement has been made in many ways. The law of causation was supposed to be a law of nature arrived at by induction. Recently it has been again interpreted in that way by J. S. Mill. He has even suggested the possibility of its not being valid in other parts of the universe. As opposed to that view, I shall merely say, for what it is worth, that there is good reason to think that the empirical proof of the law is extremely doubtful. For the number of cases in which we think we can trace perfectly the causal connection between natural processes is small as compared with the number of those in which we are absolutely unable to do so at present. The former cases belong almost exclusively to inorganic nature. The cases that are not understood include the larger part of the phenomena of organic nature. In fact, by the evidence of our own consciousness, we positively assume both in beasts and in man a principle of free will, for which we claim most decidedly complete independence of the force of the law of causation. And in spite of all theoretical speculations as to possible mistakes about this conviction, I am of the opinion that our natural consciousness will hardly ever be free from it. Thus the case of conduct itself, which we know best and most accurately, we consider as being an exception to that law. Were therefore the law of causation a law of experience, its inductive proof would seem to be in a very bad shape. The best we could say is that it was not any more valid than rules of meteorology like the law of rotation of the wind, etc. Perhaps, we could not positively controvert the vitalistic physiologists who maintain that the law of causation is valid in inorganic nature; although in the organic world they relegate it to a lower sphere of action.

Finally, the law of causation bears on its face the character of a purely logical law, chiefly because the conclusions derived from it do not concern actual experience, but its interpretation. Hence it cannot be refuted by any possible experience.[7] For if we founder anywhere in applying the law of causation, we do not conclude that it is false, but simply that we do not yet completely understand the complex of causes mutually interacting in the given phenomenon. And when at length we have succeeded in explaining certain natural processes by the law of causation, the conclusions we derive from it are that certain masses of matter exist and move in space and act on each other with certain motive forces. But the conception of both matter and force are entirely abstract in nature, as is shown by their attributes. Matter without force[8] is assumed to exist only in space, but not to act or to have any properties. Thus it would be of no importance whatever for all other affairs in the world

---

[7] Helmholtz, *Über das Sehen des Menschen, ein populär wissenschaftlicher Vortrag*. Leipzig 1855.

[8] The word *force* (*Kraft*) appears to be used here in the sense of energy; and in the same sense as it was used in the author's famous paper *Über die Erhaltung der Kraft*, read before the Physical Society of Berlin in 1847. (J.P.C.S.)

or for our perceptions. It would be practically non-existent. Force without matter is indeed said to act; but it cannot exist independently, for whatever exists is matter. Thus the two conceptions are inseparable; they are merely abstract modes of regarding the same objects of nature in various aspects. For that very reason neither matter nor force can be direct objects of observation, but are always merely the revealed causes of the facts of experience. Hence, if we conclude by proposing certain abstractions, which can never be objects of experience, as the final and sufficient bases of natural phenomena, how can we say that experience proves that the phenomena have sufficient bases?

The law of sufficient basis amounts simply to the requirement of wishing to understand everything. The process of our comprehension with respect to natural phenomena is that we try to find *generic notions* and *laws of nature.* Laws of nature are merely generic notions for the changes in nature. But since we have to assume the laws of nature as being valid and as acting independently of our observation and thinking, whereas as generic notions they would concern at first only the method of our thinking, we call them *causes* and *forces.* Hence, when we cannot trace natural phenomena to a law, and therefore cannot make the law objectively responsible as being the cause of the phenomena, the very possibility of comprehending such phenomena ceases.

However, we must try to comprehend them. There is no other method of bringing them under the control of the intellect. And so in investigating them we must proceed on the supposition that they are comprehensible. Accordingly, the law of sufficient reason is really nothing more than the *urge* of our intellect to bring all our perceptions under its own control. It is not a law of nature. Our intellect is the faculty of forming general conceptions. It has nothing to do with our sense-perceptions and experiences, unless it is able to form general conceptions or laws. These laws are then objectified and designated as causes. But if it is found that the natural phenomena are to be subsumed under a definite causal connection, this is certainly an objectively valid fact, and corresponds to special objective relations between natural phenomena, which we express in our thinking as being their causal connection, simply because we do not know how else to express it.

Just as it is the characteristic function of the eye to have light-sensations, so that we can *see* the world only as a *luminous phenomenon,* so likewise it is the characteristic function of the intellect to form general conceptions, that is, to search for causes; and hence it can *conceive (begreifen)* of the world only as being *causal* connection. We have other organs besides the eye for comprehending the external world, and thus we can feel or smell many things that we cannot see. Besides our intellect there is no other equally systematized faculty, at any rate for comprehending the external world. Thus if we are unable to *conceive* a thing, we cannot imagine it as existing.

The earlier history of the theory of the sense-perceptions is practically the same as the history of philosophy, as given at the end of §17. The investigations of the physiologists of the seventeenth and eighteenth centuries generally did not go beyond the image on the retina, for they supposed that when it was formed, everything was settled. Hence they were little troubled by the questions as to why we see objects erect and why we see them single, in spite of two inverted retinal images.

Among philosophers Descartes was the first to take any deep interest in visual perceptions as related to the knowledge of his time. He considered the qualities of sensation as being essentially subjective, but he regarded the ideas of the quantitative relations of size, form, motion, position, duration, number of objects, etc., as something that could be correctly perceived objectively. However, in order to explain the correctness of these ideas, he assumes, as the idealistic philosophers did who came after him, a system of *innate ideas* which are in harmony with the things. This theory was subsequently developed in its most logical and purest form by Leibnitz.

Berkeley made a profound study of the influence of memory on the perceptions and their concomitant inductive conclusions. He says concerning them that they take place so quickly that we are not aware of them unless we are deliberately on the watch for them. It is true, this empirical basis led him to assert that not only the qualities of sensation but the perceptions also were mainly merely internal processes having no correspondence with anything outside. What led him into making this false conclusion was the error contained in the proposition that the cause (the object perceived) must be of the same kind as its effect (the idea), that is, must be a mental entity also, and not a real object.

In his theory of the human understanding, Locke denied the existence of innate ideas and attempted to establish an empirical basis for all understanding; but this attempt ended in Hume's denying all possibility of objective knowledge.

The most essential step for putting the problem in its true light was taken by Kant in his *Critique of Pure Reason*, in which he derived all real content of knowledge from experience. But he made a distinction between this and whatever in the form of our apperceptions and ideas was conditioned by the peculiar ability of our mind. Pure thinking a priori can yield only formally correct propositions, which, while they may certainly appear to be absolutely binding as necessary laws of thought and imagination, are, however, of no real significance for actuality; and hence they can never enable us to form any conclusion about facts of possible experience.

According to this view perception is recognized as an effect produced on our sensitive faculty by the object perceived; this effect, in its minuter determinations, being just as dependent on what causes the effect as on the nature of that on which the effect is produced. This point of view was applied to the empirical relations especially by Joh. Müller in his theory of the Specific Energy of the Senses.[9]

The subsequent idealistic systems of philosophy associated with the names of J. G. Fichte, Schelling and Hegel all emphasized the theory that idea is essentially dependent on the nature of the mind; thus neglecting the influence which the thing causing the effect has on the effect. Consequently, their views have had slight influence on the theory of the sense-perceptions.

Kant had briefly represented space and time as given forms of all apperception, without going further and investigating how much might be derived from experience in the more minute formation of individual apperceptions of space and time. This investigation was outside of his special work. Thus, for example, he regarded the geometrical axioms as being propositions in space-apperception which were given to start with;— a view which is not at all settled yet.[10] His lead was followed by Joh. Müller and the group of physiologists who tried to develop the *intuition theory* of space-apperception. Joh. Müller himself assumed that the retina might "sense" itself in its space-extension by virtue of an innate ability for it, and that the sensations of the two retinas are fused together in this case. The one who has recently tried to carry out this view in its most logical form and to adapt it to newer discoveries is E. Hering.

Prior to Müller, Steinbuch had tried to explain individual apperceptions of space by means of the movements of the eye and of the body. Among the philosophers, Herbart, Lotze, Waitz and Cornelius attacked the same problem. From the empirical side, it was Wheatstone especially who, by inventing the stereoscope, gave a powerful incentive to the investigation of the influence of experience on our visual apperceptions. In addition to minor contributions which I myself have made to the solution of this problem in various works, attempts to give an *empirical* view may be found in the writings of Nagel, Wundt and Classen. In the succeeding chapters, more will be said with reference to these investigations and the points of controversy.

REFERENCES

1637. Cartesius, *Dioptrice*. See Tome V. of V. Cousin's edition of his Works.
1644. Cartesius, *Principia Philosophiae*, T. III.
1703. Leibnitz, *Nouveaux essais sur l'entendment humain*. See Vol. 1, p. 194 of his *Opera philos.* editied by Erdmann.
1709. Berkeley, *Theory of vision*. London.
1720. Locke, *Essay on the human understanding*.
    Hume, *Untersuchungen über den menschlichen Verstand*.
1787. J. Kant, *Kritik der reinen Vernunft*. 2. Aufl. Riga 1787.
1811. Steinbuch, *Beiträge zur Physiologie der Sinne*. Nürnberg.
1816. J. F. Herbart, *Lehrbuch zur Psychologie*. See Vol. V of his Works published by Hartenstein, Leipzig 1850.
1825. Herbart, Psychologie als Wissenschaft. *Sämtliche Werke*. Bd. VI.
1826. Joh. Müller, *Zur vergleichenden des Gesichtssinns*. Leipzig.
1849. Th. Waitz, *Lehrbuch der Psychologie als Naturwissenschafl*. Braunschweig.
1852. H. Lotze, *Medizinische Physiologie*. Leipzig.
1856. H. Lotze, *Mikrokosmus*. Leipzig.
1861. Cornelius, *Die Theorie des Sehens und räumlichen Vorstellens*. Halle.
    M. J. Schleiden, *Zur Theorie des Erkennens durch den Gesichtssinn*. Leipzig.
    A. Nagel, *Das Sehen mit zwei Augenund die Lehre von den identischen Netzhautstellen*. Leipzig u. Heidelberg.
1861–64. E. Hering, *Beiträge zur Physiologie*. Leipzig.
1862. W. Wundt, *Beiträge zur Theorie der Sinneswahrnehmung*. Leipzig u. Heidelberg. *Reprinted from the Zeitschrift für rationelle Medizin* 1858–1862.
1863. A. Classen, *Das Schlussverfahren des Sehaktes*. E. Rostock. Hering über Dr. A. Classens Beitrag zur physiologischen Optik. *Archiv für pathol. Anatomie und Physiologie*. VIII. 2. p. 179.
1864. C. S. Cornelius, *Zur Theorie des Sehens*. Halle.
    J. Dastich, *Über die neueren physiologisch-psychologischen Forschungen im Gebiete der menschlichen Sinne*. Prag.
1866. H. Ulrici, *Gott und der Mensch. I. Leib und Seele, Grundzüge einer Psychologie des Menschen*. Leipzig.

---

[9]See E. Minkowski, zur Müllerschen Lehre von spezifischen Sinnesenergien. *Zft. f. Sinnesphysiol.*, 45 (1911), 129–152. (J. P. C. S.)

[10]As is well known, Helmholtz subsequently defended the empirical value of the axioms of geometry with very much greater determination and in opposition to Kant. In another place we shall discuss more in detail the relation between apriority, as Kant intended, and Helmholtz's empiricism.— K.

Introduction to Reading 2

Psychophysics is the branch of psychology invented by Gustav Fechner in 1860 that is concerned with measuring the relationship between the intensity and quality of a physical stimulus (e.g., the intensity of a light or the frequency of a tone) and the perceptual experience caused by that stimulus (brightness or pitch, respectively). The goal is to use the behavioral measurements to develop and test theories of how the sensory system in question captures environmental energy and transduces it into an internal perceptual representation.

At the most basic level, psychophysics has revealed that there are lights that are too dim to see and sounds that are too quiet to hear because our eyes and ears are not sensitive enough to detect them. Similarly, there are *differences* between the brightnesses of lights or the loudnesses of tones that are not detectable because they are too small to be discriminated by our sensory systems. These failures of detection and discrimination turn out to be extremely informative in the process of discovering how the senses work.

To give just one example, consider the problem of color vision (see the Introduction to Reading 7 for the story of how two different theories of color vision—both correct—came to be developed using psychophysical methods). The surface of the earth is continuously bombarded with electromagnetic radiation that varies in its wavelength from 10^6 meters (radio waves), to 10^{-14} meters (cosmic rays). A tiny segment of this spectrum, with wavelengths between about 400 and 700 nanometers (a nanometer is 10^{-9} meters), is visible to humans as light. As the wavelength of a light is varied from 400 to 700 nm, the perceived color changes from blue to green to yellow to red (and everything between).

Psychophysics permits one to precisely measure the sensitivity of the visual system to different wavelengths of light. For example, people with normal color vision are more sensitive to greenish light than to bluish light (that is, they require a blue light to be physically more intense than a green light in order to just barely detect both; or, put another way, when viewing a blue and a green light with the same physical intensity, they will judge the blue as dimmer). Fechner devised several now-classic methods to perform these measurements, methods that have been improved and perfected over the last 140 years. However, until the 1950s, all the methods had one property in common: they dictated that a stimulus be presented on every trial to the observer, and they assumed that the observer was unbiased: that is, the observer would say "yes, I detect the light" or "no, I do not detect a difference in the loudness of the two tones" in a completely reliable and unbiased fashion.

Tanner and Swets, in this selection, argue that this assumption about the lack of bias in psychophysical judgements may often be incorrect, or at the very least that one should attempt to empirically verify whether it is correct. When viewing near-threshold stimuli (i.e., stimuli that are just barely detectable), observers are confronted with a decision making problem that arises because sensory systems (or, more generally, all biological systems) contain *noise*. For example, imagine participating in a psychophysical experiment in which you are to detect a very low-amplitude tone while you are sitting in a soundproof booth wearing headphones. In this situation, you will not experience absolute silence; your auditory system will occasionally produce spontaneous neural signals that might be indistinguishable from a real sound. Such spontaneous events constitute sensory noise. The problem observers face is to categorize such spontaneous events as "noise" and other events that are triggered by actual sounds as "signals."

Tanner and Swets described a new psychophysical approach, now most commonly called Signal Detection Theory (SDT), that provides a systematic framework for characterizing this decision-making problem. The theory was initially developed by mathematicians and engineers as a framework for analyzing general signal detectability problems in telecommunications (e.g., Peterson, Birdsall, & Fox, 1954). According to the theory as applied to vision, there exists a hypothetical continuum of perceptual experience magnitudes that are produced by noise and signal events. A "noise event" will, over trials, produce a range of perceptual experiences that vary randomly but are generally quite small in magnitude. A "signal event" will also evoke a range of perceptual experiences that vary randomly but that are on average greater in magnitude than those produced by noise events. The decision-making problem for observers is most acute when these two ranges of perceptual experience overlap considerably. In this case, the theory assumes that a criterion is adopted by the observer that is used to categorize trials into target and noise events. A bit of mathematics then permits one to separately estimate the observer's true sensitivity to a stimulus or stimulus difference, and the observer's decision criterion, which reflects response bias. For a revealing application of SDT, see Reading 10: Newsome et al.

This contribution to the collection of psychophysical tools has had a profound affect on how psychologists think about perception (and, for that matter, about many other domains in which a decision has to be based on a weak or noisy signal, including memory and nonperceptual decision making) and about how to carry out psychophysical experiments. Green and Swets (1966) subsequently published a much more detailed analysis of SDT, and a continuing stream of work to further advance the usefulness and applicability of SDT has appeared over the last few decades (e.g., Macmillan & Creelman, 1991).

REFERENCES

Fechner, G. T. (1860). *Elemente der Psychophysik*. Leipzig: Breitkopf and Härtel. (Translated by H. E. Adler, *Elements of Psychophysics*. New York: Holt, Rinehart, & Winston, 1966)

Green & Swets (1966). *Signal detection theory and psychophysics*. New York: John Wiley & Co.

Macmillan, N. A., & Creelman, C. D. (1991). *Detection theory: A user's guide*. Cambridge: Cambridge University Press.

Peterson, W. W., Birdsall, T. G., & Fox, W. C. (1954). The theory of signal detectability. *Transactions of the IRE Professional Group on Information Theory, 4*, 171–212.

A Decision-Making Theory of Visual Detection

W. P. Tanner, Jr. and J. A. Swets • University of Michigan

This paper is concerned with the human observer's behavior in detecting light signals in a uniform light background. Detection of these signals depends on information transmitted to cortical centers by way of the visual pathways. An analysis is made of the form of this information, and the types of decisions which can be based on information of this form. Based on this analysis, the expected form of data collected in "yes-no" and "forced-choice" psychophysical experiments is defined, and experiments demonstrating the internal consistency of the theory are presented.

As the theory at first glance appears to be inconsistent with the large quantity of existing data on this subject, it is wise to review the form of these data. The general procedure is to hold signal size, duration, and certain other physical parameters constant, and to observe the way in which the frequency of detection varies as a function of intensity of the light signal. The way in which data of this form are handled implies certain underlying theoretical viewpoints.

In Fig. 2.1 the dotted lines represent the form of the results of hypothetical experiments. Consider first a single dotted line. Any point on the line might represent an experimentally determined point. This point is corrected for chance by application of the usual formula:

$$p = \frac{p' - c}{1 - c}, \qquad [1]$$

where p' is the observed proportion of positive responses, p is the corrected proportion of positive responses, and c is the intercept of the dotted curve at $\Delta I = 0$.

Justification of this correction depends on the validity of the assumption that a "false alarm" is a guess, independent of any sensory activity upon which a decision might be based. For this to be the case it is necessary to have a mechanism which triggers when seeing occurs and which becomes incapable of discriminating between quantities of neural activity when seeing does not occur. Only under such a system would a guess be equally likely in the absence of seeing for all values of signal intensity. The application of the chance correction to data from both yes-no and forced-choice experiments is consistent with these assumptions.

The solid curve represents a "true" curve onto which each of the dotted, or experimental, curves can be mapped by using the chance correction and proper estimates of "c." The parameters of the solid curve are assumed to be characteristic of the physiology of the individual's sensory system, independent of psychological control. The assumption carries with it the notion that if some threshold of

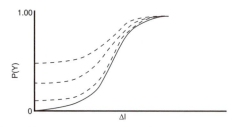

FIGURE 2.1 ■ Conventional Seeing Frequency or Betting Curve

neural activity is exceeded, phenomenal seeing results.

To infer that the form of the curve representing the frequency of seeing as a function of light intensity is the same as the curve representing the frequency of seeing as a function of neural activity is to assume a linear relationship between neural activity and light intensity. Efforts to fit seeing frequency curves by normal probability functions suggest a predisposition toward accepting this assumption.

A New Theory of Visual Detection

The theory presented in this paper differs from conventional thinking about these assumptions. First, it is assumed that false-alarm rate and correct detection vary together. Secondly, neural activity is assumed to be a monotonically increasing function of light intensity, not necessarily linear. A more specific statement than this is left for experimental determination.

Figure 2.2 is a block diagram of the visual pathways showing the major stages of transmission of visual information. All the stages prior to that labelled "cortex" are assumed to function only in the transmission of information, presenting to the cortex a representation of the environment. The function of interpreting this information is left to mechanisms at the cortical level.

In this simplified presentation, the displayed information consists of neural impulse activity. In the case under consideration, in which a signal is presented at a specified time in a known spatial location, the same restrictions are assumed to exist for the display. Thus, if the observer is asked to state whether a signal exists in location A at time B, he is assumed to consider only that information in the neural display which refers to location A at time B.

A judgment on the existence of a signal is presumably based on a measure of neural activity.

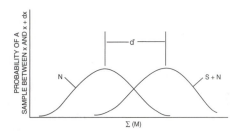

FIGURE 2.3 ■ Hypothetical Distributions of Noise and Signal Plus Noise

There exists a statistical relationship between the measure and signal intensity. That is, the more intense the signal, the greater is the average of the measures resulting. Thus, for any signal there is a universe distribution which is in fact a sampling distribution. It includes all measures which might result if the signal were repeated and measured an infinite number of times. The mean of this universe distribution is associated with the intensity level of the signal. The variance may be associated with other parameters of the signal such as duration or size, but this is beyond the scope of this paper.

Figure 2.3 shows two probability distributions: N represents the case where noise alone is sampled—that is, no signal exists—and $S + N$, the case where signal plus noise exists. The mean of N depends on background intensity; the mean of $S + N$ on background plus signal intensity. The variance of N depends on signal parameters, not background parameters in the case considered here; that is, where the observer knows a priori that if a signal exists then it is a particular signal. From the way the diagram is conceptualized, the greater the measure, $\Sigma(M)$, the more likely it is that this sample represents a signal. But one can never be sure. Thus, if an observer is asked if a signal exists, he is assumed to base his judgment on the quantity of neural activity. He makes an observation, and then attempts to decide whether this observation is more representative of N or of $S + N$. His task is, in fact, the tasking of testing a statistical hypothesis.

The ideal behavior, that which makes optimum use of the information available in this task, is defined mathematically by Peterson and Birdsall (1953). The mathematics and symbols used are theirs, unless otherwise stated. The first case con-

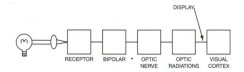

FIGURE 2.2 ■ Block Diagram of the Visual Channel

sidered is the yes-no psychophysical experiment in which a signal is presented at a known location during a well-defined interval in time. This corresponds to Peterson and Birdsall's case of the signal known exactly.

For mathematical convenience, it is assumed that the distributions shown in Fig. 2.3 are Gaussian, with variance equal for N and all values of $S + N$. Experimental results suggest that equal variance is not a true assumption, but that the deviations are not great enough to justify the inconvenience of a more precise assumption for the purpose of this analysis.

It is also assumed that there is a cutoff point such that any measure of neural activity which exceeds that cutoff is in the criterion; that is, any value exceeding cutoff is accepted as representing the existence of a signal, and any value less than the cutoff represents noise alone. Again, for mathematical convenience, the cutoff point is assumed to be well defined and stable. The justification for accepting this convenience is twofold: first, such behavior is statistically optimum, and second, if absolute stability is physically impossible, any lack of definition or random instability throughout an experiment has the same effect mathematically as additional variance in the sampling distributions.

Now, consider the way in which the placing of the cutoff affects behavior in the case of a given signal. In the lower right-hand corner of Fig. 2.4 the distributions N and $S + N$ are reproduced for a

value of $d' = 1$. The parameter d' is the square root of Peterson and Birdsall's d. The square root of d is more convenient here; d' is the difference between the means of N and $S + N$ in terms of the standard deviation N. The criterion scale is also calibrated in terms of the standard deviation of N. On the abscissa there is $P_N(A)$, the probability that, if no signal exists, the measure will be in the criterion, and on the ordinate, $P_{SN}(A)$, the probability that if a signal exists, the measure will be in the criterion.

If the cutoff is at $-\infty$, all measures are in the criterion: $P_N(A) = P_{SN}(A) = 1$. At -1 standard deviation, $P_N(A) = .84$, and $P_{SN}(A) = .98$. At 0, $P_N(A) = .5$ and $P_{SN}(A) = .84$. At $+1$, $P_N(A) = .16$ and $P_{SN}(A) = .5$; and for $+\infty$ $P_N(A) = P_{SN}(A) = 0$. Thus, for $d' = 1$ this is the curve showing possible detections for each false-alarm rate. The curve represents the best that can be done with the information available, and the mirror image is the curve of worst possible behaviors.

The maximum behavior in any given experiment is a point on this curve at which the slope is β where

$$\beta = \frac{1 - P(SN)}{P(SN)} \frac{(V_{N\cdot CA} + K_{N\cdot A})}{(V_{SN\cdot A} + K_{SN\cdot CA})} \qquad [2]$$

$P(SN)$ is the a priori probability that the signal exists, $V_{N\cdot CA}$ is the value of a correct rejection, $K_{N\cdot A}$ the cost of a false alarm, $V_{SN\cdot A}$ the value of a correct detection, and $K_{SN\cdot CA}$ is the cost of a miss. Thus, as $P(SN)$ or $V_{SN\cdot A}$ increases, or $K_{N\cdot A}$ decreases, β becomes smaller, and it is worth while to accept a higher false-alarm rate in the interest of achieving a greater percentage of correct decisions.

Figure 2.5 shows a family of curves of $P_{SN}(A)$ vs. $P_N(A)$ with d' as a parameter. For values of d' greater than 4, detection is very good. This is to be compared with the predictions of the conventional theory shown in Fig. 2.6 with $P_N(A)$ assumed to represent guesses. For each value of d' it is assumed that there is a true value of $P_{SN}(A)$ either for $P_N(A) = 0$ or for some very small value. The chance correction should transform each of these to horizontal lines.

Another way of comparing the predictions of this theory with those of conventional theory is to construct the so-called betting curves, or curves showing the predicted shape of the psychophysical function. These are shown in Fig. 2.7, where $P(A)$, the probability of acceptance, is plotted as a function of d'. These curves will not map onto the

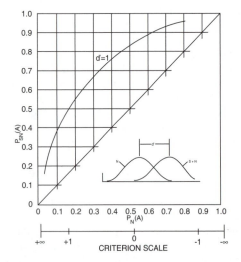

FIGURE 2.4 ■ $P_{SN}(A)$ vs. $P_N(A)$. The Criterion scale shows the corresponding criteria expressed in terms of σ_N from M_N.

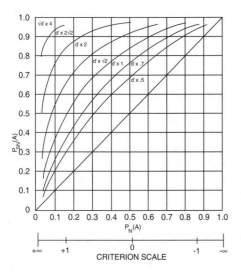

FIGURE 2.5 ■ $P_{SN}(A)$ vs. $P_N(A)$

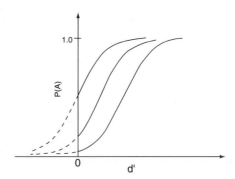

FIGURE 2.7 ■ $P(A)$ as a Function of d' Assuming the Theory

same curve by the application of the chance correction. The shift is horizontal rather than vertical. The dotted portions of the curve show that we are dealing with only a part of the curve, and thus, in the terms of this theory, it is improper to apply a normalizing procedure such as the chance-correction formula to that part of the curve.

In the forced-choice psychophysical experiment, maximum behavior is defined in a different way. In the general forced-choice experiment, the observer knows that the signal will occur in one of n intervals, and he is forced to choose in which of these intervals it occurs. The information upon which his decision is based is contained in the same display as in the case of the yes-no experiment, and, presumably, the values of d' for any given light intensity must be the same. While the solution of this problem is not contained in their study, Peterson and Birdsall have assisted greatly in determining this solution. The probability that a correct answer $P(C)$ will result for a given value of d' is the probability that one sample from the $S + N$ distribution is greater than the greatest of $n - 1$ samples from the distribution of noise alone. The case in which four intervals are used is the basis for Fig. 2.8. This figure shows the probability of one sample from $S + N$ being greater than the greatest of three from N. For a given value of d' this is

$$P(C) = \int_{x=-\infty}^{+\infty} F(x)^3 g(x) dx, \qquad [3]$$

where $F(x)$ is the area of N and $g(x)$ is the ordinate of $S + N$. In Fig. 2.8 $P(C)$, as determined by this integration, is plotted as a function of d' for the equal-variance case.

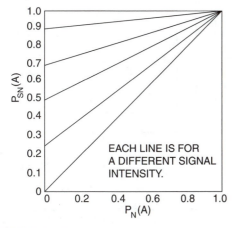

FIGURE 2.6 ■ $P_{SN}(A)$ vs. $P_N(A)$ as a Function of d' Assuming the Guessing Hypothesis

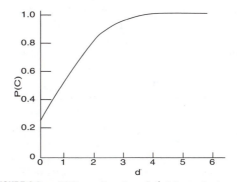

FIGURE 2.8 ■ $P(C)$ as a Function of d'. A theoretical curve.

Criterion of Internal Consistency

These two sets of predictions are for the standard experimental situations. They are based on the same neurological parameters. Thus, if the parameters, that is, d's, are estimated from one of the experiments, these estimates should furnish a basis for predicting the data for the other experiment if the theory is internally consistent. An equivalent criterion of internal consistency is that both experiments yield the same estimates of d'.

Experimental Design

Experiments were conducted to test this internal consistency, using three Michigan sophomores as observers. All the experiments employed a circular target 30 minutes in diameter, 1/100 second in duration, on a 10-foot-lambert background. Details of the experimental procedure and the laboratory have been published by Blackwell, Pritchard, and Ohmart (1954).

The observers were trained in the temporal forced-choice experiment. The signal appeared in a known location at one of four specified times, and the observers were forced to choose the time at which they thought the signal occurred. Five light intensity increments were used here, with 50 observations per point per experimental session. The last two of these sessions were the test sessions, so that each forced-choice point in the analysis is based on 100 experimental observations.

Following the forced-choice experiments, there was a series of yes-no experiments under the same experimental conditions, except that only four light intensity increments were used. These were the same as the four greatest intensities used in the forced-choice experiments, reduced by adding a .1 fixed filter. In the first four of these sessions, two values of a priori probabilities, $P(SN)$ equal to .8 and .4, were used. The observers were informed of the value of $P(SN)$ before each experimental session. No values or costs were incorporated in these four sessions, which were thus excluded from the analysis as practice sessions.

The test experiments consisted of 12 sessions in each of which all of the information necessary for the calculation of a β (the best best possible decision level) was furnished the observers. While they did not know the formal calculation of β, that they knew the direction of cutoff change indicated

by a change in any of these factors was suggested by the fact that the obtained values of $P_N(A)$ varied approximately with changes in the information given them. The values and costs were made real to the observers, for they were actually paid in cash. It was possible for them to earn as much as two dollars extra in a single experimental session as a result of this payment.

The first four sessions each carried the same value of β as $P(SN) = .8$ and the same payment was maintained. A high value of $P_N(A)$, or false-alarm rate, resulted. In the next four sessions with $P(SN)$ held at .8, $K_{N \cdot A}$ and $V_{N \cdot CA}$ were gradually increased from session to session (not within sessions) until $P_N(A)$ dropped to a low value. When $P(SN)$ was dropped to .4, and K_{NA} and $V_{N \cdot CA}$ were reduced so that for the thirteenth session $P_N(A)$ stayed low. The last three sessions successively involved increases in $V_{S \cdot NA}$ and $K_{SN \cdot CA}$ again forcing $P_N(A)$ toward a higher value.

Results

Figures 2.9 and 2.10 show scatter diagrams of $P_{SN}(A)$ vs. $P_N(A)$ for a particular intensity or signal and for a single observer. These scatter diagrams can be used to estimate d'. In Fig. 2.9 the estimate of d' is .7. In Fig. 2.10, the estimate of d' is 1.3. Each d' estimated in this way is based on 560 observations. A procedure similar to this was used for the d's for each of four signals for each of the four observers.

In the forced-choice experiment the estimates

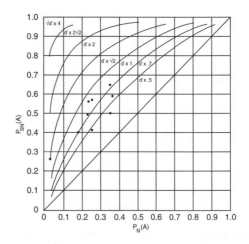

FIGURE 2.9 ■ A Scatter Diagram of $P_{SN}(A)$ vs. $P_N(A)$

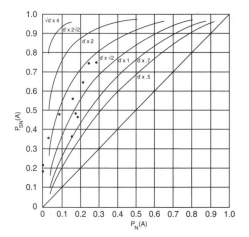

FIGURE 2.10 ■ A Scatter Diagram of $P_{SN}(A)$ vs. $P_N(A)$

of d' are made by entering our forced-choice curve (Fig. 2.8), using the observed percentage correct as an estimate of $P(C)$. Figure 2.11 shows log d' as a function of log signal intensity for the first observer, the estimates of d' being from both forced-choice and yes-no experiments. In general the agreement is good. The deviation of the forced-choice point at the top can be explained on the basis of inadequate experimental data for the determination of the high probability involved. The deviation of the low point is unexplained. Figure 2.12 is the same plot for the second observer, showing about the same picture. Figure 2.13 is for the third observer, showing not quite as good a fit, but nevertheless satisfactory for psychological experiments. For this observer, the lowest point for forced choice is off the graph to the right of the line.

Figures 2.14, 2.15, and 2.16 show the predictions for forced-choice data (when yes-no data are used to estimate d') for the three observers. Note that the lowest point is on the curve in both of the first two cases suggesting that the deviation which appeared on the curves in Figures 2.11, 2.12, and 2.13 is not significant.

Discussion

The results satisfy the criterion of internal consistency. The theory also turns out to be consistent with the vast amount of data in the literature, for, when the d' vs. ΔI function for any one of the observers is used to predict probability of detection as a function of ΔI in terms of this theory, the re-

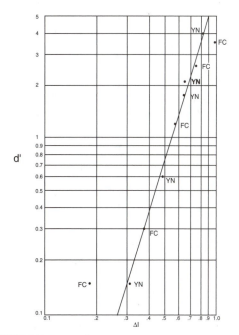

FIGURE 2.11 ■ Log d' vs. Log ΔI for Observer 1

sult closely approximates the type of curve frequently reported. Shapes of curves thus furnish no basis for selecting between the two theories, and a decision must rest on the other arguments.

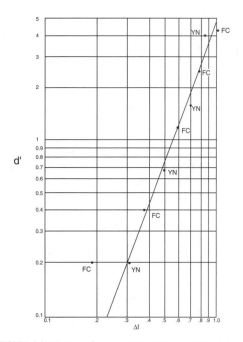

FIGURE 2.12 ■ Log d' vs. Log ΔI for Observer 2

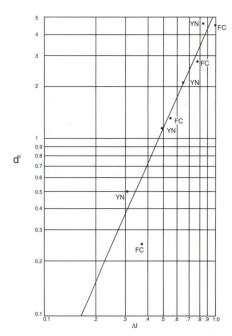

FIGURE 2.13 ■ Log d' vs. Log ΔI for Observer 3

According to conventional theory, application of the chance correction should yield corrected values of $P_{SN}(A)$ which are independent of $P_N(A)$, or should yield corrected thresholds in the conventional sense which are independent of $P_N(A)$. Rank-order correlations for the three observers between $P_N(A)$ and corrected thresholds (.30, .71, .67) are highly significant; the combined $p \ll .001$. This is a result consistent with theory presented here.

Another method of comparison is to fit the scatter diagrams (Figures 2.9 and 2.10) by straight lines. According to the independence theory, these straight lines should intercept the point (1.00, 1.00). Sampling error would be expected to send some of the lines to either side of this point. There are 12 of these scatter diagrams, and all 12 of these lines intersect the line $P_{SN}(A) = 1.00$ at values of $P_N(A)$ between 0 and 1.00 in an order which would be predicted if these lines were arcs of the curves $P_{SN}(A)$ as defined by the theory of signal detectability.

Two additional sessions were run in which the observers were permitted three categories of response (yes, no, and doubtful), and were told to be sure of being correct if they responded either yes or no. Again, two a priori probabilities (.8 and .4) were employed, and again $P_N(A)$ was corre-

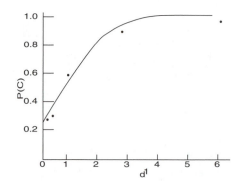

FIGURE 2.14 ■ Prediction of Forced-Choice Data from Yes-No Data for Observer 1

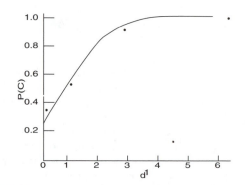

FIGURE 2.15 ■ Prediction of Forced-Choice Data from Yes-No Data for Observer 2

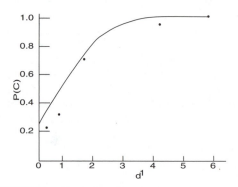

FIGURE 2.16 ■ Prediction of Forced-Choice Data from Yes-No Data for Observer 3

lated with $P(SN)$. The observers, interviewed after these sessions, reported that their "yes" responses were based on "phenomenal" seeing.

This does not mean that the observers were abnormal because they hallucinated. It suggests, on the other hand, that phenomenal seeing develops through experience, and is subject to change with experience. Psychological as well as physiological factors are involved. Psychological "set" is a function of β, and after experience with a given set one begins to see, or not to see, rather automatically. Change the set, and the level of seeing changes. The experiments reported here were such that the observers learned to adjust rapidly to different sets.

Conclusions

The following conclusions are advanced: (*a*) The conventional concept of a threshold, or a threshold region, needs re-evaluation in the light of the present theory that the visual detection problem is the problem of detecting signals in noise. (*b*) The hypothesis that false alarms are guesses is rejected on the basis of statistical tests. (*c*) Change in neural activity is a power function of change in light intensity. (*d*) The mathematical model of signal detection is applicable to problems of visual detection. (*e*) The criterion of seeing depends on psychological as well as physiological factors. In the experiments reported here the observers tended to use optimum criteria. (*f*) The experimental data support the assumption of a logical connection between forced-choice and yes-no techniques developed by the theory.

REFERENCES

Blackwell, H. R., Pritchard, B. S., & Ohmart, T. G. Automatic apparatus for stimulus presentation and recording in visual threshold experiments. *J. Opt. Soc. Amer.*, 1954, 44, 322–326.

Peterson, W. W., & Birdsall, T. G. The theory of signal detectability. Electronic Defense Group, Univer. of Michigan, *Tech. Rep.*, No. 13, Sept., 1953.

Introduction to Reading 3

While some of the most astounding discoveries about how the brain implements vision were being made in the 1960s and early 1970s (see Reading 7: Hubel and Wiesel), vision scientists were beginning to wonder how best to interpret what was being observed. Clearly neural firing rates are related to perceptual experience in some way, but what about the details?

In this selection, Barlow articulates a "neuron doctrine" for understanding the neural basis of perception. This can be seen as a functional extension of the discovery by the great neuroanatomist Santiago Ramon y Cajal around the turn of the century that the basic unit of brain structure is the individual neuron (Cajal, 1937). The ideas articulated in this selection provided a crucial grounding that has helped motivate research in the neurophysiology of vision for more than a quarter-century. The essential idea is that one can best understand the role of any given neuron in perception by determining just what sort of stimuli cause that neuron to fire. A cell in area V4 of the Macaque monkey brain might respond most vigorously to a red bar of light oriented 45° from the upright appearing at the fovea. One can think of this cell as serving to detect that feature in the image. Furthermore, as Zeki (1974) and others found, certain brain regions contain a predominance of cells that are selective for a particular property. In area V4, for example, that property is color; in MT, motion. According to the neuron doctrine, one can then conclude that V4 and MT are responsible for representing color and motion, respectively. Several dozen anatomically distinct visual areas in the primate brain have been discovered (Felleman & Van Essen, 1991) and the functional properties of many of these areas have been described (e.g., Livingstone & Hubel, 1988; Zeki, 1984). Along with the idea of specificity of function within cortical regions came the proposal that the visual system contained a number of functionally distinct parallel pathways, including the X- and Y-pathways in the cat (Enroth-Cugell & Robson, 1966), and the parvocellular and magnocellular pathways (Schiller, 1986), and the ventral "what" and dorsal "where" pathways (Reading 17: Mishkin et al.) in primates. Each of these pathways was thought to carry information about specific visual properties, such as color, form, and motion.

This view of the visual system, in which perceptual attributes such as color, orientation, motion, depth, and texture are represented in specialized neurons and projected via specialized pathways to specialized cortical areas, provides a global framework that has guided research in the neural basis of vision for several decades. However, it also raises a serious problem. If visual scenes are analyzed into their component features, how are the features recombined so as to yield the subjective experience of coherent objects? This is known as the binding problem, and its solution is currently hotly debated (see Roskies et al., 1999 and Reading 21: Triesman & Gelade).

Despite the enormous influence of the neuron doctrine in neurophysiological research, most neurophysiologists today would agree that the strongest form of the doctrine (that there is a one-to-one correspondence between the behavior of single neurons or cortical areas on the one hand and perceptual experience on the other) is probably not correct. First, many cortical cells are tuned to multiple properties simultaneously; that is, they are multiplexors. A given cell might respond to motion, to a particular range of orientations in the absence of motion, to a particular range of colors even when the stimulus is round, etc. (Schiller, 1996). Second, many visual attributes are represented by the joint activity of large populations of neurons, each of which is tuned to a fairly wide range of feature values surrounding the "best" feature. For example, the first stage of color representation consists of the relative activity of the three types of broadly-tuned retinal cones (see the introduction to Reading 7: Hurvich & Jamison). Similarly, the orientation of a luminance edge is represented in primary visual cortex by strong responses from cells whose tuning functions are centered on the location and orientation of the edge, and by weaker responses from cells whose preferred locations and orientations are near that of the edge. The distributed activity of many broadly-tuned cells can yield quite precise representations of properties like orientation or color.

Thus, an emerging view of the neural basis of vision is that the brain consists of both special- and general-purpose components. The ubiquity of feedback and crosstalk in cortex makes it nearly impossible to suppose that a given cell serves only a single function. This is not to say that there is no specialization at all: clearly cortical regions in the occipital lobe perform qualitatively different functions than those in prefrontal cortex, and some areas, such as MT, do seem to be quite specialized for processing a particular visual property (in this case, motion). However, as we learn more about the functional properties of the brain, an increasingly complex view of specialized and generalized function will be required. Despite these complexities, however, the neuron doctrine remains a potent idea in contemporary visual neuroscience (Lee, 1999).

REFERENCES

Cajal, S. R. (1937). *Recollections of my life.* Cambridge, MA: MIT Press.

Enroth-Cugell, C., & Robson, J. G. (1966). The contrast sensitivity of retinal ganglion cells of the cat. *Journal of Physiology, London, 18*, 517–552.

Felleman, D. J., & Van Essen, D. C. (1991). Distributed hierarchical processing in the primate cerebral cortex. *Cerebral Cortex, 1*, 1–47.

Lee, B. B. (1999). Single units and sensation: A retrospect. *Perception, 28,* 1493–1508.

Livingstone, M., & Hubel, D. (1988). Segregation of form, color, movement, and depth: Anatomy, physiology, and perception. *Science, 240*, 740–749.

Roskies, A. L., et al. (1999) The binding problem. *Neuron, 24*, 7–125.

Schiller, P. H. (1986). The central visual system. *Vision Research, 26*, 1351–1386.

Schiller, P. H. (1996). On the specificity of neurons and visual areas. *Behavioural Brain Research, 76*, 21–35.

Stone, J. (1984). *Parallel processing in the visual system.* New York: Plenum Press.

Zeki, S. (1974). Functional specialization in the visual cortex of the rhesus monkey. *Nature, 274*, 423–428.

Single Units and Sensation:
A Neuron Doctrine for Perceptual Psychology?

H. B. Barlow • University of California, Berkeley

The problem discussed is the relationship between the firing of single neurons in sensory
pathways and subjectively experienced sensations. The conclusions are formulated as the
following five dogmas:

1. To understand nervous function one needs to look at interactions at a cellular level, rather
   than either a more macroscopic or microscopic level, because behaviour depends upon the
   organized pattern of these intercellular interactions.
2. The sensory system is organized to achieve as complete a representation of the sensory
   stimulus as possible with the minimum number of active neurons.
3. Trigger features of sensory neurons are matched to redundant patterns of stimulation by
   experience as well as by developmental processes.
4. Perception corresponds to the activity of a small selection from the very numerous high-level
   neurons, each of which corresponds to a pattern of external events of the order of complexity
   of the events symbolized by a word.
5. High impulse frequency in such neurons corresponds to high certainty that the trigger feature
   is present.

The development of the concepts leading up to these speculative dogmas, their experimental
basis, and some of their limitations are discussed.

Introduction

In this article I shall discuss the difficult but challenging problem of the relation between our subjective perceptions and the activity of the nerve cells in our brains. Results obtained by recording from single neurons in sensory pathways have aroused a lot of interest and obviously tell us something important about how we sense the world around us; but what exactly have we been told? In order to probe this question, ideas that fit current knowledge as well as possible must be formulated, and they must be stated clearly enough to be tested to see if they are right or wrong; this is what I have tried to do. The central proposition is that our perceptions are caused by the activity of a rather small number of neurons selected from a very large population of predominantly silent cells. The activity of each single cell is thus an important perceptual event and it is thought to be related quite simply to our subjective experience. The subtlety and sensitivity of perception results from the mechanisms determining when a single cell becomes active, rather than from complex combinatorial rules of usage of nerve cells.

In order to avoid vagueness, I have formulated this notion in five definite propositions, or dogmas, and the reader who wishes to see the trend of this article can glance ahead. Some of the dogmas will be readily accepted by most people who hope to find a scientific basis for human thought processes, but I felt they required statement and discussion in spite of their widespread tacit acceptance. Others are more original, will be challenged by many, and have the nature of extrapolations from the current trend of results rather than conclusions reasonably based upon them. Before these dogmas are stated the developments that have led to them will be briefly reviewed. The literature is extensive, and much of it will have been incorporated into the reader's common knowledge. My aim, therefore, is to pick out the conceptual turning points in order to show the direction we are headed. After stating the dogmas, criticisms and alternatives will be discussed in an attempt both to justify them and to clarify them further.

Recording from Single Neurons

Peripheral Nerves

In the twenties and thirties methods were developed for amplifying and recording the weak transient electrical potentials associated with the activity of nerve fibres, and Adrian and his colleagues used these methods to record the all-or-none impulses of single nerve fibres connecting the sense organs to the brain (Adrian, 1926a, 1926b; Adrian and Zotterman, 1926a, 1926b; Adrian, 1928). They showed, for example, that each fibre coming from the skin responded to a particular type of stimulus, such as pressure, temperature change, or damage, applied to a specific region or receptive field. The frequency of the impulses depended upon the intensity of the stimulus, but it was clear that the character of the sensation (touch, heat, or pain) depended upon the fibre carrying the message, not the nature of the message, since this consisted of trains of similar impulses in all fibres. Nerves had long been recognized as the link between physical stimulus and sensation, so these results provided physiological flesh and blood to the skeleton that anatomical studies had revealed a long time earlier.

Most of the results confirmed another ancient idea, namely Müller's doctrine of specific nerve energies: the specificity of different sensations stems from the responsiveness of different nerve fibres to different types of stimulus. The chemical senses proved to be a little different (Pfaffman, 1941, 1955; Ganchrow and Erickson, 1970), but in spite of the fact that they did not quite fall in line, the concept that resulted from two decades of recording from peripheral fibres and following their connections in the brain was of a simple mapping from sense organs to sensorium, so that a copy of physical events at the body surface was presented to the brain (Bard, 1938; Marshall et al., 1941; Adrian, 1941, 1947). Some modification was recognized to occur, for sensory nerves usually adapt to a constant stimulus, and therefore signal sudden changes of stimulus energy better than sustained levels. Neighbouring receptive fields and modalities were also known to overlap, but when the activity of neurons at higher levels in sensory pathways was recorded it became obvious that something was happening more complex and significant than could be fitted into the concept of simple mapping with overlap and adaptation.

Sensory Neurons of the Retina

Starting with Granit (Granit and Svaetichin, 1939; Granit, 1947) and Hartline (1938; 1940a, 1940b) in the retina, and Galambos and Davis (Galambos and Davis, 1943; Galambos, 1944; Galambos and Davis, 1948) at the periphery of the pathway for hearing, a generation of physiologists has studied sensory neurons in the central nervous system; all this obviously cannot be reviewed here, but we shall concentrate on the results that expanded the conceptual frame built on the earlier work. Previously it was possible for physiologists to be satisfied with describing how the sense organs and their nerves present a picture of the external world to the brain, and they were happy to leave it to the psychologists to discuss what happened next; but these next things started to happen around the physiologist's micro-electrodes, and he has to join the discussion.

The realization that physiological experiments can answer questions of psychological interest first dawned on me personally when I was working on the frog's retina. A vigorous discharge can be evoked from retinal ganglion cells by stimulating the appropriate region of the retina—the ganglion cell's "receptive field" (Hartline, is simultaneously stimulated the response of 1940a); but if the surrounding region is simultaneously stimulated the response of the cell is diminished or completely abolished (Barlow, 1953). This phenomenon is called lateral inhibition, or peripheral suppression, and such a physiological mechanism had already been postulated in order to account for simultaneous brightness and Mach bands (Mach, 1886; Fry, 1948). Thus the physiological experiment was really providing evidence in support of a psychological hypothesis.

The invasion of psychological territory did not stop at this point. If one explains the responsiveness of single ganglion cells in the frog's retina using hand-held targets, one finds that one particular type of ganglion cell is most effectively driven by something like a black disc subtending a degree or so moved rapidly to and fro within the unit's receptive field. This causes a vigorous discharge which can be maintained without much decrement as long as the movement is continued. Now, if the stimulus which is optimal for this class of cells is presented to intact frogs, the behavioural response is often dramatic: they turn towards the target and make repeated feeding responses consisting of a jump and snap. The selectivity of the retinal neurons, and the frog's reaction when they are selectively stimulated, suggest that they are "bug detectors" (Barlow, 1953) performing a primitive but vitally important form of recognition.

This result makes one suddenly realize that a large part of the sensory machinery involved in a frog's feeding responses may actually reside in the retina rather than in mysterious "centres" that would be too difficult to understand by physiological methods. The essential lock-like property resides in each member of a whole class of neurons, and allows the cell to discharge only to the appropriate key pattern of sensory stimulation. Lettvin et al. (1959) suggested that there were five different classes of cell in the frog, and Levick, Hill and I (Barlow et al., 1964) found an even larger number of categories in the rabbit. We called these key patterns "trigger features," and Maturana et al. (1960) emphasized another important aspect of the behaviour of these ganglion cells: a cell continues to respond to the same trigger feature in spite of changes in light intensity over many decades. The properties of the retina are such that a ganglion cell can, figuratively speaking, reach out and determine that something specific is happening in front of the eye. Light is the agent by which it does this, but it is the detailed pattern of the light that carries the information, and the overall level of illumination prevailing at the time is almost totally disregarded.

It is true that Ingle (1968, 1971), Grüsser and Grüsser–Cornehls (1968), and Ewert (1970) have shown that it is too simple to suppose that feeding automatically and inevitably follows the activation of a certain class of retinal ganglion cells by their trigger features; higher coordinating mechanisms are also involved. Just as light is only an intermediate agent allowing a retinal ganglion cell to detect its trigger feature, so these optic nerve impulses must doubtless be regarded as intermediate agents enabling the higher centres to perform their tasks. We shall proceed to discuss these problems, but we have gained two important concepts from the frog's retina: it transmits a map, not of the light intensities at each point of the image, but of the trigger features in the world before the eye, and its main function is not to transduce different luminance levels into different impulse frequencies, but to continue responding invariantly to the same external patterns despite changes of average luminance.

Sensory Neurons of the Cerebral Cortex

The function of the visual area of the mammalian cerebral cortex is obviously more relevant to the problem of our own subjective perceptions than is the frog's retina, and Hubel and Wiesel (1959) early discovered examples of selectivity for pattern in the responsiveness of cells in the visual cortex of cats. They found that a light or dark line, or a dark–light border, was required to evoke a vigorous response even in the simplest first-order cells. Furthermore the stimulus had to be at a rather precise orientation and position in the visual field and in addition it usually had to be moving, often in a specific direction. Hubel and Wiesel (1962) also made a distinction between these cells and other classes with more elaborate stimulus requirements, which they believed corresponded to cells at later stages of information processing. They called these "complex" and "hypercomplex" units, and showed that they had properties suggesting that the input to each was from the simpler category of cells. The fascination of this analysis depends to a large extent upon successfully following the way units become selective for more and more complex properties at each stage. Some doubts have been cast on their hierarchical scheme (Stone, 1972), but it certainly gave new insight into how higher levels of categorization are developed from lower levels.

As well as the hierarchical concept, this work provided evidence for a new type of invariance. In the cat, as in the frog, the retina is mainly responsible for ensuring that the message sent to the brain is not much perturbed by changes in ambient illumination. In the cortex Hubel and Wiesel (1962) found that some of the higher level neurons responded to the same trigger feature over a considerable range of positions. The modality specificity of peripheral neurons indicates how one can, for instance, detect warmth at any point on the body surface, and we now see that the organized pattern specificity of a set of cortical neurons can in the same way produce positional invariance for pattern perception. This was previously one of the great puzzles, and, although we certainly do not understand how recognition is invariant for position, size, and perspective transformations, at least a start has been made.

Later experiments have shown that the primary neurons of the visual cortex are more specific in one respect than Hubel and Wiesel originally thought. They showed that most neurons are fed by inputs from both eyes, and they emphasized that the dominance of ipsi- or contra-lateral eye varied from cell to cell. Now it can be shown that a binocular stimulus often has to be very precisely positioned in both eyes in order to evoke the most vigorous response (Barlow et al., 1967; Pettigrew et al., 1968), and a more important variable than dominance emerges from the exact relative positions in the two eyes. Consider what must happen when the eyes are converged on some point in front of the cat and appropriate visual stimuli are presented; it is easy to position this stimulus correctly for either eye by itself, but, if it is to be correctly positioned for both, it will have to be at some specific distance from the cat. When the precise positioning for different units is studied, it is found that this specific distance for optimal response varies in different units in the same cortex, and among units serving the same region of visual space. Conversely, the selection of units which are activated provides the cat with some information about the distances of the various stimulus objects.

In uncovering this aspect of the pattern selectivity of sensory neurons we again get the sense that a central neuron is reaching out to discover something important about what is happening in the real objective world. One even wonders if the line and edge detectors of Hubel and Wiesel may not have, as their main function, the linking together of information about the same object in the two retinal images in order to determine the object's most important coordinate—its distance from the animal. At all events, as in the case of the frog's bug-detector, the importance of the information abstracted from the retinal images gives some insight into the purpose or direction of the physiological mechanisms.

Something is known about these first steps of information processing in the visual cortex; what about the later stages? Results suggesting greater and greater specificity of response requirements have been obtained, and a nice example is the unit described by Gross et al. (1972) in the infero-temporal cortex of macaques; this responded best to stimulation by a figure with many of the specific characteristics of a monkey's hand, and the requirements of one such unit are well documented.

Work in this area is not easy to repeat, for one can readily see that it is largely a matter of chance to find a trigger feature of this order of complexity. Also, the possibility that cells may retain to adulthood the modifiable properties of immature cells that will be described later makes the prospect of investigating the sensory association areas an intimidating one.

Cortical neurons receive selective excitatory and inhibitory inputs from other neurons and thereby possess selective responsiveness for some characteristics and invariances for changes in other characteristics. This seems to have the potentiality of being a powerful information processing system.

Single Units and Psychophysics

The neurophysiological discoveries outlined above of course made a deep impression on those investigating sensation psychophysically, but although there are many superficial points of contact it has not proved easy to link sensations securely to specific patterns of neurophysiological activity. The topics I have chosen are again ones which seem to have implications about how we conceptualize this neuropsychic relationship.

Lateral Inhibition and Simultaneous Contrast

The relation between lateral inhibition in the retina and simultaneous contrast has already been mentioned, but there is a large gap between the physiological level and the subjective effects shown in textbook illustrations, and it is too big to be bridged by a single simple statement. It is quite easy to show that frog and cat retinal ganglion cells demonstrate relevant effects, since their antagonistic surrounds (Barlow, 1953; Kuffler, 1953) make their responses depend upon contrast rather than absolute luminance. Hence on-centre cells respond to spots we would call white, off-centre cells to spots we would call black, even when the so-called black spot has a higher luminance than the white spot (Barlow et al., 1957). But subjective contrast effects also hold for conditions where one cannot make such easy comparisons, for instance at the centre of an area which is much too large to fill the centre of a retinal receptive field. Of course, one can postulate some "filling in" process (Yarbus, 1965), but the necessity of introducing ad hoc assumptions makes many explanations of subjective effects in terms of single units unconvincing.

The concept that enables one to escape this difficulty is to concentrate on the informational flow rather than on the direct subjective-physiological comparison. Information discarded in a peripheral stage of processing cannot be accurately added back centrally, and in the present case it helps to talk about "attenuating low spatial frequencies" instead of "signalling spatial contrast." To say that some of the low-frequency attenuation of the whole visual system is performed by the opposed centre-surround organisation of the retinal ganglion cell (Campbell and Green, 1965; Enroth-Cugell and Robson, 1966) is more accurate than to say that all simultaneous contrast effects originate there.

Colour

In the field of colour vision De Valois has looked for relationships between various psychophysically measurable aspects of colour and the properties of single unit responses recorded at the level of the lateral geniculate nucleus. The main results provided a startling confirmation of Hering's long-standing hypothesis about the reciprocal organisation of colour systems (Svaetichin and MacNicholl, 1958; De Valois, 1960; Hurvich and Jameson, 1960; Wagner et al., 1960), but the details are important. He has been able to establish neuro-psychic parallels using what may be called the "lower envelope" or "most sensitive neuron" principle. A monkey's ability to discriminate hue and saturation (De Valois et al., 1966, 1967) is very close to what one would expect if the monkey only pays attention to the most sensitive of the optic nerves conveying information about these qualities of the stimulus. Thus the psychophysical performance follows the lower envelope of the performance of individual fibres. It is particularly interesting to see that a continuous psychophysical function, hue discrimination as a function of wavelength, is served by a different type of neuron in different ranges; over the long wavelength range the red–green opponent system was much more sensitive to wavelength shift, whereas the blue–yellow system was more sensitive at short wavelengths.

This result again fits in with the concept that neurophysiology and sensation are best linked by looking at the flow of information rather than simpler measures of neuronal activity. For instance it might be suggested that sensation follows the average neural activity, and it would be easy to justify this on the neurophysiological grounds that post-synaptic potentials are usually additive. However, this oversimple suggestion is proved false by the fact that psychophysical hue discrimination does not follow the average response of the red–green and blue–yellow systems, but instead follows the lower envelope. Now when two noisy channels are both conveying information about a signal, the channel with the highest signal/noise ratio dominates the situation; the low signal/noise ratio channel can be used to improve performance slightly, but it is a very small contribution except where its signal/noise ratio is nearly as high as that of the more sensitive channel. Thus the "most-sensitive neuron" principle again fits the concept that, to link neurophysiological activity and sensation, one should look at the flow of information.

Touch

Another example is given by the work of Mountcastle and his colleagues (Talbot et al., 1968), in which they studied the responses at a number of levels to vibratory stimuli applied to the glabrous skin of the hand. First they recorded from cutaneous afferents in the monkey, then the cortical responses in the same species, finally they made psychophysical measures of sensory responses in humans to the same stimuli. As with the work on colour, they established that the sensory response depends simply upon the category of nerve fibre with the lowest threshold.

The fact that the subjective sensation in both the colour and touch systems seems to follow the lower envelope of the responses of the various types of sensory neuron may give an important clue to the way in which these neurons represent sensations. It is as if the screen on which sensations appear is completely blank until a sensory pathway is activated, but when this happens a point lights up and becomes instantly visible. This is not what one would expect if there was a lot of ongoing activity in all pathways, or if the magnitude of the signal was a linear function of intensity, nor is it what one would expect if sensation depended in a complex combinatorial way upon the activity of many units. Rather it suggests the concept that the magnitude of the signal directly represents the signal/noise ratio, for then the insignificant signals will automatically be small, and the neuron firing most will automatically be the most sensitive. This concept receives some support in the next section and is taken up in the fifth dogma and its discussion.

Adaptation After-effects

The fact that one is almost unaware of the constant pressure applied to the skin by the chair one is sitting on presumably results, at least in part, from the rapid decline in frequency of the volley of sensory impulses initiated by contact (Adrian, 1928). Central neurons that respond to specific patterns of sensory input also give a decreased response when the pattern is sustained or repeatedly presented, though there have actually been surprisingly few investigations of this effect. These adaptation, habituation, or fatigue effects lead to plausible explanations for many well-known sensory illusions.

For example the rate of discharge in the directionally selective neurons of the rabbit retina declines if a stimulus is continuously moved through the receptive field in the preferred direction, and following cessation of movement the maintained discharge is found to be suppressed (Barlow and Hill, 1963). The resulting imbalance between neurons signalling opposite directions

seems to provide a ready explanation of the apparent reversed movement of stationary objects following prolonged inspection of moving objects (the so-called "waterfall effect"), and provides another example of an ancient psychophysical hypothesis (Wohlgemuth, 1911) being confirmed neurophysiologically. One must bear in mind that these neural effects were described in the rabbit's retina, whereas in the human, as in the cat and monkey, neurons are probably not directionally selective until the level of the visual cortex (Barlow and Brindley, 1963), but the same type of explanation may well apply to neurons at this level.

It has been suggested that one can make inverse inferences from the existence of an after-effect to the presence of neurons with particular selective responses. This is no place to argue whether the after-effects of adaptation to gratings imply a Fourier-type analysis (Blakemore and Campbell, 1969), or whether they can be satisfactorily accounted for by families of different-sized neurons with conventional Hubel–Wiesel-type receptive fields, but there is certainly room for argument, and this makes selective adaptation a difficult tool to use to discover later stages of information processing.

Instead, I think the importance of sensory adaptational effects, and of the corresponding neurophysiological phenomena, lies in the support both these phenomena lend to the concept put forward at the end of the last section. If sensory messages are to be given a prominence proportional to their informational value, mechanisms must exist for reducing the magnitude of representation of patterns which are constantly present, and this is presumably the underlying rationale for adaptive effects.

Noisiness or Reliability of Single Units

It used to be commonly held that nerve cells were unreliable elements, much perturbed by metabolic or other changes and perhaps also by random disturbances of more fundamental origin (McCulloch, 1959; Burns, 1968). The fairly high degree of reliability that the nervous system achieves as a whole was explained by the supposed redundancy of neural circuits and appropriate rules for averaging and combining them. Developments in the study of human vision at the absolute threshold and of the absolute sensitivity of retinal ganglion cells in the cat now indicate that nerve cells are not intrinsically unreliable and that noise often originates externally.

Signal detection theory has familiarized psychologists with the problem of detecting signals in the presence of noise (Tanner and Swets, 1954; Green and Swets, 1966), and I think the assumed prevalence of internally generated noise was a major reason why this was thought to be an important new approach. But psychophysical studies have actually shown that the senses and the brain can operate with astonishing intrinsic reliability. Noise may always be present, but to an amazing extent it originates outside the nervous system. This was originally implied by the results of Hecht et al. (1942) on the absolute threshold of vision; they showed that about 100 quanta at the cornea, leading to 10 or less absorptions in the retina, were sufficient to give a sensation of light. But their most revolutionary finding was that the frequency-of-seeing curve, describing the breadth of the threshold zone, is mainly accounted for by quantum fluctuations, not internal sloppiness or random variations of the threshold criterion as had previously been thought. That is not to say that "intrinsic retinal noise" or "dark-light" is nonexistent or unimportant, for it is probably the main factor determining how many quanta are required for reliable detection (Barlow, 1956). It now appears probable that this originates in the photoreceptors and, in some subjects at least, is low enough to allow the conscious detection of the sensation caused by absorption of a single quantum (Sakitt, 1972); similar sensations occur in the absence of light stimuli, but at a lower frequency. In addition, the subjects can apparently discriminate between the sensory messages resulting from 2, 3, 4, etc. quantal absorptions, each being detected progressively more clearly and reliably.

This psychophysical work shows that the human brain, acting as a whole, can distinguish between the disturbances caused by small numbers of quantal absorptions. These must of course originate from single molecular events in single cells, but possibly the disturbance is thereafter diffused through many cells and abstracted in some way from a redundant neural representation. It therefore becomes very interesting to go into the neurophysiology and find how the absorption of a few quanta is signalled.

A sensitive example of a retinal ganglion cell of the cat, with its associated bipolar cells, receptors, amacrine and horizontal cells, will give a readily detectable discharge of impulses to as few as 2 or 3 quanta of light absorbed in the retina (Barlow et al., 1971). Such a stimulus will give rise to an average of 5 to 10 extra impulses. Thus a single quantal absorption causes as many as 3 extra impulses, two quanta cause about 6 impulses, and so on. The addition of 3 impulses to the maintained discharge is detectable on average, though, like the absorption of a single quantum in the human, it cannot be reliably detected on a single trial. There is of course some intrinsic noise, as shown by the maintained discharge, but its level is extraordinarily low when one considers that a single ganglion cell is connected to more than 100 rods containing a total of some 10^{10} molecules of rhodopsin, each poised ready to signal the absorption of a quantum. The important point is that quantitative knowledge of the noise level and reliability of single retinal ganglion cells enables one to see that the performance of the whole visual system can be attributed to a single cell: averaging is not necessary.

Individual nerve cells were formerly thought to be unreliable, idiosyncratic, and incapable of performing complex tasks without acting in concert and thus overcoming their individual errors. This was quite wrong, and we now realise their apparently erratic behaviour was caused by our ignorance, not the neuron's incompetence. Thus we gain support from this neuropsychical comparison for the concept of a neuron as a reliable element capable of performing a responsible role in our mental life, though we need not of course go to the other extreme and assume that mental errors are never caused by malfunctioning, ill-educated, or noisy neurons.

Modifiability of Cortical Neurons

The most recent conceptual change about the neural basis of our sensations has arisen from a reinspection of the origin of the selective responsiveness of cortical neurons.

Evidence for Modifiability

Hubel and Wiesel (1963) at first thought they had shown that the whole of the elaborate organization responsible for the selectivity of neurons in the primary visual cortex was developed solely under genetic control. They reported that they found cortical neurons with normal adult-type specificity of responsiveness in young kittens which had not opened their eyes, or which had been deprived of visual experience by suture of their eyelids. In later investigations (Wiesel and Hubel, 1963, 1965; Hubel and Wiesel, 1965) they found that abnormal visual experience, such as unilateral eye-suture, or prevention of simultaneous usage of the eyes by alternating occlusion or surgically induced strabismus, caused the development of an abnormal population of cortical cells. In accordance with their earlier findings they attributed this to a disruption of the preformed organization, and they discovered the very important fact that abnormal experience only modifies the cortex if it occurs during a particular "sensitive" period—about 3 to 12 weeks in cats (Hubel and Wiesel, 1970).

Recent developments have extended these seminal findings, but they lead to somewhat different conclusions about the relative importance of experience and genetic factors in determining the selectivity of cortical neurons. First it was shown that kittens brought up with the two eyes exposed to different stimuli, one to vertical stripes, the other to horizontal, had a corresponding orientation selectivity of the receptive fields connected to each eye (Hirsch and Spinelli, 1970, 1971). This was confirmed in kittens exposed only to vertically or horizontally striped environments; these had no neurons sensitive to horizontally or vertically oriented stimuli respectively (Blakemore and Cooper, 1970). Evidence has been obtained that cats raised with a vertical displacement of the images in one eye induced by prisms also have abnormal vertical disparities of the pairs of receptive fields of cortical neurons connected to both eyes (Shlaer, 1971). Again, the cortex of a kitten exposed only to bright dots, with no contours or edges, contained units of an abnormal type responding well to small spots of light and showing little of the customary preference for lines (Pettigrew and Freeman, forthcoming). Furthermore it appears that a very brief period of exposure, as little as an hour, can have very pronounced effects on the subsequent selectivity of neurons in the visual cortex (Blakemore and Mitchell, 1973).

Such results could still possibly have been explained by disruption of the innately-determined highly-specific connections that were originally thought to underlie response specificity, but a re-examination of the properties of cortical neurons of kittens with no visual experience shows that they do not actually have fully-developed adult-type specificity (Barlow and Pettigrew, 1971). This is certainly the case with regard to disparity selectivity and, although there is directional preference and may be some weak orientation selectivity, they are not as narrowly selective as adult cells (Pettigrew, forthcoming). The anatomy of the developing cortex shows that only a small fraction of the normal complement of synapses is present before the critical period, and it is hard to believe that the cells could have adult properties (Cragg, 1972). It will take more work to determine the limits within which the pattern selectivity of cortical neurons can be modified, but the results already make it impossible to believe Hubel and Wiesel's original claim that many cells of the visually inexperienced kitten have the full adult-type selectivity.

Type of Modification Caused

It is instructive to look at the way in which experience modifies selectivity. In all cases the cortex of animals whose visual experience has been modified lacks neurons selectively responsive to patterns of excitation which a normal animal receives, but which have been excluded by the experimental modification. Thus unilateral lid suture led to a cortex with very few neurons excitable from the lid-sutured eye; likewise, alternating occlusion or strabismus, which decreases the probability of simultaneous excitation of corresponding neurons in the two eyes, decreased the proportion of neurons responding to both eyes. The same is true of the kittens reared in striped environments, or with a vertically deviating prism over one eye, or in an environment with point sources but no lines; in all these cases the rule holds that neurons are found for patterns of excitation that occur in the modified environment, but normally occurring types of selectivity are rare or absent if the patterns they would respond to have not been experienced in the modified environment.

This rule seems to amount to a striking confirmation of the speculation (Barlow, 1960) that a prime function of sensory centres is to code efficiently the patterns of excitation that occur, thus developing a less redundant representation of the environment. Previous examples of redundancy-reducing codes could be explained as genetically determined features of neural connectivity, but the above discoveries are definite examples of a modified code developed in response to a modified environment.

If on this page we have begun the correct story for simple cells of area 17, one can see that a book has been opened with regard to the properties of cells higher in the hierarchy, which are presumably themselves experience-dependent and are fed by information from these experience-dependent neurons at the lower cortical levels. Even a small degree of modifiability would be extraordinarily significant in a hierarchically organized system, just as, in evolution, weak selection pressure is effective over many generations.

Current Concept of the Single Neuron

The cumulative effect of all the changes I have tried to outline above has been to make us realise that each single neuron can perform a much more complex and subtle task than had previously been thought. Neurons do not loosely and unreliably map the luminous intensities of the visual image onto our sensorium, but instead they detect pattern elements, discriminate the depth of objects, ignore irrelevant causes of variation, and are arranged in an intriguing hierarchy. Furthermore, there is evidence that they give prominence to what is informationally important, can respond with great reliability, and can have their pattern selectivity permanently modified by early visual experience. This amounts to a revolution in our outlook. It is now quite inappropriate to regard unit activity as a noisy indication of more basic and reliable processes involved in mental operations; instead, we must regard single neurons as the prime movers of these mechanisms. Thinking is brought about by neurons, and we should not use phrases like "unit activity reflects, reveals, or monitors thought processes," because the activities of neurons, quite simply, *are* thought processes.

This revolution stemmed from physiological work and makes us realize that the activity of each single neuron may play a significant role in perception. I think that more clearly stated hypotheses are now needed about these roles in order to allow our psychological knowledge and intuitions about our perceptions to help us plan future experiments.

Five Propositions

The following five brief statements are intended to define which aspect of the brain's activity is important for understanding its main function, to suggest the way that single neurons represent what is going on around us, and to say how this is related to our subjective experience. The statements are dogmatic and incautious because it is important that they should be clear and testable.

First Dogma

A description of that activity of a single nerve cell which is transmitted to and influences other nerve cells, and of a nerve cell's response to such influences from other cells, is a complete enough description for functional understanding of the nervous system. There is nothing else "looking at" or controlling this activity, which must therefore provide a basis for understanding how the brain controls behaviour.

Second Dogma

At progressively higher levels in sensory pathways information about the physical stimulus is carried by progressively fewer active neurons. The sensory system is organized to achieve as complete a representation as possible with the minimum number of active neurons.

Third Dogma

Trigger features of neurons are matched to the redundant features of sensory stimulation in order to achieve greater completeness and economy of representation. This selective responsiveness is determined by the sensory stimulation to which neurons have been exposed, as well as by genetic factors operating during development.

Fourth Dogma

Just as physical stimuli directly cause receptors to initiate neural activity, so the active high-level neurons directly and simply cause the elements of our perception.

Fifth Dogma

The frequency of neural impulses codes subjective certainty: a high impulse frequency in a given neuron corresponds to a high degree of confidence that the cause of the percept is present in the external world.

First Dogma: Significant Level of Description

This dogma asserts that a picture of how the brain works, and in particular how it processes and represents sensory information, can be built up from knowledge of the interactions of individual cells. At the moment single-unit electrical recording is the only tool with temporal and spatial resolution adequate to locate the effect of a particular sensory stimulus in a particular cell. Other tools (biochemical, electron microscopy, etc.) can obviously provide essential information about these interactions, but the dogma may be criticized more fundamentally; it may be suggested that the whole problem should be approached at a different level. One could attack from either side, suggesting either that one should look at grosser signs of nervous activity, such as the weak extracellular potentials that result from the activity of many neurons, or that one should approach the problem at a more microscopic level, studying synaptic and molecular changes.

Interest in evoked potentials and electroencephalography has waned partly because their study led to slow progress compared with single-unit recording, but also because the rationale for their use was undermined. A prime reason for attending to these macroscopic manifestations of nervous activity was the belief that individual cells were too unreliable to be worthy of attention singly, and hence it was better to look at a sign of activity that resulted from many of them. Here, it was thought, may be a property of a group of cells analogous to temperature or pressure as a property of a collection of molecules that individually behave randomly. The demonstration that single nerve cells have diverse and highly specific responsiveness to sensory stimuli, and are astonishingly reliable, showed the fallacy of this analogy.

The search for a molar property of a mass of working nerve cells is certainly not worthless. Physiologists, and all biologists for that matter, tend to be emotionally divided into globalists and atomists. The globalists are amazed at the perfection of functioning of the whole animal, and they observe that the atomists' analytical investigations of living matter always leave unexplained many of the most remarkable attributes of the intact animal. As a result the globalist can play a crucially important role in pointing out where the atomists' explanations are incomplete. Now the brain does much more interesting things than produce weak extracellular potentials: it controls behaviour, and this is surely the global product that, at our present state of understanding, really does appear greater than the sum of its parts. It would be no use looking at single neurons if it will be forever impossible to explain overall behaviour in terms of the actions and interactions of these subunits; if that were so, the globalists' despair would be justified. On the other hand it is precisely because rapid progress has been made that this article is being written; it no longer seems completely unrealistic to attempt to understand perception at the atomic single-unit level.

The second criticism, that one should approach the problem at a more microscopic level, is really only answerable by saying, "Go ahead and do it," for undoubtedly there is much to be learned at a synaptic and molecular level. But the important question here is whether lack of this knowledge will impede a major advance in our conception of how the brain works. The dogma asserts that it is the intercellular actions and interactions that possess the elaborate organization responsible for behaviour; hence it asserts that knowledge at a more-microscopic intracellular level is not a prerequisite for understanding such organization.

Second Dogma: The Economical Representation of Sensory Messages

The main task in this section is to discern the principles that underlie the changes in characteristic responsiveness of single units at successive levels in sensory pathways. The aim is to understand how sensory information is represented or "displayed." The successive levels to be considered will be peripheral photoreceptors and cutaneous afferents; retinal ganglion cells of the cat, frog, or rabbit, the latter of which seem to exemplify a more complex type of processing; and the visual cortex of cats. Obviously these are not an ideal series for comparisons and extrapolations, but they are the best we can do.

The discussion initially revolves around three issues: changes in the degree of specificity and generality of the stimuli to which the cells respond; changes in the number of parallel categories of selectively sensitive cells that carry the information; and changes in the number of the cells that one may expect to be activated by normal visual scenes. What emerges is that, at the higher levels, fewer and fewer cells are active, but each represents a more and more specific happening in the sensory environment.

Specificity and Generality of Responsiveness

The pattern specificity of sensory neurons is the aspect that is most widely emphasized: it was spectacular to discover single neurons in the retina responding to movement of the image in a specific direction, cortical neurons responding only to slits of light at a particular orientation, and a unit in the infero-temporal cortex that responds best to a monkey's hand. But the invariance of the response to changes in the stimulus is equally remarkable. A retinal unit continues to respond to direction of motion in spite of many decades of change in input luminance or contrast, in fact in spite of reversal of contrast (Barlow, 1969a). At the cortical level a complex cell insists that a stimulus is appropriately oriented, but will respond in spite of wide variations of position (Hubel and Wiesel, 1962). And the monkey-paw unit similarly retains its pattern specificity over a large part of the visual field (Gross et al., 1972).

In talking about these properties of sensory neurons actual examples are perhaps more informative than the words specific and general. A single receptor containing a red-sensitive pigment is specific in the sense that long-wavelength light must be present at a particular part of the image in order to excite it, and it is general in the sense that all images with this property will excite it. In contrast to this type of specificity and generality, the high-level neurons are no longer limited to purely local attributes of the image. They are selective for pattern, which requires that a considerable region of the image is taken into account. But there are other aspects of their specific selectivity that also need to be considered.

Number of Selective Categories

At the level of receptors there are a small number of different sensory modalities picking up, in parallel, information from different positions. This is the case both for the half dozen types of cutaneous sensation, and for the smaller number of retinal receptor types responding to the visual image. At the level of ganglion cells the number of sub-modalities or selective categories has greatly increased. Consider the rabbit, where there are the following (Barlow et al., 1964; Levick, 1967): two concentric types (on- and off-centre); four on–off type directionally selective (for movements up, down, antero–posterior, and postero–anterior); three directions for slow, on-type, directionally selective; one type sensitive to fast movement; one type sensitive to "uniformity"; and, confined to the visual streak, two types of orientation-selective neurons, neurons selective for slow-moving small objects, and neurons selective for edges. This makes a total of 15 different selective categories. In addition there must be units signaling colour, since the rabbit shows behavioural evidence for it, but these have not yet been found in the retina.

Now move up to the simple cells in area 17 of cat cortex. These vary in position, orientation, disparity, and size, as well as being selective for light bars, dark bars, or edges. The evidence is not sufficient to say how many distinct selective categories these form, but for each of the first three variables the resolution of a single neuron is good, in the sense that small departures from the preferred position, orientation, or disparity cause large decreases of response amplitude (Bishop, 1970). These variables already define four dimensions, and we have not yet considered size specificity, velocity specificity, nor the additional complexities of light, dark, or edge detectors, and of course colour. There are certainly several orders of magnitude more neurons in the primary projection area than there are input fibres, or resolvable points in the visual field, and it is abundantly clear that the number of selective categories has increased enormously. Activity of a particular neuron signifies much more than the presence of light at a particular locus in the visual field; its activity signifies a great deal about the nature of the pattern of light at that locus.

The fact that many parallel communication channels are used in the nervous system has been widely recognised, but here we see an enormous expansion of the number of parallel paths, and this occurs without much redundant reduplication of channels, for each neuron seems to have a different specific responsiveness. It is as if, at high levels, the size of the alphabet available for representing a sensory message was enormously increased. Perhaps it would be better to say that, if the activity of a low-level neuron is like the occurrence of a letter, that of a high-level neuron is like the occurrence of a word—a meaningful combination of letters. But to understand this better we must look at the third aspect of the way sensory messages are represented at different levels, namely the proportion of neurons that are usually active. If the pattern of activity caused by a visual scene has, on average, K neurons active out of the total of N neurons, then we have seen above that N increases at high levels; can one say anything about how K changes?

Number of Active Cells

If one considers the retinal cones under typical photopic conditions, the vast majority must be partially active. They may be nearer the depolarized than the hyperpolarized limit of their dynamic range, but the majority will be somewhere well within it. For the retinal ganglion cells of a cat the situation is a little different; while a few units, those corresponding to the brightest and dimmest parts of the scene, will be vigorously active, the majority, corresponding to the parts of the scene near the mean luminance, will be discharging at rates close to their maintained discharge level, which in its turn is near the low-frequency end of their dynamic range. Thus there will be a lot of units with low degrees of activity and a few which are vigorously active. Recoding in the retina changes the distribution of activity so that low impulse frequencies are common, high impulse frequencies rare.

Now consider the rabbit, with its more elaborate retinal processing, and greater richness of pattern–feature signalling neurons. It is characteristic of the more specific of these neurons that they have a very low maintained discharge, and are extremely hard to excite until their exact trigger feature has been found. One flashes lights, waves wands, and jiggles "noise figures" in the appropriate part of the visual field for many minutes, maybe hours, before finding the right combination for excitation. It is reasonably certain that the right combination does not occur often in the natural environment either, and therefore these units must spend only a small fraction of the time in an active state. Low impulse frequencies are even commoner, high impulse frequencies even rarer, than in cat retina.

For the cat cortex this trend is carried further, and one can see another aspect emerging. If one takes a small region of the visual field, it either does contain a bright bar, dark bar, or edge, or, much more likely, it does not. Thus, like the rabbit units, the cells with these specific responsivities must be only infrequently active. But in addition, on the rare occasions when one of the appropriate trigger features is present, it is one of a set which tend to be mutually exclusive: a bright bar cannot be a dark bar, and it can have only one orientation and disparity. The stimulus selects which cell to activate from a range of many possible cells, and it is pretty well impossible to activate simultaneously more than a small fraction of this number.

The picture developing is that at low levels visual information is carried by the pattern of joint activity of many elements, whereas at the upper levels of the hierarchy a relatively small proportion are active, and each of these says a lot when it is active. But, although we clearly see that the proportion active, K/N, decreases, we cannot tell whether it decreases as rapidly as N increases, and thus we still do not know how K itself changes. The second dogma goes beyond the evidence, but it attempts to make sense out of it. It asserts that the overall direction or aim of information processing in higher sensory centres is to represent the input as completely as possible by activity in as few neurons as possible (Barlow, 1961, 1969b). In other words, not only the proportion but also the actual number of active neurons, K, is reduced, while as much information as possible about the input is preserved.

By how much can one reasonably expect K to be reduced? One requires the concepts of channel capacity and redundancy from information theory (Shannon and Weaver, 1949; Woodward, 1953) to make a rough estimate. Some reduction can be accomplished without any loss of information simply by the increase of N. K/N is the probability of a fibre being active, and, if it is the same for all neurons, the information capacity of a set of N neurons, either active or not active, is $-K\log_2(K/N) - (N-K)\log_2[(N-K)/N]$. If K/N is small, the second term contributes little; the capacity then is, approximately, the number of active neurons times the information provided by each active neuron, and this increases directly as the negative logarithm of the probability of it being active, $-\log(K/N)$. Hence the number active can be reduced as N increases without loss of information capacity, but by itself this does not allow K to be reduced very much: for instance, if we suppose that ¼ of the 2×10^6 optic nerve fibres are active and that there are 10^8 cortical neurons receiving this information, then one finds that $1·5 \times 10^5$ cortical neurons must, on average, be active in order to have the same information capacity as the 5×10^5 active optic nerve fibres. But this applies only to capacity, and a substantial reduction in K is possible on the basis of another principle.

Visual information is enormously redundant, and it has been suggested previously that sensory coding is largely concerned with exploiting this redundancy to obtain more economical representation of the information. If the argument is correct, the number of active neurons can be reduced, but it is very difficult even to guess how big a reduction in K such recoding can achieve; if it is $1/10$ up to the cortex, and another factor of $1/10$ achieved in visual I, II and III, one would end up with about 1000 active fibres carrying the information provided by 5×10^6 active optic nerve fibres; though the reductions might be substantially greater or less, this is the order of magnitude of the reduction contemplated.

According to dogma, these 1000 active neurons represent the visual scene, but it is obvious that each neuron must convey an enormously larger share of the picture than, say, one point out of the quarter million points of a television picture. Perhaps a better analogy is to recall the 1000 words that a picture is proverbially worth; apparently an active neuron says something of the order of complexity of a word. It seems to me not unreasonable to suppose that a single visual scene can be represented quite completely by about 1000 of such entities, bearing in mind that each one is selected from a vast vocabulary and will in addition carry some positional information.

Third Dogma: Selectivity Adapted to Environment

Evolutionary Adaptation

Some economies of the type indicated above can be achieved by exploiting forms of redundancy which are present in all normal environments. Levels of sensory stimulation do not range at random over the whole scale of possible values, and it makes sense to regard adaptation of peripheral receptors as a measure to achieve economy by signalling changes from the mean instead of absolute values. Similarly in most situations

neighbouring points on a sensory surface are more likely to be similar than distant points, and it thus makes sense to regard contrast enhancement by lateral inhibition as another economy measure. The argument can be carried on to cover the redundancy-reducing value of movement, edge, or disparity detectors (Barlow, 1969b), but, if these are genetically-determined redundancy-reducing codes, they must be fixed once and for all during development, and they could only work for redundant properties of all sensory environments. The hypothesis becomes more interesting when one considers the possible mechanisms for achieving economy by exploiting the redundancy of particular sensory scenes, for this requires storage of information and plasticity of the neural structures involved.

Reversible Adaptation

The neural changes of dark and light adaptation may be regarded as a simple example of reversible plasticity achieving this end. The luminance corresponding to zero impulses is affected by the past history of illumination and by the surrounding luminances in such a way that the majority of fibres are responding at low frequencies. But, even though this involves definite changes in the synaptic transfer properties of retinal neurons, the statistical characteristic of visual images that enables this to achieve economy is always the same, namely the fact that the distribution of luminances is grouped around local and temporal mean values, so that small deviations from the mean are commoner than large deviations (Barlow, 1969a). Hence the most commonly occurring luminances require fewest impulses.

Permanent Adaptation

The effects permanently impressed on the visual system during the sensitive period are the first example of plasticity for a particular type of redundancy. The distribution of orientational selectivity of primary neurons is biased in favour of the orientations the individual experienced during this critical time. If the analogy of a neuron's signal resembling the utterance of a word is recalled, this result suggests that the kitten's cortex only develops words for what it has seen. This could be brought about by either selection or modification: are the dictionary words there, only the ones experienced becoming permanently connected; or do the cells themselves determine that a frequently experienced pattern, such as lines of a particular range of orientations, are events for which words are desirable? The evidence favours modification, and the idea to which it leads of the successive hierarchical construction of a dictionary of meaningful neurons has enormous appeal. For the present we can only justify the third dogma by saying the evidence suggests such a dictionary may be built up, though we are far from being able to look into its pages by physiological methods. In the next section we turn to the subjective view of this dictionary.

Fourth Dogma: Origin of Perceptions

Personal Perception

In order to delimit more accurately what this dogma does and does not say it may be useful to define and separate three mysteries of perception. The first is the personal, subjective, aspect of my experience of, say, the red pencil with a blue eraser in my hand. There does not seem to be anything that could be said about the activity of nerve cells accompanying this experience that would in any way "explain" the aspect of it that is mysterious, personal, and subjective. I think this part of the experience is something that one must be content to leave on one side for the moment, but it is important that this part of subjective experience almost always accompanies electrical stimulation of a peripheral sensory nerve, and usually accompanies electrical stimulation of the sensory areas of the brain, for this implies that the full subjective experience, including this mysterious personal element, accompanies the neural events of sensation, however these are caused. This fact strongly suggests that it is no waste of time to look into these neural events: beauty is a mysterious attribute of a work of art, but that does not imply that you cannot create a beautiful painting by non-mysterious material means.

Conscious Perception

The second mystery is that we are not consciously aware of much that goes on in our brains, so the inverse of the fourth dogma is certainly not true: not every cortical neuron's activity has a simple perceptual correlate. Even at high mental levels much neural business is conducted without conscious awareness, and my own belief is that the conscious part is confined to experiences one communicates to other people, or experiences one is contemplating communicating to other people. This immediately introduces a social element into individual consciousness, for communication is impossible without a channel being open to a recipient. However, for present purposes we need only point out that interesting aspects of consciousness of this sort are by no means incompatible with the fourth dogma. An element of perception can possess a simple neural cause without it necessarily being the case that all simple neural events cause perception. There is therefore plenty of room for social, historical, or moral influences on perception, because these can influence the selection of the neural events that enter conscious perception.

Validity of Perceptions

The third mystery about perceptions is why they are generally "true": why are they so extraordinarily useful in guiding our actions and helping us to make decisions? This is the aspect that the second and third dogmas help one to understand. The economical and fairly complete representation of visual scenes by a reasonably small number of active neurons makes it much easier to visualize how they can be used for these purposes. The key point is that the active neurons carry the bulk of the information, and the vast number of inactive ones need not be taken into consideration. The difficulty of detecting among our sense impressions the entities we use for rational thought has always been baffling: "water," "men," "sheep," and even the simple letter "A" represent particular logical functions of activity among the sensory neurons, but the number of possible logical functions is so vast that we are mystified how particular ones are realized, or why particular ones are selected for realization. The representation suggested by the second and third dogmas would allow relatively simple logical combinations to have properties approaching those required for the literal symbols of Boole (1854), the subjects of our conceptions. By using such symbols together with operational signs he founded mathematical logic, but the title of his major work, *The Laws of Thought*, clearly states his claim that his inquiries had "probable intimations concerning the nature and constitution of the human mind." It is gratifying to approach closer to an intuitively plausible neural realization of what he symbolized.

The notion that what we sense is a point by point representation of the physical signals impinging on our body has been rejected for psychological and philosophical reasons (see Boring, 1942), and more recent physiological evidence clearly supports this rejection. But this same evidence suggests that it should be replaced, not by return to a subjectively constructed phenomenology (Dreyfus, 1972), nor by the notion that we sense the world in terms of rigidly preordained "structures," but by the deeper and more adaptive ideas of dogmas two and three; our sensorium is presented with a fairly small number of communications, each representing the occurrence of a group of external events having a word-like order of complexity, and, like words, having the special property that they lead to an economical representation of these physical events.

Fifth Dogma: Signalling Subjective Certainty

There is one way in which the properties of neurons do not match up to the way Boole used symbols, for he insisted on their binary nature, or "duality." This is the property Aristotle called the principle of contradiction, and without it Boole's symbolic representation of logic would have been impossible. In contrast to this duality the response of a sensory nerve cell to its trigger feature consists of a volley of impulses lasting $\frac{1}{10}$ to 1 second, during which time the neuron can discharge any number of impulses between zero and nearly 1000. Therefore the response is graded, and it is not legitimate to consider it as a Boolean binary variable. The essential notion expressed in the fifth dogma is that a neuron stands for an idealization of reality whose complement can be formulated as a null hypothesis, and it is this that has the required Boolean logical property of duality. The idealizations should not be thought of as Kantian or Platonic, but rather as abstractions that model reality in the manner suggested by Craik (1943). The ideal populations of a statistician come even closer, for the parameters of such distributions model reality, and they are used to calculate whether or not a particular sample belongs within it. The process of idealizing the complement of the trigger feature will be clarified by a simple example.

Suppose we have a sensory neuron whose trigger feature is a simple physical event, such as the increase of light intensity at a specific position in the visual field. We are examining the suggestion that the graded responses this neuron gives to visual stimuli represent some function of the degree of certainty that the light did in fact increase, estimated from the physical events accessible to the neuron. For simplicity assume that a record is available of the total numbers of quanta absorbed in the receptive field of the sensory neuron during successive periods of about $\frac{1}{10}$ second duration up to and including the period about which it is to signal centrally. It is in principle possible to calculate the probability of occurrence of the observed number of quantal absorptions on the hypothesis that there was no change in the light intensity, and this is the test a statistician would apply to determine whether or not the trigger feature was present. On this view impulse frequency signals some function of the significance level of a test of this sort, low probabilities corresponding to high impulse frequencies. Notice that the trigger feature is "an increase of light," the idealization is "there was no increase," and this idealization is based on observation of what has recently happened and therefore incorporates a model of the recent past.

The responses actually obtained to varying intensities of incremental stimulus fit quite well into this scheme (Barlow, 1969a), as do some less obvious features. The low-frequency maintained discharge could well represent the results, of low significance, obtained by testing the null hypothesis when no stimulus has been applied. Although individual fibres would not reach significance, information about quantal absorptions would be retained, and changes insignificant singly could be combined centrally to reach significance.

In the above example a high value of P and low impulse frequency would result from a shadow falling on the receptive field. The detection of this shadow might be of great survival significance for the animal, but the on-centre unit's trigger feature, null hypothesis, and statistical tests would be a poor way of detecting and signalling this important event. A different type of unit is required whose null hypothesis should be "There has been no *decrease* in the quantal absorption rate"; these would fire when the hypothesis is disproved by the quantal absorption rate dropping below the normal range of variation. Obviously these are the off-centre units, and it seems that the existence of complementary "on" and "off" systems fits the notion quite well. When there are a large number of neurons with trigger features that cannot coexist, as in area 17, these correspond to a large number of mutually exclusive hypotheses to be tested.

The fifth dogma clearly requires more development and testing, but it provides a possible answer to the question "What variable corresponds to impulse frequency in a high level sensory neuron?" Furthermore the answer ties it to a rather definitely felt subjective quantity—the sense of certainty.

Criticisms and Alternatives

Single-unit recording hints at this probabilistic, adaptive, many-levelled, system for processing and displaying sensory information, but can we believe that what we perceive is the activity of a relatively small selection of upper-level units of this hierarchy? This is certainly a big jump beyond the present physiological evidence. We do not know how perspective transformations are disregarded, enabling us to perceive the same object irrespective of our angle of view, nor do we understand the mechanisms underlying size constancy, yet these mechanisms must intervene between the highest neurons we know about and quite simple perceptions. I think we have seen enough of what can be achieved in a few stages of neural image processing to believe that a few more stages could reach the point where a single neuron embodies, by virtue of its peripheral connections and their properties, an elementary percept, but let us examine an alternative and the evidence adduced in its support.

Combinational or Holographic Representations

The key suggestion about the organization of sensory processing that the second dogma asserts is that the information is carried by progressively fewer active neurons at progressively higher levels in the hierarchy. The brain receives complex patterns of activity in nerve fibres from the sensory receptors, and it generates complex patterns of outgoing commands to the muscles. It could be held that the patterns are equally complex at all the intervening stages as well, and this would mean that the significance of a single unit's activity

would be virtually undecipherable without knowing what was going on in a host of other units. Certainly one would make little progress in understanding a computer's operation by following the status of a single bit in its central processor, so this criticism is partly met by pointing to the success that has been achieved in the visual system by looking at the activity of units singly, one at a time. But we should also look critically at the main evidence advanced in favour of the combinatorial or holographic scheme.

Mass Action and Resistance to Damage

The main argument that has been levelled against the view that individual cells play an important role in perception and in favour of a holographic representation is the reported fact that large parts of the cortex can be damaged with only minor resultant changes in behaviour or learning (Lashley, 1929, 1950). This led to Lashley's doctrine of "cerebral mass action," but repetition of the original experiments and refinements in methods of testing, some of it by Lashley himself, have considerably weakened the original evidence in its favour (Zangwill, 1961). However, it certainly is remarkable that a mechanism with as much interdependence between its parts as the brain can function at all after it has been extensively damaged. A computer would not usually survive brain surgery or gunshot wounds, and it is therefore worthwhile considering the implications of the fact that the cortex is relatively immune to quite extensive injury.

The whole of a visual scene can be reconstructed from a small part of a hologram, with only slight loss of resolution and degradation of signal/noise ratio (Gabor et al., 1971), so it has been claimed that the cortex must operate by some analogous principle in order to account for its resistance to damage. What is not widely appreciated is the fact that holography differs from ordinary image-recording photography not only in principle, but also in the materials used, for it requires photographic emulsions with resolutions of the order of the wavelength of light (Gabor et al., 1971). With such materials a good quality 35 mm picture could easily be reproduced and repeated in every 1 mm^2 of the plate, and a plate containing such a reduplicated image would have to be pulverized into tiny pieces to prevent reconstructibility of the original from every fragment. The mass-action-like resistance to damage of the hologram is partly due to the enormous informational capacity of the materials that are required; immunity to damage is easy to achieve when such high redundancy is permissible, and this argument carries little weight in favour of holographic views of nervous operation.

Codes can be given error-correcting properties much less wastefully, and the argument can be turned around to favour the representation hypothesized in dogmas two and three. Because the few active cells have a fixed significance, and because the inactive ones are thought to carry so little information that they can be neglected, the only result of removing part of the cortex would be to eliminate some of the active neurons, and hence some of the perceptual entities, when a given scene is viewed. The "meaning" of the active units in the undamaged cortex would remain the same, and might provide a sufficient basis for decision and action. This is very different from the situation where a neuron's activity has totally different significance depending upon the pattern of activity of which it forms a part, for if any of this pattern was in a damaged region the significance of activity in the undamaged part would be altered. Hence damage immunity is really an argument for neurons having an invariant meaning not dependent upon the activity of other neurons.

It should also be pointed out that very limited replication of "percept neurons" would give considerable damage immunity: if a given neuron is replicated half a dozen times in different cortical regions there is a good chance of at least one of them surviving an extensive cortical ablation. This sixfold redundancy is enormously less than the holographic scheme possesses, and it can be concluded that the mass action argument rebounds against the extensive combinatorial usage of neurons and actually favours the hypothesis of this article.

Pontifical Cells

Sherrington (1941) introduced the notion of "one ultimate pontifical nerve-cell, . . . the climax of the whole system of integration" and immediately rejected the idea in favour of the concept of mind as a "million-fold democracy whose each unit is a cell." Those who like the notion of perception as a cooperative or emergent property of many cells dismiss the suggestion that the activity of a single

neuron can be an important element of perception by saying that, carried to its logical conclusion, it implies there must be a single "pontifical cell" corresponding to each and every recognizable object or scene. First, notice that the current proposal does not say that each distinct perception corresponds to a different neuron being active, if perception is taken to mean the whole of what is perceived at any one moment; it says there is a simple correspondence between the elements of perception and unit activity. Thus the whole of subjective experience at any one time must correspond to a specific combination of active cells, and the "pontifical cell" should be replaced by a number of "cardinal cells." Among the many cardinals only a few speak at once; each makes a complicated statement, but not, of course, as complicated as that of the pontif if he were to express the whole of perception in one utterance.

Two important difficulties arise from the notion of pontifical cells; first, if a separate neuron is needed for each of our perceptions, there are not enough to account for their almost incredible variety; second, the activity of a single isolated element would not convey anything of a perception's great richness, the connection between one perception and others. The "grandmother cell" might respond to all views of grandmother's face, but how would that indicate that it shares features in common with other human faces, and that, on a particular occasion, it occurs in a specific position surrounded by other recognizable objects? Our perceptions simply do not have the property of being isolated unique events as one would expect if each corresponded to the firing of a unique neuron. Instead, they overlap with each other, sharing parts which continue unchanged from one moment to another, or recur at later moments in different contexts. I think the "cardinal cell" representation surmounts these problems without any difficulty; if a critic can say how many different perceptions we are capable of, and how rich a network of relatedness exists between these perceptions, then one might be able to estimate how many cardinals' voices were required to represent these perceptions. But there is a misleading feature of the ecclesiastical analogy.

Most organizational hierarchies are pyramids: there are many members of the church, fewer priests, only a select number of cardinals, and a single pope. The hierarchy of sensory neurons is very different. It is true that there are more retinal receptors than ganglion cells, but the number of cortical neurons in area 17 is certainly orders of magnitude greater than the number of incoming fibres. The numbers at succeeding levels may be somewhat fewer, but a high proportion of the nerve cells in the brain must be capable of being influenced by vision, so if the hierarchical organization is pyramidal it is inverted rather than erect, divergent rather than convergent, if one uses the term "'cardinal cell," one must be sure to remember that the college of these cardinals outnumbers the church members and must include a substantial fraction of the 10^{10} cells of the human brain.

After-thoughts

It is sufficiently obvious that these propositions are incomplete, that there are aspects of the sensory problem left untouched, and that the dogmas go considerably beyond the evidence. I have said, in essence, that the cells of our brain are each capable of more than had previously been supposed, and that what their activities represent may be more simply related to the elements of our conscious perceptions than had previously been thought. But clever neurons are not enough. The simplest computer program with its recursive routines and branch points has more subtlety than the simple hierarchy of clever neurons that I have here proposed as the substrate of perception.

I think one can actually point to the main element that is lacking. We have seen that some properties of the environment can be represented, or modelled, in a system of the type proposed; I feel that a corresponding model is also needed for our own motor actions and their consequences. Such motor and sensory models could then interact and play exploratory games with each other, providing an internal model for the attempts of our ever-inquisitive perceptions to grasp the world around us. A higher-level language than that of neuronal firing might be required to describe and conceptualize such games, but its elements would have to be reducible to, or constructible from, the interactions of neurons.

The five dogmas do not impede developments in this direction. My claim for them is that they are a simple set of hypotheses on an interesting topic, that they are compatible with currently known facts, and that, if any are disproved, then knowledge in this field will be substantially advanced.

REFERENCES

Adrian, E. D., 1926a, "The impulses produced by sensory nerve-endings", Pt.1, *J. Physiol., 61,* 49–72.

Adrian, E. D., 1926b, "The impulses produced by sensory nerve-endings", Pt. 4, J. Physiol., 62, 33–51.

Adrian, E. D., 1928, *The Basis of Sensation* (Christophers, London; also Hafner, New York, 1964).

Adrian, E. D., 1941, "Afferent discharges to the cerebral cortex from peripheral sense organs", *J. Physiol., 100,* 159–191.

Adrian, E. D., 1947, *The physical background of perception* (Clarendon Press, Oxford).

Adrian, E. D., Zotterman, Y., 1926a, "The impulses produced by sensory nerve-endings, Pt.2, The response of a single end-organ", *J. Physiol., 61,* 151–171.

Adrian, E. D., Zotterman, Y., 1926b, "The impulses produced by sensory nerve-endings, Pt.3, Impulses set up by touch and pressure", *J. Physiol., 61,* 465–493.

Bard, P., 1938, "Studies on the cortical representation of somatic sensitivity", *Harvey Lectures 1938* (Academic Press, New York), pp.143–169.

Barlow, H. B., 1953, "Summation and inhibition in the frog's retina", *J. Physiol., 119,* 69–88.

Barlow, H. B., 1956, "Retinal noise and absolute threshold", *J. Opt. Soc. Amer., 46,* 634–639.

Barlow, H. B., 1960, "The coding of sensory messages" in *Current Problems in Animal Behaviour*, Eds. W. H. Thorpe, O. L. Zangwill (Cambridge University Press, Cambridge), pp. 331–360.

Barlow, H. B., 1961, "Possible principles underlying the transformations of sensory messages" in *Sensory Communication*, Ed. W. A. Rosenblith (MIT Press, Cambridge, Mass. and John Wiley, New York), pp. 217–234.

Barlow, H. B., 1969a, "Pattern recognition and the responses of sensory neurons", *Ann. N. Y. Acad. Sci., 156,* 872–881.

Barlow, H. B., 1969b, 'Trigger features, adaptation, and economy of impulses", in *Information Processing and the Nervous System*, Ed. K. N. Leibovic (Springer-Verlag, New York), pp. 209–226.

Barlow, H. B., Blakemore, C., Pettigrew, J. D., 1967, "The neural mechanism of binocular depth discrimination", *J. Physiol., 193,* 327–342.

Barlow, H. B., Brindley, G. S., 1963, "Interocular transfer of movement aftereffects during pressure binding of the stimulated eye", *Nature, 200,* 1346–1347.

Barlow, H. B., FitzHugh, R., Kuffler, S. W., 1957, "Change of organization in the receptive fields of the cat's retina during dark adaptation", *J. Physiol., 137,* 338–354.

Barlow, H. B., Hill, R. M., 1963, "Evidence for a physiological explanation of the waterfall phenomenon and figural after-effects", *Nature, 200,* 1345–1347.

Barlow, H. B., Hill, R. M., Levick, W. R., 1964, "Retinal ganglion cells responding selectively to direction and speed of image motion in the rabbit"; *J. Physiol.; 173;* 377–407.

Barlow, H. B., Levick, W. K., Yoon, M., 1971, "Responses to single quanta of light in retinal ganglion cells of the cat", *Vision Research, 11,* Suppl. 3, 87–102.

Barlow, H. B., Pettigrew, J. D., 1971, "Lack of specificity of neurones in the visual cortex of young kittens", *J. Physiol., 218,* 98–100.

Bishop, P. O., 1970, "Beginning of form vision and binocular depth discrimination in cortex", in *The Neurosciences: Second Study Program*, Ed. F. O. Schmitt (Rockefeller University Press, New York), pp. 471–485.

Blakemore, C., Campbell, F. W., 1969, "On the existence of neurones in the human visual system selectively sensitive to the orientation and size of retinal images", *J. Physiol., 203,* 237–260.

Blakemore, C., Cooper, G. F., 1970, "Development of the brain depends on the visual environment", *Nature, 228,* 477–478.

Blakemore, C., Mitchell, D. E., 1973, "Environmental modification of the visual cortex and the neural basis of learning and memory", *Nature, 241,* 467–468.

Boole, G., 1854, *An Investigation of the Laws of Thought* (Dover Publications Reprint, New York).

Boring, E. G., 1942, *Sensation and perception in the history of experimental psychology* (Appleton Crofts, New York).

Burns, B., 1968, *The uncertain nervous system* (Edward Arnold, London).

Campbell, F. W., Green, D. G., 1965, "Optical and retinal factors affecting visual resolution", *J. Physiol., 181,* 576–593.

Cragg, B. G., 1972, "The development of synapses in cat visual cortex", *Investigative Ophthalmology, 11,* 377–385.

Craik, K. J. W., 1943, *The Nature of Explanation* (Cambridge University Press, Cambridge).

De Valois, R. L., 1960, "Color vision mechanisms in the monkey", *J. Cen. Physiol., 45,* Suppl., 115–128.

De Valois, R. L., Abramov, I., Jacobs, G. H., 1966, "Analysis of response patterns of in LGN cells", *J. Opt. Soc. Am., 56,* 966, 977.

De Valois, R. L., Abramov, I., Mead, W. R., 1967, "Single cell analysis of wavelength discrimination at the lateral geniculate nucleus in the macaque", *J. Neurophysiol, 30,* 415–433.

Dreyfus, H. L., 1972, *What Computers Can't Do* (Harper and Row, New York).

Enroth-Cugell, C., Robson, J. G., 1966, "The contrast sensitivity of retinal ganglion cells of the cat", *J. Physiol., 187,* 517–552.

Ewert, J. P., 1970, "Neural mechanisms of prey-catching and avoidance behavior in the toad (*Bufo bufo L.*)", *Brain Behav. Evol., 3,* 36–56.

Fry, G. A., 1948, "Mechanisms subserving simultaneous brightness contrast", *Am. J. Optom., 25,* 162–178.

Gabor, D., Kock, W. E., Stroke, G. W., 1971, "Holography", *Science, 173,* 11–23.

Galambos, R., 1944, "Inhibition of activity in single auditory nerve fibers by acoustic stimulation", *J. Neurophysiol., 7,* 287–303.

Galambos. R., Davis, H., 1943, "The response of single auditory-nerve fibres to acoustic stimulation", *J. Neurophysiol., 7,* 287–303.

Galambos, R., Davis, H., 1948, "Action potentials from single auditory-nerve fibres?" *Science, 108,* 513.

Ganchrow, J. K., Erickson, R. P., 1970, "Neural correlates of gustatory intensity and quality", *J. Neurophysiol., 33,* 768–783.

Granit, R., 1947, *The Sensory Mechanisms of the Retina* (Oxford University Press, Oxford).

Granit, R., Svaetichin, G., 1939, "Principles and technique of the electrophysiological analysis of colour reception with the aid of microelectrodes", Upsala Läkaref Färh., 65, 161–177.

Green, D. M., Swets, J. A., 1966, *Signal Detection Theory and Psychophysics* (John Wiley, New York).

Gross, C. G., Rocha-Miranda, C. E., Bender, D. B., 1972, "Visual properties of neurons in inferotemporal cortex of the macaque", *J. Neurophysiol., 35,* 96–111.

Grüsser, O.-J., Grüsser-Cornehls, U., 1968, "Neurophysiologische Grundlagn visueller angeborener Auslösemechanismen beim Frosch", *Zeitschrift für vergleichende Physiologie, 59,* 1–24.

Hartline, H. K., 1938, "The response of single optic nerve fibres of the vertebrate eye to illumination of the retina", *Am. J. Physiol., 121,* 400–415.

Hartline, H. K., 1940a, "The receptive fields of optic nerve fibers", *Am. J. Physiol., 130,* 690–699.

Hartline, H. K., 1940b, "The effects of spatial summation in the retina on the excitation of the fibers of the optic nerve", *Am. J. Physiol., 130,* 700–711.

Hecht, S., Shlaer, S., Pirenne, M., 1942, "Energy, quanta, and vision", *J. Gen. Physiol., 25,* 819–840.

Hirsch, H. V. B., Spinelli, D. N., 1970, "Visual experience modifies distribution of horizontally and vertically oriented receptive fields in cats", *Science, 168,* 869–871.

Hirsch, H. V. B., Spinelli, D. N., 1971, "Modification of the distribution of receptive field orientation in cats by selective visual exposure during development", *Exp. Brain Res., 13,* 509–527.

Hubel, D. H., Wiesel, T. N., 1959, "Receptive fields of single neurons on the cat's striate cortex", *J. Physiol., 160,* 106–154.

Hubel, D. H., Wiesel, T. N., 1962, "Receptive fields, binocular interaction, and functional architecture in the cat's visual cortex", *J. Physiol., 148,* 574–591.

Hubel, D. H., Wiesel, T. N., 1963, "Receptive fields of cells in striate cortex of very young, visually inexperienced kittens", *J. Neurophysiol., 26,* 994–1002.

Hubel, D. H., Wiesel, T. N., 1965, "Binocular interaction in striate cortex of kittens reared with artificial squint", *J. Neurophysiol., 28,* 1041–1059.

Hubel, D. H., Wiesel, T. N., 1970, "The period of susceptibility to the physiological effects of unilateral eye closure in kittens", *J. Physiol., 906,* 419–436.

Hurvich, L. M., Jameson, D., 1960, "Perceived color, induction effects, and opponent-response mechanisms", *J. Gen. Physiol., 43,* Suppl., 66–80.

Ingle, D., 1968, "Visual release of prey-catching behaviour in frogs and toads", *Brain, Behaviour and Evolution, 1,* 500–518.

Ingle, D., 1971, "Prey-catching behaviour of anurans toward moving and stationary objects", *Vision Research,* Suppl. No. 3, 447–456.

Kuffler, S. W., 1953, "Discharge patterns and functional organization of mammalian retina", *J. Neurophysiol., 16,* 37–68.

Lashley, K. S., 1929, *Brain Mechanisms and Intelligence: A Quantitative Study of Injuries to the Brain* (University of Chicago Press, Chicago).

Lashley, K. S., 1950, "In search of the Engram physiological mechanisms in animal behaviour", in *Symposium of the Society for Experimental Biology,* Ed. J. F. Danielli and R. Brown (Cambridge University Press, Cambridge).

Lettvin, J. Y., Maturana, H. R., McCulloch, W. S., Pitts, W. H., 1959, "What the frog's eye tells the frog's brain", *Proc. Inst. Rad. Eng., 47,* 1940–1951.

Levick, W. R., 1967, "Receptive fields and trigger features of ganglion cells in the visual streak of the rabbit's retina", *J. Physiol., 188,* 285–307.

Mach, E., 1886, *The Analysis of Sensations, and the Relation of the Physical to the Psychial*. Translation of first edition (1886) revised from fifth German edition by S. Waterlow (Open Court, Chicago and London, 1914) Ed. C. M. Williams. (Also Dover Publications, New York, 1959.)

Marshall, W. H., Woolsey, C. N., Bard, P., 1941, "Observations on cortical somatic sensory mechanisms of cat and monkey", *J. Neurophysiol., 4,* 1–24.

Maturana, H. R., Lettvin, J. Y., McCulloch, W. S., Pitts, W. H., 1960, "Anatomy and physiology of vision in the frog (*Rana Pipiens*)", *J. Gen. Physiol., 43,* Suppl. No.2, Mechanisms of Vision,

McCulloch, W. S., 1959, "Agatha Tyche: of nervous nets— the lucky reckoners," in *Mechanisation of Thought Processes: Proceedings of a Symposium Held at the National Physical Laboratory, Vol.2* (HMSO, London), pp. 611–634.

Pettigrew, J. D. (forthcoming), "The effect of visual experience on the development of stimulus specificity by kitten cortical neurones".

Pettigrew, J. D., Freeman, R. (forthcoming), "Visual experience without lines: Effect on developing cortical neurones".

Pettigrew, J. D., Nikara, T., Bishop, P. O., 1968, "Binocular interaction on single units in cat striate cortex: simultaneous stimulation by single moving slit with receptive fields in correspondence", *Exp. Brain Res., 6,* 391–410.

Pfaffman, C., 1941, "Gustatory afferent impulses", *J. Cell. Comp. Physiol., 17,* 243–258.

Pfaffman, C., 1955, "Gustatory nerve impulses in rat, cat, and rabbit", *J. Neurophysiol., 18,* 429–440.

Sakitt, B., 1972, "Counting every quantum", *J. Physiol., 222,* 131–150.

Shannon, C. E., Weaver, W., 1949, *The mathematical theory of communication* (University of Illinois Press, Urbana).

Sherrington, C. S., 1941, *Man on His Nature* (Cambridge University press, Cambridge).

Shlaer, R., 1971, "Shift in binocular disparity causes compensatory change in the cortical structure of kittens", *Science, 173,* 638–641.

Stone, J., 1972, "Morphology and physiology of the geniculocortical synapse in the cat: The question of parallel input to the striate cortex", *Invest. Ophthal., 11,* 338–346.

Svaetichin, G., MacNichol, E. R., Jr.,1958, "Retinal mechanisms for chromatic and achromatic vision", *Ann. N. Y. Acad. Sci. 74,* 385–404.

Talbot, W. H., Darian-Smith, I., Kornhuber, H. H., Mountcastle, V. B., 1968, "The sense of flutter-vibration: Comparison of human capacity with response patterns of mechano-receptive afferents from the monkey hand", *J. Neurophysiol., 31,* 301–334.

Tanner, W. P., Jr., Swets, J. A., 1954, "A decision making theory of visual detection", *Psychol. Review, 61,* 401–409.

Wagner, H. G., MacNichol, E. R., Wolbarsht, M. L., 1960, "The response properties of single ganglion cells in the goldfish retina", *J. Gen. Physiol, 43,* Suppl., 115–128.

Wiesel, T. N., Hubel, D. H., 1963, "Single cell responses in striate cortex of kittens deprived of vision in one eye", *J. Neurophysiol., 26,* 1004–1017.

Wiesel, T. N., Hubel, D. H., 1965, "Comparison of the effects of unilateral and bilateral eye closure on cortical unit responses in kittens", *J. Neurophysiol., 28,* 1029–1040.

Wohlgemuth, A., 1911, "On the after-effect of seen movement", *Brit. J. Psychol.,* Monograph. Suppl., 1, 1–17.

Woodward, P. M., 1953, *Probability and Information Theory with Applications to Radar* (Pergamon Press, Oxford).

Yarbus, A. L., 1965, *Eye Movements and Vision*, Translated from Russian by Basil Haigh (Plenum Press, New York).

Zangwill, O. L., 1961, "Lashley's concept of cerebral mass action", in *Current Problems in Animal Behaviour*, Eds. W. H. Thorpe, O. L. Zangwill (Cambridge University Press, Cambridge).

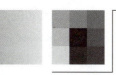

Introduction to Reading 4

J. J. Gibson (1904–1979) was one of the most influential perceptual psychologists of the 20th century. Over a period of three decades, he developed a rich theoretical framework for understanding perception that presented a powerful and controversial challenge to main-stream ideas. I refer to Gibson's contribution as a "theoretical framework" rather than as a theory because he advocated a set of very broad principles to guide one's thinking about perception rather than a specific set of proposals that may apply to specified domains, although he is known for his incisive analysis of important perceptual problems, such as the perception of depth or of optic flow. His central ideas, including *direct perception, ecological optics, invariants*, and *affordances* have deep implications for the sorts of experiments one will be led to carry out and the sorts of explanations that should be developed to account for data.

In a collection like this one, each of the selections provides only a small glimpse of the underlying themes that motivated and carried beyond the work in question. Perhaps more than any other selection in this volume, this reading fails to capture adequately the scope of Gibson's ideas. However, it does provide a flavor for his style of discourse and reasoning, and it gives an introduction to the notion of information pickup. A sketch of some of Gibson's other ideas follows.

The scientific Zeitgeist among perception theorists in the 1950s and 60s, when Gibson began the development of his most influential theoretical ideas (and continuing today), was that of constructivism. Perception is indirect in the sense that the organism engages in a sort of "perceptual thought" as Irvin Rock (1983) put it. Helmholtz's idea of unconscious inference (Reading 1) is a major source of constructivism.

Gibson came to reject the foundation of constructivism: in particular, he viewed the organism and the world as inseparable, and he held that perception was direct and unmediated by inference or "perceptual thought." The connection between an organism and its environment is the central idea of evolutionary biology: organisms adapt to their environments so as to support reproductive success. Organisms are optimized for survival; they exist only because they have successfully adapted. Among these adaptations (for most organisms) is the ability to know the local conditions so as to obtain food or avoid predators. This aspect of Gibson's world view, although not as central a part of most contemporary theories of perception as it is for Gibson, is nevertheless uncontroversial.

In contrast, the notion of direct perception, and the ecological optics that support it, is a radical departure. Ecological optics begins from the observation that the world consists of surfaces that structure the ambient light (through reflection). The organism intercepts a small segment of the ambient array of light, which contains information that specifies various properties of visible surfaces (color, texture, depth, slant, shape). A major goal of Gibson's research program was to analyze the information contained in the optic array, in order to understand what properties about surfaces it contained. Gibson emphasizes that the optic array must be considered as a whole in what it specifies about surfaces. For example, the perceived size of an object depends not only on the retinal image size of the object and its perceived distance, but also on such factors as the amount of ground texture it occludes. Movement of the observer within the environment provides rich information about the relative positions of objects and surfaces. Thus, says Gibson, it is inadequate to assume that the stimulus is an object in isolation; one must analyze the optic array as a whole.

Invariants in a scene provide information about a wide variety of scene properties. Dynamic invariants like optic flow provide information about the observer's motion within the environment and about where and when a collision will occur; structural invariants like the texture gradient on a slanted surface (assuming the surface has a roughly uniform texture, which is almost always the case) provide information about surface orientation. Gibson emphasized that perception is active and involves an interaction between the organism and the environment. Organisms evolved to actively extract invariants from the environment.

Perhaps the most radical idea in Gibson's body of work is that of the direct perception of *affordances*. Objects and surfaces have meanings that are relevant for action: chairs afford sitting, stairs afford climbing, a stone affords grasping and throwing, a ledge affords support for standing, and so forth. Gibson held that such environmental meanings are directly "picked up" by the organism. He sometimes used the analogy of a radio being tuned to a particular portion of the electromagnetic spectrum, and resonating to the signal there. Similarly, an organism resonates to certain invariants in the optic array that directly specify what actions the local environment affords. The details of just how this takes place, what specific brain mechanisms carry out this function, is something Gibson never addressed.

Gibson's ideas have inspired the work of ecological perception theorists; the community of skeptics, however, is larger. One detailed articulation of a skeptic's viewpoint, along with a number of brief replies both pro and con, can be found in Ullman (1980). Michaels & Carello (1981) provide an exellent introduction to the theory of direct perception. However, the richest source are the many writings of Gibson himself (e.g., 1950, 1966, 1979; Reed & Jones, 1982).

REFERENCES

Gibson, J. J. (1950). *Perception of the visual world*. Boston: Houghton Mifflin.

Gibson, J. J. (1966). *The senses considered as perceptual systems*. Boston: Houghton Mifflin.

Gibson, J. J. (1979). *The ecological approach to visual perception*. Boston: Houghton Mifflin.

Michaels, C. F., & Carello, C. (1981). *Direct perception*. Englewood Cliffs, NJ: Prentice-Hall.

Reed, E., & Jones, R. (Eds.) (1982). *Reasons for realism: Selected essays of James J. Gibson*. Hillsdale, NJ: Lawrence Erlbaum Associates.

Rock, I. (1983). *The logic of perception*. Cambridge, MA: MIT Press.

Ullman, S. (1980). Against direct perception. *Behavioral and Brain Sciences, 3*, 373–415.

The Theory of Information Pickup and its Consequences

J. J. Gibson • Cornell University

In this book the traditional theories of perception have been abandoned. The perennial doctrine that two-dimensional images are restored to three-dimensional reality by a process called depth perception will not do. Neither will the doctrine that the images are transformed by the cues for distance and slant so as to yield constancy of size and shape in the perception of objects. The deep-seated notion of the retinal image as a still picture has been abandoned.

The simple assumption that perceptions of the world are caused by stimuli from the world will not do. The more sophisticated assumption that perceptions of the world are caused when sensations triggered by stimuli are supplemented by memories will not do either. Not even the assumption that a sequence of stimuli is converted into a phenomenal scene by memory will do. The very notion of stimulation as typically composed of discrete stimuli has been abandoned.

The established theory that exteroception and proprioception arise when exteroceptors and proprioceptors are stimulated will not do. The doctrine of special channels of sensation corresponding to specific nerve bundles has been abandoned.

The belief of empiricists that the perceived meanings and values of things are supplied from the past experience of the observer will not do. But even worse is the belief of nativists that meanings and values are supplied from the past experience of the race by way of innate ideas. The theory that meaning is attached to experience or imposed on it has been abandoned.

Not even the current theory that the inputs of the sensory channels are subject to "cognitive processing" will do. The inputs are described in terms of information theory, but the processes are described in terms of old-fashioned mental acts: recognition, interpretation, inference, concepts, ideas, and storage and retrieval of ideas. These are still the operations of the mind upon the deliverances of the senses, and there are too many perplexities entailed in this theory. It will not do, and the approach should be abandoned.

What sort of theory, then, will explain perception? Nothing less than one based on the pickup of information. To this theory, even in its undeveloped state, we should now turn.

Let us remember once again that it is the perception of the environment that we wish to explain. If we were content to explain only the perception of forms or pictures on a surface, of nonsense figures to which meanings must be attached, of discrete stimuli imposed on an observer willy-nilly, in short, the items most often presented to an observer in the laboratory, the traditional theories might prove to be adequate and would not have to be abandoned. But we should not be content with that limited aim. It leaves out of account the eventful world and the perceiver's awareness of being in the world. The laboratory does not have to be limited to simple stimuli, so-called. The experiments reported in Chapters 9 and 10 showed that information can be displayed.

What is New about the Pickup of Information?

The theory of information pickup differs radically from the traditional theories of perception. First, it involves a new notion of perception, not just a new theory of the process. Second, it involves a new assumption about what there is to be perceived. Third, it involves a new conception of the information for perception, with two kinds always available, one about the environment and another about the self. Fourth, it requires the new assumption of perceptual systems with overlapping functions, each having outputs to adjustable organs as well as inputs from organs. We are especially concerned with vision, but none of the systems, listening, touching, smelling, or tasting, is a channel of sense. Finally, fifth, optical information pickup entails an activity of the system not heretofore imagined by any visual scientist, the concurrent registering of both persistence and change in the flow of structured stimulation. This is the crux of the theory but the hardest part to explicate, because it can be phrased in different ways and a terminology has to be invented.

Consider these five novelties in order, ending with the problem of detecting variants and invariants or change and nonchange.

A Redefinition of Perception

Perceiving is an achievement of the individual, not an appearance in the theater of his consciousness. It is a keeping-in-touch with the world, an experiencing of things rather than a having of experiences. It involves awareness-of instead of just awareness. It may be awareness of something in the environment or something in the observer or both at once, but there is no content of awareness independent of that of which one is aware. This is close to the act psychology of the nineteenth century except that perception is not a mental act. Neither is it a bodily act. Perceiving is a psychosomatic act, not of the mind or of the body but of a living observer.

The act of picking up information, moreover, is a continuous act, an activity that is ceaseless and unbroken. The sea of energy in which we live flows and changes without sharp breaks. Even the tiny fraction of this energy that affects the receptors in the eyes, ears, nose, mouth, and skin is a flux, not a sequence. The exploring, orienting, and adjusting of these organs sink to a minimum during sleep but do not stop dead. Hence, perceiving is a stream, and William James's description of the stream of consciousness (1890, Ch. 9) applies to it. Discrete percepts, like discrete ideas, are "as mythical as the Jack of Spades."

The continuous act of perceiving involves the coperceiving of the self. At least, that is one way to put it. The very term *perception* must be redefined to allow for this fact, and the word *proprioception* must be given a different meaning than it was given by Sherrington.

A New Assertion about What is Perceived

My description of the environment and the changes that can occur in it implies that places, attached objects, objects, and substances are what are mainly perceived, together with events, which are changes of these things. To see these things is to perceive what they afford. This is very different from the accepted categories of what there is to perceive as described in the textbooks. Color, form, location, space, time, and motion—these are the chapter headings that have been handed down through the centuries, but they are not what is perceived.

Places. A *place* is one of many adjacent places that make up the habitat and, beyond that, the whole environment. But smaller places are nested within larger places. They do not have boundaries, unless artificial boundaries are imposed by surveyors (my piece of land, my town, my country, my state). A place at one level is what you can see from here or hereabouts, and locomotion consists of going from place to place in this sense (Chapter 11). A very important kind of learning for animals and children is place-learning—learning the affordances of places and learning to distinguish among them—and way-finding, which culminate in the state of being oriented to the whole habitat and knowing where one is in the environment.

A place persists in some respects and changes in others. In one respect, it cannot be changed at all—in its location relative to other places. A place cannot be displaced like an object. That is, the adjacent order of places cannot be permuted; they cannot be shuffled. The sleeping places, eating places, meeting places, hiding places, and falling-off places of the habitat are immobile. Place-learning is therefore different from other kinds.

Attached Objects. I defined an *object* in Chapter 3 as a substance partially or wholly surrounded by the medium. An object attached to a place is only partly surrounded. It is a protuberance. It cannot be displaced without becoming detached. Nevertheless, it has a surface and enough of a natural boundary to constitute a unit. Attached objects can thus be counted. Animals and children learn what such objects are good for and how to distinguish them. But they cannot be separated from the places where they are found.

Detached Objects. A fully detached object can be displaced or, in some cases, can displace itself. Learning to perceive it thus has a different character from learning to perceive places and attached objects. Its affordances are different. It can be put side by side with another object and compared. It can therefore be grouped or classed by the manipulation of sorting. Such objects when grouped can be rearranged, that is, permuted. And this means not only that they can be counted but that an abstract number can be assigned to the group.

It is probably harder for a child to perceive "same object in a different place" than it is to perceive "same object in the same place." The former requires that the information for persistence-despite-displacement should have been noticed, whereas the latter does not.

Inanimate detached objects, rigid or nonrigid, natural or manufactured, can be said to have features that distinguish them. The features are probably not denumerable, unlike the objects themselves. But if they are compounded to specify affordances, as I argued they must be, only the relevant compounds need to be distinguished. So when it comes to the natural, nonrigid, animate objects of the world whose dimensions of difference are overwhelmingly rich and complex, we pay attention only to what the animal or person affords.

Persisting Substances. A *substance* is that of which places and objects are composed. It can be vaporous, liquid, plastic, viscous, or rigid, that is, increasingly "substantial." A substance, together with what it affords, is fairly well specified by the color and texture of its surface. Smoke, milk, clay, bread, and wood are polymorphic in layout but invariant in color-texture. Substances, of course, can be smelled and tasted and palpated as well as seen.

The animal or child who begins to perceive substances, therefore, does so in a different way than one who begins to perceive places, attached objects, and detached objects. Substances are formless and cannot be counted. The number of substances, natural compositions, or mixtures is not fixed. (The number of chemical elements is fixed, but that is a different matter.) We discriminate among surface colors and textures, but we cannot group them as we do detached objects and we cannot order them as we do places.

We also, of course, perceive changes in otherwise persisting substances, the ripening of fruit, and the results of boiling and baking, or of mixing and hardening. But these are a kind of event.

Events. As I used the term, an *event* is any change of a substance, place, or object, chemical, mechanical, or biophysical. The change may be slow or fast, reversible or nonreversible, repeating or nonrepeating. Events include what happens to objects in general, plus what the animate objects make happen. Events are nested within superordinate events. The motion of a detached object is not the prototype of an event that we have been led to think it was. Events of different sorts are perceived as such and are not, surely, reducible to elementary motions.

The Information for Perception

Information, as the term is used in this book (but not in other books), refers to specification of the observer's environment, not to specification of the observer's receptors or sense organs. The qualities of objects are specified by information; the qualities of the receptors and nerves are specified by sensations. Information about the world cuts right across the qualities of sense.

The term *information* cannot have its familiar dictionary meaning of *knowledge communicated to a receiver*. This is unfortunate, and I would use another term if I could. The only recourse is to ask the reader to remember that picking up information is not to be thought of as a case of communicating. The world does not speak to the observer. Animals and humans communicate with cries, gestures, speech, pictures, writing, and television, but we cannot hope to understand perception in terms of these channels; it is quite the other way around. Words and pictures convey information, carry it, or transmit it, but the information in the sea of energy around each of us, luminous or mechanical or chemical energy, is not conveyed. It is simply there. The assumption that information can be transmitted and the assumption that it can be stored are appropriate for the theory of communication, not for the theory of perception.

The vast area of speculation about the so-called media of communication had a certain discipline imposed on it some years ago by a mathematical theory of communication (Shannon and Weaver, 1949). A useful measure of information transmitted was formulated, in terms of "bits." A sender and receiver, a channel, and a finite number of possible signals were assumed. The result was a genuine discipline of communications engineering. But, although psychologists promptly tried to apply it to the senses and neuropsychologists began thinking of nerve impulses in terms of bits and the brain in terms of a computer, the applications did not work. Shannon's concept of information applies to telephone hookups and radio broadcasting in elegant ways but not, I think, to the firsthand perception of being in-the-world, to what the baby gets when first it opens its eyes. The information for perception, unhappily, cannot be defined and measured as Claude Shannon's information can be.

The information in ambient light, along with sound, odor, touches, and natural chemicals, is inexhaustible. A perceiver can keep on noticing facts about the world she lives in to the end of her life without ever reaching a limit. There is no threshold for information comparable to a stimulus threshold. Information is not lost to the environment when gained by the individual; it is not conserved like energy.

Information is not specific to the banks of photoreceptors, mechanoreceptors, and chemoreceptors that lie within the sense organs. Sensations are specific to receptors and thus, normally, to the kinds of stimulus energy that touch them off. But information is not energy-specific. Stimuli are not always imposed on a passive subject. In life one *obtains* stimulation in order to extract the information (Gibson, 1966b, Ch. 2). The information can be the same, despite a radical change in the stimulation obtained.

Finally, a concept of information is required that admits of the possibility of illusion. Illusions are a theoretical perplexity in any approach to the study of perception. Is information always valid and illusion simply a failure to pick it up? Or is the information picked up sometimes impoverished, masked, ambiguous, equivocal, contradictory, even false? The puzzle is especially critical in vision.

In Chapter 14 of *The Senses Considered as Perceptual Systems* (Gibson, 1966b) and again in this book I have tried to come to terms with the problem of misperception. I am only sure of this: it is not one problem but a complex of different problems. Consider, first, the mirage of palm trees in the desert sky, or the straight stick that looks bent because it is partly immersed in water. These illusions, together with the illusion of Narcissus, arise from the regular reflection or refraction of light, that is, from exceptions to the ecological optics of the scatter-reflecting surface and the perfectly homogeneous medium. Then consider, second, the misperception in the case of the shark under the calm water or the electric shock hidden in the radio cabinet. Failure to perceive the danger is not then blamed on the perceiver. Consider, third, the sheet of glass mistaken for an open doorway or the horizontal sheet of glass (the optical cliff) mistaken for a void. A fourth case is the room composed of trapezoidal surfaces or the trapezoidal window, which look normally rectangular so long as the observer does not open both eyes and walk around. Optical misinformation enters into each of these cases in a different way. But in the last analysis, *are* they explained by misinformation? Or is it a matter of failure to pick up *all* the available information, the inexhaustible reservoir that lies open to further scrutiny?

The misperceiving of affordances is a serious matter. As I noted in Chapter 8, a wildcat may look like a cat. (But *does* he look just like a cat?) A malevolent man may act like a benevolent one. (But *does* he exactly?) The line between the pickup of misinformation and the failure to pick up information is hard to draw.

Consider the human habit of picture-making, which I take to be the devising and displaying of optical information for perception by others. It is thus a means of communication, giving rise to mediated apprehension, but it is more like direct pickup than word-making is. Depiction and its consequences are deferred until later, but it can be pointed out here that picture-makers have been experimenting on us for centuries with artificial displays of information in a special form. They enrich or impoverish it, mask or clarify it, ambiguate or disambiguate it. They often try to produce a discrepancy of information, an equivocation or contradiction, in the same display. Painters invented the cues for depth in the first place, and psychologists looked at their paintings and began to talk about cues. The notions of counterbalanced cues, of figure-ground reversals, of equivocal perspectives, of different perspectives on the same object, of "impossible" objects—all these come from artists who were simply experimenting with frozen optical information.

An important fact to be noted about any pictorial display of optical information is that, in contrast with the inexhaustible reservoir of information in an illuminated medium, it cannot be looked at close up. Information to specify the display as such, the canvas, the surface, the screen, can always be picked up by an observer who walks around and looks closely.

The Concept of a Perceptual System

The theory of information pickup requires perceptual systems, not senses. Some years ago I tried to prove that a perceptual system was radically different from a sense (Gibson, 1966b), the one being active and the other passive. People said, "Well, what I mean by a sense is an *active* sense." But it turned out that they still meant the passive inputs of a sensory nerve, the activity being what occurs in the brain when the inputs get there. That was not what I meant by a perceptual system. I meant the activities of looking, listening, touching, tasting, or sniffing. People then said, "Well, but those are responses to sights, sounds, touches, tastes, or smells, that is, motor acts resulting from sensory inputs. What you call a perceptual system is nothing but a case of feedback." I was discouraged. People did not understand.

I shall here make another attempt to show that the senses considered as special senses cannot be reconciled with the senses considered as perceptual systems. The five perceptual systems correspond to five modes of overt attention. They have overlapping functions, and they are all more or less subordinated to an overall orienting system. A system has organs, whereas a sense has receptors. A system can orient, explore, investigate, adjust, optimize, resonate, extract, and come to an equilibrium, whereas a sense cannot. The characteristic activities of the visual system have been described in Chapter 12 of this book. The characteristic activities of the auditory system, the haptic system, and the two related parts of what I called the "chemical value system" were described in Chapters 5–8 of my earlier book (Gibson, 1966b). Five fundamental differences between a sense and a perceptual system are given below.

1. A special sense is defined by a bank of receptors or receptive units that are connected with a so-called projection center in the brain. Local stimuli at the sensory surface will cause local firing of neurons in the center. The adjustments of the organ in which the receptors are incorporated are not included within the definition of a sense.

    A perceptual system is defined by an organ and its adjustments at a given level of functioning, subordinate or superordinate. At any level, the incoming and outgoing nerve fibers are considered together so as to make a continuous loop.

    The organs of the visual system, for example, from lower to higher are roughly as follows. First, the lens, pupil, chamber, and retina comprise an organ. Second, the eye with its muscles in the orbit comprise an organ that is both stabilized and mobile. Third, the two eyes in the head comprise a binocular organ. Fourth, the eyes in a mobile head that can turn comprise an organ for the pickup of ambient information. Fifth, the eyes in a head on a body constitute a superordinate organ for information pickup over paths of locomotion. The adjustments of accommodation, intensity modulation, and dark adaptation go with the first level. The movements of compensation, fixation, and scanning go with the second level. The movements of vergence and the pickup of disparity go with the third level. The movements of the head, and of the body as a whole, go with the fourth and fifth levels. All of them serve the pickup of information.

2. In the case of a special sense, the receptors can only receive stimuli, passively, whereas in the case of a perceptual system the input-output loop can be supposed to obtain information, actively. Even when the theory of the special senses is liberalized by the modern hypothesis of receptive units, the latter are supposed to be triggered by complex stimuli or modulated in some passive fashion.

3. The inputs of a special sense constitute a rep-

ertory of innate sensations, whereas the achievements of a perceptual system are susceptible to maturation and learning. Sensations of one modality can be combined with those of another in accordance with the laws of association; they can be organized or fused or supplemented or selected, but *no new sensations can be learned*. The information that is picked up, on the other hand, becomes more and more subtle, elaborate, and precise with practice. One can keep on learning to perceive as long as life goes on.

4. The inputs of the special senses have the qualities of the receptors being stimulated, whereas the achievements of the perceptual systems are specific to the qualities of things in the world, especially their affordances. The recognition of this limitation of the senses was forced upon us by Johannes Müller with his doctrine of specific "nerve energies." He understood clearly, if reluctantly, the implication that, because we can never know the external causes of our sensations, we cannot know the outer world. Strenuous efforts have to be made if one is to avoid this shocking conclusion. Helmholtz argued that we must deduce the causes of our sensations because we cannot detect them. The hypothesis that sensations provide clues or cues for perception of the world is similar. The popular formula that we can interpret sensory signals is a variant of it. But it seems to me that all such arguments come down to this: we can perceive the world only if we already know what there is to be perceived. And that, of course, is circular. I shall come back to this point again.

The alternative is to assume that sensations triggered by light, sound, pressure, and chemicals are merely incidental, that information is available to a perceptual system, and that the qualities of the world in relation to the needs of the observer are experienced directly.

5. In the case of a special sense the process of attention occurs at centers within the nervous system, whereas in the case of a perceptual system attention pervades the whole input-output loop. In the first case attention is a consciousness that can be focused; in the second case it is a skill that can be educated. In the first case physiological metaphors are used, such as the filtering of nervous impulses or the switching of impulses from one path to another. In the second case the metaphors used can be terms such as *resonating, extracting, optimizing, or symmetricalizing* and such acts as orienting, exploring, investigating, or adjusting.

I suggested in Chapter 12 that a normal act of visual attention consists of scanning a whole feature of the ambient array, not of fixating a single detail of the array. We are tempted to think of attention as strictly a narrowing-down and holding-still, but actually this is rare. The invariants of structure in an optic array that constitute information are more likely to be gradients than small details, and they are scanned over wide angles.

The Registering of Both Persistence and Change

The theory of information pickup requires that the visual system be able to detect both persistence and change—the persistence of places, objects, and substances along with whatever changes they undergo. Everything in the world persists in some respects and changes in some respects. So also does the observer himself. And some things persist for long intervals, others for short.

The perceiving of persistence and change (instead of color, form, space, time, and motion) can be stated in various ways. We can say that the perceiver separates the change from the nonchange, *notices* what stays the same and what does not, or sees the continuing identity of things along with the events in which they participate. The question, of course, is how he does so. What is the information for persistence and change? The answer must be of this sort: The perceiver extracts the invariants of structure from the flux of stimulation while still noticing the flux. For the visual system in particular, he tunes in on the invariant structure of the ambient optic array that underlies the changing perspective structure caused by his movements.

The hypothesis that invariance under optical transformation constitutes information for the perception of a rigid persisting object goes back to the moving-shadow experiment (Gibson and Gibson, 1957). The outcome of that experiment was paradoxical; it seemed at the time that a changing form elicited the perception of a constant form with a changing slant. The solution was to postulate invariants of optical structure for the persisting object, "formless" invariants, and a particular disturbance of optical structure for the motion of the object, a perspective transformation. Separate terms needed to be devised for physical motions and for the optical motions that specified them, for events in the world and for events in the array, for geometry did not provide the terms. Similarly, different terms need to be invented to describe invariants of the changing world and invariants of the changing array; the geometrical word *form* will not do. Perhaps the best policy is to use the terms *persistence* and *change* to refer to the environment but *preservation* and *disturbance* of structure to refer to the optic array.

The stimulus-sequence theory of perception, based on a succession of discrete eye fixations, can assume only that the way to apprehend persistence is by an act of comparison and judgment. The perception of what-it-is-now is compared with the memory of what-it-was-then, and they are judged *same*. The continuous pickup theory of perception can assume that the apprehension of persistence is a simple act of invariance detection. Similarly, the snapshot theory must assume that the way to apprehend change is to compare what-it-is-now with what-it-was-then and judge *different*, whereas the pickup theory can assume an awareness of transformation. The congruence of the array with itself or the disparity of the array with itself, as the case may be, is picked up.

The perception of the persisting identity of things is fundamental to other kinds of perception. Consider an example, the persisting identity of another person. How does a child come to apprehend the identity of the mother? You might say that when the mother-figure, or the face, is continually fixated by the child the persistence of the sensation is supported by the continuing stimulus. So it is when the child clings to the mother. But what if the mother-figure is scanned? What if the figure leaves and returns to the field of view? What if the figure goes away and comes back? What is perceived when it emerges from the distance or from darkness, when its back is turned, when its clothing is changed, when its emotional state is altered, when it comes back into sight after a long interval? In short, how is it that the phenomenal identity of a person agrees so well with the biological identity, despite all the vicissitudes of the figure in the optic array and all the events in which the person participates?

The same questions can be asked about inanimate objects, attached objects, places, and substances. The features of a person are invariant to a considerable degree (the eyes, nose, mouth, style of gesture, and voice). But so are the analogous features of other things, the child's blanket, the kitchen stove, the bedroom, and the bread on the table. All have to be identified as continuing, as persisting, as maintaining existence. And this is not explained by the constructing of a concept for each.

We are accustomed to assuming that successive stimuli from the same entity, sensory encounters with it, are united by an act of recognition. We have assumed that perception ceases and memory takes over when sensation stops. Hence, every fresh glimpse of anything requires the act of linking it up with the memories of that thing instead of some other thing. The judgment, "I have seen this before," is required for the apprehension of "same thing," even when the observer has only turned away, or has only glanced away for an instant. The classical theory of sense perception is reduced to

THE EFFECTS OF PERSISTENT STIMULATION ON PERCEPTION

We have assumed that perception stops when sensation stops and that sensation stops when stimulation stops, or very soon thereafter. Hence, a persisting stimulus is required for the perception of a persisting object. The fact is, however, that a truly persisting stimulus on the retina or the skin specifies only that the observer does not or cannot move his eye or his limb, and the sense perception soon fades out by sensory adaptation (Chapter 4). The persistence of an object is specified by invariants of structure, not by the persistence of stimulation.

The seeing of persistence considered as the picking up of invariants under change resolves an old puzzle: the phenomenal identity of the spots of a retinal pattern when the image is transposed over the retina stroboscopically. The experiments of Josef Ternus first made this puzzle evident. See Gibson (1950, p. 56 ff.) for a discussion and references.

I used to think that the aftereffects of persisting stimulation of the retina obtained by the prolonged fixation of a display could be very revealing. Besides ordinary afterimages there are all sorts of perceptual aftereffects, some of which I discovered. But I no longer believe that experiments on so-called perceptual adaptation are revealing, and I have given up theorizing about them. The aftereffects of prolonged scrutiny are of many sorts. Until we know more about information pickup, this field of investigation will be incoherent.

an absurdity by this requirement. The alternative is to accept the theory of invariance detection.

The quality of familiarity that can go with the perception of a place, object, or person, as distinguished from the quality of unfamiliarity, is a fact of experience. But is familiarity a result of the percept making contact with the traces of past percepts of the same thing? Is unfamiliarity a result of not making such contact? I think not. There is a circularity in the reasoning, and it is a bad theory. The quality of familiarity simply accompanies the perception of persistence.

The perception of the persisting identity of places and objects is more fundamental than the perception of the differences among them. We are told that to perceive something is to categorize it, to distinguish it from the other types of things that it might have been. The essence of perceiving is discriminating. Things differ among themselves, along dimensions of difference. But this leaves out of account the simple fact that the substance, place, object, person, or whatever has to last long enough to be distinguished from other substances, places, objects, or persons. The detecting of the invariant features of a persisting thing should not be confused with the detecting of the invariant features that make different things similar. Invariants over time and invariants over entities are not grasped in the same way.

In the case of the persisting thing, I suggest, the perceptual system simply extracts the invariants from the flowing array; it *resonates* to the invariant structure or is attuned to it. In the case of substantially distinct things, I venture, the perceptual system must abstract the invariants. The former process seems to be simpler than the latter, more nearly automatic. The latter process has been interpreted to imply an intellectual act of lifting out something that is mental from a collection of objects that are physical, of forming an abstract concept from concrete percepts, but that is very dubious. Abstraction is invariance detection across objects. But the invariant is only a similarity, not a persistence.

Summary of the Theory of Pickup

According to the theory being proposed, *perceiving* is a registering of certain definite dimensions of invariance in the stimulus flux together with definite parameters of disturbance. The invariants are invariants of structure, and the disturbances are disturbances of structure. The structure, for vision, is that of the ambient optic array.

The invariants specify the persistence of the environment and of oneself. The disturbances specify the changes in the environment and of oneself. A perceiver is aware of her existence in a persisting environment and is also aware of her movements relative to the environment, along with the motions of objects and nonrigid surfaces relative to the environment. The term *awareness* is used to imply a direct pickup of the information, not necessarily to imply consciousness.

There are many dimensions of invariance in an ambient optic array over time, that is, for paths of observation. One invariant, for example, is caused by the occluding edge of the nose, and it specifies the self. Another is the gradient of optical texture caused by the material texture of the substratum, and it specifies the basic environment. Equally, there are many parameters of disturbance of an ambient optic array. One, for example, is caused by the sweeping of the nose over the ambient optic array, and it specifies head turning. Another is the deletion and accretion of texture at the edges of a form in the array, and it specifies the motion of an object over the ground.

For different kinds of events in the world there are different parameters of optical disturbance, not only accretion-deletion but also polar outflow-inflow, compression, transformation, substitution, and others. Hence, the same object can be seen undergoing different events, and different objects can be seen undergoing the same event. For example, an apple may ripen, fall, collide, roll, or be eaten, and eating may happen to an apple, carrot, egg, biscuit, or lamb chop. If the parameter of optical disturbance is distinguished, the event will be perceived. Note how radically different this is from saying that if stimulus-event A is invariably followed by stimulus-event B we will come to expect B whenever we experience A. The latter is classical association theory (or conditioning theory, or expectancy theory). It rests on the stimulus-sequence doctrine. It implies that falling, colliding, rolling, or eating are not units but sequences. It implies, with David Hume, that even if B has followed A a thousand times there is no certainty that it will follow A in the future. An event is only known by a conjunction of atomic sensations, a contingency. If this recurrent sequence is experienced again and again, the observer will begin to anticipate, or have faith, or learn by induction, but that is the best he can do.

The process of pickup is postulated to depend on the input-output loop of a perceptual system. For this reason, the information that is picked up cannot be the familiar kind that is transmitted from one person to another and that can be stored. According to pickup theory, information does not have to be stored in memory because it is always available.

The process of pickup is postulated to be very susceptible to development and learning. The opportunities for educating attention, for exploring and adjusting, for extracting and abstracting are unlimited. The increasing capacity of a perceptual system to pick up information, however, does not in itself constitute information. The ability to perceive does not imply, necessarily, the having of an idea of what can be perceived. The having of ideas is a fact, but it is not a prerequisite of perceiving. Perhaps it is a kind of extended perceiving.

The Traditional Theories of Perception: Input Processing

The theory of information pickup purports to be an alternative to the traditional theories of perception. It differs from all of them, I venture to suggest, in rejecting the assumption that perception is the processing of inputs. *Inputs* mean sensory or afferent nerve impulses to the brain.

Adherents to the traditional theories of perception have recently been making the claim that what they assume is the processing of information in a modern sense of the term, not sensations, and that therefore they are not bound by the traditional theories of perception. But it seems to me that all they are doing is climbing on the latest bandwagon, the computer bandwagon, without reappraising the traditional assumption that perceiving is the processing of inputs. I refuse to let them pre-empt the term *information*. As I use the term, it is not something that has to be processed. The inputs of the receptors have to be processed, of course, because they in themselves do not specify anything more than the anatomical units that are triggered.

All kinds of metaphors have been suggested to describe the ways in which sensory inputs are processed to yield perceptions. It is supposed that sensation occurs first, perception occurs next, and knowledge occurs last, a progression from the lower to the higher mental processes. One process

is the filtering of sensory inputs. Another is the organizing of sensory inputs, the grouping of elements into a spatial pattern. The integrating of elements into a temporal pattern may or may not be included in the organizing process. After that, the processes become highly speculative. Some theorists propose mental operations. Others argue for semilogical processes or problem-solving. Many theorists are in favor of a process analogous to the decoding of signals. All theorists seem to agree that past experience is brought to bear on the sensory inputs, which means that memories are somehow applied to them. Apart from filtering and organizing, the processes suggested are cognitive. Consider some of them.

Mental Operations on the Sensory Inputs

The a priori categories of understanding possessed by the perceived, according to Kant
The perceiver's presuppositions about what is being perceived
Innate ideas about the world

Semilogical Operations on the Sensory Inputs

Unconscious inferences about the outer causes of the sensory inputs, according to Helmholtz (the outer world is deduced)
Estimates of the probable character of the "distant" objects based on the "proximal" stimuli, according to Egon Brunswik (1956), said to be a quasirational, not a fully rational, process

Decoding Operations on the Sensory Inputs

The interpreting of the inputs considered as signals (a very popular analogy with many variants)
The decoding of sensory messages
The utilizing of sensory cues
The understanding of signs, or indicators, or even *clues*, in the manner of a police detective

The Application of Memories to the Sensory Inputs

The "accrual" of a context of memory images and feelings to the core of sensations, according to E. B. Titchener's theory of perception (1924)

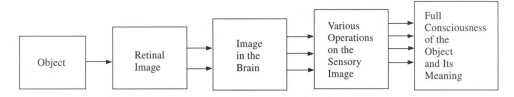

FIGURE 4.1 ■ The Commonly Supposed Sequence of Stages in the Visual Perceiving of an Object

This last hypothetical process is perhaps the most widely accepted of all, and the most elaborated. Perceptual learning is supposed to be a matter of enriching the input, not of differentiating the information (Gibson and Gibson, 1955). But the process of combining memories with inputs turns out to be not at all simple when analyzed. The appropriate memories have to be retrieved from storage, that is, aroused or summoned; an image does not simply accrue. The sensory input must fuse in some fashion with the stored images; or the sensory input is assimilated to a composite memory image, or, if this will not do, it is said to be assimilated to a class, a type, a schema, or a concept. Each new sensory input must be categorized—assigned to its class, matched to its type, fitted to its schema, and so on. Note that categories cannot become established until enough items have been classified but that items cannot be classified until categories have been established. It is this difficulty, for one, that compels some theorists to suppose that classification is a priori and that people and animals have innate or instinctive knowledge of the world.

The error lies, it seems to me, in assuming that either innate ideas or acquired ideas must be applied to bare sensory inputs for perceiving to occur. The fallacy is to assume that because inputs convey no knowledge they can somehow be made to yield knowledge by "processing" them. Knowledge of the world must come from somewhere; the debate is over whether it comes from stored knowledge, from innate knowledge, or from reason. But all three doctrines beg the question. Knowledge of the world cannot be explained by supposing that knowledge of the world already exists. All forms of cognitive processing imply cognition so as to account for cognition.

All this should be treated as ancient history. Knowledge of the environment, surely, develops as perception develops, extends as the observers travel, gets finer as they learn to scrutinize, gets longer as they apprehend more events, gets fuller as they see more objects, and gets richer as they notice more affordances. Knowledge of this sort does not "come from" anywhere; it is got by looking, along with listening, feeling, smelling, and tasting. The child also, of course, begins to acquire knowledge that comes from parents, teachers, pictures, and books. But this is a different kind of knowledge.

The False Dichotomy between Present and Past Experience

The division between present experience and past experience may seem to be self-evident. How could anyone deny it? Yet it is denied in supposing that we can experience both change and nonchange. The difference between present and past blurs, and the clarity of the distinction slips away. The stream of experience does not consist of an instantaneous present and a linear past receding into the distance; it is not a "traveling razor's edge" dividing the past from the future. Perhaps the present has a certain duration. If so, it should be possible to find out when perceiving stops and remembering begins. But it has not been possible. There are attempts to talk about a "conscious" present, or a "specious" present, or a "span" of present perception, or a span of "immediate memory," but they all founder on the simple fact that there is no dividing line between the present and the past, between perceiving and remembering. A special sense impression clearly ceases when the sensory excitation ends, but a perception does not. It does not become a memory after a certain length of time. A perception, in fact, does not *have* an end. Perceiving goes on.

Perhaps the force of the dichotomy between present and past experience comes from language, where we are not allowed to say anything intermediate between "I see you" and "I saw you" or "I am seeing you" and "I was seeing you." Verbs can take the present tense or the past tense. We have no words to describe my continuing awareness of you, whether you are in sight or out of sight. Language is categorical. Because we are led to separate the present from the past, we find ourselves involved in what I have called the "muddle of memory" (Gibson, 1966a). We think that the past ceases to exist unless it is "preserved" in memory. We assume that memory is the bridge between the past and the present. We assume that memories accumulate and are stored somewhere; that they are images, or pictures, or representations of the past; or that memory is actually physiological, not mental, consisting of engrams or traces; or that it actually consists of neural connections, not engrams; that memory is the basis of all learning; that memory is the basis of habit; that memories live on in the unconscious; that heredity is a form of memory; that cultural heredity is another form of memory; that any effect of the past on the present is memory, including hysteresis. If we cannot do any better than this, we should stop using the word.

The traditional theories of perception take it for granted that what we see now, present experience, is the sensory basis of our perception of the environment and that what we have seen *up to now*, past experience, is added to it. We can only understand the present in terms of the past. But what we see *now* (when it is carefully analyzed) turns out to be at most a peculiar set of surfaces that happen to come within the field of view and face the point of observation. It does not comprise what we see. It could not possibly be the basis of our perception of the environment. What we see *now* refers to the self, not the environment. The perspective appearance of the world at a given moment of time is simply what specifies to the observer where he is at that moment. The perceptual process does not begin with this peculiar projection, this momentary pattern. The perceiving of the world begins with the pickup of invariants.

Evidently the theory of information pickup does not need memory. It does not have to have as a basic postulate the effect of past experience on present experience by way of memory. It needs to explain learning, that is, the improvement of perceiving with practice and the education of attention, but not by an appeal to the catch-all of past experience or to the muddle of memory.

The state of a perceptual system is altered when it is attuned to information of a certain sort. The system has become sensitized. Differences are noticed that were previously not noticed. Features become distinctive that were formerly vague. But this altered state need not be thought of as depending on a memory, an image, an engram, or a trace. An image of the past, if experienced at all, would be only an incidental symptom of the altered state.

This is not to deny that reminiscence, expectation, imagination, fantasy, and dreaming actually occur. It is only to deny that they have an essential role to play in perceiving. They are kinds of visual awareness other than perceptual. Let us now consider them in their own right.

A New Approach to Nonperceptual Awareness

The redefinition of *perception* implies a redefinition of the so-called higher mental processes. In the old mentalistic psychology, they stood above the lower mental processes, the sensory and reflex processes, which could be understood in terms of the physiology of receptors and nerves. These higher processes were vaguely supposed to be intellectual processes, inasmuch as the intellect was contrasted with the senses. They occurred in the brain. They were operations of the mind. No list of them was ever agreed upon, but *remembering, thinking, conceiving, inferring, judging, expecting*, and, above all, *knowing* were the words used. *Imagining, dreaming, rationalizing*, and *wishful thinking* were also recognized, but it was not clear that they were higher processes in the intellectual sense. I am convinced that none of them can ever be understood as an operation of the mind. They will never be understood as reactions of the body, either. But perhaps if they are reconsidered in relation to ecological perceiving they will begin to sort themselves out in a new and reasonable way that fits with the evidence.

To perceive is to be aware of the surfaces of the environment and of oneself in it. The interchange between hidden and unhidden surfaces is essential to this awareness. These are existing surfaces; they are specified at some points of observation. Perceiving gets wider and finer and longer and richer and fuller as the observer explores the environment. The full awareness of surfaces includes their layout, their substances, their events, and their affordances. Note how this definition includes within perception a part of memory, expectation, knowledge, and meaning—some part but not all of those mental processes in each case.

One kind of remembering, then, would be an awareness of surfaces that have ceased to exist or events that will not recur, such as items in the story of one's own life. There is no point of observation at which such an item will come into sight.

To expect, anticipate, plan, or imagine creatively is to be aware of surfaces that do not exist or events that do not occur but that could arise or be fabricated within what we call the limits of possibility.

To daydream, dream, or imagine wishfully (or fearfully) is to be aware of surfaces or events that do not exist or occur and that are outside the limits of possibility.

These three kinds of nonperceptual awareness are not explained, I think, by the traditional hypothesis of mental imagery. They are better explained by some such hypothesis as this: a perceptual system that has become sensitized to certain invariants and can extract them from the stimulus flux can also operate without the constraints of the stimulus flux. Information becomes further detached from stimulation. The adjustment loops for looking around, looking at, scanning, and focusing are then inoperative. The visual system visualizes. But this is still an activity of the system, not an appearance in the theater of consciousness.

Besides these, other kinds of cognitive awareness occur that are not strictly perceptual. Before considering them, however, I must clarify what I mean by *imaginary* or *unreal*.

The Relationship between Imagining and Perceiving

I assume that a normal observer is well aware of the difference between surfaces that exist and surfaces that do not. (Those that do not have ceased to exist, or have not begun to, or have not and will not.) How can this be so? What is the information for existence? What are the criteria? It is widely believed that young children are not aware of the differences, and neither are adults suffering from hallucinations. They do not distinguish between what is "real" and what is "imaginary" because perception and mental imagery cannot be separated. This doctrine rests on the assumption that, because a percept and an image both occur in the brain, the one can pass over into the other by

gradual steps. The only "tests for reality" are intellectual. A percept cannot validate itself.

We have been told ever since John Locke that an image is a "faint copy" of a percept. We are told by Titchener (1924) that an image is "easily confused with a sensation" (p. 198). His devoted student, C. W. Perky, managed to show that a faint optical picture secretly projected from behind on a translucent screen is sometimes not identified as such when an observer is imagining an object of the same sort on the screen (Perky, 1910). We are told by a famous neurosurgeon that electrical stimulation of the surface of the brain in a conscious patient "has the force" of an actual perception (Penfield, 1958). It is said that when a feeling of reality accompanies a content of consciousness it is marked as a percept and when it does not it is marked as an image. All these assertions are extremely dubious.

I suggest that perfectly reliable and automatic tests for reality are involved in the working of a perceptual system. They do not have to be intellectual. A surface is seen with more or less definition as the accommodation of the lens changes; an image is not. A surface becomes clearer when fixated; an image does not. A surface can be scanned; an image cannot. When the eyes converge on an object in the world, the sensation of crossed diplopia disappears, and when the eyes diverge, the "double image" reappears; this does not happen for an image in the space of the mind. An object can be scrutinized with the whole repertory of optimizing adjustments described in Chapter 11. No image can be scrutinized—not an afterimage, not a so-called eidetic image, not the image in a dream, and not even a hallucination. An imaginary object can undergo an *imaginary* scrutiny, no doubt, but you are not going to discover a new and surprising feature of the object this way. For it is the very features of the object that your perceptual system has already picked up that constitute your ability to visualize it. The most decisive test for reality is whether you can discover new features and details by the act of scrutiny. Can you obtain new stimulation and extract new information from it? Is the information inexhaustible? Is there more to be seen? The imaginary scrutiny of an imaginary entity cannot pass this test.

A related criterion for the existence of a thing is reversible occlusion. Whatever goes out of sight as you move your head and comes into sight as you move back is a *persisting* surface. Whatever comes into sight when you move your head is *pre-existing* surface. That is to say, it exists. The present, past, or future tense of the verb *see* is irrelevant; the fact is perceived without words. Hence, a criterion for *real* versus *imaginary* is what happens when you turn and move. When the infant turns her head and creeps about and brings her hands in and out of her field of view, she perceives what is real. The assumption that children cannot tell the difference between what is real and what is imaginary until the intellect develops is mentalistic nonsense. As the child grows up, she apprehends more reality as she visits more places of her habitat.

Nevertheless, it is argued that dreams sometimes have the "feeling" of reality, that some drugs can induce hallucinations, and that a true hallucination in psychosis is proof that a mental image can be the same as a percept, for the patient acts as if he were perceiving and thinks he is perceiving. I remain dubious (Gibson, 1970). The dreamer is asleep and cannot make the ordinary tests for reality. The drug-taker is hoping for a vision and does not want to make tests for reality. There are many possible reasons why the hallucinating patient does not scrutinize what he says he sees, does not walk around it or take another look at it or test it.

There is a popular fallacy to the effect that if you can touch what you see it is real. The sense of touch is supposed to be more trustworthy than the sense of sight, and Bishop Berkeley's theory of vision was based on this idea. But it is surely wrong. Tactual hallucinations can occur as well as visual. And if the senses are actually perceptual systems, the haptic system as I described it (Gibson, 1966b) has its own exploratory adjustments and its own automatic tests for reality. One perceptual system does not *validate* another. Seeing and touching are two ways of getting much the same information about the world.

A New Approach to Knowing

The theory of information pickup makes a clear-cut separation between perception and fantasy, but it closes the supposed gap between perception and knowledge. The extracting and abstracting of invariants are what happens in both perceiving and knowing. To perceive the environment and to conceive it are different in degree but not in kind. One is continuous with the other. Our reasons for supposing that seeing something is quite unlike knowing something come from the old doctrine that seeing is having temporary sensations one after another at the passing moment of present time, whereas knowing is having permanent concepts stored in memory. It should now be clear that perceptual seeing is an awareness of persisting structure.

Knowing is an *extension* of perceiving. The child becomes aware of the world by looking around and looking at, by listening, feeling, smelling, and tasting, but then she begins to be *made* aware of the world as well. She is shown things, and told things, and given models and pictures of things, and then instruments and tools and books, and finally rules and short cuts for finding out more things. Toys, pictures, and words are aids to perceiving, provided by parents and teachers. They transmit to the next generation the tricks of the human trade. The labors of the first perceivers are spared their descendants. The extracting and abstracting of the invariants that specify the environment are made vastly easier with these aids to comprehension. But they are not in themselves knowledge, as we are tempted to think. All they can do is facilitate knowing by the young.

These extended or aided modes of apprehension are all cases of information pickup from a stimulus flux. The learner has to hear the speech in order to pick up the message; to see the model, the picture, or the writing; to manipulate the instrument in order to extract the information. But the information itself is largely independent of the stimulus flux.

What are the kinds of culturally transmitted knowledge? I am uncertain, for they have not been considered at this level of description. Present-day discussions of the "media of communication" seem to me glib and superficial. I suspect that there are many kinds merging into one another, of great complexity. But I can think of three obvious ways to facilitate knowing, to aid perceiving, or to extend the limits of comprehension: the use of instruments, the use of verbal descriptions, and the use of pictures. Words and pictures work in a different way than do instruments, for the information is obtained at second hand. Consider them separately.

Knowing Mediated by Instruments

Surfaces and events that are too small or too far away cannot be perceived. You can of course increase the visual solid angle if you approach the item and put your eye close to it, but that procedure has its limits. You cannot approach the moon by walking, and you cannot get your eye close enough to a drop of pond water to see the little animals swimming in it. What can be done is to *enlarge* the visual solid angle from the moon or the water drop. You can convert a tiny sample of the ambient optic array at a point of observation into a magnified sample by means of a telescope or a microscope. The structure of the sample is only a little distorted. The surfaces perceived when the eye is placed at the eyepiece are "virtual" instead of "real," but only in the special sense that they are very much closer to the observer. The invariants of structure are nearly the same when a visual angle with its nested components is magnified. This description of magnification comes from ecological optics. For designing the lens system of the instrument, a different optics is needed.

The discovery of these instruments in the seventeenth century enabled men to know much more about very large bodies and very small bodies than they had before. But this new knowledge was almost like seeing. The mountains of the moon and the motions of a living cell could be observed with adjustments of the instrument not unlike those of the head and eyes. The guarantees of reality were similar. You did not have to take another person's word for what he had seen. You might have to learn to use the instrument, but you did not have to learn to interpret the information. Nor did you have to judge whether or not the other person was telling the truth. With a telescope or a microscope you could look for yourself.

All sorts of instruments have been devised for mediating apprehension. Some optical instruments merely enhance the information that vision is ready to pick up; others—a spectroscope, for example—require some inference; still others, like the Wilson cloud chamber, demand a complex chain of inferences.

Some measuring instruments are closer to perception than others. The measuring stick for counting units of distance, the gravity balance for counting units of mass, and the hourglass for time are easy to understand. But the complex magnitudes of physical science are another matter. The voltmeters, accelerometers, and photometers are hard to understand. The child can see the pointer and the scale well enough but has to learn to "read" the instrument, as we say. The direct perception

THE UNAIDED PERCEIVING OF OBJECTS IN THE SKY

Objects in the sky are very different from objects on the ground. The heavenly bodies do not come to rest on the ground as ordinary objects do. The rainbow and the clouds are transient, forming and dissipating like mists on earth. But the sun, the moon, the planets, and the stars seem permanent, appearing to revolve around the stationary earth in perfect cycles and continuing to exist while out of sight. They are immortal and mysterious. They cannot be scrutinized.

Optical information for direct perception of these bodies with the unaided eye is lacking. Their size and distance are indeterminate except that they rise and set from behind the distant horizon and are thus very far away. Their motions are very different from those of ordinary objects. The character of their surfaces is indefinite, and of what substances they are composed is not clear. The sun is fiery by day, and the others are fiery at night, unlike the textured reflecting surfaces of most terrestrial objects. What they afford is not visible to the eye. Lights in the sky used to look like gods. Nowadays they look like flying saucers.

of a distance is in terms of whether one can jump it. The direct perception of a mass is in terms of whether one can lift it. Indirect knowledge of the metric dimensions of the world is a far extreme from direct perception of the affordance dimensions of the environment. Nevertheless, they are both cut from the same cloth.

Knowing Mediated by Descriptions: Explicit Knowledge

The principal way in which we save our children the trouble of finding out everything for themselves is by describing things for them. We transmit information and convey knowledge. Wisdom is handed down. Parents and teachers and books give the children knowledge of the world at second hand. Instead of having to be extracted by the child from the stimulus flux, this knowledge is communicated to the child.

It is surely true that speech and language convey information of a certain sort from person to person and from parent to child. Written language can even be stored so that it accumulates in libraries. But we should never forget that this is information that has been put into words. It is not the limitless information available in a flowing stimulus array.

Knowledge that has been put into words can be said to be *explicit* instead of *tacit*. The human observer can verbalize his awareness, and the result is to make it communicable. But my hypothesis is that there has to be an awareness of the world before it can be put into words. You have to see it before you can say it. Perceiving precedes predicating.

In the course of development the young child first hears talk about what she is perceiving. Then she begins herself to talk about what she perceives. Then she begins to talk to herself about what she knows—when she is alone in her crib, for example. And, finally, her verbal system probably begins to verbalize silently, in much the same way that the visual system begins to visualize, without the constraints of stimulation or muscular action but within the limits of the invariants to which the system is attuned. But no matter how much the child puts knowledge into words all of it cannot be put into words. However skilled an explicator one may become one will always, I believe, see more than one can say.

Consider an adult, a philosopher, for example, who sees the cat on the mat. He knows *that* the cat is on the mat and believes the proposition and can say it, but all the time he plainly sees all sorts of wordless facts—the mat extending without interruption behind the cat, the far side of the cat, the cat hiding part of the mat, the edges of the cat, the cat being supported by the mat, or resting on it, the horizontal rigidity of the floor under the mat, and so on. The so-called concepts of extension, of far and near, gravity, rigidity, horizontal, and so on, are nothing but partial abstractions from a rich but unitary perception of *cat-on-mat*. The parts of it he can name are called concepts, but they are not all of what he can see.

Fact and Fiction in Words and Pictures

Information about the environment that has been put into words has this disadvantage: The reality testing that accompanies the pickup of natural information is missing. Descriptions, spoken or written, do not permit the flowing stimulus array to be scrutinized. The invariants have already been extracted. You have to trust the original perceiver; you must "take his word for it," as we say. What he presents may be fact, or it may be fiction. The same is true of a depiction as of a description.

The child, as I argued above, has no difficulty in contrasting real and imaginary, and the two do not merge. But the factual and the fictional may do so. In storytelling, adults do not always distinguish between true stories and fairy stories. The child herself does not always separate the giving of an account from the telling of a story. Tigers and dragons are both fascinating beasts, and the child will not learn the difference until she perceives that the zoo contains the former but not the latter.

Fictions are not necessarily fantasies. They do not automatically lead one astray, as hallucinations do. They can promote creative plans. They can permit vicarious learning when the child identifies with a fictional character who solves problems and makes errors. The "comic" characters of childhood, the funny and the foolish, the strong and the weak, the clever and the stupid, occupy a great part of children's cognitive awareness, but this does not interfere in the least with their realism when it comes to perceiving.

The difference between the real and the imaginary is specified by two different modes of operation of a perceptual system. But the difference between the factual and the fictional depends on the social system of communication and brings in complicated questions. Verbal descriptions can be true or false as predications. Visual depictions can be correct or incorrect in a wholly different way. A picture cannot be true in the sense that a proposition is true, but it may or may not be true to life.

Knowing and Imagining Mediated by Pictures

Perceiving, knowing, recalling, expecting, and imagining can all be induced by pictures, perhaps even more readily than by words. Picture-making and picture-perceiving have been going on for twenty or thirty thousand years of human life, and this achievement, like language, is ours alone. The image makers can arouse in us an awareness of what they have seen, of what they have noticed, of what they recall, expect, or imagine, and they do so *without converting the information into a different mode*. The description puts the optical invariants into words. The depiction, however, captures and displays them in an optic array, where they are more or less the same as they would be in the case of direct perception. So I will argue, at least. The justification of this theory is obviously not a simple matter, and it is deferred to the last chapters of this book, Part IV.

The reality-testing that accompanies unmediated perceiving and that is partly retained in perceiving with instruments is obviously lost in the kind of perceiving that is mediated by pictures. Nevertheless, pictures give us a kind of grasp on the rich complexities of the natural environment that words could never do. Pictures do not stereotype our experience in the same way and to the same degree. We can learn from pictures with less effort than it takes to learn from words. It is not like perceiving at first hand, but it is *more* like perceiving than any verbal description can be.

The child who has learned to talk about things and events can, metaphorically, talk to himself silently about things and events, so it is supposed. He is said to have "internalized" his speech, whatever that might mean. By analogy with this theory, a child who has learned to draw might be supposed to picture to himself things and events without movement of his hands, to have "internalized" his picturemaking. A theory of internal language and internal images might be based on this theory. But it seems to me very dubious. Whether or not it is plausible is best decided after we have considered picturemaking in its own right.

Summary

When vision is thought of as a perceptual system instead of as a channel for inputs to the brain, a new theory of perception considered as information pickup becomes possible. Information is conceived as available in the ambient energy flux, not as signals in a bundle of nerve fibers. It is information about both the persisting and the changing features of the environment together. Moreover, information about the observer and his movements is available, so that self-awareness accompanies perceptual awareness.

The qualities of visual experience that are specific to the receptors stimulated are not relevant to information pickup but incidental to it. Excitation and transmission are facts of physiology at the cellular level.

The process of pickup involves not only overt movements that can be measured, such as orienting, exploring, and adjusting, but also more general activities, such as optimizing, resonating, and extracting invariants, that cannot so easily be measured.

The ecological theory of direct perception cannot stand by itself. It implies a new theory of cognition in general. In turn, that implies a new theory of noncognitive kinds of awareness—fictions, fantasies, dreams, and hallucinations.

Perceiving is the simplest and best kind of knowing. But there are other kinds, of which three were suggested. Knowing by means of instruments extends perceiving into the realm of the very distant and the very small; it also allows of metric knowledge. Knowing by means of language makes knowing explicit instead of tacit. Language permits descriptions and pools the accumulated observations of our ancestors. Knowing by means of pictures also extends perceiving and consolidates the gains of perceiving.

The awareness of imaginary entities and events might be ascribed to the operation of the perceptual system with a suspension of reality-testing, Imagination, as well as knowledge and perception, can be aroused by another person who uses language or makes pictures.

These tentative proposals are offered as a substitute for the outworn theory of past experience, memory, and mental images.

REFERENCES

Brunswick, E. (1956). *Perception and the representative design of psychological experiments.* Berkeley: University of California Press.

Gibson, J. J. (1950). *The perception of the visual world.* Boston: Houghton Mifflin.

Gibson, J. J. (1966a). The problem of temporal order in stimulations and perception. *Journal of Psychology, 62,* 141–149.

Gibson, J. J. (1966b). *The senses considered as perceptual systems.* Boston: Houghton Mifflin.

Gibson, J. J. (1970). On the relation between hallucination and perception. *Leonardo, 3,* 425–427.

Gibson, J. J., & Gibson, E. J. (1955). Perceptual learning: Differentiation or enrichment? *Psychological Review, 62,* 32–41.

James, W. (1890). *The principles of psychology,* Vol. 1. New York: Henry Holt.

Penfield, W. (1958). Some mechanisms of consciousness discovered during electrical stimulation of the brain. *Proceedings of the National Academy of Science, 44,* 51–66.

Perky, C. W. (1910). An experimental study of imagination. *American Journal of Psychology, 21,* 422–452. Routledge and Kegan Paul.

Shannon, C. E., & Weaver, W. (1949). *The mathematical theory of communication.* Urbana: University of Illinois Press.

Titchener, E. B. (1924). *A textbook of psychology.* New York: Macmillan.

Introduction to Reading 5

David Marr (1945–1980) was a neurobiologist and computer scientist who, with the publication of *Vision* in 1982, provided a sudden insight that changed the way many vision scientists thought about their work. In fact, Marr's contribution was twofold: he provided a theoretical analysis of vision as a scientific problem (an analysis that yielded principles that he thought should guide theory development), and, together with several colleagues, he proposed theories of vision, guided by those principles, in several domains, including the detection of edges (Marr & Hildreth, 1980) and the perception of depth (Marr & Poggio, 1979) and shape (Marr & Nishihara, 1978). This work was partly inspired by what was perhaps the first effort to treat vision as a computational problem by Koenderink and van Doorn (1976).

The selection reprinted here is the first chapter of *Vision*, which describes the principles that characterize different aspects of vision as a scientific problem. The distinctions he makes between the computational, algorithmic/representational, and implementational levels of analysis have guided the thinking of vision scientists ever since; one could argue that these ideas have been more influential than the domain-specific models themselves.

The computational level of analysis concerns the goals and purpose of the system under investigation. A computational analysis of a system attempts to characterize, in an abstract way, what the system is designed to do. Palmer (1999) draws an instructive analogy with a household thermostat to clarify this idea: a computational analysis of a thermostat specifies the quantitative relationships among its inputs (the current temperature and the temperature setting) and its outputs (a signal to the furnace to turn on or off). The method by which these mathematical relations are achieved is not part of the analysis, nor are the specific properties of the device that will implement the method. In the case of vision, a computational analysis is concerned with specifying the properties of the optic array of light that has been structured by the surfaces in the environment, and the information that must be extracted from that array (e.g., surface depth and orientation). In many ways, Gibson's theory of direct perception (Reading 4) is a computational analysis of vision. It emphasizes the information contained in the optic array, including a variety of dynamic and structural invariants, and it states that affordances are extracted so as to guide actions.[1]

The algorithmic level is concerned with specifying an algorithm or procedure for carrying out the purpose specified by the computational level. In Palmer's (1999) thermostat analogy, the algorithm would include encoding the ambient temperature in the house and the temperature dial setting, comparing them, and then sending the appropriate signal depending on whether the temperature is greater or less than the setting. Other possible algorithms are possible (although this one seems pretty straightforward). The nature of the representation of the relevant entities (in this case, the temperature, the setting, and the control signal) is crucial, because the representation will constrain what sorts of algorithms are possible. For example, if the temperature and setting are represented as words ("sixty-three"), then the comparison will require different steps than if they are represented as numerals. No specification of how this algorithm is to be carried out is made at this level. An example from vision is the algorithm for detecting edges proposed by Marr and Hildreth (1980). They specify that a two-dimensional second derivative of the image intensities must be computed, and that the points where this function passes from negative to positive or vice-versa (so-called "zero-crossings") are where luminance edges exist. This is one

possible algorithm; it can be carried out in a number of different ways (e.g., by a network of neurons in a visual system or by a digital computer made of silicon chips).

The most concrete level of analysis is the implementation. The thermostat in Palmer's analogy is a physical device with parts that can represent the relevant information and carry out the algorithm. It may have a dial to specify the setting, a bimetallic strip that changes its shape depending on the temperature, a power source, and wires that connect it to the furnace. Many other implementations are possible. In fact, one can purchase many different thermostats that all carry out essentially the same algorithm in service of essentially the same purpose, but that do so in a variety of ways. The implementational level in vision is, of course, the brain and its billions of neurons and connections, but vision scientists often simulate the algorithms that are thought to be carried out in the brain using digital computers in order to analyze their adequacy, under the assumption that the algorithm's performance does not depend on how the algorithm is implemented.

These ideas for thinking about the problem of vision provided some needed order in cases where theoretical issues were inadvertently spanning levels. By being clear about just what was being explained, theoretical and empirical developments were greatly clarified. Viewing vision as a computational problem has also facilitated communication between disciplines such as psychophysics, neuroscience, and computer science, and has thus contributed substantially to progress in all these areas.

---

[1]It is important to point out, however, that Marr did not view Gibson's theory as fully adequate. "The fatal shortcoming [of Gibson's analysis] . . . results from a failure to realize two things. First, the detection of physical invariants, like image surfaces, is exactly and precisely an information-processing problem, in modern terminology. And second, he vastly underrated the sheer difficulty of such detection" (Marr, 1982, p. 30).

REFERENCES

Koenderink, J. J., & van Doorn, A. J. (1976). Geometry of binocular vision and a model for stereopsis. *Biological Cybernetics, 21*, 29–35.

Marr, D., & Hildreth, E. C. (1980).Theory of edge detection. *Proceedings of the Royal Society of London B, 207*, 187–217.

Marr, D., & Nishihara, H. K. (1978). Representation and recognition of the spatial organization of three-dimensional shapes. *Proceedings of the Royal Society of London B, 200*, 269–294.

Marr, D., & Poggio, T. (1979). A computational theory of human stereo vision. *Proceedings of the Royal Society of London B, 204*, 301–328.

Palmer, S. E. (1999). *Vision science: Photons to phenomenology.* Cambridge, MA: MIT Press.

The Philosophy and the Approach

D. Marr • Massachusetts Institute of Technology

Background

The problems of visual perception have attracted the curiosity of scientists for many centuries. Important early contributions were made by Newton (1704), who laid the foundations for modern work on color vision, and Helmholtz (1910), whose treatise on psychological optics generates interest even today. Early this century, Wertheimer (1912, 1923) noticed the apparent motion not of individual dots but of wholes, or "fields," in images presented sequentially as in a movie. In much the same way we perceive the migration across the sky of a flock of geese: the flock somehow constitutes a single entity, and is not seen as individual birds. This observation started the Gestalt school of psychology, which was concerned with describing the qualities of wholes by using terms like *solidarity* and *distinctness*, and trying to formulate the "laws" that governed the creation of these wholes. The attempt failed for various reasons, and the Gestalt school dissolved into the fog of subjectivism. With the death of the school, many of its early and genuine insights were unfortunately lost to the mainstream of experimental psychology.

Since then, students of the psychology of perception have made no serious attempts at an overall understanding of what perception is, concentrating instead on the analysis of properties and performance. The trichromatism of color vision was firmly established (see Brindley, 1970), and the preoccupation with motion continued, with the most interesting developments perhaps being the experiments of Miles (1931) and of Wallach and O'Connell (1953), which established that under suitable conditions an unfamiliar three-dimensional shape can be correctly perceived from only its changing monocular projection.*

The development of the digital electronic computer made possible a similar discovery for binocular vision. In 1960 Bela Julesz devised computer-generated random-dot stereograms, which are image pairs constructed of dot patterns that appear random when viewed monocularly but fuse when viewed one through each eye to give a percept of shapes and surfaces with a clear three-dimensional structure. An example is shown in Figure 5.1. Here the image for the left eye is a matrix of black and white squares generated at random by a computer program. The image for the right eye is made by copying the left image, shifting a square-shaped region at its center slightly to the left, and then providing a new random pattern to fill the gap that the shift creates. If each of the eyes sees only one matrix, as if the matrices were both in the same physical place, the result is the sensation of a square floating in space. Plainly, such percepts are caused solely by the stereo disparity between matching elements in the images presented to each eye; from such experiments, we know that the analysis of stereoscopic information, like the analysis of motion, can proceed independently in the absence of other information.

---

* The two dimensional image seen by a single eye.

FIGURE 5.1 ■ A Random-Dot Stereogram of the Type Used Extensively By Bela Julesz. The left and right images are identical except for a central square region that is displaced slightly in one image. When fused binocularly, the images yield the impression of the central square floating in front of the background.

Such findings are of critical importance because they help us to subdivide our study of perception into more specialized parts which can be treated separately. I shall refer to these as independent modules of perception.

The most recent contribution of psychophysics has been of a different kind but of equal importance. It arose from a combination of adaptation and threshold detection studies and originated from the demonstration by Campbell and Robson (1968) of the existence of independent, spatial-frequency-tuned channels—that is, channels sensitive to intensity variations in the image occurring at a particular scale or spatial interval—in the early stages of our perceptual apparatus. This paper led to an explosion of articles on various aspects of these channels, which culminated ten years later with quite satisfactory quantitative accounts of the characteristics of the first stages of visual perception (Wilson and Bergen, 1979). I shall discuss this in detail later on.

Recently a rather different approach has attracted considerable attention. In 1971, Roger N. Shepard and Jacqueline Metzler made line drawings of simple objects that differed from one another either by a three-dimensional rotation or by a rotation plus a reflection (see Figure 5.2). They asked how long it took to decide whether two depicted objects differed by a rotation and a reflection or merely a rotation. They found that the time taken

depended on the three-dimensional angle of rotation necessary to bring the two objects into correspondence. Indeed, the time varied linearly with this angle. One is led thereby to the notion that a mental rotation of sorts is actually being performed—that a mental description of the first shape in a pair is being adjusted incrementally in orientation until it matches the second, such adjustment requiring greater time when greater angles are involved.

The significance of this approach lies not so much in its results, whose interpretation is controversial, as in the type of questions it raised. For until then, the notion of a representation was not one that visual psychologists took seriously. This type of experiment meant that the notion had to be considered. Although the early thoughts of visual psychologists were naive compared with those of the computer vision community, which had had to face the problem of representation from the beginning, it was not long before the thinking of psychologists became more sophisticated (see Shepard, 1979).

But what of explanation? For a long time, the best hope seemed to lie along another line of investigation, that of electrophysiology. The development of amplifiers allowed Adrian (1928) and his colleagues to record the minute voltage changes that accompanied the transmission of nerve signals. Their investigations showed that the character of the sensation so produced depended on which

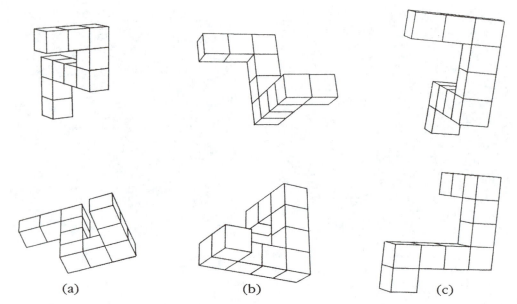

FIGURE 5.2 ■ Some Drawings Similar to Those Used in Shepard and Metzler's Experiments on Mental Rotation. The ones Shown in (a) are identical, as a clockwise turning of this page by 80° will readily prove. Those in (b) are also identical, and again the relative angle between the two is 80°. Here, however, a rotation in depth will make the first coincide with the second. Finally, those in (c) are not at all identical, for no rotation will bring them into congruence. The time taken to decide whether a pair is the same was found to vary linearly with the angle through which one figure must be rotated to be brought into correspondence with the other. This suggested to the investigators that a stepwise mental rotation was in fact being performed by the subjects of their experiments.

fiber carried the message, not how the fiber was stimulated—as one might have expected from anatomical studies. This led to the view that the peripheral nerve fibers could be thought of as a simple mapping supplying the sensorium with a copy of the physical events at the body surface (Adrian, 1947). The rest of the explanation, it was thought, could safely be left to the psychologists.

The next development was the technical improvement in amplification that made possible the recording of single neurons (Granit and Svaetichin, 1939; Hartline, 1938; Galambos and Davis, 1943). This led to the notion of a cell's "receptive field" (Hartline, 1940) and to the Harvard School's famous series of studies of the behavior of neurons at successively deeper levels of the visual pathway (Kuffler, 1953; Hubel and Wiesel, 1962, 1968). But perhaps the most exciting development was the new view that questions of psychological interest could be illuminated and perhaps even explained by neurophysiological experiments. The dearest early example of this was Barlow's (1953) study of ganglion cells in the frog retina, and I cannot put it better than he did:

If one explores the responsiveness of single ganglion cells in the frog's retina using handheld targets, one finds that one particular type of ganglion cell is most effectively driven by something like a black disc subtending a degree or so moved rapidly to and fro within the unit's receptive field. This causes a vigorous discharge which can be maintained without much decrement as long as the movement is continued. Now, if the stimulus which is optimal for this class of cells is presented to intact frogs, the behavioural response is often dramatic; they turn towards the target and make repeated feeding responses consisting of a jump and snap. The selectivity of the retinal neurons and the frog's reaction when they are selectively stimulated, suggest that they are "bug detectors" (Barlow 1953) performing a primitive but vitally important form of recognition.

The result makes one suddenly realize that a large part of the sensory machinery involved in a frog's feeding responses may actually reside in the retina rather than in mysterious "centres" that would be too difficult to understand by physiological methods. The essential lock-like property resides in each member of a whole class of neurons and allows the cell to discharge only to the appropriate key pattern of sensory stimulation. Lettvin et al. (1959) suggested that there were five different classes of cell in the frog, and Barlow, Hill and Levick (1964) found an even larger number of categories in the rabbit. [Barlow et al.] called these key patterns "trigger features" and Maturana et al. (1960) emphasized another important aspect of the behaviour of these ganglion cells; a cell continues to respond to the same trigger feature in spite of changes in light intensity over many decades. The properties of the retina are such that a ganglion cell can, figuratively speaking, reach out and determine that something specific is happening in front of the eye. Light is the agent by which it does this, but it is the detailed pattern of the light that carries the information, and the overall level of illumination prevailing at the time is almost totally disregarded. (p. 373)

Barlow (1972) then goes on to summarize these findings in the following way:

The cumulative effect of all the changes I have tried to outline above has been to make us realise that each *single neuron can perform a much more complex and subtle task than had previously been thought* (emphasis added). Neurons do not loosely and unreliably remap the luminous intensities of the visual image onto our sensorium, but instead they detect pattern elements, discriminate the depth of objects, ignore irrelevant causes of variation and are arranged in an intriguing hierarchy. Furthermore, there is evidence that they give prominence to what is informationally important, can respond with great reliability, and can have their pattern selectivity permanently modified by early visual experience. This amounts to a revolution in our outlook. It is now quite inappropriate to regard unit activity as a noisy indication of more basic and reliable processes involved in mental operations: instead, we must regard single neurons as the prime movers of these mechanisms. Thinking is brought about by neurons and we should not use phrases like "unit activity reflects, reveals, or monitors thought processes," because the activities of neurons, quite simply, are thought processes.

This revolution stemmed from physiological work and makes us realize that the activity of each single neuron may play a significant role in perception. (p. 380)

This aspect of his thinking led Barlow to formulate the first and most important of his five dogmas: "A description of that activity of a single nerve cell which is transmitted to and influences other nerve cells and of a nerve cell's response to such influences from other cells, is a complete

enough description for functional understanding of the nervous system. There is nothing else "looking at" or controlling this activity, which must therefore provide a basis for understanding how the brain controls behaviour" (Barlow, 1972, p. 380).

I shall return later on to more carefully examine the validity of this point of view, but for now let us just enjoy it. The vigor and excitement of these ideas need no emphasis. At the time the eventual success of a reductionist approach seemed likely. Hubel and Wiesel's (1962, 1968) pioneering studies had shown the way; single-unit studies on stereopsis (Barlow, Blakemore, and Pettigrew, 1967) and on color (DeValois, Abramov, and Mead, 1967; Gouras, 1968) seemed to confirm the close links between perception and single-cell recordings, and the intriguing results of Gross, Rocha-Miranda, and Bender (1972), who found "hand-detectors" in the inferotemporal cortex, seemed to show that the application of the reductionist approach would not be limited just to the early parts of the visual pathway.

It was, of course, recognized that physiologists had been lucky: If one probes around in a conventional electronic computer and records the behavior of single elements within it, one is unlikely to be able to discern what a given element is doing. But the brain, thanks to Barlow's first dogma, seemed to be built along more accommodating lines—people *were* able to determine the functions of single elements of the brain. There seemed no reason why the reductionist approach could not be taken all the way.

I was myself fully caught up in this excitement. Truth, I also believed, was basically neural, and the central aim of all research was a thorough functional analysis of the structure of the central nervous system. My enthusiasm found expression in a theory of the cerebellar cortex (Marr, 1969). According to this theory, the simple and regular cortical structure is interpreted as a simple but powerful memorizing device for learning motor skills; because of a simple combinatorial trick, each of the 15 million Purkinje cells in the cerebellum is capable of learning over 200 different patterns and discriminating them from unlearned patterns. Evidence is gradually accumulating that the cerebellum is involved in learning motor skills (Ito, 1978), so that something like this theory may in fact be correct.

The way seemed clear. On the one hand we had new experimental techniques of proven power, and on the other, the beginnings of a theoretical approach that could back them up with a fine analysis of cortical structure. Psychophysics could tell us what needed explaining, and the recent advances in anatomy—the Fink-Heimer technique from Nauta's laboratory and the recent successful deployment by Szentagothai and others of the electron microscope—could provide the necessary information about the structure of the cerebral cortex.

But somewhere underneath, something was going wrong. The initial discoveries of the 1950s and 1960s were not being followed by equally dramatic discoveries in the 1970s. No neurophysiologists had recorded new and clear high-level correlates of perception. The leaders of the 1960s had turned away from what they had been doing—Hubel and Wiesel concentrated on anatomy, Barlow turned to psychophysics, and the mainstream of neurophysiology concentrated on development and plasticity (the concept that neural connections are not fixed) or on a more thorough analysis of the cells that had already been discovered (for example, Bishop, Coombs, and Henry, 1971; Schiller, Finlay, and Volman, 1976a, 1976b), or on cells in species like the owl (for example, Pettigrew and Konishi, 1976). None of the new studies succeeded in elucidating the *function* of the visual cortex.

It is difficult to say precisely why this happened, because the reasoning was never made explicit and was probably largely unconscious. However, various factors are identifiable. In my own case, the cerebellar study had two effects. On the one hand, it suggested that one could eventually hope to understand cortical structure in functional terms, and this was exciting. But at the same time the study has disappointed me, because even if the theory was correct, it did not much enlighten one about the motor system—it did not, for example, tell one how to go about programming a mechanical arm. It suggested that if one wishes to program a mechanical arm so that it operates in a versatile way, then at some point a very large and rather simple type of memory will prove indispensable. But it did not say why, nor what that memory should contain.

The discoveries of the visual neurophysiologists left one in a similar situation. Suppose, for example, that one actually found the apocryphal grandmother cell.* Would that really tell us anything much at all? It would tell us that it existed—Gross's hand-detectors tell us almost that—but not why or even how such a thing may be constructed from the outputs of previously discovered cells. Do the single-unit recordings—the simple and complex cells—tell us much about how to detect edges or why one would want to, except in a rather general way through arguments based on economy and redundancy? If we really knew the answers, for example, we should be able to program them on a computer. But finding a hand-detector certainly did not allow us to program one.

As one reflected on these sorts of issues in the early 1970s, it gradually became clear that something important was missing that was not present in either of the disciplines of neurophysiology or psychophysics. The key observation is that neurophysiology and psychophysics have as their business to *describe* the behavior of cells or of subjects but not to *explain* such behavior. What are the visual areas of the cerebral cortex actually doing? What are the problems in doing it that need explaining, and at what level of description should such explanations be sought?

The best way of finding out the difficulties of doing something is to try to do it, so at this point I moved to the Artificial Intelligence Laboratory at MIT, where Marvin Minsky had collected a group of people and a powerful computer for the express purpose of addressing these questions.

The first great revelation was that the problems are difficult. Of course, these days this fact is a commonplace. But in the 1960s almost no one realized that machine vision was difficult. The field had to go through the same experience as the machine translation field did in its fiascoes of the 1950s before it was at last realized that here were some problems that had to be taken seriously. The reason for this misperception is that we humans are ourselves so good at vision. The notion of a feature detector was well established by Barlow and by Hubel and Wiesel, and the idea that extracting edges and lines from images might be at all difficult simply did not occur to those who had not tried to do it. It turned out to be an elusive problem: Edges that are of critical importance from a three-dimensional point of view often cannot be found at all by looking at the intensity changes in an image. Any kind of textured image gives a multitude of noisy edge segments; variations in reflectance and illumination cause no end of

---

* A cell that fires only when one's grandmother comes into view.

trouble; and even if an edge has a clear existence at one point, it is as likely as not to fade out quite soon, appearing only in patches along its length in the image. The common and almost despairing feeling of the early investigators like B.K.P. Horn and T.O. Binford was that practically anything could happen in an image and furthermore that practically everything did.

Three types of approach were taken to try to come to grips with these phenomena. The first was unashamedly empirical, associated most with Azriel Rosenfeld. His style was to take some new trick for edge detection, texture discrimination, or something similar, run it on images, and observe the result. Although several interesting ideas emerged in this way, including the simultaneous use of operators* of different sizes as an approach to increasing sensitivity and reducing noise (Rosenfeld and Thurston, 1971), these studies were not as useful as they could have been because they were never accompanied by any serious assessment of how well the different algorithms performed. Few attempts were made to compare the merits of different operators (although Fram and Deutsch, 1975, did try), and an approach like trying to prove mathematically which operator was optimal was not even attempted. Indeed, it could not be, because no one had yet formulated precisely what these operators should be trying to do. Nevertheless, considerable ingenuity was shown. The most clever was probably Hueckel's (1973) operator, which solved in an ingenious way the problem of finding the edge orientation that best fit a given intensity change in a small neighborhood of an image.

The second approach was to try for depth of analysis by restricting the scope to a world of single, illuminated, matte white toy blocks set against a black background. The blocks could occur in any shapes provided only that all faces were planar and all edges were straight. This restriction allowed more specialized techniques to be used, but it still did not make the problem easy. The Binford–Horn line finder (Horn, 1973) was used to find edges, and both it and its sequel (described in Shirai, 1973) made use of the special circumstances of the environment, such as the fact that all edges there were straight.

These techniques did work reasonably well, however, and they allowed a preliminary analysis of later problems to emerge—roughly, what does one do once a complete line drawing has been ex-

tracted from a scene? Studies of this had begun sometime before with Roberts (1965) and Guzman (1968), and they culminated in the works of Waltz (1975) and Mackworth (1973), which essentially solved the interpretation problem for line drawings derived from images of prismatic solids. Waltz's work had a particularly dramatic impact, because it was the first to show explicitly that an exhaustive analysis of all possible local physical arrangements of surfaces, edges, and shadows could lead to an effective and efficient algorithm for interpreting an actual image. Figure 5.3 and its legend convey the main ideas behind Waltz's theory.

The hope that lay behind this work was, of course, that once the toy world of white blocks had been understood, the solutions found there could be generalized, providing the basis for attacking the more complex problems posed by a richer visual environment. Unfortunately, this turned out not to be so. For the roots of the approach that was eventually successful, we have to look at the third kind of development that was taking place then.

Two pieces of work were important here. Neither is probably of very great significance to human perception for what it actually accomplished—in the end, it is likely that neither will particularly reflect human visual processes—but they are both of importance because of the way in which they were formulated. The first was Land and McCann's (1971) work on the retinex theory of color vision, as developed by them and subsequently by Horn (1974). The starting point is the traditional one of regarding color as a perceptual approximation to reflectance. This allows the formulation of a clear computational question, namely, How can the effects of reflectance changes be separated from the vagaries of the prevailing illumination? Land and McCann suggested using the fact that changes in illumination are usually gradual, whereas changes in reflectance of a surface or of an object boundary are often quite sharp. Hence by filtering out slow changes, those changes due to the reflectance alone could be isolated. Horn devised a clever parallel algorithm for this, and I suggested how it might be implemented by neurons in the retina (Marr, 1974a).

---

* *Operator* refers to a local calculation to be applied at each location in the image, making use of the intensity there and in the immediate vicinity.

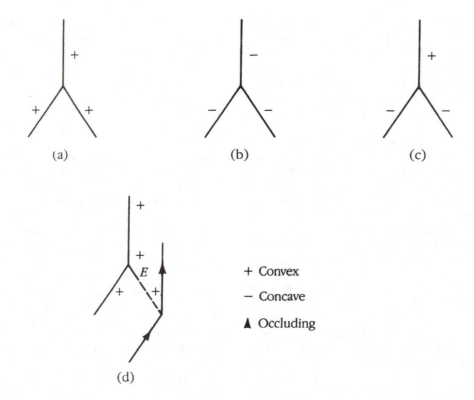

FIGURE 5.3 ■ Some configurations of edges are physically realizable, and some are not. The trihedral junctions of three convex edges (a) or of three concave edges (b) are realizable, whereas the configuration (c) is impossible. Waltz catalogued all the possible junctions, including shadow edges, for up to four coincident edges. He then found that by using this catalog to implement consistency relations [requiring, for example, that an edge be of the same type all along its length like edge E in (d)], the solution to the labeling of a line drawing that included shadows was often uniquely determined.

I do not now believe that this is at all a correct analysis of color vision or of the retina, but it showed the possible style of a correct analysis. Gone are the ad hoc programs of computer vision; gone is the restriction to a special visual miniworld; gone is any explanation *in terms of* neurons—except as a way of implementing a method. And present is a clear understanding of what is to be computed, how it is to be done, the physical assumptions on which the method is based, and some kind of analysis of algorithms that are capable of carrying it out.

The other piece of work was Horn's (1975) analysis of shape from shading, which was the first in what was to become a distinguished series of articles on the formation of images. By carefully analyzing the way in which the illumination, surface geometry, surface reflectance, and viewpoint conspired to create the measured intensity values in an image, Horn formulated a differential equation that related the image intensity values to the surface geometry. If the surface reflectance and illumination are known, one can solve for the surface geometry (see also Horn, 1977). Thus from shading one can derive shape.

The message was plain. There must exist an additional level of understanding at which the character of the information-processing tasks carried out during perception are analyzed and understood in a way that is independent of the particular mechanisms and structures that implement them in our heads. This was what was missing—the analysis of the problem as an information-processing task. Such analysis does not usurp an understanding at the other levels—of neurons or of computer programs—but it is a necessary complement to them, since without it there can be no real understanding of the function of all those neurons.

This realization was arrived at independently and formulated together by Tomaso Poggio in Tübingen and myself (Marr and Poggio, 1977; Marr, 1977b). It was not even quite new—Leon D. Harmon was saying something similar at about the same time, and others had paid lip service to a similar distinction. But the important point is that if the notion of different types of understanding is taken very seriously, it allows the study of the information-processing basis of perception to be made *rigorous*. It becomes possible, by separating explanations into different levels, to make explicit statements about what is being computed and why and to construct theories stating that what is being computed is optimal in some sense or is guaranteed to function correctly. The ad hoc element is removed, and heuristic computer programs are replaced by solid foundations on which a real subject can be built. This realization—the formulation of what was missing, together with a clear idea of how to supply it—formed the basic foundation for a new integrated approach, which it is the purpose of this book to describe.

Understanding Complex Information-Processing Systems

Almost never can a complex system of any kind be understood as a simple extrapolation from the properties of its elementary components. Consider, for example, some gas in a bottle. A description of thermodynamic effects—temperature, pressure, density, and the relationships among these factors—is not formulated by using a large set of equations, one for each of the particles involved. Such effects are described at their own level, that of an enormous collection of particles; the effort is to show that in principle the microscopic and macroscopic descriptions are consistent with one another. If one hopes to achieve a full understanding of a system as complicated as a nervous system, a developing embryo, a set of metabolic pathways, a bottle of gas, or even a large computer program, then one must be prepared to contemplate different kinds of explanation at different levels of description that are linked, at least in principle, into a cohesive whole, even if linking the levels in complete detail is impractical. For the specific case of a system that solves an informa-

tion-processing problem, there are in addition the twin strands of process and representation, and both these ideas need some discussion.

Representation and Description

A *representation* is a formal system for making explicit certain entities or types of information, together with a specification of how the system does this. And I shall call the result of using a representation to describe a given entity a *description* of the entity in that representation (Marr and Nishihara, 1978).

For example, the Arabic, Roman, and binary numeral systems are all formal systems for representing numbers. The Arabic representation consists of a string of symbols drawn from the set (0, 1, 2, 3, 4, 5, 6, 7, 8, 9), and the rule for constructing the description of a particular integer n is that one decomposes n into a sum of multiples of powers of 10 and unites these multiples into a string with the largest powers on the left and the smallest on the right. Thus, thirty-seven equals $3 \times 10^1 + 7 \times 10^0$, which becomes 37, the Arabic numeral system's description of the number. What this description makes explicit is the number's decomposition into powers of 10. The binary numeral system's description of the number thirty-seven is 100101, and this description makes explicit the number's decomposition into powers of 2. In the Roman numeral system, thirty-seven is represented as XXXVII.

This definition of a representation is quite general. For example, a representation for shape would be a formal scheme for describing some aspects of shape, together with rules that specify how the scheme is applied to any particular shape. A musical score provides a way of representing a symphony; the alphabet allows the construction of a written representation of words; and so forth. The phrase "formal scheme" is critical to the definition, but the reader should not be frightened by it. The reason is simply that we are dealing with information-processing machines, and the way such machines work is by using symbols to stand for things—to represent things, in our terminology. To say that something is a formal scheme means only that it is a set of symbols with rules for putting them together—no more and no less.

A representation, therefore, is not a foreign idea at all—we all use representations all the time. However, the notion that one can capture some aspect of reality by making a description of it using a symbol and that to do so can be useful seems to me a fascinating and powerful idea. But even the simple examples we have discussed introduce some rather general and important issues that arise whenever one chooses to use one particular representation. For example, if one chooses the Arabic numeral representation, it is easy to discover whether a number is a power of 10 but difficult to discover whether it is a power of 2. If one chooses the binary representation, the situation is reversed. Thus, there is a trade-off; any particular representation makes certain information explicit at the expense of information that is pushed into the background and may be quite hard to recover.

This issue is important, because how information is represented can greatly affect how easy it is to do different things with it. This is evident even from our numbers example: It is easy to add, to subtract, and even to multiply if the Arabic or binary representations are used, but it is not at all easy to do these things—especially multiplication—with Roman numerals. This is a key reason why the Roman culture failed to develop mathematics in the way the earlier Arabic cultures had.

An analogous problem faces computer engineers today. Electronic technology is much more suited to a binary number system than to the conventional base 10 system, yet humans supply their data and require the results in base 10. The design decision facing the engineer, therefore, is, Should one pay the cost of conversion into base 2, carry out the arithmetic in a binary representation, and then convert back into decimal numbers on output; or should one sacrifice efficiency of circuitry to carry out operations directly in a decimal representation? On the whole, business computers and pocket calculators take the second approach, and general purpose computers take the first. But even though one is not restricted to using just one representation system for a given type of information, the choice of which to use is important and cannot be taken lightly. It determines what information is made explicit and hence what is pushed further into the background, and it has a far-reaching effect on the ease and difficulty with which operations may subsequently be carried out on that information.

Process

The term *process* is very broad. For example, addition is a process, and so is taking a Fourier trans-

form. But so is making a cup of tea, or going shopping. For the purposes of this book, I want to restrict our attention to the meanings associated with machines that are carrying out information-processing tasks. So let us examine in depth the notions behind one simple such device, a cash register at the checkout counter of a supermarket.

There are several levels at which one needs to understand such a device, and it is perhaps most useful to think in terms of three of them. The most abstract is the level of *what* the device does and *why*. What it does is arithmetic, so our first task is to master the theory of addition. Addition is a mapping, usually denoted by +, from pairs of numbers into single numbers; for example, + maps the pair (3, 4) to 7, and I shall write this in the form (3 + 4) → 7. Addition has a number of abstract properties, however. It is commutative: both (3 + 4) and (4 + 3) are equal to 7; and associative: the sum of 3 + (4 + 5) is the same as the sum of (3 + 4) + 5. Then there is the unique distinguished element, zero, the adding of which has no effect: (4 + 0) → 4. Also, for every number there is a unique "inverse," written (– 4) in the case of 4, which when added to the number gives zero: [4 + (– 4)1 → 0.

Notice that these properties are part of the fundamental *theory* of addition. They are true no matter how the numbers are written—whether in binary, Arabic, or Roman representation—and no matter how the addition is executed. Thus part of this first level is something that might be characterized as *what* is being computed.

The other half of this level of explanation has to do with the question of *why* the cash register performs addition and not, for instance, multiplication when combining the prices of the purchased items to arrive at a final bill. The reason is that the rules we intuitively feel to be appropriate for combining the individual prices in fact define the mathematical operation of addition. These can be formulated as *constraints* in the following way:

1. If you buy nothing, it should cost you nothing; and buying nothing and something should cost the same as buying just the something. (The rules for zero.)
2. The order in which goods are presented to the cashier should not affect the total. (Commutativity.)
3. Arranging the goods into two piles and paying for each pile separately should not affect the

total amount you pay. (Associativity; the basic operation for combining prices.)

4. If you buy an item and then return it for a refund, your total expenditure should be zero. (Inverses)

It is a mathematical theorem that these conditions define the operation of addition, which is therefore the appropriate computation to use.

This whole argument is what I call the *computational theory* of the cash register. Its important features are (1) that it contains separate arguments about what is completed and why and (2) that the resulting operation is defined uniquely by the constraints it has to satisfy. In the theory of visual processes, the underlying task is to reliably derive properties of the world from images of it; the business of isolating constraints that are both powerful enough to allow a process to be defined and generally true of the world is a central theme of our inquiry.

In order that a process shall actually run, however, one has to realize it in some way and therefore choose a representation for the entities that the process manipulates. The second level of the analysis of a process, therefore, involves choosing two things: (1) a *representation* for the input and for the output of the process and (2) an *algorithm* by which the transformation may actually be accomplished. For addition, of course, the input and output representations can both be the same, because they both consist of numbers. However this is not true in general. In the case of a Fourier transform, for example, the input representation may be the time domain, and the output, the frequency domain. If the first of our levels specifies what and why, this second level specifies *how*. For addition, we might choose Arabic numerals for the representations, and for the algorithm we could follow the usual rules about adding the least significant digits first and "carrying" if the sum exceeds 9. Cash registers, whether mechanical or electronic, usually use this type of representation and algorithm.

There are three important points here. First, there is usually a wide choice of representation. Second, the choice of algorithm often depends rather critically on the particular representation that is employed. And third, even for a given fixed representation, there are often several possible algorithms for carrying out the same process. Which one is chosen will usually depend on any particularly desirable or undesirable characteristics that the algorithms may have; for example, one algorithm may be much more efficient than another, or another may be slightly less efficient but more robust (that is, less sensitive to slight inaccuracies in the data on which it must run). Or again, one algorithm may be parallel, and another, serial. The choice, then, may depend on the type of hardware or machinery in which the algorithm is to be embodied physically.

This brings us to the third level, that of the device in which the process is to be realized physically. The important point here is that, once again, the same algorithm may be implemented in quite different technologies. The child who methodically adds two numbers from right to left, carrying a digit when necessary, may be using the same algorithm that is implemented by the wires and transistors of the cash register in the neighborhood supermarket, but the physical realization of the algorithm is quite different in these two cases. Another example: Many people have written computer programs to play tic-tac-toe, and there is a more or less standard algorithm that cannot lose. This algorithm has in fact been implemented by W. D. Hillis and B. Silverman in a quite different technology, in a computer made out of Tinkertoys, a children's wooden building set. The whole monstrously ungainly engine, which actually works, currently resides in a museum at the University of Missouri in St. Louis.

Some styles of algorithm will suit some physical substrates better than others. For example, in conventional digital computers, the number of connections is comparable to the number of gates, while in a brain, the number of connections is much larger ($\times 10^4$) than the number of nerve cells. The underlying reason is that wires are rather cheap in biological architecture, because they can grow individually and in three dimensions. In conventional technology, wire laying is more or less restricted to two dimensions, which quite severely restricts the scope for using parallel techniques and algorithms; the same operations are often better carried out serially.

The Three Levels

We can summarize our discussion in something like the manner shown in Figure 5.4, which illustrates the different levels at which an information-processing device must be understood before one

Computational theory	Representation and algorithm	Hardware implementation
What is the goal of the computation, why is it appropriate, and what is the logic of the strategy by which it can be carried out?	How can this computational theory be implemented? In particular, what is the representation for the input and output, and what is the algorithm for the transformation?	How can the representation and algorithm be realized physically?

FIGURE 5.4 ■ The three levels at which any machine carrying out an information-processing task must be understood.

can be said to have understood it completely. At one extreme, the top level, is the abstract computational theory of the device, in which the performance of the device is characterized as a mapping from one kind of information to another, the abstract properties of this mapping are defined precisely, and its appropriateness and adequacy for the task at hand are demonstrated. In the center is the choice of representation for the input and output and the algorithm to be used to transform one into the other. And at the other extreme are the details of how the algorithm and representation are realized physically—the detailed computer architecture, so to speak. These three levels are coupled, but only loosely. The choice of an algorithm is influenced for example, by what it has to do and by the hardware in which it must run. But there is a wide choice available at each level, and the explication of each level involves issues that are rather independent of the other two.

Each of the three levels of description will have its place in the eventual understanding of perceptual information processing, and of course they are logically and causally related. But an important point to note is that since the three levels are only rather loosely related, some phenomena may be explained at only one or two of them. This means, for example, that a correct explanation of some psychophysical observation must be formulated at the appropriate level. In attempts to relate psychophysical problems to physiology, too often there is confusion about the level at which problems should be addressed. For instance, some are related mainly to the physical mechanisms of vision—such as afterimages (for example, the one you see after staring at a light bulb) or such as the fact that any color can be matched by a suitable

mixture of the three primaries (a consequence principally of the fact that we humans have three types of cones). On the other hand, the ambiguity of the Necker cube (Figure 5.5) seems to demand a different kind of explanation. To be sure, part of the explanation of its perceptual reversal must have to do with a bistable neural network (that is, one with two distinct stable states) somewhere inside the brain, but few would feel satisfied by an account that failed to mention the existence of two different but perfectly plausible three-dimensional interpretations of this two-dimensional image.

For some phenomena, the type of explanation required is fairly obvious. Neuroanatomy, for example, is clearly tied principally to the third level, the physical realization of the computation. The same holds for synaptic mechanisms, action potentials, inhibitory interactions, and so forth. Neurophysiology, too, is related mostly to this level, but it can also help us to understand the type of representations being used, particularly if one accepts something along the lines of Barlow's views that I quoted earlier. But one has to exercise extreme caution in making inferences from neurophysiological findings about the algorithms and representations being used, particularly until one has a clear idea about what information needs to be represented and what processes need to be implemented.

Psychophysics, on the other hand, is related more directly to the level of algorithm and representation. Different algorithms tend to fail in radically different ways as they are pushed to the limits of their performance or are deprived of critical information. As we shall see, primarily psychophysical evidence proved to Poggio and myself that our first stereo-matching algorithm (Marr and

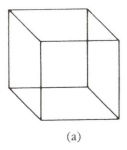
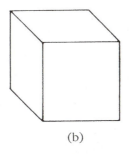
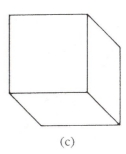

(a)   (b)   (c)

FIGURE 5.5 ■ The so-called Necker illusion, named after L. A. Necker, the Swiss naturalist who developed it in 1832. The essence of the matter is that the two-dimensional representation (a) has collapsed the depth out of a cube and that a certain aspect of human vision is to recover this missing third dimension. The depth of the cube can indeed be perceived, but two interpretations are possible, (b) and (c). A person's perception characteristically flips from one to the other.

Poggio, 1976) was not the one that is used by the brain, and the best evidence that our second algorithm (Marr and Poggio, 1979) *is* roughly the one that is used also comes from psychophysics. Of course, the underlying computational theory remained the same in both cases, only the algorithms were different.

Psychophysics can also help to determine the nature of a representation. The work of Roger Shepard (1975), Eleanor Rosch (1978), or Elizabeth Warrington (1975) provides some interesting hints in this direction. More specifically, Stevens (1979) argued from psychophysical experiments that surface orientation is represented by the coordinates of slant and tilt, rather than (for example) the more traditional (*p, q*) of gradient space (see Chapter 3). He also deduced from the uniformity of the size of errors made by subjects judging surface orientation over a wide range of orientations that the representational quantities used for slant and tilt are pure angles and not, for example, their cosines, sines, or tangents.

More generally, if the idea that different phenomena need to be explained at different levels is kept clearly in mind, it often helps in the assessment of the validity of the different kinds of objections that are raised from time to time. For example, one favorite is that the brain is quite different from a computer because one is parallel and the other serial. The answer to this, of course, is that the distinction between serial and parallel is a distinction at the level of algorithm; it is not fundamental at all—anything programmed in parallel can be rewritten serially (though not necessarily vice versa). The distinction, therefore, provides no grounds for arguing that the brain operates

so differently from a computer that a computer could not be programmed to perform the same tasks.

Importance of Computational Theory

Although algorithms and mechanisms are empirically more accessible, it is the top level, the level of computational theory, which is critically important from an information-processing point of view. The reason for this is that the nature of the computations that underlie perception depends more upon the computational problems that have to be solved than upon the particular hardware in which their solutions are implemented. To phrase the matter another way, an algorithm is likely to be understood more readily by understanding the nature of the problem being solved than by examining the mechanism (and the hardware) in which it is embodied.

In a similar vein, trying to understand perception by studying only neurons is like trying to understand bird flight by studying only feathers: It just cannot be done. In order to understand bird flight, we have to understand aerodynamics; only then do the structure of feathers and the different shapes of birds' wings make sense. More to the point, as we shall see, we cannot understand why retinal ganglion cells and lateral geniculate neurons have the receptive fields they do just by studying their anatomy and physiology. We can understand how these cells and neurons behave as they do by studying their wiring and interactions, but in order to understand *why* the receptive fields are as they are—why they are circularly symmetrical and why their excitatory and inhibitory regions have characteristic shapes and distributions—we have to know a little of the theory of differential operators, band-pass channels, and the mathematics of the uncertainty principle (see Chapter 2).

Perhaps it is not surprising that the very specialized empirical disciplines of the neurosciences failed to appreciate fully the absence of computational theory; but it is surprising that this level of approach did not play a more forceful role in the early development of artificial intelligence. For far too long, a heuristic program for carrying out some task was held to be a theory of that task, and the distinction between what a program did and how it did it was not taken seriously. As a result, (1) a style of explanation evolved that invoked the use of special mechanisms to solve particular problems, (2) particular data structures, such as the lists of attribute value pairs called property lists in the LISP programing language, were held to amount to theories of the representation of knowledge, and (3) there was frequently no way to determine whether a program would deal with a particular case other than by running the program.

Failure to recognize this theoretical distinction between *what* and *how* also greatly hampered communication between the fields of artificial intelligence and linguistics. Chomsky's (1965) theory of transformational grammar is a true computational theory in the sense defined earlier. It is concerned solely with specifying what the syntactic decomposition of an English sentence should be, and not at all with how that decomposition should be achieved. Chomsky himself was very clear about this—it is roughly his distinction between competence and performance, though his idea of performance did include other factors, like stopping in midutterance—but the fact that his theory was defined by transformations, which look like computations, seems to have confused many people. Winograd (1972), for example, felt able to criticize Chomsky's theory on the grounds that it cannot be inverted and so cannot be made to run on a computer; I had heard reflections of the same argument made by Chomsky's colleagues in linguistics as they turn their attention to how grammatical structure might actually be computed from a real English sentence.

The explanation is simply that finding algorithms by which Chomsky's theory may be implemented is a completely different endeavor from formulating the theory itself. In our terms, it is a study at a different level, and both tasks have to be done. This point was appreciated by Marcus (1980), who was concerned precisely with how Chomsky's theory can be realized and with the kinds of constraints on the power of the human grammatical processor that might give rise to the structural constraints in syntax that Chomsky found. It even appears that the emerging "trace" theory of grammar (Chomsky and Lasnik, 1977) may provide a way of synthesizing the two approaches—showing that, for example, some of the rather ad hoc restrictions that form part of the computational theory may be consequences of weaknesses in the computational power that is available for implementing syntactical decoding.

The Approach of J. J. Gibson

In perception, perhaps the nearest anyone came to the level of computational theory was Gibson (1966). However, although some aspects of his thinking were on the right lines, he did not understand properly what information processing was, which led him to seriously underestimate the complexity of the information-processing problems involved in vision and the consequent subtlety that is necessary in approaching them.

Gibson's important contribution was to take the debate away from the philosophical considerations of sense-data and the affective qualities of sensation and to note instead that the important thing about the senses is that they are channels for perception of the real world outside or, in the case of vision, of the visible surfaces. He therefore asked the critically important question, How does one obtain constant perceptions in everyday life on the basis of continually changing sensations? This is exactly the right question, showing that Gibson correctly regarded the problem of perception as that of recovering from sensory information "valid" properties of the external world. His problem was that he had a much oversimplified view of how this should be done. His approach led him to consider higher-order variables—stimulus energy, ratios, proportions, and so on—as "invariants" of the movement of an observer and of changes in stimulation intensity.

"These invariants," he wrote, "correspond to permanent properties of the environment. They constitute, therefore, information about the permanent environment." This led him to a view in which the function of the brain was to "detect invariants" despite changes in "sensations" of light, pressure, or loudness of sound. Thus, he says that the "function of the brain, when looped with its perceptual organs, is not to decode signals, nor to interpret messages, nor to accept images, nor to *organize* the sensory input or to *process* the data, in modern terminology. It is to seek and extract information about the environment from the flowing array of ambient energy" and he thought of the nervous system as in some way "resonating" to these invariants. He then embarked on a broad study of animals in their environments, looking for invariants to which they might resonate. This was the basic idea behind the notion of ecological optics (Gibson, 1966, 1979).

Although one can criticize certain shortcomings in the quality of Gibson's analysis, its major and, in my view fatal shortcoming lies at a deeper level and results from a failure to realize two things. First, the detection of physical invariants, like image surfaces, is exactly and precisely an information-processing problem, in modern terminology. And second, he vastly underrated the sheer difficulty of such detection. In discussing the recovery of three-dimensional information from the movement of an observer, he says that "in motion, perspective information alone can be used" (Gibson, 1966, p. 202). And perhaps the key to Gibson is the following:

> The detection of non-change when an object moves in the world is not as difficult as it might appear. It is only made to seem difficult when we assume that the perception of constant dimensions of the object must depend on the correcting of sensations of inconstant form and size. The information for the constant dimension of an object is normally carried by invariant relations in an optic array. Rigidity is *specified*. (emphasis added)

Yes, to be sure, but *how*? Detecting physical invariants is just as difficult as Gibson feared, but nevertheless we can do it. And the only way to understand how is to treat it as an information-processing problem.

The underlying point is that visual information processing is actually very complicated, and Gibson was not the only thinker who was misled by the apparent simplicity of the act of seeing. The whole tradition of philosophical inquiry into the nature of perception seems not to have taken seriously enough the complexity of the information processing involved. For example, Austin's (1962) *Sense and Sensibilia* entertainingly demolishes the argument, apparently favored by earlier philosophers, that since we are sometimes deluded by illusions (for example, a straight stick appears bent if it is partly submerged in water), we see sense-data rather than material things. The answer is simply that usually our perceptual processing does run correctly (it delivers a true description of what is there), but although evolution has seen to it that our processing allows for many changes (like inconstant illumination), the perturbation due to the refraction of light by water is not one of them. And incidentally, although the example of the bent stick has been discussed since Aristotle, I have seen no philosophical inquiry into the nature of the perceptions of, for instance, a heron, which is a bird that feeds by pecking up fish first seen from above the water surface. For such birds the visual correction might be present.

Anyway, my main point here is another one. Austin (1962) spends much time on the idea that perception tells one about real properties of the external world, and one thing he considers is "real shape," (p. 66), a notion which had cropped up earlier in his discussion of a coin that "looked elliptical" from some points of view. Even so,

> it had a real shape which remained unchanged. But coins in fact are rather special cases. For one thing their outlines are well defined and very highly stable, and for another they have a known and a nameable shape. But there are plenty of things of which this is not true. What is the real shape of a cloud?...or of a cat? Does its real shape change whenever it moves? If not, in what posture *is* its real shape on display? Furthermore, is its real shape such as to be fairly smooth outlines, or must it be finely enough serrated to take account of each hair? *It is pretty obvious that there is no answer to these questions—no rules according to which, no procedure by which, answers are to be determined* (emphasis added). (p. 67)

But there *are* answers to these questions. There are ways of describing the shape of a cat to an arbitrary level of precision (see Chapter 5), and there are rules and procedures for arriving at such descriptions. That is exactly what vision is about, and precisely what makes it complicated.

A Representational Framework for Vision

Vision is a process that produces from images of the external world a description that is useful to the viewer and not cluttered with irrelevant information (Marr, 1976; Marr and Nishihara, 1978). We have already seen that a process may be thought of as a mapping from one representation to another, and in the case of human vision, the initial representation is in no doubt—it consists of arrays of image intensity values as detected by the photoreceptors in the retina.

It is quite proper to think of an image as a representation; the items that are made explicit are the image intensity values at each point in the array, which we can conveniently denote by $I(x,y)$ at coordinate (x,y). In order to simplify our discussion, we shall negect for the moment the fact that there are several different types of receptor, and imagine instead that there is just one, so that the image is black-and-white. Each value of $I(x,y)$ thus specifies a particular level of gray; we shall refer to each detector as a picture element or *pixel* and to the whole array I as an image.

But what of the output of the process of vision? We have already agreed that it must consist of a useful description of the world, but that requirement is rather nebulous. Can we not do better? Well, it is perfectly true that, unlike the input, the result of vision is much harder to discern, let alone specify precisely, and an important aspect of this new approach is that it makes quite concrete proposals about what that end is. But before we begin that discussion, let us step back a little and spend a little time formulating the more general issues that are raised by these questions.

The Purpose of Vision

The usefulness of a representation depends upon how well suited it is to the purpose for which it is used. A pigeon uses vision to help it navigate, fly, and seek out food. Many types of jumping spider use vision to tell the difference between a potential meal and a potential mate. One type, for example, has a curious retina formed of two diagonal strips arranged in a V. If it detects a red V on the back of an object lying in front of it, the spider has found a mate. Otherwise, maybe a meal. The frog, as we have seen, detects bugs with its retina; and the rabbit retina is full of special gadgets, including what is apparently a hawk detector, since it responds well to the pattern made by a preying hawk hovering overhead. Human vision, on the other hand, seems to be very much more general, although it clearly contains a variety of special-purpose mechanisms that can, for example, direct

the eye toward an unexpected movement in the visual field or cause one to blink or otherwise avoid something that approaches one's head too quickly.

Vision, in short, is used in such a bewildering variety of ways that the visual systems of different animals must differ significantly from one another. Can the type of formulation that I have been advocating, in terms of representations and processes, possibly prove adequate for them all? I think so. The general point here is that because vision is used by different animals for such a wide variety of purposes, it is inconceivable that all seeing animals use the same representations; each can confidently be expected to use one or more representations that are nicely tailored to the owner's purposes.

As an example, let us consider briefly a primitive but highly efficient visual system that has the added virtue of being well understood. Werner Reichardt's group in Tübingen has spent the last 14 years patiently unraveling the visual flight-control system of the housefly, and in a famous collaboration, Reichardt and Tomaso Poggio have gone far toward solving the problem (Reichardt and Poggio, 1976, 1979; Poggio and Reichardt, 1976). Roughly speaking, the fly's visual apparatus controls its flight through a collection of about five independent, rigidly inflexible, very fast responding systems (the time from visual stimulus to change of torque is only 21 ms). For example, one of these systems is the landing system; if the visual field "explodes" fast enough (because a surface looms nearby), the fly automatically "lands" toward its center. If this center is above the fly, the fly automatically inverts to land upside down. When the feet touch, power to the wings is cut off. Conversely, to take off, the fly jumps; when the feet no longer touch the ground, power is restored to the wings, and the insect flies again.

In-flight control is achieved by independent systems controlling the fly's vertical velocity (through control of the lift generated by the wings) and horizontal direction (determined by the torque produced by the asymmetry of the horizontal thrust from the left and right wings). The visual input to the horizontal control system, for example, is completely described by the two terms

$$r(\psi)\dot{\psi} + D(\psi)$$

where r and D have the form illustrated in Figure 5.6. This input describes how the fly tracks an ob-

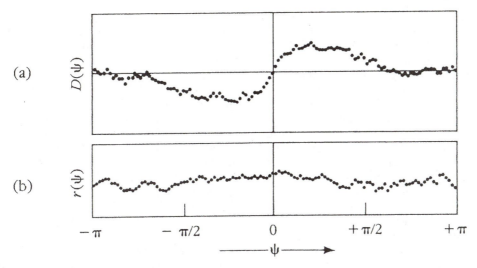

FIGURE 5.6 ■ The horizontal component of the visual input R to the fly's flight system is described by the formula $R = D(\psi) - r(\psi)\dot{\psi}$, where ψ is the direction of the stimulus and $\dot{\psi}$ is its angular velocity in the fly's visual field. $D(\psi)$ is an odd function, as shown in (a), which has the effect of keeping the target centered in the fly's visual field; $r(\psi)$ is essentially constant as shown in (b).

ject that is present at angle ψ in the visual field and has angular velocity $\dot{\psi}$. This system is triggered to track objects of a certain angular dimension in the visual field, and the motor strategy is such that if the visible object was another fly a few inches away, then it would be intercepted successfully. If the target was an elephant 100 yd away, interception would fail because the fly's built-in parameters are for another fly nearby, not an elephant far away.

Thus, fly vision delivers a representation in which at least these three things are specified: (1) whether the visual field is looming sufficiently fast that the fly should contemplate landing; (2) whether there is a small patch—it could be a black speck or, it turns out, a textured figure in front of a textured ground—having some kind of motion relative to its background; and if there is such a patch, (3) ψ and $\dot{\psi}$ for this patch are delivered to the motor system. And that is probably about 60% of fly vision. In particular, it is extremely unlikely that the fly has any explicit representation of the visual world around him—no true conception of a surface, for example, but just a few triggers and some specifically fly-centered parameters like ψ and $\dot{\psi}$.

It is clear that human vision is much more complex than this, although it may well incorporate subsystems not unlike the fly's to help with spe-

cific and rather low-level tasks like the control of pursuit eye movements. Nevertheless, as Poggio and Reichardt have shown, even these simple systems can be understood in the same sort of way, as information-processing tasks. And one of the fascinating aspects of their work is how they have managed not only to formulate the differential equations that accurately describe the visual control system of the fly but also to express these equations, using the Volterra series expansion, in a way that gives direct information about the minimum possible complexity of connections of the underlying neuronal networks.

Advanced Vision

Visual systems like the fly's serve adequately and with speed and precision the needs of their owners, but they are not very complicated; very little objective information about the world is obtained. The information is all very much subjective—the angular size of the stimulus as the fly sees it rather than the objective size of the object out there, the angle that the object has in the fly's visual field rather than its position relative to the fly or to some external reference, and the object's angular velocity, again in the fly's visual field, rather than any assessment of its true velocity relative to the fly or to some stationary reference point.

One reason for this simplicity must be that these facts provide the fly with sufficient information for it to survive. Of course, the information is not optimal and from time to time the fly will fritter away its energy chasing a falling leaf a medium distance away or an elephant a long way away as a direct consequence of the inadequacies of its perceptual system. But this apparently does not matter very much—the fly has sufficient excess energy for it to be able to absorb these extra costs. Another reason is certainly that translating these rather subjective measurements into more objective qualities involves much more computation. How, then, should one think about more advanced visual systems—human vision, for example. What are the issues? What kind of information is vision really delivering, and what are the representational issues involved?

My approach to these problems was very much influenced by the fascinating accounts of clinical neurology, such as Critchley (1953) and Warrington and Taylor (1973). Particularly important was a lecture that Elizabeth Warrington gave at MIT in October 1973, in which she described the capacities and limitations of patients who had suffered left or right parietal lesions. For me, the most important thing that she did was to draw a distinction between the two classes of patient (see Warrington and Taylor, 1978). For those with lesions on the right side, recognition of a common object was possible *provided* that the patient's view of it was in some sense straightforward. She used the words *conventional* and *unconventional*—a water pail or a clarinet seen from the side gave "conventional" views but seen end-on gave "unconventional" views. If these patients recognized the object at all, they knew its name and its semantics—that is, its use and purpose, how big it was, how much it weighed, what it was made of, and so forth. If their view was unconventional—a pail seen from above, for example—not only would the patients fail to recognize it, but they would vehemently deny that it *could* be a view of a pail. Patients with left parietal lesions behaved completely differently. Often these patients had no language, so they were unable to name the viewed object or state its purpose and semantics. But they could convey that they correctly perceived its geometry—that is, its shape—even from the unconventional view.

Warrington's talk suggested two things. First, the representation of the shape of an object is stored in a different place and is therefore a quite different kind of thing from the representation of its use and purpose. And second, vision alone can deliver an internal description of the shape of a viewed object, even when the object was not recognized in the conventional sense of understanding its use and purpose.

This was an important moment for me for two reasons. The general trend in the computer vision community was to believe that recognition was so difficult that it required every possible kind of information. The results of this point of view duly appeared a few years later in programs like Freuder's (1974) and Tenenbaum and Barrow's (1976). In the latter program, knowledge about offices—for example, that desks have telephones on them and that telephones are black—was used to help "segment" out a black blob halfway up an image and "recognize" it as a telephone. Freuder's program used a similar approach to "segment" and "recognize" a hammer in a scene. Clearly, we do use such knowledge in real life; I once saw a brown blob quivering amongst the lettuce in my garden and correctly identified it as a rabbit, even though the visual information alone was inadequate. And yet here was this young woman calmly telling us not only that her patients could convey to her that they had grasped the shapes of things that she had shown them, even though they could not name the objects or say how they were used, but also that they could happily continue to do so even if she made the task extremely difficult visually by showing them peculiar views or by illuminating the objects in peculiar ways. It seemed clear that the intuitions of the computer vision people were completely wrong and that even in difficult circumstances shapes could be determined by vision alone.

The second important thing, I thought, was that Elizabeth Warrington had put her finger on what was somehow the quintessential fact of human vision—that it tells about shape and space and spatial arrangement. Here lay a way to formulate its purpose—building a description of the shapes and positions of things from images. Of course, that is by no means all that vision can do; it also tells about the illumination and about the reflectances of the surfaces that make the shapes—their brightnesses and colors and visual textures—and about their motion. But these things seemed secondary; they could be hung off a theory in which the main job of vision was to derive a representation of shape.

To the Desirable via the Possible

Finally, one has to come to terms with cold reality. Desirable as it may be to have vision deliver a completely invariant shape description from an image (whatever that may mean in detail), it is almost certainly impossible in only one step. We can only do what is possible and proceed from there toward what is desirable. Thus we arrived at the idea of a sequence of representations, starting with descriptions that could be obtained straight from an image but that are carefully designed to facilitate the subsequent recovery of gradually more objective, physical properties about an object's shape. The main stepping stone toward this goal is describing the geometry of the visible surfaces, since the information encoded in images, for example by stereopsis, shading, texture, contours, or visual motion, is due to a shape's local surface properties. The objective of many early visual computations is to extract this information.

However, this description of the visible surfaces turns out to be unsuitable for recognition tasks.

There are several reasons why, perhaps the most prominent being that like all early visual processes, it depends critically on the vantage point. The final step therefore consists of transforming the viewer-centered surface description into a representation of the third-dimensional shape and spatial arrangement of an object that does not depend upon the direction from which the object is being viewed. This final description is object centered rather than viewer centered.

The overall framework described here therefore divides the derivation of shape information from images into three representational stages: (Table 5.1): (1) the representation of properties of the two-dimensional image, such as intensity changes and local two-dimensional geometry; (2) the representation of properties of the visible surfaces in a viewer-centered coordinate system, such as surface orientation, distance from the viewer, and discontinuities in these quantities; surface reflectance; and some coarse description of the prevailing illumination; and (3) an object-centered representation of the three-dimensional structure and

TABLE 5.1. Representational Framework for Deriving Shape Information from Images

Name	Purpose	Primitives
Image(s)	Represents intensity.	Intensity value at each point in the image
Primal sketch	Makes explicit important information about the two-dimensional image, primarily the intensity changes there and their geometrical distribution and organization.	Zero-crossings Blobs Terminations and discontinuities Edge segments Virtual lines Groups Curvilinear organization Boundaries
2½-D sketch	Makes explicit the orientation and rough depth of the visible surfaces, and contours of discontinuities in these quantities in a viewer-centered coordinate frame.	Local surface orientation (the "needles" primitives) Distance from viewer Discontinuities in depth Discontinuities in surface orientation
3-D model representation	Describes shapes and their spatial organization in an object-centered coordinate frame, using a modular hierarchical representation that includes volumetric primitives (i.e., primitives that represent the volume of space that a shape occupies) as well as surface primitives.	3-D models arranged hierarchically, each one based on a spatial configuration of a few sticks or axes, to which volumetric or surface shape primitives are attached

of the organization of the viewed shape, together with some description of its surface properties.

This framework is summarized in Table 5.1. Chapters 2 through 5 give a more detailed account.

REFERENCES

Adrian, E. D. (1928). *The Basis of Sensation*. London: Christophers. (Reprint ed. New York: Hafner, 1964).

Adrian, E. D. (1947). *The Physical Background of Perception*. Oxford: Clarendon.

Austin, J. L. (1962). *Sense and Sensibilia*. Oxford: Clarendon Press.

Barlow, H. B. (1953). Summation and inhibition in the frog's retina. *J. Physiol. (Lond)* 119, 69–88.

Barlow, H. B. (1972). Single units and sensation: a neuron doctrine for perceptual psychology? *Perception 1*, 371–394.

Barlow, H. B., Blakemore, C. & Pettigrew, J. D. (1967). The neural mechanism of binocular depth discrimination. *J. Physiol. (Lond)* 133, 327–342.

Barlow, H. B., Hill, R. M. & Levick, W. R. (1964). Retinal ganglion cells responding selectively to direction and speed of image motion in the rabbit. *J. Physiol. (Lond.)* 173, 377–407.

Bishop, P. O., Coombs, J. S., & Henry, G. H. (1971). Responses to visual contours: Spatio-temporal aspects of excitation in the receptive fields of simple striate neurons. *J. Physiol. (Lond.)* 219, 625–657.

Brindley, G. S. (1970). *Physiology of the Retina and Visual Pathway*. Physiological Society Monograph no. 6. London: Edwin Arnold.

Campbell, F. W. C. & Robson, J. (1968). Application of Fourier analysis to the visibility of gratings. *J. Physiol. (Lond.)* 197, 551–566.

Chomsky, N. (1965). *Aspects of the Theory of Syntax*. Cambridge, Mass.: MIT Press.

Chomsky, N., & Lasnik, H. (1977). Filters and control. *Linguistic Inquiry 8*, 425–504.

DeValois, R. L., Abramov, I., & Mead, W. R. (1967). Single cell analysis of wavelength discrimination at the lateral geniculate nucleus in the macaque. *J. Neurophysiol. 30*, 415–433.

Fram, J. R., & Deutsch, E. S. (1975). On the quantitative evaluation of edge detection schemes and their comparison with human performance. *IEEE Transactions on Computers C–24*, 616–628.

Freuder, E. C. (1974). A computer vision system for visual recognition using active knowledge. MIT A.I. Lab Tech. Rep. 345.

Galambos, R., & Davis, H. (1943). The response of single auditory-nerve fibres to acoustic stimulation. *J. Neurophysiol. 7*, 287–303.

Gibson, J. J. (1966). *The Senses considered as Perceptual Systems*. Boston: Houghton Mifflin.

Gibson, J. J. (1979). *The Ecological Approach to Visual Perception*. Boston: Houghton Mifflin.

Gouras, P. (1968). Identification of cone mechanisms in monkey ganglion cells. *J. Physiol. (Lond)* 199, 533–547.

Granit, R., & Svaetichin, G. (1939). Principles and technique of the electrophysiological analysis of colour reception with the aid of microelectrodes. *Upsala Lakraef Fath. 65*, 161–177.

Gross, C. G., Rocha-Miranda, C. E., & Bender, D. B. (1972). Visual properties of neurons in inferotemporal cortex of the macaque. *J. Neurophysiol. 35*, 96–111.

Guzman, A. (1968). Decomposition of a visual scene into three-dimensional bodies. In *AFIPS Conf. Proc. 33*, 291–304. Washington, D.C.: Thompson.

Hartline, H. K. (1938). The response of single optic nerve fibres of the vertebrate eye to illumination of the retina. *Am. J. Physiol. 121*, 400–415.

Hartline, H. K. (1940). The receptive fields of optic nerve fibers. *Am. J. Physiol. 130*, 690–699.

Helmholtz, H. L. F. von. (1910). *Treatise on Physiological Optics*. Translated by J. P. Southall, 1925. New York: Dover.

Horn, B. K. P. (1973). The Binford-Horn LINEFINDER. MIT A.I. Lab. Memo 285.

Horn, B. K. P. (1974). Determining lightness from an image. *Computer Graphics and Image Processing 3*, 277–299.

Horn, B. K. P. (1975). Obtaining shape from shading information. In *The Psychology of Computer Vision*, P. H. Winston, ed., 115–155. New York: McGraw-Hill.

Horn, B. K. P. (1977). Understanding image intensities. *Artificial Intelligence 8*, 201–231.

Hubel, D. H., & Wiesel, T. N. (1962). Receptive fields, binocular interaction and functional architecture in the cat's visual cortex. *J. Physiol. (Lond.) 166*, 106–154.

Hubel, D. H., & Wiesel, T. N. (1968). Receptive fields and functional architecture of monkey striate cortex. *J. Physiol. (Lond.) 195*, 215–243.

Hueckel, M. H. (1973). An operator which recognizes edges and lines. *J. Assoc. Comput. Mach. 20*, 634–647.

Ito, M. (1978). Recent advances in cerebellar physiology and pathology. In *Advances in Neurology*, R. A. P. Kark, R. N. Rosenberg, and L. J. Shut, eds., 59–84. New York: Raven Press.

Kuffler, S. W. (1953). Discharge patterns and functional organization of mammalian retina. *J. Neurophysiol. 16*, 37–68.

Land, E. H., & McCann, J. J. (1971). Lightness and retinex theory. *J. Opt Sec. Am. 61*, 1–11.

Lettvin, J. Y., Maturana, R. R., McCulloch, W. S., & Pitts, W. H. (1959). What the frog's eye tells the frog's brain. *Proc. Inst. Rad. Eng. 47*, 1940–1951.

Mackworth, A. K. (1973). Interpreting pictures of polyhedral scenes. *Art. Intel. 4*, 121–137.

Marcus, M. P. (1980). *A Theory of Syntactic Recognition for Natural Language*. Cambridge, Mass.: MIT Press.

Marr, D. (1969). A theory of cerebellar cortex. *J. Physiol. (Lond.) 202*, 437–470.

Marr, D. (1974a). The computation of lightness by the primate retina. *Vision Res. 14*, 1377–1388.

Marr, D. (1974b). A note on the computation of binocular disparity in a symbolic, low-level visual processor. MIT A.I. Lab. Memo 327.

Marr, D. (1976). Early processing of visual information. *Phil. Trans R. Soc. Lond. B 275*, 483–524.

Marr, D. (1977a). Analysis of occluding contour. *Proc. R. Soc. Lond. B 197*, 441–475.

Marr, D. (1977b). Artificial intelligence—a personal view. *Artificial Intelligence 9*, 37–48.

Marr, D., & Nishihara. H. K. (1978). Representation and recognition of the spatial organization of three-dimensional shapes. *Proc. R. Soc. Lond. B 200*, 269–294.

Marr, D., & Poggio, T. (1976). Cooperative computation of stereo disparity. *Science 194*, 283–287.

Marr, D., & Poggio, T. (1977). From understanding computation to understanding neural circuitry. *Neurosciences Res. Prog. Bull. 15*, 470–488.

Marr, D., & Poggio, T. (1979). A computational theory of human stereo vision. *Proc. R. Soc. Lond. B 204*, 301–328.

Maturana, H. R., Lettvin, J. Y., McCulloch, W. S., & Pitts, W. H. (1960). Anatomy and physiology of vision in the frog (*Rana Pipiens*). *J. Gen. Physiol. 43* (suppl. no. 2, Mechanisms of Vision), 129–171.

Miles, W. R. (1931). Movement in interpretations of the silhouette of a revolving fan. *Am. J. Psychol. 43*, 392–404.

Newton, I. (1704). *Optics.* London.

Pettigrew, J. D., & Konishi, M. (1976). Neurons selective for orientation and binocular disparity in the visual wulst of the barn owl (*Tyto alba*). *Science 193*, 675–678.

Poggio, T., & Reichardt, W. (1976). Visual control of orientation behavior in the fly. Part II. Towards the underlying neural interactions. *Quart. Rev. Biophys. 9*, 377–438.

Reichardt, W., & Poggio, T. (1976). Visual control of orientation behavior in the fly. Part I. A quantitative analysis, *Quart. Rev. Biophys. 3*, 311–375.

Reichardt, W., & Poggio, T. (1979). Visual control of flight in flies. In *Recent Theoretical Developments in Neurobiology,* W. E. Reichardt, V. B. Mountcastle, and T. Poggio, eds.

Roberts, L. G. (1965). Machine perception of three-dimensional solids. In *Optical and electro optical infomation processing*, ed. J. T. Tippett et at., 159–197. Cambridge, Mass.: MIT Press.

Rosch, E. (1978). Principles of categorization. In *Cognition and categorization*, E. Rosch and B. Lloyd, eds., 27–48. Hillsdale, N.J.: Lawrence Erlbaum Associates.

Rosenfeld, A., & Thurston, M. (1971). Edge and curve detection for visual scene analysis. *IEEE Trans. Comput. C-20*, 562–569.

Schiller, P. H., Finlay, B. L., & Volman, S. F. (1976b). Quantitative studies of single-cell properties in monkey striate cortex. II. Orientation specificity and ocular dominance. *J. Neurophysiol. 39*, 1320–1333.

Shepard, R. N. (1975). Form, formation and transformation of internal representations. In *Information Processing and Cognition: The Loyola Symposium*, R. Solso, ed., 87–122. Hillsdale, N.J.: Lawrence Erlbaum Associates.

Shepard, R. N., & Metzler, J. (1971). Mental rotation of three-dimensional objects. *Science, 171,* 701–703.

Shirai, Y. (1973). A context-sensitive line finder for recognition of polyhedra. *Artificial Intelligence 4*, 95–120.

Stevens, K. A. (1979). Surface perception from local analysis of texture and contour. Ph.D. dissertation, MIT. (Available as The information content of texture gradients. *Biol. Cybernetics 42* (1981), 95–105; also, The visual interpretation of surface contours. *Artificial Intelligence 17* (1981), 47–74.)

Tenenbaum, J. M., & Barrow, H. G. (1976). Experiments in interpretation-guided segmentation. Stanford Research Institute Tech. Note 123.

Wallach, H., & O'Connell, D. N. (1953). The kinetic depth effect. *J. Exp. Psychol. 45*, 205–217.

Waltz, D. (1975). Understanding line drawings of scenes with shadows. In *The Psychology of Computer Vision*, P. H. Winston, ed., pp. 19–91. New York: McGraw-Hill.

Warrington, E. K. (1975). The selective impairment of semantic memory. *Quart. J. Exp. Psychol. 27*, 635–657.

Warrington, E. K., & Taylor, A. M. (1973). The contribution of the right parietal lobe to object recognition. *Cortex 3*, 152–164.

Warrington, E. K., & Taylor, A. M. (1978). Two categorical stages of object recognition. *Perception 7*, 695–705.

Wertheimer, M. (1912). Experimentelle Studien uber das Sehen von Bewegung. Zeitschrift f. Psychol. 61, 161–265.

Wilson, H. R., & Bergen, J. R. (1979). A four mechanism model for spatial vision. *Vision Res. 19*, 19–32.

Winograd, T. (1972). *Understanding Natural Language.* New York: Academic Press.

PART 1

Theoretical Perspectives

Discussion Questions

1. Although Marr and Gibson appear to be at opposite theoretical extremes (for example, Marr emphasized the importance of internal representations and algorithms, while Gibson emphasized the richness of the optic array and the extent to which it directly specified properties of the world), one could argue that Gibson's theory is a rare example of what Marr would call a computational theory of vision. Is there a sense in which Gibson and Marr were kindred souls?

2. At which of Marr's three levels (implementation, algorithm and representation, computational) does Gregory's *neuron doctrine* reside? Is the scientific value of a theory linked to its level (e.g., is a theory that is "merely" implementational less valuable than one that is computational)?

3. It is not always possible to clearly identify which of Marr's three levels characterizes each of the articles in the other sections of this book. Is this a shortcoming of the article in question or of Marr's approach?

4. Is signal detection theory, as discussed by Tanner and Swets, a computational theory, an algorithm, or both? Would Helmholtz be sympathetic to this approach? Gibson?

Suggested Readings

Gregory, R. L. (1980). Perceptions as hypotheses. *Philosophical Transactions of the Royal Society of London, B, 290*, 181–197. A modern constructivist in the tradition of Helmholtz makes the case for perception as a form of implicit reasoning.

Fodor, J. A. (1983). *The modularity of mind.* Cambridge, MA: MIT Press. Philosopher Jerry Fodor reviews the evidence for functional specialization, particularly at the perceptual or input end of cognition, and he analyzes the consequences of a modular design for our understanding of the mind.

Fodor, J. A., & Pylyshyn, Z. (1981). How direct is visual perception? Some reflections on Gibson's ecological approach. *Cognition, 9*, 139–196. A detailed analysis of one of the cornerstones of Gibson's influential approach to perception.

Teller, D. Y. (1984). Linking propositions. *Vision Research, 24*, 1233–1246. Teller discusses the often implicit assumptions that are made in drawing conclusions about the neural basis of vision from psychophysical evidence.

PART 2

Early Vision

Introduction to Reading 6

In the nineteenth century, Sir Thomas Young (1802) first proposed a theory of color vision that assumed the existence of three light sensitive detectors; one each for red, green, and blue light. This idea was independently proposed by Hermann von Helmholtz (1867), and it came to be called the Young-Helmholtz trichromatic theory of color vision. According to the theory, color vision is the result of the neural activity caused by three classes of retinal detectors, which we now know to be three types of cone photoreceptors, each of which has a distinct pattern of sensitivity to different wavelengths of light (see the introduction to Reading 2 for more on light and color). For example, the S-cones respond best to short-wavelength (blueish) light, and less well to yellow or red light; M-cones respond best to medium wavelength light, and so forth. All three cone classes are broadly tuned, however, and respond to some degree throughout the visible spectrum. Trichromatic theory was able to explain the results of behavioral experiments in which observers are asked to match a mixture of three monochromatic comparison lights to a single monochromatic test light. Such a match in color appearance between two physically different lights is called a *metameric match*, and the two patches of light so matched are said to be *metamers* of one another. Trichromatic theory provided an excellent account of such experiments, and was further corroborated by the much later finding, using microspectrophotometry, that there are indeed exactly three different types of retinal cones in people with normal color vision (Brown & Wald, 1964). The theory also provides a complete and compelling account of the three types of dichromatic color blindness, in which one of the three types of receptors is missing due to a genetic abnormality.

In the late nineteenth century, Ewald Hering (1878) proposed an alternative theory of color vision that was prompted by a number of observations that seemed to present problems for the trichromatic theory. For example, Hering noted that the afterimage produced when one views a red patch of light for several minutes is green (and vice-versa) and the afterimage produced by a blue light is yellow (and vice-versa). Furthermore, when observers are asked to sort a wide range of colors into categories, they tend to produce four categories (red, yellow, green, and blue), and not three. Certain color combinations cannot be produced or even imagined (e.g., a reddish-green or a bluish-yellow). All of these facts suggested to Hering that there are four primary colors, and that they are detected by pairs of opponent mechanisms: a red-green mechanism and a blue-yellow mechanism.

Debates arose during the succeeding century about whether the Young-Helmholtz trichromatic theory or Hering's opponent process theory was correct. The undeniable success of trichromatic theory, together with the apparently subjective nature of Hering's observations, led many to adopt trichromatic theory as the "correct" theory of color vision (although many exceptions to this general trend can be found throughout the first half of the 20th century).

In this reading, Leo Hurvich and Dorothea Jameson achieved a synthesis of the two theories by proposing that they both are correct, but reflect different levels of color processing. According to this dual-process account, trichromatic theory correctly describes the operation of the retinal photoreceptors—the cones—while the opponent process theory accounts for the operation of a later mechanism in the lateral geniculate nucleus and in visual cortex that combines the output of the cones in a subtractive fashion. This selection describes the synthesis and the experiments they conducted to achieve it. The authors used an elegant hue-cancellation method to measure psychophysically the sensitivity of the opponent mechanism.

Subsequent neurophysiological experiments confirmed the existence of neurons in the primate brain that exhibit the properties required to implement the opponent-process mechanism of Hering (e.g., Lennie, Krauskopf, & Sclar, 1990). The dual-process account is now well accepted among vision scientists.

REFERENCES

Brown, P. K., & Wald, G. (1964). Visual pigments in single rods and cones of human retina. *Science, 144,* 45–52.

Helmholtz, H. von (1867/1925). *Treatise on physiological optics.* Translated from the 3rd German edition. New York: Dover Publications.

Hering, E. (1878/1964). *Outlines of a theory of the light sense.*

(L. M. Hurvich & D. J. Jameson, Trans.). Cambridge, MA: Harvard University Press.

Lennie, P., Krauskopf, J., & Sclar, G. (1990). Chromatic mechanisms in striate cortex of macaque. *Journal of Neuroscience, 10,* 649–669.

Young, T. (1802). *On the theory of light and colors.* London: The Society.

An Opponent-Process Theory of Color Vision

L. M. Hurvich and D. Jameson • Eastman Kodak Company

The two major theoretical accounts of color vision are those classified as the Young-Helmholtz and the Hering types of theories. For many years the former has been judged by most workers in the field to provide the simplest explanation of the way in which light stimuli give rise to color sensations. The advantages that appear to favor the Young-Helmholtz three-component hypothesis are two: it is parsimonious, and its postulates are easily quantifiable and hence subject to precise experimental test. In its parsimonious and easily quantifiable form, the theory is simple: in addition to the rods which subserve twilight vision, the eye contains three kinds of cone photoreceptors; each type of cone contains a differently selective photochemical substance; each is associated with its own specific nerve fiber; and each cone-photochemical-nerve fiber system is correlated with one of the three specific "fundamental" color sensations, namely, red, green, and blue (or violet). All sensations are considered as compounded of varying amounts of these three excitatory systems, with white arising from equal and simultaneous excitation of all three, and yellow from equal red and green excitations.

The Young-Helmholtz three-cone, three-nerve, three-sensation theory derives directly from the basic fact of color mixture, namely, that all visible hues can be matched by the mixture, in proper proportions, of only three physical light stimuli. Based squarely on this fact, the theory is readily quantified in terms of the three measurable variables of color mixture experiments. But the three measured variables, it must be emphasized, are the three physical light stimuli used in the color mixture experiments; they are not the postulated three "fundamental" color sensations, for with each different stimulus triad used for color matching a different and equally valid triad of color mixture functions is obtained. Consequently, throughout some hundred years since the original formulation of the idea, a continued series of attempts has been made to find the proper transformation of the three measured color mixture curves that will bridge the gap and yield the unique spectral distribution curves of the desired physiological correlates of the three postulated "fundamental" color sensations. An infinity of such transformations is available for trial, and almost every serious adherent of the theory has proposed at least one new set of "fundamental sensation curves" (48, pp. 368–372). The search, however, continues, because serious defects have been found in every proposal made thus far. When the explanatory or predictive power of the theory in any given quantified form is tested it cannot handle more than a limited number of facts satisfactorily (11, p. 805).

Moreover, some facts of color experience seem unassimilable into the framework of the simple Young-Helmholtz theory with its three independent, fundamental, process-sensation systems. How can this system of three independent processes be made to account, for example, for the apparent linkages that seem to occur between specific pairs of colors as either the stimulus conditions or the conditions of the human observer are varied? Why should the red and green hues in the spectrum predominate at low stimulus levels, and the yellow and blue hue components increase concomitantly as the spectrum is increased in luminance (43)? Why, as stimulus size is greatly decreased, should discrimination between yellow and blue hues become progressively worse than that between red and green (4, 10)? Why should the hues drop out in pairs in instances of congential color defect, or when the visual system is impaired by disease (29, 31)? On the other hand, since the sensation of white is granted no special physiological process in this parsimonious theory, but occurs as the fusion product of three equally large fundamental hue sensations, how account for the large degree of independence of white and chromatic qualities when the adaptation of the visual system is varied (37, 41)?

As more and more ad hoc hypotheses are added to the original Young-Helmholtz formulation in order to answer these and other problems forced by the increasing accumulation of experimental data, we naturally find the formulation becoming less and less precise and quantifiable, and obviously less parsimonious. We also find, however, that exactly those phenomena that require modification and extension of the simple "three-color theory" remind us more and more of its chief theoretical rival, the Hering theory of three paired, opponent color processes.

In view of this situation, it seems highly desirable that we take a close second look at Hering's alternative approach to an understanding of color phenomena. The vast accumulation of psychophysical data for which any adequate theoretical proposal must account requires that the basic postulates of the theory, as outlined qualitatively by Hering (13, 14), be restated in quantitative terms for such a critical scrutiny to be most meaningful. This paper will review our attempt to provide such a quantitative restatement, and will summarize briefly some of the critical comparisons between the theoretical deductions and relevant psychophysical data. (Detailed quantitative accounts are given in 21, 22, 23, 25, 26, 27.)

Basic Schema for the Hering Theory

The Three Variables

The Hering theory is like the Young-Helmholtz theory in that it, too, postulates three independent variables as the basis for color vision, but the

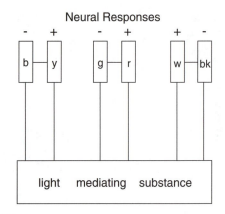

FIGURE 6.1 ▪ Basic Schema for Hering Opponent-Colors Mechanism.

Hering variables are three pairs of visual processes directly associated with three pairs of unique sensory qualities. The two members of each pair are opponent, both in terms of the opposite nature of the assumed physiological processes and (in terms of the mutually exclusive sensory qualities. These paired and opponent visual qualities are yellow-blue, red-green, and white-black.

The basic schema for the opponent-colors mechanism is shown diagrammatically in Fig. 6.1. The three paired opponent response systems are labeled *y-b*, *r-g*, and *w-bk*. The convention of positive and negative signs is used to indicate that each neural system is capable of two modes of response that are physiologically opponent in nature, and that the paired sensory qualities correlated with these opposed modes of response are also mutually opponent or exclusive. That is, we may experience red-blues or green-blues but never yellow-blues, and we see yellow-greens or blue-greens, but never red-greens, and so on. In the absence of any external visual stimulus, the state of the visual system is assumed to be a condition of active equilibrium, and this equilibrium condition is associated with the neutral, homeogeneous "gray" sensation perceived after a long stay in complete darkness. This sensation is quite different from the black experience of the white-black opponent pair. Blackness arises neither by direct light stimulation nor in the simple absence of light, but rather by way of either simultaneous or successive contrast during, or following, light stimulation of some part of the retina.

Properties of Paired Systems

The three pairs of visual response processes are independent of each other; that is, they have different response thresholds, they follow different laws of increase with increase in strength of stimulation, and probably have different time constants. The achromatic system is the most sensitive; that is, the amount of photochemical absorption necessary to excite the achromatic white response is less than the amount of photochemical activity required to stimulate either the y-b or r-g chromatic pairs. This characteristic accounts for the existence of the so-called achromatic interval, i.e., the fact that spectral lines appear achromatic at the absolute threshold for visibility (42, p. 167). Similarly, the red-green system has a lower threshold than the yellow-blue one. The failure of the yellow-blue system to respond at near-threshold levels that are sufficient to activate the red-green system exhibits itself in the facts of so-called "small field dichromasy," in which the eye behaves, with respect to stimuli that are very small in area as well as of low intensity, in a manner similar to the congenital tritanope, i.e., a specific type of "color blind" individual for whom yellow and blue discriminations are impossible and the only hues seen are reds and greens (4, 49).

With increase in level of stimulation the different paired systems also show differences in rate of response increase, such that the achromatic response increase is probably the most rapid of the three, with the result that at very high intensities all spectral stimuli show a strong whitening, or desaturation, relative to their appearance at some intermediate luminance level (42, p. 168). Of the two chromatic pairs, the yellow-blue system, although exhibiting a higher threshold, shows a more rapid rate of increase in response with increase in luminance than does the red-green system. Thus, the mixed hues of the spectrum—the violets, blue-greens, yellow-greens, and the oranges—all vary systematically with increase in spectral luminance, and all show a tendency to be more blue or yellow, respectively, at high luminances, and more red or green at the lower luminance levels (the Bezold-Brücke hue shift phenomenon).

The opponent systems show a tendency toward restoring the balanced equilibrium condition associated with the neutral "gray" sensation. Thus excitation, say, of the r process in the r-g system results in a decrease with time in r responsiveness, and in an increase in the responsiveness of the opponent g process. It we think of the r process as perhaps associated with the building up of an electrical potential in the neural system, and of the g process as associated with the collapse of the potential during impulse firing, then it is easy to see that as the neural potential is increased to higher values there will be a tendency to resist further build up, and also an increased disposition of the tissue toward impulse firing in order to restore the potential to its normal equilibrium value. Although we are not at all ready to ascribe a specific neural correlate of this sort to the postulated opponent processes at this time, the neurophysiological parallels are useful for conceptualizing the opponent-process notion as a real biological phenomenon.

To return to our example, if the responsiveness of the opponent g process tends to increase as r excitation is continued, then when the r stimulus is removed we can expect g activity to be released, strongly at first, then more slowly, and ultimately fading out as equilibrium is again approached. The sensory correlate of this reversal of opponent activities with removal of stimulation is, of course, the familiar phenomenon of the complementary afterimage. If the stimulus (of constant magnitude) is not removed but continues to act for a considerable length of time, then the r process, whose responsiveness is being continuously decreased, will eventually cease to respond further, and a new equilibrium state will be reached. The disappearance of a sensory response with continued constant stimulation can be observed either by the *Ganzfeld* technique, in which the whole retina is uniformly illuminated by diffuse light (18), or by the "painted image" technique, in which optical means are used to fix a well defined image on the retina in such a way that its retinal position remains constant and independent of eye movements (39). By either method the eventual result of continued steady stimulation is a disappearance of the visual experience: the light seems to have gone out in the *Ganzfeld* situation, or, in the fixed-image situation, the perceived object simply fades out of view.

Not only are the visual responses modified by changes in time in the excitabilities of the opponent processes, but they are also importantly affected by spatial interaction among the various elements of the visual field. Within certain limits there is evidence of summation of similar kinds of activity in adjacent elements, as in threshold responses for small stimulus areas (5, pp. 846–852). But perhaps more important for the over-all functioning of the visual system are the antagonistic interactions, such that *r* activity in one area induces *g* activity in adjacent areas, and similarly for the yellow-blue and white-black paired response systems. These opponent spatial induction effects are evident in all the familiar color and brightness contrast phenomena (35, pp. 138–142). They are probably also primarily responsible for the great visual-image clarity that characterizes vision in spite of the fact that the optical system of the eye is obviously imperfect, and that consequently the light image formed on the retinal surface lacks sharply defined boundaries (17, pp. 151–159). The spatial interaction causing intensification of opponent qualities at adjacent surfaces would seem an ideal crispening device to sharpen up the initially blurred retinal image.

Photochemical Postulates

In addition to the various temporal and spatial induction effects, which are assumed to be based in the neural visual-response tissue, visual adaptation probably also involves changes in the photochemical activities that initiate the neural responses, since a certain amount of photochemical bleaching is expected to occur with continued exposure of the photosensitive materials to a retinal light stimulus. In order for the three paired opponent-response systems to be selectively stimulated, there must, of course, be more than one substance available for photochemical mediation between the incident light and the neural excitation. Whatever the specific nature of the photosensitive materials, they must form a link in the system of three independent variables, and hence we have postulated three independent photosensitive materials, which we may call α, β and γ.

Our schematic model now takes the form shown in Fig. 6.2A or 6.2B. The three independent photosensitive materials may be contained in discrete retinal units with complex interconnections to the neural response systems, as shown in Fig. 6.2A, or two or more of these materials may be combined in receptor units having simpler connections to the neural response systems, as diagrammed in Fig. 6.2B. There is no way of differentiating these models in terms of visual behavior; and however the three photochemicals may be segregated or combined in the retina, and whatever the number

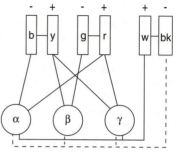

Neural Responses

Photochemical Absorptions

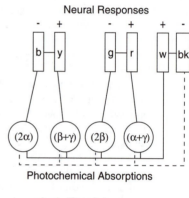

Neural Responses

Photochemical Absorptions

$$y\text{-}b = k_1\,(\beta+\gamma-2\alpha)$$
$$r\text{-}g = k_2\,(\alpha+\gamma-2\beta)$$
$$w\text{-}bk = k_3\,(\alpha+\gamma+\beta) - k_4(\alpha+\beta+\gamma)$$

FIGURE 6.2 ■ Schematic Diagram Showing Relations Between Photosensitive Materials α, β, and γ and Neural Opponent Resonse Processes *y–b*, *r–g*, and *w–bk*.

of different photoreceptor units, there remain only three independent photosensitive materials, and the theory remains a three-variable, opponent-colors schema.

Quantification of Opponents Theory

Since our aim is to present this schema in quantitative terms, one of the first questions that has to be asked is this: Is it possible to obtain by psychophysical experiment direct measurements of the spectral distributions of the three basic response variables of the Hering theory?

Measures of Achromatic and Chromatic Responses

It can fairly be assumed that the achromatic, white response is closely connected with the distribution of the brightness quality throughout the visible spectrum, and Fig. 6.3 therefore shows two functions (which we have measured by a threshold technique) that give the whiteness distribution of an equal energy spectrum for two observers (20). The induced rather than directly stimulated black component of the achromatic white-black response pair has this same distribution, but of opposite sign, since the strength of the black contrast response is directly related to the magnitude of either the surrounding or the preceding whiteness or brightness.

A method for determining the spectral distributions of the paired chromatic responses is implicit in the opponents theory itself. Since the two members of each hue pair are mutually opponent or exclusive, then a yellow response of given strength should be exactly canceled by a stimulus that, taken alone, elicits the same magnitude of blue response, and a similar relation should hold between red and green responses. Thus a null method, based on the antagonism of the two members of each hue pair, can be used to measure the spectral distributions of the chromatic responses. In brief, a wave length is first selected that evokes, say, a blue hue response. The observer then views, in turn, a series of spectral wave lengths that appear yellowish in hue (yellow-greens, yellow, and yellow-reds). To each of these yellow stimuli just enough of the previously selected blue stimulus is then added exactly to cancel the yellow hue without introducing any blueness. The observer simply reports when the test field appears neither yellow nor blue;

the hue remainder that he sees may be green, neutral, or red, depending on the test wave length. Knowing the energies of the series of spectral yellow stimuli, and having determined experimentally the energy of the blue stimulus of fixed wave length that is required for the hue cancellation in each case, we can now plot the distribution of the relative magnitudes of yellow hue response evoked by the various test wave lengths. The procedure is simply reversed to obtain the distribution of the blue component of the yellow-blue pair; that is, varying amounts of a fixed wave length of yellow hue are used to cancel the blue hue quality of a series of "blue" test wave lengths. By using a red stimulus of fixed wave length and variable energy to cancel the greens, and a green stimulus to cancel the reds, the spectral distribution of the red-green pair of chromatic responses is similarly determined.

Two sets of paired chromatic response vs. wave length functions that were measured in this way (25), together with the achromatic spectral functions shown in Fig. 6.3, are plotted in Fig. 6.4 for an equal energy spectrum. The opponent members of each hue pair have been given arbitrary positive and negative designations, to correspond with their opponent characteristics. Thus the positive values of the red-green function indicate redness, and the negative values greenness. Similarly, the positive values of the yellow-blue function indicate yellowness, and the negative values blueness.

These are the psychophysical functions that represent the spectral distributions of the three independent variables of the Hering opponent-colors theory for these two observers. They are assumed to be directly correlated with the response activity of the visual nervous tissue (retina, optic nerve, and visual centers), and should not be taken as photochemical absorption spectra, about which these data tell us nothing.

Brightness, Hue, and Saturation

The psychophysical opponent-response functions shown in Fig. 6.4 provide a direct description of the appearance of the spectrum, for these observers, for a neutral condition of bright adaptation and at the moderate level of luminance for which the functions were obtained. Thus, all wave lengths evoke some whiteness as well as hue; the whiteness and brightness of an equal energy spectrum is relatively small at the two spectral extremes and relatively high at the intermediate wave lengths.

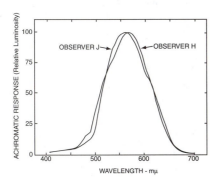

FIGURE 6.3 ■ Whiteness Distribution of an Equal Energy Spectrum for Two Observers.

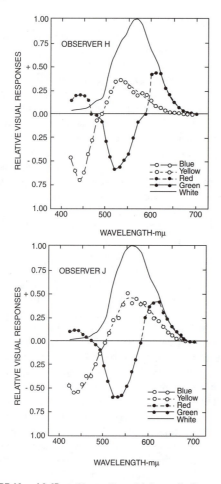

FIGURE 4A and 6.4B ■ Chromatic and Achromatic Response Functions for Equal Energy Spectrum for Two Observers.

The short wave lengths appear as red-blue hues (violets); there is a narrow band of pure or unique blue where the red-green function is equal to zero; then come the blue-greens, followed by a narrow band of unique green at the wave length where the yellow-blue function is equal to zero; this is followed by the yellow-greens, and then pure yellow occurs at the second intersection of the red-green function with the zero ordinate value; and finally the yellow-red hues appear in the long wave length region (19). A quantitative expression for hue, a "hue coefficient," can be obtained by taking the value of one of the chromatic responses, say, the yellow value at 550 mμ, relative to the total of all chromatic responses at that wave length, in this case, yellow plus green.

The saturation of the color depends on the rela-

tive amounts of chromatic and achromatic responses. At the two spectral extremes where the chromatic responses are large relative to the white response, the spectral saturation is high. Where the reverse is true, spectral saturation is low. This can be expressed quantitatively in the form of a "saturation coefficient." To use the same example, the total of the yellow-plus-green values relative to the white plus yellow plus green is relatively low at 550 mμ and this wave length appears much less saturated than does, say, either 440 mμ or 670 mμ.

Color Mixture

Since color-mixture experiments simply involve matching the three perceived qualities evoked by one stimulus by the proper mixture of three other stimuli, it is possible to determine the color-mixture relations that are inherent in the response curves of Fig. 6.4 for any three arbitrarily selected mixture primaries. That is, the red-green value, the yellow-blue value and the white value of the total visual response to any wave length of unit energy are matched by the totals of the three corresponding values for the three mixture primaries when the latter stimuli are combined in the proper ratios. On paper, the color equations for most spectral matches require the admission of negative values for one of the mixture primaries. In actual color-mixture experiments, these negative values are realized by removing one of the mixture primaries from the matching field and adding it to the test stimulus.

To calculate, for example, the amounts of energy required for a color match to a given wave length λ by the mixture of the spectral primaries 460 mμ, 530 mμ and 650 mμ, let a = the energy at 460 mμ, b = the energy at 530 mμ, and c = the energy at 650 mμ. The three equations to be solved for these three unknowns a, b, and c are then:

$$a(r_{460}) + b(r_{530}) + c(r_{650}) = r\gamma$$
$$a(y_{460}) + b(y_{530}) + c(y_{650}) = y\gamma$$
$$a(w_{460}) + b(w_{530}) + c(w_{650}) = w\gamma$$

The values for r (or for $-r$ when the response function is negative, indicating that the hue is green rather than red), for y (or for $-y$ when the response is blue rather than yellow), and for w are then read from the response functions for unit energy for each wave length in question. (See Fig. 6.4.) The values $r\gamma$, $y\gamma$ and $w\gamma$ represent the unit energy response values for any spectral wave length for which a color-mixture equation is to be calculated. Solving this set of three equations for the three unknowns a, b, and c, we then have a color-mixture equation of the form

$$a_{460} + b_{530} + c_{550} = 1$$

This equation, which is expressed in energy units, may be converted to photometric units in the usual way by multiplying each energy value by the relative luminosity (given by the achromatic response function) at the given wave length.

Color-mixture relations calculated in this manner for wave lengths λ from 420 mμ through 700 mμ from smoothed visual response data for two observers are shown in Fig. 6.5. The two additional sets of color-mixture functions (for the same three mixture primaries) that are shown for comparison in the figure are the results of actual color mixture experiments by W. D. Wright and L. C. Thomson (24, 47).

Since the relations between the measured response functions and the color-mixture data are, as we have just seen, known for two individual observers, it is now also possible (by assuming specific spectral loci for the unique hues) to reverse the procedure and derive opponent-response functions from the color-mixture data for Wright and Thomson, or for any other observer whose color-mixture data are available. Since it seems preferable to develop a general theoretical model on the basis of a representative average, rather than a small number of individual observers, we have used for the model chromatic and achromatic response functions derived from the average color-mixture data for the CIE international standard observer (30). These derived functions are shown in Fig. 6.6. (The details of the derivation are given in 22.) They are, of course, smoother and more regular than the individual, measured functions, but in other respects they are quite similar (compare Fig. 6.4).

Photochemical Distributions

The specific set of α, β, and γ photosensitive absorption functions that have been assumed for the theoretical model are shown in Fig. 6.7. These curves have not been measured, and they have the particular forms shown and the high degree of

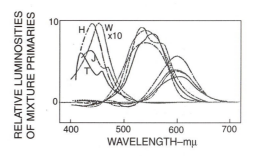

FIGURE 6.5 ■ Calculated Color Mixture Functions for Observers H and J and Experimental Color Mixture Functions for Observers T and W (24, 47).

overlap exhibited because of the specific interrelations that we have postulated a priori between the photochemical events and the neural response activities of the visual opponent mechanisms. Once the photopigments actually present in the human retina have been identified by the biochemists, the visual theorist will have no need to make such a priori postulates, and the specific interrelations required between the identified photosensitive materials and the neural processes underlying the color responses can easily be deduced. As matters now stand, however, the functions shown in Fig. 6.7 meet the basic demands of the known facts, and any changes in these theoretical absorption functions that will no doubt be required by results of photochemical researches will not importantly affect any of the basic postulates of the theoretical model. The broadness and similarity of shape of all three selective functions that we have assumed are characteristic of all visual pigments so far identified in a variety of animal species (2).

These assumed photopigment distributions do not enter into the consideration of color phenomena, in normal vision, until we come to an examination of some of the phenomena of chromatic adaptation in which selective photochemical bleaching seems to act as one of the important determinants. The other determinants are, of course, the spatial and temporal induction effects in the neural opponent response processes that have been mentioned earlier.

Dependence of Hue and Saturation on Both Wave Length and Luminance

What are the visual phenomena for which the model can account? As we have already indicated,

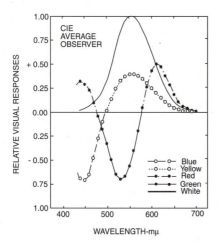

FIGURE 6.6 ▪ Theoretical Chromatic and Achromatic Response Functions for Equal Energy Spectrum for CIE Average Observer.

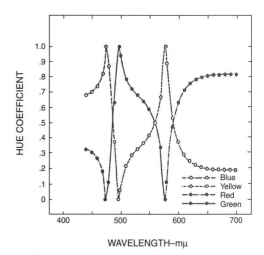

FIGURE 6.8 ▪ Spectral Hue Coefficients; Moderate Luminance.

the measured chromatic and achromatic response functions provide a direct and quantifiable description of the color sensations evoked by any stimulus of specified wave-length composition (23). The achromatic, white function is taken as a direct expression of spectral brightness. Spectral hue, which is determined by the chromatic responses evoked by each wave length, can also be expressed quantitatively as a coefficient value relating the magnitude of response of one chromatic system to the total of all chromatic responses at that wave length. An example of such a hue coefficient function for a moderate level of luminance is shown in Fig. 6.8. It is clear, from the varying rate of change in

the hue coefficient function from one region of the spectrum to the next, that an observer's ability to discriminate among neighboring wave lengths on the basis of hue changes alone will also differ for the different regions of the spectrum. This discriminative capacity is obviously also quantifiable in terms of the amount of wave-length change required to elicit a threshold change of fixed amount in the value of the hue coefficient. With change in the luminance at which the spectrum is presented, these coefficient functions will be altered, in the sense that the yellow-blue values will increase at the higher luminances, and will be diminished at the lower luminances. This is so because, in accordance with the different energy-vs.-response function postulated for the yellow-blue system as compared with the red-green one, as the excitation level is increased, the yellow and blue spectral responses will be uniformly magnified relative to the red and green ones at the higher levels, and uniformly diminished at the lower levels. Although the exact differential between the two paired systems is not known, under certain circumstances an over-all difference in response magnitudes of approximately 20 per cent seems to occur for a log unit change in luminance. Thus, at some wave length for which, say, the red and yellow responses are equal at a luminance of 10 mL, the yellow will be about 20% greater than the red at 100 mL, and about 20% less at a luminance of only 1 mL. If we assume this 20% differential between y-b and r-g response magnitudes per log unit

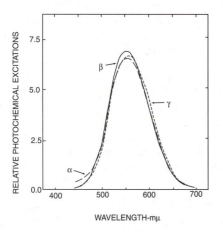

FIGURE 6.7 ▪ Spectral Distribution Curves for Assumed Photosensitive Materials.

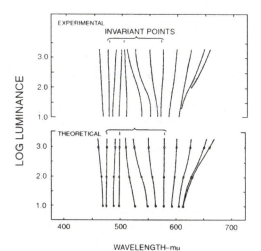

FIGURE 6.9 ■ Constant Hue Contours as Measured by Purdy (38) and as Predicted by Theory.

of luminance change as a reasonable value, and compute the spectral hue coefficients for a range of approximately three log units of luminance variation, then we can specify the amount of hue shift associated with a change in intensity of any wave length. Conversely, we can also specify the wave length changes necessary to maintain a constant hue sensation (constant hue coefficient value) as the luminance is increased or decreased. The latter procedure has been used to obtain the functions shown in Fig. 6.9, and the curves in the upper part of the figure are functions measured by Purdy in an actual experiment of this sort (38).

These hue phenomena do not involve the achromatic response pair at all, and depend only on the two paired chromatic response systems. Whatever the chromatic response to a given stimulus, the perceived color saturation clearly will also depend on the extent to which the white system is simultaneously responding. For any given amount of chromatic response, the color will obviously appear less saturated if there is a large magnitude of white response to dilute the color, and more saturated if the white component of the total response is relatively small. The perceived saturation of the spectrum is also expressed as a quantitative coefficient function. (See Fig. 6.10.) Here the value taken as the saturation coefficient is the ratio of the total chromatic to the chromatic-plus-white responses at each wave length. The relatively high values at the spectral extremes and the minimal value in the pure yellow region are perfectly consistent both with qualitative reports and with

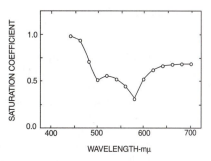

FIGURE 6.10 ■ Spectral Saturation Coefficients; Moderate Luminance.

the experimental data on this problem (e.g., 28). Again, as in the hue functions, the rate of change of the saturation coefficient from one spectral region to the next is indicative of a varying discriminative capacity with respect to wave length; and, again, the form of the function as shown applies to a moderate luminance level and varies in a determinable manner with change in the level of excitation in accordance with the different energy-vs.-response rates of the three independent response systems.

In view of the variations in the hue and saturation functions with change in luminance, we should expect that discrimination functions that depend on changes in these two color attributes, such as discrimination of one wave length from the next in an equal brightness spectrum, would also reflect such a dependence on luminance. Figure 6.11 shows, in the upper half, a set of wave-

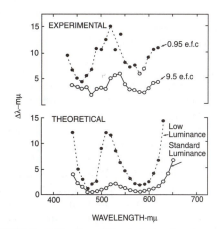

FIGURE 6.11 ■ Wave-length Discrimination Functions for Two Luminance Levels as Measured by Weale (45) and as Predicted by Theory.

length discrimination functions obtained at two luminance levels by Weale (45). The higher values of difference threshold obtained at the low luminance level may be explained by a general reduction of discriminative capacity in dim light. The shift of the midspectral maximum toward lower wave lengths, and the relatively greater heightening of the minimum in the yellow region, cannot, however, be attributed to such a generalized reduction in discriminatory capacity. The selectively greater loss in yellow and blue responses at the low-luminance level that is one of the postulates of our model does, however, account for changes of exactly this sort in the form of the function. This is shown by the two theoretical functions computed from pairs of spectral hue and saturation functions that are associated with the two specified luminance levels. Since brightness is kept constant in such experiments, only the hue and saturation variables need be considered in our analysis of these functions (22).

Chromatic Adaptation

The phenomena that we have treated thus far all refer to the individual with normal color vision in a neutral state of adaptation. What of his color perception after the visual system has been exposed for some time to a strongly colored illuminant? For analytical purposes, the simplest situation of this sort is the one in which the eye has been exposed to a large surround field of given color and luminance, and the test stimuli are viewed at the same level of luminance as the surround. Under these circumstances, the three photochemical receptor substances will probably have undergone some selective bleaching, and because of the similar brightness of the surround and test fields, spatial induction effects in the neural response processes will probably be fairly constant. To simplify the treatment for these particular conditions, therefore, we may ignore the constant neural inductions and consider the photosensitive changes as exercising a controlling influence on the response systems.

We know that under these circumstances the color-mixture data do not change. That is, with uniform chromatic adaptation, any change in the perceived color of one side of a bipartite color-mixture field will also occur on the other side, and to exactly the same extent. Thus a color equation that has been made with the eye adapted to a neu-

tral white light will also be a valid equation when the eye is adapted to a colored illuminant (15). These important constancies of color equations mean that whatever photochemical changes occur with adaptation must occur in a very specific way. That is, the spectral distribution functions representing the three selective photochemicals may be selectively multiplied or reduced by a constant factor, but no one of them can change its form (44, pp. 211–212). In other words, any single substance cannot lose a greater percentage of its absorption at one wave length than it loses at another wave length. Thus, exposure to a colored light can cause any one of the postulated photochemical functions shown in Fig. 6.7 to be multiplied or divided by a constant amount, but this is the only alteration in the photosensitive functions that is consistent with the fact that color equations are invariant with chromatic adaptation.

The extent to which the three substances are selectively attenuated as a result of exposure to colored light is clearly controlled by the light stimulus itself. That substance which initially absorbs most of the adapting light will suffer the greatest relative bleaching, and the substance which absorbs relatively little of the adapting light

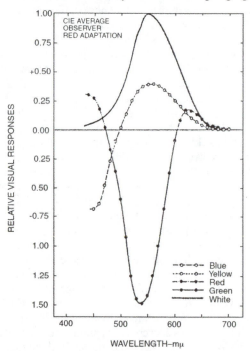

FIGURE 6.12 ■ Chromatic and Achromatic Visual Response Functions for Red Adaptation as Predicted by Theory.

will be relatively little affected by it. Thus, by determining their relative absorptions of the adapting light, we can compute the relative changes in the heights of the photosensitive distribution functions for the three photopigments that we have postulated. Since the excitations of the opponent response systems depend on these photochemical light absorptions (see Fig. 6.2), we can now also determine the forms and magnitudes of the chromatic and achromatic response functions for the new condition of adaptation. In spite of the close overlap of the photosensitive functions that we have postulated, the "adapted" chromatic response functions determined in this way change in striking fashion relative to the functions for the neutral adaptation condition. The achromatic function changes too, but relatively very little. These theoretically computed adaptation changes are consistent with the kinds of change known to occur in situations of this sort. If the eye that has been adapted to white light is exposed for some time to a saturated red equal in brightness to the white, the normally red end of the spectrum does not become excessively dark, but the amount of redness seen is strongly reduced, and the greens become greatly supersaturated (3, pp. 133–137). Also, the wave length that formerly appeared pure yellow is now strongly greenish, and this is also true for the wave length that formerly appeared pure blue. These changes can be determined from the functions shown in Fig. 6.12 that have been computed for a given red adaptation, in comparison with the functions for the neutral state that were given in Fig. 6.6.

From this new set of "adapted" opponent response functions the hue and saturation coefficients and the discrimination data for this new state can also now be determined (26).

These "adapted" response functions are specified, as we said above, for a circumscribed set of conditions for which the photochemical adaptation changes could be taken as primary. As soon as the relative luminance conditions are altered, however, then the neural inductions enter importantly into the complex picture. For example, if a test stimulus seen within a strongly colored (say, red) surround looks neutral when its luminance is the same as that of the surround, then it will probably appear somewhat reddish at a higher luminance, and the complementary green at a lower luminance (12). (The test stimulus is assumed also to be of predominantly long wave length compo-

sition.) In terms of opponent inductions this phenomenon is readily understood. If the red process excited by the red surround induces an opponent green process in the test area, then at an intermediate luminance this green induction is just strong enough to cancel the red-process activity aroused by the test stimulus itself. When the test stimulus is made brighter and the red response to it increases, the unchanged green induction from the surround becomes inadequate to cancel completely the increased red response to the stronger test stimulus, and the red test hue is now seen. At a much lower luminance of test stimulus, the red process is activated to a much lesser extent, and the green induction from the surround, which is still unchanged in strength, is now sufficient to impart a green hue to the perceived test area. These phenomena are not only consistent with the opponent induction postulate, but they also make it clear why attempts to treat the problem of chromatic adaptation exclusively as a matter of photochemical bleaching are foredoomed to failure (e.g., 1, 33).

Color Anomalies and Color Blindness

When we come to consider individuals who do not have normal color vision we find that their color vision can depart from the normal in two general ways. Their color perceptions may be distorted relative to the normal, or they may exhibit specific color weaknesses or losses. Also, they may show both types of these deviant characteristics at the same time. By distorted color perceptions we mean, for example, the perceptions of the particular type of anomalous individual who has the following characteristics: he sees a distinct orange in the spectral region described normally as pure yellow or nearly so; he needs three stimuli for color mixture; he makes color matches with high precision but uses quite different proportions of the mixture stimuli than does the normal observer. An individual of this type does not seem to have lost any of the efficiency of his neural visual response processes, and it seems reasonable to assume that his color distortions have their basis in the photochemical complex responsible for selective light absorption.

The particular assumptions that we have made concerning the kinds of deviation that the photosensitive materials may exhibit stem from a generalization made by Dartnall (2), on the basis of his researches concerned with the identification of visual photopigments in a variety of lower organisms. Dartnall has found that when the absorption curves of the various visual pigments are plotted as a function of the vibration frequency of the incident light (the reciprocal of the more usual wave-length specification), all the absorption curves have very nearly the same shape, and they can be made to coincide simply by shifting the curves so that they all reach an absorption maximum at the same frequency. In other words, a single template representing amount of absorption as ordinate, against frequency of radiant energy as abscissa, can be used to fit the absorption function of any visual pigment, whatever the locus of its absorption maximum. It seems reasonable to expect that this same generalization will apply to the photosensitive distributions of anomalous individuals with respect to the population of observers with normal color responses. We have conse-

quently assumed that, in congenital abnormalities of the visual system, the normal photopigments can undergo changes that result in a uniform shift of the entire set of photosensitive distribution functions as a group along the frequency scale. These shifts are assumed to occur in either of two directions: toward higher frequencies (shorter wave lengths) resulting in the type of anomalous color vision identified as *protanomaly*, or toward lower frequencies (longer wave lengths) relative to the normal absorption loci, resulting in the second major type of anomalous color vision known as *deuteranomaly*. The amount of these displacements may also vary in different degrees of congenital anomaly.

Since the absorption of light by the photosensitive materials provides the stimulus for the neural chromatic and achromatic response systems, the visual response functions thus controlled by the deviant photosensitive materials will necessarily be altered, too, and in a systematic manner. Examples of theoretically derived anomalous response functions based on these assumptions are given in Fig. 6.13. The set of functions in the center block are those for the observer with normal photosensitive materials; those in the upper block are for a protanomalous type whose visual pigment absorptions are assumed to be shifted toward the shorter wave lengths by an amount equal to about 15 mμ from the normal peak of about 550 mμ. This type of individual will have a luminosity function (described by the achromatic, white response function) that peaks at a shorter wave length than the normal and will show considerable loss of luminosity at the red end of the spectrum (48, Ch. 25). The spectral hues will also be altered, with a distinctly reddish yellow occurring where the normal individual sees a unique or pure yellow, whereas the protanomalous observer's pure yellow occurs at a wave length described by the normal as quite greenish. In making color matches, such as a match between 589 mμ on one side of a bipartite field and a mixture of 530 mμ and 670 mγ on the other, this observer will require a much greater proportion of 670 mμ in the mixture than will the average observer with normal color vision (27, 46). This particular match, the Rayleigh equation, is the earliest and best known diagnostic test for anomalous color vision. In this same test, the anomalous individual whose response functions are shown in the lower block in Fig. 6.13 will deviate from the normal in the opposite way;

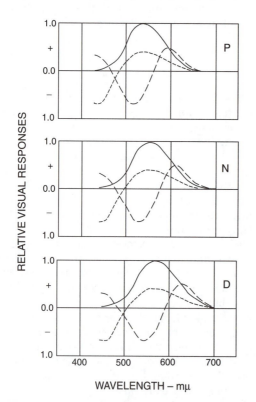

FIGURE 6.13 ■ Theoretical Chromatic and Achromatic Response Functions for Equal Energy Spectrum. For observers with protanomalous, normal, and deuteranomalous photoreceptor systems and with normal strength visual response processes.

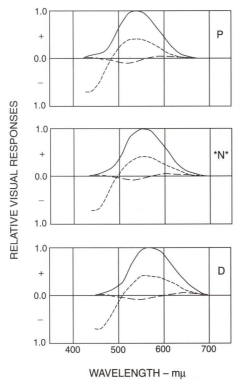

FIGURE 6.14 ■ Theoretical Chromatic and Achromatic Response Functions for Equal Energy Spectrum. For observers with protanomalous, normal, and deuteranomalous photoreceptor systems, and with impaired red-green response processes.

that is, he will require a much greater proportion of 530 mμ in the mixture for the Rayleigh equation (46). This type of anomalous individual (deuteranomalous) is assumed to have photopigment absorptions that are shifted toward the longer wave lengths, and he will see greenish-yellows where the normal sees yellow, yellows where the normal sees orange, etc. Since the neural response processes of both types of anomalies of this sort are assumed to be operating at the normal efficiency, these individuals will show high precision in making their distorted color matches, and their discriminatory capacities will also be good. As a matter of fact, anomalous individuals of this sort have understandably high confidence in their own color capability, and they are extremely resistant toward accepting the results of diagnostic tests which indicate that their visual capacities are deviant from (with the implication of "inferior to") those of the normal population (36, pp. 235–238).

Not all anomalous individuals are as fortunate as the types shown in Fig. 6.13, however. Many give evidence of real color weakness, in addition to distortions of the kinds already discussed (40). These color-weak individuals seem to have been deprived of some of the efficiency of the neural response processes, particularly of the red-green opponent pair, and their systems may be represented in terms of the theory by the kinds of response functions given as examples in Fig. 6.14. The visual pigments of these three types of individuals are taken to be the same as those shown in the preceding figure, respectively, but the red-green paired system is reduced to one-tenth of the normal strength. Such observers have real losses in color discrimination in addition to possible color distortions, and their color matches are imprecise as well as deviant. Individuals with congenitally abnormal color systems are frequently of this general type, and cases of acquired color blindness caused by degenerative disease invariably show this kind of color weakness at some stage in the development of the neural disorder (31).

When the weaknesses become extreme, whether in congenital or acquired disorders, the red-green system seems to be entirely lost to normal function, and a condition of dichromasy, or so-called "color-blindness," results. That is, the visual system becomes a two-variable one, as shown in Fig. 6.15. Here the yellow-blue and the white-black neural systems remain intact and functioning, but there

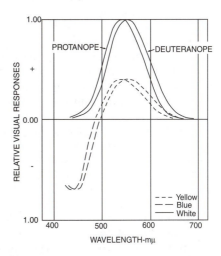

FIGURE 6.15 ■ Theoretical Chromatic and Achromatic Response Functions for Equal Energy Spectrum. For observers with nonfunctioning red-green response processes.

is no red-green response function. If the red-green loss occurs without changes in the visual pigments, the remaining yellow-blue and white-black response functions are like those of the normal individual; but, since there is no red-green system, the spectrum is divided into only two hue sections for these individuals. The short wave lengths which normally vary from violet through blue and blue-green to pure green all appear as blue, but of varying saturations, with a neutral region where the normal pure green occurs. Beyond this wave length the remainder of the spectrum appears yellow, in varying saturations, out to the extreme long-wave limit of visibility. The luminosity function is the same as for the observer with normal color vision. Individuals who fit this response pattern would be classified as *deuteranopes* (29). If the visual pigments are altered, so as to produce an absorption shift toward the short wave lengths in addition to the complete red-green neural loss, then the spectrum is again divided into a shortwave blue and a long-wave yellow section, but the neutral region that divides the spectrum into the two major hues occurs at a shorter wave length than for the deuteranopes. The luminosity function is also displaced in this type of dichromasy, as it is for the anomalous individuals with similar photopigment changes, and the type of "color-blind" vision associated with this pattern is called *protanopia* (29).

These two theoretically assumed kinds of deviation from the normal system—i.e., photopigment changes and neutral losses or weaknesses of the paired red-green response system—permit us to assemble a systematic picture of the many various manifestations of abnormal red-green vision that defy understanding in terms of any model of the visual system that assumes a one-to-one correspondence between light absorption in the retinal receptors and the resulting color sensations (22, 27).

Defects or losses may also occur in the yellow-blue neural response system, although such defects seem to be much more rare than the red-green defects. Again, these yellow-blue neural losses may take place either with or without changes in the photosensitive materials in the retina. Examples of the remaining red-green and white-black response functions in two types of yellow-blue blindness are given in Fig. 6.16. In each type of this disorder, the yellow-blue neural response function is missing, and the total gamut of colors for these individuals includes only neutral and reds and

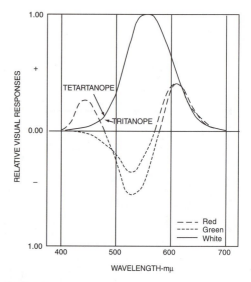

FIGURE 6.16 ■ Theoretical Chromatic and Achromatic Response Functions for Equal Energy Spectrum. For observers with nonfunctioning yellow-blue response processes.

greens of various saturations. If there is no simultaneous photopigment disorder, there are two neutral points in the spectrum, one in the region where the normal sees a pure yellow, and another in the region where the normal sees a pure blue. Yellow-blue blindness of this sort is called *tetartanopia*, and only a few cases of it have been reported in the literature (e.g., 34, pp. 68–92). Slightly more common is the second type of yellow-blue blindness, known as *tritanopia* (49), in which not only the neural yellow-blue system is lost, but also the short-wave photopigment seems to be missing. Observers of this type have a neutral point in the normally yellow-green region of the spectrum, but there is no second neutral point, and the green hues extend into the short-wave region that appears violet to the person with normal color vision.

For all these types of deviant color vision, calculation from the theoretical spectral response functions of discrimination curves, color mixture equations, and other psychophysical relations are in good agreement with the experimental data that are available for the various kinds of defective color systems (22, 27).

Opponents-Theory and Neurophysiology

The conceptual model for the opponent-colors theory as originally presented by Hering drew its sharpest criticism on the grounds of being bad physiology. Some of this criticism was based on an erroneous interpretation of Hering's views, an interpretation that incorrectly assigned the opponent processes to the photochemical activities in the retinal cells. Hering's own concept of mutually opponent neural processes, each capable of being activated by external stimulation, was also, however, far ahead of the knowledge of neurophysiology at the time it was proposed (16). But this concept now turns out to be perfectly consistent with the picture of neural function that is only just recently beginning to build up from electrophysiological studies of the visual neural apparatus.

It has become clear that nerves do not simply respond or fail to respond when a stimulus is presented to the appropriate end-organ. Rather, they may respond according to any of a number of quite specific patterns. For example, a nerve fiber may (a) discharge at the onset of stimulation and subsequently gradually become quiet; (b) discharge at both onset and cessation of stimulation with a quiet period in between; or (c) cease any spontaneous activity when first stimulated and during continued stimulation, but respond with a burst of electrical impulses when the stimulus ceases to act (7). The on- and off-phases of discharge are mutually inhibitory processes, they are associated with slow electrical potentials of opposite sign, and they cancel each other when the experimental conditions are so manipulated as to cause both on- and off-discharges to impinge simultaneously on the same ganglion cell (6). In Granit's opinion (6), the evidence from electrophysiology provides a "belated vindication of Hering's view" that the visual system is characterized by mutually opponent neural processes.

The concept of mutual interaction among the various elements of the physiological field is also basic to the theory and is critical to an understanding of both areal effects and simultaneous contrast phenomena. Here again, we find the researches in electrophysiology indicating that individual nerve elements never act independently, and that visual function must be thought of in terms of the integrated action of all the units of the neural visual system (8). Hartline (9) has found that, even in the very simple Limulus eye, the discharge of impulses in any one optic nerve fiber depends not only upon the stimulus to the specific receptor unit from which that fiber arises but also upon the stimulation over the entire population of mutually interacting elements. Both excitatory and inhibitory interactions of the sort to be expected by theory have actually been demonstrated in the neural responses of the vertebrate visual system by Hartline (8), Kuffler (32), and Granit (6).

The way in which the postulated three independent systems of paired opponent processes (y-b, r-g, w-bk) are differentiated neurally is still a matter for conjecture. Hering thought it was a matter of process specificity, but was willing to use the concept of material, or structural, specificity, which he guessed would be more readily comprehended by most interested readers of his views at the time. Our own theoretical preference at this time is the conjecture that a particular color quality is more probably determined by a particular state of the nervous tissue than by activity of a particular structural element in the nervous network. Thus, we would be inclined to look for a difference between yellow-blue vs. red-green processes, rather than toward isolation of yellow-blue or red-green fibers or nerve cells.

Summary

This paper has presented a summary of our progress to date in providing a quantitative formulation for the Hering opponent-colors theory, and in relating the postulated visual mechanism to specific problems of color sensation, color mixture and color discrimination; to the dependence of these functions on the physical variables of both stimulus wave length and energy level; to their further dependence on adapting and surround stimulation; and to the changes in these functions that occur in various kinds of abnormal color vision. It is our conclusion that the opponent-colors theory serves as a fruitful working hypothesis by bringing a systematic coherence to the mass of isolated color phenomena that have been reported and subjected to quantitative experiment throughout the years. The physiological concepts basic to the theory are also shown to be consistent with recent findings in neurophysiology.

REFERENCES

1. Brewer, W. L. (1954). Fundamental response functions and binocular color matching. *J. Opt. Soc. Amer, 45,* 207–212.
2. Dartnall, H. J. A. (1953). The interpretation of spectral sensitivity curves. *Brit. med. Bull., 9,* 24–30.
3. Evans, R. M. (1948). *An introduction to color.* New York: Wiley.

4. Farnsworth, D. (1955). Tritanomalous vision as threshold function. *Die Farbe*, 185–196.
5. Graham, C. H. (1934). Vision: III. Some neural correlations. In C. Murchinson (Ed.), *A handbook of general experimental psychology* (pp. 829–879).
6. Grant, R. (1955). *Receptors and sensory perception.* New Haven: Yale University Press.
7. Hartline, H. K. (1938). The response of single optic nerve fibers of the vertebrate eye to illumination of the retina. *Amer. J. Physiol., 121,* 400–415.
8. Hartline, H. K. (1941). The neural mechanisms of vision. *Harvey Lectures, 1941–42, 37,* 39–68.
9. Hartline, H. K., Wagner, H. C., & Ratcliff, F. (1956). Inhibition in the eye of limulus. *J. gen. Physiol, 39,* 651–673.
10. Hartridge, H. (1949). The polychromatic theory. *Documenta Ophthal., 3,* 166–193.
11. Hecht, S. (1934). Vision: II. The nature of the photoreceptor process. In C. Murchison (Ed.), *A handbook of general experimental psychology* (pp. 704–828). Worcester: Clark University Press.
12. Helson, H. (1938). Fundamental problems in color vision. I. The principle governing changes in hue, saturation, and lightness of non-selective samples in chromatic illumination. *J. Exp. Psychol., 23,* 439–426.
13. Hering, E. (1878). *Zur Lehre vom Lichtsinne.* Berlin.
14. Hering, E. (1880). Zur Erklärung der Farbenblindheit aus der Theorie der Gegenfarben. *Lotos, Jb. f. Naturwiss., 1,* 76–107.
15. Hering, E. (1887). Ueber Newton's Gesetz der Farbenmischung. *Lotos, Jb. f. Naturwiss., 7,* 177–268.
16. Hering, E. (1888). *Zur Theorie der Vorgänge in der lebendigen Substanz.* Prague. (English translation by F. Welby, in *Brain*, 1897, *20,* 232–258.)
17. Hering, E. (1920). *Grundzüge der Lehre vom Lichtsinn.* Berlin: Springer.
18. Hochberg, J. E., Treibel, W., & Seaman, G. (1951). Color adaptation under conditions of homogeneous visual stimulation (Ganzfeld). *J. Exp. Psychol., 41,* 153–159.
19. Hurvich, L. M., & Jameson, D. (1951). The binocular fusion of yellow in relation to color theories. *Science, 114,* 199–202.
20. Hurvich, L. M., & Jameson, D. (1953). Spectral sensitivity of the fovea. I. Neutral adaptation. *J. Opt. Soc. Amer., 43,* 485–494.
21. Hurvich, L. M., & Jameson, D. (1955). A quantitative theoretical account of color vision. *Trans. N. Y. Acad. Sci., 18,* 33–38.
22. Hurvich, L. M., & Jameson, D. (1955). Some quantitative aspects of an opponent-colors theory. II. Brightness, saturation, and hue in normal and dichromatic vision. *J. Opt. Soc. Amer., 45,* 602–616.
23. Hurvich, L. M., & Jameson, D. (1956). Some quantitative aspects of an opponent-colors theory. IV. A psychological color specification system. *J. Opt. Soc. Amer., 46,* 416–421.
24. Ishak, I. G. H. (1952). Determination of the tristimulus values of the spectrum for eight Egyptian observers and one British observer. *J. Opt. Soc. Amer, 42,* 844–849.
25. Jameson, D., & Hurvich, L. M. (1955). Some quantitative aspects of an opponent-colors theory. I. Chromatic responses and spectral saturation. *J. Opt. Soc. Amer., 45,* 546–552.
26. Jameson, D., & Hurvich, L. M. (1956). Some quantitative aspects of an opponent-color theory. III. Changes in brightness, saturation, and hue with chromatic adaptation. *J. Opt. Soc. Amer., 46,* 405–415.
27. Jameson, D., & Hurvich, L. M. (1956). Theoretical analysis of anomalous color vision. *J. Opt. Soc. Amer, 46,* 1015–1089.
28. Jones, L. A., & Lowry, E. M. (1926). Retinal sensibility to saturation differences. *J. Opt. Soc. Amer., 13,* 25–34.
29. Judd, D. B. (1949). Current views on colour blindness. *Documenta Ophthal., 3,* 251–288.
30. Judd, D. B. (1951). Basic correlates of the visual stimulus. In S. S. Stevens (Ed.), *Handbook of experimental psychology* (pp. 811–867). New York: Wiley.
31. Köllner, H. (1912). *Die Störungen des Farbensinnes.* Berlin: S. Karger.
32. Kuffler, S. W. (1953). Discharge patterns and functional organization of mammalian retina. *J. Neurophysiol., 16,* 33–68.
33. MacAdam, D. L. (1956). Chromatic adaptation. *J. Opt. Soc. Amer., 46,* 500–513.
34. Müller, G. E. (1924). *Darstellung und Elblärung der verschiedenen Typen der Farbenblindheit.* Göttingen: Vandenhoech and Ruprecht.
35. Parsons, J. H. (1924). *An introduction to the study of colour vision.* (2nd ed.) Cambridge: Cambridge University Press.
36. Pickford, R. W. (1951). *Individual differences in colour vision.* London: Routledge and Kegan Paul.
37. Piéron, H. (1939). La dissociation de l'adaptation lumineuse et de l'adaptation chromatique et ses conséquences théoriques. *Année psychol., 40,* 1–14.
38. Purdy, D. M. (1937). The Bezold-Brücke phenomenon and contours for constant hue. *Amer. J. Psychol., 49,* 513–315.
39. Riggs, L. A., Ratliff, F., Cornsweet, J. C., & Cornsweet, T. N. (1953). The disappearance of steadily fixed visual test objects. *J. Opt. Soc. Amer., 43,* 495–501.
40. Rosmanit, J. (1914). *Anleitung zur Festellungcztslc der Farbentüchtigkeit.* Leipzig: Deuticke.
41. Troland, L. T. (1916). Apparent brightness: Its conditions and properties. *Trans. Illum. Engr. Soc, 11,* 957–966.
42. Troland, L. T. (1930). The principles of psychopsyiology. Vol. 2. *Sensation.* New York: D. Van Nostrand.
43. von Bezold, W. (1873). Ueber das Gesetz der Farbenmischung und die physiologischen Grundfarben. *Ann. Phys. u. Chem., 150,* 221–241.
44. von Kries, J. (1905). Die Gesichtsempfindungen. In W. Nagel (Ed.), *Handbuch der Pbysiolosic des Menschen* (pp. 109–282). Brunswick: Vieweg.
45. Weale, R. A. (1951). Hue-discrimination in paracentral parts of the human retina measured at different luminance levels. *J. Physiol., 113,* 115–122.
46. Willis, M. P., & Farnsworth, D. (1952). Comparative evaluation of anomaloscopes. *Med. Res. Lab. Rep. No. 190, 11,* No. 7, 1–89.
47. Wright, W. D., & Pitt, F. H. G. (1935). The colour-vision characteristics of two trichromats. *Proc. Phys. Soc.* (London), *47,* 205–217.
48. Wright, W. D. (1947). *Researches on normal and defective colour vision.* St. Louis: Mosby.
49. Wright, W. D. (1952). The characteristics of tritanopia. *J. Opt. Soc. Amer., 42,* 509–521.

Introduction to Reading 7

The modern study of the neural basis of visual perception can be traced to a series of seminal papers that appeared between 1938 and 1968. Hartline (1938) first described the pattern of neural discharge produced in the optic nerve when spots of light were presented to the eye of the frog and of the horseshoe crab *Limulus*. Hartline coined the term "receptive field," which refers to the region of the sensory surface (in the case of vision, the retina) that, when stimulated, causes a change in the response of the neuron in question. The measurements required to define the receptive field of a neuron involve inserting an electrode in or near its axon and presenting stimuli of various sorts (e.g., small spots of light) at different locations on the retina. The frequency of neural discharge will depend on the location and other properties (e.g., orientation, color, shape, speed and direction of motion) of the stimulus.

Subsequently, Kuffler (1953) and Barlow (1953) investigated the receptive field properties of optic nerve fibers in the cat and the frog, respectively. Kuffler discovered that the receptive field of a retinal ganglion cell is roughly circular; in "on-center" cells, the receptive field has a central excitatory region (that when stimulated causes an increase in the cell's discharge), surrounded by a donut-shaped inhibitory region. Off-center cells exhibited the reverse polarity—a central inhibitory region surrounded by an excitatory region.

David Hubel and Torsten Wiesel were young research scientists working in the laboratory of Stephen Kuffler in the Wilmer Institute at Johns Hopkins University in the late 1950s when they began their remarkable measurements of the receptive field properties of neurons in the cortex of the cat and, later, the monkey. These were the first such measurements ever taken of visual cortical cells; there was no way for Hubel and Wiesel to predict what they would find. Their initial expectation was that the cortical cell receptive fields would be similar to circular on- and off-center fields of the optic nerve fibers that had been measured by Kuffler. As described by Hubel (1982) in his Nobel Lecture, he and Wiesel met with frustration at first, because the small spots of light that had served to map the receptive fields of the optic nerve were quite ineffective in driving cortical cells. It was only by accident that they discovered, as they were inserting and removing from their projection instrument the opaque slides containing the visual stimuli, that an oriented edge passing over a particular location on the retina caused the cell to fire. This chance observation eventually led them to realize that most cells in primary visual cortex prefer edges with a particular orientation in a particular location.

Some years earlier, Mountcastle (1957) observed (in somatosensory cortex of the cat) that cortex was organized into an array of functional columns, with all the cells in a column having similar receptive field properties. Hubel and Wiesel discovered that the columnar organiza-tion applied in the primate visual system as well. In fact, they provided evidence for two independent columnar organizations in vision. First, they found orientation columns in which the cells within a column respond to stimuli with approximately the same orientation and in about the same location (these columns were not arranged randomly: adjacent columns represented similar orientations). They also found *ocular dominance columns* that are organized according to the eye from which their input comes.

Many of these early discoveries are reported in this selection. This work began a flood of investigations of the neural basis of visual perception, confirming and extending these initial observations. For example, Grinvald et al. (1986) used optical imaging techniques to more directly reveal the surface structure of the orientation columns that were inferred by Hubel & Wiesel's laborious single-cell recordings. These and hundreds of other studies can be traced to the pioneering results reported in this article.

REFERENCES

Barlow, H. B. (1953). Summation and inhibition in the frog's retina. *Journal of Physiology 119*, 69–88.

Grinvald, A., Lieke, E., Frostig, R. D., Gilbert, C. D., & Wiesel, T. N. (1986). Functional architecture of cortex revealed by optical imaging of intrinsic signals. *Nature, 324*, 361–364.

Hartline, H. K. (1938). The response of single optic nerve fibers of the vertebrate eye to illumination of the retina. *American Journal of Physiology, 121*, 400–415.

Hubel, D. H. (1982). Exploration of the primary visual cortex, 1955–78. *Nature, 299,* 515–524.

Hubel, D. H., & Wiesel, T. N. (1962). Receptive fields, binocular interactions and functional architecture in the cat's visual cortex. *Journal of Physiology, 160*, 106–154.

Kuffler, S. W. (1953). Discharge patterns and functional organization of mammalian retina. *Journal of Neurophysiology, 16*, 37–68.

Mountcastle, V. B. (1957). Modality and topographic properties of single neurons of cat's somatic sensory cortex. *Journal of Neurophysiology, 20*, 408–434.

Receptive Fields and Functional Architecture of Monkey Striate Cortex

D. H. Hubel and T. N. Wiesel • Harvard Medical School

Summary

1. The striate cortex was studied in lightly anesthetized macaque and spider monkeys by recording extracellularly from single units and stimulating the retinas with spots or patterns of light. Most cells can be categorized as simple, complex, or hypercomplex, with response properties very similar to those previously described in the cat. On the average, however, receptive fields are smaller, and there is a greater sensitivity to changes in stimulus orientation. A small proportion of the cells are colour coded.

2. Evidence is presented for at least two independent systems of columns extending vertically from surface to white matter. Columns of the first type contain cells with common receptive-field orientations. They are similar to the orientation columns described in the cat, but are probably smaller in cross-sectional area. In the second system cells are aggregated into columns according to eye preference. The ocular dominance columns are larger then the orientation columns, and the two sets of boundaries seem to be independent.

3. There is a tendency for cells to be grouped according to symmetry of responses to movement; in some regions the cells respond equally well to the two opposite directions of movement of a line, but other regions contain a mixture of cells favouring one direction and cells favouring the other.

4. A horizontal organization corresponding to the cortical layering can also be discerned. The upper layers (II and the upper two-thirds of III) contain complex and hypercomplex cells, but simple cells are virtually absent. The cells are mostly binocularly driven. Simple cells are found deep in layer III, and in IV A and IV B. In layer IV B they form a large proportion of the population, whereas complex cells are rare. In layers IV A and IV B one finds units lacking orientation specificity; it is not clear whether these are cell bodies or axons of geniculate cells. In layer IV most cells are driven by one eye only; this layer consists of a mosaic with cells of some regions responding to one eye only, those of other regions responding to the other eye. Layers V and VI contain mostly complex and hypercomplex cells, binocularly driven.

5. The cortex is seen as a system organized vertically and horizontally in entirely different ways. In the vertical system (in which cells lying along a vertical line in the cortex have common features) stimulus dimensions such as retinal position, line orientation, ocular dominance, and perhaps directionality of movement, are mapped in sets of superimposed but independent mosaics. The horizontal system segregates cells in layers by hierarchical orders, the lowest orders (simple cells monocularly driven) located in and near layer IV, the higher orders in the upper and lower layers.

Introduction

Over the past ten years we have studied the sequential processing of visual information in the cat by examining the responses of single cells at various points along the visual pathway. In extending this work it seemed natural to turn to the monkey, an animal that comes close to man in its visual capabilities, especially its high acuity and well developed colour vision. In contrast with the cat, moreover, most primates have a visual pathway that is further differentiated, with a rod-free fovea, a six-layered geniculate, and a striate cortex that lends itself well to studies of functional architecture, being conspicuously laminated and well demarcated from neighbouring cortical areas.

In this paper we present the results of a series of recordings from the monkey striate cortex. The study may be regarded as a continuation of previous work on the monkey optic nerve (Hubel & Wiesel, 1960) and lateral geniculate body (Wiesel & Hubel, 1966). The early experiments were done in the cortex of the spider monkey (*Ateles*), but the rhesus (*Macaca mulatta*) was used in all of the more recent work.

Methods

Six spider monkeys and sixteen macaques were used. Details of stimulating and recording procedures have been published elsewhere (Hubel & Wiesel, 1962; Wiesel & Hubel, 1966). Animals, 2–3 kg in weight, were anaesthetized with thiopental sodium, and light anaesthesia was maintained throughout the experiment. Since intravenous succinylcholine alone was often insufficient to prevent all eye movements, gallamine triethiodide (2–3 mg/kg) was also usually given intramuscularly at half-hour intervals.

When only one or two penetrations were planned in a single animal, a small hole was drilled in the skull, the dura incised keeping the arachnoid intact, and the electrode introduced through a hollow 19-gauge stainless-steel needle, which was cemented into the hole to make a closed chamber. In a few experiments designed to explore a wider area of cortex a modified Davies chamber was cemented to the skull (Hubel & Wiesel, 1963). Micro-electrodes were sharpened tungsten wire insulated with a clear vinyl lacquer (Hubel, 1957).

To help reconstruct the electrode tracks, one or several lesions were made in each penetration by passing direct current through the electrode (Hubel, 1959). In the monkey cortex 2 μA for 2 sec (electrode negative) was usually sufficient. All brains were fixed in formalin, photographed, embedded in celloidin, sectioned serially at 20μ, and stained for Nissl substance with cresyl violet.

Results

Receptive Field Types

This study is based upon recordings of 150 cells in seven penetrations in sixteen spider monkeys, and 272 cells in twenty-five penetrations in sixteen macaque monkeys. Most of the penetrations were made in cortical regions subserving the 0–4° parafoveal region; a few passed through buried cortical folds subserving the mid or far periphery, and in two laterally placed penetrations the fields were in the fovea. The approximate recording sites in the sixteen rhesus experiments are shown for a representative brain in Fig. 7.1.

We begin by describing the various types of receptive fields that can be distinguished in the monkey striate cortex, emphasizing especially any dif-

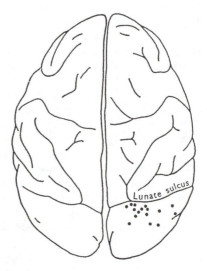

FIGURE 7.1 ■ Recording Sites for the Sixteen Rhesus Experiments. Diagram of monkey brain viewed from above; anterior is up. Many of the dots represent several closely spaced penetrations in a single monkey. Several deep penetrations went into buried folds of striate and non-striate cortex.

ferences between monkey and cat. Implicit in these descriptions is the possibly over-simplified concept of a hierarchical system dependent on anatomical wiring, in which geniculate cells with concentric fields converge on simple cortical cells, simple cells in turn converge upon complex cells, and complex on hypercomplex. The evidence for such connexions (Hubel & Wiesel, 1962, 1965a) is derived from the properties of the fields themselves, and also from the functional architecture of the cortex.

Simple cells. As in the cat, these cells are defined as having receptive fields with spatially distinct "on" and "off" areas separated by parallel straight lines (Hubel & Wiesel, 1959). Twenty-five of the 272 cells studied in rhesus were definitely established as simple, and a similar proportion was seen in the spider monkey. This small number almost certainly does not reflect the actual proportion of simple cells in striate cortex, since judging from spike size and difficulties in isolation these cells are mostly small. Moreover, some penetrations stopped short of the layers where simple cells are most populous. In a typical penetration through the full cortical thickness, when the electrode was fine enough to isolate cells easily, three or four out of thirty or so cells could be expected to be simple. An example of such a penetration is described in detail in the next section.

Even in this small sampling, we found representatives of all of the "simple" receptive field subtypes described in the cat (Hubel & Wiesel, 1962, Fig. 2). The commonest simple fields were those with long narrow "on"-centres sandwiched between two more extensive "off" regions, and those with an "on" and an "off" region lying side by side, but a few examples of each of the other types were also seen. Knowing the exact configuration of a field made it possible to predict the optimum stimulus: its size, shape, orientation, and position on the retina. As described below, and in contrast with what we found in the cat, most simple cells were driven by one eye only. Six of the twenty-five cells showed opponent-colour properties, suggesting that the proportion of colour coded cells may be higher in simple cells than in complex.

Complex cells. Complex cells are the commonest of all types, making up 177 of the 272 cells in the rhesus. The properties of these cells were similar to those we have described for the cat (Hubel & Wiesel, 1962). By definition, there was no sepa-

ration of receptive fields into excitatory and inhibitory parts. As for simple cells, a line stimulus (slit, dark bar, or edge) in a particular orientation evoked optimum responses, and as the orientation was varied the responses fell off, usually failing long before an angle 90° to the optimum was reached. Prolonging the line in either direction did not reduce the response. But whereas for the simple cell the position of stimulus was crucial, in the complex a response was evoked on shining the correctly oriented line on any part of the field, or by moving the line over the field. As in the cat, about half of the cells showed highly asymmetrical responses to diametrically opposite directions of movement, while the rest showed little or no directional preference. Even when responses were highly asymmetrical, the less effective direction of movement usually evoked some minimal response (see Fig. 7.2), but there were a few examples in which the maintained activity was actually suppressed.

Individual complex cells differed markedly in their relative responsiveness to slits, edges, or dark bars. The majority responded very much better to one than to the other two, but some reacted briskly to two of them, and a few to all three. For a cell that was sensitive to slits, but not to edges, the responses increased as slit width was increased up to some optimal value, and then they fell off sharply; the optimum width was always a small fraction of the width of the whole field. For complex cells that responded best to edges, some reacted to one configuration and also to its mirror image, while others responded only to one edge configuration. In the first type a broad slit or dark bar usually gave more vigorous responses than an edge, as though it combined the advantages of the two types of edge. On narrowing the stimulus down to a width that might be close to the optimum for the usual slit or dark-bar complex cell, the response usually failed. Presumably the two types of cells are connected to simple cells in entirely different ways.

A complex cell that responded best to a moving dark bar is illustrated in Fig. 7.2. Here the optimally oriented stimulus (Fig. 7.2) gave very different responses to the two different directions of movement, with a minimal, inconstant discharge to movement down and to the left. The rate of decline of this cell's responses as the stimulus orientation deviated from the optimum was fairly typical; while the decline varied to some extent from

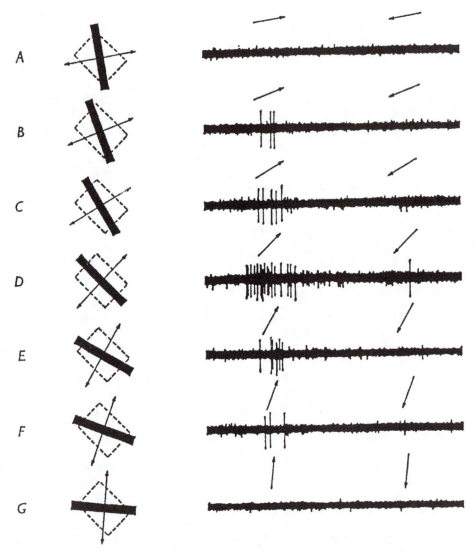

FIGURE 7.2 ■ Responses of a Complex Cell in Right Striate Cortex (layer IV A) to Various Orientations of a Moving Black Bar. Receptive field in the left eye indicated by the interrupted rectangles; it was approximately 3/8 × 3/8° in size, and was situated 4° below and to the left of the point of fixation. Ocular-dominance group 4. Duration of each record, 2 sec. Background intensity 1·3 $\log_{10}$ cd/m², dark bars 0·0 log cd/m².

cell to cell (see below), it was generally steeper in the monkey than in the cat. Most field orientations could be specified to within 5–10°, as compared to 10–15° in the cat.

Hypercomplex cells. Fifty-three of the 272 cells recorded from the rhesus were lower-order hypercomplex. For these, extending the line (slit, edge or dark bar) beyond the activating part of the receptive field in one or both directions caused a marked fall-off in the response, and there was usu-

ally no response at all if the line was made long enough. The proportion of hypercomplex cells occurring here may well be higher than our figures suggest, since in the early monkey experiments we did not know that such cells existed and did not systematically vary the lengths of the stimuli. We have recently found hypercomplex cells in the cat striate cortex, but they seem to be less common then in the monkey.

Responses of a typical hypercomplex cell are

shown in Fig. 7.3. The more or less square central activating region, indicated by interrupted lines, was flanked by a weak antagonistic region above and by a stronger one below, so that to evoke a consistent response a line (edge or bar) had to be terminated within the rectangle or at its borders (Fig. 7.3A–D). When it extended beyond them, as in Fig. 7.3E–G, the response was reduced or obliterated. Another example is shown in Fig. 7.4; here the most powerful stimulus was an obliquely ori-

ented slit moving in either direction across the region marked by broken lines. Lengthening the stimulus in both directions again greatly reduced the response, though this time the suppression was not complete.

No higher-order hypercomplex cells were seen in monkey striate cortex (Hubel & Wiesel, 1965a).

Sizes of receptive fields. For comparable regions of the visual field, simple receptive fields in the monkey were on the average much smaller than in

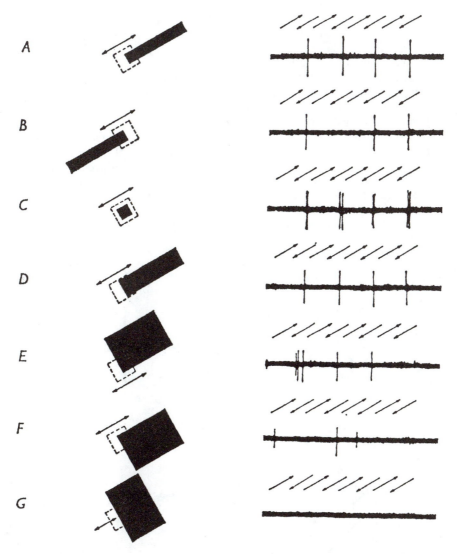

FIGURE 7.3 ■ Responses of a Hypercomplex Cell from Layer III of Monkey Striate Cortex. (This was cell 9 in Figs. 7 and 8). 'Activating' portion of receptive field (3/8 × 3/8°) is outlined by interrupted lines. Stimulus of this region by a moving edge activates cell (*A–D*). Below this region, and to some extent above it, are regions appropriate stimulation of which suppresses the response to an edge (*E–G*). Duration of each record 5 sec. Stimulus intensities as in Fig. 2.

the cat. At 1–4° from the centre of gaze, for example, fields ranged from ¼ × ¼° up to ½ × ¾°, as against about ½ × ½° up to about 4 × 4° for the cat. Complex and hypercomplex fields in the monkey were likewise smaller than in the cat, perhaps about one quarter the size in linear dimensions. They tended to be somewhat larger than the simple fields, perhaps 1½ to 2 times as big, in linear dimensions.

In the two experiments made in the region representing the fovea one or two simple fields were less than ¼ × ¼°, but their exact boundaries were not determined. Surprisingly, the range of sizes of complex and hyercomplex fields was not very different from that seen a few degrees further out. As we have discussed elsewhere (Hubel & Wiesel, 1962), acuity is probably not closely related to over-all receptive field dimensions, but rather to the widths of optimally shaped stimuli.

Units lacking orientation specificity. In layer IV we usually recorded monocularly driven units whose receptive fields were similar to those of geniculate cells. The spikes of these units were small and negative, being quite different from the typical spikes of myelinated fibres seen in optic tract and radiations, and corpus callosum (Hubel,

1959; Hubel & Wiesel, 1967). The field properties and localization of these IVth layer units makes one suspect that they are axons or axon-terminals of geniculate cells, but they could be cortical cells, and it will probably be necessary to stimulate electrically the subcortical optic radiations to settle the question. Some units with concentric receptive fields had more complex responses to coloured stimuli than anything we saw in the lateral geniculate; these are discussed below.

Cells with specific colour responses. In the rhesus lateral geniculate body, the majority of the dorsal-layer cells have opponent-colour properties, light exciting them at some wave-lengths, inhibiting them at others, diffuse white light evoking little or no response (De Valois, Jacobs & Jones, 1963; Wiesel & Hubel, 1966). For cortical cells, we expected that with this input there might be a similar emphasis on wave-length discrimination. Motokawa, Taira & Okuda (1962) have in fact described opponent cells in monkey cortex. It was surprising to us, however, that the great majority of cells could discriminate precisely the orientation or direction of movement of a stimulus, but had no marked selectivity regarding wave-length. There were interesting and striking exceptions to

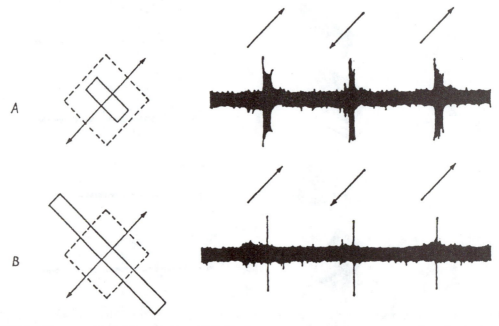

FIGURE 7.4 ■ Hypercomplex Cell Recorded from Right Striate Cortex, Layer II. *A*: stimulus of left eye by moving slit within activating region (1/4 × 3/8°); *B*: similar stimulation with slit extending beyond activating region. Background, log 0·0 cd/m²; stimulus, log 1·3 cd.m². Duration of each record 10 sec.

this, which are described below, but on the whole the colour responses seen in area 17 have been disappointing: for a high proportion of cells the response to a given stimulus shape was qualitatively the same—firing being increased or firing being suppressed—regardless of wave-length, and the optimum stimulus shape was independent of wave-length. Even in the two penetrations in the region representing fovea most cells seemed to be relatively unconcerned with colour, though here the proportion of cells with colour specific responses seemed higher than it was 2–4° from the fovea.

Of the twenty-five simple cells recorded in rhesus, six had more specific colour-coded behaviour, the excitatory and inhibitory parts of the receptive field differing in spectral sensitivity in the manner of geniculate Type I cells (Wiesel & Hubel, 1966). All six fields were similar in organization, with a long narrow excitatory region with highest sensitivity to long wave-lengths, flanked on either side by more extensive inhibitory regions with relatively greater blue-green sensitivity. These cells behaved as though they received input from a set of Type I red on-centre, green off-surround geniculate cells, the commonest variety found in the dorsal geniculate layers. Certain features of two of the cells were not so easily explained, however: one responded well to a properly positioned red slit but not at all well to a white slit; another failed to respond to diffuse white light, as expected, but also responded poorly to diffuse red. Obviously it will be necessary to sample many more cells of this type, and to study them more thoroughly.

Complex and hypercomplex cells with colour selectivity. Of the 177 complex cells examined in rhesus, only twelve (about 7 %) were identified as having clear colour specificity. Not all cells were studied with monochromatic stimuli, but enough were to be reasonably sure that colour coded cells are a small minority, probably not more than 10 % for regions 2–4° from the fovea. Four cells gave responses to coloured stimuli that were qualitatively similar to their responses to white stimuli, but only over an unusually restricted band of wave-lengths. A cell might respond actively in the blue-violet (or the red), but not to light at the other end of the spectrum.

Six cells showed still more specific reactions to coloured stimuli. They responded actively to a properly oriented slit at some wave-lengths but not

others, and gave little or no response to a similarly oriented white slit at any intensity. An example is illustrated in Fig. 7.5 and Fig. 7.6. This cell had typical complex properties, favouring up-and-left movement of a 1 o'clock oriented slit and showing no response to a slit oriented at right angles to this. The only stimuli that evoked brisk responses were blue ones, and it was striking that white slits produced by removing the interference filter from the light path were completely ineffective. The other five cells behaved in a similar way, but favoured long wave-lengths.

Three cells, finally, had opponent-colour properties like the ones just mentioned, favouring monochromatic slits over white, but also had hypercomplex characteristics, in that a long slit was distinctly less effective than one of limited length.

Cells with concentric fields and dual-opponent systems. Under this heading we group a very few cells with centre-surround receptive-field organization, but with more complex behavior than anything we have seen in the geniculate. The fields appeared to be organized in centre-surround fashion. With centre-size spots the cells were excited by long-wave lengths and inhibited by short, with

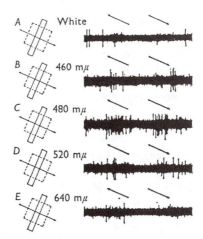

FIGURE 7.5 ■ Complex Cell with Colour Coded Properties Recorded in Layer II of Striate Cortex. Responses to movement of optimally oriented slits of white light and monochromatic light at various wave-lengths. Monochromatic light made by interposing interference filters in a beam of white light: stimulus energies are greatest for *A*, and progressively less for *E, D, C,* and *B*. None of the responses was improved by lowering the intensity. Size of receptive field 1/2 × 1/2°. Ocular dominance group 1. Background and white stimulus intensities as in Fig. 4. Time for each record 5 sec.

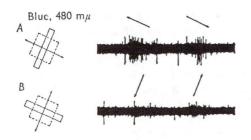

Blue, 480 mμ

A

B

FIGURE 7.6 ■ Same Cell as Fig. 5. Responses to Two Orthogonal Stimulus Orientations at 480 mμ.

little response to white light. On the other hand a large spot was almost completely ineffective regardless of wavelength, suggesting that the surround was red-off green-on, i.e. the reverse of the centre. It was as if two Type III (non opponent-colour) geniculate fields, an on-centre with maximum sensitivity in the red, and an off-centre with maximum sensitivity in the blue-green, had been superimposed. Since these cells were influenced from one eye only it is possible that they were axons of geniculate cells. We saw nothing this complicated in the rhesus geniculate, but our sampling there was small enough so that a relatively rare type could easily have been missed. Ganglion cells with somewhat similar fields have been described recently by Daw (1967) in the retina of the goldfish. In the units described above, however, the situation seems somewhat simpler, there being a single boundary between centre and surround instead of a separate boundary for each of the two opponent systems, as was found in the goldfish.

In summary, cells with interesting colour properties occur in the cortex but are in the minority, and, as in the geniculate, seem very diverse in type, with fields ranging in their spatial characteristics from non-oriented to hypercomplex. This survey is intended only to suggest the diversity; a satisfactory study will probably mean recording from thousands, rather than hundreds of cortical cells.

Functional Architecture

A REPRESENTATIVE PENETRATION THROUGH STRIATE CORTEX (AREA 17)

As shown in Fig. 7.1, most of the penetrations through area 17 were made from the smooth exposed part of the occipital lobe a few millimetres behind the lunate sulcus, i.e. just behind the 17–18 border, which runs parallel to and just behind the sulcus. In all rhesus experiments the brain was sectioned in the parasagittal plane, which has the advantage of intersecting the lunate sulcus and the 17–18 boundary at right angles. The convention of numbering the layers (Pl. 7.1) combines that of von Bonin (1942) for layers I–IV, and that of Lorente de Nó (1943) and Brodmann (1909) for V and VI. In this system each layer can be identified easily in a Nissl preparation, except for the poorly defined II–III boundary, which we place arbitrarily between the upper ⅓ and the lower ⅔ of the cell-rich layer making up II and III. The pale layer beneath III is termed IV A, and the alternating cell-rich, pale, and cell-rich layers are termed IV B, V, and VI.

In the penetration to be described, three small lesions 50–70μ in diameter were made at roughly ½ mm intervals, to help estimate shrinkage during fixation and embedding, and to increase the accuracy of estimating positions of the cells encountered (Fig. 7.7; Pl. 7.1). Except for cells tagged specifically by lesions, or cells very close to lesions, estimations made by this method are nevertheless only approximate. Sometimes, for example, the position of a superficial lesion corresponded poorly with depths calculated from two or more deeper lesions, possibly because of uneven shrinkage, or possibly due to dimpling of the cortex in the first part of some penetrations. The security with which one can assign a cell to a particular layer thus varies widely from cell to cell even in the same penetration, and statistics are difficult to compile. Specific questions can, nevertheless, often be answered with some certainty by placing lesions near cells of a particular type in penetration after penetration (see Fig. 7.11 and 7.12 below). The penetration of Fig. 7.7 and 7.8 was exploratory, and lesions were not placed according to any particular plan.

In Figs. 7.7 and 7.8 the first nine cells were situated in layers II and III, lesion 1 marking the position of unit 9. Six of the nine cells were complex and, as in the cat, some showed highly asymmetrical responses to diametrically opposite directions of movement (cells 1 and 2), while the others showed no such directional preference. Cell 9 of this penetration was lower-order hypercomplex, and has already been illustrated in Fig. 7.3.

In layer IV A four complex cells were recorded, 10 and 11 responding best to dark bars, 12 and 13 to slits.

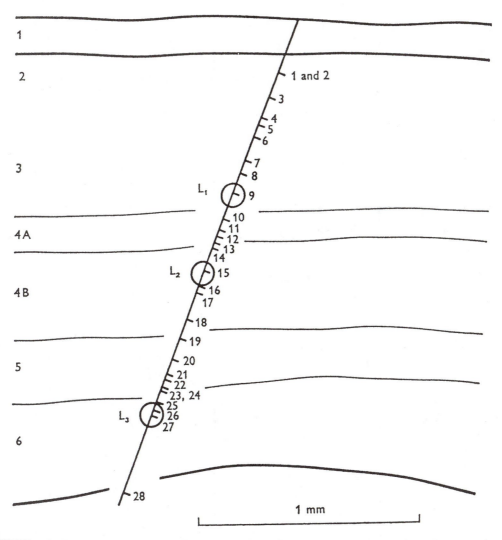

FIGURE 7.7 ■ Positions of Twenty-eight Units Recorded in a Single Penetration through Rhesus Striate Cortex. Positions of three lesions (L_1–L_2) are indicated by circles (see also Pl. 1 and Fig.8).

In IV B the fields of four successively recorded cells were simple in type. The second of these (unit 15) was marked by lesion 2. In three of the simple cells (14, 16, and 17) the long narrow excitatory region was most sensitive to light of long wavelengths, with hardly any responses in the green and blue, whereas the inhibitory flanks were most sensitive in the greens and blues with little response to red. It was as if these cells had received input only from a group of red on-centre green off-surround geniculate cells. In contrast to these opponent-colour cells, unit 15, whose field was similar geometrically, seemed identical to the usual simple

cell in cat cortex, with no hint of opponent colour properties.

The remaining cells in this penetration were complex. The only one with remarkable colour features was No. 20, which lacked any opponent colour properties but favoured short wave-lengths strongly, as though it had its entire input from blue-sensitive cones.

The sequence of receptive field orientations seen in this penetration was less regular than in most, but as usual there were runs of cells in which the fields all had identical orientation, for example, cells 10, 11; 12–14; 16–18. At the beginning of

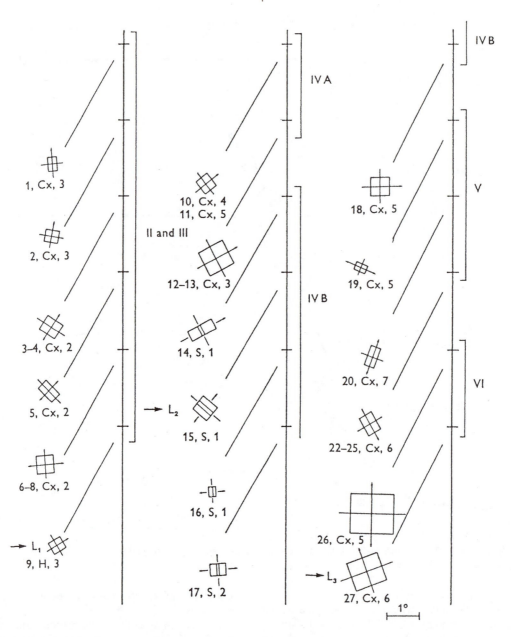

FIGURE 7.8 ■ Receptive-field Diagrams for Units Recorded in the Penetration of Fig. 7. Approximate positions and shapes of each field, referred to the fovea, are indicated by rectangles. Foveas are indicated separately for each field by the short horizontal lines intersecting the three long vertical lines. Responses to a moving line are shown for every field by arrows; a single arrowhead indicates strong directional preference. Square brackets refer to cortical layers. For each field the first number is the unit number; S, Cx and H mean simple, complex and hypercomplex; the last number refers to ocular-dominance groups. Cells of group 1 were driven only by the contralateral eye; for cells of group 2 there was marked dominance of the contralateral eye; for group 3, slight dominance. For cells in group 4 there was no obvious difference between the two eyes. In group 5 the ipsilateral eye dominated slightly; in group 6 markedly, and in group 7 the cells were driven only by the ipsilateral eye.

the penetration, the sequence of cells 1–8 is of particular interest as an example of several small shifts of field orientation all in the same direction (see below).

Many of the cells in this penetration were driven from both eyes. Cells 1–17 were dominated by the left (contralateral) eye, except for No. 11, which favoured the right eye slightly; from 18 to 27 all cells favoured the right eye. The tendency for neighbouring cells to favour the same eye was thus very pronounced, more so then is usual in the cat (Hubel & Wiesel, 1962).

This penetration illustrates several architectural features of the striate cortex which will be taken up in more detail in the remainder of the paper: (1) a tendency to aggregation of certain physiological cell types according to anatomical layering; (2) an aggregation of cells according to receptive field orientation; and (3) an independent clustering of cells according to eye dominance.

VERTICAL ORGANIZATION

Given a set of properties of a cell, such as receptive-field position or orientation, eye preference, presence or absence of symmetry of responses to opposite directions of movement, colour coding, and so on, one can examine neighbouring cells to see whether or not they share certain of these properties. If, for example, the same value of a stimulus variable is optimal for all cells in a small region, it can be asked whether that value changes steadily or in discrete steps as one progresses through the cortex. Where the steps are discrete one can try to discover the shape and extent of the regions.

In the visual cortex a number of variables remain unchanged, or at least show no systematic trend, in penetrations extending vertically from surface to white matter. The host fundamental are the two position co-ordinates by which the retinal surface is mapped on to the cortex. This mapping is continuous. Besides this, in the monkey striate cortex, as in that of the cat, each small area dealing with a particular part of the retina is subdivided by sets of vertical partitions into several independent systems of discrete cell aggregations. One of these systems is defined by receptive-field orientation, another by ocular dominance. It seems very likely that these aggregations are columnar, with walls parallel to the vertically running fibre bundles and perpendicular to the layering pattern.

The evidence for this is chiefly that sequences of cells with common physiological characteristics tend to be long in penetrations that are perpendicular or almost perpendicular to the cortical surface, and short in oblique penetrations. In the cat the most direct evidence that aggregations were columnar in shape came from multiple closely spaced parallel penetrations in which a lesion was made at each change of receptive field orientation (Hubel & Wiesel, 1963). This type of experiment was not done in the monkey, but we have no reason to think that the results would be different.

Retinotopic representation. Neighbouring cells in area 17 invariably have receptive fields in roughly the same part of the retina, and movement along the cortex corresponds to movement along the retina according to the well known retinotopic representation. We have not tried to make a detailed topographic mapping, but in a limited exploration of the dorsal convexity and ten or so additional penetrations through the buried calcarine fissure, our results agree well with Talbot & Marshall's early survey of the convexity (1941), and the subsequent extensive mapping by Daniel & Whitteridge (1961). This detailed topographic representation does not hold at a microscopic level. As in the cat (Hubel & Wiesel, 1962), the fields of successively recorded cells in a perpendicular track are not precisely superimposed: instead there is an irregular variation in field position from cell to cell, small enough so that the fields overlap, and large enough so that, in a perpendicular penetration with fifteen or twenty fields super-imposed, the area covered is about 2–4 times that of the average receptive field. In a long oblique penetration one finds some drift in field position corresponding to the gross topography, but when the component of movement along the surface is only a millimetre or so, for the part of the cortex subserving regions of retina within about 5° of the fovea, the drift is considerably less then the random staggering, and is obscured by it. In the peripheral retina the topographic representation becomes coarser, but to compensate for this the receptive fields become larger, and the situation is therefore similar.

This topographic representation does not by itself constitute a columnar system even though the retinal position co-ordinates remain virtually constant in a penetration perpendicular to the cortical surface. The term "column" as first used by Mountcastle (1957) and as it is used here, refers to a discrete aggregation of cells, each aggregation being separated from its neighbours by vertical walls that intersect the surface (or a given layer) in a mosaic. In the retinotopic projection the representation is continuous; there are no sudden jumps as the surface is traversed. It is upon this continuous topographic map that the column-systems described below are engrafted.

Receptive-field orientation. Sequences of cells with identical receptive-field orientations can be seen in Fig. 7.8, 7.10, 7.11, and 7.12. The sequences tended to be shorter than in the cat, and penetrations in which the same orientation was maintained from surface to white matter were somewhat less common, occurring only when the track was normal to the cortical surface or almost so. An example can be seen in Fig. 7.12, penetration 1. Some idea of the cross-sectional size of a column can be obtained by projecting the distance spanned by a single sequence on to the cortical surface. This projected distance was seldom more than about ¼ mm, and most sequences were considerably shorter, an average being more like 0•1–0•2 mm (see Fig. 7.10).

Ordered orientation columns. In several experiments in the cat certain regions of the striate cortex seemed to be highly organized, with changes in orientation from column to column taking place in small regular progressive steps, all in the same direction, either clockwise or counterclockwise. Hints of such organization were seen in many penetrations in the monkey, but the sequences tended to be short. For example, in the first six cells of Fig. 7.7, five orientations are represented, each shifted about 20° clockwise compared with the previous. Following such a sequence there was often a shift of orientation in the reverse direction, perhaps followed by a resumption of the sequence for a few more steps and then another similar interruption. Large shifts, of 45–90°, while not rare, were less common than small ones.

By far the most impressive example of orderly sequences was seen in one experiment in the spider monkey, illustrated in Fig. 7.9. The penetration entered area 17 very close to the 17–18 border, at an angle of about 30° to the normal. Fields of the first cells were oriented almost vertically. Subsequent cells and unresolved unit activity

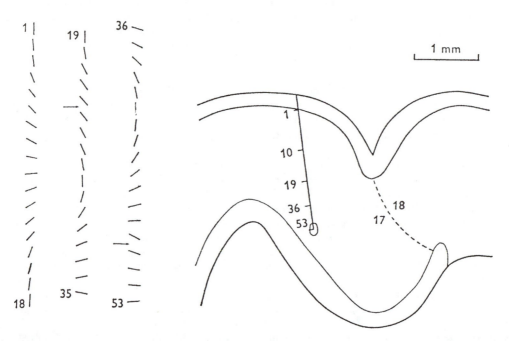

FIGURE 7.9 ■ Reconstruction of a Penetration Through Striate Cortex about 1 mm from 17–18 Border, Near Occipital Pole of Spider Monkey. To the left of the figure the lines indicate orientations of columns traversed; each line represents one or several units recorded against a rich unresolved background activity. Arrows indicate reversal of directions of shifts in orientation. Histological section through first part of this penetration is shown in Pl. 2.

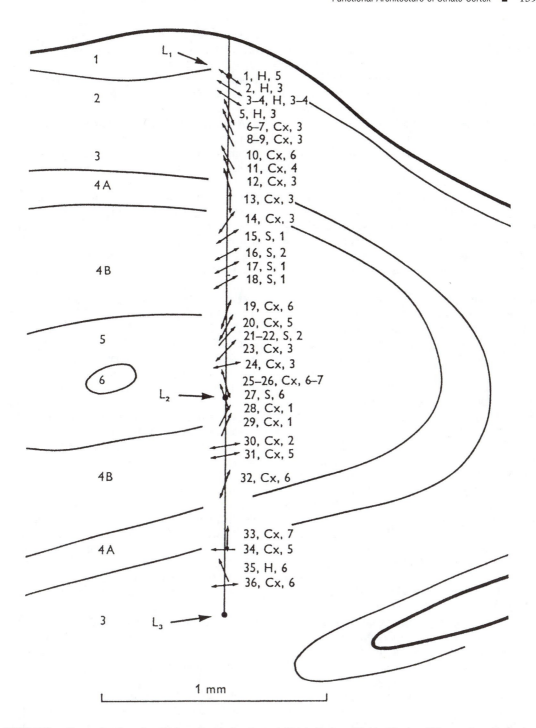

1
2
3
4 A
4 B
5
6
4 B
4 A
3

L$_1$
L$_2$
L$_3$

1, H, 5
2, H, 3
3–4, H, 3–4
5, H, 3
6–7, Cx, 3
8–9, Cx, 3
10, Cx, 6
11, Cx, 4
12, Cx, 3
13, Cx, 3
14, Cx, 3
15, S, 1
16, S, 2
17, S, 1
18, S, 1
19, Cx, 6
20, Cx, 5
21–22, S, 2
23, Cx, 3
24, Cx, 3
25–26, Cx, 6–7
27, S, 6
28, Cx, 1
29, Cx, 1
30, Cx, 2
31, Cx, 5
32, Cx, 6
33, Cx, 7
34, Cx, 5
35, H, 6
36, Cx, 6

1 mm

FIGURE 7.10 ■ Reconstruction of an Oblique Penetration through Striate Cortex of Spider Monkey. This experiment indicates laminar groupings of cells according to complexity, and aggregation according to orientation, directionality of movement, and ocular-dominance. As in Fig. 8, 19 Cx 6 means 'Unit 19, complex, ocular-dominance group 6'.

showed regular small shifts in orientation, consistently in a counter-clockwise direction, so that at a depth of about 1 mm, after eighteen shifts, the orientation had revolved through 180° and was again vertical. The progression continued in a counter-clockwise direction for another 45°, and then, at the point marked by the first arrow, the direction of shifts suddenly reversed. Now fifteen clockwise changes in orientation took place in the next 180°, followed by another ten clockwise shifts through almost another 180°. Finally, near the end, the process seemed to be reversing itself again, with counter-clockwise shifts beginning at the second arrow. There were, in all, 52 shifts in orientation, the smallest being about 6° and the largest around 20°, and in the course of the penetration each orientation was represented about 4 times. The field positions of the final cells were in exactly the same place as those of the first, indicating that the distance traversed in a direction parallel to the surface had been too small to produce a measurable shift in receptive field position.

In this penetration the average shift was about 13°, associated with an average electrode movement of 40μ, or, given the obliquity of 30°, a movement parallel to the cortical surface of 20μ. From the higher-power photomicrograph of the cortex in the area of this penetration, shown in Plate 7.2, 20μ seems to be the order of magnitude of the widths of the vertical pallisades of cells in this area. The vertically orientated striations may thus represent the actual columns of cells, at least in this experiment, and the columns must have close to the minimum possible width, since the pallisades are only one or a very few cells wide. From this degree of orderliness and the probability that a similar order would have held for any direction of horizontal movement across the cortical surface, it seems likely that columns have the form of parallel sheets rather than pillars. In the cat this sort of geometry was also suggested in one surface-mapping experiment (Hubel & Wiesel, 1963, Fig. 4 and Pl. 2).

Ocular dominance. In the monkey there was a marked tendency for successively recorded cells to have the same eye-preference (Figs. 7.8, 7.10, 7.11 and 7.12). Neighbouring cells did not necessarily fall into the same ocular-dominance group, but they usually favoured the same eye. Since there were several vertical penetrations from surface to white matter in which there was no change in eye preference, it is likely that the aggregations of cells are columnar. It is also evident that these regions

of common eye-preference have nothing to do with orientation columns, the two systems apparently having entirely independent borders. Of the two types of columns, those associated with eye dominance seem to be larger, often including several orientation columns.

Aggregation of cells according to ocular dominance was first established in the cat striate cortex (Hubel & Wiesel, 1962; 1965b), but in the cat organization was less clear cut, since, besides regions in which all cells had similar eye preference, there were regions of mixed allegiance, in which cells of all ocular-dominance groups, including group 4, were mingled. (For definitions of ocular-dominance groups see legend of Fig. 7.8.) These mixed regions tended to obscure the parcellation into columns in the cat (Hubel & Wiesel, 1962, p. 140), and indeed it was not until the columns had been accentuated by raising cats with strabismus that we became fully convinced of their existence (Hubel & Wiesel, 1965b). In the monkey the parcellation is far more obvious: the columns are possibly larger, mixed columns are rarer if they exist at all, and cells of dominance groups 1, 2, 6 and 7 make up a larger proportion of the population.

Direction of movement. As noted above, the monkey striate cortex resembles that of the cat in that complex cells tend to respond actively to a moving stimulus, with great cell-to-cell variation on directional selectivity—some firing actively to diametrically opposed directions, others responding to one direction and hardly at all to the other, and still others with various degrees of intermediate directional asymmetry. There is some intermixing between these groups, in that two simultaneously recorded cells are often driven by opposite directions of movement (Hubel, 1958). In the present series there nevertheless appeared to be some grouping of cells according to the presence or absence of directional preference. In most penetrations there were sequences, sometimes long ones, in which all cells showed strong directional preference, followed by sequences in which the cells all responded well to both directions of movement. This is seen in Fig. 7.10, which illustrates a penetration cutting across a gyrus in the spider monkey. Cells 1–5, 13–20, 23–27, 30–33, were all bidirectional, whereas those of sequence 6–12 were unidirectional. There may thus be another independent, perhaps columnar system of cortical subdivisions, this one dependent on symmetric vs. asymmetric responses to movement.

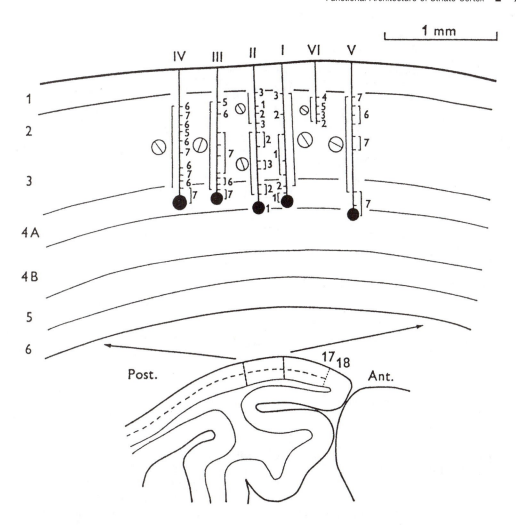

FIGURE 7.11 ■ Six Closely Spaced Parallel Penetrations through Rhesus Striate Cortex Made to Determine the Layer in which Background and Some Units Lacked Orientation Specificity, and in which most Cells were Driven by One Eye Exclusively. Lesion made in these regions are indicated by black circles. Lines within the open circles indicate optimum stimulus orientation. Numbers to right of each penetration refer to ocular dominance group of each isolated unit.

Finally, there was some indication of a grouping of cells according to their preference for stimulus form—slits, edges, or dark bars. Colour coded cells similarly often came in clusters. The shape of the aggregations for these systems is not clear: they could be nests or columns.

HORIZONTAL ORGANIZATION

The most conspicuous anatomical feature of the striate cortex is its rich layering—indeed it was so named for that reason. From the outset it has been

clear that there are differences from layer to layer in the physiological properties of cells in area 17. These differences are more prominent than in the cat, just as the histological differences in layers are more prominent. In five experiments done specifically to investigate the layering differences, fourteen penetrations were made, six through the full cortical thickness and eight to the 4th layer. Two experiments, to be discussed in more detail below, are illustrated in Figs. 7.11 and 7.12, and the results from all rhesus experiments are tabulated in the histograms of Figs. 7.13 and 7.14.

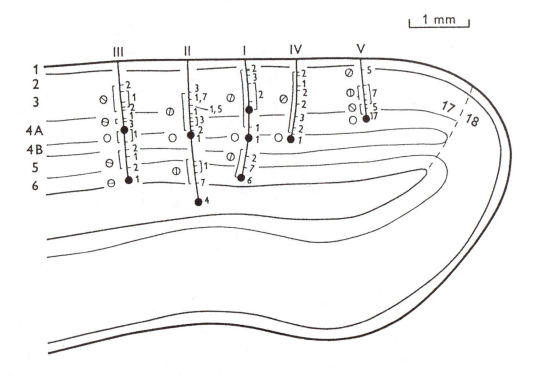

FIGURE 7.12 ■ Five Close-spaced Penetrations in Rhesus Area 17. Open circles indicate a lack of background orientation specificity; other conventions as in Fig. 11.

Receptive field organization. In the second layer and upper part of the third almost all of the cells were complex or hypercomplex, and as a rule the optimum stimulus orientation was precisely defined. We found no simple cells in layer II, and in III they occurred only in the deepest parts, close to IV. On entering this border zone and crossing into upper IV the first simple cells appeared, hypercomplex cells were no longer seen, and in complex cells the orientation specificity began to relax, with brisk responses over a wider range of orientations to either side of the optimum, but still no response at 90° to the optimum.

Usually in IV A, but sometimes only on entering IV B, a sudden change took place in the unresolved background activity: it became more prominent, higher in pitch, and lost all trace of orientation preference. Figure 7.11 and Pl. 7.3 illustrate an experiment done expressly to determine the depth at which the background lost its orientation specificity. In each penetration this point was marked by a lesion, shown as a filled circle. All lesions were in IV A or near the IV A–IV B border. A

similar experiment, with the same outcome, is illustrated in Fig. 7.12. Here the points of appearance of non-oriented background are shown to the left of each penetration by open circles.

Throughout IV B there was a mixture of simple cells and units which lacked orientation specificity. This was the layer with the fewest complex units and the most non-oriented ones (Fig. 7.13). In V and VI the background again became selectively responsive to specifically oriented lines, and the units were mainly complex, with some hypercomplex ones intermixed.

Some of these laminar differences in field types are illustrated also in Fig. 7.10.

Binocular interaction. One marked difference between layers was related to binocular interaction. This is illustrated in the histograms of Fig. 7.14, and in Figs. 7.11 and 7.12. At the beginning of a typical penetration one eye or the other was consistently dominant, and through layer II and most or all of III one encountered a mixture of cells in groups 2 and 3 with a few from group 1, or else a mixture of 5 and 6 with an occasional group 7.

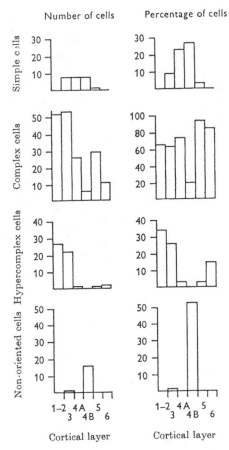

FIGURE 7.13 ■ Histograms of 272 Cortical Cells Showing Numbers of the Different Cell Categories, in Each Layer. Only the cells from the rhesus monkeys are included. In the right-hand set of histograms, cells are expressed as a percentage of the total number in a given layer.

At some stage, usually in upper IV, but occasionally as deep as the border of IV A and IV B, the eye that had been non-dominant would drop out completely, and through the remainder of layer IV cell after cell would be in group 1 instead of 2 or 3, or group 7 instead of 5 or 6. This was just the point at which the background became poorly oriented (i.e. the regions marked by lesions in Figs. 7.11 and 7.12). Simple cells recorded here were almost always groups 1 or 7, but a few exceptions were seen in groups 2 and 6 and there was a single group 4 simple cell. In penetrations that extended through most of the cortical thickness, binocularly driven units remained scarce as layer IV was traversed, but reappeared abruptly in layer V, and persisted throughout V and VI.

Finally, ocular-dominance differed markedly with cell type (Fig. 7.14). This is not surprising since both ocular dominance and cell type tended to vary from layer to layer. There was an increase in binocular interaction in going from simple to complex and from complex to hypercomplex, with groups 1 and 7 becoming rarer, and the intermediate groups more common. But in general cells driven equally by the two eyes were less common in the monkey than in the cat, most monkey cells falling in groups 1, 2, 6 and 7. The ocular-dominance distribution of cells in the cat is closer to that of monkey area 18, than to monkey 17 (unpublished). These results suggest that in monkey striate cortex impulses from the two eyes probably converge not so much on the simple cell, as occurs in the cat, but chiefly on the complex cell.

Discussion

From this and previous studies it is clear that any small region of the striate cortex analyses some small part of the visual field in terms of the direction of light-dark contours (in particular, the tan-

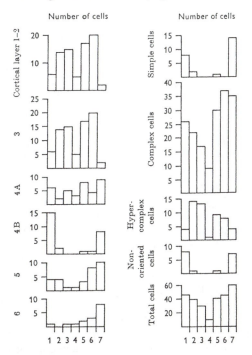

FIGURE 7.14 ■ Left: Distribution of 272 Rhesus Cells among the Various Layers according to Ocular-dominance Group. Right: Distribution of 272 cells among the different cell-classes, according to ocular-dominance group.

gent to the contour lines), a detection of movement of the contours, a registration of the type of contour (light against dark, edge, and the like), and, at the hypercomplex level, a detection of any change in direction (curvature) of the contours. At any one time only a small proportion of cells are likely to be influenced (activated or suppressed), since contours of inappropriate orientation and diffuse light have little or no effect on a cell.

Hypercomplex cells, which we had thought occurred only in 18 and 19 in the cat, turn out to be fairly common in 17, both in cat and monkey. Presumably in early studies their presence was not detected because they gave no response to a line that was too long, or perhaps they were classed as complex when they responded well to a line that happened to be the correct length. For these cells the proportion responding to a given contour must be extremely small, since even an appropriately oriented line is ineffective if it maintains that orientation over too great a distance.

The elaboration of simple cortical fields from geniculate concentric fields, complex from simple, and hypercomplex from complex is probably the prime function of the striate cortex—unless there are still other as yet unidentified cells there. One need not assume, of course, that the output consists entirely of the axons of hypercomplex cells, the other types being merely interposed as links between input and output. We know, for example, that in the cat the posterior corpus callosum contains axons of all three cell types (Hubel & Wiesel, 1967).

A second function of the striate cortex concerns the convergence upon single cells of input from the two eyes. At the geniculate level any binocular interaction must be relatively subtle, since no one has yet mapped out receptive fields in the two eyes for a single geniculate cell, as can be done routinely for cortical cells. In the cortex stimulation of both eyes in corresponding parts of the receptive fields usually gives a greater response than stimulation of either eye alone. In the monkey as in the cat, this convergence takes a special form in which the influence of the two eyes is combined in varying proportions in different cells. Indeed, in the monkey the process of amalgamation of the two inputs is further delayed, so that interaction is minimal for simple cells, distinctly more for complex, and possibly still more for hypercomplex.

Given that contour analysis and binocular convergence are two prime functions of striate cor-

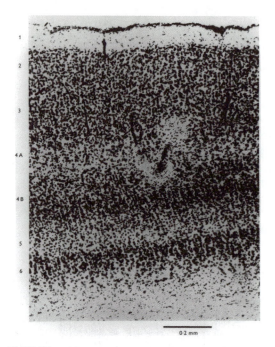

PLATE 7.1 ■ Nissl-stained section corresponding to the experiment of Figs. 7 and 8, showing part of penetration and two lesions. Layers are indicated to left.

tex, the parallel and independent manner in which the processes are carried out by this structure is worth noting. For both functions columns are the units of organization. In a given "eye-preference" column one eye is emphasized, in the next the other eye. In a superimposed but quite independent system, one "orientation" column subserves one orientation, another column a different one. In both types of column the contour analysis and binocular convergence occur in a vertically interconnected system of layers, with the earliest stages in IV B, the latest ones in II and III, and probably also in V and VI. Thus IV B is made up chiefly of simple cells and units (possibly afferent fibres) that show no orientation preference, and these are almost all monocularly driven, whereas in II and III one finds complex and hypercomplex cells, mostly binocularly driven. This difference by layers in complexity of responses and in binocular interaction is entirely consistent with the Golgi type anatomy of Cajal (1911) and Lorente do Nó (1943), since in terms of connexions cells of layer IV are closest to the input, and the upper and lower layers are furthest away. It is hardly surprising that physiologically the populations of individual layers are not pure, in view of the mixture of morphological cell types in each layer, and the presence of axons passing up and down from other layers. In the cat the layering is less distinct, and the tendency for each layer to contain a mixture of cell types seems to be greater—in any case the physiological evidence for segregation of different cell types in different layers, while suggestive in the cat (Kubel & Wiesel, 1962), was not nearly as clear as in the monkey. The present demonstration of a clear difference in function between cells in different cortical layers is, of course, only a first step toward the goal of correlating histologically defined cell types with function.

The form taken by the two systems of columns deserves some comment. The existence of regions in which orientation columns are highly ordered continues to be baffling, for if there are two kinds of striate cortex, one ordered and the other not, the anatomy gives no hint of this. There is a suggestion that the narrow orderly columns may sometimes correspond to the radial fascicles seen microscopically, but these are seen everywhere in 17, and the ordered regions seem not to be present everywhere. Where columns are ordered, it seems likely that they are very long narrow slabs, perhaps not straight, but swirling, if one can judge from the reversals in shifts seen in Fig. 7.9. It is possible that these ordered regions may be more common than we realize, for their detection depends on rather ideal recording conditions in which the electrode moves forward steadily rather than in jumps, and records activity at all times. The possible purpose served by such an ordered system of columns has been discussed elsewhere (Hubel & Wiesel, 1963).

In view of the recent work of Campbell & Kulikowski (1966) showing a difference in ability of humans to discriminate between horizontal or vertical lines and oblique lines, we have looked for any differences in the occurrence of horizontally and vertically oriented fields as opposed to oblique fields, but have seen none, in cat or in monkey. The problem is presumably one comparing the frequency or size of the various orientation columns, and our series is doubtless too small to permit this, especially if one wishes to detect a difference of a few per cent. At least it is clear that horizontal and vertical orientations are not many times more common than others.

In the binocular columnar system the columns seem to be coarser, and take a special form. At the level of layer IV B there is a mosaic of alternating

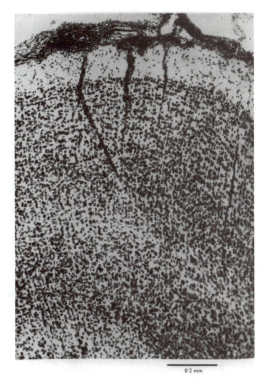

PLATE 7.2 ■ Nissl-stained section corresponding to the experiment of Fig. 9, showing first part of the track outlined by inflammatory reaction.

left-eye and right-eye representation, each apparently almost pure. This presumably simply reflects the tendency for afferents to the cortex to be grouped (Hubel & Wiesel, 1965b), as is so for the columns of the somatosensory cortex described by Mountcastle (1957). As the visual input is transmitted over several stages to the more complex cells in the upper and lower layers, there must be progressively more intermixing between the eyes, presumably by interconnexions that run obliquely. The columns nevertheless remain discrete, with almost all cells in one column favouring one eye, though no longer dominated completely by it. There do not seem to be regions of mixed dominance, as one finds in the cat. For the binocular columns the physiological evidence thus indicates that there is some interchange between one column and its immediate neighbours, minimal in layer IV, but increasing in the superficial and deep layers. (By definition two adjacent binocular columns must favour opposite eyes.) This is in sharp contrast to the orientation columns, since for these there is no evidence to suggest any cross talk be-

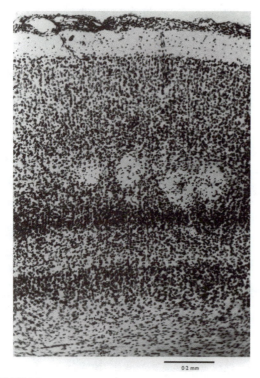

0·2 mm

PLATE 7.3 ■ Nissl section showing four of the five lesions of Fig. 11.

tween one column and its immediately adjoining neighbours. There is of course no reason why an orientation column should not have rich connexions with another column of identical field orientation even though the two may be separated by as many as 15–18 different columns. Indeed, if eye-preference columns are interconnected, and if one eye-preference column does contain many orientation columns, then the interconnexions must be highly specific, one orientation column being connected to another some distance away. These suggestions depend of course on rather indirect inferences from physiological experiments, but they may have some value in indicating certain patterns of connexions to look for with morphological techniques.

If there are indications that the orientation columns take the form of parallel pillars, or, in more ordered areas, parallel slabs, we have no hints at all about the shape of the eye-preference columns. They differ from the orientation columns in being of just two types, instead of more than a dozen, and the two should be about equally prominent, given the lack of any marked dominance of one

eye or other in the cortex as a whole. One would therefore expect a patchwork of alternating columns like a checker board, or a confluent matrix of one type with pillars of the other type embedded within it, or a series of parallel slabs. These possibilities are mentioned here because the term "column" itself implies a series of pillarlike structures, which is probably the least likely form in this case.

The columnar system seems to represent a method by which many areas of cortex—somatosensory (Mountcastle, 1957) visual including 17, 18 and 19, and perhaps motor (Asanuma & Sakata, 1967)—deal with multidimensional problems using a two-dimensional surface. In the visual system the two co-ordinates of the visual field are mapped on the two surface co-ordinates; other variables, notably line orientation, eye dominance, possibly movement directionality, are handled by subdividing this surface into overlapping mosaics which are independent, just as the picture of a jigsaw puzzle is independent of the borders separating the pieces. With two such mosaics known and a third suspected, it will not be surprising if more are found in the future.

To conclude, it is easy to draw up a large list of gaps still to be filled in our understanding of this structure. To mention only a few, the binocular interaction we have described tells us nothing about mechanisms for handling stereoscopic depth perception. Bishop's group in Sydney and Barlow's in California have evidence for horizontal non-correspondence of some cells in cat area 17, and the relation of these to the binocular mechanisms described here for the monkey will be most interesting. Our knowledge of cortical colour mechanisms is still very sketchy. Anatomically one is just beginning to understand the layering of the cortex, and some features, such as the significance of layers I, V and VI are still a complete mystery. At a synaptic level the correlation of structure with physiology, as is now being done in the retina (Dowling & Boycott, 1966), is still lacking in the cortex. The part, if any, that area 17 plays in attention mechanisms in conscious animals is completely obscure. But despite the large areas still unexplored, in broad outline the function of area 17 is probably now relatively well understood. One knows roughly how the output differs from the input, and it is possible to make guesses that can be tested concerning the circuits that underlie these transformations. Knowing what image is falling on the retina at any given moment, one can predict with some confidence what most types of cells will be doing.

Specialized as the cells of 17 are, compared with rods and cones, they must, nevertheless, still represent a very elementary stage in the handling of complex forms, occupied as they are with a relatively simple region-by-region analysis of retinal contours. How this information is used at later stages in the visual path is far from clear, and represents one of the most tantalizing problems for the future.

REFERENCES

Asanuma, H., & Sakata, H. (1967). Functional organization of a cortical efferent system examined with focal depth stimulation in cats. *J. Neurophysiol., 30,* 35–54.

Brodmann, K. (1909). *Vergleichende Lokalisationslehre der Grosshirnrinde.* Leipzig: J. A. Barth.

Cajal, S., & Ramon, Y. (1911). *Histologie du système nerveux de l'homme et des vertébrés,* vol. 2. Paris: Maloine.

Campbell, F. W., & Kulikowski, J. J. (1966). Orientational selectivity of the human visual system. *J. Physiol., 187,* 437–418.

Daniel, P. M. & Whitteridge, D. (1961). The representation of the visual field on the cerebral cortex in monkeys. *J. Physiol., 159,* 203–221.

Daw, N. W. (1967). Color coded units in the goldfish retina. Ph.D. Thesis, Johns Hopkins University, Baltimore.

De Valois, R. L., Jacobs, G. H. & Jones, A. E. (1963). Responses of single cells in primate red-green color vision system. *Optik, 20,* 87–98.

Dowling, J. E., & Boycott, B. B. (1966). Organization of the primate retina: Electron microscopy. *Proc. R. Soc. B, 166,* 80–111.

Hubel, D. H. (1967). Tungsten microelectrode for recording from single units. *Science, N. Y., 125,* 549–550.

Hubel, D. H. (1958). Cortical unit responses to visual stimuli in unanesthetized cats. *Am. J. Ophthal., 46,* 110–121.

Hubel, D. H. (1959). Single unit activity in striate cortex of unrestrained cats. *J. Physiol., 147,* 226–238.

Hubel, D. H., & Wiesel, T. N. (1959). Receptive fields of single neurones in the cat's striate cortex. *J. Physiol., 148,* 574–591.

Hubel, D. H., & Wiesel, T. N. (1960). Receptive fields of optic nerve fibres in the spider monkey. *J. Physiol., 154,* 572–580.

Hubel, D. H., & Wiesel, T. N. (1962). Receptive fields, binocular interaction and functional architecture in the cat's visual cortex. *J. Physiol., 160,* 106–154.

Hubel, D. H., & Wiesel, T. N. (1963). Shape and arrangement of columns in cat's striate cortex. *J. Physiol., 165,* 559–588.

Hubel, D. H., & Wiesel, T. N. (1965a). Receptive fields and functional architecture in two non-striate visual areas (18 and 19) of the cat. *J. Neurophysiol., 28,* 229–289.

Hubel, D. H., & Wiesel, T. N. (19656). Binocular interaction in striate cortex of kittens reared with artificial squint. *J. Neurophysiol., 28,* 1041–1059.

Hubel, D. H., & Wiesel, T. N. (1967). Cortical and callosal connections concerned with the vertical meridian of visual fields in the cat. *J. Neurophysiol.* (In press)

Lorente De Nó, R. (1943). Cerebral cortex: architecture, intracortical connections, motor projections. In *Physiology of the Nervous System,* ed. Fulton, J. F., 2nd edn., pp. 274–301. New York: Oxford University Press.

Motokawa, K., Taira, N., & Okuda, J. (1962). Spectral responses of single units in the primate visual cortex. *Tohoku J. Exp. Med., 78,* 320–337.

Mountcastle, V. B. (1957). Modality and topographic properties of single neurons of cat's somatic sensory cortex. *J. Neurophysiol., 20,* 408–434.

Talbot, S. A., & Marshall, W. R. (1941). Physiological studies on neural mechanisms of visual localization and discrimination. *Am. J. Ophthal., 24,* 1255–1263.

von Bonin, G. (1942). The striate area of primates. *J. Comp. Neurol., 77,* 405–429.

Wiesel, T. N., & Hubel, D. H. (1966). Spatial and chromatic interactions in the lateral geniculate body of the rhesus monkey. *J. Neurophysiol., 29,* 1115–1156.

Introduction to Reading 8

Spatial vision has always been of special interest to perceptual theorists, because it holds the key to the perception of object shape, which is among the most crucial functions of vision. A wide variety of approaches to spatial vision have been proposed, and these proposals are aimed at quite different levels of analysis. For example, the approach to object recognition offered by Biederman (Reading 20) proposes that one extracts object parts and the relations among the parts (e.g., "on top of"), and then matches the derived *structural description* to stored representations in memory.

The approach taken by Blakemore and Campbell in this reading is quite different. The authors argue that the visual system consists of an array of analyzers or filters each of which is tuned to a particular orientation (as had been reported by Hubel and Wiesel, Reading 7) and spatial frequency. The spatial frequency of a pattern is a measure of its spatial scale or size. This measure of spatial scale depends on a mathematical tool called *Fourier analysis*, named for its inventor, the French mathematician Jean Fourier.

According to Fourier's theorem, any pattern, and in particular any spatial pattern such as a visual image, can be analyzed into a set of underlying sinusoidal components. A sinusoidal component looks like a set of black and white bars of some fixed width such that the variation in luminance across the image varies sinusoidally, increasing and then decreasing smoothly in a repeating pattern (see Plate 1 in the article). Three properties of a sinusoidal grating determine its appearance: the orientation of the grating, its contrast (i.e., the difference in luminance between the peaks and troughs of the luminance sinusoid) and its spatial frequency (i.e., the number of bars per unit of distance in the image). A grating with a low spatial frequency has wide bars, and a grating with a high spatial frequency has thin bars. Spatial frequency is measured in terms of the number of cycles (one pair of dark and bright bars is one cycle) per degree of visual angle (a measure of distance on the retina), abbreviated c/deg. Fourier's theorem states that one can recreate any given spatial pattern by simply adding together an appropriately selected set of sinusoidal components. To discover what these components are, one can apply a computational algorithm called Fourier analysis that yields the contrast, orientation, and phase (relative position) of each of the visible spatial frequencies that are present in the image; this is a mathematically complete representation of that image.

Campbell and Robson's idea, then, is that the visual system represents images by performing a biological Fourier analysis of that image. It does so by employing a large number of detectors (i.e., neurons) each of which measures the degree to which the particular spatial frequency to which it is tuned is present in the image. For example, there might be an image containing a small number of large fuzzy objects, spaced far apart, each with a smooth and patternless surface. Such an image contains a predominance of low spatial frequencies and relatively little power in the higher spatial frequencies, and it will tend to activate neurons with large receptive fields that are tuned to coarse spatial frequencies. On the other hand, an image consisting of a large number of tiny pebbles, each with an intricate pattern on its surface, would have more power in the high spatial frequencies and little or none in the low spatial frequencies. In practice, images will tend to have at least some power in almost all spatial frequencies, and it is the relative power at each spatial frequency that permits one to distinguish one image from another.

The initial psychophysical evidence for this idea is described in this selection. Blakemore and Campbell exploited a phenomenon known as *spatial frequency*

adaptation to investigate the implications of their proposal. Adaptation refers to the fact that any neuron will, upon being stimulated by its preferred stimulus for an extended period of time, become fatigued and thus respond less effectively to continued stimulation. Psychophysically, this is reflected in reduced sensitivity to a stimulus that has been presented over an extended period of time; a stronger stimulus is therefore required at threshold than if no adaptation had taken place.

In the case of spatial frequency adaptation, the observer views a high-contrast adapting grating of a fixed spatial frequency for one minute and then the spatial frequency contrast threshold is estimated for a range of spatial frequencies. The key discovery in this reading is that spatial frequency adaptation affects only a narrow range of spatial frequencies surrounding the frequency of the adapting grating (Figure 6). This strongly suggests that there exist units that are tuned to specific spatial frequencies. This is precisely what one would expect to find if spatial patterns were represented in terms of their underlying Fourier spectrum.

Corroborating evidence for such a system of spatial vision subsequently emerged from several sources. For example, Graham and Nachmias (1971) noted that a square-wave grating (a repeating pattern of bars with sharp boundaries) is mathematically equivalent to a sinusoid with the same spatial frequency (called the fundamental frequency), plus an infinite sequence of additional gratings of increasing frequency and decreasing amplitude (these additional gratings are called the *harmonics,* which in this case consist of all the odd multiples of the fundamental frequency). If the square wave really is represented as the combined separate activation of the fundamental and all the harmonics, then there should exist some high-spatial-frequency square waves that appear to be identical to a sine wave with the same spatial frequency, because the harmonics of the square wave should be invisible if the fundamental frequency of that square wave is high enough. This prediction, and several others, were confirmed in their experiments (see also the experiment described in p. 186).

Another source of corroborating evidence came from neurophysiology: single cells differ in the sizes of their receptive fields, and any given cell should respond best to a particular spatial frequency, with its response falling off as the spatial frequency of the image departs from its preferred frequency. De Valois, Albrecht, and Thorell (1982) identified cells in the cortex of the macaque monkey that had just these properties. However, because the receptive fields of these cells are limited in spatial extent, they must be described as carrying out a local, piecewise, Fourier analysis of the scene.

This approach to spatial vision is appealing because it can in principle permit one to predict the response of the pattern vision system by characterizing the responses of a few relatively simply units, and then adding up their responses appropriately for any given visual stimulus (Graham, 1989). This is a powerful idea. However, it also has its limitations. Perhaps most importantly, this kind of mechanism treats a scene as a single pattern, and it does not provide a mechanism for decomposing a complex scene into its constituent objects, particularly when the scene contains several overlapping and partly occluded objects (as most scenes do). Edge-based algorithms for scene perception (e.g., Marr & Hildreth, 1980), for example, provide explicit representation of potential surface boundaries, which could be useful for segmenting a scene into objects. However, a hybrid approach involving local spatial frequency analysis together with edge-based or other algorithms offers a rich framework for explaining spatial vision.

REFERENCES

De Valois, R. L., Albrecht, D. G., & Thorell, L. G. (1982). Spatial frequency selectivity of cells in macaque visual cortex. *Vision Research, 22,* 545–559.

Graham, N. (1989). *Visual pattern analyzers.* Oxford: Oxford University Press.

Graham, N., & Nachmias, J. (1971). Detection of grating pat-
terns containing two spatial frequencies: A comparison of single-channel and multiple-channel models. *Vision Research, 11,* 251–259.

Marr, D., & Hildreth, E. C. (1980). Theory of edge detection. *Proceedings of the Royal Society of London B, 207,* 187–217.

On the Existence of Neurones in the Human Visual System Selectively Sensitive to the Orientation and Size of Retinal Images

C. Blakemore and F. W. Campbell • University of Cambridge, England

Summary

1. It was found that an occipital evoked potential can be elicited in the human by moving a grating pattern without changing the mean light flux entering the eye. Prolonged viewing of a high contrast grating reduces the amplitude of the potential evoked by a low contrast grating.

2. This adaptation to a grating was studied psychophysically by determining the contrast threshold before and after adaptation. There is a temporary fivefold rise in contrast threshold after exposure to a high contrast grating of the same orientation and spatial frequency.

3. By determining the rise of threshold over a range of spatial frequency for a number of adapting frequencies it was found that the threshold elevation is limited to a spectrum of frequencies with a bandwidth of just over an octave at half amplitude, centered on the adapting frequency.

4. The amplitude of the effect and its bandwidth are very similar for adapting spatial frequencies between 3 c/deg. and 14 c/deg. At higher frequencies the bandwidth is slightly narrower. For lower adapting frequencies the peak of the effect stays at 3 c/deg.

5. These and other findings suggest that the human visual system may possess neurones se-
lectively sensitive to spatial frequency and size. The orientational selectivity and the interocular transfer of the adaptation effect implicate the visual cortex as the site of these neurones.

6. This neural system may play an essential preliminary role in the recognition of complex images and generalization for magnification.

Introduction

Recently, attempts have been made to apply Fourier theory in describing the transmission of spatial information through the visual system. Using this approach it has been possible to compare and contrast, quantitatively, the role in this process of the retinal, geniculate and cortical neurones, as well as the preceding optics.

Not only has this simple approach been of value in the quantitative study of single units, it has also proved useful in the treatment of psychophysical responses from human observers, providing a unifying mathematical description of the threshold for non-repetitive patterns, such as lines and bars (Campbell, Carpenter & Levinson, 1969), as well as for gratings of simple and complex wave form (Campbell & Robson, 1968).

These studies raise the question of how the brain deals with spatial information and interprets the retinal image. Campbell & Robson (1968) have proposed that there may exist in the visual nervous system a number of elements each selectively sensitive to a limited range of spatial frequency i.e. a system of neurones encoding the dimensions of retinal images. However, they made no attempt to measure quantitatively the properties of these elements. But such measurements have been made on single units in the cat cortex and these are presented in the preceding article, where it is reported that the cat does possess cells each of which responds to a narrow range of spatial frequency (Campbell, Cooper & Enroth-Cugell, 1969).

In this paper we attempt to measure the properties of these neurones in man and compare them with those found previously in the cat. To achieve this we have used a recently discovered, spatial-adaptation effect.

Gilinsky (1968) found that an observer's acuity for a striped pattern is lowered by adaptation to a pattern of identical orientation and bar width but of higher mean luminance. She also found that this adaptation effect decreases as the orientation of the acuity grating is altered relative to the adapting grating.

Blakemore & Campbell (1969) noticed this adaptation phenomenon during a study of the occipital evoked potential and went on to confirm its orientation selectivity psychophysically. They used gratings with sinusoidal light distribution and measured the elevation in threshold by varying the contrast of the grating while keeping its space-average luminance constant. In addition, they discovered that the effect is maximal when the test and adapting gratings are identical in spatial frequency. Pantle & Sekuler (1968) also found that this psychophysical adaptation is frequency dependent.

This phenomenon cannot be due to a conventional after-image, because it occurs even when the subject does not fixate steadily upon the high contrast grating but permits his gaze to roam over the pattern. Furthermore, under those conditions no after-image of the grating is perceived when a uniform surface is viewed after adaptation.

In Part I of this paper we establish the characteristics of this adaptation effect and in Part II we use the phenomenon to detect the presence and measure the properties of neurones selectively sensitive to spatial frequency.

Methods

Stimulus. Gratings, the luminance profile of which varied sinusoidally along the horizontal meridian, were generated on an oscilloscope using a method described by Campbell & Green (1965). The space-average luminance was kept constant at about 100 cd/m². The pattern could be switched on and off, or its phase displaced by 180°, without changing the mean luminance. The contrast was varied by a logarithmic attenuator and a potentiometer in series. The contrast was monitored by measuring the amplitude of the signal to the oscilloscope by means of a logarithmic converter (Hewlett-Packard, type 7561A). The output of the log converter was monitored by a digital voltmeter or displayed on x-y plotter. The viewing distance was 114 in. and the diameter of the screen 3 in. (subtending 1·5 deg. at the eye) except for the experiment described in the legend of Fig. 8.12.

During all psychophysical measurements of contrast threshold the pattern was turned on and off twice per second, without change in mean luminance.

Recording of evoked potential. One electrode was applied to the inion and the other 2½ cm temporally. Signals were differentially amplified with an earthed electrode applied to the forehead. High and low pass filters with corner frequencies of 8 and 25 c/sec were used in the amplifier and the output was led to a computer of averaged transients (Enhancetron). The evoked potential was averaged for 200 sweeps. To provide a time-dependent patterned stimulus which would evoke a potential, the phase of the grating was changed by 180° at a rate of 8 times per second. Care was taken to avoid signals arising from nearby muscles by suitable positioning and training of the subject.

Results

Part I: The pattern adaptation effect

EVOKED POTENTIAL EVIDENCE

It is important to note that, in this experiment, the flux of light reaching the eye did not change as the phase of the stimulus was switched. An evoked potential can, therefore, be generated solely by a change in retinal position of a pattern, as reported by Cobb, Ettlinger & Morton (1968).

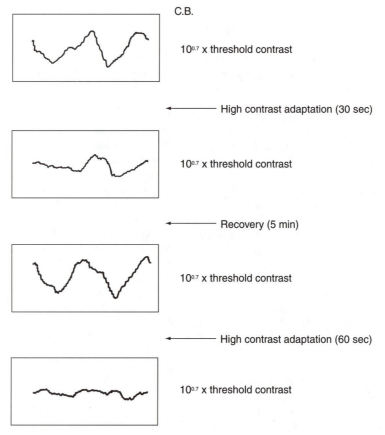

FIGURE 8.1 ■ The Effects of Spatial Adaptation on the Evoked Potential for Subject C. B. A sine-wave grating pattern (12 c/deg.) was shifted in phase by 180°, eight times per second, and the occipital potential evoked was summed 200 times on the Enhancetron to produce the records shown in boxes on the left. The stimulus was identical for each record. Each trace shows the potential for two phase shifts. The first record is for a low contrast grating, $10^{0.7}$ times the threshold contrast for this spatial frequency. C. B. then viewed a high contrast grating (1·5 log units above threshold) for 30 sec and the potential for the same low contrast grating was immediately re-measured. This second trace is clearly rather lower in amplitude than the first. After 5 min recovery the low contrast grating produced a record (3rd box) very similar to that of the original. The final record taken after 60 sec exposure to the high contrast grating has no distinguishable signal. The failure to record the potential was accompanied by subjective elevation of threshold.

During this study of the human occipital potential evoked by a moving patterned stimulus, we discovered that the amplitude of the potential generated by a low contrast moving grating is markedly reduced if the subject has recently viewed a similar pattern of high contrast. The results are shown in Fig. 8.1. The failure to record objectively an evoked potential after adaptation to a high contrast grating was accompanied by subjective fading of the low contrast pattern. We found it impracticable to collect detailed information about this effect using the evoked potential technique and

we therefore decided to study it using psychophysical methods.

PSYCHOPHYSICAL EVIDENCE

Time course of recovery. The subject used a potentiometer to set the contrast of the grating on the oscilloscope to his own threshold before and after adapting to a high contrast pattern. After logarithmic conversion the contrast settings were displayed against time. A typical result is shown for subject F.W.C. in Fig. 8.2. The record to the left of

F.W.C.

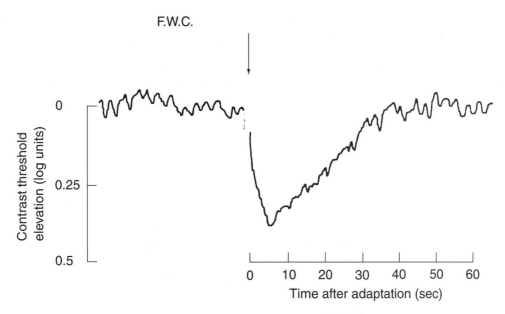

FIGURE 8.2 ■ The Time Course of Recovery from Adaptation. F.W.C. turned a potentiometer to adjust the contrast of the grating (12·5 c/deg.) until it was just visible. His searching movements oscillate around threshold in the first part of this record from an x–y plotter, after logarithmic conversion. The arrow indicates a period of 60 sec during which the record was stopped and F.W.C. viewed a high contrast grating (1·5 log units above threshold). The trace re-starts as he searches for his elevated threshold and gradually tracks the recovery back to normal contrast sensitivity, which is complete in about 60 sec.

the arrow was obtained before adaptation. The fluctuations represent the subject's attempts to estimate and re-estimate the contrast at which the grating appeared and disappeared. Their amplitude is about 0·05 log units and clearly oscillate about some steady threshold value. The arrow indicates the lapse of 60 sec during which the contrast of the pattern on the screen was increased by the experimenter to 1·5 log units above the subject's threshold. The subject viewed this adapting pattern continuously, allowing his eye to wander over the screen to avoid the formation of an after-image.

At the end of this period, the experimenter reduced the contrast of the grating and instructed the observer again to set the contrast to threshold. The record to the right of the arrow describes the time course of the recovery of the contrast sensitivity. It will be noted that initially, the subject took a few seconds to locate his elevated threshold and thereafter he steadily tracked the slow recovery until he reached the original setting where the record reaches a plateau.

The logarithm of the contrast is being recorded and, since the phase is approximated by a linear slope, we conclude that the recovery function is exponential. The time constant of this function in this example is about 20 sec. There was no significant variation in this time constant for five subjects nor over a wide variety of stimulus conditions, with the short adaptation times used here.

For most of the remaining experiments we found it unnecessary to record the complete recovery phase and instead decided that it was convenient and sufficient to measure the initial, elevated threshold, immediately after the adapting period. The subject was therefore instructed to adjust the contrast as quickly as possible to his new threshold. Thereupon, he pressed a switch and the output of the logarithmic converter was displayed on a 4-digit voltmeter.

Time course of induction. The results shown in Fig. 8.3 were obtained by having an observer (F.W. C.) view a sinusoidal grating of 15 c/deg. (cycles per degree subtended at the eye) for various periods of time and determining his rise of threshold immediately after each adaptation period. A recovery time of at least 3 min was allowed between each reading. For the upper curve the adapting grating was set at a contrast of 1·25 log units above the normal contrast threshold for this grating. For

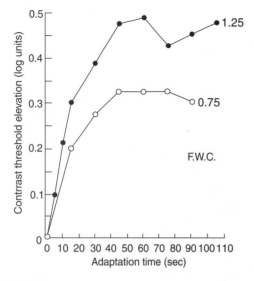

FIGURE 8.3 **FIGURE 8.3** ■ The Effect of Adapting Time. The initial elevation of threshold for F.W.C. is plotted against the adaptation time. For the filled circles the adapting grating of 15 c/deg. was 1·25 log units above threshold. For the open circles it was 0·75 log units above threshold.

spatial frequency. These slopes are approximately parallel for all but the highest spatial frequencies (20 c/deg., 28·3 c/deg.). However, since there was only a limited range of supra-threshold contrast available for these frequencies too much significance should not be attached to this finding. The first point on each curve is the contrast threshold for that spatial frequency with no previous adaptation. The position of each curve on the ordinate is clearly directly related to the more familiar contrast sensitivity function, an example of which is shown in Fig. 8.5.

In the experiments described in Part II we chose to adapt with grating at 1·5 log units above their contrast threshold. This was done in order to produce as large an effect as possible without excluding comparable measurements at all but the highest spatial frequencies.

the lower curve the grating was 0·75 log units above threshold. It is evident that, although the effect is greater for the higher contrast grating, the time course is similar for the two examples and that in both cases the adaptation effect reaches a plateau after viewing for about 1 min.

Therefore in all subsequent experiments an initial adaptation period of at least 60 sec was used in order to reach the equilibrium level. In cases where a number of threshold determinations were required under the same adaptation conditions, the subject viewed the screen continuously, the first reading being made after initial adaptation for 1 min. Subsequent estimates were made after at least 10 sec of re-adaptation each time. After the initial adaptation the low contrast test pattern was exposed and a threshold setting made as quickly as possible. The high contrast pattern was then substituted for the periods of re-adaptation between subsequent readings. This period was found to be sufficient to maintain the adaptation at the equilibrium level.

The contrast of the adapting pattern. Fig. 8.4 shows the result of an experiment in which pattern adaptation was measured for gratings of a number of spatial frequencies over a range of adapting contrast. The points are joined for each

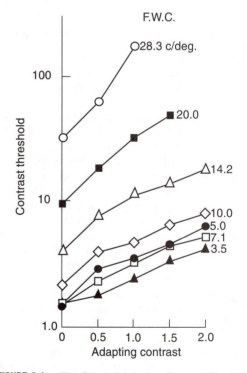

FIGURE 8.4 ■ The Effect of Adapting Contrast. The initial contrast threshold for F.W.C. after a period of adaptation, is plotted, on an arbitrary logarithmic scale, against the contrast of the adapting pattern in log units. Results are shown for a number of spatial frequencies: in each case adapting and test grating were of the same frequency. The data points for zero adapting contrast are, of course, the normal contrast threshold values.

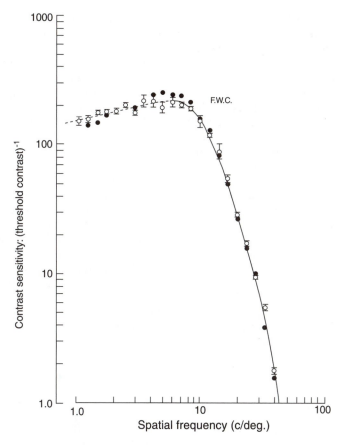

FIGURE 8.5 ■ The Contrast Sensitivity Function for F.W.C. Contrast sensitivity is plotted on an arbitrary logarithmic scale against spatial frequency. The open circles and vertical bars show initial threshold estimates with 1 s.e. (*n* = 6). The filled circles are repeat determinations at the end of the series of adaptation experiments. The continuous curve is the function e⁻ ᶠ and the interrupted portion was fitted by eye to the low frequency data points. During threshold determinations the pattern was turned on and off twice per second, without changing mean luminance.

Binocular transfer of pattern adaptation. To find out whether this adaptation effect transfers from one eye to the other we performed the following experiment. Initially the contrast threshold of each eye was independently determined in subject F.W.C. for a spatial frequency of 10 c/deg. The left eye alone was then adapted as in the previous experiment to a grating of this frequency, 1·5 log units above the left eye's threshold. The contrast threshold was then re-determined for each eye separately. Ten readings were taken for each eye, the high contrast grating being substituted in the left eye between each reading to maintain adaptation.

As expected, there was the usual elevation of threshold in the adapted eye. Moreover, there was a significant rise of threshold ($P < 0.001$) in the right eye which had not been adapted. However, the rise of threshold in the adapted eye was 1·6 times greater than that in the unadapted.

We therefore conclude that there is definite, but incomplete, interocular transfer of the adaptation phenomenon.

Part II: Spatially Selective Channels

CONTRAST SENSITIVITY CHARACTERISTIC BEFORE ADAPTATION

Initially we determined the contrast sensitivity for a series of spatial frequencies spaced at one quarter octave intervals. These results are shown in Fig.

8.5 as open circles, which are the mean of six readings, with vertical lines representing 1 S.E. At the end of the experiments described below contrast sensitivity was redetermined in order to assess any possible equipment drift or change in the observer's threshold criterion. These second determinations are shown as filled circles and it is evident that no consistent difference has occurred. The high frequency portion of the curve drawn through the data is the best fitting value of e^{-f} (f = spatial frequency), a function which previous studies have shown to be appropriate (Campbell, Kulikowsky & Levinson, 1966). The interrupted portion of the curve, through the low frequency data, was fitted by eye.

CONTRAST SENSITIVITY CHARACTERISTIC AFTER ADAPTATION

The curve fitted to the data in Fig. 8.5 is reproduced in Fig. 8.6A.

As described earlier the subject continually viewed a grating of 7·1 c/deg., 1·5 log units above threshold for that frequency. While this adaptation was maintained, the contrast threshold for frequencies from 2·1 to 23·8 c/deg., at one quarter octave steps, was determined by briefly interpolating the low contrast test grating which the subject set to threshold.

The results are shown with their S.E. ($n = 6$). It is clear that the sensitivity has been dramatically depressed in the region of 7·1 c/deg. but that there is practically no effect beyond the frequencies 2·5 and 11·9 c/deg. It is conceivable that adaptation at one specific frequency might have affected contrast threshold at all measurable spatial frequencies. If such were the case the over-all contrast sensitivity curve should have been uniformly lowered. This is not so, and we therefore conclude that the adapting pattern is principally depressing the sensitivity of some "channel," independently of others, and that this channel is adapted by a limited range of spatial frequency.

In order to define its characteristics more spe-

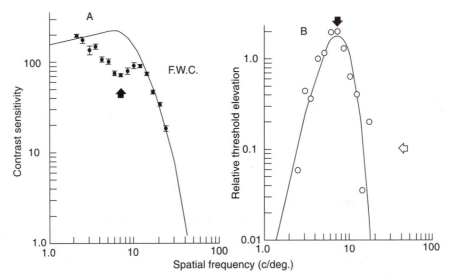

FIGURE 8.5 ■ The effect of Adapting at 7·1 c/deg. A. The continuous curve from Fig. 5 is reproduced. The filled circles and vertical bars are the means and s.e. ($n = 6$) for re-determinations of contrast sensitivity at a number of spatial frequencies while F.W.C. was continuously adapting to a grating of 7·1 c/deg., 1·5 log. units above threshold. The exact procedure is described in the text.

B. The depression in sensitivity due to adaptation at 7·1 c/deg. is plotted, with open circles, as relative threshold elevation against spatial frequency. The vertical difference between each point and the smooth curve in Fig. 6A is the ratio of sensitivity before and after adaptation. The relative threshold elevation is the antilogarithm of this difference minus 1, so that no change in threshold would give a value of zero on the ordinate. The continuous curve is the funtion $[e^{-f^2}-e^{-(2f)^2}]^2$, fitted by eye to the data points. The filled arrows show the adapting frequency of 7·1 c/deg. The open arrow marks the value on the ordinate for a threshold elevation equivalent to $2\sqrt{2}$ times an average s.e. for determining contrast sensitivity.

cifically we have reduced the data as follows. We took the difference between each data point and the smooth curve in Fig. 8.5, at each spatial frequency. This difference is the ratio of sensitivity before and after adaptation (since the ordinate is logarithmic). If there be no effect of adaptation on the contrast sensitivity then this ratio should theoretically be 1. If there is a depression of sensitivity after adaptation the ratio will be greater than 1. For example, at 7·1 c/deg. in Fig. 8.6 the ratio was 3·0 as the depression in contrast sensitivity was 0·48 log units. For mathematical convenience in describing the effect, we subtracted 1 from each ratio in order to express the depression as a positive increment above zero, so in this example the relative threshold elevation at 7·1 c/deg. is 2·0. In Fig. 8.6B we plot the log adaptation effect, derived in this manner, against log spatial frequency.

Naturally, due to the statistical variations in determining the mean contrast sensitivity, both before and after adaptation, some of the ratios which have values close to zero will be negative after this transformation. As no negative values of statistical significance were found, these points do not help us to define the shape of the curve and they have therefore been omitted. Indeed, probably some of the positive values which are plotted between 0·01 and 0·1 may not be significantly different from zero and little emphasis should be placed on them. An average standard error for redetermining contrast sensitivity without adaptation was about 0·02 log units. The ratio of twice the standard error of the difference to the original mean would give a value of about 0·1 on the ordinate of Fig. 8.6B. An open arrow marks this average significance level on the graph.

The curve fitted to these results is the simple function

$$[e^{-f^2} - e^{-(2f)^2}]^2.$$

ADAPTATION CHARACTERISTICS AT OTHER SPATIAL FREQUENCIES

The middle frequencies. The above experiment was repeated using adapting gratings of the following spatial frequencies, 3·5, 5·0, 7·1, 10·0 and 14·2 c/deg. These results are shown in Fig. 8.7, plotted as in Fig. 8.6B. It is clear that the effect is maximal at the spatial frequency used for adaptation and that the magnitude, that is the position on the ordinate, is similar in all cases.

To express the similarity of shape for these curves we reproduce the results normalized for the spatial frequency of the adapting grating. This transformation is shown in Fig. 8.8. This method of pooling the data illustrates that the individual curves are very similar and that good superposition of the results does not require displacement of these individual curves on the ordinate. Because of the similarity of functions relating threshold elevation to the contrast of the adapting grating, whatever the spatial frequency of the latter (see Fig. 8.4), this result was not unexpected. The maximum elevation of threshold is determined by the contrast of the adapting grating, whatever its spatial frequency. It can be seen that the function

$$[e^{-f^2} e^{-(2f)^2}]^2$$ fits all the pooled data.

High spatial frequencies. At higher spatial frequencies the contrast sensitivity decreased rapidly (see Fig. 8.5) and inevitably there is little reserve of suprathreshold contrast available for adaptation. Thus we were unable to adapt with gratings of 1·5 log units above threshold, as in the preceding experiments, we were forced to use only 1·25 log units for adaptation at 20 c/deg. and 1·0 log units for 28·3 c/deg. Therefore these results, shown in Fig. 8.9, cannot strictly be compared with the results of the previous section. In this figure the adaptation data for these two high spatial frequencies are displayed as in Fig. 8.7. The smooth curves are the same function fitted to all the previous results, at the same position on the ordinate. Clearly this function does not fit high frequency data. The adaptation characteristics appear to be narrower and the maximum effect greater than at lower spatial frequencies, despite the lower adapting contrasts used. This latter point is illustrated in another way in Fig. 8.4 where it may be seen that the threshold elevation *versus* adapting contrast functions are steeper for 20 and 28·3 c/deg. than for other spatial frequencies.

Low spatial frequencies. The low spatial frequency results must be treated separately because of an unexpected observation. We found that for adapting frequencies lower than 3 c/deg. the maximum adaptation effect did not occur, as in the previous experiments, at the same frequency as the adapting grating. Figure 8.10 shows the effect of adapting to gratings of 2·5, 1·8, 1·5 and 1·3 c/deg. It will be noted that, as the spatial frequency of the adapting grating is lowered the magnitude of the adaptation effect is decreased without, however, its position changing on the frequency scale. All the curves peak at about 3 c/deg. When we

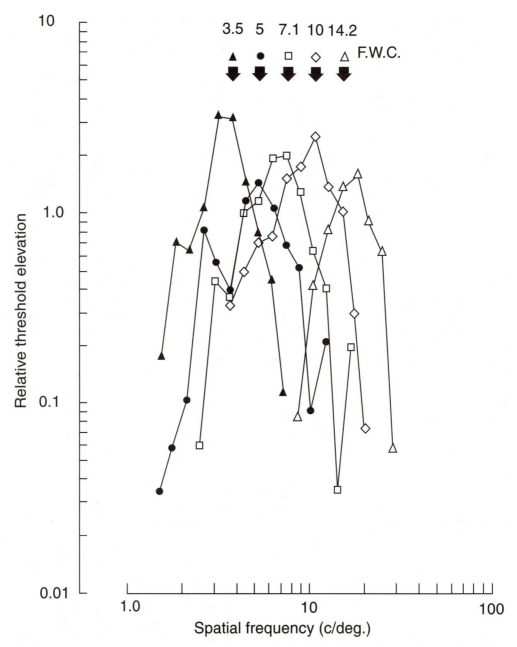

FIGURE 8.7 ■ Adaptation Characteristics Derived as in Fig. 6 for Five Adapting Spatial Frequencies. Each arrow marks the frequency of adaptation and above it is the symbol used for the relative threshold elevation caused by the adaptation. Points are joined in order of spatial frequency. The adapting frequencies were 3·5, 5·0, 7·1, 10·0 and 14·2.

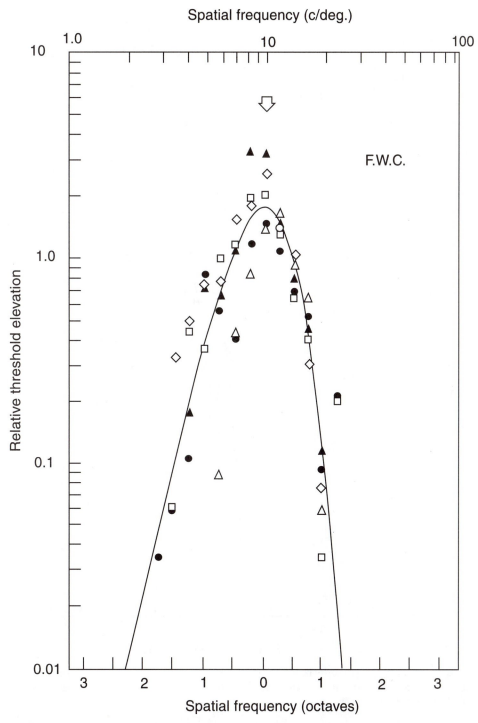

FIGURE 8.8 ■ Adaptation Characteristics Normalized for Spatial Frequency. The data points of Fig. 7 have been shifted along the abscissa so that all the adapting frequencies superimpose at 10 c/deg., shown by the arrow. The abscissa is also expressed, on the lower scale, as octaves of spatial frequency on either side fo the adapting frequency. There is no normalization on the ordinate and the continuous curve is the function fitted in Fig. 6 *B*, at the same position on the ordinate.

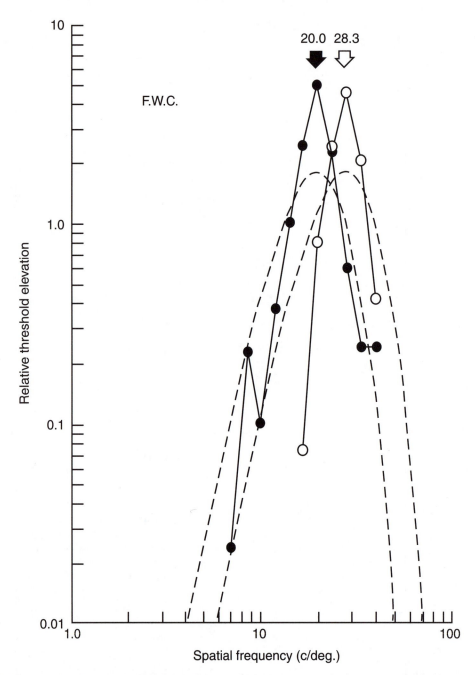

FIGURE 8.9 ■ Threshold Elevation for Adaptation at 20 c/deg. (filled circles) and 28·3 c/deg. (open circles). The symbols are joined. The interrupted curves are the same function fitted in Fig. 6*B* at the same position on the ordinate as in Fig. 6*B*, 7 and 8, and with the peak at the adapting frequency.

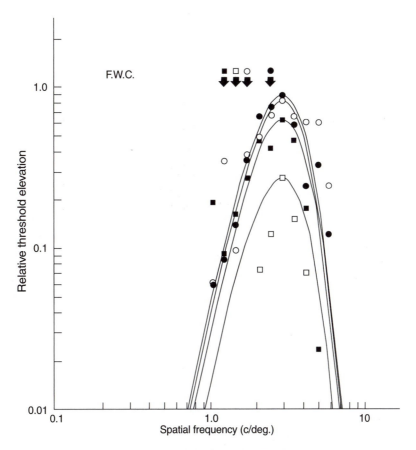

FIGURE 8.10 ■ The Effect of Adapting at 2·5 (●), 1·8 (O), 1·5 (■) and 1·3 (□) c/deg. Arrows with appropriate symbols above show these frequencies. The smooth curves are the function fitted in Fig. 6*B,* normalized on the abscissa and with the peak passing through the data point at 3·0 c/deg., since this is the frequency of maximum threshold elevation for all these adapting frequencies.

attempted to adapt to spatial frequencies less than 1·3 c/deg. there was no significant elevation of threshold at any spatial frequency.

THE EFFECT OF CONTRAST ON SPATIAL SELECTIVITY

In the prior experiments, the contrast of the adapting grating was usually set at 1·5 log units above threshold at each discrete spatial frequency. It is evident from Fig. 8.4 that the elevation of threshold at the same spatial frequency as the adapting pattern increases with the contrast of the latter. Could it be that the shape of the whole adaptation characteristic depends upon the contrast of adaptation? We tested this speculation at a frequency of 10 c/deg. by adapting at contrast levels of 0·5,

1·0, 1·5 and 2·0 log units above threshold, and measuring the change of threshold for neighbouring frequencies as in the previous experiments.

The results are shown in Fig. 8.11A. It may be seen that the position of each curve on the ordinate does depend, as we expected, on the contrast of the adapting pattern. However, the shape appears to be remarkably similar in each instance. This point is better illustrated by normalizing on the ordinate for data points at the central spatial frequency (10 c/deg). This transformation is shown in Fig. 8.11B. The continuous curve is the function previously found to give a good fit (Fig. 8.8).

It thus appears that within the middle frequency range the shape of the adaptation characteristic is independent of both the frequency of the adapting pattern (Fig. 8.8) and its contrast (Fig. 8.11).

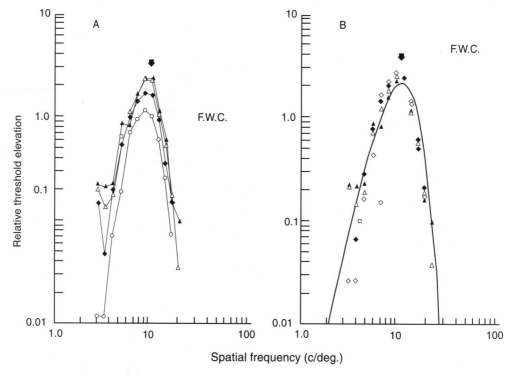

FIGURE 8.11 ■ *A*. Each set of points shows the effect of adapting at 10 c/deg. The different symbols refer to different contrasts of the adapting pattern, as shown below. Symbols are joined. The arrow marks the adapting frequency.

B. The data points for adapting contrasts of 1·5, 1·0 and 0·5 log units above threshold have been shifted up until the points at the adapting frequency all super-impose on that for 2·0 log units of adapting contrast. The smooth curve is the function from Fig. 6B, at the same position on the ordinate and centred at 10 c/deg.

▲, 2·0 log units; △, 1·5 log units; ◆, 1·0 log units; ◇, 0·5 log units.

CONTRIBUTION OF INDIVIDUAL MECHANISMS TO CONTRAST SENSITIVITY CHARACTERISTIC

It is clear from Fig. 8.5 and Fig. 8.8 that the adaptation characteristic is restricted to a narrow band of spatial frequency compared with the broad band of frequencies that can be detected by the visual system.

Consider the hypothesis that the adaptation characteristics established in Fig. 8.7 reflect the presence of neurones each selectively sensitive to a limited range of spatial frequency. If this be so, the shape of the over-all contrast sensitivity could be due to the combination of the sensitivity characteristics of individual narrow-band detectors.

The presence of these narrow band detection characteristics dispersed throughout the spectrum of spatial frequency might lead to minor irregularities in the contrast sensitivity function, particu-

larly if they were few in number or regularly spaced along the frequency domain. Indeed Patel (1966) has suggested that the contrast sensitivity function of man may have such irregular "bumps" and Nye (1968) has reported them on the contrast sensitivity function of the pigeon.

In order to be confident of such excursions in the over-all sensitivity function it is necessary to sample contrast sensitivity at much closer frequency intervals than has been used heretofore. It is also essential to avoid small instrumental artifacts in generating gratings of different spatial frequency which might arise, for example, from small variations in the time-base trigger point. We chose, therefore, to measure contrast sensitivity initially at frequency intervals of ¹/₁₀ octave and to produce these various spatial frequencies by changing the viewing distance for a pattern of constant frequency generated on the oscilloscope. Two runs

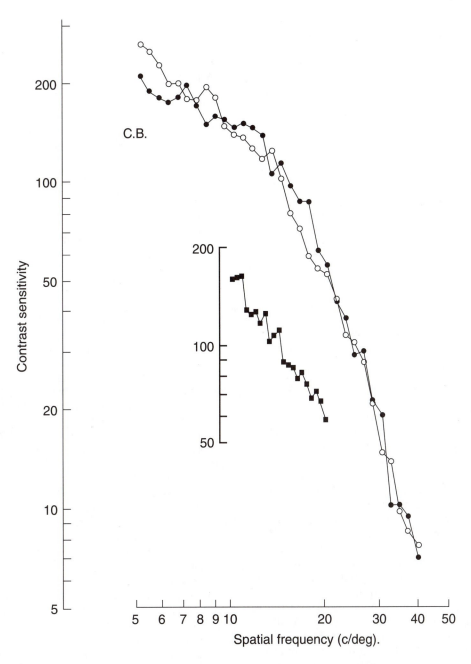

FIGURE 8.12 ■ Normal Contrast Sensitivity for C.B. The frequency on the screen was fixed at 13·3 c/in. and the screen diameter was 3 in. Spatial frequency at the eye was varied in one tenth octave steps by changing the viewing distance. This manoeuvre also altered the angular subtense of the screen at each spatial frequency. The filled circles are the means of initial determinations (*n* = 6) of contrast sensitivity, plotted on an arbitrary logarithmic scale. The open circles are means of redeterminations under identical conditions (*n* = 6). The filled squares are further estimates of contrast sensitivity from 10 to 20 c/deg., at one twentieth of an octave steps. These points have been displaced downwards by half of one log unit and the inset ordinate is appropriate.

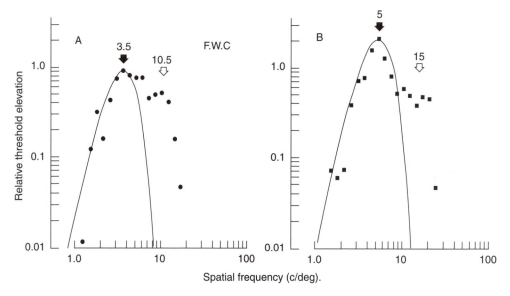

FIGURE 8.13 ■ Adaptation with a Square-wave Grating. In each case the filled arrow marks the spatial frequency of the square-wave grating, 1·5 log units above threshold, which was viewed for adaptation. The open arrow shows the third harmonic frequency, three times the fundamental frequency. In Fig. 13A the fundamental is 3·5 c/deg., in 13B it is 5·0 c/deg. The function from Fig. 6B is positioned with its peak at the data point for the fundamental frequency.

were made at ¹⁄₁₀ octave intervals over a range of 3 octaves from 5 to 40 c/deg. with six readings at each frequency for each run. The means are plotted in Fig. 8.12. It can be seen that although there are slight excursions in the contrast sensitivity within one run, these bumps are not correlated on the frequency scale in the two runs. We therefore conclude that there are no significant excursions from a smooth contrast sensitivity function.

To be doubly sure of this conclusion, in a third run, we sampled a one octave range (from 10 to 20 c/deg.) at ¹⁄₂₀ octave intervals. The results are shown in Fig. 8.12 as squares and, to avoid confusion, they have been displaced downwards from the data for the first two runs by one half a log unit on the contrast sensitivity ordinate. These results again indicate that, if there are significant bumps, they are very small in amplitude, or closer than about one tenth of an octave in frequency, and therefore not detected by us.

ADAPTATION WITH A SQUARE-WAVE GRATING

Campbell & Robson (1968) and Robson & Campbell (1964) have shown that if contrast sensitivity is measured with a square-wave grating, the harmonic content plays an essential role in

determining the contrast activity for such gratings. The first higher harmonic in a square-wave grating is the third and it has an amplitude of one third that of the fundamental frequency; this third harmonic, three times the spatial frequency of the fundamental, is the only one which need be considered here, for the higher odd harmonics have a relatively small effective magnitude.

We might predict that the elevation of threshold for a sine wave at the third harmonic frequency might be substantially elevated after adaptation to a square-wave grating, if indeed these spatially selective mechanisms are operating independently. We measured the adaptation characteristic in the normal way after adapting to square-wave gratings of 3·5 c/deg. (Fig. 8.13A) and 5 c/deg. (Fig. 8.13B).

In each case the usual curve is fitted to the data, normalizing it to the fundamental frequency on the abscissa and the data point at that frequency on the ordinate. These results should be compared with Fig. 8.8, where sine-wave gratings were used for adaptation. The arrows indicate the fundamental and third harmonic frequencies. Clearly the harmonic component of the square wave pattern has caused a substantial elevation of threshold in the region of the third harmonic frequency.

Discussion

In the paper by Campbell et al. (1969), cells were found in the visual cortex of the cat each of which responded to a relatively narrow range of spatial frequency. A neurone responds to a limited band of spatial frequency and the position of this range varies over 4 octaves from unit to unit. In the present study on man we have found that prolonged viewing at one spatial frequency causes a depression of contrast sensitivity over a limited range of neighbouring frequencies. We suggest that the spatially sensitive mechanisms revealed by this adaptation reflect the properties of neurones in the human visual system, similar to those found in the cat, which are involved in the encoding of the spatial characteristics of the retinal image. Moreover, our initial observations on the human evoked potential clearly suggest that the adaptation phenomenon is associated with depression of neural activity.

In the cat cortex it was found that the spatial sensitivity function was surprisingly similar, at its high frequency end, from neurone to neurone whatever its position in the frequency spectrum. Likewise, psychophysically, we have found that for adapting spatial frequencies of 3·5–14·2 c/deg. the adaptation characteristic is remarkably constant. At very high spatial frequencies (20 and 28·3 c/deg.), beyond the resolution of the cat visual system, the human adaptation characteristic is somewhat narrower (Fig. 8.9). The functional significance of this latter finding is not yet clear.

On the evidence we have it is not possible to argue quantitatively from the response characteristics of the cat cortical neurones to the human adaptation characteristic, since we do not know, for example, how the responses of individual neurones combine when more than one neurone is activated by a particular spatial frequency. Therefore, at this stage no particular emphasis should be placed on the function we have arbitrarily chosen to fit the data and to compare one set of data with another. The striking finding is that one function describes so well the adaptation characteristic for a wide variety of adapting frequencies and contrasts.

This study of spatial adaptation has, in effect, been restricted to the fovea by the use of a centrally fixated field of 1·5° diameter. Under these experimental conditions the results of Fig. 8.10 suggest that there are no adaptable channels which have peak sensitivities of lower then 3 c/deg. It seems unlikely that the field size alone accounts for this observation since, at 3 c/deg., there were nearly 5 cycles of the grating present on the screen. It therefore appears that the size-detecting channels of central vision are handling a range of 3–4 octaves of spatial frequency.

A number of properties of the adaptation effect point to its central origin in the visual system. First, the adaptation is orientationally specific (Blakemore & Campbell, 1969), matching the orientation selectivity of units in the cat and monkey cortex (Hubel & Wiesel, 1962, 1968; Campbell, Cleland, Cooper & Enroth-Cugell, 1968). Secondly, we have shown that spatial adaptation through one eye causes threshold elevation through the other, suggesting that the effect occurs after binocular combination. We therefore suggest that the adaptation effect exposes the properties of central human neurones beyond the optic radiation. Strength would be added to this argument by evidence that individual neurones in the cat or monkey cortex do indeed adapt in a manner that would be predicted by this phenomenon.

Adaptation phenomena of this type might be of value in crossing the species barrier and allowing a description of the neurophysiology of man for many stimulus-coding mechanisms. An elegant example of this approach is Barlow & Hill's (1963) comparison of the after effect of seen motion and the depression of spontaneous activity after exposure to moving stimuli in the direction-selective units of the rabbit retina.

In this study we have intentionally used the simplest optical stimulus (Hopkins, 1962). The sine-wave grating is simple because it contains only one spatial frequency presented in one meridian. The most complex stimulus in Fourier terms is a single sharp disk of light for it contains a very wide band of spatial frequencies and they are present at all orientations. The "bandwidth" of the individual spatial mechanisms revealed by adaptation is quite narrow (about 1 octave at half amplitude; see Fig. 8.6*B*). Therefore any complex pattern of light on the retina, containing a wide spectrum of Fourier components, will cause activity in many mechanisms. We should like to suggest that the pattern of responses from the family of mechanisms may serve to encode the spatial content of the particular retinal image and thus lead, in an unknown manner, to its identification.

Is there any evidence to support this hypoth-

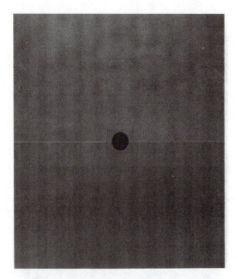

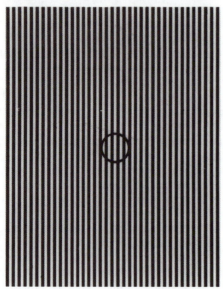

Explanation of Plate 8.1 The upper section consists of two low contrast gratings, one with a sinusoidal and the other a square-wave form. From a distance of about 1 m the wave forms should be clearly distinguishable. The lower section is a high contrast square-wave grating with a spatial frequency three times that of the upper.

The high contrast grating should be viewed for about 45 sec, allowing the gaze to wander around the circle. The dot in the upper section should now be fixated and an attempt made to discriminate the low contrast sine and square wave forms.

The low contrast gratings are photographs of the oscilloscope face. The high frequency pattern has been drawn with maximum contrast to facilitate adaptation.

esis? The experimental results shown in Fig. 8.13, where a square wave was used to produce adaptation, indicate that the sensitivity of two mechanisms was depressed (one at the fundamental spatial frequency and one at the third harmonic) by a single grating pattern.

The reader may perform the complementary experiment by viewing Plate 8.1 from a distance of about 1 m. The lower half of the upper square consists of a square-wave grating and directly above it is a sine wave of the same spatial frequency. At their contrast levels the difference is clearly distinguishable. The lower square is a high contrast grating with a spatial frequency three times that of the upper pair. The reader should view this high contrast grating, allowing his gaze to wander around the fixation circle. After about 45 sec the gaze should be transferred to the fixation point in the centre of the upper square and it will be noted that sine- and square-wave gratings are temporarily indistinguishable.

A further piece of evidence which supports the idea that spatially selective mechanisms contribute to the perception of complex spatial patterns is described by C. Blakemore & P. Sutton (1969, in preparation). They find that adaptation to one spatial frequency causes disturbance in the appearance of neighbouring frequencies, lower spatial frequencies appear to decrease and higher to increase their apparent frequencies. This suggests that adaptation of one mechanism disturbs the distribution of activity in the population of such mechanisms activated by a nearby spatial frequency.

An advantage of a system based on frequency analysis might be that it simplifies recognition of familiar objects presented at unfamiliar magnifications. Consider a child who has just learned to differentiate the letters of the alphabet and suppose that it is asked to recognize letters presented at quite different magnifications. It does this readily even although it has never observed the letters at these specific magnifications. We know that if we are so close to an object that we cannot perceive it in entireity it cannot be readily identified; "we cannot see the wood for the tree." Conversely, an object that subtends too small an angle cannot be recognized. Sutherland (1968) has lucidly reviewed the literature on size invariance and concludes 'that many species have the capacity to classify a shape as the same shape regardless of changes in size, at least over a considerable range, and that this capacity is innate."

There must be a limited range of spatial dimensions which the system can handle with facility and speed. If it analyses the distribution of spatial frequencies in an object into independent channels covering its range of operation and then uses the ratios of these frequencies to identify the object, it would render the absolute size of the object redundant for the purpose of image recognition, for the relative harmonic content is independent of absolute size. Only the harmonic content would have to be stored in the memory system and this would require a much smaller storage than if the appearance of every familiar object had to be learned at every common magnification. This generalization for size, and therefore distance would greatly facilitate the process of learning to recognize images in a natural environment. This system might then be analogous to the auditor system where we can identify a musical interval (fre-

quency ratio) independently of its position in the auditory spectrum (Helmholtz, 1877) .

Such a mechanism for analysing spatial frequencies would be difficult to envisage if it had to operate simultaneously in two dimensions. It may well be significant that the visual system also transmits the input signal through a number of separate orientationally selective channels, each of which can then analyse the spatial frequency content of the object over a narrow range of orientations (Campbell & Kulikowski, 1966). Although this arrangement would lead to a further economy in the size of the memory store it would also carry the penalty that one would be restricted to recognizing familiar objects only if they were presented at the learned orientation.

HERE IS THE EVIDENCE

We cannot generalize for orientation as we can do so remarkably well for magnification.

REFERENCES

Barlow, H. B. & Hill, R. M. (1963). Evidence for a physiological explanation of the waterfall phenomenon and figural after-effects. *Nature, Lond. 200*, 1345–347.

Blakemore, C. & Campbell, F. W. (1969). Adaptation to spatial stimuli. *J. Physiol. 200*, 11–13.

Campbell, F. W., Carpenter, R. H. S., & Levinson, J. Z. (1969). Visibility of aperiodic patterns compared with that of sinusoidel gratings. *J. Physiol.* (In the Press.)

Campbell, F. W., Cleland, B. C., Cooper, G. F., & Enroth-Cugell, C. (1968). The selectivity of visual cortical cells to moving gratings. *J. Physiol., 198*, 237–250.

Campbell, F. W., Cooper, G. F., & Enroth-Cugell, C. (1969). The spatial selectivity of the visual cells of the cat. *J. Physiol., 203*, 223–236.

Campbell, F. W. & Green, D. G. (1965). Optical and retinal factors affecting visual resolution. *Physiol., 181*, 576–593.

Campbell, F. W. & Kulikowski, J. J. (1966). Orientational selectivity of the human visual system. *J. Physiol., 181*, 437–446.

Campbell, F. W., Kulikowski, J. J., & Levinson, J. (1966). The effect of orientation on the visual resolution of gratings. *J. Physiol., 187*, 427–436.

Campbell, F. W. & Robson, J. G. (1988). Application of Fourier analysis to the visibility of gratings. *J. Physiol. 197*, 561–566.

Cobb, W. A., Ettlinger, G., & Morton, H. B. (1968). Cerebral potentials evoked in man by pattern reversal and their suppression in visual rivalry. *J. Physiol., 195*, 33P.

Dilinsky, A. S. (1968). Orientation-specific effects of patterns of adapting light on visual acuity. *J. Opt. Soc. Am., 58.* 13–18.

Helmholtz, H. (1877). *On the Sensations of Tone*. New York: Dover Publications Inc. (reprinted 1954)

Hopkins, H. H. (1962). 21st Thomas Young Oration. The application of frequency response techniques in optics. *Proc. Phys. Soc., 79*, 889–919.

Hubel, D. H. & Wiesel, T. N. (1962). Receptive fields, binocular interaction and functional architecture in the cat's visual cortex. *J. Physiol., 160*, 106–154.

Hubel, D. H. & Wiesel, T. N. (1968). Receptive fields and functional architecture of monkey striate cortex. *J. Physiol., 195*, 216–243.

Nye, P. W. (1968). Binocular acuity of the pigeon measured in terms of the modulation transfer function. *Vision Res., 8*, 1023–1041.

Pantle, A. & Sekuler, R. (1968). Size-detecting mechanisms in human vision. *Science, N.Y., 162*, 1146–1148.

Patel, A. S. (1966). Spatial resolution by the human visual system. The effect of mean retinal illumination. *J. Opt. Soc. Am., 56*, 689–694.

Robson, J. G. & Campbell, F. W. (1984). A threshold contrast function for the visual system. *Symposium on the Physiological Basis for Form Discrimination*, pp. 44–48. Hunter Laboratory of Psychology, Brown University, Providence, R.I.

Sutherland, N. S. (1988). Outlines of a theory of visual pattern recognition in animals and man. *Proc. R. Soc. B, 171*, 297–317.

Introduction to Reading 9

For well over a century, studies of the perceptual deficits suffered by people who had experienced brain damage due to stroke or to closed head injury had provided the best available evidence about the functional architecture of the human brain. There are many fascinating, and sometimes sad, case descriptions of patients who have lost the ability to recognize faces or objects, to see color or motion, or to notice objects in certain parts of the visual field (e.g., Sacks, 1985; Zeki, 1993; see Reading 16 by Lissauer for a detailed description of a case of visual agnosia, the inability to recognize objects following brain injury). These studies revealed, long before neurophysiological and neuroimaging techniques were available for direct measurements, that most visual functions are carried out in the posterior brain (in the occipital and parts of the temporal and parietal lobes), and that visual functions appear to be roughly modular: that is, local brain damage can have a highly specific perceptual effect (e.g., it can cause a deficit in seeing visual motion but leave color and form vision intact; Zihl, von Cramon, & Mai, 1983). However, because neuropsychology depends on "experiments of nature," precise correlation between structure and function were hard to come by.

The advent of neurophysiological techniques in the 1940s and 50s led to direct measurements of single-cell discharge first in invertebrates, then in vertebrates, in mammals such as cats, and finally in non-human primates. In the 1970s, single-cell recording in monkeys revealed visual areas that appeared to be functionally specialized (e.g., Zeki, 1974). Brains of rhesus and macaque monkeys are similar in many respects to human brains, but they are by no means identical. Thus, while invasive neurophysiological investigations of the monkey brain can yield important hints as to the structure and function of the human brain, they necessarily provide only an approximation.

In the 1980s and 90s, new techniques emerged for measuring the function of the intact human brain. The first of these to come into wide use was positron emission tomography (PET). In this method, a radioactive isotope is introduced to a volunteer's bloodstream (e.g., by inhaling air containing $C^{15}O_2$, radioactive carbon dioxide). Brain regions that are highly active during a particular task require oxygen and glucose, and will therefore demand an increased supply of oxygenated blood. A PET scanner can measure the average cerebral blood flow (CBF) over a several minute interval by detecting local concentrations of radioactivity. The resulting 3-D map of cortical blood flow can be subtracted from a corresponding map when the subject is either resting or performing a baseline task, and this difference image represents regions of increased activity associated with the perceptual task in question.

In this selection, Zeki and colleagues wished to determine what parts of the brain are active during the perception of color and of motion. At the time the study was undertaken, studies of achromatopsia (cortical color blindness; Meadows, 1974) and akinetopsia (cortical motion blindness; Zihl et al., 1983), together with studies of single-cell discharges in monkeys had provided clear hints about what brain region should be expected to respond to these stimuli. However, no evidence from the intact human brain had been collected.

This study confirmed that the two areas that had been implicated by previous neuropsychological and neurophysiological studies were also present in the human brain. The outcome was not unexpected. However, the application of this approach to investigating the functional properties of the brain was a crucial first step in opening up this promising new technique for further applications. Reading 23 by O'Craven et al. illustrates the use of functional magnetic resonance imaging (fMRI), a second imaging technology that was developed in the early 1990s, to further extend understanding of the neural basis of perception.

REFERENCES

Meadows, J. C. (1974). Disturbed perception of colors associated with localized cerebral lesions. *Brain, 97*, 615–632.

Sacks, O. (1985). *The man who mistook his wife for a hat and other clinical tales.* New York: Summit Books.

Zeki, S. M. (1974). Functional organization of a visual area in the posterior bank of the superior temporal sulcus of the rhesus monkey. *Journal of Physiology, 236*, 549–573.

Zeki, S. (1993). *A vision of the brain.* Oxford: Blackwell.

Zihl, J., von Cramon, D., & Mai, N. (1983). Selective disturbance of movement vision after bilateral brain damage. *Brain, 106*, 313–340.

READING 9

A Direct Demonstration of Functional Specialization in Human Visual Cortex

S. Zeki, J. D. G. Watson, C. J. Lueck, K. J. Friston, C. Kennard,
and R. S. J. Frackowiak

We have used positron emission tomography (PET), which measures regional cerebral blood flow (rCBF), to demonstrate directly the specialization of function in the normal human visual cortex. A novel technique, statistical parametric mapping, was used to detect foci of significant change in cerebral blood flow within the prestriate cortex, in order to localize those parts involved in the perception of color and visual motion. For color, we stimulated the subjects with a multicolored abstract display containing no recognizable objects (Land color Mondrian) and contrasted the resulting blood flow maps with those obtained when subjects viewed an identical display consisting of equiluminous shades of gray. The comparison identified a unique area (area V4) located in the lingual and fusiform gyri of the prestriate cortex. For motion, blood flow maps when subjects viewed moving or stationary black and white random-square patterns were contrasted. The comparison identified a unique area located in the region of the temporo-parieto-occipital junction (area V5). We thus provide direct evidence to show that, just as in the macaque monkey, different areas of the human prestriate visual cortex are specialized for different attributes of vision. The striate cortex (V1) and the contiguous visual area (V2), which in the monkey brain feed both the homologous areas, were active in all 4 conditions. This pattern of activity allowed us to use an extension of the approach to assess the functional relationship between the 3 areas during color and motion stimulation. This is based on an hypothesis-led analysis of the covariance structure of the blood flow maps and promises to be a powerful tool for inferring anatomical pathways in the normal human brain. In this study, we were able to demonstrate a positive functional relationship between areas V1/V2 and V4 during color vision and areas V1/V2 and V5 during motion stimulation, reflecting the anatomical connections between these areas in the macaque monkey.

The concept of functional specialization in the cerebral cortex can be traced back to the beginnings of modern neurology in the middle of the last century when Broca (1861) in France and Fritsch and Hitzig (1870) in Germany firmly established its foundations by showing that the integrity of specific, separate cortical areas is necessary for the production of articulate speech and voluntary movement. Subsequent work charting and defining the many cortical areas associated with different functions has been a triumph of neurology. By the 1930s, Lashley could write that "in

193

the field of neurophysiology no fact is more firmly established than the functional differentiation of various parts of the cerebral cortex. . . . No one today can seriously believe that the different parts of the cerebral cortex all have the same functions or can entertain for a moment the proposition of Hermann that because the mind is a unit the brain must also act as a unit" (Lashley, 1931).

Yet, it is the very unitary nature of the visual image in the brain, one in which the different attributes of the visual scene—form, color, motion, depth—are seen in precise spatiotemporal registration, that was to conceal the profound division of labor within the visual cortex. The error was reinforced by the anatomical organization of the visual pathways. The cortical input from the retina is funneled through the striate cortex [Henschen's "cortical retina" (1930)], lesions in which lead to absolute blindness, usually without dissociation of visual submodalities. It therefore seemed natural to Holmes (1918, 1945) and others (Monbrun, 1939; Teuber et al., 1960; Duke-Elder, 1971) to consider that the striate cortex (area V1) was the sole visual "perceptive center" in humans, while the cortex surrounding it associated the "received" visual "impressions," contrasting them with previous "impressions" of a similar kind (for review, see Zeki, 1990a). Thus, the suggestion, based on imperfect early clinical evidence (Verrey, 1888; Mackay and Dunlop, 1899), that a specific region of this "association" cortex in the lingual and fusiform gyri (which, at that time, were considered by some to be part of the primary visual receptive center) may be specialized for color, considered to be a visual impression, seemed improbable. Henschen (1930) wrote that, if this view were true, then "with the striate cortex destroyed and with cortex of that other gyrus [lingual and fusiform] intact, a patient would have to be absolutely blind and yet be able to see colors, which makes no sense." Further evidence in favor of functional specialization in the occipital cortex was repeatedly discounted and, indeed, the concept "vanished" from the clinical literature (Damasio, 1985).

The concept of functional specialization in the visual cortex is therefore more recent (Zeki, 1974a, 1978a). It is based on studies of the macaque monkey, which show that, of the many visual areas (Cragg, 1969; Zeki, 1969, 1971) that lie outside the striate cortex, one area (V5) is specialized for visual motion, while another, anatomically distinct area (V4) is specialized for color (Zeki, 1973, 1974b, 1977). Following this discovery, renewed attempts have been made to chart the specialized visual areas in the human brain. However, the recent evidence in favor of dissociation of color and movement processing in the cerebral cortex of humans is still indirect. It is based, in part, on naturally occurring cortical lesions that give rise to an inability to see colors (achromatopsia, e.g., Pearlman et al., 1979; Damasio et at., 1980; Kolmel, 1988) or to cerebral motion blindness (Zihl et al., 1983; Thurston et al., 1988). Unfortunately, such lesions are uncontrolled and uncontrollable in their extent. It is also based, in part, on psychophysical evidence which shows that human subjects find that the perception of motion becomes difficult, and even incoherent, when asked to discriminate moving stimuli distinguished from the background on the basis of color alone, in other words, that the motion system is "color blind" (Ramachandran and Gregory, 1978; Carney et al., 1987; Ramachandran, 1987).

In this study, we wanted to demonstrate functional specialization in the normal human visual cortex directly and to chart the anatomy of the areas involved. Obviously, this requires the use of at least 2 different visual stimuli, representing 2 different submodalities, in the same study. We used the same 2 submodalities, motion and color, that were used to establish functional specialization in the monkey visual cortex (Zeki, 1973, 1974b). Our approach was to use positron emission tomography (PET) to detect significant regional changes in cerebral blood flow (rCBF) in the brains of normal human subjects when they viewed stimuli chosen to emphasize color or motion. We were encouraged by the earlier experiments of Fox et al. (1986), who showed that PET can provide an accurate picture of the position and topographic organization of the primary visual, or striate, cortex.

Preliminary reports of these results have been published (Lueck et al., 1989; Cunningham et al., 1990).

Materials and Methods

Nine normal volunteers were studied. All were male, 7 were right handed, and their ages ranged from 21 to 43 yr (mean, 29 yr). Two experiments were performed. In the first, 6 subjects were stimulated with colored and isoluminant gray-shaded abstract displays occupying the central 40° of the field of view. In the second, the other 3 subjects were presented with a random array of stationary or moving small black and white squares. All subjects gave informed written consent, and the studies were approved by the Hammersmith Hospital Ethics Committee. Permission to administer radiation was obtained from the Administration of Radioactive Substances Advisory Committee of the Department of Health, U.K.

Paradigm design. Both experiments involved 6 sequential measurements of rCBF during the presentation of different visual stimuli. Also in both experiments, 3 different stimuli were presented in balanced order (ABCCBA) to remove time and habituation effects. The stimuli were as follows.

Experiment 1. Stimulus A: Eyes closed. Stimulus B: Eyes open, with the central 40° occupied by an abstract display of 15 multicolored squares and rectangles (Land color Mondrian; Land, 1974). Stimulus C: Eyes open, with the central field occupied by an isoluminant gray shaded version of the colored Mondrian presented in stimulus B.

Experiment 2. Stimulus A: eyes closed. Stimulus B: Eyes open, with the central field occupied by a stationary display of black and white random squares. Stimulus C: Eyes open, with the same display moving in a random direction every 5 sec.

The visual stimuli. Displays were generated on a high-resolution AMIGA monitor (Commodore Computers Inc.), presented at a viewing distance of 47 cm and occupying the central 40° of the field of view. The Mondrian we used was a collage of 15 squares and rectangles of different shapes and colors, assembled to form an abstract scene with no recognizable objects, thus minimizing the role of memory and learning. No area of the Mondrian was surrounded by another area of single color only, thus eliminating any effects that might be attributable to induced colors or to color contrasts. The isoluminant gray values were determined in a separate calibration experiment in which each of the colors from the Mondrian was individually displayed in the form of a vertical grating alternating temporally with a gray grating at a frequency of 5 Hz. The luminance of the gray grating was gradually varied until the illusory perception of motion ceased. This was taken to be the isoluminant value for that color (Anstis and Cavanagh, 1983). The procedure was repeated for

each color in turn, and a gray replica of the color Mondrian was thus constructed. With each rectangle isoluminant with its color counterpart, the only difference between the color and the gray displays was the absence of color in the latter.

For motion, we used 2 versions of a black and white random-square pattern in which an array of approximately 100 small black squares, each subtending 1°, were displayed on a white background. The display could be stationary or moving. When in motion, all the squares moved constantly at a rate of 6°/sec, in 1 of 8 directions, ranging from 0° to 315° in steps of 45°. The direction of motion was changed every 5 sec. To prevent visual adaptation and fading, subjects were asked to move their eyes back and forth slowly along a horizontal boundary line subtending approximately 5° over the central part of the field of view in the color experiment, and to fixate on a small stationary square during the motion experiment.

Blood flow measurement. Cerebral blood flow was measured with the dynamic/integral technique described by Lammertsma et al. (1990), of which a brief account follows. Subjects inhaled trace quantities of $C^{15}O_2$, provided at a concentration of 6 MBq/ml and a flow rate of 500 ml/min through a standard oxygen face mask for a period of 2 min. The effective dose equivalent of each administration was 1.2 mSv. Twenty-one successive dynamic PET scans were collected within a period of 3.5 min, starting 0.5 min before administration of the flow tracer ($C^{15}O_2$). Stimuli were administered throughout the period of scanning, though the blood flow maps were constructed only from the integral of tissue activity recorded for the 2 min after commencing administration of tracer. Absolute blood flow measurements could then be calculated from the second-by-second radioactivity measurements recorded from a small radial artery cannula during scanning, corrected by reference to the series of dynamic PET scans. The latter is necessary to correct for the distortion of the radial artery counts relative to the true activity profile entering the brain due to dispersion and delay of the blood in the brachial artery and cannula before it reaches the radiation detector. The corrected arterial input function and the integrated counts in the brain were used to derive the quantitative parametric images of rCBF. Scanning of activity in the tissues of the brain was performed using a CTI 931/08/12 PET scanner (CTI Inc., Knoxville, TN), whose physical characteristics have been described elsewhere (Spinks et al., 1988). The scanner collects data in 15 planes covering an axial field of view of 10.13 cm, with no interplane dead space. This permits imaging of the brain from cerebellum to vertex with a resolution of 8.5 × 8.5 × 7.0 mm at full width half-maximum (FWHM), following reconstruction with a Hanning filter of cutoff frequency 0.5. The reconstructed data of each plane were displayed in a 128 × 128-pixel format, with each pixel 2.05 × 2.05 mm.

Image analysis. All calculations and image matrix manipulations were carried out on Sun 3/60 computers (Sun Computers Inc.) using ANALYZE image display software (BRU, Mayo Foundation) and PROMALAB (Mathworks Inc.).

The 15 original scan slices of each data set (6.75-mm interplane distance) were transformed using bilinear interpolation into a standard stereotactic space, corresponding to the atlas of Talairach and Tournoux (1988). The intercommissural line was identified directly from the PET images according to a previously described method (Friston et al., 1989). To increase the signal-to-noise ratio and to allow summation between locally dispersed sites of activation from different individuals each image was smoothed using a Gaussian filter (FWHM, 10 pixels). This dispersion is due, in large part, to normal variations in gyral shape and direction between subjects. In the standard stereotactic space, each pixel was 2 mm^2, and the interplane distance corresponded to 4 mm.

Statistical analysis. Because of the confounding effect of global changes in cerebral blood flow (CBF), the differences in global CBF between subjects were removed using an analysis of covariance (ANCOVA), as previously described (Friston et al., 1990). All analyses were performed on a pixel-by-pixel basis. This generated 6 adjusted group means and the associated error variance for each pixel. Planned comparisons of these means were performed using the t statistic, the hypothesis being that some specific regions of the brain would be preferentially activated with specific types of visual stimulation. The t distribution was transformed into the standard normal distribution to render the statistical parametric maps (SPMs) Gaussian. Under the null hypothesis that there will be no regional difference during visual stimulation, the SPMs are stationary; that is, their autocorrelation function (the degree of interdependency of adjacent pixel values) is the same over the entire map. The SPMs were thresholded to make a correction for the effective number of independent measures in the SPM. This is less than the number of pixels because of the smoothness resulting from reconstruction, filtering, and averaging of the images. The threshold was set to give an expected false positive every 20 planes. This threshold was determined by measuring smoothness empirically and modeling the SPM as a stationary Gaussian process (K. J. Friston et al., unpublished observations). Significant pixels ($p < 0.05$) were then displayed on coronal, sagittal, and transverse views of the brain.

The only comparable method of image analysis in the literature is that described by Fox et al. (1986). The similarities between the above approach and that of Fox et al. include the following: Both use a standard stereotactic coordinate space and attempt to remove the confounding effects of global differences in cerebral blood flow. Both are done pixel by pixel and attempt to assess significance of change using an estimate of error variance. The major differences include the following: our approach removes global variance statistically, by an analysis of covariance, rather than by a simple proportional normalization, by division of pixel values by whole-brain mean flow. Our estimation of error variance is longitudinal, across subjects for each stimulus, and performed independently for each pixel in the image. Our approach thus accounts for regional changes in error variance, or the "reliability" of the regional responses to physiological activation. The resultant images (SPMs), reflecting differences in activation, are statistical in a formal sense in that they reflect significance of local change irrespective of changes elsewhere. Finally, the findings are accepted as significant only if they survive a correction for the effective number of pixels analyzed. In contrast, the method of Fox et al. (1986) determines the variance in pixels across the entire brain resulting from the subtraction of 2 conditions. It is tested in a global sense for deviation from the normal distribution, and if a significant difference is found, outliers are identified by thresholding.

Planned comparison of differences. Two planned comparisons were made in each experiment (color and motion). First, a comparison was made of the condition with the key visual component, color or motion, and the corresponding control, gray or stationary. Second, a comparison of vision with nonvision, that is, the middle 4 condition means with the first and last, was performed. These comparisons were intended to identify specific cortical areas critically concerned with the modality in question (color or motion) and also the cortex implicated more generally in vision.

To estimate the size, as opposed to significance, of the increases, the adjusted group rCBFs for the different stimuli were compared at locations identified by maxima in the SPM. Because the original scans were smoothed, these adjusted pixel values correspond to the adjusted mean rCBF of a 20-mm region centered on the chosen pixel.

Analysis of covariance structure. In order to investigate further the relationship of distributed brain systems underlying vision, covariance SPMs were generated. Our aim was to make inferences about anatomical connections between the areas activated in the study. The maps were designed to show which areas covaried systematically with the rCBF variation of a reference pixel in a chosen area, for example, V4. This analysis assumes that the brain is composed of certain regions whose activity is specifically perturbed (up or down) by aspects of vision and of other areas whose activity is independent, with no relation to the visual stimuli presented. With a particular function such as vision, regions collectively involved must constitute a highly covarying network. By choosing a reference pixel in one region within this system, the remaining components of the system should be identified in the corresponding covariance SPM. Clearly, this approach is descriptive and must be hypothesis led.

Five reference pixels were identified, their locations indicated by the position of maxima in the contrast SPMs. These pixels were in the striate cortex (V1), the color centers (V4), and the motion centers (V5) in both hemispheres.

Results

Comparison of Conditions

The cortical areas activated nonspecifically by vision were centered on, and coextensive with, the striate and immediate peristriate cortex. Because we could not distinguish a boundary between V1 and the contiguous visual area V2, we refer to this zone as V1/V2 in this paper. No other brain re-

gions showed increased rCBF of such high significance. The results of this first comparison for the color and the motion study were qualitatively equivalent, and therefore only the SPM from the color study is shown in Color Plate 9.1.

In the first experiment, comparison of color and gray scans demonstrated a focal, bilateral activation in the lingual and fusiform gyri on the inferior and medial aspects of the occipital lobes (Color Plate 9.2). We refer to this area as area V4. Although both sides are clearly shown, the statistical analysis indicates a lateralization of function to the left, as suggested in our preliminary communication on 3 subjects (Lueck et al., 1989).

In the second experiment, comparison of moving and stationary displays demonstrated a focal, bilateral activation at the confluence of temporal, parietal, and occipital cortices situated laterally on the cortical convexity (Color Plate 9.3), approximately at the junction of Brodmann's areas 19 and 37. We refer to this area as area V5.

The dissociation between areas that were maximally active during color and visual motion stimulation is direct evidence of functional parcellation in the human prestriate visual cortex.

Quantitative Changes in rCBF

Locations of V1/V2, V4, and V5 (right and left) were identified from maxima in the SPMs (Color Plates 9.1–9.3). These locations were used to tabulate the adjusted mean rCBF for each condition in each area. The stereotactic and rCBF data are presented in Tables 9.1 and 9.2. The activity in the primary visual cortex was different in the 2 experiments. In the first experiment, the increase in rCBF in area V1/V2 was 17%, and, in the second, the rCBF increased by 24%, presumably reflecting the difference in stimulation of the striate cortex by the Mondrians and the random-pattern stimuli.

Covariance Structure

In the first experiment, when the reference pixel was placed in either of the color centers (V4), positive covariance was demonstrated in the striate and peristriate regions (V1/V2) and contralateral color area (Color Plate 9.4). Similarly, in the second experiment, the primary visual areas (V1/V2) covaried with the motion area (V5), as did the contralateral motion center. This suggests that V1 sends independent parallel outputs to V4 and to V5 and that areas V4 and V5 in one hemisphere are connected with their counterparts in the other, points taken up in the Discussion.

Discussion

The neurobiologist has obtained much information about cortical function from anatomical and single-cell electrophysiological experiments, and such experiments were the basis for the demonstration of functional specialization in the macaque monkey visual cortex (Zeki, 1974a, 1978a). To study the human brain in such detail is more difficult, but the advent of PET has made it possible to record activity simultaneously from the entire human brain, though with limited spatial and temporal resolution. Nevertheless, the capacity to observe all cerebral areas participating in the performance of a task, or subtending a physiological function, allows us not only to localize function, but also to make inferences about functional anatomical connections. In this way, we can study an isolated system in the healthy human brain.

The main difficulty we faced in investigating the visual system was choosing appropriately specific stimuli that would activate the striate and certain prestriate visual areas, but not others. The problem was awkward because most visual stimuli will contain attributes of possible relevance to many specialized visual areas. For example, in addition to its potential effects on V4, a Mondrian contains oriented boundaries that, in the monkey, will activate cells in areas V3 and V3A that are orientation selective, even though they are indifferent to the color of the stimulus (Zeki, 1978c). The solution chosen was to contrast scans obtained with stimuli identical in all respects save the one of interest. The stimuli we used, Land's Mondrian display and the moving random pattern, were designed for and had been effectively used in animal studies and human psychophysical experiments. They allowed us to demonstrate separate motion and color centers in the human prestriate visual cortex well outside the striate area, thus proving that functional specialization is an important feature of the organization of the human visual cortex. Our results also indicate that previous conclusions about the organization of the visual cortex drawn from anatomy and single-cell recording in

the monkey, which is unable to communicate a percept such as color verbally, are valid for the human brain.

The Color Center (area V4)

The data show that, when comparing brain activity during color and gray stimulation, the only area showing a significant change of activity was in the region of the lingual and fusiform gyri. This area lies outside the striate cortex and is the same area implicated in achromatopsia (cerebral color blindness) by clinical studies (Verrey, 1888; Mackay and Dunlop, 1899; Lenz, 1921; Pearlman et al., 1979; Damasio et al., 1980; Kolmel, 1988; Sacks et al., 1988). The clinical literature is unclear as to whether the color center lies in both gyri or is restricted to only one. Verrey (1888) located it in both, which he mistakenly considered to be part of the primary visual cortex. Mackay and Dunlop (1899), on the other hand, located it in the fusiform gyrus. A similar location can be inferred from the work of Lenz (1921), whose patient was examined postmortem in the greatest detail. Unfortunately, our data do not clarify the problem further, except that the coordinates of the area of maximal change of rCBF lie in the fusiform gyrus. In the macaque monkey, V4 is well removed from V1 by other areas, in particular area V2, throughout most of its extent. It comes closest to V1 in the region of foveal representation of the latter (Zeki, 1971). The topographical arrangement of visual areas is somewhat different in humans, but it would be reasonable to expect that V2, which surrounds human V1 throughout most of its extent (Horton and Hedley-Whyte, 1984), would be one area interposed between V1 and the human homologue of V4. If so, then the inferior portion of V2 should lie in the lingual gyrus, because the striate cortex emerges inferiorly from the calcarine sulcus onto it. Hence, the fusiform gyrus is a more likely location for the color center, but the precise localization difficulty is magnified by the variability of the sulcal and gyral pattern in this part of the occipital lobe from subject to subject.

The motion center (area V5)

As shown in the second experiment, the area of significantly changed rCBF during motion stimulation was well removed from area V4. It was lo-

TABLE 9.1. Experiment 1: Color Versus Gray

Region	CBF (adjusted group means; ml dl⁻¹ min⁻¹)			Talairach coordinates[a]	Z score
	Rest	Gray	Color		
Right V4	59	62	64	+20, −66, −4	2.90*
Left V4	65	65	68	−26, −68, −8	3.93
Mean	62	63	66		
Right V5	51	51	52		
Left V5	46	49	48		
Mean	49	50	50		
V1/V2	62	72	72	−4, −90, 0	13.0

Adjusted group mean rCBF for each condition (averaged from 2 estimations for each of the 3 physiological states) in the areas indicated in the SPMs to have shown significant rCBF change (at $p < 0.05$ level) for color versus gray. Flow values have been normalized by ANCOVA to a mean flow of 50 ml dl⁻¹ min⁻¹. Loci were identified on the SPM in which V4 was activated. V1/V2 was identified in this experiment, and the coordinates were confirmed on the SPM from the second experiment (see Table 9.2).

[a] Talairach coordinates are stated as mm x, y, z from the anterior ACPC line and correspond to the stereotactic conventions of the atlas of Talairach and Tournoux (1988).

*Score not significant at $p < 0.05$, corrected for multiple comparisons.

cated more laterally and superiorly, at the junction of parietal and occipital cortices (the junction of Brodmann's cytoarchitectonic areas 19 and 37). As far as we can tell, this is similar to the site of activation reported in abstract by Miezin et al. (1987).

The topographical separation between V5 and V4 is impressive. It allows us to determine directly, with certainty, that functional specialization is an organizational feature of the human visual cortex. V5, as demonstrated in this study, was much smaller than the extent of the lesion leading to cerebral motion blindness in the unique patient of Zihl et al. (1983). Macaque V5 is surrounded by satellite areas also involved with visual motion, but in different ways (Zeki, 1980; Desimone and Ungerleider, 1986; Komatsu and Wurtz, 1988; Tanaka et al., 1986). It is possible that, with the use of a greater repertoire of specific stimuli, motion-sensitive cortex surrounding V5 may be demonstrated in the future.

While we refer to human V4 and V5 as the color and motion centers, respectively, we do not wish to imply that the processing of color or motion is necessarily their only function, or that these are the only areas involved with those submodalities of vision. We state only that color and motion are among their chief functions. Indeed, in the

macaque monkey, both V4 and V5 are parts of more extensive pathways that include other areas. The motion pathways include areas V1 and V2 in addition to V5, as well as areas in the parietal and temporal cortices. In addition to V4, the color pathways include V1 and V2 and other regions of the temporal and parietal cortices (Zeki and Shipp, 1988). That the parietal and inferior temporal cortices were not significantly activated in our experiments almost certainly reflects the fact that we chose the simplest possible visual stimuli. For color, the stimuli were designed to minimize any effect of memory and learning, both of which may be important functions of the inferior temporal cortex. For motion, factors such as absolute and relative position, important functions of the parietal cortex, were controlled out. Corbetta et al. (1990) have shown that the use of attention directed to a specific visual submodality, at least for shape and color, activates many areas, including the areas defined in our present and previous study (Lueck et al., 1989). This implies that precise localization of the perception of attributes of vision cannot be adequately demonstrated when factors such as attention are added to appropriate visual stimulation. The use of more sophisticated stimuli may, in the future, give us insights into the nature and role of the target projection fields of V4 and V5 in human vision.

Area V1 (the striate cortex)

Not surprisingly, area V1 was active in all our experiments when the eyes were open. The spatial resolution of the scanner was not high enough to determine its boundaries with the precision possible with Nissl- or myelin-stained sections. It is interesting that the increase in activity in V1 was higher in the motion study, regardless of whether the "motion" stimulus was moving or stationary (Table 9.2). Why this should be so is not entirely clear. The pattern of random small black dots contained many more boundaries of higher contrast than the 15 rectangles forming the color Mondrian, and the total luminance of the 2 displays was not equivalent. It might therefore have been a more powerful stimulus for a visual area that contains many more orientation-selective than wavelength-selective cells. This explanation derives some support from the observation that the presence of motion in the stimulus gave rise only to a minimal increase in striate rCBF.

TABLE 9.2. Experiment 2: Motion Versus Static

Region	CBF (adjusted group means; ml dl⁻¹ min⁻¹)			Talairach coordinates[a]	Z score
	Rest	Static	Motion		
Right V4	61	66	66		
Left V4	64	66	64		
Mean	63	66	65		
Right V5	49	48	52	+38, −62, +8	5.58
Left V5	47	49	53	−38, −74, +8	4.51
Mean	48	49	52		
VI/V2	55	68	69	−4, −90, 0	

Adjusted group mean rCBF for each condition (averaged from 2 estimations for each of the 3 physiological states) in the areas indicated in the SPMs to have shown significant rCBF range (at $p < 0.05$ level) for motion versus static. Flow values have been normalized by ANCOVA to a mean flow of 50 mi dl⁻¹min⁻¹. Loci were identified on the SPM in which V5 was activated. V1/V2 was identified in the first experiment (see Table 1), and the coordinates were confirmed on the SPM from this experiment. [a]Talairach coordinates are stated as mm x, y, z from the anterior end of the ACPC line and correspond to the stereotactic conventions of the atlas of Talairach and Tournoux (1988).

Area V2

While we have been able to demonstrate unambiguously that V4 and V5 are 2 separate, functionally specialized visual areas, we were unsuccessful in distinguishing between areas V1 and V2. We suppose that the area of high activity at the occipital pole found in all our scans represents area V2 in addition to V1. The human studies of Burkhalter and Bernardo (1989) show that, as in the macaque, V2 surrounds V1 and is connected to it. There are 2 major difficulties in separating the 2 areas. One is the current spatial resolution of PET studies, and the other is that both areas were probably active in all conditions, given that, at least in the monkey, all submodalities of vision are represented in both (Baizer et al., 1977; Zeki, 1978d; DeYoe and Van Essen, 1985; Shipp and Zeki, 1985).

Human V1 and V2 are very similar to that of the macaque in terms of cytochrome oxidase architecture (Horton and Hedley-Whyte, 1984; Burkhalter and Bernardo, 1989). However, at least in the macaque, the nature of the functional grouping is different in the 2 areas, with color and motion signals being segregated in different layers of V1 as opposed to different stripes in V2 (Livingstone and Hubel, 1984; DeYoe and Van Essen, 1985; Shipp and Zeki, 1985). One might

therefore expect that, with higher resolution in the functional images, the differences between the 2 areas and therefore their boundaries should be resolvable. Even allowing for the limited resolution of our PET SPMs, the region of high activity in the posterior part of the occipital lobe is too widespread to be confined to V1 (Color Plate 9.1). This suggests that a visual area adjoining V1, located in the lingual gyrus inferiorly and the cuneus superiorly, is active in addition to V1, and we suppose that part of this area corresponds to human V2.

Functional Connections of Human Visual Cortex: Parallel Outputs from Area V1 to Areas V4 and V5 in the Human Brain

Confidence that the areas we have demonstrated are visual in function is supported by the fact that their rCBF covaried consistently with rCBF changes in the striate cortex. This contrasted with other areas, for example, the primary motor cortex, whose rCBF did not covary systematically with V1/V2. Covariation between areas must indicate a functional and hence anatomical connection between them, either directly or through intervening areas, which would then also be expected to covary with the others. This method of analysis may therefore be used to provide powerful, though indirect, evidence of functional anatomical connections in the normal human brain.

Anatomical evidence in the macaque monkey shows that V1 is connected with V5, both directly (Zeki, 1969, 1971; Lund et al., 1975) and through V2 (Zeki, 1971; Shipp and Zeki, 1985, 1989a,b). V1 is also connected with V4. This connection is mainly through V2 (Zeki, 1971; DeYoe and Van Essen, 1985; Shipp and Zeki, 1985; Zeki and Shipp, 1989), but there is also a direct output to V4 from the foveal representation in V1 (Zeki, 1978b; Yukie and Iwai, 1985). Compatible with this is the finding that, during motion stimulation, V1/V2 covaries with V5, and during color stimulation, it covaries with V4. In addition to demonstrating indirectly the connections between V1/V2 and these 2 areas, the results show that, as in the macaque monkey, the outputs must be in parallel, because V4 was not active in the motion study, nor was V5 in the color study.

The demonstration of parallel outputs from the monkey striate cortex led to the conclusion that V1 must act as a segregator, parceling out different signals to different prestriate areas (Zeki, 1975), a conclusion since confirmed (Livingstone and Hubel, 1984). In a similar way, our demonstration of parallel outputs from human V1/V2 leads to the conclusion that V1/V2 of the human brain also acts functionally as a segregator. This is a safe conclusion because it is based on a large body of anatomical results from the monkey visual cortex. The importance of the demonstration of this similarity in the organization of monkey and human brain lies in the fact that, by analogy, one may be able to make predictions about other, as yet uncharted, human cortical areas, just as predictions about the internal functional organization of areas in monkeys can be made by studying their anatomical connections (Zeki and Shipp, 1988; Zeki, 1990b). A second conclusion is that there is much information in the PET scans from which one can make functional and anatomical deductions.

In summary, a detailed analysis of the PET data reported here allows us to demonstrate parallelism in the human visual cortex and to infer connections between the visual areas. This goes well beyond our initial aim to obtain direct evidence for functional specialization in human visual cortex. We had no notion when we started of how rich a source of information such noninvasive studies could be, especially when coupled with detailed knowledge gained from experimental studies in primates. The success of the approach encourages us to use the method extensively to inquire more deeply into the strategies used by the cerebral cortex to construct the visual image in the human brain.

REFERENCES

Anstis, S., & Cavanagh, P. (1983). A minimum motion technique for judging equiluminance. In J. D. Mellon & L. T. Sharpe (eds.), *Colour vision*, pp. 155–166. London: Academic.

Baizer, J. S., Robinson, D. L., & Dow, B. M. (1977). Visual responses of area 18 neurons in awake, behaving monkey. *J Neurophysiol, 40*, 1024–1037.

Broca, P. P. (1861). Perte de la parole, ramollissement chronique et déstruction partielle du lobe antérieur gauche du cerveau. *Bull Soc Anthropol* (Paris) 2:235.

Burkhalter, A., & Bernardo, K. L. (1989). Organization of cortico-cortical connections in human visual cortex. *Proc Natl Acad Sci USA 86*, 1071–1075.

Carney, T., Shadlen, M., & Witskes, E. (1987). Parallel processing of motion and colour information. *Nature, 328*, 647–649.

Corbetta, M., Miezin, F. M., Dobmeyer, S., Shulman, G. L., & Petersen, S. E. (1990). Attentional modulation of neural processing of shape, color, and velocity in humans. *Science, 248*, 1556–1559.

Cragg, B. G. (1969). The topography of the afferent projections in circumstriate visual cortex (C.V.C.) of the monkey studied by the Nauta method. *Vision Res, 9*, 733–747.

Cunningham, V. J., Deiber, M-P., Frackowiak, R. S. J., Friston, K. J., Kennard, C., Lammertsma, A. A., Lueck, C. J., Romaya, J., & Zeki, S. (1990). The motion area (area V5) of human visual cortex. *J Physiol (Lond), 423*, 101P.

Damasio, A. (1985). Disorders of complex visual processing: Agnosias, achromatopsia, Balint's syndrome, and related difficulties of orientation and construction. In M. M. Mesulam (ed.) *Principles of behavioral neurology*, pp. 259–288. Philadelphia: Davis.

Damasio, A., Yamada, T., Damasio, H., Corbett, J., & McKee, J. (1980). Central achromatopsia: behavioral, anatomic and physiologic aspects. *Neurology, 30*, 1064–1071.

Desimone, R., & Ungerleider, L. G. (1986). Multiple visual areas in the caudal superior temporal sulcus of the macaque. *J Comp Neurol, 248*, 164–189.

DeYoe, E. A., & Van Essen, D. C. (1985). Segregation of efferent connections and receptive held properties in visual area V2 of the macaque. *Nature, 317*, 58–61.

Duke-Elder, S. (1971). A system of ophthalmology, Vol 12. London: Churchill.

Fox, P. T., Miutum, M. A., Raichle, M. E., Miezin, F. M., Allman, J. M., & Van Essen, D. C. (1986). Mapping human visual cortex with positron emission tomography. *Nature, 323*, 806–809.

Friston, K. J., Passingham, R. E., Nutt, J. G., Heather, J. D., Sawle, G. V., & Frackowiak, R. S. J. (1989) Localization in PET images: Direct fitting of the intercommissural (AC-PC) line. *J Cereb Blood Flow Metab, 9*, 690–695.

Friston, K. J., Frith, C. D., Liddle, P. F., Dolan, R. J., Lammertsma, A. A., & Frackowiak, R. S. J. (1990). The relationship between global and local changes in PET scans. *J Cereb Blood Flow Metab, 10*, 458–466.

Fritsch, G., & Hitzig, E. (1870). Über die elektrische Erregbakeit des Grosshirns. *Arch Anat Physiol Wiss Med, 37*, 300–332.

Henschen, S. E. (1930). Pathologie des Gehirns. 8, Stockholm.

Holmes, G. (1918). Disturbances of vision by cerebral lesions. *Br J Ophthalmol, 2*, 253–285.

Holmes, G. (1945). The Ferrier Lecture: The organization of the visual cortex in man. *Proc R Soc Lond [Biol], 132*, 348–361.

Horton, J. C., & Hedley-Whyte, E. T. (1984). Mapping of cytochrome oxidase patches and ocular dominance columns in human visual cortex. *Philos Trans R Soc Lond [Biol], 304*, 255–272.

Kolmel, H. (1988). Pure homonymous hemiachromatopsia. *Eur Arch Psychiatry Neurol Sci, 237*, 237–243.

Komatsu, H., & Wurtz, R. H. (1988). Relation of cortical areas MT and MST to pursuit eye movements. I. Localization and visual properties of neurons. *J Neurophysiol, 60*, 580–603.

Lammertsma, A. A., Cunningham, V. J., Deiber, M-P., Heather, J. D., Bloomfield, P. M., Nutt, J., Frackowiak, R. S. J., & Jones, T. (1990). Combination of dynamic and integral methods for generating reproducible functional CBF images. *J Cereb Blood Flow Metab, 10*, 675–686.

Land, E. H. (1974). The retinex theory of colour vision. *Proc R Inst Gr Brit 47*, 23–58.

Lashley, K. S. (1931). Mass action in cerebral function. *Science 73*, 245–254.

Lenz, G. (1921). Zwei Sektionsfalle doppelseitiger zentraler Farbenhemianopsia. *Z Ges Neurol Psychiatr, 71*, 135–186.

Livingstone, M. S., & Hubel, D. H. (1984). Anatomy and physiology of a color system in primate visual cortex. *J Neurosci, 4*, 309–356.

Lueck, C. J., Zeki, S., Friston, K. L., Deiber, M-P., Cope, P., Cunningham, V. J., Lammertsma, A. A., Kennard, C., & Frackowiak, R. S. J. (1989). The colour centre in the cerebral cortex of man. *Nature, 340*, 386–389.

Lund, J. S., Lund, R. D., Hendrickson, A. E., Bunt, A. H., & Fuchs, A. F. (1975). The origin of efferent pathways from the primary visual cortex (area 17) of the macaque as shown by the retrograde transport of horseradish peroxidase. *J Comp Neurol, 164*, 287–304.

Mackay, G., & Dunlop, J. C. (1899). The cerebral lesions in a case of complete acquired colour blindness. *Scott Med Surg J, 5*, 503–512.

Miezin, F. M., Fox, P. T., Raichle, M. E., & Allman, J. M. (1987). Localized responses to low contrast moving random dot patterns in human visual cortex monitored with positron emission tomography. *Soc Neurosci Abstr, 13*, 631.

Monbrun, A. (1939). Les affections des voies optiques rétrochiasmatiques et de l'écorce visuelle. In: *Traité d'ophtalmologie*, pp. 903–905. Paris: Masson et Cie.

Pearlman, A. L., Birch, J., & Meadows, J. C. (1979). Cerebral color blindness: An acquired defect in hue discrimination. *Ann Neurol, 5*, 253–261.

Ramachandran, V. S. (1987). Interaction between colour and motion in human vision. *Nature, 328*, 645–647.

Ramachandran, V. S., & Gregory, R. L. (1978). Does colour provide an input to human motion perception? *Nature, 275*, 55–56.

Sacks, O., Wasserman, R. L., Zeki, S., & Seigel, R. M. (1988). Sudden color blindness of cerebral origin. *Soc. Neurodci Abstr, 14*, 1251.

Shipp, S., & Zeki, S. (1985). Segregation of pathways leading from area V2 to areas V4 and V5 of macaque monkey visual cortex. *Nature, 315*, 322–325.

Shipp, S., & Zeki, S. (1989a). The organization of connections between areas V1 and V5 of macaque monkey visual cortex. *Eur J Neurosci, 1*, 309–332.

Shipp, S., & Zeki, S. (1989b). The organization of connections between areas V5 and V2 in macaque monkey visual cortex. *Eur J Neurosci, 1*, 333–354.

Spinks, T. J., Jones, T., Gilardi, M. C., & Heather, J. D. (1988). Physical performance of the latest generation of commercial positron scanner. *IEEE Trans Nucl Sci, 35*, 721–725.

Talairch, J. & Tournoux, P. (1988). *Co-planar stereotaxic atlas of the human brain*. Stuttgart: Thieme.

Tanaka, K., Hirosaka, K., Saito, H-A., Yukie, M., Fukada, Y., & Iwai, E. (1986). Analysis of local and wide field movements in the superior temporal visual areas of the macaque monkey. *J Neurosci, 6*, 134–144.

Teuber, H. L., Battersby, W. S., & Bender, M. B. (1960). *Visual field defects after penetrating missile wounds of the brain*. Cambridge, MA: Harvard

Thurston, S. E., Leigh, R. J., Crawford, T., Thompson, A., & Kennard, C. (1988). Two distinct deficits of visual tracking caused by unilateral lesions of cortex in humans. *Ann Neurol, 23*, 266–273.

Verrey (1888). Hémiachromatopsie droite absolue. *Arch Ophthalmol (Paris) 14*, 422–434.

Yukie, M., & Iwai, E. (1985). Laminar origin of direct projection from area V1 to V4 in the rhesus monkey. *Brain Res, 346*, 383–386.

Zeki, S. M. (1969). Representation of central visual fields in prestriate cortex of the monkey. *Brain Res, 14*, 271–291.

Zeki, S. M. (1971). Cortical projections from two prestriate areas in the monkey. *Brain Res, 34*, 19–35.

Zeki, S. M. (1973). Colour coding in the rhesus monkey prestriate cortex. *Brain Res, 53*, 422–427.

Zeki, S. M. (1974a). The mosaic organization of the visual cortex in the monkey. In R. Bellairs & E. G. Grey, (eds.), *Essays on the nervous system*, pp. 327–343. Oxford: Clarendon.

Zeki, S. M. (1974b). Functional organization of a visual area in the posterior bank of the superior temporal sulcus of the rhesus monkey. *J Physiol (Lond) 236*, 549–573.

Zeki, S. M. (1975). The functional organization of projections from striate to prestriate visual cortex in the rhesus monkey. *Cold Spring Harbor Symp Quant Biol, 40*, 591–600.

Zeki, S. M. (1977). Colour coding in the superior temporal sulcus of rhesus monkey visual cortex. *Proc R Soc Lond [Biol] 197*, 195–223.

Zeki, S. M. (1978a). Functional specialization in the visual cortex of the rhesus monkey. *Nature, 274*, 423–428.

Zeki, S. M. (1978b). The cortical projections of foveal striate cortex in the rhesus monkey. *J Physiol (Lond), 277*, 227–244.

Zeki, S. M. (1978c). The third visual complex of rhesus monkey prestriate cortex. *J Physiol (Lond), 277*, 245–272.

Zeki, S. M. (1978d). Uniformity and diversity of structure and function in rhesus monkey prestriate visual cortex. *J Physiol (Lond), 277*, 273–290.

Zeki, S. (1980). The responses of cells in the anterior bank of the superior temporal sulcus in macaque monkeys. *J Physiol (Lond) 308*, 35P.

Zeki, S. (1990a). A century of cerebral achromatopsia. *Brain 113*, 1721–1777.

Zeki, S. (1990b). The motion pathways of the visual cortex. In C. Blakemore (ed.). *Vision: Coding and efficiency*, pp. 321–345. Cambridge: Cambridge UP.

Zeki, S., & Shipp, S. (1988). The functional logic of cortical connections. *Nature, 335*, 311–317.

Zeki, S., & Shipp, S. (1989). Modular connections between areas V2 and V4 of macaque monkey visual cortex. *Eur J Neurosci, 1*, 494–506.

Zihl, J., von Cramon, D., & Mai, N. (1983). Selective disturbance of movement vision after bilateral brain damage. *Brain 106*, 313–340.

Introduction to Reading 10

A major goal of neurophysiological research is to relate three domains: visual objects and events in the world, the brain, and the perceptual capacities and experiences of observers. Many lines of investigation (for example, Reading 7 by Hubel and Wiesel; Reading 9 by Zeki et al.) have focused on the relation between stimulus properties and the functional organization of the brain. Psychophysics has been used to investigate the relation between physical stimuli and perceptual judgements (e.g., Reading 6 by Hurvich and Jameson; Reading 8 by Blakemore and Campbell).

However, these investigations provide only part of the story. In order to fully understand perception, one must come to grips with the relation between the brain and perceptual experience. In this selection, Newsome, Britten, and Movshon explore the neural basis of a perceptual decision. This relationship had been investigated previously, but in these earlier cases, neural and psychophysical performance had been measured at different times. The experiment reported here is distinguished by the fact that the investigators were able to compare the performance of the observer and the performance of individual neurons at the same time under identical circumstances.

At the time the experiment was conducted, there was good reason to believe that cortical area MT played an important role in motion perception. Cells in this area respond briskly and selectively to bars or dots moving within their receptive fields (Zeki, 1974); furthermore, when the cells in this area are destroyed, significant impairments in detecting motion are observed (Newsome & Paré, 1988). Many cells in MT respond selectively to the direction of visual motion. For example, a given cell might respond well to rightward motion, but quite poorly or not at all to leftward motion.

In this experiment, monkeys were shown a *random-dot kinematogram*, consisting of a field of dots, most of which moves randomly; a small proportion of the dots, however, move coherently in the same direction. When the coherence is small, the predominant direction of motion is difficult to see, but as the proportion of dots moving in the same direct increases, the direction of motion becomes easier to detect. The monkey in this experiment was trained to indicate the perceived direction of motion by moving his eyes in that direction. As the proportion of coherently moving dots increased, the probability of correctly reporting (with an eye movement) the direction of movement also increased. The discharge of single neurons in area MT was also measured while this task was performed. By applying the methods of signal detection theory (see Reading 3 by Tanner and Swets), an estimate of the neuron's "decision" could be made. This was done by assuming that the monkey adopts a criterion for judging when the neural response produced by a particular display was due to dots moving in the cell's preferred direction or due to spontaneous neural activity (and not related to the stimulus). Because the range of neural responses for these two cases overlaps when the proportion of coherently moving dots is small, the decision will necessarily be correct on only some of the trials; the degree of overlap in the range of neural responses during coherent motion in the preferred and null directions determines how often one can be expected to make a correct decision. The estimated proportion correct for a neuron could then be compared to the monkey's behavioral response (Figure 1b). The match was quite good and suggests that the behavioral decision could in principle have been based on the response of a single neuron.

This relation between neural and behavioral performance could, of course, be merely correlational and not causal; that is, both the behavioral response and the neural response might be caused by some other part of the brain. A subsequent study by Salzman et al. (1992) established a more direct causal link: by electrically stimulating a small population of neurons in MT that had a known directional selectivity, the authors were able to bias perceptual judgements in the motion discrimination task; in other words, the stimulation could cause an increase in the monkey's reports (via eye movement) that he saw motion in the stimulated cell's preferred direction. This result suggests that the behavioral response is based directly on the behavior of these neurons. The authors found that microstimulation during the inter-trial interval, when the monkeys were not doing the task, never elicited eye movements; this result makes it unlikely that the stimulation applied by the experimenters simply affected the eye-movement control system directly.

Unfortunately, the monkeys could not be asked what they saw during stimulation. However, these experiments come about as close as can be hoped to demonstrating a direct link between neural activity and perceptual experience. (For a related experiment addressing the correlation between neural activity and awareness, see Reading 25 by Sheinberg and Logothetis).

REFERENCES

Newsome, W. T., & Paré, E. B. (1988). A selective impairment of motion perception following lesions of the middle temporal visual area (MT). *Journal of Neuroscience, 8,* 2201–2211.

Salzman, C. D., Murasugi, C. M., Britten, K. H., & Newsome, W. T. (1992). Microstimulation in visual area MT: Effects on direction discrimination performance. *Journal of Neuroscience, 12,* 2331–2355.

Zeki, S. (1974). Functional organisation of a visual area in the posterior bank of the superior temporal sulcus of the rhesus monkey. *Journal of Physiology, 236,* 549–573.

Neuronal Correlates of a Perceptual Decision

W. T. Newsome and K. H. Britten • SUNY Stony Brook
J. A. Movshon • New York University

The relationship between neuronal activity and psychophysical judgement has long been of interest to students of sensory processing. Previous analyses of this problem have compared the performance of human or animal observers in detection or discrimination tasks with the signals carried by individual neurons, but have been hampered because neuronal and perceptual data were not obtained at the same time and under the same conditions (1–4). We have now measured the performance of monkeys and of visual cortical neurons while the animals performed a psychophysical task well matched to the properties of the neurons under study. Here we report that the reliability and sensitivity of most neurons on this task equalled or exceeded that of the monkeys. We therefore suggest that under our conditions, psychophysical judgements could be based on the activity of a relatively small number of neurons.

Our general methods for monitoring unit activity and eye position in alert, behaving monkeys are derived from those devised by Wurtz et al. (5) and our psychophysical methods were based on those described by Newsome and Paré (6). In brief, animals were trained to report the direction of motion of a random dot display in which some dots moved coherently while the remainder moved at random. We varied the strength of the motion signal by varying the proportion of the dots moving coherently: at 0% correlation, all the motion was random; at 100% correlation, all the motion was coherent. Near threshold, the stimulus resembled the dynamic noise seen on a domestic television set tuned between stations, combined with a barely perceptible sensation of global motion. We recorded single neuron activity from area MT (V5), a region of the extrastriate visual cortex concerned with motion processing, where most neurons respond optimally to visual stimuli of a particular direction and speed of motion (7–10). Because efficient extraction of motion signals from this stimulus requires considerable integration over space, it seemed likely that neurons in MT, which have relatively large receptive fields, would be particularly suited to this task. Newsome and Paré (6) have recently shown that lesions of MT elevate perceptual thresholds for this task.

We used a two-alternative forced-choice procedure to measure thresholds. We placed our stimulus so that it just covered the receptive field of the neuron under study, and adjusted the speed to match that preferred by the neuron. Motion was presented either in the neuron's preferred direction or in the "null" direction 180° away. On an individual trial, the monkey was required to hold fixation for 2 seconds while the motion stimulus was presented. At the end of the trial, the monkey indicated his judgment by transferring his gaze to one of two small light-emitting diodes, corresponding to the preferred or null direction of motion. We presented at least 30 trials (15 in each direction) for each of several correlation values chosen to elicit performance that varied from chance to near perfection, and compiled these data into psychometric functions. Recalling that performance would be 50% correct by chance, we defined the threshold as the correlation required for the monkey to judge the direction of motion correctly on 82% of the trials.

While measuring the psychophysical threshold, we recorded the activity of the MT neuron for which the stimulus parameters were optimized. The computer counted the action potentials elicited on each trial, and compiled distributions like those shown for a typical neuron in Fig. 10.1a. In these distributions, filled bars represent trials in which the motion was in the null direction, and cross-hatched bars indicate trials for the preferred direction. It is evident that at a correlation of 0.8% the two distributions were not different, whereas at a correlation of 12.8%, where the neuron was strongly direction-selective, they barely overlapped. To compare these neuronal data with the psychophysical data, we postulated that performance depended on a comparison between the activity of two neurons, the one under study and another differing only in that it preferred the opposite direction of motion. Under this assumption, we could use the distributions in Fig. 10.1a to represent the responses of the neuron under study and its "antineuron"; we simply reversed the preferred and null directions for the antineuron. On any individual trial, therefore, the observer would compare a response drawn from the distribution represented by the hatched bars in Fig. 10.1a with one drawn from the distribution represented by the solid bars. The direction chosen would be the preferred direction of the neuron giving the larger response. The performance of an MT neuron could then be characterized as the probability that a randomly selected response from the hatched distribution in Fig. 10.1a was larger than a randomly selected response from the solid distribution. We chose this method for analysing physiological data because it most directly related neuronal performance to the directional discrimination task that the monkey was engaged in.

For the data in Fig. 10.1a, at a correlation of 0.8%, this decision rule chose the correct direction only on about half the trials (random performance), whereas at a correlation of 12.8% it performed nearly perfectly. We used a method based on signal detection theory (11) to estimate this choice probability for each correlation value, and plotted the results as "neurometric functions" for-

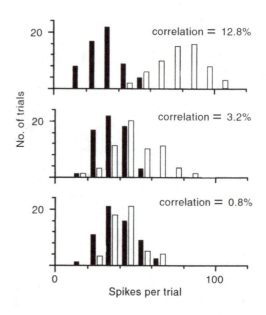

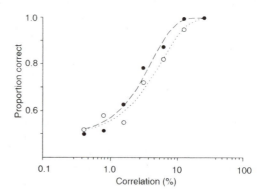

FIGURE 10.1 ■ Physiological and Psychophysical Data Obtained Simultaneously from a rhesus monkey. *a.* The responses of a directionally selective MT neuron at three different motion correlations spanning physiological threshold. The hatched bars represent responses to motion in the neuron's preferred direction; the solid bars indicate responses to motion in the null direction (180° opposite to the preferred). Sixty trials were performed in each direction for each of the three correlation levels. Response distributions for a range of correlation levels were used to compute a "neurometric" function that characterized the neuron's sensitivity to the motion signal and could be compared with the psychometric function computed from the monkey's behavioural responses. *b.* Comparison of simultaneously recorded psychometric and neurometric functions. Psychophysical performance of the monkey, ○: performance of the neuron ●. Psychophysical performance at each correlation is given by the proportion of trials on

mally equivalent to the psychometric functions representing the psychophysical data (2,4). The two functions for this example neuron are shown in Fig. 10.1b; filled circles represent neurometric data, open circles represent psychometric data. Evidently the two curves are very similar, with the neurometric data points lying slightly to the left of the psychometric data points; in this case the neuronal threshold was slightly lower than the psychophysical one. We used a likelihood-ratio statistic to test the hypothesis that the psychometric and neurometric functions were the same. For this neuron, this hypothesis could not be rejected ($P > 0.05$).

We performed this analysis for 45 neurons recorded from one monkey, and 15 neurons from a second. Fig. 10.2 shows a histogram of the distribution of the ratio of neurometric to psychometric thresholds for these 60 neurons. Values of this ratio of <1 represent cases where the neuron's threshold was lower than the monkey's; values >1 represent cases where the monkey's performance was better than the neuron's. Intuitively, it might be expected that the behavioural threshold would be lower than any particular neuronal threshold but, in most cases, neuronal thresholds and perceptual thresholds were similar. Indeed in some cases, neuronal thresholds were substantially lower than perceptual thresholds. For 20 of the 60 neurons in our sample, the psychometric and neurometric functions were statistically indistinguishable ($P>0.05$); in 18 of the 40 remaining cases, neuronal thresholds were lower than perceptual thresholds. In other words, if the monkeys were able to select and measure the discharge of some of these neurons as we did, their performance could have been better than it actually was.

An inability to select the most informative signals can be considered as a kind of perceptual uncertainty, of the kind modelled by Pelli (13).

which the monkey correctly identified the direction of motion. Neuronal performance is calculated from distributions of responses like those in Fig. 1a using a signal-detection method described in the text. The physiological and psychophysical data form similar curves, but the data for the neuron lie to the left of the data for the monkey, meaning that the neuron was somewhat more sensitive than the monkey. We fit the data with smooth functions of the form introduced to psychophysics by Quick[12]. Threshold, defined as the correlation for which the direction of motion was identified correctly on 82% of the trials, was 6.1% for the monkey and 4.4% for the neuron.

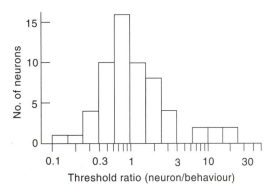

FIGURE 10.2 ■ Comparison of Psychophysical and Physiological Thresholds Obtained for 60 MT Neurons in Two Rhesus Monkeys. The frequency histogram shows the distribution of the ration of the physiological threshold to the psychophysical threshold for all the neurons for which we obtained data. A value of 1 represents perfect correspondence between psychophysical and physiological thresholds; values < 1 indicate that the physiological threshold was lower than the physiological threshold, whereas values > 1 indicate the converse. The directional preferences of the 60 neurons were roughly uniformly distributed and there was no reliable association between a neuron's direction or speed preference and its threshold relative to the perceptual threshold.

Obliged to monitor signals from many sources less informative than the one perfectly tuned to the visual target, the animal's perceptual performance would be degraded, because each sub-optimal source would contribute more noise than signal. Neuronal performance would then exceed psychophysical performance. Our results suggest, however, that this effect is not large. Substantial uncertainty would make the psychometric function steeper than the neurometric function (13), but as was the case for the example shown in Fig. 10.1B, the slopes of these two functions are usually similar. We thus conclude that under our conditions, the monkey's perceptual decision is not greatly affected by irrelevant signals introduced by uncertainty.

The apparent absence of uncertainty leads, however, to another question: if a perceptual decision can be based with relative certainty on the discharge of the most informative neurons, why is behavioural performance not further enhanced by using a pooled signal derived from many such informative neurons? If enough such neurons were present, such pooling would substantially improve psychophysical performance by averaging out the noise that obscures weak signals. Our data show that in most cases, the neuronal and psychophysical performances are similar, indicating that signals from many neuronal sources are not pooled to reduce perceptual thresholds.

One way to account for the absence of either pooling or uncertainty effects is to suggest that the variability in the responses of similarly tuned neurons is correlated. Both pooling and uncertainty act as we have stated only if different neuronal signals are perturbed by independent sources of variation. If the sources are not *independent*, then uncertainty does no damage and pooling provides no benefit, because different neurons are carrying similar signals. The rich network of shared connections that link MT neurons with the retina might well produce correlation among neurons with related selectivities, but this possibility has not been studied. Our lack of information about the degree of shared variability makes it impossible for us to assert that the neurons whose responses we have recorded are the ones that contribute to the monkey's perceptual judgements. Nonetheless, our results show that a reasonable account of the monkey's performance can be constructed, using

a simple decision rule, from signals carried by small numbers of neurons whose selectivities are well matched to the demands of the perceptual task.

NOTES

1. Barlow, H. B., & Levick, W. R. J. (1969). *J. Physiol.,* *200*, 1–24.
2. Tolhurst, D. J., Movshon, J. A., & Dean, A. F. (1983). *Vision Res., 23,* 775–785.
3. Parker, A. J., & Hawken, M. J. (1985). *J. Opt. Soc. Am., A2,* 1101–1114.
4. Bradley, A., Skottun, B. C., Ohzawa, I. Sclar, G., & Freedman, R. D. (1987). *J. Neurophysiol., 55,* 1308–1327.
5. Mikami, A., Newsome, W. T., & Wurtz, R. H. (1986). *J. Neurophysiol., 55,* 1308–1327.
6. Newsome, W. T., & Paré, E. B. (1988). *J. Neurosci., 8,* 2201–2211.
7. Dubner, R., & Zeki, S. M. (1971). *Brain Res., 35,* 528–532.
8. Zeki, S. M. (1974). *J. Physiol., 236,* 549–573.
9. Maunsell, J. H. R., & Van Essen, D. C. (1983). *J. Neurophysiol., 49,* 1127–1147.
10. Albright, T. D. (1984). *J. Neurophysiol., 52,* 1106–1130.
11. Green, D. M., & Swets, J. A. (1966). *Signal Detection Theory and Psychophysics.* New York: Wiley.
12. Quick, R. F. (1974). *Kybernetik, 16,* 65–67.
13. Pelli, D. G. (1985). *J. Opt. Soc. Am., A2, 1508–1532.*

Early Vision

Discussion Questions

1. Would Gibson find any of the articles in this section of value? What about Marr?
2. The articles by Hurvich and Jamison and by Blakemore and Campbell use psychophysical (i.e., behavioral) methods to make inferences about underlying physiological mechanisms. Would a physiological technique such as single-cell recording or functional neuroimaging be a more direct and convincing approach to these problems? What can psychophysics reveal that a purely physiological approach cannot, and vice-versa?
3. To what extent is the Zeki et al. article an extension of the Hubel and Weisel discoveries, and to what extent does it strike out in a new direction? Are Zeki and Barlow working in a common theoretical tradition toward the same end?
4. The Newsome et al. article is concerned with identifying a neural basis for perceptual decisions. Does it belong with the other articles in this section, or should it have been placed with articles on attention and awareness? Why?

Suggested Readings

Cornsweet, T. (1970). *Visual Perception*. New York: Academic Press. Chapter II: The Experiment of Hecht, Schlaer, and Pirenne (pp. 6–26). The Cornsweet chapter describes with exceptional clarity and detail a landmark experiment which provided psychophysical evidence for the absolute sensitivity of a single retinal photoreceptor. Cornsweet beautifully lays out the authors' reasoning and the many implications of their experiment. The experiment itself is well worth reading, though most will benefit from studying Cornsweet's treatment first.

Hecht, S., Schlaer, S., & Pirenne, M. H. (1942). Energy, quanta, and vision. *Journal of General Physiology, 25,* 819–840.

Hartline, H. K. (1940). The receptive fields of optic nerve fibers. *American Journal of Physiology, 130*, 690–699.

Barlow, H. B. (1953). Summation and inhibition in the frog's retina. *Journal of Physiology, 119*, 69–88.

Kuffler, S. W. (1953). Discharge patterns and functional organization of mammalian retina. *Journal of Neurophysiology, 16*, 37–68.

Lettvin, J. Y., Maturana, H. R., McCulloch, W. S., & Pitts, W. H. (1959). What the frog's eye tells the frog's brain. *Proceedings of the Institute of Radio Engineers, 47*, 1940–1951.

Ratliff, F., & Hartline, H. K. (1959). The responses of limulus optic nerve fibers to patterns of illumination on the receptor mosaic. *Journal of General Physiology, 42,* 1241–1255. The previous five articles are among the pioneering works that provided initial evidence about the receptive field properties of cells in the retina and optic nerve. They provided some of the context in which Hubel and Weisel were able to make their seminal discoveries in cortex.

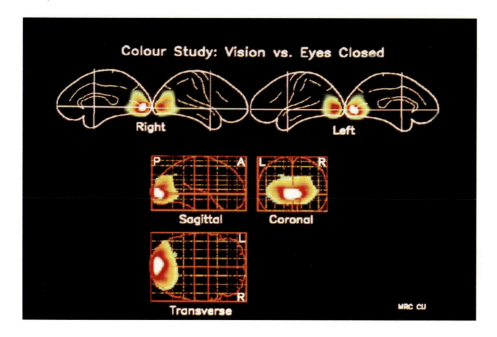

COLOR PLATE 9.1 ■ Projections onto the Lateral and Medial Surfaces of the Brain (top) and Coronal, Sagittal, and Transverse Projections (bottom) of Statistical Parametric Maps Obtained by Planned Comparison of Means Between Conditions with Eyes Closed (rest) and Those with Eyes Open (color and gray). All areas of significant increase in rCBF are shown in the *lower images*, projected onto the transverse, coronal, and sagittal planes. The grid is the standard proportional stereotactic grid of Talairach and Tournoux (1988), which defines the 3-D space into which all the subjects' brains have been rescaled (normalized). The contours of the brain in the transverse plane at the level of the ACPC line (*bottom*), the midsagittal plane (*upper left*), and the coronal plane at the midpoint of the ACPC line are shown on the respective grids. This display permits rapid inspection and localization of all the data. The *white* and *red* end of the color scale (distributed over 255 levels) shows areas of maximally significant rCBF change, and the *blue* and *green* end shows the threshold of $p < 0.05$. The striate and prestriate areas show highly significant changes in rCBF. The *upper images* are projected onto the medial and lateral surfaces of the brain to illustrate more clearly the extent of significant change in rCBF. It is clear that, in addition to the striate area, the cuneate gyrus above and the fusiform and lingual gyri below have been stimulated, as has the immediate peristrate area back to the occipital pole. Parts of this area have been identified as responsible for color perception, others represent the primary visual cortex, and the remainder (or a major part of it) must represent the human equivalent of V2.

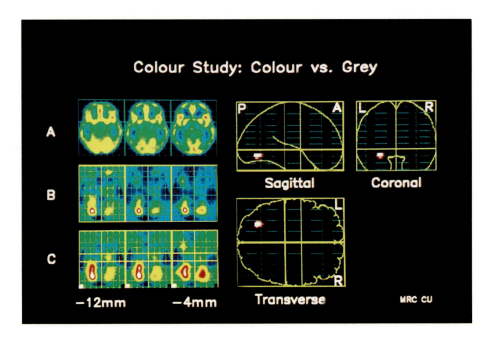

COLOR PLATE 9.2 ■ Data from the Color Experiment. On the *left* are transverse images of the brain at planes −12, −8, and −4 mm relative to the ACPC line. *A*, Anatomical features averaged from the 6 subjects to Talairach space. *B*, The arithmetical differences between adjusted mean blood flows for color and gray stimuli. *C*, The SPMs derived from a formal comparison of the adjusted mean blood flows and variances for each of the 2 conditions. The color-coding conventions are arbitrary and similar to Color Plate 9.1. On the *right* are the orthogonal projections of the statistical comparison at a threshold of $p < 0.05$ (corrected for multiple comparisons). The areas showing increased flow, subserving the perception of color, are located inferiorly and medially in the occipital cortex (V4).

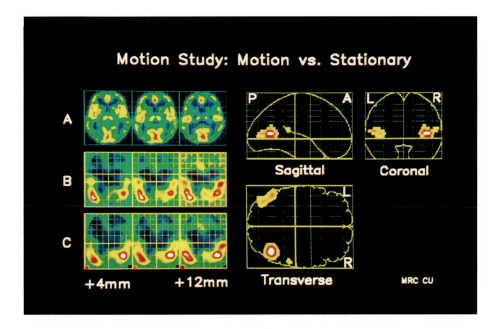

COLOR PLATE 9.3 ■ Data from the Visual Motion Experiment, with Conventions Identical to Color Plate 9.2 and Spanning Planes +4 to +12 mm Relative to the ACPC Line. The map shows areas specifically subserving the perception of movement in the visual scene (V5). The areas are located on the convexity of the prestriate cortex at the junction of areas 19 and 37 of Brodmann.

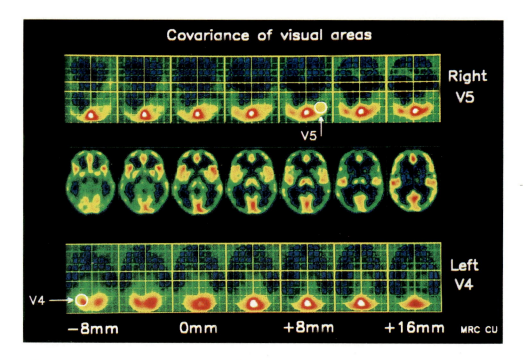

COLOR PLATE 9.4 ■ Transverse Sections of Covariance Maps for Motion (*top*) and Color (*bottom*) Experiments. In the middle row, to orient with respect to anatomical detail, is the average of the PET images for the 6 color subjects, for all conditions. To generate these covariance maps, a pixel within the ringed areas (V4 or V5) was chosen as the reference point (coordinates in Tables 1 and 2). The positive covariation of other pixels with the chosen pixel was used to generate the maps. For example, when the chosen pixel was within V4 (*lower row*), the positive covariation was with its homologue on the other side and the V1/V2 complex. No other cortical area covaried positively. When the chosen pixel was in the right V5, the positive covariation was only with its opposite homologue and the V1/V2 complex. Identical results were obtained if the reference pixel was placed in the right V4 or the left V5.

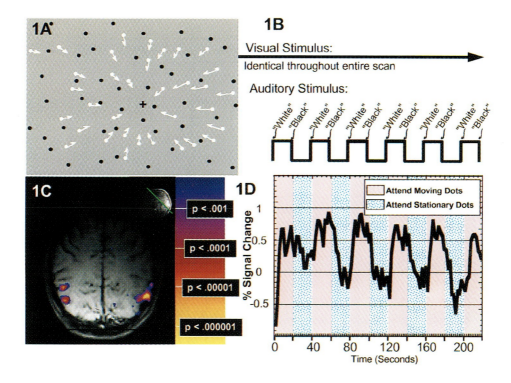

COLOR PLATE 23.5 ■ Experiment 1: Constant Stimulus

(A) The critical visual stimulus consisted of both stationary dots and dots moving toward a central fixation cross. The arrows indicate motion and were not present in the actual stimuli.

(B) The diagram indicates that the visual stimulus continued unchanged throughout the scan, and an auditory stimulus alerted subjects to direct their attention alternately to the white (moving) or black (stationary) subset of dots.

(C) A KS statistical map comparing the two attention conditions shows a region consistent with MT–MST, which is more active during attention to moving dots. The colored bar is a key to the P values. The small inset indicates the slice orientation.

(D) The average time course of activation for that region (three subjects; eight runs total).

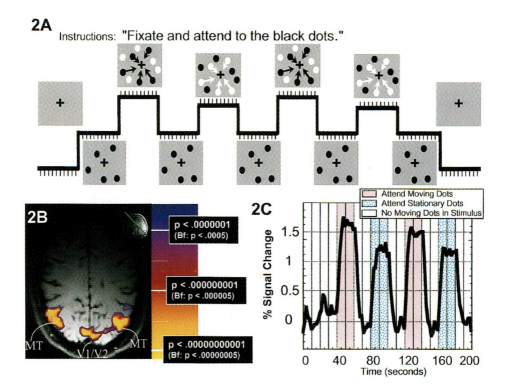

2A

Instructions: "Fixate and attend to the black dots."

2B

p < .0000001
(Bf: p < .0005)

p < .000000001
(Bf: p < .000005)

p < .00000000001
(Bf: p < .00000005)

MT   MT
V1/V2

2C

Attend Moving Dots
Attend Stationary Dots
No Moving Dots in Stimulus

% Signal Change

1.5

1

0.5

0

0   40   80   120   160   200
Time (seconds)

COLOR PLATE 23.6 ■ Experiment 2: Comparison of Stimulus-Driven and Attention-Driven Effects

(A) A cartoon of one stimulus sequence for Experiment 2, in which the subject was instructed to attend to the black dots throughout the entire scan. Each small tick mark indicates the acquisition of an image.

(B) The KS map shows regions that are significantly more active when the display includes moving stimuli than when it contains stationary dots alone.

(C) The average time course for the lateral regions (MT–MST) demonstrates both the effect of the stimulus and the effect of attention. During time periods indicated by white bars, the subjects viewed stationary dots alone. They viewed the critical "moving and stationary dots" stimulus during the times indicated by closed bars (when they attended to the moving dots) and hatched bars (when they attended to the stationary dots). Mean values for the percent change from the stationary dot baseline (designated 0%) were 1.14% for the attend stationary condition and 1.51% for the attend moving condition. The difference is a measure of the attentional effect. The sensory effect was three to four times as large as the attentional effect, depending on which of the two moving dot conditions is used as a re.erent. The colored bar is a key to the *P* values (and *P* values when Bonferroni corrected for multiple comparisons). Because the sensory effect is much larger than the attentional effect shown in Color Plate 23.5, a more stringent threshold is used here.

Perceptual Organization and Constancy

Introduction to Readings 11 and 12

The following two readings were written almost contemporaneously, about a decade after the Gestalt movement in perception began with the publication of another of Wertheimer's seminal works (Wertheimer, 1912). In that earlier paper, Wertheimer analyzed the phenomenon of apparent motion and how various perceptual experiences may be evoked by a stimulus consisting of multiple elements in stationary alternation. The perceptual laws of proximity and similarity were already evident in this earlier writing, but in Reading 11 by Wertheimer, the principles (or "factors") of perceptual organization are discussed in much more detail for static configurations of items. These principles are now a standard part of every introductory perception text and in many introductory psychology texts. The analysis by Rubin of how figure and ground are experienced, and in which the now-classic Rubin face-vase figure is introduced, was similarly influential and typical of the insights that were then emerging during a time of excitement in perceptual psychology.

The principles of perceptual organization articulated by Wertheimer and by Rubin are often misunderstood by students. They are seen as rather obscure lists of arbitrary rules that happen to characterize how it is we see configurations of seemingly arbitrary elements like disks, squares, and the like. The relation between the laws of organization as applied to these abstract displays on the one hand, and to real perception on the other, is not always clear.

The most important thing a modern reader must keep in mind when studying these writings is that the Gestalt approach was a reaction to the structuralist movement of the late 19th and early 20th century. The structuralists viewed perception as a sort of "mental chemistry," and believed that one could completely explain perception by first determining the elements of perception (e.g., that there are some number of brightnesses that can be discriminated, and some number of colors, and so forth) and then assessing how those elements are combined in a scene. They worked very hard to train themselves to see the retinal image "as it is," in terms of the perceptual elements, and not to be influenced by the observer's interpretation of the objects and surfaces in the scene. For example, when confronted with a rectangular book on a table, they would describe the front cover the book as a parallelogram of a particular shape, rather than as a rectangle. This is close to the antithesis of Gibson's view of perception (Reading 4); Helmholtz (Reading 1) also viewed this sort of approach with skepticism.

The Gestalt psychologists, in contrast, viewed perception as a way of seeing what was actually there. In Wertheimer's words, "I do not see an arrangement of 66 plus 40 [brightnesses]. . . . In reality I see two faces!" The principles of perceptual organization characterize how the visual system has, through learning within one's lifetime and through evolution across generations, internalized certain regularities in the world that are necessary consequences of geometry and physics. For example, consider the principle of common fate (or, as it is unhelpfully translated here, the "Factor of Uniform Density"). When two or more elements in an image move together, there are two possible states of the world that could have caused this. The first possibility is that those elements belong to the same moving rigid object (or to two rigidly connected objects). The second possibility is that those elements are independently moving and it is just a coincidence that they are moving in the same way. The former possibility is much more likely than the latter, and so, in the absence of any additional information, it is prudent to interpret the scene in this way. The visual system does just this by default.

Consider another example. When viewing a garden through Venetian blinds, the foliage is fragmented by the horizontal slats of the blinds. Yet the collinear fragments of a branch are seen as part of a single continuous object. The visual system has internalized a fact about the world: two contours that are collinear in the image are likely (though by no means certain) to belong to the same object. It could be, of course, that two separate objects just happen to be aligned in such a way that the two edges in question are collinear. However, this is much less likely than that they are parts of one object. Once again, the visual system interprets the scene according to the most likely state of the world to have given rise to the retinal image. A similar argument can be made for the principle of similarity: image regions with similar brightnesses, colors, and depths are more likely to be part of a single common surface than to be independent of one another. This is precisely the sort of view that Helmholtz (Reading 1) advocated.

The illustrations provided by Wertheimer are laboratory abstractions that permit one to examine the principles in isolation under controlled circumstances. However, the principles did not evolve in order to permit organisms to perceive arrays of dots and circles. They evolved to enable the perception of real scenes containing real objects.

Rubin's analysis of figure and ground begins with the observation that a common border between two regions has the effect of shaping only one of the regions—that of the figure—and having little or no effect on the ground, which is seen to extend unhindered behind the figure. (Wertheimer makes the same point near the end of his paper.) The demonstration offered in Rubin's Figure 1 provides incisive and immediate intuition about the effect of seeing a region as figure and then as ground. As he states in the text, the concentric rings are seen as continuous when they are part of the ground, extending behind the radially marked arms of the cross serving as ground (what Albert Michotte [e.g., Michotte et al., 1991], would later called "amodal completion"), but when the organization is reversed, the rings are immediately terminated at the edge of the arms of the cross they mark. Rubin notes that the figure is seen as more "thinglike" (with a shape, for example), and the ground as more "substancelike" (like flour or sand). The figure is seen as closer to the observer than the ground (in part because its contours are seen as occluding the ground).

In addition to their careful demonstrations of the principles of perceptual organization, some Gestalt theorists offered neurophysiological explanations of the principles. Unfortunately, these turned out to be quite wrong. Nevertheless, the principles themselves endure to this day. Modern treatments of perceptual organization (see, for example, Nakayama et al., 1995) echo many of the ideas first articulated by Wertheimer, Koffka (1935), Köhler (1947), and their contemporaries.

REFERENCES

Koffka, K. (1935). *Principles of gestalt psychology*. New York: Harcourt, Brace and Co.

Köhler, W. (1947). *Gestalt psychology*. New York: Liveright.

Michotte, A., Thinès, G., & Crabbé, G. (1991). Amodal completion of perceptual structures (E. Miles & T. R. Miles, Trans.). In G. Thinès, A. Costall, & G. Butterworth (Eds.), Michotte's experimental phenomenology of perception (pp. 140–167). Hillsdale, NJ: Erlbaum. (Original work published 1964)

Nakayama, K., He, Z. J., & Shimojo, S. (1995). Visual surface representation: A critical link between lower-level and higher-level vision. In S. M. Kosslyn, & D. N. Osherson (Eds.), *Visual Cognition: An invitation to cognitive science* (2nd Ed., Vol.. 2, pp. 1–70). Cambridge, MA: MIT Press.

Wertheimer, M. (1912). Experimental studies on the seeing of motion. Reprinted in T. Shipley (1961). *Classics in Psychology*. New York: Philosophical Library.

Laws of Organization in Perceptual Forms

M. Wertheimer

I stand at the window and see a house, trees, sky. Theoretically I might say there were 327 brightnesses and nuances of colour. Do I *have* "327"? No. I have sky, house, and trees. It is impossible to achieve "327" as such. And yet even though such droll calculation were possible—and implied, say, for the house 120, the trees 90, the sky 117—I should at least have *this* arrangement and division of the total, and not, say, 127 and 100 and 100; or 150 and 177.

The concrete division which I *see* is not determined by some arbitrary mode of organization lying solely within my own pleasure; instead I see the arrangement and division which is given there before me. And what a remarkable process it is when some other mode of apprehension *does* succeed! I gaze for a long time from my window, adopt after some effort the most unreal attitude possible. And I *discover* that part of a window sash and part of a bare branch together compose an *N*.

Or, I look at a picture. Two faces cheek to cheek. I see one (with its, if you will, "57" brightnesses) and the other ("49" brightnesses). I do not see an arrangement of 66 plus 40 nor of 6 plus 100. There *have* been theories which would require that I see "106." In reality I see two faces !

Or, I hear a melody (17 tones) with its accompaniment (32 tones). I hear the melody and accompaniment, not simply "49"—and certainly not 20 plus 29. And the same is true even in cases where there is no stimulus continuum. I hear the melody and its accompaniment even when they are played by an old-fashioned clock where each tone is separate from the others. Or, one sees a series of discontinuous dots upon a homogeneous ground not as a sum of dots, but as figures. Even though there may here be a greater latitude of possible arrangements, the dots usually combine in some "spontaneous," "natural" articulation—and any other arrangement, even if it can be achieved, is artificial and difficult to maintain.

When we are presented with a number of stimuli we do not as a rule experience "a number " of individual things, this one and that and that. Instead larger wholes separated from and related to one another are given in experience; their arrangement and division are concrete and definite.

Do such arrangements and divisions follow definite principles? When the stimuli *abcde* appear together what are the principles according to which *abc/de* and not *ab/cde* is experienced? It is the purpose of this paper to examine this problem, and we shall therefore begin with cases of discontinuous stimulus constellations.

I. A row of dots is presented upon a homogeneous ground. The alternate intervals are 3 mm. and 12 mm.

•• •• •• •• •• •• •• (i)

Normally this row will be seen as *ab/cd*, not as *a/bc/de*. As a matter of fact it is for most people impossible to see the whole series simultaneously in the latter grouping.

We are interested here in what is actually *seen*. The following will make this clear. One sees a row of groups obliquely tilted from lower left to upper right (*ab/cd/ef*). The arrangement *a/bc/de* is extremely difficult to achieve. Even when it can be seen, such an arrangement is far less certain than the other and is quite likely to be upset by eye-movements or variations of attention.

(ii) • • • • • •
· · · · · ·

This is even more clear in (iii).

(iii)
· · · · · · ·
· · · · · · ·
· · · · · · ·

I.e. :—
    c   f   i   l   o
  b   e   h   k   n   etc.
  a   d   g   j   m

Quite obviously the arrangement *abc/def/ghi* is greatly superior to *ceg/fhj/ikm*.

Another, still clearer example of spontaneous arrangement is that given in (iv). The natural grouping, of course, *a/bcd/efghi*, etc.

(iv)

                                    j
                          e   k
                  b   f   l
  · · · · a   c   m
                  d   g h n
                          i   o
                                    p

Resembling (i) but still more compelling is the row of three-dot groupings given in (v). One sees *abd/def*, and not some other (theoretically possible) arrangement.

(v) • • •   • • •   • • •   • • •   • • •

Another example of seeing what the objective arrangement dictates is contained in (vi) for vertical, and in (vii) for horizontal groupings.

(vi)
· · · · ·
· · · · ·
· · · · ·
· · · · ·
· · · · ·

In all the foregoing cases we have used a relatively large number of dots for each figure. Using fewer we find that the arrangement is not so imperatively dictated as before, and reversing the more obvious grouping is comparatively easy. Example: (viii)–(x).

It would be false to assume that (viii)–(x) lend themselves more readily to reversal because fewer stimulus points (dots) are involved. Such incorrect reasoning would be based upon the proposi-

(viii) • • • • •   • •   • •   • •

· · · · · (vii)

(ix) · · · · (scattered dots)

(x) · · · · · (scattered dots)

tion: "The more dots, the more difficult it will be to unite them into groups." Actually it is only the unnatural, artificial arrangement which is rendered more difficult by a larger number of points. The natural grouping (cf., e.g., (i), (ii), etc.) is not at all impeded by increasing the number of dots. It never occurs, for example, that with a long row of such dots the process of " uniting" them into pairs is abandoned and individual points seen instead. It is not true that fewer stimulus points "obviously" yield simpler, surer, more elementary results.

In each of the above cases that form of grouping is most natural which involves the smallest interval. They all show, that is to say, the predominant influence of what we may call *The Factor of Proximity*. Here is the first of the principles which we undertook to discover. That the principle holds also for auditory organization can readily be seen by substituting tap-tap, pause, tap-tap, pause, etc. for (i), and so on for the others.

II. Proximity is not, however, the only factor involved in natural groupings. This is apparent from the following examples. We shall maintain an identical proximity throughout but vary the colour of the dots themselves:—

O O • • O O • • O O • • O O • • O O • • (xi)

Or, again:—

(xii)
O • O • O • O • O • O •
O • O • O • O • O • O •
O • O • O • O • O • O •
O • O • O • O • O • O •
O • O • O • O • O • O •
O • O • O • O • O • O •
O • O • O • O • O • O •
O • O • O • O • O • O •
O • O • O • O • O • O •
O • O • O • O • O • O •

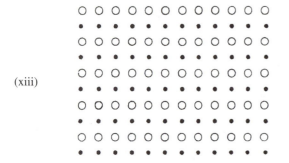

(xiii)

Or, to repeat (v) but with uniform proximity:—

(xiv) ○ ○ ○ ● ● ● ○ ○ ○ ● ● ● ○ ○ ○ ● ● ● ○ ○ ○ ● ● ●

Thus we are led to the discovery of a second principle—viz. the tendency of like parts to band together—which we may call *The Factor of Similarity*. And again it should be remarked that this principle applies also to auditory experience. Maintaining a constant interval, the beats may be soft and loud (analogous to (xi)) thus: .. ! ! .. ! ! etc. Even when the attempt to hear some other arrangement succeeds, this cannot be maintained for long. The natural grouping soon returns as an overpowering "upset" of the artificial arrangement.

In (xi)–(xiv) there is, however, the possibility of another arrangement which should not be overlooked. We have treated these sequences in terms of a *constant* direction from left to right. But it is also true that a continual *change* of direction is taking place between the groups themselves: viz. the transition from group one to group two (soft-to-loud), the transition from group two to group three (loud-to-soft), and so on. This naturally involves a special factor. To retain a constant direction it would be necessary to make each succeeding pair louder than the last. Schematically this can be represented as:—

(xv)

Or, in the same way:—

(xvi)

This retention of constant direction could also be demonstrated with achromatic colours (green background) thus: white, light grey, medium grey, dark grey, black. A musical reproduction of (xv) would be C, C, E, E, F#; F#, A, A, C, C, . . . ; and similarly for (xvi): C, C, C, E, E, E, F#, F#, F#, A, A, A, C, C, C, . . .

Thus far we have dealt merely with a special case of the general law. Not only similarity and dissimilarity, but more and less dissimilarity operate to determine experienced arrangement. With tones, for example, C, C#, E, F, G#, A, C, C#...will be heard in the grouping *ab/cd* . . . and C, C#, D, E, F, F#, G#, A, A#, C, C#, D . . . in the grouping *abc/def* . . . Or, again using achromatic colours, we might present these same relationships in the manner suggested (schematically) by (xvii) and (xviii).

(xvii)

(xviii)

(It is apparent from the foregoing that quantitative comparisons can be made regarding the application of the same laws in regions—form, colour, sound—heretofore treated as psychologically separate and heterogeneous.)

III. What will happen when *two* such factors appear in the same constellation? They may be made to co-operate; or, they can be set in opposition—as, for example, when *one* operates to favour *ab/cd* while the *other* favours */bc/de*. By appropriate variations, either factor may be weakened or stengthened. As an example, consider this arrangement:—

● ○   ○ ●   ● ○   ○ ● (xix)

where both similarity and proximity are employed. An illustration of opposition in which similarity is victorious despite the preferential status given to proximity is this:—

(xx)
```
O  •   O  •   O  •   O  •
  •  O   •  O   •  O   •  Q
```

A less decided victory by similarity:—

(xxi)
```
•  O  •  O  •  O  •  O  •
O  •  O  •  O  •  O  •  O
  •  O  •  O  •  O  •  O  •
```

Functioning together towards the same end, similarity and proximity greatly strengthen the prominence here of verticality:—

(xxii)
```
•  O  •  O  •
•  O  •  O  •
•  O  •  O  •
•  O  •  O  •
•  O  •  O  •
•  O  •  O  •
```

Where, in cases such as these, *proximity* is the predominant factor, a gradual increase of interval will eventually introduce a point at which *similarity* is predominant. In this way it is possible to test the strength of these Factors.

IV. A row of dots is presented:—

```
•  •  •      •  •  •      •  •  •      •  •  •
a  b  c      d  e  f      g  h  i      j  k  l
```

and then, without the subject's expecting it, but before his eyes, a sudden, slight shift upward is given, say, to *d, e, f* or to *d, e, f,* and *j, k, l* together. *This* shift is "pro-structural," since it involves an entire group of naturally related dots. A shift upward of, say, *c, d, e* or *c, d, e* and *i, j, k* would be "contra-structural" because the common fate (i.e. the shift) to which these dots are subjected does *not* conform with their natural groupings.

Shifts of the latter kind are far less "smooth" than those of the former type. The former often call forth from the subject no more than bare recognition that a change has occurred; not so with the latter type. Here it is as if some particular "opposition" to the change had been encountered. The result is confusing and discomforting. Sometimes a revolt against the originally dominant Factor of Proximity will occur and the shifted dots themselves thereupon constitute a new grouping whose common fate it has been to be shifted above the original row. The principle involved here may be

designated *The Factor of Uniform Destiny* (or of *"Common Fate"*).

V. Imagine a sequence of rows of which this would be the first:—

Row A.
```
••      ••      ••      ••      ••
a b    c d     e f     g h     i j
```

The intervals between *a-b*, *c-d*, etc. (designated hereafter as S_1) are in this row 2 mm.; those between *b-c*, *d-e*, etc. (S_2) are 20 mm. We shall hold *a, c, e, g,* and *i* while varying the horizontal position of *b, d, f, h,* and *j,* thus:—

	$S_1 + S_2 = 22$	
Row A	$S_1 = 2$ mm.	$S_2 = 20$ mm.
B	5	17
C	8	14
D	11	11
E	14	8
F	17	5
G	20	2

Experimentally we now present these rows *separately.*[1] It will be found that there are three major constellations: The dominant impression in Row A is *ab/cd*, and in Row G it is */bc/de*. But in the middle row (represented in our schema by D) the predominant impression is that of uniformity. These three constellations thus constitute "unique regions" and it will be found that intervening rows are more indefinite in character and their arrangement less striking; indeed they are often most easily seen in the sense of the nearest major constellation. Example: intermediate rows in the vicinity of D will be seen *as* "not quite equally spaced" (even when the difference between intervals S_1 and S_2 is clearly supraliminal).

Or to take another example. Suppose one side of an angle is held horizontal and the other passes through an arc from 30° to 150°. No more here than in the preceding case is *each* degree of equal value psychologically. Instead there are three principal stages : acute, right, and obtuse. The "right angle," for example, has a certain region such that an angle of 93° appears *as* a (more or less inad-

---

[1]The above classification of but 7 rows is intended merely as a schema. In actual experimentation many more than 7 (with correspondingly more minute variations of intervals) are needed.

equate) right angle. Stages intermediate between the major ones have the character of indefiniteness about them and are readily seen in the sense of one *or* the other adjacent *Prägnanzstufen*.[2] This can be very clearly demonstrated by tachistoscopic presentations, for in this case the observer frequently *sees* a right angle even when objectively a more acute or more obtuse angle is being presented. Although the observer may report that it was "not quite correct," "somehow wrong," etc., he is usually unable to say in which direction the "error" lies.

In general we may say, as in the case above where the location of *b* between *a* and *c* was varied, that our impressions are not psychologically equivalent for all positions of *b*. Instead there are certain *Prägnanzstufen* with their appropriate realms or regions, and intermediate stages typically appear "in the sense of" one of these characteristic regions.

VI. Suppose now that the variations from A to G are carried out before the observer's eyes. This procedure leads to a discovery of *The Factor of Objective Set [Einstellung]*. As one proceeds from A towards G from G towards A the *original* grouping in each case (i.e. *ab/cd* in the former, */bc/de* in the latter) tends to maintain itself even beyond the middle row. Then there occurs an upset and the opposite grouping becomes dominant. The constellation of Row C, for example, will be different when preceded by A and B from what it would be when preceded by G, F, E. This means that the row is *a part in a sequence* and the law of its arrangement is such that the constellation resulting from *one* form of sequence will be different from that given by some *other* sequence. Or, again, a certain (objectively) ambiguous arrangement will be perfectly definite and unequivocal when given as a part in a sequence. (In view of its great strength this Factor must in all cases be considered with much care.)

Parenthetically: it is customary to attribute influences such as these to purely subjective (meaning by this "purely arbitrary") conditions. But our examples refer only to *objective* factors: the presence or absence of a certain row of dots in a sequence is determined solely by objective condi-

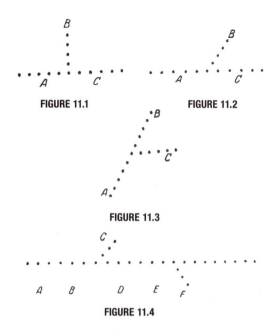

FIGURE 11.1   FIGURE 11.2

FIGURE 11.3

FIGURE 11.4

tions. It is objectively quite different whether a Row M is presented after Row L or after Row N; or, whether the presentations follow one another immediately or occur on different days. When several rows are simultaneously presented it is of course possible to select one row or another quite according to one's (subjective) fancy; or any certain row may be compared with another just above or below it. But this special case is not what we are here concerned with. Such subjectively determined arrangements are possible *only* if the rows of dots permit of two or more modes of apprehension. Curiously enough, however, it has been just this special case (where objective conditions do not themselves compel us to see one arrangement rather than another) which has usually been thought of as *the* fundamental relationship. As a matter of fact we shall see below how even purely subjective factors are by no means as arbitrary in their operations as one might suppose.

VII. That spatial proximity will not alone account for organization can be shown by an example such as Fig. 11.1. Taken individually the points in B are in closer proximity to the individual points

---

[2] ["*Stufen*" = steps or stages; the term "*Prägnanz*" cannot be translated. In the present usage "*Prägnanzstufen*" means *regions* of figural stability in a sense which should be clear from the text.]

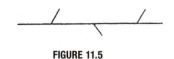

FIGURE 11.5

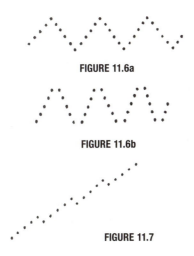

FIGURE 11.6a

FIGURE 11.6b

FIGURE 11.7

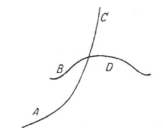

FIGURE 11.11

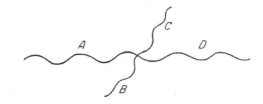

FIGURE 11.12

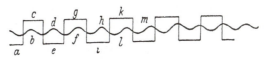

FIGURE 11.13

of A (or C) than the points of A and C are to each other. Nevertheless the perceived grouping is not AB/C or BC/A, but quite clearly, "a horizontal line and a vertical line"—i.e. AC/B. In Fig. 11.2 the spatial proximity of B and C is even grater, yet the result is still AC/B—i.e. horizontal-oblique. The same is true of the relationship AB/C in Fig. 11.3. As Figs. 11.4–11.7 also show we are dealing now with a new principle which we may call *The Factor of Direction*. That direction may still be uneqivocally given even when curved lines are used is of course obvious (cf. Figs. 11.8–11.12). The dominance of this Factor in certain cases will be especially clear if one attempts to see Fig. 11.13 (*abefil . . .*) (*cdghkm . . .*) instead of (*acegik . . .*) (*bdfhlm . . .*).

Suppose in Fig. 11.8 we had only the part designated as A, and suppose any two other lines were to be added. Which of the additional ones would join A as its continuation and which would appear as an appendage? As it is now drawn AC constitutes the continuity, B the appendage. Figs. 11.14–

11.19 represent a few such variations. Thus, for example, we see that AC/B is still the dominant organization even in Fig. 11.15 (where C is tangent to the circle implied by A). But in Fig. 11.16, when B is tangent to A, we still have AC/B. Naturally, however, the length of B and C is an important consideration. In all such cases there arise the same questions as those suggested above in our discussion of *Prägnanzstufen*. Certain arrangements are stronger than others, and seem to "triumph"; interme-

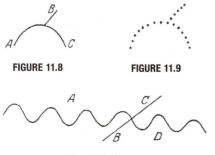

FIGURE 11.8

FIGURE 11.9

FIGURE 11.10

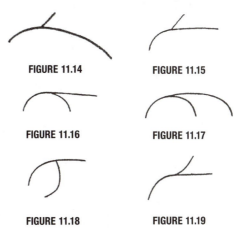

FIGURE 11.14

FIGURE 11.15

FIGURE 11.16

FIGURE 11.17

FIGURE 11.18

FIGURE 11.19

diate arrangements are less distinctive, more equivocal.

On the whole the reader should find no difficulty in *seeing* what is meant here. In designing a pattern, for example, one has a feeling how successive parts should follow one another; one knows what a "good" continuation is, how "inner coherence" is to be achieved, etc.; one recognizes a resultant "good Gestalt" simply by its own "inner necessity." A more detailed study at this juncture would require consideration of the following: Additions to an incomplete object (e.g. the segment of a curve) may proceed in a direction opposed to that of the original, or they may *carry on* the principle "logically demanded" by the original. It is in the latter case that "unity" will result. This does not mean, however, that "simplicity" will result from an addition which is (piecewise considered) "simple." Indeed even a very "complicated" addition may promote unity of the resultant whole. "Simplicity" does not refer to the properties of individual parts; simplicity is a property of wholes. Finally, the addition must be viewed also in terms of such characteristic "whole properties" as closure, equilibrium, and symmetry.[3]

From an inspection of Figs. 11.20–11.22 we are led to the discovery of still another principle: *The Factor of Closure.* If A, B, C, D are given and *AB/ CD* constitute two self-enclosed units, then *this* arrangement rather than *AC/BD* will be apprehended. It is not true, however, that closure is necessarily the dominant Factor in all cases which satisfy these conditions. In Fig. 11.23, for example, it is not three self-enclosed areas but rather *The Factor of the "Good Curve"* which predominates.

It is instructive in this connection to determine the conditions under which two figures will appear as *two* independent figures, and those under which they will combine to yield an entirely different (single) figure. (Examples: Fig. 11.24–

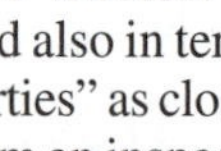

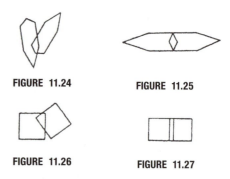

FIGURE 11.24   FIGURE 11.25

FIGURE 11.26   FIGURE 11.27

11.27.) And this applies also to surfaces. The reader may test the influence of surface wholeness by attempting to see Fig. 11.24 as three separate, closed figures. With coloured areas the unity of naturally coherent parts may be enhanced still more. Fig. 11.28 is most readily seen as an oblique deltoid (*bc*) within a rectangle (*ad*). Try now to see on the left side a hexagon whose lower right-hand corner is shaded, and on the right side another hexagon whose upper left-hand corner is shaded [viz. Figs., 11.28*a* and 11.28*b*].

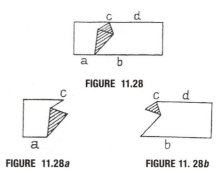

FIGURE 11.28

FIGURE 11.28*a*   FIGURE 11. 28*b*

Once more we observe (as with the curves of Figs. 11.9–11.12) the influence of a tendency towards the "good" Gestalt, and in the present case it is probably easier than before to grasp the meaning of this expression. Here it is clearly evident that a unitary colour tends to bring about uniformity of colouring within the given surface.[4]

Taking any figure (e.g. Fig. 11.29) it is instructive to raise such questions as the following: By means of what additions can one so alter the fig-

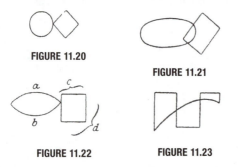

FIGURE 11.20

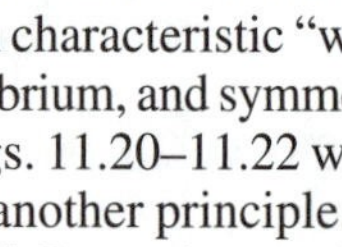

FIGURE 11.21

FIGURE 11.22   FIGURE 11.23

---

[3]Symmetry signifies far more than mere similarity of parts; it refers rather to the logical correctness of a part considered relative to the whole in which that part occurs.

[4]The Factor of similarity can thus be seen as a special instance of *The Factor of the Good Gestalt.*

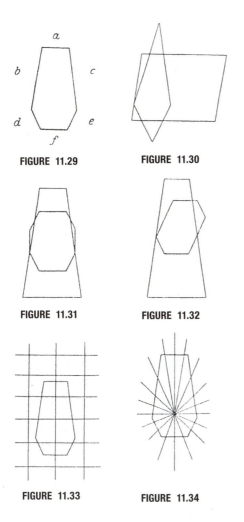

FIGURE 11.29

FIGURE 11.30

FIGURE 11.31

FIGURE 11.32

FIGURE 11.33

FIGURE 11.34

ure that a spontaneous apprehension of the original would be impossible? (Figs. 11.30–11.32 are examples.) An excellent method of achieving this result is to complete certain "good subsidiaries" in a manner which is "contra-structural" relative to the original. (But notice that not all additions to the original will have this effect. Figs. 11.33–11.34, for example, represent additions which we may call "indifferent" since they are rather "pro-structural" not "contra-structural.")

Let us call the original (Fig. 11.29) *O* and any contra-structural addition *C*, while any pro-structural addition we shall call *P*. For our purposes, then, *O* is to be thought of as a subsidiary of some more inclusive whole. Now *O* whether taken alone or as part of *OP* is different from what it would be in *OC*. It is of the first importance for *O* in *which* constellation it appears.[5] (In this way a person thor-

oughly familiar with O can be made quite blind to its existence. This applies not only to recognition but to perception in general.)

VIII. Another Factor is that of past experience or habit. Its principle is that if *AB* and *C* but not *BC* have become habitual (or "associated") there is then a tendency for *ABC* to appear as *AB/C*. Unlike the other principles with which we have been dealing, it is characteristic of this one that the contents *A, B, C* are assumed to be independent of the constellation in which they appear. Their arrangement is one principle determined merely by extrinsic circumstances (e.g. drill).

There can be no doubt that some of our apprehensions are determined in this way.[6] Often arbitrary material can be arranged in arbitrary form and, after a sufficient drill, made habitual. The difficulty is, however, that many people are inclined to attribute to this principle the fundamental structure of *all* apprehension. The situation in §VII, they would say, simply involves the prominence of habitual complex. Straight lines, right angles, the arcs of circles, squares—all are familiar from everyday experience. And so it is also with the intervals between parts (e.g. the spaces between written words), and with uniformity of coloured surfaces. Experience supplies a constant drill in such matters,

And yet, despite its plausibility, the doctrine of past experience brushes aside the real problems of apprehension much too easily. Its duty should be to demonstrate in each of the foregoing cases (1) that the dominant apprehension was due to earlier experience (and to nothing else); (2) that non-dominant apprehensions in each instance had *not* been previously experienced; and, in general, (3) that in the *amassing* of experience none but the adventitious factors need ever be involved. It should be clear from our earlier discussions and examples that this programme could not succeed. A single example will suffice to show this. Right angles surround us from childhood (table, cupboard, window, corners of rooms, houses). At first this seems quite self-evident. But does the child's environment consist of nothing but man-made objects? Are there not in nature (e.g. the branches of trees) fully as many obtuse and acute angles? But far more important than these is the following

---

[5]Compare *Selections 9a* and *9b*.

[6]Example: 314 cm. is apprehended as *abc/de*, not as *ab/cde*—i.e. as 314 cm., not 31/4 cm. nor as 314c/m.

consideration. Is it *true* that cupboards, tables, etc., actually present right angles to the child's eye ? If we consider the literal reception of stimuli upon the retina, how often are *right angles* as such involved? Certainly less often than the *perception of angles*. As a matter of fact the conditions necessary for a literal "right angle" stimulation are realized but rarely in everyday life (viz. *only* when the table or other object appears in a frontal parallel plane). Hence the argument from experience is referring not to repetition of literal stimulus conditions, but to repetition of phenomenal experience—and the problem therefore simply repeats itself.

Regardless of whether or not one believes that the relationships discussed in §VII depend upon past experience, the question remains in either case: Do these relationships exhibit the operations of intrinsic laws or not, and if so, which laws? Such a question requires experimental inquiry and cannot be answered by the mere expression "past experience." Let us take two arrangements which have been habitually experienced in the forms *abc* and *def* many thousands of times. I place them together and present *abcdef*. Is the result sure to be *abc/def*? Fig. 11.35, which is merely the combination of a W and an M, may be taken as an example. One ordinarily sees not the familiar letters W and M, but a situation between two symmetrically curved uprights. If we designate parts of the W from left to right as *abc* and those of the M as *def,* the figure may be described *ad/be/cf* (or as */be/* between */ad/* and */cf/*); *not*, however, as *abc/def.*

FIGURE 11.35

But the objection might be raised that while we are familiar enough with W and M, we are not accustomed to seeing them in *this* way (one above the other) and that this is why the other arrangement is dominant. It would certainly be false, however, to consider this an "explanation." At best this mode of approach could show only why the arrangement W-M is *not* seen; the positive side would still be untouched. But apart from this, the objection is rendered impotent when we arrange *abc* and *def* one above the other (Fig. 11.36) in a fashion quite as unusual as that given in Fig. 11.35. Nor is the argument admissible that the arrangement */ad/* and not */be/* and */cf/* in Fig. 11.35 are themselves familiar from past experience. It simply is

FIGURE 11.36

not true that as much experience has been had with */be/* as with the *b* in *abc* and the *e* in *def*.

IX. When an object appears upon a homogeneous field there must be stimulus differentiation (inhomogeneity) in order that the object may be perceived. A perfectly homogeneous field appears as a total field *[Ganzfeld]* opposing subdivision, disintegration, etc. To effect a segregation within this field requires relatively strong differentiation between the object and its background. And this holds not only for ideally homogeneous fields but also for fields in which, e.g., a symmetrical brightness distribution obtains, or in which the "homogeneity" consists in a uniform dappled effect. The best case for the resulting of a figure in such a field is when in the total field a closed surface of simple form is different in colour from the remaining field. Such a surface figure is not one member of a duo (of which the total field or "ground" would be the other member); its contours serve as boundary lines only for *this* figure. The background is not limited by the figure, but usually seems to continue unbroken beneath that figure.

Within this figure there may be then further subdivision resulting in subsidiary wholes. The procedure here as before is in the direction "from above downward" and it will be found that the Factors discussed in §VII are crucial for these subdivisions.[7] As regards attention, fixation, etc., it follows that they are *secondarily* determined relative to the natural relations already given by whole constellations as such. Consider, e.g., the difference between some artificially determined concentration of attention and that spontaneously resulting from the pro-structural emphasis given by a figure itself. For an approach "from above downward," i.e. from whole-properties downward towards subsidiary wholes and parts, individual parts ("elements") are not primary, not pieces to be combined in and-summations, but are *parts of wholes*.

---

[7]Epistemologically this distinction between "above" and "below" is of great importance. The mind and the psychophysiological reception of stimuli do *not* respond after the manner of a mirror or photographic apparatus receiving individual "stimuli" *qua* individual units and working them up "from below" into the objects of experience. Instead response is made to articulation as a whole—and this after the manner suggested by the Factors of § VII. It follows that the apparatus of reception cannot be described as a piecewise sort of mechanism. It must be of such a nature as to be able *to grasp the inner necessity* of articulated wholes. When we consider the problem in this light it becomes apparent that pieces are not even experienced as such but that apprehension itself is characteristically "from above."

Figure and Ground

E. Rubin

The Fundamental Difference between Figure and Ground. We shall here attempt to clarify the difference in the appearance of an area when it is seen as figure and when it is seen as ground.

This difference has several aspects. The most important of these is that what is perceived as figure and what is perceived as ground do not have shape in the same way. In a certain sense, the ground has no shape. A field which had previously been experienced as ground can function in a surprising way when experienced as figure. This effect depends on the new shape, which had not previously been in awareness, and which is now experienced for the first time.

In several cases, in which the change from seeing an area as ground to seeing it as figure occurred rather slowly, I experienced how the ground gradually took on a certain shape and became figure. In German, there is an expression which is perhaps strikingly appropriate: "wie der Grund gestaltet wird" ("How the ground becomes structured"). Something happens to the ground when it goes over into figure. Especially when it proceeds slowly, it seems that there is something new added to the area which was ground and is becoming figure. The experienced object becomes enriched while changing. This impression is also clear when the reversal of figure and ground occurs suddenly.

To characterize the fundamental difference between figure and ground it is useful to consider the contour, which is defined as the common boundary of the two fields. One can then state as a fundamental principle: when two fields have a common border, and one is seen as figure and the other as ground, the immediate perceptual experience is characterized by a shaping effect which emerges from the common border of the fields and which operates only on one field, or operates more strongly on one than on the other.

The field which is most affected by this shaping process is figure; the other field is ground. In principle, two limiting cases are possible: both fields may become figure simultaneously (in which case both are equally affected by the shaping process of the contour), or neither field may be affected by this shaping process, and therefore neither becomes figure.

It must be emphasized that one does not sense this shaping process as such, but only its effect, the emergence of a shaped surface. Therefore, it might be more correct to say, instead of "a shaping effect emerges from the contour," that it is *as though* a shaping effect emerges from the contour. Then the expression "the shaping effect of the contour" is regarded as figurative. Whatever one chooses, it is certain that the contour can have a completely different significance for the two fields. It often happened that when the subjects were asked to describe the ground, they said that they had the impression that it extended behind the figure.

With the help of Fig. 12.1, the reader can make observations along these lines. One can experience alternately a radially marked or concentrically marked cross. If the concentric cross is seen as figure after the radial one, it is possible to note a characteristic change in the concentric markings which depends on whether they belong to the fig-

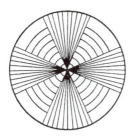

FIGURE 12.1

ure or the ground. When they are part of the ground, they do not appear interrupted. On the contrary, one has the impression that concentric circles continue behind the figure. Nothing of this kind is noticed when the concentrically marked sectors compose that which is seen as figure.

By cutting a nonsense figure out of cardboard and placing it at a slant in front of a frontal-parallel homogeneously colored wall, a very clear example is obtained of both how a common border can only affect the shape of one surface, and how the other surface seems to extend behind it. If one observes such a piece of cardboard, it will clearly emerge as figure, and it hides a part of the wall. It is, so to speak, obvious that the wall continues behind the cardboard. An interesting task is to try to determine how the visible portion of the wall, which is not covered by the cardboard, would look if *it* were seen as figure. If one tries this, one will discover that the task is very difficult. Furthermore, it is extremely foreign and "unnatural," which proves that it does not occur in everyday life. It almost seems impossible to get the contour that wall and cardboard have in common to exert its shaping effect on the wall surface.

Observations of this kind on the continuous extension of the ground behind the figure can easily be made on almost any object—preferably not too regular—which stands in front of a wall or surface. In effect, the common contour indicates this is the end of the object, and seems to concern the ground to such a small degree that the ground can quietly continue on past behind the figure. Subjects have frequently pointed this out.

It must be noted that the impression that the ground extends behind the border, or that the figure ends at the border, is not a matter of an abstract knowing or an abstract assumption, but of an immediate impression which occurs *in spite of* knowledge. If an irregular black area, e.g., a piece

of black paper, is placed on the center of a piece of white paper lying on the floor and the white area emerges as figure, it is easy to get the impression that the black is a dark hole which continues behind the opening. Under these conditions, when I wanted to alter the figure in such a way as to get stronger white "tongues" extending into the "hole," I had to pull myself together to pick up the black piece of paper in order to cut it. In spite of my knowledge of the stimulus, the impression that the border common to the black and the white was the end of the white object was so striking that it seemed to me as though my behavior were absurd: to cut a hole smaller, in order to make the white field in which the hole was, larger. The peculiar conflict which one can experience here between what one knows, and what one sees with one's own eyes, is so interesting that it is recommended that the reader try the experiment himself. Further, if one places the white paper on a patterned rug and reduces the illumination to a very low level, one can experience something very remarkable: the rug pattern is seen in the hole—through the black and the white paper! The awareness that the experienced object is a hole, and that one can look through holes, is responsible for the result, but only in a suggestive way. I must add that I have only had this experience under exceptional conditions, and it occurred only rarely in my subjects. I have a strong recollection of having read a treatise in which something similar was described, but I have been unable to locate it again.

The "Thing-Character" of the Figure and the "Substance-Character" of the Ground. When a reversal of figure and ground occurs, one can observe that the area affected by the shape-giving function of the contour at the same time obtains a characteristic which is similar to that which leads one to call objects "things." The experienced shape is essential to the object, and the contour is the edge of this object. When we talk of the thing-character of the figure, we do not intend to say that the particular figure is similar to a particular thing like a hairbrush. Even when the figure does not look like any known thing, it can still have this thing-character. By "thing-character" we mean a similarity to what is common in all experienced objects to which can legitimately be attached the predicate, "thing."

In contrast with this characteristic of the figure, the ground—or the background—which is unaffected by the shape-giving of the contour, has a characteristic which is more like a "substance," like flour, sand, iron, etc. This does not mean that the substance of which the ground is composed, e.g., the paper, comes clearly into awareness, but that the experienced ground, as such, has a characteristic in common with all the referents of the word "substance."

The function of the individual character of the figure shows a close relation to the principle that the difference between two fields is essentially greater when the experienced objects are both figures than when they are both grounds. A field experienced as figure is a richer, more differentiated structure than the same field experienced as ground.

Subjective Color Differences between Figure and Ground. I have noticed in many different situations that the color seems more substantial and more compact in the figure than in the ground. Dr. Katz had the same impression in several experiments. One subject, in some experiments in which she was asked to describe the difference between figure and ground, confirmed these findings. (She had read Katz's work, and was herself engaged in research on color.) She clearly expressed in her description of the ground the indefinite localization which is characteristic of film colors according to Katz.[1] That this impression was also present in other subjects, but did not enter their protocols because they were unaware of the concepts and descriptions, can be surmised from their uncertain statements when asked about the localization of the ground.

That excellent observer, Hering, has described an experiment[2] in which an open-topped box with a blackened inside and covered by a piece of white cardboard with a ragged-edged hole cut in it, can be seen in two ways. Either one sees a hole in the cardboard and, behind the plane of the hole, a dark space, or one sees a black spot, the shape of the hole, on top of the white cardboard. The percept in the two cases is entirely different. In the first case the percept of the dark stimulus is a space-filling one, spread out in depth. In the second, the dark stimulus appears surface-like, and is squeezed into a surface, and looks like the color of a surface. When the experiment succeeds, the difference is very striking.

A good procedure for making observations similar to Hering's is the following. I sketched an octagon in the middle of a large piece of white cardboard, cut out one of the systems of sectors (as in

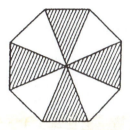

FIGURE 12.2

Fig. 12.2), and stood the cardboard in an open window so that the dark night could be seen through the openings. If I viewed the white sector-systems as figure, the dark or black areas had the character of a weak, space-filling film color behind the piece of cardboard. If I viewed the dark system as figure, I saw a pitch-black surface, lying on the cardboard. Not only did the film color become more compact and substantial, but at the same time it became more decidedly black. There was a weak light from a lamp in the room.

At this point we can also refer back to the experiment mentioned above, in which a black field was surrounded by a white. When the white field is seen as figure, the black piece of paper stops looking like a black surface. Usually it is seen as a dark, weak, space-filling color. One can say briefly, though not quite precisely, that in this case something which actually is the surface color of an object is experienced as a space-filling color, while in Hering's experiment something which actually is a space-filling color is experienced as a surface color.

It appears as though the greater structural solidity of the color of a field when seen as figure can be noticed not only in direct perception but also in after-images and in visual images.

Difference between Figure and Ground in Apparent Localization. It has already been indicated that a difference can appear in the localization of figure and ground in the third dimension, in that the ground is often less clearly localized than the figure. In addition to this relatively qualitative difference, a non-objective but more quantitative difference is very frequently noticed. This difference is based on the strong tendency to localize the area seen as figure closer than that seen as ground. Since

---

[1] *Die Erscheinungsweisen der Farben*, etc. *Zeitschr. f. Psychologie*, Ergänz. Band 7. [See also Katz, Selection 6. Eds.]

[2] *Hermanns Handbuch der Phsyiologie*, Vol. 3, Part 1, pp. 574f.

often only very uncertain estimates are obtained of the greater distance of the ground, one can only speak of a certain order of magnitude of this difference in distance, and this order of magnitude can vary widely between one meter and one mm. Often the difference is only that the figure lies on the ground, without any real difference in distance.

In Relation to the Ground, the Figure Is More Impressive and More Dominant. Everything about the figure is remembered better, and the figure brings forth more associations than the ground.

As a rule there is a further difference when an area is seen as figure or as ground, in that when it is experienced as figure it is in general more impressive than when it is experienced as ground. It dominates consciousness; consequently in descriptions, the figure is usually mentioned before the ground.

If one has sufficient practice in observations of this kind, the following conditions demonstrate effectively that a figure is more impressive and dominant than the ground. First look simply and naturally at a piece of rectangular white paper, and then quickly place a small black figure in its center. You can then observe, almost directly, how the white surface recedes from the center of consciousness, while the black figure takes over. The form of the white surface, determined by the contour it has in common with the table-top, is no longer as clear. This last effect surely contributes to the phenomenon that the experienced white area loses some of its thing-character even though you fully realize that it is a piece of white paper that is before you.

Another illustration of the dominance of the figure is that if a subject is asked to make judgments about the familiarity or unfamiliarity of a series of figures of the same color, on a uniformly colored ground, he speaks about the figure and not the ground. This fact could be explained in that the grounds on which the figures lie are less different, since they are less affected by the influence of the contour they have in common with the figure. The ground seems to merge into the general environment, a circumstance which is hardly taken into account in judgments about familiarity or unfamiliarity.

It seems to be relatively unimportant for the recognition of a figure whether it is seen on one or another ground. In this connection, there is a kind of figural autonomy. In experiments in which the ground was yellow with strong black parallel stripes, recognition of the figures was 58% when the stripes were similarly oriented during training and test (either vertical both times or horizontal both times), and was 46.5% when their orientation was different in training and test. Probably the small difference in these numbers can be accounted for by an indirect effect (emphasized by special instructions) of the stripes in the ground on the character of the perceived figure.

In comparison judgments between two fields, each of which contains figure and ground, subjects report that the figures are similar or different; they do not talk about the grounds. This is true of judgments of differences. A natural explanation of why this is also true of judgments of similarity (in addition to the factor that figures in general are more impressive than grounds) is that the grounds in general do not seem as different as the figures. In consequence, statements of similarity between two grounds are practically meaningless.

That the figure is as a whole more impressive and dominates consciousness also implies that everything about the figure is recalled better than characteristics of the ground. When I held a separate nonsense figure in my hand, I often caught myself noticing, in the moment after I had looked at it, that I did not have the slightest notion over which ground I had held the figure. In the experiments just mentioned, with figures on yellow, striped grounds, the subjects did not mention that in half the figures the stripes had been turned 90°, an indication that the direction of the stripes had not been strongly learned during training.

The rule that more is remembered about the figure than about the ground holds for immediate, natural attitudes; this does not suggest that under special conditions one cannot set oneself to remember more about the ground.

For that matter, it is not easy to decide whether the fact that details about the ground are difficult to reproduce later is due to nothing about such details ever having been in consciousness or to something having been there but forgotten. Even if one assumes that something *was* there, it can be difficult to decide what this "something" was.

In experiments with nonsense figures subjects often "read into" the figures. This can involve known objects, birds, animals, and people, flowers, or coffee-cans, crochet hooks, etc., but sometimes also more abstract forces, tendencies, directions, and movements. In addition, verbal naming as well as loosely connected conceptions are sometimes used in thinking about the figure. It must be emphasized that in experiments with nonsense figures there was not a single instance in which such associations occurred in regard to the part of the field that was seen as ground. . . .

When something is read into a figure, this process is based on a similarity in shape between the figure and the particular thing. This explains why things are not read into the ground. Since the contour's shaping effect is absent or less strong on the ground than the figure, no particular shape similarity exists between the ground and the particular thing. In Fig. 12.3 the reader has the opportunity not only to convince himself that the ground is perceived as shapeless but also to see that a meaning read into a field when it is figure is not read in when the field is seen as ground.

The Relation between Figure and Ground with Regard to Affect. In experiments on figure and ground the opportunity sometimes arose to observe relations connected with affective experience. Some of these are not special to these experiments, such as that the subjects get tired of the experiments, or that they feel satisfied when they think they have accomplished the task set for them by the instructions, etc. Other affective relations are more closely related to the special conditions of these experiments. This holds of feelings associated with what is read into the figure. This is a function of the fact that feelings are attached to figures and not to grounds, and these feelings are an aspect of the relation implied in the statement that the figure dominates in consciousness. In the first place, the remarkable or unexpected that the subjects see in the figures can amuse them. In the second place, the particulars that they read into the figure can arouse certain feelings related to what is read in. If a figure looks like a beloved and admired professor from the homeland, this may remind the subject of the pleasure in having met him again as he stopped by on the way to Göttingen. If a figure looks like a beautiful female torso, this also indubitably calls forth certain feelings.

In addition to feelings of this kind, feelings of an aesthetic character can also occur. The autonomy of the figure relative to the ground has the consequence that, independently of the ground on which it lies, a figure can arouse an aesthetic impression. In contrast, the objective figure which constitutes the ground is usually aesthetically indifferent. This is obvious as long as it is not experienced as figure, but is worth mentioning since it

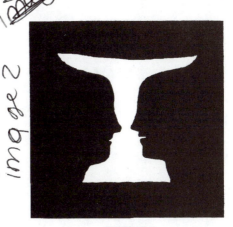

FIGURE 12.3

plays no small role in art. When one succeeds in experiencing as figure areas which are intended as ground, one can sometimes see that they constitute aesthetically displeasing forms. If one has the misfortune in pictures of the Sistine Madonna to see the background as figure, one will see a remarkable lobster claw grasping Saint Barbara, and another odd pincer-like instrument seizing the holy sexton. These figures are hardly beautiful. Ornaments frequently become aesthetically displeasing when the part intended as ground is seen as figure. . . .

Rules for the Probability That a Surface Is Seen as Figure. When two fields adjoin one another, what are the characteristic qualities of these fields which make it probable that one will be seen as figure and the other as ground? The following principle is fundamental: if one of the two homogeneous, different colored fields is larger than and encloses the other, there is a great likelihood that the small, surrounded field will be seen as figure. . . .

Conscious intent can also play an important role. . . .

Further, there is a certain tendency to uniformity. In a design in which the same motifs are repeated, there is a tendency to see the repetition in the same way. There is a tendency to experience a cohesive, homogeneously colored field either entirely as figure or entirely as ground. . . .

In experiments with reciprocal cross figures (as Fig. 12.2) presented squarely to the subject, the cross whose sectors are horizontal and vertical is more easily seen as figure than is the other cross. In general, it is easiest to see as figure that sector system which appears "straightest."

Introduction to Reading 13

Visual illusions have always provided rich sources of evidence about the normal workings of the visual system. However, insight about what a given illusion really means is not always immediate. Among the most interesting and most persistently puzzling of these is the moon illusion. The nature of the illusion is stated quite clearly and concisely in the opening sentences of this reading by Kaufman and Rock: "When the moon hangs low over the horizon, it looks much bigger than when it is high in the sky. Yet in photographs, its image has essentially the same size no matter where the camera finds it." Why does our perceptual experience of the moon's size depend on its position in the sky? More detailed accounts of this work may be found in Kaufman & Rock (1962; Rock & Kaufman, 1962).

Kaufman and Rock's studies attempt to adjudicate between two competing accounts of the illusion: the apparent-distance account and the angle-of-regard account. The first idea is a natural consequence of the idea that the size of an object is "unconsciously inferred" (in the words of Helmholtz, see Reading 1) from retinal size and perceived distance. If we assume that retinal size is always registered correctly (it is, after all, the proximal stimulus), then illusions of size must reflect incorrectly registered distance to the object. Holway and Boring (1941) provided ample evidence that when distance cues are impoverished, then judgements of size increasingly rely on the size of the retinal image. However, Boring (1943) rejected this idea because when he asked people to directly estimate the distance to the moon, they tended to judge it as *closer* when it was near the horizon than when it was high in the sky.

The alternative angle of regard theory, though highly implausible at first sight (by what mechanism could it operate?) was nevertheless supported by Boring's original experiments. However, using better methods, Kaufman and Rock were able to show that while angle of regard may have a small effect, it is by no means large enough to provide a satisfactory account of the illusion, and that the apparent-distance explanation does accord with empirical observation. Kaufman and Rock's explanation for the fact that observers judge the horizon moon as closer than the zenith moon assumes that the distance judgement is based on subjects' judgment of the moon's size (the large horizon moon is assumed to be closer because it looks larger) and not on the (presumably unconscious) distance estimate that seems to give rise to the illusion in the first place.

More recently, Hershenson (1989) has edited a collection of work proposing and testing several additional theories of the moon illusion. Some of these are less plausible than others, but their very existence a quarter of a century after Kaufman and Rock first tackled this problem attests to the difficulty of achieving a completely satisfactory explanation.

REFERENCES

Boring, E. G. (1943). The moon illusion. *American Journal of Physics, 11*, 55–60.

Hershenson, M. (Ed.) (1989). *The Moon Illusion*. Hillsdale, NJ: Erlbaum.

Holway, A. F., & Boring, E. G. (1941). Determinants of apparent visual size with distance variant. *American Journal of Psychology, 54*, 21–37.

Kaufman, L., & Rock, I. (1962). The moon illusion. *Science, 136*, 953–961.

Rock, I., & Kaufman, L. (1962). The moon illusion, II. *Science, 136*, 1023–1031.

The Moon Illusion

L. Kaufman • Sperry Gyroscope Co.

I. Rock • Yeshiva University

When the moon is near the horizon, it looks bigger than when it is at the zenith. Is this because the observer raises his eyes to see the zenith moon or because he views the horizon moon over terrain?

When the moon hangs low over the horizon, it looks much bigger than when it is high in the sky. Yet in photographs its image has essentially the same size no matter where the camera finds it. Of course this is equally true of the images in the eye. The change in size is not an optical effect but a psychological one. It is therefore known as the moon illusion.

Men have recognized the moon illusion (as well as the corresponding sun illusion) since antiquity. Many explanations for it have been advanced, but only two deserve serious consideration. One can be called the apparent-distance theory and the other the angle-of-regard theory. According to the former the horizon moon looks bigger because it seems farther away; according to the latter the high moon looks smaller because the viewer raises his eyes or head to look at it.

The apparent-distance theory seems to be the older, going back at least to the second-century astronomer and geometer Ptolemy. He proposed that any object seen through filled space, such as the moon seen across terrain at the horizon, is perceived as being more distant than an object just as far away but seen through empty space, such as the moon at the zenith. If the images of these objects in the eye are in fact of equal size, the one that appears farther away will seem larger.

This follows from the geometrical relationship between size and distance (see Fig. 13.1). If two objects at unequal distances from the observer form images of the same size on the retina, the more remote object must be the larger. It is well known to psychologists that an observer perceiving two equal images, and receiving sensory information that one object is farther away than the other, correctly sees the farther one to be the larger (Fig. 13.2). The reader can demonstrate this fact for himself by looking at a sharply contrasted object against a uniform background long enough to form a clear, persistent afterimage on the retina. This afterimage is of course constant in size. But when the gaze is shifted between two surfaces at different distances, the image appears larger when it is projected on the farther surface.

Similarly, if the moon seems farther away when it is on the horizon than when it is higher in the sky, it should look larger (see Figs. 13.3 and 13.4). Some years ago Edwin G. Boring and his colleagues at Harvard University subjected the apparent-distance theory to what he considered a critical test. He asked people to judge the relative distances of the zenith and horizon moons. Most of his subjects said the horizon moon seemed nearer—the opposite of what the theory called for. So Boring sought another explanation.

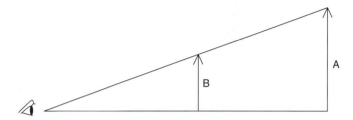

FIGURE 13.1 ■ Distance and Size are Related in the Manner Shown Here. Although Arrows *A* and *B* subtend the same visual angle at the observer's eye and therefore produce images of the same size on his retina, arrow *A* is seen to be farther away and hence actually to be larger.

He proposed that the postural changes involved in looking at the zenith moon might somehow be responsible for the moon illusion (the angle-of-regard theory). Although he could find no explanation of why this might be so, he and his colleagues carried out a series of experiments that seemed to connect the apparent size of the moon with the elevation of the observers' eyes. They used a number of methods; the major one was designed to measure the illusion as follows. The subjects were asked to match the moon, as they saw it, with one of a series of disks of light projected on a nearby screen. Looking at the horizon moon with eyes level, most observers selected a disk one and a half or two times larger than the one they chose when their eyes were raised 30 degrees to view the zenith moon. When they tilted their heads so that they could look at the zenith moon with eyes level, their choice indicated that they experienced no illusion. Two subjects lay supine so that they could see the zenith moon "straight ahead," and, by bending their necks backward, could see the horizon moon with eyes "elevated." For them the illusion was reversed, the zenith moon appearing the larger.

In spite of the apparent persuasiveness of these results, the authors of the present article, working

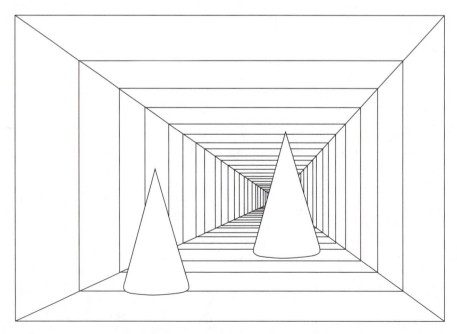

FIGURE 13.2 ■ Distance-size relationship is automatically taken into account by an observer. If two objects that are actually the same size are perceived as being at different distances, the one that seems to be farther away will look larger. The figure at the right is perceived as being larger than the identical figure at the left only because it seems to be farther away.

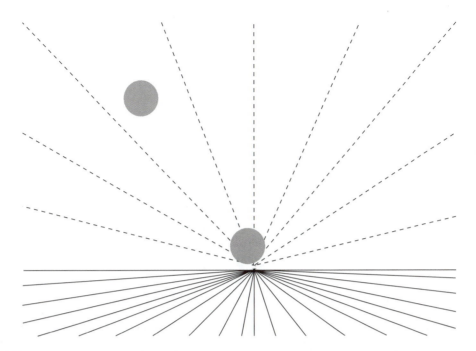

FIGURE 13.3 ■ Apparent-distance theory holds that this is what happens in the case of the moon illusion. The horizon appears to be farther away, although it is not. The viewer automatically takes the apparent distance into account. He then unconsciously applies the rule that, of two objects forming images of equal size, the more distant must be the larger.

at the New School for Social Research and at Yeshiva University, decided some five years ago to reopen the subject. For one thing, we ourselves saw no significant change in size whether we looked at the moon with our eyes level or elevated. For another, we questioned Boring's method of determining the moon's apparent size.

In effect he was asking his subjects to compare things that are not really commensurable. It is difficult to say how large the moon appears to be. Its virtually infinite distance gives it a large but more or less indeterminate size. The comparison disks, on the other hand, were nearby, so that the observer could easily make a judgment as to their actual size. He then had to match a circle of indeterminate size with one having a diameter of some specific number of inches. We felt that such a comparison was extremely difficult to make.

We decided to try a more direct approach, in which two artificial moons seen against the sky could be compared with each other. (The actual illusion involves the same sort of comparison, although the two real moons are separated by a considerable interval of time as well as space.) In our artificial moon apparatus light rays from a lamp

pass through a circular aperture and are made parallel by a lens. The parallel rays fall on a piece of glass or a half-silvered mirror tilted at an angle of 45 degrees. An observer looking into the glass sees a bright disk against the sky, which is also visible through the glass (see Fig. 13.5).

With two such devices, one pointed toward the horizon and the other pointed toward the zenith, we could test the illusion both qualitatively and quantitatively. Each device was equipped with a set of circular apertures of different sizes; thus the aperture in one could be changed until the subject said that the size of the "moon" matched that in the other. The ratio of the zenith aperture to the horizon aperture gave a numerical value for the illusion. A ratio of one would mean no illusion; a ratio greater than one would indicate that the illusion was present in its usual form.

First we set out to test the eye-elevation hypothesis by our new method. In one experiment 10 subjects viewed the artificial horizon moon normally and compared it with a zenith moon that they saw either with eyes elevated or, by tilting their heads, with their eyes level. We obtained an illusion both ways. The ratio of the horizon moon's

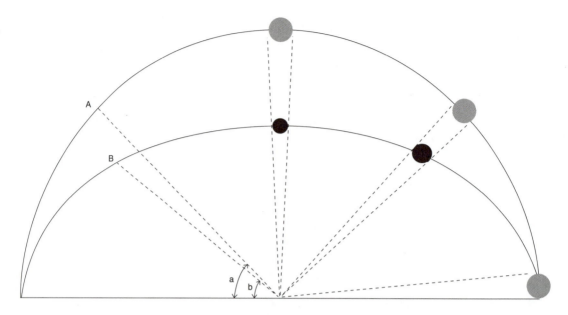

FIGURE 13.4 ■ Effect of apparent distance on the moon's apparent size is diagramed. The true positions of the moon are along the upper curve; its apparent positions, if the horizon seems more distant than the zenith, would be along the lower curve. The perceived size of the moon would accordingly vary as shown by the darker disks. Measurement of the half-arc angles (a, b) to the mid-points (A,B) of the actual and apparent arcs from zenith to horizon indicates that most people see the sky as "flattened," confirming the theory.

apparent diameter to that of the zenith moon was 1.48 with eyes elevated and 1.46 without eye elevation—an insignificant difference. Then we had the subjects compare two moons in the same region of the sky, one viewed with eyes level and the other with eyes elevated. The ratio between the sizes of the two moons was only 1.04. There was no illusion to speak of. We concluded that Boring's findings on eye elevation were peculiar to the methods employed.

Before abandoning the angle-of-regard theory completely, we rechecked one other phenomenon that seemed to support it. Many years ago the German psychologist Erna Schur found she could produce the illusion indoors, in a large dark space such as a zeppelin hangar, by projecting disks of light on the wall and ceiling. Moreover, Boring and Alfred H. Holway reported a sun illusion even when the subject looked at the sun through a dense filter that blanked out everything but the bright disk itself. In both cases no terrain was visible to differentiate horizon from zenith. We repeated Schur's experiment in the Hayden Planetarium in New York and got a ratio of only 1.03 between horizon and zenith. Next we set up our artificial

moon apparatus in a totally dark room and repeated our eye-elevation experiment. In this case the moons were each seen at optical infinity, one at the zenith and one straight ahead. Again the ratio turned out to be 1.03. Considering that T. G. Hermans of the University of Washington has recently reported approximately the same ratio in studying the effect of eye elevation in apparent size, and that we came very close to it (1.04) in our outdoor observations of two moons in the same part of the sky, eye elevation would appear to exert a slight effect. Why this should be so is by no means clear, but in any case it cannot really account for the moon illusion.

We therefore turned to the apparent-distance theory. Boring had rejected it because his subjects said that the horizon moon appeared to be nearer than the zenith moon. But, we wondered, did they really see the horizon moon as nearer? Or were they judging it to be nearer precisely because it looked bigger, effectively turning the reasoning upside down? In that case the reported distance would be a secondary phenomenon, an artifact of the very illusion it was supposed to test. To check this possibility we showed our subjects pairs of artificial moons of different diameters and in-

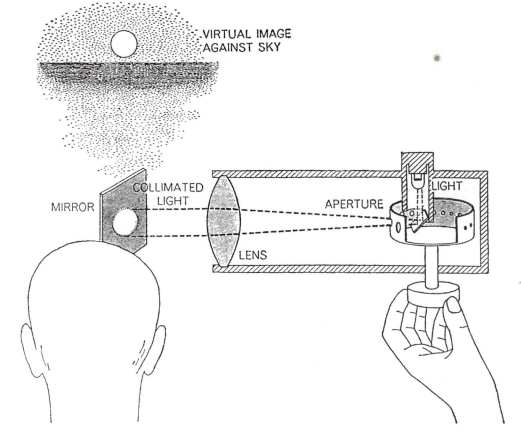

FIGURE 13.5 ■ Moons were simulated by an optical apparatus, shown here schematically. Light passing through one of a series of apertures of different sizes is collimated (rendered parallel) by a lens and falls on a half-silvered mirror. An observer looking into the mirror sees against the sky, as if at an infinite distance, a virtual image of the luminous aperture.

structed them to compare their relative distances. Whenever the zenith moon was larger, the subjects said it was nearer than the horizon moon; when it was smaller, they said it was farther away.

Therefore we next undertook to elicit a judgment of distance without regard to the moon. We asked people to scan a moonless sky and to try to see it as a surface. Then they were to say whether the surface seemed farther away immediately over the horizon or at the zenith. Nine out of 10 observers answered that the horizon sky was the more distant; the tenth could see no difference. From this experiment we conclude that the horizon sky does appear farther away whether the observer realizes it or not when the moon is present.

This evidence is supported by a number of observations, dating back to the English mathematician Robert Smith in 1738, on the "half-arc angle."

Most people, when they are asked to point along the line that bisects the arc of sky from horizon to zenith, indicate a direction considerably less than 45 degrees from the horizontal. The vault of the heavens looks flattened, like a semiellipsoid, rather than hemispherical. Accordingly the horizon seems farther away than the zenith. If the moon is perceived on the "surface" of the semiellipsoid, it too will appear more distant, and therefore larger, at the horizon [see Fig. 13.4]. All this convinced us that the apparent-distance theory was perfectly tenable on logical grounds, and we set out to test it directly.

Pointing our artificial-moon apparatus at the horizon, we had observers view the "moon" through a hole in a sheet of cardboard that masked the terrain. Under these circumstances the illusion vanished: the horizon moon looked no larger than

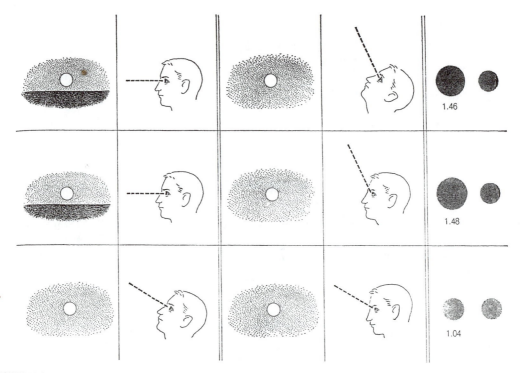

FIGURE 13.6 ■ Eye-elevation hypothesis was tested by having subjects view simulated horizon and zenith moons in various ways. A horizontal moon was compared with a zenith moon seen with eyes level (*top row*) and also with eyes elevated (*middle row*). As shown by the ratios between the perceived sizes of the horizon and zenith moons (*right*), the illusion was present in both cases and was almost the same in spite of the different angles of regard. Then subjects were asked to compare two moons in the same part of the sky, raising their heads so that their eyes were level in one case and lowering their heads so that their eyes were elevated in the other case (*bottom row*). Changing the angle of regard had no significant effect on the size of the two moons, as shown by the 1.04 ratio.

the zenith moon. Then we pointed two of our devices at the horizon; in one the moon was viewed through a mask and in the other the moon was seen over unobstructed terrain. The illusion appeared, just as the apparent-distance theory predicts; to make the two disks appear equal the masked aperture had to be made 1.34 times larger than the aperture of the moon over terrain [see Figs. 13.6 and 13.7]. This was quite comparable with the ratios that were obtained in the ordinary illusion experiment carried out at the same site with different subjects.

If, as was beginning to seem likely, the horizon moon looks larger only because it is seen over terrain, it should be possible to reverse the illusion by moving the terrain overhead with a mirror or prism. We arranged a mirror at a 45-degree angle so that by looking into it a subject could see the horizon and its moon high in the sky. By looking straight ahead into another mirror he saw an image of the zenith sky and moons in a horizontal direction. As we had expected, the illusion did reverse: the moon on an overhead horizon appeared to be larger than the moon at a horizontal zenith, with a ratio of 1:34 [Figs. 13.8 and 13.9].

At this point we could no longer doubt that terrain plays the major role in the moon illusion, but the nature of its role had not been established. Perhaps it was acting in some way other than by giving a sense of greater distance. We now located our apparatus at a site where the visible horizon was about two miles away in one direction and no more than 2,000 feet away 30 degrees to the left, providing a direct test of the effect of distance. The illusion was distinctly greater when the low-lying artificial moon was seen over the more distant horizon.

In this same experiment we also controlled for cloud conditions. Hermann von Helmholtz and others had speculated that cloudiness might in-

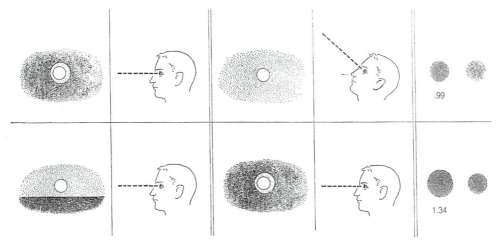

FIGURE 13.7 ■ Effect of terrain was shown by an experiment in which the landscape beneath the horizon moon could be masked, leaving the moon visible through an aperture. When this masked horizon moon was compared with a zenith moon, there was no illusion (*top row*). When a normal horizon moon with terrain was compared with the masked horizon moon, substantial illusion resulted (*bottom row*).

crease the apparent flattening of the sky, and in fact recent observations have indicated that the half-arc angle varies inversely with the degree of cloudiness. If the effect exists, and if the apparent-distance theory is correct, then cloudiness should magnify the moon illusion.

Accordingly we split our experiment into three parts. One group of subjects viewed the artificial moons against a completely overcast sky, one against partial cloud cover and one against a clear sky. The illusion increased significantly both with distance to the horizon and with the degree of cloudiness. Taking all cloud conditions together, the illusion for the far horizon was 1.51 and for the near horizon 1.36. Combining the observations on far and near horizons, the illusion averaged 1.52 in an overcast, 1.45 under partial clouds and 1.34 in a clear sky.

A further test of the apparent-distance theory was provided by turning the horizon upside down with prisms. Inversion is known to lessen the impression of distance, and so we expected it to reduce the size of the moon illusion. Here too our expectations were confirmed: with the horizon inverted the ratio of horizon to zenith moon was 1.28; for the same set of observers under normal conditions it was 1.66. The result probably explains why people have noted a reduced illusion when they view the moon with head down, looking backward

between their legs. The image would be inverted. Our inversion observations, incidentally, were carried out on a New York City rooftop, with the horizon moon seen framed between tall buildings. The high value of the ratio for the normal illusion supports the idea that a framing effect can enhance the size the horizon moon, as many city dwellers have speculated.

The apparent-distance theory was by now supported by a considerable body of experimental evidence, but it remained to be shown that no other factors are involved in the illusion. Two that have been frequently proposed are color and brightness. Often the horizon moon is much redder than the zenith moon because of the selective scattering by the atmosphere of the shorter wavelengths of light. Many people have suggested that the color difference produces a difference in apparent size. We tried putting a minus-blue filter in front of our artificial horizon moon and found that the resulting reddening had no effect on the illusion.

The Irish metaphysician George Berkeley, among others, attributed the illusion to the dimness of the full horizon moon in the twilight sky compared with the brighter zenith moon in the dark night sky. Again we duplicated the conditions in our apparatus. Neither decreasing the relative brightness of the artificial horizon moon nor increasing the contrast of the zenith moon against its background had any measurable effect on this illusion.

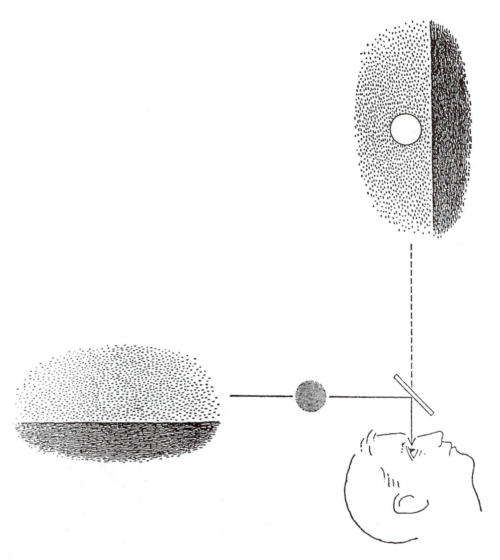

FIGURE 13.8 ■ Terrain's importance was confirmed by using mirrors to reverse the positions of the horizon and zenith moons. By looking up into a mirror the observer saw the horizon terrain and its moons overhead.

In sum, we have demonstrated that the moon illusion depends on the presence of terrain and specifically on the distance effect of the terrain. Eye elevation, color and apparent brightness evidently have nothing to do with the phenomenon.

The theory we have been defending should not be confused with a deceptively similar explanation that has often been ventured. The horizon moon, it is said, can be compared with objects adjacent to its image along the terrain. If the moon is seen next to a distant house and if its image is about the same size as the house, then it appears as large as a house; since the house is quite large, the moon must be large. This explanation is incorrect because the illusion can be obtained over water or desert, where there are no familiar terrestrial objects for comparison. The apparent-distance theory, on the other hand, stresses the impression of distance created by the terrain considered merely as a plane extending outward from the observer—a distance

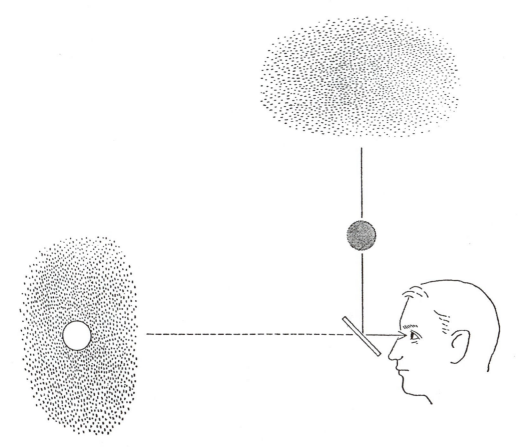

FIGURE 13.9 ■ Looking into mirror he saw a patch of zenith sky and its moon, but in a horizontal direction. The illusion was thereupon reversed from Fig 13.8: the overhead moon appeared 1.34 times larger than the one seen straight ahead.

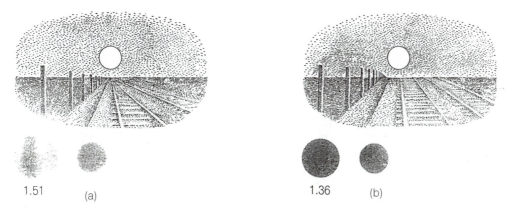

1.51   (a)   1.36   (b)

FIGURE 13.10 ■ Effect of distance was tested more directly by comparing two horizon moons with a zenith moon. One horizon moon was placed where the visible horizon was far off (a); the other was over a nearby horizon (b). The illusion varied significantly with distance. (The railroad tracks, added here to emphasize the difference in distance, were not actually in the experimental scene.)

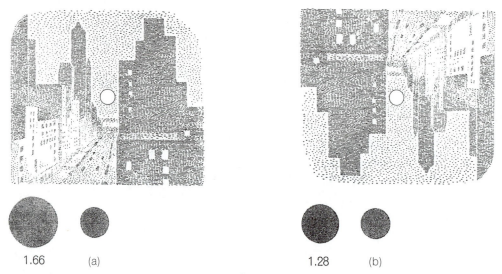

1.66   (a)   1.28   (b)

FIGURE 13.11 ■ Impression of distance is known to be lessened by inversion of a scene. Two horizon moons were compared with a zenith moon. In one case the horizon moon was seen normally between tall buildings (a); in the other case the skyline was inverted by a prism (b). The moon illusion was significantly smaller in the case of the inverted skyline, confirming the importance of distance as a factor.

impression that in turn affects the moon's apparent size according to well-understood relationships.

Eighteen hundred years after Ptolemy we have tested his hypothesis and provided evidence that it is correct. Oddly enough, there is no part of our technique that could not have been carried out centuries ago. But experimentation in psychology is a fairly recent development. So too is the theory of size perception, in which apparent distance is now understood to play a basic role.

Introduction to Readings 14 and 15

The purpose of vision is to provide veridical information about the layout and properties of objects and surfaces in the local environment. That is, vision should provide us with accurate estimates of the size, shape, location, color, and texture of objects. In fact, it does this quite well.

But this ability to correctly represent surface properties presents us with a puzzle. The puzzle is most easily understood by considering a simple example. A white piece of paper diffusely reflects about 85% of the light that strikes it (the reflectance, R, of the paper is 0.85). If we view the paper outside on a bright, sunny day (where the illumination I is very large), the amount of light reflected by the paper into our eyes (the luminance $L = R*I$) is many orders of magnitude greater than if we were to view that same paper indoors under incandescent lighting (where I is much smaller). Yet we unhesitatingly would judge the paper as white (i.e., with a reflectance of about 0.85) on both occasions. We would not be fooled into thinking that the paper is white in the one case and gray in the other.

This remarkable ability to correctly recover surface properties like lightness or color despite variation in the proximal stimulus (i.e., the retinal image) is called *perceptual constancy*. Correct judgements of surface lightness as in the example of the white sheet of paper are instances of lightness constancy. Correct judgements about surface color despite variations in the wavelength composition of the illuminant (e.g., judging the white piece of paper as such when it is illuminated with either a flourescent or an incandescent lightbulb, which have easily discriminable colors) are instances of color constancy. Correctly judging the shape of the page on which these words are written as rectangular, despite the fact that the retinal image is probably trapezoidal (unless you happen to be holding this book exactly perpendicular to your line of sight), is an instance of shape constancy. Correctly judging the size of a basketball when it is thrown toward you despite a dramatic change in the size of the retinal image is called size constancy (see Reading 15: Kaufman and Rock). Explaining perceptual constancy has been a major goal of philosophers and psychologists over the centuries.

Every instance of perceptual constancy involves some interaction between two factors, one of which is relevant—the object or surface property in question—and one of which is irrelevant—some relation between the object or surface and the environment that affects the measurement taken by the eye. In the case of lightness constancy, the relevant property is surface reflectance, which determines surface lightness and color, and the irrelevant factor is the brightness and color of the illumination, which can vary over a wide range. In the case of size constancy, the relevant property is the object's size, and the irrelevant factor is its distance from the observer. In shape constancy, the relevant property is object shape, and the irrelevant factor is the observer's viewpoint relative to the object.

In these two readings, the question of lightness constancy is investigated. One approach to the problem is to assume that the brightness of the illuminant is somehow estimated and then "factored out" when interpreting the amount of light that is reflected into the eye from the surface. However, as Wallach points out, the only means to estimate the brightness of the illuminant is via the light reflected from surfaces that have unknown surface reflectance; this solution is therefore circular.

Wallach's solution, inspired in part by an earlier experiment reported by Gelb (1929), is that lightness constancy depends on the visual system's relying on the *ratio* of the brightnesses of adjacent regions in the image. The intuition is that the visual system assumes (and

usually this assumption is perfectly valid), that adjacent surface regions are illuminated by the same amount of light. Thus the luminance ratio automatically factors out the illuminant and provides an invariant cue to surface color ($L_1/L_2 = R_1{}^*I/R_2{}^*I = R_1/R_2$).[1] Gelb's experiment cleverly violated the constant-illumination assumption by using a hidden spotlight to illuminate a black piece of paper suspended in a dimly-illuminated room, so that the illumination of the paper and of its immediate surround were quite different. In this case, the black paper appeared white, because even a black piece of paper with reflectance of 10% reflects a large amount of light when the illuminant is bright. The moment a white paper was placed in the spotlight's path, partly overlapping the black paper, the luminance ratio exhibited by the white and black papers could be perceived correctly, and the true color of both surfaces was apprehended. Wallach's experiments show that the ratio principle provides an excellent account of people's judgements of surface lightness

It turns out, however, that the ratio principle cannot account for all instances of lightness constancy. Different mechanisms are required to deal with lightness judgments that are required by the presence of reflectance edges in the image (that is, edges that are due to changes in surface reflectance) and by the presence of illumination edges (i.e., edges that are due to changes in illumination,

---

[1] Two brief clarifying comments about the Wallach selection: First, the author uses the word "color" to refer to shades of white, gray, and black. Second, the unfamiliar term "episcotister" (p. 249) refers to a device for continuously varying the brightness of a beam of light passing through it. It consists of an opaque, rapidly rotating disk with a wedge-shaped aperture in it that can be varied in size. A aperture of 180° means that half the disk is open to pass light. If the disk rotates rapidly enough, the light passing through the aperture appears to be continuous because the eye's ability to detect flicker is limited (this fact makes the apparent continuity of television and motion pictures possible). The amount of light passing through the episcotister depends directly on the size of the aperture, measured in degrees.

such as the presence of a shadow). Gilchrist (1988) showed that these two kinds of edges produce dramatically different judgments of surface lightness, judgments that nevertheless reflect almost perfect lightness constancy in each case. Somehow the visual system must classify edges as being due to reflectance or illumination changes before estimating lightness.

The experiment of Rock and colleagues is a clever variation on an earlier study by Rock and Brosgole (1964), who asked whether perceptual grouping by proximity (see Reading 11: Wertheimer) occurs before or after the relative depths of various objects in the scene are registered. They showed observers an array of luminous beads suspended in a frame by a grid of transparent wire; the beads were closer together in the vertical than in the horizontal direction, so that when viewed head-on, the beads appeared to form vertical columns as a result of grouping by vertical proximity. The frame was then tilted horizontally away from the viewer so that the right side of the frame was further away than the left side. Under these conditions, the retinal projections of the beads were closer together in the horizontal direction than in the vertical direction due to foreshortening. If perceptual

grouping is "early," that is, if it is based on the retinal image before relative depth is computed, then one would expect the beads to form horizontal rows as a result of grouping by horizontal proximity. However, this is not what happened: the observers continued to see the beads as forming columns. This implies that the relative depth of the frame was registered before grouping occurred, suggesting that in this case grouping is a relatively "late" perceptual process.

In their article, Rock and colleagues ask whether perceptual grouping by similarity (again, see Reading 11: Wertheimer) occurs before or after lightness constancy is achieved. The idea is simple: if grouping is based on retinal illumination, then the items in the central column of Fig. 15.2 should be perceived as belonging to the luminance-matched group, but if grouping is based on a post-constancy representation, then the central column should be judged as belonging to the reflectance-matched group. The result is equally simple: grouping is based on a post-constancy representation in which similarity of surface reflectance determines the percept; in other words, grouping by similarity is a relatively "late" perceptual process.

REFERENCES

Epstein, W. (1977). *Stability and constancy in visual perception: Mechanisms and processes.* New York: John Wiley & Sons.

Gelb, A. (1929). Die Farbenkonstanzder Sehdinge. In A. Bethe, G. V. Bergmann, G. Embden, & A. Ellinger (Eds.). *Handbuch der normalen und pathologischen physiologie* (Vol. 12, pp. 594–678). Berlin: Springer–Verlag.

Gilchrist, A. L. (1988). Lightness contrast and failures of constancy: A common explanation. *Perception & Psychophysics, 43*, 415–424.

Rock, I. & Brosgole, L. (1964). Grouping based on phenomenal proximity. *Journal of Experimental Psychology, 67*, 531–538.

Brightness Constancy and the Nature of Achromatic Colors

H. Wallach • Swarthmore College

Part I

The problem of brightness constancy arises through the following circumstances. The amount of light which is reflected by an opaque object and which stimulates the eye depends not only upon the color of the object but just as much upon the amount of light which falls on the object, that is upon the illumination in which the object is seen. When in spite of this, the seen colors are in agreement with the object colors, when a given object appears to have the same color in various illuminations, we speak of brightness constancy.

The majority of investigators who aim at all at functional explanations understand this problem to mean: How is illumination registered and in what way is it taken into account so that the experienced colors remain constant when the illumination is varied? In this version the problem is a difficult one at the outset, for illumination is never directly or independently given but is represented in stimulation only in as much as it affects the amount of light which is reflected by the objects. To be sure, we perceive illumination as well as surface color; a spot of light here, a shadow there, a brightly lighted region near the window or the dim light of dusk on everything. But the fact remains that both variables, object color and objective illumination, affect the eye through the same medium, the varying amount of reflected light. If the seen illumination were found to be in agree-

ment with the objective illumination, in principle the same problem would arise which we face regarding the surface colors. There is only one stimulus variable to represent two objective variables each of which seems to have its counterpart in experience. Under these circumstances investigation has largely consisted in the study of factors by which illumination could be recognized and in the demonstration of their effectiveness in bringing about constancy.

The following observations suggested a radically different approach to the writer. They concern some variations of an experiment by A. Gelb which demonstrated brightness constancy in a most impressive way. Gelb's experiment[1] is most conveniently performed by opening the door of a dimly lighted room and by suspending in the frame a piece of black paper. This paper is illuminated by a strong projection lantern which stands on the floor or on a low table and is tilted upwards so that the part of its beam which is not intercepted by the black paper passes through the open door onto the ceiling of the adjacent room where it is invisible to the observer. In the light of the strong lantern the paper may look white instead of black. When a white piece of paper is held up in front of the black paper so that it too reflects the strong light of the lantern, the black paper assumes a black

---

[1]Described in W. D. Ellis, *A source book of gestalt psychology.* New York: Harcourt, Brace, 1939, p. 207.

color. According to the usual interpretation it looks first white because no cues for the special strong illumination are available when this illumination affects only one visible surface. With the introduction of the white paper into the beam a special brilliant illumination becomes visible and constancy is restored: the two papers are perceived with their real color.

The arrangement of Gelb's experiment lends itself to a still more impressive demonstration. When the black paper is presented alone, reducing the intensity of the lantern light by small steps to zero causes the perceived color of the paper to vary all the way from white through gray to black. Every change in illumination is accompanied by a corresponding change in the perceived color. However, when a larger white paper is fastened behind the black paper so that the latter is seen surrounded by white, the same changes in illumination do not at all affect the seen colors which remain white and black throughout. Paired in this way the colors are immune to changes in illumination and remain "constant." It is rather a change in the perceived illumination which now accompanies the change in the objective illumination.

The question arises: what determines the color with which the black paper is seen at a given intensity of the lantern light when the paper is presented alone? Do we deal in this situation with an absolute relation between the intensity of the light which stimulates a portion of the retina and the resulting perceived color? In considering this question we have to remember that there is another variable in the situation, the dim general illumination of the room. When this is varied it becomes immediately clear that this general illumination also affects the color of the black paper. When, with a high intensity of the lantern light, the general illumination is raised, the color of the black paper changes from white to gray, and this in spite of the fact that the paper too now reflects light of a somewhat higher intensity than before. Only *relatively*, that is in relation to the light which comes from other surfaces, has the light reflected by the black paper become less intense.

Such dependence of the perceived color on the *relative* intensity of the perceived light should be demonstrable in a simpler form, and this is the case.

In a dark room a white screen is illuminated by the light of two slide projectors. In one of the projectors an opaque card with a circular hole of ½ in. diameter is inserted, and the bright image of the hole is focused on the screen. The slide for the other projector consists of a blank glass covered with an opaque card with a circular hole of one in. diameter and with a ½ in. cardboard disk which is pasted concentrically into the hole. Focused on the screen this slide produces a bright ring. The two projectors are so adjusted that this ring surrounds the image of the ½ in. hole so that the edge of the latter coincides with the inner edge of the ring. The light intensity of the projectors can be changed by running them on variable transformers or by letting their beams pass through episcotisters.

We have then on the screen a circular region (disk) and surrounding it a ringshaped region which reflect light intensities that can be separately controlled. When the intensity of the disk is kept constant and that of the ring is widely varied, the color of the disk may change all the way from white to dark gray. The disk looks dark gray when the light reflected from the ring is of high intensity and it becomes white when the brightness of the ring is greatly lowered. When the light intensity of the disk is varied and that of the ring is kept constant, the color of the disk, of course, undergoes similar changes. Again it is quite clear that the color which appears in one region, namely in that of the disk, depends on the relation of the light intensity of this region to that of its surroundings. This is true also of the ring. It can be shown in corresponding fashion that its color depends on the relation of the intensity of the ring to that of the disk.

When the ring is altogether omitted so that the disk is seen in completely dark surroundings, it ceases to look white or gray and assumes instead a luminous appearance similar to that of the moon at dusk. Lowering the intensity of the disk greatly does not change this mode of appearance, provided the rest of the room is really dark; the disk looks merely dimmer. The same observation can be made with the ring when it is presented without the disk, or with both the ring and the disk when they are placed far from each other on the screen. Opaque colors which deserve to be called white or gray, in other words "surface colors," will make their appearance only when two regions of different light intensity are in contact with each other, for instance when the ring surrounds the disk or when two oblongs have the longer edges as their common border.

The importance of a close contact for the emergence of surface colors becomes strikingly clear in the following observation. The intensity of the disk is adjusted to be one quarter that of the ring, which makes the color of the disk a medium gray. An opaque object is moved from the side into the beam of the lantern which projects the ring so that part of it is blotted out by the shadow of that object.

When this happens the gray color disappears almost simultaneously from that part of the disk which is adjacent to the shadow. It looks as if the dense gray there were dissolving leaving the screen transparent to let a light behind it shine through. Brought about in this fashion, the change from surface color to a luminous appearance is quite impressive. That side of the disk which is still well surrounded by a brighter ring continues to show the gray color, and between it and the luminous side the disk shows a steady gradient in the density of the gray.

These observations make it clear that, at least under these conditions, surface colors occur in our experience when regions of different light intensity are in contact with each other and that the particular surface colors which come about depend on the relation of these light intensities. They are apparently the product of nervous processes of limited scope, for close spatial contact between the regions of different light intensity is required for their emergence. Moreover, the degree to which surface color is present in a certain region depends on the intimacy of the contact between this region and its partner. This is easily demonstrated by the following observations.

No matter what the brightness relation between ring and disk be, the ring will always show a less dense surface color and have more of a luminous appearance than the disk. This becomes quite clear when two pairs of such regions are presented for comparison which are so chosen that the intensity of the ring in one pair equals that of the disk in the other one, and vice versa. Even the region of lower light intensity in each pair, which is perceived as a gray, has a more luminous appearance where it occurs in the ring than where it occurs in the disk. The most obvious explanation for this difference in the mode of appearance is that the disk is more under the influence of the ring than vice versa, in as much as the disk is completely surrounded by

the ring, whereas the ring is in contact with the disk only on one side. This explanation agrees well with the observation reported earlier that the elimination of part of the ring rendered that part of the disk more luminous which was then no longer enclosed by a region of different light intensity.

This influence under which surface colors emerge is clearly a mutual one. Though less so, the ring does display surface color. There is a great difference in the mode of appearance between a ring which surrounds, for instance, an area of higher intensity and an equal ring presented in an otherwise dark field. Whereas the latter looks merely luminous, the former shows in addition to some luminousity a distinct gray.

The mutual influence on which the emergence of surface colors depends must also account for the fact that the particular colors which come about depend on the relation of the stimulating light intensities. It is probably best conceived of as some kind of interaction which takes place as part of the nervous process which underlies color perception.

It will be remembered that the dependence of the perceived colors on the relative intensities of the stimulating light was also evident in the variations of Gelb's experiment which were first reported. It remains to be added that the transition from surface color to a luminous mode of appearance can be demonstrated with Gelb's set-up in the following way. At first the special illumination of the black paper and the general illumination of the room are so adjusted that the black paper looks white. When now the general illumination is further reduced, the paper becomes more and more luminous, and it ceases altogether to look white when the rest of the room is completely dark. Luminosity of the paper can also be produced by excluding the general illumination from its immediate neighborhood. By such measures a rather luminous gray, not unlike that appearing in the ring, may also be achieved. Thus it is not only in projected rings and disks that luminosity appears as an alternative to surface colors when adequate differences in intensity are lacking or when the contact between those regions is diminished. Clearly discernible segregated objects as for instance a suspended piece of black paper function in the same fashion.

Part II

So far, we have become acquainted with the way in which surface colors come into existence and with the manner in which they depend on the stimulus situation. They depend on the relation of stimulus intensities on the retina which are so located with regard to each other that the subsequent nervous processes interact. Now the question arises what bearing this has on the problem of brightness constancy.

In order to answer this question, some clarification of the nature of brightness constancy is needed. One may say that brightness constancy prevails when a perceived color is in agreement with the corresponding object color. Object color is a persistent physical characteristic of a surface, the property to reflect a certain proportion of the light which falls on that surface. For instance, a surface which looks black under constancy conditions reflects about four percent of the illuminating light, and a white one about 80 percent. This property, called reflectance, is not conveyed to the eye as such. It is rather represented to the eye by light of a given intensity. This fact constitutes the problem of brightness constancy, for the intensity of the reflected light depends to the same degree on the color of the reflecting surface as on the strength of the illumination. If in our environment illumination were always and everywhere the same, the fact that our visual sense is not directly affected by reflectances but only by the reflected light intensities would not raise a problem in perception, for the reflected light could represent the object colors unequivocally. But illumination varies widely, even between different parts of the same visual field, and often very different light intensities come to represent the same reflectance to the eye and, in constancy, produce the same color in the observer's experience. When, for instance, a medium gray which reflects 20 percent of the illuminating light is presented once in an illumination of an intensity 100 and again under light of an intensity 300, the intensities of the reflected light are 20 and 60 respectively; if complete constancy prevails, both stimulus intensities lead to perception of the same medium gray. Similarly the white background on which the gray samples are shown will reflect light of the intensity 80 in the weaker illumination and of the intensity 240 where it is in the stronger illumination, and the two differently illuminated parts of the background will probably both be judged as white. At first glance no orderly connection between stimulus intensity and perceived color seems to exist.

There is, however, one feature in the stimulus situation which remains the same when the illumination is varied. The intensity of the light reflected by the gray in the weaker illumination (20) stands in a ratio of 1:4 to that reflected by the white in the weaker illumination (80), and the same ratio exists between the intensities reflected by the gray and the white in the stronger illumination (60 and 240). It is easy to see that in the case of any given set of object colors the *ratios* of the intensities of the reflected light remain the same for any change in illumination which affects all of them.[2] Thus, if the perceived colors were to depend on the ratios of the intensities of the reflected lights, they would remain unchanged when a given set of object colors were presented in changed illumination, and constancy would be assured. A medium gray may serve again as an example. Although it affects the eye with different light intensities when the illumination is changed, it would be perceived as the same color because the ratio of the intensity that it reflects to the intensity of the light reflected by the surrounding white would remain the same, for a change in illumination affects the latter in the same proportion.

At this point we have to consider the observations reported in Part I. They suggested that the perceived surface colors depend on the relation, not yet quantitatively defined, of the light intensities in interacting regions. But we now find that constancy would result, if our visual perception functioned in such a fashion that the perceived colors depended on the *ratios* of the intensities of the reflected light.

Thus, we merely have to make the assumption that the relation on which surface colors depend is one of simple proportionality to give the observations of Part I a direct bearing on the problem of brightness constancy. If this assumption were correct brightness constancy would find its explanation in the very process by which surface colors come about.

This assumption can be tested by simple experiments. If it is correct, the particular colors which are perceived in a pair of ring and disk should depend on the ratio of the intensities of the two regions, and only on that ratio. In other words, no matter what the absolute intensities of ring and disk may be, the same colors should be seen in the case of any pair of intensities which happen to

---

[2]This is a simple consequence of the fact already mentioned that object colors reflect a constant *fraction* of the illumination.

stand in the same ratio to each other. This is, in close approximation, the case, as the following report of quantitative experiments[3] shows.

Two pairs of ring and disk were used, in order to permit simultaneous comparison. The intensity of each of these four regions could be varied independently.

Four identical projections lanterns equipped with 500 watt bulbs were used for this purpose. They were arranged in two groups and each group produced on the screen a pair of ring and disk as described in Part I. They were all so adjusted that they gave their respective regions the same light intensity. This was done in the following way. First a pair of ring and disk was formed with one lantern from group I and one from group II, and the intensity of one of them was varied until the contour between the ring and the disk disappeared because of brightness equality. Then these two lanterns were restored to their respective groups and similar adjustments were made within each group by varying the light intensities of the not yet equated lanterns.

The intensity variations required by the experiments were brought about with the help of episcotisters through which the lantern beams had to pass before reaching the screen. This technique has the advantage that the episcotister apertures are a direct measure of the relative intensities in the various regions.

Measurements were made by the method of limits. Ring and disk of one pair and the ring of the other pair were kept at constant intensities, and the intensity of the remaining disk was varied in suitable steps until the S judged the colors of the two disks as equal.

In the first experiment one of the rings was given the full illumination of its lantern and the disk inside it received half of the intensity, for its light beam passed through an episocotister of 180 degrees aperture. The light for the ring of the other pair was cut down to one-eighth of full intensity by passing it through an episcotister of 45 degrees aperture. The aperture for the disk of the latter pair was varied in steps of two degrees. The following are the means of one upper and one lower limit for each of five Ss: 24, 26, 24, 23, 24 degrees with a total mean of 24.2 degrees. This result means that, on the average, a light intensity in a disk corresponding to an episcotister aperture of 24.2 degrees when it is surrounded by a ring of an intensity of 45 degrees aperture brings about in the S's experience the same gray as does a disk of an in-

tensity of 180 degrees aperture inside a ring of an intensity of 360 degrees aperture. There is only a small deviation from the value of 22.5 degrees which with 45 degrees forms the same ratio as does 180 degrees with 360 degrees. Comparing the grays in the two disks was not difficult for the Ss. The great difference in absolute intensity between the two pairs of ring and disk (8: 1) made the less intense pair look much dimmer, but that did not affect the distinctness of the disks' color. However, it made the rings look very different; though both were white, the more intense one was by far more luminous. This latter observation which was also made in most of the following experiments seems to be important, for it corresponds to a fact which can be observed in real constancy situations. When identical sets of object colors are placed in different illuminations and appear approximately the same, the set in the stronger objective illumination is often also *seen* to be more strongly illuminated. Perceived illumination and the different degree of luminous appearance which was frequently observed in our experiments seem, functionally speaking, to be closely related experiences. A detailed discussion will be presented in a later publication.

In another experiment a disk of 90 degrees intensity was shown in a ring of 360 degrees intensity. This combination which forms an intensity ratio of 4: 1 brings about a much darker gray in the disk. In the other pair, the disk whose intensity was varied was surrounded by a ring of 180 degrees intensity. The proportionate value for the disk is here 45 degrees. The averages of two upper and two lower limits for each of four Ss were 46, 52, 45, 44 degrees with a mean of 47 degrees.

In the following experiment the disk of the brighter pair was varied and a ratio of 3:1 between ring and disk was used. In the darker pair, the ring had an intensity of 180 degrees and the disk one of 60 degrees, and the variable disk was surrounded by a ring of 360 degrees intensity. Five upper and five lower limits were determined for each of three Ss. The means were 113, 115, 121 degrees. The proportionate value is here 120 degrees.

It will be noted that so far all deviations from the proportionate values were in one direction.

---

[3]These experiments were performed by the students of various seminars in Perception and classes in Experimental Psychology at Swarthmore College under the author's supervision.

They all imply that, where they occur, a disk of proportionate intensity in the dimmer pair looks darker than the disk in the pair of higher intensity; viz. in the first two experiments the disk in the less intense pair had to be given a slightly higher than proportionate intensity to give a color match and in the last experiment the disk in the more intense pair had to be made objectively darker. Thus, although these deviations are small, they deserve our attention. Experiments with an improved technique were made to find out how significant they are.

To facilitate measuring a variable episcotister was used for the determination of the limits. This device permits changing the aperture by definite amounts while it is spinning. Only when the Ss had given a judgment of equality was the episcotister stopped and its angle measured with a protractor.

It has been described above how the intensities of the four lanterns were equated at the outset of the experiments. These equations are likely to contain subliminal errors which could affect our measurements. In the experiments which follow the episcotisters were interchanged between the groups of lanterns after half the number of limits had been determined for a given S, so that the group which during the first half of an experiment produced the brighter pair of ring and disk were made to produce the dimmer pair during the second half, and vice versa. Thus, any error in the original lantern adjustment which would affect the measurements during the first half of the experiment in one direction would in the second half affect it in the opposite direction. In this manner such an error will appear in the scatter of the limit values but will not affect their mean.

The first experiment (I) done with this improved technique was one with a small difference between the brighter and the dimmer pair. The former had a ring of 360 degrees intensity and a disk of 180 degrees, and the other pair had a variable disk in a ring of 180 degrees. Four Ss took part in the experiment. For each one four upper and four lower limits were determined. Table 14.1 presents the means of these limits. The proportionate value is here 90 degrees. It will be noted that the small deviations from this value are in a direction opposite to those previously reported, for they would imply that a disk of proportionate intensity in the dimmer pair is perceived as a slightly lighter gray than the disk in the more intense pair.

This is not so with the results of the following

TABLE 14.1. Episcotister Settings in Degrees for Disk within Ring of 180 Degrees in Comparison with Disk of 180 Degrees within Ring of 360 Degrees

Subjects	Ad.	McN.	Ba.	Cl.	
Upper limit	88	86	85.5	90	
Lower limit	84	84	79.5	84.5	
Mean	86	85	82	86	Grand mean: 85

experiment (II) in which a still lighter gray was produced and in which the intensity of the dimmer ring was only one quarter of that of the brighter one. In the dimmer pair the ring had an intensity of 90 degrees and the disk was variable, while in the brighter pair the ring had 360 degrees and the disk 240 degrees of light. The results are given in Table 14.2. With the Ss Mo. and Cr., 10 upper and 10 lower limits were determined, with Ke. and Cy. only six. Individual differences are larger in this experiment. For two of the Ss there was a marked deviation from the proportionate value of 60 degrees, which implied that for them a disk of 60 degrees intensity in the dimmer pair showed a slightly darker gray than the disk in the brighter pair.

Ten Ss were employed in an experiment (III) in which the variable disk was surrounded by a ring of 360 degrees of light and the dimmer pair consisted of a ring of 90 degrees and a disk of 30 degrees intensity. Six upper and lower limits were determined for each S, except for Ss Mo. and Cr., who again supplied 10 pairs of limits each. The average of the individual means as shown in Table 14.3 was 106 degrees, a clear deviation from the proportionate value of 120 degrees. It implies that the gray in the disk of low intensity looks somewhat darker than a disk of proportionate value in the brighter pair.

The direction of the deviations from proportionate values encountered in the last two experiments was such that they could be regarded as the effect

TABLE 14.2. Episcotister Settings in Degrees for Disk within Ring of 90 Degrees in Comparison with Disk of 240 Degrees within Ring of 360 Degrees

Subjects	Mo.	Cr.	Ke.	Cy.	
Upper limit	61	62	73	74	
Lower limit	62	64	68	67	
Mean	61.5	63	70.5	70.5	Grand mean: 66.4

TABLE 14.3. Episcotister Settings in Degrees for Disk within Ring of 360 Degrees in Comparison with Disk of 30 Degrees within Ring of 90 Degrees

Subjects	Ca.	Ga.	Ha.	Ht.	Lu.	Ro.	Mo.	Cr.	Ke.	Cy.	
Upper limit	104.5	91	117.5	116.5	113	130	128	107.5	105	113	
Lower limit	92.5	91	99.5	98.5	103	112	100	103	97	95	
Mean	98.5	91	108.5	107.5	108	121	114	105	101	104	Grand mean: 106

of a slight influence of the absolute stimulus intensities on the color process which otherwise could be conceived as functioning according to a proportional law. The question arose whether these deviations reflected intrinsic properties of the color process or whether they were introduced by incidental experimental conditions. An answer cannot yet be given and must be left to further detailed investigation. However, an experiment which was performed with this question in mind will be reported below, because it will add the data of still another combination of intensities.

It was suspected that the presence of the brighter pair of ring and disk in the visual field when the gray in the disk of the dimmer pair developed was responsible for the fact that this gray looked a trifle too dark. If the high intensities of the brighter pair had an influence across the spatial interval on the colors which emerged in the dimmer pair, this is what should have happened. Such an influence can be avoided by presenting the pairs successively. This was done in the following experiment (4). The intensities in the brighter pair were 360 and 180 degrees, the ring in the dimmer pair was 90 degrees and the disk was varied. Table 14.4 shows for four Ss the means of four upper and four lower limits. Ordinarily, with an intensity ratio of 4:1 between the rings the deviation under discussion was to be expected. It did not appear. The slight deviation from the proportionate value of 45 degrees was in the opposite direction.

In another experiment, however, successive presentation failed to eliminate completely the deviation under discussion. Experiment III was repeated with three further Ss who did the experiment twice, once with successive and once with simultaneous presentation. The limits listed in Table 14.5 are the averages of four determinations each. Although successive presentation reduces the deviation from the proportionate value of 120 degrees, it does not eliminate it.

These deviations from proportionate values appear rather insignificant when one compares them with the remaining effect of the proportional law.

For example, in experiment III which showed the largest deviation, a disk of an intensity of 30 degrees aperture had on the average the same color as one of an intensity of 106 degrees aperture, that is, an intensity 3.5 times as high. The deviation from the proportionate value of 120 degrees amounts only to 12 percent.

It should be mentioned at this point that such experiments can also be done with a less elaborate set-up. Two color mixers and one projection lantern suffice for a crude demonstration of the proportional law. With the help of a large color wheel of black and white disks and a small one fastened on top of it to the same mixer one can obtain a ring-shaped and a circular region in which the intensities of the reflected light can be varied independently. On one mixer, e.g., the large wheel can be set to show a sector of 90 degrees white and the small one a sector of 45 degrees white. To the other mixer are fastened a small wheel with a white sector of 180 degrees and a large wheel of 360 degrees white. When the mixers spin in general room illumination, one sees a dark gray disk surrounded by a medium gray ring on one mixer and a light gray disk in a white ring on the other one. However, when the mixers are placed in separate strictly local illumination they look quite different. That illumination can be provided by a lantern equipped with an opaque slide which has two circular holes a good distance apart. It projects two narrow beams of light of equal intensity. When the mixers are placed each in one of the beams at such a distance from the projector that their wheels are covered by the light almost to the outer rim

TABLE 14.4. Episcotister Settings in Degrees for Disk within Ring of 90 Degrees in Comparison with Disk of 180 Degrees within Ring of 360 Degrees

Subjects	Ad.	McN.	Ba.	Cl.	
Upper limit	43	42	41	44	
Lower limit	41	40	42	44	
Mean	42	41	41.5	44	Grand mean: 42

TABLE 14.5. **Episcotister Settings in Degrees for Disk within Ring of 360 Degrees in Comparison with Disk of 30 Degrees within Ring of 90 Degrees**

Subjects Presentation	Cl.		He.		Be.	
	Sim.	Succ.	Sim.	Succ.	Sim.	Succ.
Upper limit	110.5	121	99	108.5	104	112
Lower limit	99.5	99	97.5	99	94	104
Mean	105	110	98	104	99	108

and the rest of the room is entirely dark, both color mixers show a white ring and a light gray disk much alike in color. The reason for this change is easy to understand. Under local illumination the two color mixers provide exactly the same pattern of stimulus intensities as the set-up in experiment IV, and thus the same colors develop as in that experiment. In general illumination, on the other hand, the pairs of ring and disk are surrounded by regions of other intensity, e.g., the light reflected by the wall of the room, which cooperate in determining the colors which come about in the pairs. If, for instance, light reflected by a white wall forms the stimulus intensity of the surrounding region, that intensity stands to the intensity of the dimmer ring in a ratio of 4:1, and in this relation the ring should assume a medium gray color, as indeed it did.

It was explained above how the assumption that the achromatic colors depend on the ratios of the pertinent stimulus intensities accounts for brightness constancy. On that occasion complete constancy was shown to follow from this assumption. However, complete constancy has hardly ever been demonstrated experimentally. An object color presented in reduced illumination usually looks somewhat darker than another sample of that color in full illumination, though not as much darker as the difference of the reflected light intensities would warrant if there were no constancy. Yet complete constancy would follow from a direct application of the proportional law. Deviations from proportionality which occurred in our experiments are by far too small to account for the usual lag in constancy. The difficulty resolves itself when it is realized that the proportional law cannot be applied so simply to this situation. Here the two pairs of regions, the sample and its background in full illumination and the other sample with background in reduced illumination, are not as completely separated from each other as the corresponding regions in our experiments, for the regions of dif-

ferent illumination are in contact with each other and the brighter one can have an influence on the dimmer one. In other words, we have here a case where three or more regions of different intensity interact. Such processes have not yet been sufficiently investigated, and no report can be made at this time. It seems, however, quite likely that a full investigation will furnish the rules for the prediction of the lag in constancy in individual experiments.

This report may so far have given the impression that, apart from the small deviations discussed, the proportional law permits prediction of color equations if the pertinent stimulus intensities are known. However, this is so only with important qualifications. To a certain extent also the geometrical arrangement of the regions of different intensity has an influence on what colors come about in these regions. Some brief experiments which permit a first appraisal of the importance of these conditions will be reported below.

In the measuring experiments so far reported the width of the ring was ⅝ of the diameter of the disk so that the area of the ring was four times as large as the area of the disk. A reduction of the width of the ring to ¼ of the diameter of the disk so that its area was about the same as that of the disk did not affect the color in the disk as the following experiment shows, in which the colors in two disks were compared which were surrounded by rings of different width. Both rings were given the same intensity of 120 degrees aperture; the disk in the narrow ring had an intensity of 15 degrees and appeared as a very dark gray; the disk in the ring of standard width was variable. The mean of two upper and two lower limits for a single S was also 15 degrees. A number of other observers were satisfied with that equation.

The width of the narrow ring was further reduced so that it amounted to only ¹⁄₁₆ of the diameter of the disk. The same constant intensities as in the last experiment were used. The averages of two upper and two lower limits for each of two Ss were 37 and 37 degrees. This result means that a disk of 15 degrees intensity inside the very narrow ring looked as light as a disk of 37 degrees intensity inside a ring of standard width. The outcome of this experiment was so striking that we repeated it with another combination of intensities. The intensity of the two rings remained the same, but the disk in the very narrow ring had an intensity of 60 degrees. Again a higher intensity was needed for an equation in the disk inside the standard ring. The averages of two upper and two lower limits for the same two Ss were 87 and 86 degrees. However, with this intensity ratio of 120:60, which produces a light gray, the effect of making the ring very narrow was not so great. It amounted only to 45 percent, whereas in the case of a ratio of 120:15 which normally produces a very dark gray the disk in the standard ring had to be made 145 percent more intense. On the whole it looks as if the very narrow ring which has only one-quarter of the area of the disk cannot make the disk color as dark as does a ring of sufficient width.

As just reported, no difference in the effect of a ring which has about the same area as the disk and of one which has four times the area of the disk has been found. Two further measurements were made with a much wider ring. Its width was 1.5 the diameter of the disk and its area 15 times that of the disk. In one experiment the intensity ratio between the wide ring and its disk was again 120:15. In the disk of the standard pair the averages of four upper and four lower limits for the two Ss were 17 and 16 degrees. When a ratio of 120:60 was used, averages for two pairs of limits were 66 and 63 degrees. The deviations from 15 and 60 degrees respectively are probably incidental. At any rate, they are not in the direction which would indicate an enhancement in the effectiveness of the ring with increased width. It seems that, once the ring has an area equal to that of the disk, any further increase in its width does not affect the resulting color of the disk.

It was reported in Part I that a ring looks more luminous than a disk of the same intensity in another pair in which the intensities of ring and disk are the same as in the first pair but interchanged. The question arises whether such a reversal of intensities also causes a color difference in the regions of equal intensity. Two pairs of disk and ring in which the area of the ring was the same as that of the disk were presented and the lights were so arranged that in one pair the lower intensity was in the ring and in the other pair in the disk. The two higher intensities in the two pairs amounted both to 360 degrees, the ring of lower intensity was kept at 45 degrees, and the disk of lower intensity was variable. Measurements were made with four Ss. The means of three upper and three lower limits were 54, 71, 83, 86 degrees. These figures indicate that for the same intensity ratio the lower intensity appears as a lighter gray when it is given in the ring than when it is given in the disk. A rather dark gray results from a ratio of 360:45 degrees. In the case of smaller ratios which give rise to lighter grays the differences in color which result when the intensities of ring and disk are interchanged are very much smaller. For an intensity ratio of 2:1 only a difference in luminosity can be discerned.

Summary

It was found that opaque achromatic surface colors are perceived when light of different intensity stimulates adjacent areas on the retina. The achromatic color which is seen in a particular region must be regarded as the result of stimulation received from that region *and* of stimulation from neighboring regions. Although these colors are qualities which are perceived in a given region, they are products of an interaction process, which depends on difference in stimulation in at least two areas. In the absence of a suitable difference in stimulation a color of an entirely different mode of appearance is seen. A single bright region in an otherwise dark field, for instance, looks luminous instead of white, and reducing the light intensity in that region fails to make it look gray; it continues to appear luminous and merely becomes dimmer.

The first steps were taken to investigate quantitatively the rules of this dependence in the simplest case, that of two regions of different intensities of stimulation where one region surrounds the other. The colors which come about under these circumstances depend in close approximation on the *ratios* of the intensities involved and seem independent of the absolute intensity of local stimulation. The region of higher intensity will assume the color white and that of lower intensity will show a gray (or a black) which depends on the intensity ratio of the two regions. The greater the difference in intensity the darker will be the gray which appears in the region of the lower intensity.

It can be shown that a dependence of perceived colors on the ratios of stimulus intensities accounts for the constancy of achromatic colors under varying illumination. Complete constancy would follow from this rule of interaction of two intensities. The fact that measurements of brightness constancy rarely give results which denote complete constancy presents no difficulty for this explanation. These experiments involve interaction between more than two regions of different stimulus intensity.

Grouping Based on Phenomenal Similarity of Achromatic Color

I. Rock, R. Nijhawan, S. Palmer • University of California, Berkeley
L. Tudor • Rutgers University

It is widely acknowledged that a precondition for the perception of the world of objects and events is an early process of organization, and it has generally been assumed that such organization is based on the Gestalt laws of grouping. However, the stage at which such grouping occurs, whether early or late, is an empirical question. It is demonstrated in two experiments that grouping by similarity of neutral color is based not on similarity of absolute luminance at the level of the proximal stimulus, but on phenomenal similarity of lightness resulting from the achievement of lightness constancy. An alternative explanation of such grouping based on the equivalence of luminance ratios between elements and background is ruled out by appropriate control conditions.

Introduction

It is now widely acknowledged that a precondition for the perception of the world of objects and events is a process of organization in the visual system. As Gestalt psychologists pointed out, there is no more a priori affinity within the light that reaches the retina from a single external object than there is from light some of which emanates from within that object and some of which emanates from elsewhere. Thus the experience of the world as consisting of discrete and separate things is an achievement that typically (but not always) corresponds accurately to the actual presence of separate things in the real world.

It is also widely accepted that, at least on a descriptive level, the Gestalt laws of grouping (Wertheimer 1923) and the related law about figure–ground organization (Rubin 1921) give an account of how such organization might be achieved.

Elements within the proximal stimulus are presumably grouped with one another on the basis of factors such as their relative proximity and similarity to one another, the extent to which they are smooth or "good" continuations of one another, whether or not they move in the same direction with the same speed as one another, and the like. Stimuli tend to be seen as figure rather than as ground if they are surrounded, symmetrical, or convex regions, and the like.

However, if these laws indeed account for the parsing of the field into things and non-things, they have been assumed to operate at a very early stage of processing, prior to the allocation of attention and prior to further processing that will yield constancy of object properties such as size, shape, lightness, and the like. This follows because attention and constancy mechanisms are believed to presuppose the prior existence of discrete entities or candidate objects on which to operate. But the stage at which grouping occurs is an empirical question subject to experimental analysis.

In one such study on the role of proximity in grouping, Rock and Brosgole (1964) elaborated on an earlier experiment by Corbin (1942), the latter being the first investigation with which we are familiar ever to consider the question of "level" in perceptual grouping. The basic plan was first to arrange luminous beads on invisible strings such that the beads were nearer to one another vertically than horizontally. When the array was seen in the subject's frontal plane, columns rather than rows were therefore perceived. Then the array was tilted about a vertical axis and placed at various slants such that the foreshortening between columns led to changes in the relative retinal proximity of beads along the horizontal dimension compared with the vertical dimension. Thus if grouping were based on proximity defined at the level of the retina, at some degree of tilt of the array—beyond approximately 41°—grouping should have shifted from columns to rows.

The result was that, under conditions of binocular viewing, grouping did not shift to rows until the array was tilted by such a large angle that constancy failed, namely beyond 55°. Constancy here refers to the perceived separation between beads along the horizontal axis, and separate measurements of it were obtained. However, under conditions of monocular viewing, where there were few if any effective cues to depth within the array, grouping shifted from columns to rows at about the point at which the projected horizontal separation between beads equaled the vertical separation, i.e. at a tilt of 43°. The perceived separation between beads also became equal at about this point under monocular conditions.

Thus it would seem from these results that either it is perceived proximity (rather than retinal proximity) among elements that governs grouping, or, at the very least, when the perception of relative proximity differs from retinally defined relative proximity, the former supersedes the latter as the principle of grouping. We can assume that in the monocular condition of this experiment subjects perceived the array in a frontal plane regardless of its objective tilt, and the constancy measures bear this out. [See the equidistance tendency described by Gogel (1965).] This is similar to the state of affairs that obtains in Wertheimer's demonstrations of proximity in a drawing: Retinal proximity and perceived proximity are necessarily confounded.

From the results of Rock and Brosgole (1964) one might reasonably conclude that grouping occurs at a later, post-constancy stage of processing and is not based on the state of affairs at the retinal level. However, there is other evidence to which we refer in section 4 suggesting that the story may be more complex.

The experiments we now describe bear on the issue of grouping based on similarity of neutral color when some elements in an array are lighter or darker gray than others. This leads to a strong grouping effect when all other grouping factors, such as proximity, are neutralized. However, there are two ways of looking at differences in neutral color. A light-gray element yields a retinal image of greater luminance than a darker one. But it is also perceived as lighter and could be seen as such even if it were in dimmer illumination. In fact, the illumination could be adjusted so that the lighter element would yield an image of the same luminance as a darker element in stronger illumination. So the question to be resolved by experiment is whether grouping is based on the similarity of luminance at the retinal (or proximal) level, or on the similarity of perceived lightness at the distal (or constancy) level.

In a preliminary experiment, Tudor (1987) cast shadows over rows or columns of gray circular spots on a white background as a means of varying luminance while holding perceived lightness constant. But the elongated shadow itself tended to induce grouping in the direction of its long axis, perhaps by virtue of common region (Palmer 1992a)—(see Fig. 15.1a). To eliminate this unwanted factor, in a second preliminary experiment, Tudor introduced a crisscross pattern of diagonal shadows across the entire array and this pattern favored neither columns nor rows—(see Fig. 15.1b). All spots were the same shade of gray. Grouping in this experimental condition was compared with grouping in two control conditions: in one, no shadows were introduced, and in the other, the spots that were shadowed in the experimental condition were darker gray. These darker gray spots had the same luminance as the shadowed spots in the experimental condition. A number of patterns were used in all three conditions, which

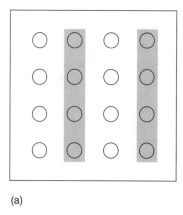

(a)   (b)

FIGURE 15.1 ■ The arrays used by Tudor in preliminary experiments. Shadows were cast along columns (or rows) of gray spots (a). This altered their luminance but not their perceived lightness since the shadows were perceived as shadows, although this is not entirely the case in this picture. In a second experiment a crisscross pattern of diagonal shadows was used (b); this favored neither columns nor rows but did alter the luminance of all spots in adjacent columns (After Tudor 1987).

varied the ratios of proximities between columns and rows, pitting lightness (luminance) against proximity.

The result was that the grouping achieved in the experimental or shadowed condition was virtually identical to that achieved in the control conditions in which all spots were unshadowed and the same shade of gray, whereas both of these conditions yielded grouping different from that achieved when alternate rows or columns were different shades of gray. Thus it appears that grouping of this kind occurs on the basis of perceived lightness and not on the basis of luminance at the level of the retina.

However, there are two shortcomings of this method. One is that the crisscross pattern is confusing and tends to obfuscate grouping into columns or rows. A second is that, for reasons to be explained, we wanted to include a control condition that simulated the luminance ratios in the shadow condition, but did not contain shadows. To do so requires the introduction of a dark strip behind a series of elements, which, needless to say, would have even more of an unwanted effect on grouping than did the elongated shadow referred to above in the first preliminary experiment. In fact, Tudor (1987) tried this out in the first preliminary experiment and obtained precisely this unwanted outcome. The current method overcomes both of these shortcomings.

Experiment 1: Cast shadow

Method

SUBJECTS

Nine students at the University of California at Berkeley participated. They were all naive concerning the theoretical issues under study.

STIMULI AND PROCEDURE

The essential idea of the method was to introduce the shadow along a column of small square elements (as in the first preliminary experiment described by Tudor) but its elongated direction was orthogonal to the grouping that was expected to occur. Thus, as shown in Figure 15.2a, given five columns of squares equidistant from one another, the question posed was whether the middle shadowed column would group with the columns on the left or on the right. If a shadow cast vertically on the middle column has the effect of creating a vertical grouping within the column it is presumably irrelevant with respect to the horizontal grouping of that column.

To address the critical question of whether grouping occurs on the basis of perceived lightness or on the basis of physically measurable luminance at the retinal level, the reflectance of the squares in the two columns to one side, let us say

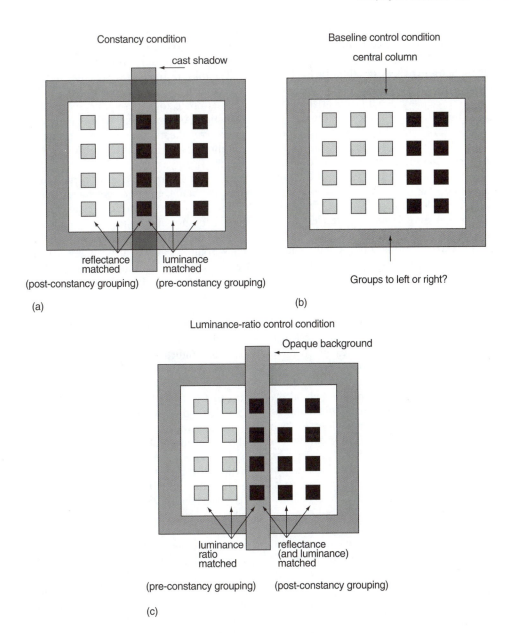

FIGURE 15.2 ■ The Arrays used in the Present Work. In the experimental array (a) a shadow is cast over the central column of light-gray squares. This creates the same luminance for these squares as for the darker ones on the right. However, it is unlikely that the reader will achieve constancy in this picture as did the subjects and thus perceive the shadow squares as the same lightness as the light-gray square. In the baseline control array (b) the squares in the central column have the same reflectance values as the corresponding ones in (a). In the luminance-ratio control array (c) the ratio of luminance of squares to background is the same in the central column on a dark-gray strip. These match the lightness of the squares on the right. However, the reader may perceive the central square as somewhat lighter than those on the right, as did the subjects. The luminance of the squares and strip in the central column matches exactly the luminance of the squares and surrounding shadow in the central column in the experimental array (a).

the right, matched the lower luminance of the shadowed squares in the middle column. However, the reflectance of the middle-column squares equaled that of the squares in the two columns on the other side, let us say the left. If constancy prevailed, these middle-column squares would appear the same lightness as those having the same reflectance, despite the presence of the shadow. Therefore, if grouping occurs on the basis of luminance, the middle column of squares should group with the columns of squares of equal *luminance* on the right; if grouping occurs on the basis of perceived lightness, the squares in the middle column should group with the squares of equal *reflectance* on the left.

To prepare the subject for the task on the critical trials, the two possible groupings of the middle column were first explained and demonstrated to them. It was illustrated first with gray squares as elements containing either vertical or horizontal yellow lines. Three columns on one side, e.g. on the right, had squares with horizontal lines and two columns on the other side, e.g. the left, had squares with vertical lines. The next illustration contained an array of three columns of red squares and two columns of green squares. In addition, a vertical rectangle (green) was placed behind the middle (red) column. Subjects were told that their task was to say "left" or "right" indicating to which side the middle column seemed to group or belong. It was explained that the grouping was to be on the basis of the squares themselves not on anything surrounding them, such as the green rectangle behind the red squares. Thus in these illustrations the grouping of the middle column was unambiguous.

After these instructions and the two illustrations, a series of six arrays of elements, each of five columns (as in the two illustrative arrays), was presented. Three of these six arrays were critical in that they concerned the property of lightness under investigation. One was the experimental array in which the middle column of gray squares was shadowed (Fig. 15.2a) as already explained. The second was a baseline control array containing three columns of light-gray squares and two of dark-gray squares, as in Fig. 15.2b. The reflectance values of these squares were the same as in the experimental array, the only difference being that the central column was not shadowed. This array should provide a baseline of grouping against which to compare responses to the other two critical arrays. We assumed that all subjects would group the middle column with the lighter two columns since these squares match on the basis of both luminance and perceived lightness.

The third critical array was the "luminance-ratio" control (Fig. 15.2c) mentioned briefly above. The rationale for this requires more detailed explanation. Assuming that in the experimental shadowed array the middle column is grouped with the columns containing the lighter (reflectance-matched) gray squares, it can be argued that the basis for such grouping is not perceived lightness after the achievement of constancy, but the ratio of the luminance of the squares to that of the immediately surrounding background. The luminance ratio of the shadowed squares to their immediate background (which is also shadowed) will be the same as that of the lighter squares to their background. After all, the shadow across the middle column does not alter the luminance ratio between squares and their background.

The rationale for this control may seem puzzling because it is now widely believed that the basis of lightness constancy, when a shadow is cast over a given surface and its surround, is precisely the preservation of the luminance ratio of that surface to its surround (Wallach 1948). However, there is now good reason to believe that this ratio will yield constancy if and only if the edge of the shadow is interpreted by the perceptual system as a shadow edge—i.e., as due to a change in illumination. If it is instead interpreted as a reflectance edge, then constancy will not be achieved (Gilchrist et al 1983; Gilchrist 1988). Therefore, what we sought to investigate in the luminance-ratio control array was whether a column of squares whose luminance ratio to their background is the same as that of the light-gray squares to their background, but that nonetheless do not appear phenomenally the same shade of gray as those lighter squares, will or will not group with columns of those lighter squares, as they (presumably) will in the experimental, shadow, condition.

We achieved this control condition by placing a dark-gray strip of paper behind the middle column of squares. The squares had the same reflectance as the dark-gray squares in the adjacent columns, as illustrated in Fig. 15.2c. The luminances of the squares and background strip in the middle column of this array precisely matched those of the squares and background in the middle column of the experimental shadowed array (shown in Fig. 15.2a). However, the edge of the strip did not look like a shadow because the strip extended beyond the cardboard containing the square elements and occluded the border, and possibly also because its edge was sharp rather than gradual as in the penumbra of the shadow in the experimental condition. It looked like a reflectance edge, which in fact it was. Hence, the darker strip and central squares did not appear to have the same lightness as the rest of the background and the squares to the left, in contrast to the experimental display for which constancy prevailed. [The exact conditions necessary for the perceptual system to discriminate between reflectance and shadow edges are not fully known (see Gilchrist et al. 1983), but for our purposes this is not essential. What matters is that we were able to create conditions where the edge in question looked like a shadow edge in our experimental condition, and thus yielded constancy, yet looked like a reflectance edge in our luminance-ratio control condition.]

Since the luminance of the middle squares in this second control array was the same as that of the squares in the experimental, shadowed array (which in turn were matched to the darker squares in the columns on the other side), the reflectance of these middle-column squares in the luminance-ratio condition was in fact the same as that of the darker squares. So the question arises whether they appeared to be the same lightness as the darker squares. The answer is that they did not; they appeared slightly lighter. The reader may perceive this in Fig. 15.2c. This is no doubt the result of simultaneous contrast, because the middle squares are on a darker background (namely the strip) than the squares in the adjacent columns.

Let us return to the sequence of the six arrays. The three critical arrays (the experimental and two control arrays) were presented within a sequence of six arrays in the first, fourth, and sixth positions. However, which of the three appeared in which of these positions was random. The second, third, and fifth arrays were fillers selected from the following unambiguous arrays: three columns of squares and two of triangles; three columns of yellow squares and two of blue; three columns of squares with holes in the center and two columns of squares without such holes. These noncritical arrays were always shown in this order. For both the critical and the noncritical arrays, the three-column–two-column arrangement was equally often in one orientation as in its mirror image.

Each array consisted of elements, generally squares, 2.5 cm × 2.5 cm, separated vertically and horizontally by 2.5 cm. There were four such elements in each of five columns. The elements were mounted on sheets of thick paper, 30.5 cm wide × 22.9 cm high; the reflectance value of the paper was 9.5 (90%) on the Munsell scale and its luminance value was 2.07 cd m^{-2}. These sheets were in turn mounted in the centers of cardboard sheets (71.1 cm × 55.9 cm), the reflectance value of which was 8.0 (59.1%) on the Munsell scale and the luminance value was 1.20 cd m^{-2}. The cardboard sheets had holes at the top so that they could be easily mounted on hooks on the wall. For the first (baseline) control array the luminance of the lighter squares in the three columns was 1.6 cd m^{-2}; the luminance of the darker squares in the remaining two columns was 0.35 cd m^{-2}. In terms of reflective values, these squares were 8.5 (68.4%) and 4.75 (17.6%) on the Munsell scale respectively. For the experimental condition, the array was the same as the one just described except that the shadow cast along the middle column rendered the luminance of these squares (which were of the same reflectance as the lighter squares) to be the same as that of the darker squares rather than as that of the lighter squares. The shadow was produced by a vertical strip of cardboard suspended between a single incandescent 40 W bulb and the array. The power output of the bulb happened to be very close to giving a luminance match between the dark squares and the shadowed squares. A finer adjustment of this was achieved by reducing the current to the bulb. The sides of the bulb were covered with black paint so as to minimize stray light which would otherwise reflect off the walls of the room. This was done to meet the single-light-source requirement as far as possible. The bulb was 155 cm behind the strip, which in turn was 15.2 cm from the array hung on the wall. For the second (luminance-ratio) control array, darker squares were placed on a dark-gray strip (30.5 cm × 5.1 cm) orientated vertically in the region of the middle column. The luminance of these squares was also 0.35 cd m^{-2} and that of the strip was 0.46 cd m^{-2}. The reflectance value of the strip was 5.5 (24.6%) on the Munsell scale. As noted above, the strip extended beyond the border of the cardboard sheet.

The observer viewed the arrays through an opening in a partition placed 61cm from the arrays on the wall. The opening, large enough to allow binocular viewing, was occluded between exposures of each array. When the experimenter had removed the preceding array and replaced it by the appropriate one in the series, the occluding cardboard was removed and the next array exposed. No time limit was imposed, but virtually all subjects responded within a few seconds, usually less than five. The subject responded "left" or "right," meaning that the central column appeared to group with or "belong" with the columns on the left or right.

RESULTS

Grouping for the three noncritical unambiguous arrays was always as expected and will not be considered further. For the baseline control array consisting of three columns of light-gray squares and two of darker-gray squares, grouping was also as would be expected under these unambiguous conditions for all nine subjects. For the experimental shadowed condition, seven of the nine subjects (78%) grouped the shadowed column with the lighter squares in the adjacent columns and two (22%) grouped the shadowed column with the darker squares in the adjacent columns on the opposite side. For the luminance-ratio control array containing the dark-gray strip, all nine subjects (100%) grouped the control squares with the dark-gray squares of equal absolute luminance. In other words, changing the background edges of the vertical rectangular region from illumination to reflectance edges reversed perceived grouping for the majority of the subjects despite the equality of the ratio of square to background in the middle column and the lighter-gray squares in the adjacent columns. This occurred despite the fact already noted that, by virtue of contrast, the central dark-gray squares on the darker-gray strip in the luminance-ratio control condition looked somewhat lighter than the dark-gray squares in the adjacent columns which were not on a strip.

Experiment 2: Transparency

Method

We sought another method to investigate the same question, namely whether grouping is based on similarity of luminance as projected to the retina, similarity of perceived lightness based on some constancy operation, or possibly on the equivalence of luminance ratios between element and background rather than on constancy per se. A method that will allow this question to be tested is based on perception of phenomenal transparency. Under certain conditions when one views a surface through a partially transparent (translucent) filter, the surface nonetheless is perceived vertically with respect to its reflectance or color. However, the luminance of that surface is also lowered by the filter.

SUBJECTS

Nine new subjects were recruited; all were naive about the theoretical issues under study.

STIMULI AND PROCEDURE

The method and procedure were essentially the same as in experiment 1 with respect to the arrays, the instructions, the procedure, and task. The two control arrays were the same as in experiment 1 except that the specific luminance values differed from those of experiment 1 but within experiment 2 they corresponded to one another and to the experimental, transparency array, analogously to experiment 1. The experimental transparency array was created by suspending a narrow, 29.0 cm × 4.5 cm neutral-density strip 15.2 cm in front of the array mounted on the wall such that from the position of the observer it was seen to be in front of the squares in the middle column only. It was 137.2 cm from the opening through which the subject looked.

The reflectance values of the light-gray and dark-gray squares in the baseline control and experimental arrays were the same as in experiment 1. Their luminance values were 49 cd m^{-2} and 13 cd m^{-2} respectively. The luminance of the light-gray squares in the middle column as viewed through the filter was 13 cd m^{-2} and thus matched that of the dark-gray squares. The luminance values of the background sheets of thick paper and the cardboard sheets were 62 cd m^{-2} and 34.5 cd m^{-2} respectively. The reflectance value of the strip used in the luminance-ratio control condition was 5.5 (24.6%) on the Munsell scale and its luminance, which matched that of the region surrounding the squares in the middle column in the experimental array, was 15.3 cd m^{-2}

With binocular vision, the filter strip was perceived to be well in front of the array in the experimental condition. Consequently a relative unambiguous constancy effect occurred. The light-gray squares in the middle column seen through the transparency strip appeared to be about the same lightness as the squares of the same reflectance seen in the adjacent columns. Figure 15.2 can serve again to illustrate the three conditions of experiment 2.

RESULTS

The results were even clearer than those of experiment 1. In the baseline control array all subjects grouped the squares in the central column with those of the same lightness in adjacent columns. In the experimental transparency array all subjects did the same thing, indicating that the altered luminance due to the translucent filter had no effect. In the luminance-ratio control array all subjects reversed their grouping; they saw the control column of squares as belonging with the dark-gray squares in the columns on the other side. Thus, despite the equivalent luminance ratio of squares to backgrounds of the middle-column squares and the light-gray squares in the adjacent columns, all subjects grouped on the basis of the reflectance of the squares themselves when they viewed this array.

Discussion

The results of both experiments indicate that grouping by similarity of neutral gray color is based on perceived lightness after the achievement of constancy, and not on the luminance of the elements at the level of the proximal stimulus. The experiments also rule out an explanation based on ratio of luminance at the level of the proximal stimulus. Such ratios can be regarded as a higher-order attribute of the proximal stimulus such as has been advocated by Gibson (1950, 1966). Of course, even if that proved to be the relevant variable in defining similarity of neutral color, it would not follow that grouping per se was explainable in terms of a higher-order attribute or direct perception theory. Grouping is the kind of process for which advocates of direct perception find no need.

In any event, by ruling out the luminance explanation and the ratio-of-luminances explanation of the similarity underlying grouping in our experiments, we are left with the post-constancy achievement of particular phenomenal shades of gray as the basis of grouping. This is not to deny that an explanation in nonphenomenological language cannot be realized eventually. Indeed the research of Gilchrist on lightness perception and related phenomena has provided a good account

of the kinds of processes underlying the perception of lightness and lightness constancy (Gilchrist 1979, 1988). But whatever these processes may be, we now have to accept the fact that grouping such as we have examined here does not occur until that stage or level of processing at which constancy is achieved.

This conclusion fits the one we drew in the introduction in describing the experiment by Rock and Brosgole (1964) on grouping by proximity. It only partially fits the findings of Olson and Attneave (1970) on the question of whether texture segregation, based on the different orientation of line elements in one quadrant of an array, results from the retinal or perceived orientation of these elements. Both factors seem to be implicated. Moreover, in a study by Beck (1975) in which the grouping of line elements by similarity was investigated, the same question of whether grouping is based on retinal or perceived orientation of elements led him to conclude that it was retinal orientation that mattered.

On the other hand, some as yet unpublished findings from our laboratory further support the conclusion that grouping occurs at a stage beyond that of the retinal input. These findings are derived from experiments in which the simple method of separating the planes in the third dimension in which the elements to be grouped are phenomenally located was used (Palmer 1992a, 1992b; Palmer and Rock, 1992). In these examples it is not so much the achievement of constancy that matters, as it is just the achievement of differential phenomenal depth. But the achievement of that depth and its utilization in grouping does imply that grouping in these cases does not occur exclusively at the very early stage of processing, as was previously assumed.

There is, therefore, a respectable amount of evidence indicating that grouping based on the Gestalt principles occurs at a relatively late level of processing. One should not then jump to the conclusion that grouping occurs only at this relatively late, post-constancy level. A more cautious—and correct—formulation would be to say simply that *grouping is affected by the perceived properties of the distal object*. One way in which this might happen is indeed if grouping occurs only at relatively late, post-constancy level. (Call this the "late only" hypothesis.) But it is also possible that grouping based on the perceived properties of the distal object merely supersedes a previously achieved grouping based on the 2-D properties of the proximal stimulus. (Call this the "both early and late" hypothesis.) How could these two hypotheses be discriminated experimentally?

One might think that this could be accomplished by presenting displays such as we used in our experiments for a very brief period, perhaps followed by a pattern mask. The underlying idea is that such a brief exposure would directly tap the initial preconstancy representation. After all, it is widely believed that image shape and size information can be extracted rapidly and simultaneously over the entire visual array (Beck 1967; Treisman and Gelade 1980; Julesz 1981), whereas perceptual constancy requires focal attention and a certain amount of additional processing time to achieve (Epstein and Lovitts 1985; Epstein and Broota 1986; Epstein and Babler 1989, 1990; Epstein et al 1992). By restricting the presentation time, one might be able to study the organization of the early pre-constancy representation. Then, assuming that the processing of achromatic color follows a similar two-stage scheme, the "both early and late" hypothesis predicts that grouping performance should change dramatically under brief presentation conditions, favoring the grouping alternative based on similarity of image luminances rather than that based on similarity of perceived lightnesses (as we found at long exposures in the experiments reported here).

Although such experiments could certainly be carried out, the difficulty arises in the theoretical interpretation of their results. Suppose that when the critical array is presented for 150 ms or less, subjects group the shadowed central column according to luminance information. Does this fact demonstrate that there is an initial preconstancy grouping based on luminance information? The key question turns out to be whether brief presentations actually tap the hypothesized pre-constancy representation or not. The luminance-based result is clearly compatible with this possibility, but it can be equally well predicted from the "late only" hypothesis. One need only assume that brief presentation causes the late, post-constancy representation to be constructed without constancy processes having had sufficient time to complete their task. Thus according to the 'late only' hypothesis grouping on brief-exposure trials would not be based on *luminance* information at all, but on nonveridically perceived *lightness*. Hence one might easily obtain the result predicted by the 'both

early and late' hypothesis without it being correct: grouping might well occur only at the late level, but appear to be based on some earlier stage if its information is passed on to later levels without achieving full constancy. We therefore find it difficult to imagine an experiment that would succeed in disentangling these two hypotheses.

In any event, the important problem that now is revealed by our findings and conclusions is this: If the Gestalt laws do not adequately explain the organization and parsing of the visual field at the earliest stage of processing, and if some organization, logically speaking, must be assumed to occur at that early stage, then what principles explain it? We suggest, as a tentative answer (Palmer and Rock, 1992), that organization of the field occurs at an early stage on the basis of a new principle, namely *uniform connectedness*. We suggest that regions of interconnected uniform stimulation, such as spots, lines, or larger areas, are interpreted by the perceptual system as signifying a single unit.

REFERENCES

Beck, J. (1967). Perceptual grouping produced by line figures. *Perception & Psychophysics, 2,* 491–495.

Beck J. (1975). The relation between similarity grouping and perceptual constancy. *American Journal of Psychology, 88,* 397–409.

Corbin, H. H. (1942). The perception of grouping and apparent movement in visual depth. *Archives of Psychology, 273.*

Epstein, W., & Babler, T. (1989). Perception of slant-in-depth is automatic. *Perception & Psychophysics, 45,* 31–33.

Epstein, W., & Babler, T. (1990). In search of depth. *Perception and Psychophysics, 48,* 68–76.

Epstein, W., Babler, T., & Bownds, S. (1992). Attentional demands of processing shape in three-dimensional space: Evidence from visual search and precuing paradigms. *Journal of Experimental Psychology: Human Perception and Performance, 18,* 503–511.

Epstein, W., & Broota, K. D. (1986). Automatic and attentional components in perception of size at a distance. *Perception & Psychophysics, 40,* 256–262

Epstein, W., & Lovitts, B. (1985). Automatic and attentional components in shape at a slant. *Journal of Experimental Psychology: Human Perception and Performance 11,* 355–366.

Gibson, J. J. (1950). *The Perception of the Visual World.* Boston, MA: Houghton Mifflin.

Gibson, J. J. (1966). *The Senses Considered as Perceptual Systems.* Boston, MA: Houghton Mifflin.

Gilchrist, A. (1979). The perception of surface blacks and whites. *Scientific American, 240,* 112–126.

Gilchrist, A. (1988). Lightness contrast and failures of constancy: A common explanation. *Perception & Psychophysics, 43,* 415–424.

Gilchrist, A., Delman, S., & Jacobson, A. (1983). The classification and integration of edges as critical to the perception of reflectance and illumination. *Perception & Psychophysics, 33,* 425–436.

Gogel, W. (1965). Equidistant tendency and its consequences. *Psychological Bulletin, 64,* 153–163.

Julesz, B. (1981). Textons, the elements of texture perception and their interactions. *Nature (London), 290,* 91–97.

Olson, R. R., & Attneave, F. (1970). What variables produce similarity grouping? *American Journal of Psychology, 83,* 1–12.

Palmer, S. E. (1992a). Common region: A new principle of perceptual grouping. *Cognitive Psychology, 24,* 436–447.

Palmer, S. E. (1992b). Similarity grouping occurs after visual completion, in preparation.

Palmer, S. E., & Rock, I. (1992). Rethinking perceptual organization: The role of uniform connectedness. *Psychonomic Bulletin & Review, 1,* 29–55.

Rock, I., & Brosgole, L. (1964). Grouping based on phenomenal proximity. *Journal of Experimental Psychology, 67,* 531–538.

Rubin, E. (1921). *Visuell wahrgenommene Figuren.* Copenhagen: Gyldenalske Boghandel. [Reprinted as "Figure and ground" in D. C. Beardslee & M. Wertheimer (eds.) *Readings in Perception* (pp. 194–203). Princeton, NJ: Van Nostrand. 1958]

Treisman, A., & Gelade, G. (1980). A feature-integration theory of attention. *Cognitive Psychology, 12,* 97–136.

Tudor, L. (1987). *Levels of Processing in Perceptual Organization.* MA thesis, Rutgers University, New Brunswick, NJ.

Wallach, H. (1948). Brightness constancy and the nature of achromatic colors. *Journal of Experimental Psychology, 38,* 310–324.

Wertheimer, M. (1923). Untersuchungen zur Lehre von der Gestalt, II. *Psychologische Forschung, 4,* 301–350

Perceptual Organization and Constancy

Discussion Questions

1. Without exception, the articles in this section rely on behavioral or psychophysical evidence to draw conclusions about perceptual organization and constancy. Is there something inherent about this topic that makes evidence from neurophysiology inappropriate or irrelevant?

2. Barlow's neuron doctrine emphasizes the receptive field properties of single cells to explain perception. In what way can this idea be applied to explain the phenomena of perceptual organization described by Wertheimer or size constancy described by Kaufman and Rock?

3. The mechanisms that give rise to perceptual constancies and perceptual organization can and do produce visual illusions (in fact, perceptual constancies and certain forms of organization *are* visual illusions). One might have thought that an organism that does not see what is "really there" is unlikely to be reproductively successful. What general properties of the world permitted such seemingly maladaptive mechanisms to evolve?

4. Rock et al. conclude, in agreement with the earlier findings of Rock and Brosgole, that perceptual organization by similarity and proximity, respectively, operates on a post-constancy representation. Many contemporary theorists would place the mechanisms of perceptual constancy and organization, along with visual attention, into a category of mechanisms termed "intermediate level vision." Is it possible to determine whether perceptual organization by similarity or proximity precedes or follows the application of attention? Describe an experiment that could do so.

5. State in as general a form as possible what the common underlying principles are that Kaufman and Rock on the one hand and Wallach on the other used to explain size and brightness constancy, respectively.

Suggested Readings

Beck, J. (1967). Perceptual grouping produced by line figures. *Perception & Psychophysics, 2*, 491–495.

Glass, L. (1969). Moiré effect from random dots. *Nature, 222*, 578–580. Beck and Glass, respectively, show how interactions among elements within a scene can cause global structures to emerge, illustrating the Gestalt psychologists' motto that "the whole is greater than the sum of its parts."

Navon, D. (1977). Forest before trees: The precedence of global features in visual perception. *Cognitive Psychology, 9*, 353–383. The author develops a method for investigating object recognition in different spatial scales within a scene.

Palmer, S.E., & Rock, I. (1994). Rethinking perceptual organization: The role of uniform connectedness. *Psychonomic Bulletin & Review, 1*, 29–35. The authors discuss the importance of a new principle of perceptual organization, extending the list first discussed by Wertheimer (Reading 11).

Kanizsa, G. (1976). Subjective contours. *Scientific American, 234*, 48–52.

Kellman, P. J., & Shipley, T. F. (1991). A theory of visual interpolation in object perception. *Cognitive Psychology, 15*, 483–524.

von der Heydt, R., Peterhans, E., & Baumgartner, G. (1984). Illusory contours and cortical neuron responses. *Science, 224*, 1260–1262. Kanizsa demonstrates the perceptual reality of illusory contours. Kellman and Shipley analyze the conditions under which one can expect to observe evidence for illusory contours and von der Heydt and colleagues provide evidence about the neural basis of the phenomenon. The latter article is a rare example of a neurophysiological study of perceptual organization.

PART 4

Object and Spatial Vision

Introduction to Reading 16[1]

The classical early paper in the history of research on agnosia is that of Lissauer, republished here in abridged form in English translation. The paper is a transcript of a talk given to the Association of East German Neurologists in Breslau (now Wroclaw, Poland) on 28 November 1888. In it Lissauer gives the first thorough clinical description of a patient whose difficulty in recognising objects was not secondary to visual sensory difficulties and dementia. He also made the most influential conceptual distinction in the history of the topic, that between apperceptive and associative agnosia. The usefulness of the distinction is accepted by most recent authors who have reviewed the field (e.g. Bauer & Rubens, 1985; Ratcliff & Newcombe, 1982; Warrington, 1985).

The conceptual distinction between apperceptive and associative agnosia is clearly drawn in the paper. Lissauer treats the apperceptive stage of the recognition process as those processes necessary for the discrimination of complex figures. For him it leads to conscious perception stripped of meaning. His view of the associative stage is particularly interesting; as the name he gave it implies, he sees it as the use of associative links to centres for sensory images in other modalities and to the object's name; a related view which has recently been returning to popularity (see Warrington & McCarthy, 1987).

In addition to the making of the seminal theoretical distinction in the history of work on the agnosias there are three other noteworthy aspects of the paper. The first is a historical point. Lissauer was only 27 years old when he gave the talk. He had been born in 1861 in Heidelberg and studied there and in Berlin and Leipzig, where he had obtained his doctorate in 1886. In 1888 he had become assistant in the University Psychiatric Clinic in Breslau

[1]Introduction by Shallice & Jackson (1988). Lissauer on agnosia. *Cognitive Neuropsychology, 5,* 153–156.

where Wernicke was the professor. Lissauer died shortly after the paper was published in 1891. Despite dying so young his work on agnosia was not his only achievement. He is known for an anatomical study on the spinal cord and also for Lissauer's paralysis, a general paralysis of rapid onset and progression (see Biographisches Lexikon, 1933).

The second noteworthy feature is the nature of the case report. In marked contrast to other neuropsychological works of that time, for instance Lichtheim (1885), the case report gives clear evidence of the detailed and systematic nature of the empirical investigations as well as of the fierce critical intelligence of its author. It must rank as one of the most adequate produced in the 19th century. It seems likely that this aspect of the investigation, like the centre/connection conceptual framework, arises from the influence of Wernicke. Kleist (1959) noted in a biography of Wernicke that when he was testing a patient for research purposes, two assistants made detailed notes of different aspects of a patient's behaviour. The extensive protocols that Lissauer provides of the patient's responses suggest that a similar procedure has been adopted in this case. Moreover, Wernicke's practical influence is clear. The patient had actually been demonstrated by Wernicke himself at a meeting of the Vaterländische Gesellschaft in Breslau in November 1888 and Lissauer, in a footnote, thanks Wernicke for allowing him to work on the patient.

The protocols form the basis for the third aspect of particular interest in this paper—the fascinating classification of the patient's errors that Lissauer provides. Error analyses are rare even in modern case descriptions of associative agnosia! The one Lissauer provides must be one of the earliest in the history of neuropsychology. Lissauer differentiates what would now be called visual, semantic, and perseverative error types. His remarks on the perseverative errors are most subtle; he suggests that they arise from the mistaken transfer of the associations of one object to the percept of another but does not speculate on the mechanism involved. This pattern of errors is now often associated with the syndrome of optic aphasia (e.g. Gil et al., 1985; Lhermitte & Beauvois, 1973). Lissauer himself notes the relation between his own explanation of associative agnosia and that given by Freund (1889) at roughly the same time in the description of the first case of optic aphasia. The relation between the two syndromes remains highly controversial to this day. It is striking that a conceptual relation was noted when they were first described.

From the perspective a hundred years inevitably provides, it is possible to criticise a number of aspects of the paper. Lissauer's treatment of apperceptive agnosia lacks a concept for the end product of the apperceptive stage; there is no idea in the paper that has the role of Warrington and Taylor's (1978) perceptual classification concept, Seymour's (1979) pictogens, or Marr's (1982) structural descriptions. In the discussion of the relation between his theory and his observations Lissauer shows no sensitivity to any possible fractionation between agnosias for different types of material (words, faces, objects, space, etc.) and so of the potential danger of making an inference from a phenomenon in one of these domains to one in another. He relies too heavily on drawing to test that the apperceptive stage is functioning properly. Finally, having differentiated associative and apperceptive agnosia theoretically in a most clear fashion, he later suggests that a pure associative agnosia may never be observed in practice in isolation; he takes a partially top-down view of the relation between associative and apperceptive processing of complex stimuli. The empirical support for his position is, however, the association of deficits found in his patient; he never considers adequately whether his patient is indeed a "pure case," a concept that was already current at the time (see e.g. Lichtheim, 1885). In fact the remarkable sophistication of the analyses Lissauer made of the many tasks employed means that a proper critique would require a very extensive commentary. In any case one cannot view the paper purely from a historical perspective. The agnosias are still far from well understood. Even the fundamental assumption on which the theoretical analysis is based, namely the existence of visual agnosia, was still being questioned 15 years ago (see Bay, 1953; Bender & Feldman, 1972)!

In the present translation no attempt has been made to change the somewhat informal style of the original but for space reasons some abridgement has been made with the deletions indicated in the text. Two principal sections have been removed. The first is half of the protocol. The second is a speculative account of the anatomy of the agnosias which is of little value. When a post mortem later became available Lissauer's expectation that the patient would have a bilateral lesion was not confirmed. The autopsy reported by Hahn (1895) (see Nielsen, 1937), showed a unilateral lesion in the left hemisphere with extensive involvement of the white matter and the cortex in the occipital and parietal regions with degeneration of the splenium which provides communication with the right hemisphere.

REFERENCES

Bauer, R. M. & Rubens. A. B. (1985). Agnosia. In K. M. Heilman & E. Valenstein (Eds.). *Clinical neuropsychology* (2nd Edition). New York: Oxford University Press.

Bay, E. (1953). Disturbances of visual perception and their examination. *Brain, 76,* 515–551.

Bender, M. B., & Feldman, M. (1972). The so-called visual agnosias. *Brain, 95,* 173–186. *Biogrophbches Lexikon hervorrogender Ärzte-Neuzeit Bd. 2* (1933). Berlin: Schwarzenberg.

Freund, D. C. (1889). Über optische Aphasie und Seelenblindheit. *Archiv für Psychiartie und Nervenkrankheiren, 20,* 276–297.

Gil, R., Pluchon, C., Toulatt, G., Michenau, D., Rogez, R., & Levevre, J. P. (1985). Disconnexion visuo-verbale (aphasie optique) pour les objets, res images les couleurs et res visages avec alexie "abstractive". *Neuropsychologia, 23,* 333–349.

Kleist, K. (1959) Carl Wernicke (1848–1905). In K. Kolle (Ed.), Grosse Nervenärzte Vol. 2. Stuttgart: Thieme.

Lhermitte, F. & Beauvois. M.-F. (1973). A visual-speech disconnexion syndrome: Report of a case with opticaphasia, agnosic alexia and colour agnosia. *Brain, 96,* 695–714.

Lichtheim, L. (1885). On aphasia. *Brain, 7,* 433–484.

Marr, D. (1982). *Vision.* San Francisco: Freeman.

Nielsen, J. M. (1937). Unilateral cerebral dominance as related to mind blindness. *Archives of Neurology and Psychiatry, 38,* 108–135.

Ratcliff, G., & Newcombe, F. (1982). Object recognition: Some deductions from the clinical evidence. In A. W. Ellis (Ed.), *Normality and pathology in cognitive function.* London: Academic Press.

Seymour, P. H. K. (1979). *Human visual cognition.* London: Collier Macmillan.

Warrington, E. K. (1985). Agnosia: The impairment of object recognition. In P. J. Vinken, G. W. Bruyn & H. L. Klawans (Eds.), *Handbook of clinical neurology, Vol. 45.* Amsterdam: Elsevier.

Warrington, E. K. & McCarthy, R. (1987). Categories or knowledge: Further fractionation and an attempted integration. *Brain 110,* 1273–1296.

Warrington, E. K., & Taylor, A. M. (1973). Two categorical stages of object recognition. *Perception, 7,* 695–705.

A Case of Visual Agnosia with a Contribution to Theory

H. Lissauer • Psychiatric Clinic Breslau, E. Germany

Translated by Marianne Jackson, National Hospital, London, UK

Since the concept of visual agnosia (Seelenblindheit) was formulated as the result of experimental work, this new "off-shoot" of physiology has been the subject of clinical research. Three years after its formulation Wilbrand (1887), in his well-known monograph, undertook to summarise the clinical history of "Seelenblindheit" and to bring it to some kind of conclusion. Having collated the data obtained so far and added his own valuable observations, he presented an extensive theory of that phenomenon which will be the main subject of the present paper.

To my knowledge there have been no clinical contributions on the specific problem of "Seelenblindheit" since Wilbrand's work, though the related fields of reading and writing disturbances and the connection between hemianopic and aphasic disturbances have been investigated by a number of authors, notably Brandenburg (1884), Batterham (1888), Bruns and Stoelting (1888), and Freund (1889). In addition, the work of Allen Starr has come to my notice. This considers the phenomenon of "Seelenblindheit" under the heading of "Apraxia and Aphasia", though it does not include detailed observations. Certainly, at this stage, it seems worthwhile to publish every unequivocally documented case of "Seelenblindheit," in particular a case such as the one described below, which in terms of the severity of its symptoms and their clear-cut manifestation cannot be surpassed by any clinical cases reported to date.

The first part of this paper deals with the case history. In the second part an attempt will be made to discuss the data from a more theoretical point of view.

Part 1

The patient, Gottlieb L., was an 80-year-old salesman. His mother, who reached an advanced age, suffered from a psychiatric illness for more than ten years. One brother died young. One sister suffered from cerebral strokes. The patient was married. He had eight children, three of whom are still alive.

Generally speaking the patient was physically fit. In his youth he had suffered an undiagnosed febrile illness, and in 1871 he contracted smallpox. He had received only an elementary education. In more recent years he lost the considerable capital which he had amassed, first as a corn merchant and later as a building contractor. He was a man of strong personality, quarrelsome, and thrifty to the point of being miserly.

For about three years the patient had experienced occasional attacks of vertigo. At times they were so severe that he fell down, and on one occasion he suffered minor injuries to the temporal areas of his head. However he always recovered quickly from these attacks and there were never any signs of paralysis or disturbances of speech or vision on these occasions. He had had psychological problems for approximately one year. In particular he had become forgetful, so that he could no longer remember the date, or how many children he had and what they were called, nor could he give his own address. The patient's daughter reported that on occasions he had mistaken her for her sister-in-law and that occasionally he had misnamed objects (. . .).

In fact the patient was able to deal with his own business affairs until the beginning of August, 1888 (. . .). On 3rd August he was able to leave the house again and he undertook a business trip to Krotoschin. He returned the same evening, unaccompanied, but very exhausted. He complained that there had been a severe storm which had blown him against a wooden fence and that he had knocked his head (. . .). He retired to bed and remained there for two to three days. He felt most unwell and complained that he was no longer able to see as well as before. However it is certain that he had supper with his family on the very day of his accident, and that they noticed nothing unusual. Indeed during the ensuing two days when he stayed in bed there was nothing in his behaviour to suggest that he had suddenly become blind. However, when he got out of bed and started to move, it was observed that he bumped into doors and protruding corners, and he was unable to find his way outside his room. He had to be accompanied whenever he ventured out of the house. The first time he went out into the street where he lived he looked around in a perplexed manner, as if things were unfamiliar to him.

In the morning, when he wanted to have a wash, the patient searched his room for the wash-stand, which was in its usual place. He also searched for his boots which were, as usual, under the bed, but he looked for these behind the stove and in the kitchen. He frequently mistook articles of clothing, for instance mistaking his jacket for his trousers. He thought that a number of pictures in his room were boxes and tried to search in them for things he had lost. When eating he mixed up pieces of cutlery. He used his spoon wrongly, by dipping the handle into the soup. Once he tried to put his hand into the food and once into a cup of coffee.

Since his accident the patient no longer read. He gave his letters to his daughter saying that his vision was not clear enough. He continuously complained about the deterioration of his eyesight. He insisted that this visual problem had started suddenly on 3rd August following his accident and fall, though in view of his weak memory one cannot rely too much on this statement. However, it is certain that at this time the patient did not recognise his daughter but called her "Oscar." He talked to her about things which were quite meaningless to her. This happened repeatedly but only for short periods of time. It is not clear whether this was just a failure of recognition or arose from more generalised confusion. However more recently the patient had been noted to be alert. He was able to give a good account of his business affairs. He managed to find his way about in the familiar environment of his own room. He was well groomed and on the whole he needed no assistance with dressing or undressing.

A few weeks after these events the patient presented himself at the eye clinic here because of his apparent loss of vision. Through the kindness of Geheimrath Förster the case was passed on to Professor Wernicke and the author, for clinical observation and treatment.

The patient was seen for the first time on 23rd September 1888. We saw a man who was physically fit for his age. However he seemed to be mentally old and slow, although he was by no means demented or depressed. He gave a generally accurate account of his illness and stated that he was no longer able to see as well as he could before the accident. This was his only complaint at that time. In fact it became immediately obvious that this man, who could give a good account of everything around him, was quite incapable of visually recognising the most common objects, although he could recognise everything by touch or hearing. Furthermore, he could see—this was established without doubt during the first examination. It was clear from the way in which he was able to look at and to handle objects that he was able to perceive visual stimuli. In the course of his examination it was established that he was not even especially weak sighted. It was also established early on that the patient could be made to draw simple unfamiliar objects placed in front of him, a clear indication that he was well able to perceive form.

Once the diagnosis of "Seelenblindheit" had been made the next step was to investigate (over as wide a range as possible) the patient's responses to visual experiences. A number of relevant protocols are given below. First I will provide an overview of all the clinical findings. These are arranged partly according to theory and partly as they arose from the method of investigation.

General Mental State

The patient had insight into his illness. He was eager to undergo all the investigations, in which he participated with satisfactory comprehension and showed decided learning ability. His main interest was in the management of his business affairs, which involved a number of legal actions. He was aware of his daughter's efforts to have him declared legally incompetent. Nevertheless he was by no means mentally intact. His memory was weak. He was frequently unable to produce well-known dates, such as the current year, and also his current address, as previously described. When talking about the past he often exaggerated and mixed up events, putting them in the wrong order, and like many old people he was often repetitive. However his memory for more recent events was less impaired. Small details were often remembered for weeks, and he was usually on time for his appointments. At no time were there the slightest signs of disorientation or confusion unless the previously described difficulties in recognising familiar persons can be cited as an example of this.

Physical Status

As noted before the patient was physically fit. Except for his visual problems, which will be discussed later, it is important to emphasise the total absence of any focal neurological signs. Using the most stringent criteria sensation and mobility of limbs were found to be intact. In the central nervous system only a moderate bilateral hearing loss was noted. Facial innervation was intact, the eye muscles worked normally, and the fundi and pupils of the eyes were normal. The absence of any dysphasic difficulties must be emphasised. The patient's speech was fluent and his vocabulary was not limited. He never used wrong words nor did he misunderstand as would have been the case had he had a receptive aphasia.

The examination of his eyesight, in this case of special interest, was of course unusually problematic since it was difficult to talk with the patient about his visual experiences because of his visual agnosia.

1. Refraction. The patient was presbyopic. His near vision was best at +8. This correction was used in all experiments and it improved acuity of near vision.

2. Visual Fields. There was a complete and dense right-sided hemianopia. The dividing line between the two halves of his visual field was a few degrees to the right of the point of fixation. This could be documented unequivocally. Central vision in both eyes was therefore preserved. The visual fields were assessed perimetrically. They appeared to be decidedly too narrow at the periphery but they may have appeared narrower than they actually were. (The left temporal field in the periphery was too narrow by 10–20°, in the upper quadrant even narrower, i.e. more than 20°; the right nasal field was less reduced.) This was due to some extent to the unsuitable light conditions at the time of testing (a chance occurrence). In addition, the patient had had very little practice. On repeated testing the limits of his visual field were found to be less narrow than on the first occasion. It is particularly important that no segmental deficits were found in his left visual half-fields.

3. Acuity. Since the patient was unable to read at first this had to be assessed by showing him larger and smaller dots on a white background. He was asked to count these dots and Bodiat's Tables were used to assess his performance. Initially even this simple test required some practice. The patient tended to overlook individual dots because of his hemianopia. However, by using this method it was possible to determine that the patient's acuity after correction of his presbyopia was ¼ to ⅕ of normal. With time the patient improved so that he was able to read small sections of print and it was then possible to use Snell's Tables. From Snell's trial III the patient could read without difficulty just as many words at a distance of 30–40cm, as he could using Snell's trials VII and VIII at a similar distance. From this it was possible to deduce that impaired reading ability rather than poor acuity was responsible for his inability to read anything correctly. It transpired from this that his visual acuity was even a little better than that reported above, i.e. approximately one third of normal. If one takes into account that visual acuity declines to half of normal with age then our patient retained nearly two thirds of the acuity that one would have expected from normal performance at his age. The statement that his visual acuity was not particularly poor was thus justified.

Incidentally the patient also gave a personal account of his visual difficulties. He reported slight blurring of his vision. Furthermore he insisted that this had originally been worse. In the first weeks after his accident it had been so bad that he had hardly been able to see at all. His description might have led to the assumption (as indeed was suggested by his first clinical symptoms) that the patient had been totally blind at least for a limited period (i.e. cortical blindness resulting from bilateral hemianopias). However, this did not seem very plausible to me. Surely it would have been noted by the people around the patient if there had been an earlier total blindness. It is more likely that because of his poor memory what the patient was in fact recalling was only his complete helplessness (for example he repeatedly reported that when out in the street he needed to be guided). This may have led him to believe that he was actually blind at that time. According to him the visual disturbance was very variable. He insisted that at times he would see everything as if through a fog, yet at other times he could see as clearly as before his accident.

It was very important to record these personal reports and they probably were related to reduced acuity and they lend support to the view that at the time of the acute onset of his visual agnosia there was also a reduction in his visual acuity.

Of course fatigue may have played a role also. In particular the patient complained of having to pause after every few words when attempting to read because of the strain of having to peer so closely at what he was trying to read. It must be emphasised that the fluctuations in the patient's self-reports of visual disturbances in no way correlated with the fluctuations in his visual agnosic difficulties. For example, on some days when the patient was particularly pleased about his clear vision he might have particular difficulties in recognising even large objects.

It is certain that neither his visual problems nor his reduced visual acuity could explain his visual agnosia.

4. *Colour Perception.* If simple colour samples were placed in front of the patient (e.g. coloured paper or wool), he would sometimes name them correctly but mostly they were incorrectly named. Typically, he would waver between two colours. There were inconsistencies if he was tested repeatedly with certain colours. If a selection of colours was put in front of him and he was given a certain colour name and asked to select this particular colour from the array, he could generally do this correctly although he still made some mistakes and often showed considerable uncertainty. He always made mistakes if he was asked to select more subtle hues, as for example with the colour of a canary or of blood. He might label a pale pink or even a deep blue a "real blood colour." With the colour of a canary he wavered between green, grey, and yellow.

All this would suggest a profound impairment of colour perception. However, a totally different picture of the patient's perception of colour was obtained if he was tested in a different way, namely not relying on the semantics of colour names. If he was presented with samples of Holmgren wools and asked to select all examples of the same shade he was able to do this without hesitation. For example he would select all the green shades and without hesitation reject all blue colours or hues tending towards yellow. If he was presented with a certain hue and asked to find its exact match, he was able to do this immediately. He would either find the closest match or report that an exact match was not available. Thus he clearly was able to differentiate between subtle hues of grey, green, and yellow.

It would appear from this that his ability to differentiate and perceive colours was well preserved and that he made mistakes only when the task required the association of a certain colour perception with a semantic or other more complicated conceptual notion. (Wilbrand in Ophthalmiatrische Beiträge zur Diagnostik der Hirnkrankheiten describes this as "amnesic colour blindness." To date this has been described only in aphasics.)

5. *Visual Estimating.* I attempted to assess this by asking the patient to bisect a fine pencil line freehand or to mark the centre of a circle with a pencil. Unexpectedly the bisection of a line was always accurate, so much so that a normal subject could not have done it better. The centre of a closed figure was marked correctly most of the time al-

though at first the patient tended to make mistakes. He was usually able to correct these mistakes as soon as he had perceived the figure as a whole. It is likely that his hemianopia made it difficult for him to keep the whole of a closed figure in his visual field.

The results of these tests suggest that his ability to estimate or measure by eye was generally good. In addition he was asked to judge the size of objects and of distances. If he was asked to mark out a length or width of a given object along the edge of the table using his hand he always managed to do this satisfactorily. However, it was different if he was asked to verbalise in inches or metres the size or distance which he had indicated correctly just before. Although his estimates were sometimes correct he made errors, which at times were the most colossal blunders. For example, he judged an umbrella to be six inches long and a piece of soap to be one foot long.

As for colour, these tests of visual estimation suggest that the patient's perception of size was apparently relatively intact but that his ability to label his estimates semantically was frequently impaired.

6. *Stereoscopic Vision.* From his ability to perceive real objects it appeared that he had not lost his stereoscopic vision. He was usually able to distinguish openings, protrusions, and irregularities on presented objects. However, I was unable to ascertain whether despite this there might have been a deterioration in his stereoscopic vision. I attempted to test this as follows: two pins were placed in front of the patient at a distance of about half a metre. One of these pins, selected at random, was then displaced in relation to the other. The patient had to judge which of the two pins was the nearer and by what distance. (As is usual with stereoscopic vision this task can be solved only by using both eyes together.) Our patient could assess the position of the pins correctly up to the point when one pin was placed about 3cm in front or behind the other. He was unable to make finer discriminations. These results are therefore not quite sufficient for me to infer that his stereoscopic vision was completely intact.

7. *Visual Memory.* The patient had a marked general memory weakness and this obviously has to be taken into account. The question arises as to whether the patient's memory for specific past or recent visual perceptions was approximately in keeping with his ability to recall general events or if it was significantly worse. First let me consider his memory for new visual impressions. This appeared to be relatively intact. During the period of these investigations the patient had many new visual experiences. He definitely remembered these. For example he had been able to learn new routes and get to know new people. During the investigations he never failed to note that an object had been presented on several occasions. For example, I showed him a selection of about 50 pictures and specifically drew his attention to 2 of these. Six days later when I saw the patient again I asked him to find these same pictures and he did this without having to think about it. He was able to do this without making a mistake. This test was repeated several times.

His memory for recent visual events therefore appeared to be relatively satisfactory; at least it was no worse than his recall for other recent experiences. A further test should be mentioned here in which only immediate and exact reproduction was important and which concerns at least partly what we call judging magnitude by eye. The test consisted of drawing on paper a line of a certain length (6–10cm). It was then covered over and the patient was asked to draw a similar line of exactly the same length. In repeated tests he did this so accurately that a normal subject could not have done better without previous special training. If more complicated designs were used such as crosses with arms of varying length there was a significant reduction in the accuracy of his reproductions, but of course the tasks were then considerably more difficult.

8. *Memory for Past Visual Experience.* His memory for past visual experiences was assessed by asking for a description of the route that had to be taken to get from one point in the town to another. Or he was asked for a description of certain well-known personalities, their style of dress, bearing, stature, colour of hair, etc. (Wilbrand [Seelenblindheit] had maps drawn from memory, a useful exercise which however was not suitable in our case because of our patient's limited education.) The patient failed most of these tests. However, it is not certain whether this was due at least to some extent to his general memory weakness or arose from a more specific visual memory deficit. Further discussion is required to decide whether the patient really had a clear visual

memory or visual imagery or whether his perception of common objects was related to concise mental pictures. As is well known, visual imagery is a variable characteristic of which few really definitive personal reports, such as Charcot's famous patient, are available. Only gross deficits in visual imagery lend themselves to clinical investigation. Although confirmation of such deficits would be of great theoretical importance, in practice they are very difficult to study. A patient can be asked to describe from memory the shape and the colour of a given object, or of an animal or a plant. In many instances our patient was able to give satisfactory descriptions. For example, he described both in words and by indicating the relative sizes what an eel looked like, a plaice, a swan, an apple, a pear, a plum, and a cherry. There was therefore no good evidence of a deficit in his ability to visualise mentally. On the other hand he was unable to give a clear and appropriate description of certain other items such as a turtle and an elephant. This form of investigation is on the whole not very productive. The number of suitable objects is not large and the information to be gained from such descriptions is rather superficial. Furthermore, one has to consider that descriptions of external attributes of objects might be produced simply as learned facts and that their verbalisation may not be accompanied by visual imagery. One can get much further by asking people to draw from memory.

Our patient was very clumsy when he attempted to draw and he became helplessly stuck on many drawing tasks after his first rather meaningless pencil lines. Of course only objects with simple outline were used (such as a table, chair, knife, fork, etc.). Some other drawings were just about recognisable but they were only of the level to be expected of a six-year-old child. For example, the patient drew two human figures in which the individual limbs could only be recognised because of the difference between male and female dress. A fork drawn by him clearly showed the handle and three pronged attachments. He also sketched a pear which showed a pointed body with the stem at one end and the remains of the flower at the other end. Thus the patient did not entirely lack internal visual representations of objects from which he could copy. However, it seemed that if compared to that of a normal adult, this skill had suffered a marked impairment, although I do not believe that this has

really been clearly demonstrated. I would prefer to regard deficiencies in his drawing ability as responsible for the poor quality of his drawings rather than an impairment of his visual memory. The assumption that the patient's visual memory was relatively intact was based on the fact that he was able to write. According to current concepts writing is no more than copying from the internal images of letters. It is, so to speak, a copying from imagery (Wernicke, 1886). Our patient could write fluently and did not make letter symbol errors. His memory for the details of letter shapes must therefore have been intact and it is unreasonable to suppose that the opposite should be true for visual memories.

I conclude therefore that there was no convincing evidence that our patient had lost his visual memory. The fact that he had retained the ability to write is an argument against such a loss.

9. Drawing

a. *Drawing real objects:* The patient was able to draw basic outlines of simple objects. He drew a pocket watch which showed the round outline of the watch, the ring attachment for the chain, and the ridged winding button. He also drew, quite accurately, a door knob, a key, and a broom, outlining correctly both the handle and the brush with its vertical bristles. He did not recognise these objects while he was drawing them. Simple drawings of objects were repeatedly copied correctly, e.g. the drawing of a fork and some printed letters which however he misinterpreted. These findings are of great importance for us. They prove that the patient was able consciously to perceive forms and they show without doubt that he could see sufficiently well to enable him to recognise all the objects involved.

Yet one cannot speak of his drawing ability being intact. Drawing was difficult for the patient and he disliked doing it. Over and over again he insisted that he had never learned or known how to draw. He tired easily and the whole procedure was very slow with many pauses. Even when at last he managed a correct drawing he often had started it off wrongly. He failed to draw many simple objects (e.g. a beer bottle, a water jug, a cup, etc.). It seemed to be easier for him to copy a simple line drawing than to draw a real object. Apparently this was because it was difficult for him to abstract from the complicated shapes and shadows of real objects those features which make up the characteristic outline which was supposed to be reproduced on paper. However, even copying from a pencil sketch was difficult for him. His drawings were usually clumsy. This might have been a longstanding problem or—and this seems more likely to me—his cerebral disorder had a specific detrimental effect on his ability to draw.

b. *Drawing from memory:* We have already discussed this. He managed to draw some things reasonably well but most things he could not draw at all. The clumsiness of his attempts was amazing. This gave rise to the following observation: the patient never drew anything in "one go" but always in a "bit by bit" fashion. He assembled the whole from individual pencil lines, often pausing to reconsider and to regroup the lines. As soon as he had drawn one part of the object according to the image in his memory this part, like all other objects in his environment, became strange to him. He was no longer able to comprehend it and therefore was unable to complete his drawing of the whole object. The problem was not one of memory impairment but of no longer being able to recognise the object or the part of the object which he had just drawn and therefore not being able to compare it with the original template in his memory. For example, if he attempted to draw a boot, the leg and foot part were there but the heel had then to be attached. This the patient realised well enough but where did it belong? At this moment he was unable to comprehend his own drawing. It might just as well have been drawn by someone else. He drew the heel first here, then there, and eventually he commented that he had no idea where it belonged. Similarly with a bottle: base, a body and neck were drawn separately, and they were then connected by quite meaningless and arbitrary pencil lines. The patient composed a human figure consisting of a head, chest, body, legs and arms, explaining this while he was drawing the parts. However in the end the result was something that was reminiscent of a primitive puppet, the individual parts having been put together in the wrong way. It was similar to the way that the patient was unable to read what he had written correctly only a mo-

ment earlier. It did not prevent him from writing spontaneously, fluently and correctly but it did interfere when he was asked to copy from a script. This was because he tended to copy the letters line by line. If he started a certain letter and then was interrupted after a few strokes of the pen and then was asked to complete the letter later the resulting letter was disjointed. I believe that it is for this reason that the drawings from this rather untalented and unskilled hand were so poor and disordered: he simply was unable to copy adequately from the template in his visual memory.

10.   Reading and Writing. The patient could write fluently both to dictation and spontaneously. He wrote individual letters as well as he did before his illness, but his writing was generally less neat and a little uneven in that he did not keep to the line and tended to exceed the margins. He often repeated what he had already written. This can be accounted for partly by his hemianopia and partly by his inability, due to his visual agnosia, to interpret what he had just written, as I have described previously in connection with drawing (. . .).

To begin with he was virtually unable to read either script or print (. . . .). He could recognise letters if he was allowed to write them passively while his hand was guided (Bruns & Stoelting, 1888). Later his reading improved considerably. In December 1888 he was able to read 4 or 5 out of 12 printed words. Longer words in particular were read incorrectly and in a distorted fashion (. . .).

11.   Form Perception. I understand this to be the ability to glance over an assembly of two-dimensional shapes in such a way that the overall impression with all its details penetrates clearly into consciousness. I believe that it is possible to test this ability quantitatively, by producing two shapes, which are designed in such a way that they are generally congruent but differ in small details. The subject has to explain whether the shapes are different and in which way. By progression from simple shapes with obvious differences to very complicated and varied shapes with minimal differences (but sufficiently different to be above the threshold of discernibility) this method can be refined to such an extent that even a normal subject would be unable (without aids such as counting or measuring) to detect the differences between the figures at one glance. The ability thus assessed appears to be in the main a function of the conscious perception of visual stimuli, that is of apperception. However, the task set, i.e. the identification and differentiation of complicated shapes, requires several skills, in particular visual memory and estimation by eye. It is of course influenced negatively or positively by visual acuity and the state of the visual fields. Nevertheless the decisive fact remains that these stimuli are not just simple ones close to the threshold of perception—as is usual when testing visual acuity—but are ones which involve easily perceivable stimuli which consciousness is supposed to control, combine, interconnect, and compare simultaneously. A certain capacity of visual perception considered to be independent of acuity is essential in this process. Acuity must of course be taken into account in the selection of the size and the quality of the test material.

I shall keep this capacity in mind when I talk about apperception of shape later in the theoretical discussion. The method of testing discussed here may be even more appropriate in cases different from ours. In our case we have already produced evidence, using the method of drawing, that the patient can perceive shapes. However, the evidence extended only to very simple objects. The above method would make it possible to determine to what extent the patient is able to draw or not. It is clear that the same method could be extended to three-dimensional shapes.

In the present case I confined myself to the following crude tests. I drew two very simple shapes, both of which could pass as a figure 3, but differing in that one had a small extra scroll at its upper end. The patient noted such differences quickly and accurately. I then drew two squares 3–4cm square. In each of these there were 12 small crosses evenly distributed but in such a way that in one square the centre was empty while in the other it was filled with one cross. In this and in similar tests (e.g. in one figure a spot was placed between the crosses) he was able to see the differences but it took time and considerable effort. Yet any normal person would have noticed the differences at the first glance. (All the objects were drawn with bold strokes of the pen so that the patient could see them clearly). Since it is difficult to produce these complicated patterns by hand I did the following: I placed before him two book covers which had identical gilded ornamental borders. He had to find on one of the covers the same ornamental

detail I had marked on the other cover. The patient performed poorly on this task. (The same tests carried out in patients with hemianopias convinced me that a hemianopia as such does not interfere with these tasks.) He found the search difficult and he always declared at the start that the shapes and ornaments placed in front of him were too complicated and that they confused him. He was able to see the general symmetry and the congruence of the forms but could not discern the details. His statement was supported by his perplexed behaviour in this test.

Another task should be mentioned in this context. It uses simple drawings of objects which have to be identified with the real original and involves the recurrence of forms which are similar but reduced in size. Thus the patient was shown drawings of a pan, scissors, a nail brush, and a bottle and each time he was given a large array of objects and he had to decide whether they were identical with one of the drawings or not. When the correct object appeared the patient could identify it with certainty, although at first he might hesitate. For example, to the patient the drawing of a bottle might have a certain similarity to the scissors or the nail brush. He definitely found it more difficult to reject an incorrect combination of drawing and object than to recognise a matching combination.

From all this I infer that under easy conditions the patient's ability to perceive and compare forms was adequate. This was shown earlier when he was copying drawings. However, compared to normal subjects this ability was much reduced.

A short comment must be added here to prepare the reader for later theoretical observations. I believe that the first demonstrated deficit can be explained to some extent by the fact that the patient had lost the symbolic meaning of his visual impressions—and indeed this is what made up his visual agnosia.

On the whole, the investigations described here appear to involve purely sensory perception and the differentiation of shapes independent of their symbolic meaning. Undoubtedly, however, in certain circumstances the symbolic meaning significantly facilitates the differentiation between shapes. Imagine, for example, two pictures which show human shapes identical in all details; however in one picture the person has a happy face and in the other a sad face. To most people this difference would be immediately obvious. However to someone for whom these human shapes were no more than a combination of meaningless squiggles requiring line-by-line comparison this difference would be difficult to discern.

12. Topographical Orientation (Indoors and Out of Doors). I emphasise this point because our patient's behaviour in respect to it was rather different from that reported from other known cases. Wilbrand's lady patient whose visual agnosia was less severe had persistent difficulty with orientation (. . .). Our patient had such difficulties with orientation both in his home and out of doors only in the first weeks after his accident. After six weeks it was already possible for him to venture out unaccompanied and soon after he was able to go for long walks in town (Breslau) without having to ask his way (. . .).

13. Reaction Times to Visual Stimuli. Under this heading I wish to mention that in the course of these investigations it was recorded if reaction times to visual stimuli were unusually prolonged. I confined myself to the simple method of asking the patient to respond by a movement of his hand, or verbally, as soon as a previously arranged visual signal had been given. Of course his reaction times would have had to be significantly delayed for it to have been observed in this way. Nevertheless, it is worth mentioning that no delay in his reaction times was noted. For obvious reasons I had to forgo more exact methods of taking measurements.

The assessment protocols which now follow are intended to give information about the most important point, namely how the patient perceived his physical environment. He was shown a range of different everyday objects and asked to describe these. If he was unable to do this he was allowed to touch the objects or, if possible, the objects were manipulated so as to produce some auditory cue. In addition to real objects he was shown and asked to interpret pictures of different sizes, either in black and white, or in colour. There were also simple outline drawings and some geometrical designs. Sometimes the patient was given a choice of descriptions from which he was asked to pick the appropriate one.

These tests showed that the patient behaved like a normal subject when he was faced with stimuli which were perceived either through touch or auditorily. In contrast, however, when objects were presented visually he was unable to recognise many of them. The ratio of objects not recognised

to objects recognised might be used to provide a measure of progression or improvement of his visual agnosia. However there were marked fluctuations in his performance. Even within one session he might recognise an object at its first presentation and misinterpret it soon after at a repeat presentation. His ability to recognise objects certainly varied from day to day (. . .). However there were some objects which he always reliably recognised. Among these were his own belongings such as his hat, his cap, his jacket, his gloves, etc., also, rather strangely, a coloured portrait of Kaiser Wilhelm I.

When the patient entered a room with a group of silent people he was aware of their presence. Sometimes he recognised an object as a whole but not a part of it, e.g. he correctly named the picture of an animal but not its head and its tail. He recognised a portrait of Bismarck but when he was asked to point to his eyes, ears, cap, etc., he made the most bizarre mistakes.

The patient's behaviour when he was unable to recognise an object in front of him is of considerable interest. Rarely did he say outright that he did not know what it was. He might say that the object was familiar but that at the moment he was unable to say anything about it. More usually, however, he would give a definite but wrong response. For example, he would call a clothes brush a pair of glasses. He mistook objects in the most bizarre way. For example, an umbrella would be seen as a plant with leaves, at another time as a pencil; a coloured apple was taken for the portrait of a lady, etc.

His answers were never given with the complete assurance with which a normal subject would make a statement about the name or characteristic of a familiar object. He usually expressed his opinion rather diffidently, half asking and with an expectant excitement about whether his reply had been correct. He might use a phrase like "Isn't it this or that?" Occasionally he might give a misinterpretation with greater conviction. Even after he had been corrected he would return again and again to the wrong interpretation. Of course sometimes an object might have been named wrongly out of embarrassment, because he had no idea what it was. However, in no way can this be seen as a plausible explanation of his misinterpretations. Not only the patient's own report but also the consistency of his misconceptions (to be discussed later) speak against this.

The patient always admitted when he had made

a mistake and had either corrected it without help or had found the correct answer, either through touching the object or because he had been given a cue. He usually made the excuse that his eyes had been mistaken. This phrase and his often strange and bizarre misinterpretations might have given rise to the suspicion that he was suffering from some form of visual hallucination. When the patient was asked whether the object in question, for example an apple, had looked different at the time he had misconceived it compared to later when the patient agreed that it was an apple, or whether the apple did not look the way he expected an apple to look, the patient denied this. He declared that the object had always looked like an apple but that he could not remember what it was called because of his weak memory. This answer was a frequent one and it was too positive a reply to be ignored. It appears to prove that the patient had made the mistake not because of visual failure but because his comprehension of what he had seen was impaired.

The method of providing a choice of interpretations often facilitated recognition. The patient confidently selected the correct interpretation which he would have been unable to provide by himself. The patient behaved much the same with pictures of objects as he did with real objects. He also mistook geometrical figures, for example a triangle for a square or even a cross.

I am unable to give psychological explanations for each individual misperception, nor can I say why the patient knew some objects and did not recognise others. For example, why did he nearly always recognise a brush but never a dust-pan? Yet the two objects belong together and are usually seen together.

Protocol

27 September 1888

Object Presented *Patient's response* (always in inverted commas)

Light: "Pencil." He describes both ends of the light as "tip and other end of the pencil". He is given the light to feel and immediately recognises it as a light.

Fountain Pen: "That's a light." What is it for? "For lighting of course." Is it lit? "No." He attempts to light it with matches at its point and is very surprised: "The light is not burning". He is asked to touch the object but is frightened to "burn" himself. He then recognises it at once as "writing pen".

Spectacles: "Lamp." After feeling it: "Spectacles".

Handkerchief: "Spectacles." After touch: "Cloth".

Carafe 1/2-filled with Water "Lamp into which you put a light", points to the stopper in the carafe. "The light goes in there." Then: "And here is water, or is it oil to burn?". After touching it the patient persists: "It is a lamp".

Metal Box: "I don't really know." After touching: "Matches".

Candle: "A piece of light."

Bread Roll: "Bread roll."

Fountain Pen: (different from above) "Candle snuffers." After touching: "Writing pen".

Piece of Paper: (folded) "Handkerchief." After touching: "Envelope".

Door Knob: "Snuffers", after some thought: "A candlestick". Manages to draw the object when asked. Persists at first: "A candlestick". It is placed in his hand, he turns it back and forth, peers into the hole of the knob, persists: "It's a candlestick". Finally he becomes doubtful, says: "It's a key".

Cigar Case: "A candlestick." Is corrected. It is something else. "It's for keeping spectacles?" "But it is too short for that." "For matches."

Cigarette: "A cigar." Is it a cigar or cigarette? "A cigarette."

Match: "A cigar or a cigarette." After touch: "A match".

2 Mark Coin: "A knife." Asked to draw it, draws an irregular curve approximately the size of a thaler (obsolete German coin). After touch: "A coin".

Purse: "A lighter, to light." The full purse is shaken close to his ear so that its contents rattle. "It's a purse."

Bunch of Keys with Several Larger Keys: "It's knives, three different knives." After he heard the rattle of keys: "It's keys".

Metal Whistle: "I have never come across that, don't know." After the whistle has been blown: "A whistle".

Pocket Watch: "A lamp", after a bit "a lighter". On request draws the watch clearly. The watch is then put to his ear. He recognises it at once: "Oh, it's a watch".

Book: "It's a watch—or a stand for the watch" "a watch holder". Is it spectacles? "No." Is it a lamp? "No." Is it a book? "Yes, perhaps that's what it is, an inkpot." Is it a pen? "No, not that." After touch: "A book".

Door Knob:	"A writing pen." Is it a watch? "No." A bread roll? "No." Is it a key? "A key perhaps." Is it a handkerchief? "No." Is it spectacles? "No." What is it then? "At most it can be a key."
Inkpot:	"An inkpot, I assume that's what it is."
Light:	"A pencil for drawing." Is it a key? "No, it's a pencil after all." Is it a bread roll? "No." Is it a light? "That's paraffin wax in it" (hesitantly).

Drawing of Figures and Numbers are Shown

A Square:	"That's a triangular thing."
A Cross:	"That's a cross."
A Triangle:	"Don't know, what is it supposed to be?"
Number 1:	"I can't decide what it is supposed to be."
Number 2:	"It's probably supposed to be a lamp." "A stand to place a lamp on." It is supposed to be a number. Is it a 1? "Yes." Is it a 2? "No." Is it a 3? "Yes, quite likely." Will you draw a 3 next to it. He does so and writes a 3 correctly. Now compare your 3 with the other number. Are they the same? "No, I see, that one is a 2."
Number 9:	"That is a 3 now." No. Is it a 4? "No." Is it a 5? "Don't know." Is it a 6? "Yes, it is a 6, but I don't like the down stroke, it does not belong there. It is not a 6." Is it a 7? "It is a 7, but that line does not belong in it." Is it an 8? "It is more likely a 7, but it is not an 8." Is it a 9? "Yes, it's the 9" (with more assurance than up to now).

29 September 1888

Watch Chain:	"It's a key."
A Blue Piece of Glass:	"A piece of wood." The glass is placed against a light which then shows through. "It is glass, could also be wood that's been lacquered." What is the colour? "It is greeney—or brown." Also red? "No." Or blue? "Yes, blue."
Pince-nez:	"Probably a ring, seems to be made of some kind of steel." Is it a ring for the finger? "No, it's the wrong shape." Is it too large or too small? "Too large." The pince-nez is opened. "Could be spectacles." Spectacles or a ring? "Spectacles."
A Green Grape:	"A pear." Apple or pear? "A pear. " Is it a plum? "No it is a pear." Is it a grape? "No." After an interval: "It seems to be a grape after all".
A Blue Grape:	"Also a grape." The same as before? "No this one is green the first was yellow."
A Cork:	"A seal." What does one use it for? "To seal something." After touch: "A cork".

A Live Grey Cat:	"A kitten." Shows head, tail, and ears correctly. The colour he calls "grey".
Walking Stick:	"A cane." Is it yours? "No, mine looks quite different."
A Clothes Brush:	"A cat." Is it the same as before? "No, the other was bigger." Do you think this is a small cat? "But it is not a real cat, it is a model of a cat." Shows an apparent head and tail at each end of the brush. Finally shows four legs along the edge of the brush, also draws on request the apparent cat as a clumsy, oblong object on which four legs are visible. When asked whether he can see legs on the object as clearly as on his drawing he is doubtful. He feels the brush and recognises it at once as a "clothes brush". (At this point it appeared as if the patient was seeing more than was actually placed in front of him. This and similar events made one think he might have hallucinations).
Piece of Soap:	"Piece of soap."
Portrait of Kaiser William I:	"Our Kaiser, the old one."
A Lamp Containing a Light:	"A figure." What does it represent? "That, I can't guess." After a pause: "It could be a man. But the figure only goes up to there" (shows the length of the light). "The other (shows the lamp) is something fixed, a base." Is it really a man and not perhaps a column? "No, here are his head and his legs." "Here is even (shows the bent wick of the light) a bent leg."
Clothes Brush:	"That is the earlier figure which was a cat." What was it really? "I have forgotten." The movement of brushing is demonstrated on his jacket. "Oh, of course a brush."
A Large Wall Mirror:	"That is a lamp made of glass I think." "A lamp." He steps close up to it. Where does the light go? "Here" He points to a corner of the mirror. What is inside it? (the reflection of the patient himself): "Seems to have a horse in it."
Umbrella (2 Feet Long):	"A lamp." How large do you estimate it to be? "8 inches." Shows on request both ends of the umbrella correctly. How long is 8 inches? Marks with his hands approximately the length of the umbrella. The umbrella is put up. Is it really a lamp? "Yes, yes, there (near the top) the light is put there." (. . .)

A Sheet of Paper with Illustrations of Animals is Shown (Not in Colour)

Donkey:	"That's Napoleon." Is it a picture? "Yes, it's a painting of Napoleon."

Horse:	"Horse." Shows head and tail correctly.
Parrot:	"Seems to be a donkey."
Swan:	"A giraffe."
Cat:	"Cat or monkey."
	The sheet of paper is turned over so that its reverse is shown: Do you see any pictures here?
	"No."

(1 protocol omitted.)

3 November 1888

Umbrella:	"An umbrella."
Clothes Brush:	"A child's small cupboard probably for children to play with." After feeling it: "A clothes brush".
Onion:	"A candle." After feeling it: "An onion".
Salt cellar:	"Also a candle to light up." Contemplating: "That can't be". Touching it: "A beer glass or something like that".
Piece of Coal:	"A beer glass." After touching: "A piece of metal". Isn't it coal? "Coal is black, this is more of a brown colour."
Piece of Cotton Wool:	"I can't see this clearly, its probably a piece of metal." After touching: "Cotton wool".
Bunch of Keys:	"Something to put on the table. You mean a paper-weight or something like that? "It can't be that. I don't really know, it's glass."
Purse:	"A lamp."
Pocket Watch:	"A lamp." After touching: "A watch".
Hat:	"A hat."

(1 protocol omitted.)

Finally, I will add part of a later protocol (end of January 1889) which is of interest in relation to the misjudgements the patient tended to make:

Key:	"Scissors to trim the light." The patient is shown real scissors: "That's also a pair of scissors to trim the light". Are both things (key and scissors) so much alike?" No they are very different! These here (points to the scissors) are ordinary scissors to trim the light with." Have you ever seen a pair of scissors like these (key) before? "I can't recall just for the moment, but it's meant for that. This is where the trimmed off bit should lie" (points to the top part of the key). Could it not be a key? "No, it's a part of a pair of scissors, it does not have a ward." ('ward', the part that goes into the lock). Takes the key into his hand: "It's a key after all: I made a mistake, I took it to be part of a pair of scissors to clean the light".

Part 2

In the following section I intend to concern myself with the explanation of the clinical manifestations of visual agnosia. This is the syndrome in which a patient is unable to name objects presented visually or indeed define their characteristics, although his ability to receive visual impressions has been shown to be sufficiently intact for him to be able to differentiate the stimuli concerned clearly. The definition of visual agnosia involves two assumptions. The first is that there has been no generalised intellectual decline such as is found in the final stages of "paralysis" (general paralysis of the insane). This does not apply in our case. The most unequivocal proof is that the patient is always able to provide the kind of accurate information about his auditory or tactile perceptions which he cannot give for visually presented objects. It is very obvious that greater alertness and in general more intelligence is required to recognise an everyday object by touch than by sight.

The second assumption is that there are no dysphasic disturbances. The way in which our patient tended to express himself could have produced the suspicion that there were some transcortical speech disturbances. In fact this was not the case. Our patient never mixed up words in a paraphasic fashion. For example, when he spoke of spectacles he meant just that: an instrument made of glass which he had put on to read or write a hundred times. However, when he said that a fork was a pair of glasses it was not that he used the wrong word for the correct concept but that the concept itself was wrong. For anyone who worked with the patient there was not the least doubt about this.

Earlier we asked for proof that the patient's visual acuity was adequate. In our case it is possible to provide this evidence with some elegance. Although it is likely that his acuity was not entirely intact, just a fraction of his actual acuity would have been sufficient to recognise most things in the environment and to prevent the kind of misperceptions observed. It is obvious that somebody who is able to draw objects from life, to read quite small print, and to count dots on a piece of paper, should not mistake a knife for scissors, etc. I am convinced that reduced acuity plays no part in these misperceptions.

It was also easy in our case to demonstrate the preservation of colour perception and there was no evidence of a central field defect. He had no difficulty in fixating. There was no impairment of eye muscle movement. We can therefore say that the sum of what might be called the subcortical tools of vision was normal, or so well preserved that our patient's visual agnosia cannot be explained in these terms. (. . .)

Since we have been unable to find a physiological explanation for our patient's visual agnosia there remains now only a discussion of the state of awareness which always has to accompany the process of recognition. In the following I shall divide this process of recognition into two stages and attempt, as far as possible, to differentiate these from each other. They are: (1) The stage of conscious awareness of a sensory impression. This I shall call apperception. (2) The stage of associating other notions with the content of this apperception. This I shall call the stage of association.

It would seem to be obvious that apperception as a special mental process should be thought of as separate from the understanding of its meaning with its manifold associations. I came to this conclusion for two reasons. First, according to the theory of localisation with which I agree completely, those processes which occur in only one modality and are therefore localised should be separated from those which involve a variety of associations and so are the product of the whole cortex. A process of the first kind involves only apperception and it must be followed by a process of the second kind before the act of recognition can be completed. Secondly my observations force me to make this distinction. There is no doubt that our patient perceived many things without comprehending them; that is, he purely apperceived some objects but did not recognise them. Therefore the first stage occurred without the second stage. Thus indeed under certain pathological conditions the first stage may occur in isolation.

How I understand the act of association and its role in recognition is simple enough: the recognition of an object can only occur when at the time of its perception a number of ideas are evoked which relate to that object. These bring into consciousness those characteristics which the mind has learned to associate with it and those conditions in which it has been experienced previously. Of course the sum total of these associations varies from one individual to another. The completeness with which the associations are recalled may also vary from one time to the next. However there are certain fundamental ideas which invariably come to mind when an object is perceived. They usually relate to the object's name and those events which have been experienced most frequently and vividly in connection with it. Memories laid down through different sensory modalities contribute to these associations but it is only when they are brought into awareness and linked with the percept that the recognition of an object becomes complete.

The associations subserving the recognition of visual objects are so manifold that their psychological analysis into individual memories is complicated. Let us take a simple example which involves all sense modalities: a musical instrument, for example a violin. For anyone who has some knowledge of this instrument, there exist a number of recollections associated with its image, its name, its sound, the sensation, and the tactile experiences which go along with handling it. In addition there will be the mental image of a violinist in his characteristic pose. It is only when the linkage between the percept of the instrument and such associated recollections occur promptly in consciousness that the individual will be able to interpret the object as a musical instrument, differentiate it from other instruments, and thus categorise it. If, however, this linkage is delayed or disrupted through some pathological process then even if the image of the violin is perceived, however precisely, it cannot be associated with prior experiences and recognition is therefore not possible. A visual agnosia which is solely due to the disruption of the link between the visual content of a perception and its various associated conceptual recollections might be called an associative agnosia.

It is rather more difficult to evaluate the concept of apperception and the definition of this concept requires a few comments first of all. My interpretation at this point and in the following is this: apperception is the physical act of perceiving a sensory stimulus quite removed from all that involves its comprehension and its conceptual processing. I am undecided whether this act should be labelled perception or apperception. Assuming that in every act of perceiving there must be a more or less lively involvement of the conscious mind, I see apperception simply as the highest level of perception in which the conscious mind takes a sensory impression with maximal intensity. Finally, on the assumption that a given individual can experience this stage of conscious sensory perception, I chose this term of apperception because I wished to define this stage as clearly and precisely as possible.

To explain this concept of apperception I can suggest nothing better than to pose the question: how in any given case can the existence of an apperception of a certain sensory impression be established? There are two methods which might be used for this purpose. The first might use active performance by the examinee, i.e. getting the subject to copy the stimulus either by drawing it or by repetition or something along these lines. In the second method the subject might be asked to describe the content of the perception but this obviously requires intact language functions. However, this method of description could be made easier and indeed independent of, say, language functions if it only involved having to make a judgement as to the congruence or incongruence of different perceptions. In this way it should be possible to demonstrate apperception in its purest form. Indeed under these circumstances apperception can be equated with the ability to detect discrepancies between sense perceptions. The amount of difference necessary for two percepts to be registered as being incongruent could provide a measure of this ability.

From this definition apperception does not appear to be something constant, present or absent as the case may be, but rather to be a capacity of variable potential which can be quantitatively graded. Furthermore, where visual perception is concerned we really ought to speak of different kinds of apperception. In particular one ought to distinguish between the abilities to perceive colour, form, and three-dimensional objects. One should also distinguish between sharpness of apperception of simple and of complex stimuli as separate capacities. The former concerns tests of visual acuity and tests such as that mentioned earlier in relation to estimation by eye. However, since errors at this level of perceptual processing may involve both subcortical organs and the conscious mind it may indeed be difficult to make distinctions here. The case of the apperception of complex forms, as discussed in connection with form perception, is of particular importance because this is a specific capacity of the cortical apparatus. It is therefore easier to assess independently of acuity which is variously affected by subcortical changes.

We now come to the question concerning the relationship which may exist between an impairment of apperception and visual agnosia. The obvious, a priori possibilities are as follows:

1. As already explained, visual agnosia can be thought of as an associative visual agnosia without pathological impairment of apperception.
2. Visual agnosia is based on an impairment of both apperception and associative functions.
3. Visual agnosia is the result of a selective impairment of apperception.

The third possibility is the only questionable one. I would like to defend this idea by introducing spatial vision into the framework of apperception as a prerequisite for any complex visual perception, even if it is justifiable to consider it an issue separate from apperception. Spatial vision is at present seen as a synthesis (Wundt) of different sensations, i.e. from the retina, from innervations of the eye muscles, and tactile ones from the area of the bulbus. It is precisely this view which requires that a complicated cortical apparatus exists for spatial vision which allows us to consider the possibility that one isolated pathological process could interrupt or limit the formation of spatial images in the conscious mind. How would a person behave whose visual impressions were limited to the perception of light and colour differences but who no longer had images of form and three-dimensional shape? The recognition of objects would become difficult and visual experiences would be chaotic and confusing such as for a person who had been born blind and whose eyesight had been restored suddenly by an operation.

We have now arrived at the possibility that there may exist both an associative and an apperceptive form of visual agnosia. I do not expect to find clinical cases representing pure examples of these two forms of agnosia. In particular I consider purely associative visual agnosia to be a contradiction in terms. It is necessary at this point to limit the strict division which has been made so far between apperceptive and associative functions. We have defined apperception as that function which enables us to give information about the differences between sensory impressions. Where simple stimuli are concerned it is easy to think of apperception as independent of the associative processes necessary for recognition. However, this way of thinking poses problems where complex stimuli are concerned. Detailed differentiation of complex stimuli and their overall comprehension is much facilitated by the linkage of the content of what has been perceived with various associated notions. I touched on this in the discussion of form perception when I cited the example of the minimal yet so obvious difference shown by the pictorial representations of two human figures, who differ only in their facial expressions. Of course the relevant details have first to be perceived before the associative ideas can ensue. These associations are necessary to bring to the percept the full illumination of the conscious mind, thus completing their apperception. Only then is it possible to give a precise description of the percept.

In relation to the process of apperception of complex visual stimuli, I would like to compare the role of association to that of a Helmholtz resonator which enables us to recognise with certainty components of a musical chord which otherwise we would have been unable to detect. From this it follows, in particular where complex visual stimuli are concerned, that the efficiency of apperception is dependent, at least to some extent, on these manifold associations. A disturbance of the latter necessarily results in some impairment of the former. Therefore we cannot expect to see an impairment of associative processes without some additional apperceptive problem, i.e. there cannot be a selective associative visual agnosia but at most a predominantly associative visual agnosia. This is also obvious in view of rather different anatomical considerations.

The above considerations are based on the assumption that the process of recognition can be divided into two, an apperceptive stage and an associative stage. Furthermore, an attempt has been made to investigate the respective contributions by these two stages of perceptual processing to the development of visual agnosia. The inference drawn from this is that an impairment of the associative process is sufficient to produce visual agnosia but that such an impairment cannot occur without simultaneous degradation of the apperceptive process. There remains the question whether a selective impairment of the apperceptive process can also result in the clinical picture of visual agnosia.

We now come to the question of how our specific case can be fitted into this framework. There can be no doubt that our patient showed an impairment of apperception. In particular, as has been described in the case history under the heading "form perception," his perception of complex vi-

sual stimuli was not intact. In contrast on simple perceptual tasks his apperception was good and this was shown on tests of visual acuity and estimation by eye. By making him draw objects from presented examples it could be shown that his perception of simple shapes was sufficiently intact to permit them to be recognised. The fact that the objects were not recognised can have been due only to a pathological disturbance of associative functions. Since this was by far the more dominant deficit it must be assumed that it was this which was responsible for the patient's misperceptions.

The existence of an impairment of the associative processes can be demonstrated even more clearly in relation to colour perception, an area which so far has not been explored in great depth. Our patient's apperception of colour, defined as the ability to differentiate between hues, was within normal limits. However the recognition of colours ultimately consists of the ability to name colours correctly, since the concept of a given colour has only two relevant components, namely its semantic label and its visual image. The correct name should be evoked by the visual impression. However, if, as in our case, this did not occur, then there must have been a disruption of the associative processes.

Finally and in conclusion, I am inclined to define the specific case of our patient L, not as a selective, but certainly a predominantly associative visual agnosia. (Three pp. omitted.)

In general it is accepted that visual agnosia is caused by moderately extensive damage to the occipital cortex. It is a fact that during the process of recognising a sensory impression that part of the cortex that has to effect recognition is activated first. There then follow a series of associative processes which elicit the various determining memory images relating to the object concerned. These memory images are distributed throughout the whole of the cortex since they involve different modalities. To activate these images it is necessary for the excitation to spread from the perceiving part of the cortex to the whole of the cortex in order to elicit throughout a specific and finely tuned reaction. This is the process in which in our case must have been mediated by the transcortical tracts of the visual cortex. A blockage of transmission along these tracts would not result necessarily in the interruption of perception, at least, there is no evidence that would support such an assumption. However the blockage would prevent a linkage between perception and those associations which are normally necessary for the process of recognition and this would result in a visual agnosia. (Two pp. omitted.)

Some other points require clarification. These concern the preservation of visual memory, or visual imagination, in visual agnosia. We have found so far that visual memory is supposed to show impairment both in cortical and in transcortical visual agnosia. In the case of L (see the case history), we noted his retained ability to write and from this we concluded that the patient continued to have at his disposal visual memory images. Even if there had been better evidence for intact memory images this would not cause difficulties for the theory. We have so far considered only one visual field as if the hemianopic field had been totally eliminated. This elimination would be complete if the existing loss of the right visual field was the result of the destruction of the visual field itself, i.e. if this was a case of visual agnosia and cortical hemianopia. In that case there would be no replacement in the hemianopic hemisphere for the loss of memory images reported in other cases of visual agnosia. It is different, however, if the hemianopia is of subcortical origin. In that case memory images of that hemisphere would be available to the conscious mind, unimpaired despite an existing visual agnosia for all visual perceptions. (Wilbrand explains the preserved visual imagery in his visual agnosic patient in this way.) (...)

Another point I wish to consider concerns the question: how is it possible that in an associative visual agnosia the ability to draw from life is preserved? In fact, copying by drawing from example is an associative process in as far as the sight of the model causes excitatory stimulation which guides the hand. In the case of absolute and complete interruption of transcortical connections, any reaction to visual perceptions including drawing would stop. In no case of visual agnosia has this been reported: only partial interruptions are involved. One could postulate that the ability to draw from example is reduced in proportion to the severity of visual agnosia. Certainly in our case a reduction of this kind has to be admitted. It is certain, that, prior to his accident, our patient was able to draw with less difficulty and less primitively and clumsily. If at times he managed to reproduce the outlines of objects without recognising them this can be explained as follows: by looking at his pencil lines and correcting his mistakes he was able to keep a check on his drawings. Also those associations, which enable us to correct the direction of a perceived line by a certain hand movement take on a special position in the sum total of the associative processes in the inner mind, and thus the problem of drawing outlines can be reduced to this elementary case. The visuo-motor innervation is very simple compared to the complicated associations involved in imagination. Furthermore, it has an anatomical advantage and can be facilitated by practice. One can assume that in the formation of spatial perception sensations of motor innervations are involved in such a way that we cannot see a shape or imagine a shape without such sensations. A fundamental rule in relation to the phenomenon of imagination is probably that whenever associations are interrupted through some pathological process those which are most familiar as a result of frequent use suffer the least. Thus it could be explained why the ability to draw simple outlines from life is not lost entirely even in cases of severe visual agnosia. (One p. omitted.)

In the following my task will be to consider the views held by other authors concerning visual agnosia and their applicability to our clinical observations.

The creator of the term "visual agnosia," Munk, wishing to explain this term, assumed that he had removed surgically the area of actual vision and with this also the seat of visual memory. This idea, which does not contradict the above, nevertheless does not fit our patient whose vision was entirely intact. This fact evidently refutes Mauthner's contradiction of the whole theory of visual agnosia. According to him all symptoms of visual agnosia could be explained by actual loss of vision. In fact the refutation of his objections justifies the existence of the concept of "Seelenblindheit" and its associated theoretical considerations. (One p. omitted.)

What is different in my presentation from those of other authors is my attempt to put special emphasis on the transcortical tracts and their importance in the manifestation of visual agnosia. This approach to the problem was suggested by the theories and systems which Wernicke and Lichtheim have postulated for the organisation of speech functions with such important consequences. More recently Freund has developed ideas much in accordance with mine. He touches on the question of visual agnosia in the conclusion of his paper about optical aphasia.

I do not wish to conclude this discussion without touching on some details of the protocols which may be of importance. I mean the frequently noted tendency of the patient to recognise objects falsely. Our discussion so far makes it comprehensible that, under certain pathological conditions, familiar objects can become so alien to the mind that they cannot be responded to. However our patient went beyond this; he made positively false statements about some of the objects he perceived, i.e. he recognised them falsely. These false statements were not motivated by his embarrassment at not knowing nor were they simply wild guesses. More likely they were the expression of an opinion, an uncertain unclear judgement, but nevertheless a real judgement. It is certainly worthwhile to have a closer look at these "misjudgements."

I have attempted to classify the various types of errors which characterised our patient's misinterpretations of visual stimuli and the following error categories were arrived at:

1. The object, and the concept under which it was mistakenly grouped, have something in common, some tangential point which to a certain degree makes the mistake comprehensible. Thus we can follow the imaginary path which led to the false interpretation. At the same time it is clear that the false concept was evoked in the conscious mind by the perception of the object. Here we have included:
   a. A real visual likeness, likeness in shape: i.e. pencil for candle, or a woven waste-paper basket for the basket work in a tailor's dummy as used to model ladies' dresses.
   b. A partial likeness, such that a specific part of the object leads to the misinterpretation of the whole: i.e. a picture of a swan for a giraffe, where apparently the long neck led to the mistake; the picture of a lion which was called a wild man because of the shaggy hair; or when a table knife was said to be a mirror because of the shiny blade.
   c. An internal relationship without any external likeness: this category of misinterpretations was not predominant but is of special interest. A typical example is the bunch of grapes for a pear, where there is no external likeness and the only relevant relationship can have been that both are in the category of fruit. It also happened that the patient at first named an object correctly, then became

doubtful and produced another identification which had some relationship to the first correct one. For example he recognised a watch, but then said that it was not a watch but a watch-stand. Similarly spectacles were eventually called a spectacle case. We can also mention here the collar which was taken to be a cuff both belonging to the category of clothing, or when a piece of caster sugar was taken to be a sweet. Of course in the latter cases, apart from the common category, there was a certain external similarity.

Although this first category of misinterpretations seems on the whole comprehensible and indeed explicable, it was decidedly less common than the two types described below.

2. The second category includes misinterpretations which appear to be rather arbitrary and incomprehensible since there is no apparent associative link between the perceived object and the concept produced to express recognition. Some of these rather arbitrary misinterpretations may well fall into the categories already mentioned because in fact they contain hidden similarities to the actual object which the patient may have perceived subconsciously. However, there emerges a completely different connection for most of these misinterpretations, namely a relationship in which we can recognise a certain rule, i.e. the rule of adherence to those notions which come to mind first at the time when the object was first presented. The patient showed a marked tendency to subsequently use a concept for other objects once it had been evoked vividly and had acquired dominance in his conscious mind. This was particularly so when after having arrived at the concept correctly through identifying a given object by vision, touch, cue, or some other means, the patient then used this same concept to misidentify other objects. There are many examples of this in the protocols and some of the errors are quite bizarre: for example an umbrella for a plant pot, a clothes brush for a cat. Similar behaviour can be observed in certain dysphasics. It is strange because the patient has only just seen, say, object (a), i.e. he has experienced it visually. He should therefore be able to distinguish it as different from a subsequent object (b). In fact sometimes the patient appeared to become aware of this. He

then seemed to think that different objects were variations of the same category of objects; for example a small moneybox key shown to him after he had seen a clock was identified as an unusual clock key.

This type of misinterpretation appears to me to be of special interest because it seems conditional on the patient finding himself in a situation where a whole range of objects different from one another is perceived by him as conceptually identical to the first seen object although in fact they are completely unrelated. It also suggests that the investigator can elicit certain misrecognitions, giving them a certain direction by selecting a suitable range of objects and thus influencing the conceptual process. Apparently some kind of psychological suggestion plays a part in this which could perhaps be likened to certain parallel manifestations in hypnotic states.

3. Finally, there is a third category of misinterpretations. The concept selected to label a given object is vaguely related to some other concept. A figurine, a pillar, a "thing" to be placed on a table, a lamp-stand, these are examples of what our patient produced in this context. However, this category is not of particular interest nor does it require further explanation. Most likely it can be accounted for in terms of embarrassment.

This largely empirical classification of the patient's misinterpretations is all I wish to offer in this connection. I dare not make a decision as to how they were arrived at. However there appear to be two separate possibilities. First, the misinterpretations may be simple misjudgements. The model for this would be that a series of notions and memory images are mistakenly transferred to the visual percept of an object (a) when in normal consciousness they would have been attached to object (b). Therefore the mistake in this case is a misplacement of the associative processes. A second possibility is that there occurred a misperception. Although the patient perceives the essential visual characteristics of the misinterpreted object, he has the idea or illusion that besides the outlines of object (a) he also has seen the outlines of object (b) and because of this he makes a false judgement, i.e. in this case he appears to "see" more than what is actually in front of him.

It is difficult to decide which of these two pos-

sibilities represents the true state of affairs. However, as I have already explained in the case history, a simple misjudgement is the most likely explanation. One might therefore be tempted to draw rather general conclusions from the misinterpretation data: from the first category of misinterpretations we may conclude that under certain pathological conditions ideas are linked in close associative relationship, which normally would be linked only if there were actual outer similarities or other conceptual associations. From the second category we may draw an even more strange conclusion that under these same pathological conditions a tendency exists to link ideas which have come to mind at the same time by chance and apart from this have no connection with each other whatsoever.

Whatever the psychological origin of misinterpretations it is certain that they are based on a deficit and this deficit is due to the fact that ideas associated with a certain sensory modality have been lost. The connection between visual agnosia and the misconception of visual impressions will become clearer as further relevant clinical observations are made public. Perhaps it will become possible from the knowledge gained of states of cerebral impairment to tackle those illusionary misinterpretations which play such an important role in the symptomatology of the so-called functional psychoses. This could well result in an important breach in the barrier which still exists between the cerebral lesion phenomena and the psychoses.

REFERENCES

Batterham, J. W. (1888). Notes on a case of amnesia. *Brain, 10,* 487–493.
Brandenburg, von (1884). Fin Fall von homonymer rechtsseitiger Hemianopsie mit Alexie und Trochlearislähmung. *Archiv. Für Ophlholmologie, 33,* 93–112.
Bruns, L., & Stoelting, B. (1888). Fin Fall von Alexie mit rechtsseitiger homonymer Hemianopsie ("Subcorticale Alexie" Wernicke). *Neurologisches Zentralblatt, 7,* 481–490.
Freund, C. S. (1889). Über optische Aphasie und Seelenblindheit. *Archiv für Psychicrtrie und Nervenkrankheiten, 20,* 276–297.
Munk, H. (1890). *Über die Funktionen der Grosshirnrinde* (17 papers 1871–1889).
Starr, A. M. (1998). The pathology of sensory aphasia. *Brain, 12,* 82–99.
Wernicke, C. (1886). Einige neuere Arbeiten über Aphasie. *Fortschritte der Medizin, IV,* 371–463.

Wilbrand, H. (1887). *Die Seelenblindheit als Herderscheinung und ihre Beziehung zur homonymen Hemianopsie, zur Alexie und Agraphie.* Bergmann: Wiesbaden.

Wilbrand, H. (1892). Fin Fall von Seelenblindheit und Hemianopsie mit Sections befund. *Deutsche Zeilschrift für Nervenheilkund, 2,* 361–387.

Introduction to Reading 17

Hubel and Wiesel (Reading 7) began their exploration of the primate visual system by investigating primary visual cortex and the receptive field properties of cells there. They found, among other things, that many cells are selectively responsive to oriented bars or edges, that they have a retinotopic organization, and that they are organized into ocular dominance and orientation columns. The decades that followed these initial discoveries saw an explosion of work delineating the neuroanatomy of the primate cortex, using techniques that permit one to detect cytoarchitectonic boundaries between adjacent brain regions (i.e., boundaries between regions containing particular cell types and connection patterns) and to assess the connectivity between areas (both feed-forward and feed-back). In parallel with these anatomical studies (many summarized, for example, in Felleman & Van Essen, 1991), investigations of the functional properties of these newly discovered anatomical regions were conducted. Cells were found that responded to variation in color, direction of motion, speed, binocular disparity (which codes depth) and spatial frequency (which codes size or spatial scale); see Reading 3 by Barlow for more details.

A crucial challenge was to discover the organizational principles that characterize connections between areas or brain systems. One such principle that proved to be extremely useful was the distinction between the parvocellular and magnocellular visual pathways. This distinction was first discovered in the lateral geniculate nucleus (LGN).

The LGN is a small part of the thalamus, which is a structure at the top of the brainstem that contains nuclei that serve as "waystations" for several different sensory systems (in particular, vision and audition). The LGN receives inputs from the optic nerves of the two eyes, and sends outputs, after a single synapse, to primary visual cortex. The LGN is a layered structure; four layers contain cells with small cell bodies (parvocellular layers, from the Latin for "small"), and two contain cells with large cell bodies (magnocellular layers, from the Latin for "large"). It was soon discovered that the flow of information through the parvo and magno (or, simply, the P and M) layers of the LGN remained distinct well into visual cortex. Morphologically distinct classes of retinal ganglion cells feed each pathway (midget cells for the P pathway and parasol cells for the M pathway). Furthermore, it was learned that there were significant functional differences between the P and M pathways. M fibers have rapid axonal conduction velocities relative to P fibers. The receptive fields of M cells tend to be larger and more eccentric, on average, than those of the P cells. M cells appear to be color-blind, while the responses of P cells depend on color.

A clear demonstration of the functional properties of the magno and parvo layers of the LGN was reported by Schiller, Logothetis, and Charles (1990). Monkeys were trained to make several different perceptual discriminations (concerning color, texture, movement, etc.). A portion of the magno or parvo layers of the LGN was destroyed, and the discrimination tasks were run again. Monkeys with magno lesions were unimpaired in color and fine pattern discrimination, but their performance on tasks requiring flicker or motion perception was impaired; in contrast, monkeys with parvo lesions could perform the motion-based tasks well, but they were impaired in making color and pattern discrimination. These observations suggested that the M pathway supports the perception of motion and flicker, while the P pathway supports the perception of pattern, form, and color.

The reading reprinted here by Mishkin, Ungerleider, and Macko provides evidence for a related organization of the primate visual system. The idea is simple: there exist two pathways that carry information about *what* and

where objects are. The ventral (lower) pathway runs from area V1 to V2, V4, and the inferior temporal cortex; this pathway represents information about static object properties like shape and color. The dorsal (upper) pathway runs from area V1 to V2, MT, and the parietal lobe; this pathway represents information about dynamic properties like motion and about relative spatial relations among objects.

This proposal has been enormously influential in helping to interpret the functional organization of visual cortex. Livingstone and Hubel (1987) proposed that the distinction between the P and M pathways in the early parts of the visual system is related to the distinction between the ventral ("what") and dorsal ("where") pathways in visual cortex. In the last decade, many complexities have been uncovered showing that the two pathways are not as distinct as once was thought, but the essential idea remains intact.

An extension of the idea of distinct "what" and "where" systems was proposed by Goodale and Milner (1992; Milner & Goodale, 1995). According to Goodale and Milner, the dorsal pathway does not merely represent spatial locations and motions of objects. Instead, it serves as the interface between the visual system and the motor system. In other words, they proposed that the dorsal and ventral pathways represent not what and where, as suggested by Ungerleider et al., but what and *how*. One crucial source of evidence for this proposal comes from an analysis of the impaired performance of a stroke victim known by her initials, D.F. The stroke (in which the blood supply to a specific brain region is disrupted, killing the neurons there) damaged portions of her ventral pathway, but left her dorsal pathway intact. When D.F. was shown an oriented slot and asked to name its orientation (vertical, horizontal, oblique) or to hold her hand in the same orientation, her performance was almost random.

However, if she was asked to insert a block of wood into the slot (as if she were posting a letter), she could do so almost flawlessly. It was as if she had no conscious access to the orientation of the edges of the relevant part of the scene (an impairment in representing *what* an object is, a ventral function that was apparently damaged by her stroke). But when D.F. was faced with using visual information to guide action (a dorsal function that was

spared by her stroke), performance was unimpaired.

Both of these proposals provide global frameworks for interpreting a wide range of studies about the functional properties of the visual system. As discussed in Reading 3 by Barlow, the functional organization of the visual system is likely to be more complex than two functional pathways. Nevertheless, these initial proposals have proven to be essential guideposts in this effort.

REFERENCES

Felleman, D. J., & Van Essen, D. C. (1991). Distributed hierarchical processing in the primate cerebral cortex. *Cerebral Cortex, 1*, 1–47.

Goodale, M. A., & Milner, A. D. (1992). Separate visual pathways for perception and action. *Trends in Neurosciences, 15*, 20–25.

Livingstone, M., & Hubel, D. (1988). Segregation of form, color, movement, and depth: Anatomy, physiology, and perception. *Science, 240*, 740–749.

Milner, A. D. & Goodale, M. A. (1995). *The visual brain in action.* Oxford: Oxford University Press.

Schiller, P. H., Logothetis, N. K., & Charles, E. R. (1990). Functions of the colour-opponent and broad-band channels of the visual system. *Nature, 343*, 68–70.

Object Vision and Spatial Vision:
Two Cortical Pathways

M. Mishkin, L. G. Ungerleider, and K. A. Macko
• National Institute of Mental Health

Evidence is reviewed indicating that striate cortex in the monkey is the source of two multisynaptic corticocortical pathways. One courses ventrally, interconnecting the striate, prestriate, and inferior temporal areas, and enables the visual identification of objects. The other runs dorsally, interconnecting the striate, prestriate, and inferior parietal areas, and allows instead the visual location of objects. How the information carried in these two separate pathways is reintegrated has become an important question for future research.

Thirty-five years ago Lashley concluded that visual mechanisms do not extend beyond the striate cortex. He was led to this view after finding that "None of the lesions in the prestriate region of the monkey has produced symptoms resembling object agnosia as described in man . . . Uncomplicated destruction of major portions of the prestriate region . . . has not been found to produce any disturbances in sensory or perceptual organization" (14).

We now know, of course, that Lashley's conclusion was wrong. Tissue essential for vision extends far beyond striate cortex to include not only the prestriate region of the occipital lobe but also large portions of the temporal and parietal lobes. Neurobehavioral studies since Lashley's (3, 6, 20–23, 28) together with converging evidence from physiological (1, 6, 10, 24, 30, 44) and anatomical studies (5, 31, 39, 41–43), indicate that these extrastriate regions contain numerous visual areas that can be distinguished both structurally and functionally. Moreover, recent work from our own laboratory (40) suggests that these multiple visual areas are organized hierarchically into two separate cortical visual pathways, one specialized for "object" vision, the other for "spatial" vision.

Two Pathways

The two cortical visual pathways are schematized in Fig. 17.1. One of them consists of a multisynaptic occipitotemporal projection system that follows the course of the inferior longitudinal fasciculus. This pathway, which interconnects the striate, prestriate, and inferior temporal areas, is crucial for the visual identification of objects (21). Subsequent links of the occipitotemporal pathway with limbic structures in the temporal lobe (36) and with ventral portions of the frontal lobe (13) may make possible the cognitive association of visual objects with other events, such as emotions and motor acts.

The other pathway consists of a multisynaptic occipitoparietal projection system that follows the course of the superior longitudinal fasciculus. This pathway, which interconnects the striate, prestriate, and inferior parietal areas, is critical for the visual location of objects (40). Subsequent links of the occipitoparietal pathway with dorsal limbic (26) and dorsal frontal cortex (13, 26) may enable the cognitive construction of spatial maps as well as the visual guidance of motor acts (8) that were initially triggered by activity in the ventral pathway. In contrast to the ventral pathway, which remains modality-specific throughout its course, the later stations in the dorsal pathway appear to receive convergent input from other modalities and so may constitute polysensory areas (10, 32).

The notion that separate neural systems mediate object and spatial vision is not new (11, 25). In previous formulations, however, these two types of visual perception were attributed to the geniculostriate and tectofugal systems, respectively, rather than to separate cortical pathways diverging from a common striate origin. The shift to the present view is in keeping with the cumulative evidence that, in primates at least, all forms of visual perception, as distinguished from visuomotor functions, are more heavily dependent on the geniculostriate than on the tectofugal system.

Object Vision

The anterior part of inferior temporal cortex, or area TE in Bonin and Bailey's terminology (2), is the last exclusively visual area in the pathway that begins in the striate cortex, or area OC, and continues through the prestriate and posterior temporal areas, OB, OA and TEO (Fig. 17.1). This ventrally directed chain of cortical visual areas appears to extract stimulus quality information from the retinal input to the striate cortex (20), processing it for the purpose of identifying the visual stimulus and ultimately assigning it some meaning through the mediation of area TE's connections

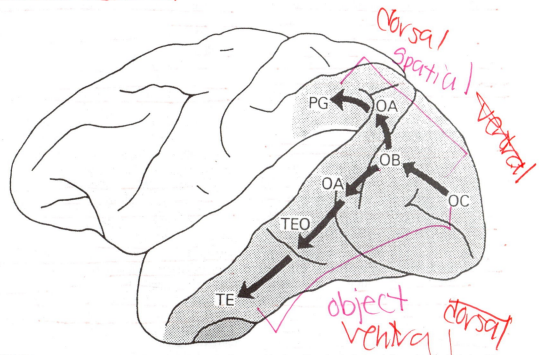

FIGURE 17.1 ■ Lateral View of the Left Hemisphere of a Rhesus Monkey. The shaded area defines the cortical visual tissue in the occipital, temporal and parietal lobes. Arrows schematize two cortical visual pathways, each beginning in primary visual cortex (area OC), diverging within prestriate cortex (areas OB and OA), and then coursing either ventrally into the inferior temporal cortex (areas TEO and TE) or dorsally into the inferior parietal cortex (area PG). Both cortical visual pathways are crucial for higher visual function, the ventral pathways for object vision and the dorsal pathway for spatial vision.

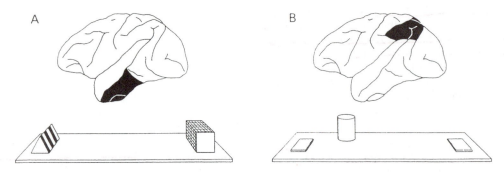

FIGURE 17.2 ■ Behavioral Tasks Sensitive to Cortical Visual Lesions in Monkeys. (A) Object discrimination. Bilateral removal of area TE in inferior temporal cortex produces severe impairment on object discrimination. A simple version of such a discrimination is a one-trial object-recognition task based on the principle of non-matching to sample, in which monkeys are first familiarized with one object of a pair in a central location (familiarization trial not shown) and are then rewarded in the choice test for selecting the unfamiliar object. (B) Landmark discrimination. Bilateral removal of posterior parietal cortex produces severe impairment on landmark discrimination. On this task, monkeys are rewarded for choosing the covered foodwell closer to a tall cylinder, the "landmark," which is positioned randomly from trial to trial closer to the left cover or closer to the right cover, the two covers being otherwise identical.

with the limbic and frontal-lobe systems (12). According to this view, the analysis of the physical properties of a visual object (such as its size, color, texture and shape) is performed in the multiple subdivisions of the prestriate–posterior temporal complex (44) and may even be completed within this tissue. Such a proposal gains support from the striking loss in pattern-discrimination ability that follows damage to the posterior temporal area (20). But the synthesis of all the physical properties of the particular object into a unique configuration appears to entail the funnelling of the outputs from the prestriate-posterior temporal region into area TE (21). This postulated integration of the coded visual properties of an object within area TE would make TE especially well suited to serve not only as the highest-order area for the visual perception of objects but also as the storehouse for their central representations and, hence, for their later recognition.

That area TE is important for the retention of some form of visual experience has been suspected for decades (18). Numerous behavioral studies (6) have demonstrated that bilateral removal of inferior temporal cortex in monkeys yields marked impairment both in the retention of visual discrimination habits acquired prior to surgery and in the postoperative acquisition of new ones. This impairment, which is exclusively visual, appears in the absence of any sensory loss and thus has long been considered a higher-order, or "visuopsychic," dysfunction.

But that the impairment is in fact a visual retention disorder was demonstrated only later when it was found that area TE lesions impair performance on visual tests that tax memory even more than they do on visual tests that tax perceptual ability (3). Now, having examined the ability of monkeys with TE lesions simply to remember the visual appearance of newly presented objects, we have uncovered what is perhaps the most dramatic impairment of all (21). After just a few days of training, normal monkeys shown an object only once will demonstrate that they recognize that object when it is presented several minutes later (Fig. 17.2A). Thus, somewhere in the visual system the single presentation of a complex stimulus leaves a trace against which a subsequently presented stimulus can be matched. If it does match, i.e. if the original neural trace is reactivated, there is immediate recognition, as demonstrated by the monkey's highly accurate performance. The area in which the neural trace appears to be preferentially established is area TE, since lesions here—but not lesions elsewhere in the cortical visual system—nearly abolish the monkey's ability to perform the recognition task. Apparently, area TE contains the traces laid down by previous viewing of stimuli, and these serve as stored central representations against which incoming stimuli are constantly being compared. In the process, old central representations may either decay, be renewed, or even be refined, while new representations are added to the store.

It is significant that by virtue of the extremely large visual receptive fields of inferior temporal neurons (6) this area seems to provide the neural basis for the phenomenon of stimulus equivalence across retinal translation (7); i.e. the ability to recognize a stimulus as the same, regardless of its position in the visual field. But a necessary consequence of this mechanism for stimulus equivalence is that within the occipitotemporal pathway itself there is a loss of information about the visual location of the objects being identified.

Spatial Vision

The neural mechanism that enables the visual location of objects also entails the transmission of information from striate through prestriate cortex; however, the prestriate route in this case, as well as the rest of the pathway for spatial vision, appears to be quite separate from the pathway for object vision (Fig. 17.1). Evidence in support of this dichotomy of cortical visual pathways has come from our studies of posterior parietal cortex.

In the initial study of the series, Pohl (28) demonstrated a dissociation of visual deficits after inferior temporal and posterior parietal lesions. That is, whereas the temporal but not the parietal lesion produced severe impairment on an object-discrimination learning task, just the reverse was found on tests in which the monkey had to learn to choose a response location on the basis of its proximity to a visual "landmark" (Fig. 17.2B). These results provided compelling evidence that "the inferior temporal cortex participates mainly in the acts of noticing and remembering an object's qualities, not its position in space. Conversely, the posterior parietal cortex seems to be concerned with the perception of the spatial relations among objects, and not their intrinsic qualities" (20).

The effective lesions in Pohl's study were large, since they included not only inferior parietal cortex, or area PG, but also dorsal prestriate tissue within area OA. To test for the possibility of a further localization of function within this region, additional experiments were performed with more restricted lesions (22). The results, however, failed to reveal any evidence of a cortical focus serving

spatial vision; rather, the severity of impairment on the landmark task was found to depend on the amount of tissue included in the lesion, completely independent of the lesion site. Since damage to the same region, no matter how extensive, failed to produce any impairment in the acquisition of a visual pattern discrimination, it appears that the entire posterior parietal region, including dorsal OA cortex, participates selectively in the processing of visuospatial as distinguished from visual object-quality information.

Our findings support the accumulating neurobiological evidence that parietal area PG, rather than being a purely tactual association area as was once thought, is a polysensory area to which both the visual and tactual modalities contribute (10, 24,30). The findings are thus consistent with the proposal (33) that area PG serves a supramodal spatial ability that subsumes both the macrospace of vision and the microspace encompassed by the hand. According to this proposal, visuospatial and tactual discrimination deficits as well as the inaccuracies in reaching that also follow inferior parietal damage, are different reflections of a single, supramodal disorder in spatial perception.

Polysensory area PG is presumed to depend for its visual input on the modality-specific prestriate area OA, which appears to serve visual spatial functions selectively. Such a hierarchical model for spatial perception suggests, in turn, that the source of the critical visual input for the entire dorsal prestriate–parietal region is, again, the striate cortex. The alternative possibility, namely, that the source of the critical input is the superior colliculus, found no support in a study of the effects of tectal lesions on performance of the landmark task; even complete bilateral destruction of the superior colliculus failed to produce a reliable loss in retention. We therefore examined the contribution of striate inputs to the visuospatial functions of posterior parietal cortex (23), using a disconnection technique analogous to the one used originally to examine the contribution of striate inputs to the object-vision functions of inferior temporal cortex (19). Our results suggested that the posterior parietal cortex, like the inferior temporal, is totally dependent on striate input for its participation in vision; but unlike the inferior temporal, the posterior parietal cortex does not seem to receive a heavy visual input via the corpus callosum. It therefore appears that each posterior parietal area may be organized largely as a substrate for contralateral spatial function, which could account in part for the symptom of contralateral spatial neglect that has so often been reported after unilateral parietal injury in man (4, 9, 17).

A second difference in the organization of visual inputs to posterior parietal and inferior temporal cortex was uncovered in an experiment that compared the effects of selective removals of striate cortex (23). In this experiment, monkeys received bilateral lesions of the striate areas representing either central vision (lateral striate) or peripheral vision (medial striate). The results indicated that while inputs from central vision are the more important ones for the object-recognition functions of inferior temporal cortex, inputs from central and peripheral vision are equally important for the visuospatial functions of posterior parietal cortex.

In summary, interactions with striate cortex are critical for the parietal just as they are for the temporal area, but the striate inputs to these two cortical targets are organized differently: relative to inferior temporal cortex, posterior parietal cortex receives a greater contribution from inputs representing both the contralateral and the peripheral visual fields. These differences, which are seen also in the visual receptive field topography of inferior temporal vs. posterior parietal neurons (6, 30), presumably reflect differences in the sensory processing required for object vs. spatial vision.

Metabolic and Anatomical Mapping

The evidence from our behavioral work demonstrates that the neural mechanisms underlying object and spatial vision depend on the relay of information from striate cortex through prestriate cortex to targets in inferior temporal and inferior parietal areas, respectively. We have now mapped the full extent of both cortical visual pathways combined, using the 2[^{14}C]deoxyglucose method (15). By comparing a blinded and a seeing hemisphere in the same monkey we have found that the entire visual system can be outlined on the basis of differential hemispheric glucose utilization during visual stimulation. Reduced glucose utilization in the blind as compared with the seeing hemisphere was seen cortically throughout the entire expanse of striate and prestriate cortex (areas OC, OB and OA), inferior temporal cortex as far forward as the temporal pole (areas TEO and TE),

and the posterior part of the inferior parietal lobule (area PG). These results, which are in remarkably close agreement with our neurobehaviorally derived model of the two cortical visual pathways, have allowed us to delineate the exact limits of the entire system (16) (Fig. 17.1).

To trace the flow of visual information within each system we undertook a series of studies using autoradiographic and degeneration tracing techniques. Our goal in these anatomical investigations was to identify the multiple visual areas within the prestriate cortex, explore their organization, and map their projections forward into both the temporal and parietal lobes.

The findings indicated that the striate cortex is indeed the source of two major cortical projection systems. The first system begins with the known striate projection to the second visual area, V2 (31, 35, 42, 43). We found that V2 in turn projects to areas V3 and V4 (38). These three prestriate areas are arranged in adjacent "belts" that nearly surround the striate cortex, and, like striate cortex, each belt contains a topographic representation of the visual field. Area V2 corresponds to prestriate area OB, while V3 and V4 are both contained within prestriate area OA, exclusive of its dorsal part. Area V4 in turn projects to both areas TEO and TE in the inferior temporal cortex (5).

The second major system begins with both striate and V2 projections to visual area MT (31, 35, 39, 41–43), which is located in the caudal portion of the superior temporal sulcus, mainly within dorsolateral OA. Area MT in turn projects to four additional areas in the upper superior temporal and the intraparietal sulci (37). Although the total extents of these four areas are not yet completely established, the more anterior one in the intraparietal sulcus clearly falls within area PG. Thus, one major system of projections out of striate cortex is directed ventrally into the temporal lobe, while a second is directed dorsally into the parietal lobe. Furthermore, the divergence between these two systems appears to begin almost immediately after striate cortex, i.e. in its initial projections.

The two multisynaptic projection systems that we have traced provide not only the anatomical substrate for our two functionally defined visual pathways but also a partial solution to the puzzle that was presented at the outset, namely, why extensive removals of prestriate cortex in monkeys have repeatedly failed to yield the expected losses in either object or spatial vision (14, 29, 40). If prestriate cortex constitutes an essential relay in both a striate-temporal and a striate-parietal pathway, then damage to this relay should yield effects at least as severe as damage to both its target areas. Yet such dramatic effects have not been found. The reason appears to be that no prestriate lesion to date has produced a total visual disconnection of the temporal and parietal lobes, since all removals have spared varying extents of prestriate tissue that could continue to relay visual information. Comparison with our anatomical maps indicates that the portions of prestriate cortex that have consistently escaped damage are those parts of both the belt areas and the MT-related areas that represent the peripheral visual fields. Thus, just as we had found from sparing in striate cortex, sparing of peripheral-field representations in prestriate cortex will protect both object and spatial vision from serious losses.

Objects in Spatial Locations

A major question posed by the present analysis is how object information and spatial information, initially carried together in the geniculostriate projections but then analysed separately in the two cortical visual pathways, are eventually reintegrated. As already noted, both pathways have further connections to the limbic system and the frontal lobe, and each of these target areas therefore constitutes a potential site of convergence and synthesis for object and spatial information. This theoretical possibility has not yet been sufficiently tested. Preliminary work does indicate, however, that one such site of reintegration may be the hippocampal formation and that one of its functions may be to enable the rapid memorization of the particular locations occupied by particular objects (27, 34). Further application of this concept of reintegration to research on the limbic system and the frontal lobe could throw new light on some old questions of local cerebral function.

NOTES

1. Allman, J. M., Baker, J. F., Newsome, W. T., & Petersen, S. E. (1981). In C. N. Woolsey (ed.), *Cortical Sensory Organization, Vol. 2: Multiple Visual Areas* (pp. 171–185). Clifton, NJ: Humana Press.
2. Bonin, G. von, & Bailey, P. (1947). *The Neocortex of Macaca Mulatta*. Urbana, IL: The University of Illinois Press.
3. Cowey, A., & Gross, C. G. (1970). *Exp. Brain Res., 11,* 128–144.
4. Denny-Brown, D., & Chambers, R. A. (1958). *Res. Publ. Assoc. Res. Nerv. Ment. Dis., 36,* 35–117.
5. Desimone, R., Fleming, J., & Gross, C. G. (1980). *Brain Res., 184,* 41–55.
6. Gross, C. G. (1973). In R. Jung (ed.), *Handbook of Sensory Physiology VII/3* (pp. 451–482). Berlin: Springer-Verlag.
7. Gross, C. G., & Mishkin, M. (1979). In S. Harnad, R. W. Doty, L. Goldstein, J. Jaynes, & G. Krauthamer (eds.), *Lateralization in the Nervous System* (pp. 109–122). New York: Academic Press.
8. Haaxma, R., & Kuypers, H. G. J. M. (1975). *Brain, 98,* 235–260
9. Heilman, K. M., & Watson, R. T. (1977). In A. Weinstein & R. P. Friedland (eds.), *Advances in Neurology, Vol. 18* (pp. 93–106). New York: Raven Press.
10. Hyvärinen, J. (1981). *Brain Res., 206,* 287–303.
11. Ingle, D., Schneider, G. E., Trevarthan. G. B., & Held, R. (1967). *Psychol. Forsch. 31,* 42–348.
12. Jones, B., & Mishkin, M. (1972). *Exp. Neurol., 36,* 362–377.
13. Kuypers, H. G. J. M., Szwarcbart, M. K., Mishkin, M., & Rosvold, H. E. (1965). *Exp. Neurol., 11,* 245–262.
14. Lashley, K. S. (1938). *Genet. Psychol. Monogr., 37,* 107–166.
15. Macko, K. A., Jarvis, C. D., Kennedy, C., Miyaoka, M., Shinohara, M., Sokoloff, L., & Mishkin, M. (1982). *Science, 218,* 394–397.
16. Macko, K. A., Kennedy, C., Sokoloff, L., & Mishkin, M. (1981). *Soc. Neurosci. Abstr., 7,* 832.
17. Mesulam. M.-M. (1981) *Ann. Neurol. 10,* 309–325.
18. Mishkin, M. (1954). *J. Comp. Physiol. Psychol., 47,* 187–193.
19. Mishkin, M. (1966). In R. Russell (ed.), *Frontiers of Physiological Psychology* (pp. 93–119). New York: Academic Press.
20. Mishkin, M. (1972). In A. G. Karczmar, & J. C. Eccles (eds.), *Behavior* (pp. 187–208). Berlin: Springer-Verlag.
21. Mishkin, M. (1982). *Philos. Trans. R. Soc. London, Ser. B, 298,* 85–95.
22. Mishkin, M., Lewis, M. E., & Ungerleider, L. G. (1982). *Behav. Brain Res., 6,* 41–55.
23. Mishkin, M., Lewis, M. E., & Ungerleider, L. G. (1982). *Behav. Brain Res., 6,* 57–77.
24. Mountcastle, V. B., Lynch, J. C., Georgopoulos, A., Sakata, H., & Acuña, C. (1975). *J. Neurophysiol., 38,* 871–908.
25. Newcombe, F., & Russell, W. R. (1969). *Neurol. Neurosurg. Psychiatry, 32,* 73–81.
26. Pandya, D. N., & Kuypers, H. G. J. M. (1968). *Brain Res., 13,* 13–36.
27. Parkinson, J. K., & Mishkin, M. (1982). *Soc. Neurosci. Abstr., 8,* 23.
28. Pohl, W. (1973). *J. Comp. Physiol. Psychol., 82,* 227–239.
29. Pribram, K. H., Spinell., D. N., & Reitz, S. L. (1969). *Brain, 92,* 301–312.
30. Robinson, D. L., Goldberg, M. E., & Stanton, G. B. (1978). *J. Neurophysiol., 41,* 910–932.
31. Rockland, K. S., & Pandya, D. N. (1981). *Brain Res., 212,* 249–270.
32. Seltzer, R., & Pandya, D. N. (1980). *Brain Res., 192,* 339–351.

33. Semmes, J. (1967). In J. G. Bosma (ed.), *Symposium on Oral Sensation and Perception* (pp. 137–148). Springfield, IL: Thomas.

34. Smith, M. L., & Milner, B. (1981). *Neuropsychologia, 19,* 781–793.

35. Tigges, J., Tigges, M., Anschel, S., Cross, N. A., Letbetter, W. D., & McBride, R. L. (1981). *J. Comp. Neurol., 202,* 539–560.

36. Turner, B. H., Mishkin, M., & Knapp, M. (1980). *J. Comp. Neurol., 191,* 515–543.

37. Ungerleider, L. G., Desimone, R., & Mishkin, M. (1982). *Soc. Neurosci. Abstr.* 8, 680.

38. Ungerleider, L. G., Gattass, R., Sousa, A. P. B., & Miskin, M. (1983). *Soc. Neurosci. Abstr. 9.*

39. Ungerleider, L. G., & Mishkin, M. (1979). *J. Comp. Neurol., 188,* 347–366.

40. Ungerleider, L. G., & Mishkin, M. (1982). In D. J. Ingle, M. A. Goodale, & R. J. W. Mansfield (eds.), *Analysis of Visual Behavior.* Cambridge, MA: The MIT Press.

41. Van Essen, D. C., Maunsell, J. H. R., & Bixby, J. L. (1981). *J. Comp. Neurol., 199,* 293–326.

42. Weller, R. E., & Kaas, J. H. (1981). In C. N. Woolsey (ed.), *Cortical Sensory Organization, Vol. 2: Multiple Visual Areas,* pp. 121–155. Clifton, NJ: Humana Press.

43. Zeki, S. M. (1969). *Brain Res., 14,* 271–291.

44. Zeki, S. M. (1978). *Nature (London) 274,* 423–428.

Introduction to Reading 18

The perception of visual motion is generally thought to involve two successive stages of neural processing. At the first stage, motion is sensed in a local region of the retina; in the second stage, these local motion measurements are integrated into a global motion signal for objects and surfaces in the scene.

Let us first consider the local motion sensing stage. Motion consists of spatial translation over time, and requires that measurements be taken at two or more locations. Reichardt (1961) proposed a simple neural mechanism that could represent local retinal motion. Consider a motion-selective cell (call it M) that is tuned to a specific speed of motion, s (for concreteness, let's call this 10 mm/sec retinal velocity). M receives input from retinal detectors (e.g., cones) at nearby locations on the retina (let's say this distance is 1 mm). The signal from one of these detectors (detector A) is delayed by a fixed interval ($\Delta t = 0.1$ sec)—it passes through a neuron that serves as a brief memory—before it arrives at M. The signal from the other detector (detector B) is sent to M with no delay. If a spot of light moves across the retina in the correct direction at a speed of 10 mm/sec, it will first stimulate detector A and then, after 0.1 sec, it will have traveled 1 mm to stimulate detector B. The signals from the two detectors will arrive at M simultaneously, because of the 0.1-sec delay in the signal from detector A, and this maximizes the probability that M will discharge. If the light moves faster or slower than 10 mm/sec, then the two signals will arrive at M at different points in time and will be less likely to cause M to fire. Similarly, if the light moves from detector B to detector A, in a direction opposite to the preferred direction of M, then it similarly will be unlikely to fire. Any desired speed and direction of local motion can be represented in this way. Several more detailed proposals of this type were proposed in the mid-1980s (e.g., Van Santen & Sperling, 1984; Adelson & Bergen, 1985; Watson & Ahumada, 1985).

However, the measurement of local motion is not sufficient to capture the motion of objects in the world; this is because of what has come to be called the *aperture problem*. The problem, in essence, is that the local motion of a 1-dimensional contour is necessarily ambiguous. Consider the edge of a piece of cardboard that is placed behind a larger piece of opaque paper so that it can only be viewed through a circular window or aperture (see Figure 1). If the cardboard is moved in a direction perpendicular to its orientation, from southeast to northwest, the contour will move within the aperture. As the contour moves from the position indicated by the solid line to the position indicated by the dotted line, it could be perceived (correctly) as moving from southeast to northwest, as indicated by the central arrow, or it could be perceived as moving directly upward, or it could even be seen as moving up and to the right. Any of the motion trajectories shown in the figure is possible. With a circular aperture, the contour will tend to be seen as moving perpendicular to its orientation, even if the true motion is otherwise. If the aperture is elongated, then motion tends to be seen as parallel to the direction of elongation. This

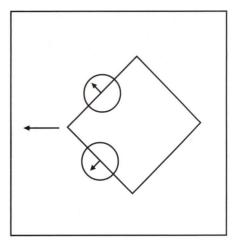

FIGURE 2

latter phenomenon is also sometimes called the *barber pole illusion*: on a barber pole, the true direction of motion of the oblique contour of the red stripe is right to left due to rotation of the pole, but the perceived direction of motion is upward, because the barber pole is equivalent to a vertically oriented rectangular aperture. In this situation, the point at which the stripes intersect the boundary of the aperture provides a reference point that is unambiguously moving upward, and this tends to dominate what is seen.

The motion detectors proposed by Reichardt are subject to the aperture problem because they "monitor" only a local region of the retina (see Figure 2). The circles represent the local region of the scene from which each of two motion detectors receive input. As the diamond moves from right to left, the contours at its leading edge will be seen locally as moving to the upper left and lower left, respectively. Yet we routinely and effortlessly perceive objects like these as moving directly to the left. The question is how this global motion information is extracted from the local image motions.[1]

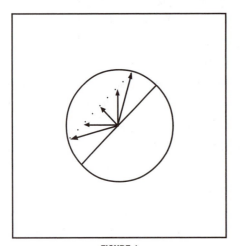

FIGURE 1

---

[1]Note that the aperture problem disappears when an object feature such as a corner enters the aperture; the motion direction of such a two-dimensional feature is unambiguous and can reveal the direction of the object as a whole.

In this reading, Adelson and Movshon investigate this question. They presented plaid patterns to observers consisting of two superimposed moving gratings (a grating is a pattern of light and dark bars in which luminance varies sinusoidally in a direction perpendicular to the orientation of the grating; see Reading 8 by Blakemore and Campbell). Any given grating, when viewed through an aperture, is consistent with a locus of velocities (where the velocity specifies speed and direction) that fall along the dotted line in Figure 18.1*a* of the article, called the *constraint line*. When two gratings are superimposed, they each specify a locus of possible velocities, and if the two gratings cohere (that is, if they are seen as part of a single rigidly-moving pattern), then the motion of the combined pattern is specified by the intersection of the two constraint lines (as in Figures 18.1*b* and 18.1*c* of the article). The intersection of the constraint lines for the diamond shape correctly recovers the "true" velocity of the diamond, moving from right to left. Coherence depends on the similarity between the two components. If coherence is not achieved because the components are too different,

then they are seen as sliding transparently over one another.

The distinction between perception of local retinal motion and coherent object motion is mirrored in the response of cortical motion-selective cells. In cortical area V1, most cells are motion-selective (that is, they respond best to a particular direction of motion and their response falls off as the direction of motion departs from the preferred one). These cells are clearly representing local motion signals. In area MT, the situation is different. As in V1, many cells are motion-selective and directionally tuned. However, when component pairs of gratings such as those used by Adelson and Movshon are presented, two different classes of cells are observed (Movshon, Adelson, Gizzi, & Newsome, 1985). Some cells behave like V1 cells: that is, they respond only to the directions perpendicular to the individual component gratings; these are termed component cells. About 25% of the cells respond to the component direction, suggesting that they are able to integrate the motions represented by the component cells. These representations are likely to be crucial in the perception of object motion.

REFERENCES

Adelson, E. H., & Bergen, J. R. (1985). Spatiotemporal energy models for the perception of motion. *Journal of the Optical Society of America A, 2,* 284–299.

Movshon, J. A., Adelson, E. H., Gizzi, M. S., & Newsome, W. T. (1985). The analysis of moving visual patterns. In C. Chagas, R. Gattass, & C. Gross (Eds.), *Pattern recognition mechanisms* (pp. 117–151). New York: Springer-Verlag.

Reichardt, W. (1961). Autocorrelation, a principle for the evaluation of sensory information by the central nervous system. In W. A. Rosenblith (Ed.), *Sensory Communication* (pp. 303–317). New York: John Wiley & Sons.

Van Santen, J. P., & Sperling, G. (1984). Temporal covariance model of human motion perception. *Journal of the Optical Society of America A, 1,* 451–473.

Watson, A. B., & Ahumada, A. J. (1985). Model of human visual-motion sensing. *Journal of the Optical Society of America A, 2,* 322–341.

Phenomenal Coherence of Moving Visual Patterns

E. H. Adelson and J. A. Movshon • New York University

When a moving grating is viewed through an aperture, only motion orthogonal to its bars is visible, as motion parallel to the bars causes no change in the stimulus. Because there is a family of physical motions of various directions and speeds that appear identical, the motion of the grating is ambiguous. In contrast, when two crossed moving gratings are superimposed, the resulting plaid pattern usually moves unambiguously and predictably. In certain cases, however, two gratings do not combine into a single coherent percept, but appear to slide across one another. We have studied the conditions under which coherence does and does not occur, and we report here that it depends on the relative contrasts, spatial frequencies and directions of motion of the gratings. These effects may reveal the previously unstudied properties of a higher order stage of motion analysis.

Figure 18.1*a* illustrates the problem of ambiguity (1, 2). The grating moves behind a circular aperture. Any of the physical motions indicated by the arrows will appear the same when viewed through the aperture. The situation can be depicted graphically in "velocity space," a space in which each vector represents a velocity: the length of a vector corresponds to speed, and its angle corresponds to direction. As shown in Fig. 18.1*a*, the motion of a single grating is consistent with a family of motions that lies along a line in velocity space; this line is parallel to the grating's bars and orthogonal to the vector representing its "primary" motion. If two moving gratings are superimposed, the resulting "plaid" pattern moves with a speed and direction which can be exactly predicted from the velocity space construction: the two loci of possible motions intersect at a single point, corresponding to the motion of the coherent pattern (Fig. 18.1*b*). This solution to the "aperture problem" is

similar to that proposed (in a rather different context) by Fennema and Thompson (3). It has advantages over that advanced by Marr and Ullman (4), which can only infer a range of possible directions from the limited information provided by a pair of gratings.

The velocity space combination rule is also different from a vector sum or vector average. In Fig. 18.1*c*, two gratings move downward and rightward with different speeds and directions. A vector sum or average would predict a pattern motion that was also downward and rightward, but the velocity space solution is a motion upward and rightward, the motion that observers report when the gratings are seen to cohere (5). Of course, nothing requires that coherent motion be seen, and instead of a single rigidly moving plaid, the two gratings are sometimes seen sliding "incoherently" over each other. We have studied the stimulus conditions under which coherence occurs, in order to

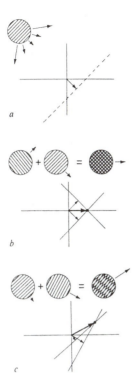

FIGURE 18.1 ■ The Velocity-space Representation of Some Moving Patterns. In each panel, a vector represents a motion in a direction given by the vector's angle at a speed given by the vector's length. *a,* A single grating moves behind an aperture. The broklen line indicates the locus of velocities compatible with the motion of the grating. *b,* A plaid composed of two orthogonal gratings moving at the same speed. The lines give the possible motion of each grating alone. Their intersection is the only shared motion, and corresponds to what is seen. *c,* A plaid composed of two oblique gratings, one moving slowly and the other more rapidly. Both gratings move down and to the right, but the pattern moves up and to the right.

characterize the mechanisms that underlly the coherent percept and resolve the ambiguity of one-dimensional motion.

Observers viewed a circular cathode ray tube display subtending 5°; the luminance of the display was constant on average, but was modulated by signals from a PDP11 computer to produce a superimposed pair of sinusoidal gratings that could each be varied in orientation, direction and speed of motion, contrast and spatial frequency. Observers were strictly instructed not to make judgements unless their eyes were steadily fixated on a small black circle in the centre of the display. Subjects

under this kind of instruction are capable of stable and reliable fixation (6). After each 1.5-s exposure, the observer indicated whether the pattern appeared "coherent" or "incoherent."

Contrast strongly affects coherence, even when both gratings are easily visible. Figure 18.2*a* shows a psychometric function for detection and a similar function for coherence, when the contrast of one of the gratings in a plaid was varied (the other grating's contrast was fixed at 0.3). The gratings were of the same spatial frequency, and moved at an angle of 135° to one another. Open symbols show the probability of detecting the low-contrast grating in the presence of its high-contrast mate. Filled symbols show the probability of a coherent percept. Both detection and coherence become more likely as contrast increases, but reliable coherence only occurs at contrasts where both gratings are clearly visible.

In further experiments, we used this contrast dependence to measure the relative tendency of different pairs of gratings to cohere. We fixed the contrast of one grating at 0.3, and used a staircase procedure to vary the contrast of the other grating until the observer saw coherent motion on half the trials. The gratings' speed, orientation and spatial frequency all affected the strength of coherence. Coherence decreased as the speed of the component gratings increased, as the angle between their "primary" directions increased, and as the difference between their spatial frequencies increased.

Figure 18.2*b* shows the effect of relative spatial frequency on coherence. Filled symbols illustrate a case in which the spatial frequency of the high-contrast grating was fixed at 1.2 cycles deg[-1], while the spatial frequency and contrast of the second grating were varied; open symbols illustrate a case where the spatial frequency of the first grating was fixed at 2.2 cycles deg[-1]. As the frequencies of the two gratings were made different, the tendency to cohere was reduced, and the contrast needed for coherence was increased. This spatial frequency dependence suggests that coherent motion, like many other visual properties, is analysed by mechanisms that are selective for spatial frequency.

There are two kinds of model that might account for our results. The first relies on the presence in our patterns of localizable blob-like features where the peaks and troughs of the crossed gratings intersect. Some process based on direction selective elements not selective for orientation might de-

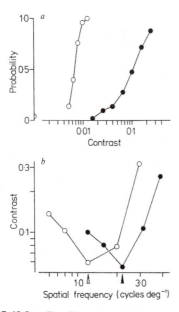

FIGURE 18.2 ■ Two Parameters Influencing Perceptual Coherence. *a*,The influence of contrast on the detectability and coherence of two crossed sinusoidal gratings. One grating was fixed in contrast at 0.3. The other was of variable contrast, and moved at an angle of 135° to the first; both had a spatial frequency of 1.6 cycles deg-1, and moved at 3 deg s-1. Filled symbols show the probability that the observer judged the two gratings to be "coherent"; open symbols show the probability that the observer detected the presence of the lower contrast grating. The half-circle on the ordinate shows the probability that the observer judged the second grating to be present when its contrast was zero— "false-positive rate" for detection; the false-positive rate for coherence judgments was zero. Subject, E.H.A. *b*,the influence of spatial frequency on coherence. The standard grating again had a contrast of 0.3 and moved at 3 deg s-1. The test gratings moved at an angle of 135° to the standard, also at 3 deg s-1. Open symbols show the results for a range of test spatial frequencies when the standard grating had a spatial frequency of 1.2 cycles deg-1 (open arrow). Filled symbols show the results when the standard grating had a spatial frequency of 2.2 cycles deg-1 (filled arrow). Subject, P.A.

tect and signal the motion of these "blobs," which is of course identical to the motion of the pattern as a whole. We have evidence to suggest that such a scheme is incorrect. We superimposed one-dimensional dynamic random visual noise (a rapidly changing pattern of random-width lines) (7) on our test patterns. A non-oriented mechanism that responds directly to the motion of blobs should be most affected by noise oriented at right angles

to the coherent motion. But a mechanism that combines the outputs of oriented channels should be most affected when those channels are most affected—when the noise is oriented at right angles to the primary motion of one or the other of the component gratings. Our results support the orientation-based model. Coherence is strongly reduced when the noise mask is perpendicular to a component's motion (and thus parallel to the component's orientation), but is almost unaffected when the mask is perpendicular to the coherent motion of the pattern. This suggests that some orientation-selective process must precede the analysis of coherent motion, and our second model incorporates this feature.

There is abundant evidence that visual analysing mechanisms selective for orientation and spatial frequency exist at a relatively early stage in the visual pathway (8–12). It is clear that such mechanisms are often sensitive to the direction of motion of one-dimensional contours (8, 9, 13–15), but they also seem unable to signal the true direction of motion of two-dimensional patterns (16–19). The perceptual coherence of two gratings into

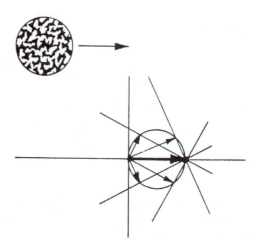

FIGURE 18.3 ■ The Velocity-space Representation of a Random-texture Field Moving to the Right. The field contains components of all orientations, and the primary motor vector for each ends on the circle passing through the origin; the common motion "implied" is the rightward motion given by the bold arrow. This circular locus of primary motions represents all the motions that can exist in a single rightward-moving pattern. As such, the locus could represent the preferences of a family of primary motion analysers whose outputs are combined to signal coherent two-dimensional motion (see text).

a single moving plaid may therefore represent the action of an additional stage of visual processing beyond those usually considered to be involved in analysing motion. At this second stage, the outputs of several "one-dimensional" motion analysers would be combined. Coherence phenomena may offer an approach to studying the properties of this postulated second-stage motion analyser.

Figure 18.3 shows how the velocity space construct helps to assign motion to more complex patterns, such as a horizontally moving random-texture field. The texture contains components of many orientations; their motions are represented in velocity space by the arrows in Fig. 18.3. As the speed of each component is proportional to the cosine of the angle between its direction and horizontal, the vectors all end on a circle that passes through the origin. Note also that the motion "families" associated with the various components all pass through the common point corresponding to the horizontally directed pattern motion.

A given vector in Fig. 18.3 could represent the preference of a one-dimensional motion detector, and the circle might represent the "receptive field" in velocity space of a second-stage motion analyser. If it combined the outputs of one-dimensional analysers corresponding to points on the circle by an operation akin to a logical "and," the second-stage analyser would respond only to a particular direction of motion of the two-dimensional stimulus. Our results on perceptual coherence might reflect the relative strengths of the different inputs to such a motion analyser. They would suggest that this analyser computes the weighted combination of signals arising from a collection of one-dimensional motion analysers having different velocity preferences but similar spatial frequency preferences.

NOTES

1. Wolhgemuth, A. (1911). *Br. J. Psychol.* Monogr. Suppl. 1.
2. Wallach, H. (1935). *Psychol. Forsch., 20,* 325–380.
3. Fennema, C. L., & Thompson, W. N. (1979). *Comp. Graph. Image Proc., 9,* 301–315.
4. Marr, D., & Ullman, S. (1981). *Proc. R. Soc., B211,* 151–180.
5. Adelson, E. H., & Movshon, J. A. (1980). *J. Opt. Soc. Am., 70,* 1605.
6. Murphy, B. J., Kowler, E., & Steinman, R. M. (1975). *Vision Res, 15,* 1263–1268.
7. Stromeyer, C. F., & Julesz, B. J. (1972). *J. Opt. Soc. Am., 62,* 1221–1232.
8. Hubel, D. H., & Weisel, T. N. (1962). *J. Physiol. Lond., 160,* 106–154.
9. Hubel, D. H., & Weisel, T. N. (1968). *J. Physiol. Lond., 195,* 215–243.
10. Robson, J. G. (1975). In E. C. Carterette & M. P. Friedman, M. P. (eds.), *Handbook of Perception,* pp. 81–116. New York: Academic.
11. Campbell, F. W., & Robson, J. G. (1968). *J. Physiol. Lond., 197,* 551–556.
12. Blakemore, C., & Campbell, F. W. (1969). *J. Physiol. Lond., 203,* 237–260.
13. Henry, G. H., Bishop, P. O., & Dreher, B. (1974). *Vision Res., 14,* 767–777.
14. Levinson, E., & Sekuler, R. (1975). *J. Physiol. Lond., 250,* 347–366.
15. Watson, A. B., Thompson, P. G., Nachmias, J., & Murphy, B. (1980). *Vision Res., 20,* 341–347.
16. Hammond, P. (1978). *J. Physiol. Lond., 285,* 479–491.
17. De Valois, R. L., De Valois, K. K., & Yund, W. S. (1979). *J. Physiol. Lond., 291,* 483–505.
18. Movson, J. A., Davis, E. T., & Adelson, E. H. (1980). *Soc. Neurosci. Abstr., 6,* 670.
19. Adelson, E. H., & Movshon, J. A. (1981). *Invest. Ophthalmol. Vis. Sci. Suppl., 20,* 17.

Introduction to Reading 19

Mental imagery has been a topic of great interest to psychologists and philosophers for centuries. One reason for this fascination comes from the fact that the experience of mental imagery is necessarily private and subjective. The role of mental images in perception and mental life more generally was hotly debated in the late 19th century, but the debate was never resolved because it relied almost exclusively on introspective reports that were not subject to scientific verification. With the rise of behaviorism, the study of imagery fell into disrepute, and it was not revisited as a scientific problem until the 1970s. Among the first of these modern efforts to investigate imagery was a proposal by Paivio (1969) according to which images were viewed as uninterpreted "pictures in the head."

This account was quickly countered by Pylyshyn (1973), who challenged the analog representation of pictorial information. He proposed instead that such information should be viewed as being represented propositionally—in terms of symbolic, language-like collections of propositions that captured the content of the represented information, including its metric properties such as size, orientation, and spatial relations among the parts, but that bore no resemblance to the represented entity. In other words, Pylyshyn proposed that objects and their representations are generally nonisomorphic . This proposal began what came to be called the analog-propositional debate, which raged throughout the 1970s and early 80s.

Shepard and Metzler's study of mental rotation was the first study to measure directly the efficiency of mental transformations, and it inspired a generation of other studies. With an experiment that was exceedingly simple and that yielded extremely clear results, they showed that the transformation (in this case, rotation) of an internal representation of a complex three-dimensional object could be quantified, and more importantly, that this transformation was smooth and continuous just as the transformation of a real object would be. Subsequent studies provided further details about the properties of mental transformation (e.g., Shepard & Cooper, 1982).

In one well-known example, Kosslyn, Ball, & Reiser (1978) first had participants memorize the layout of geographic features on a hypothetical island (e.g., beach, swamp, rock, etc.). The map was then removed, and participants were asked to imagine one landmark (e.g., the beach), and mentally scan to another (e.g., the rock); they were to press a button when they "arrived" at the destination. The observed response times were a remarkably linear function of the physical distance between the two landmarks on the memorized map. That the inspection and transformation of mental images had this continuous, analog property was just as predicted by analog theories of mental imagery.

Further support for this perspective has been provided more recently by brain imaging studies of imagery, showing that regions of the occipital cortex that are part of the early visual pathways are active during mental imagery tasks (e.g., Kosslyn, 1994). The argument runs as follows: Functional neuroimaging studies have shown that imagery and vision appear to share common neural substrates, meaning they must have common representational formats. Because the representational format of early vision is retinotopic and spatial, and because the formats of imagery and early vision are the same, imagery must be retinotopic and spatial (i.e., analog).

Proponents of the propositional account need not surrender completely, however. The evidence that mental imagery is, at some level, analog, does not rule out the possibility that the memory representations that are used to generate mental images are propositional. Indeed, structural description theories of visual object recognition (see Reading 20 by Biederman) are instances of quasi-propositional theories. So while the analog-propositional debate has subsided, the current theoretical landscape contains elements of both accounts.

REFERENCES

Kosslyn, S. M., Ball, T. M., & Reiser, B. J. (1978). Visual images preserve metric spatial information: Evidence from studies of image scanning. *Journal of Experimental Psychology: Human Perception & Performance, 4,* 47–60.

Kosslyn, S. M. (1994). *Image and brain: The resolution of the imagery debate.* Cambridge, MA: MIT Press.

Paivio, A. (1969). Mental imagery in associate learning and memory. *Psychological Review, 76,* 241–263.

Pylyshyn, Z. (1973). What the mind's eye tells the mind's brain: A critique of mental imagery. *Psychological Bulletin, 80,* 1–24.

Shepard, R. N., & Cooper, L. A. (1982). *Mental images and their transformations.* Cambridge, MA: MIT Press.

Mental Rotation of Three-Dimensional Objects

R. N. Shepard and J. Metzler • Stanford University

The time required to recognize that two perspective drawings portray objects of the same three-dimensional shape is found to be (i) a linearly increasing function of the angular difference in the portrayed orientations of the two objects and (ii) no shorter for differences corresponding simply to a rigid rotation of one of the two-dimensional drawings in its own picture plane than for differences corresponding to a rotation of the three-dimensional object in depth.

Human subjects are often able to determine that two two-dimensional pictures portray objects of the same three-dimensional shape even though the objects are depicted in very different orientations. The experiment reported here was designed to measure the time that subjects require to determine such identity of shape as a function of the angular difference in the portrayed orientations of the two three-dimensional objects.

This angular difference was produced either by a rigid rotation of one of two identical pictures in its own picture plane or by a much more complex, nonrigid transformation, of one of the pictures, that corresponds to a (rigid) rotation of the three-dimensional object in depth.

This reaction time is found (i) to increase linearly with the angular difference in portrayed orientation and (ii) to be no longer for a rotation in depth than for a rotation merely in the picture plane. These findings appear to place rather severe constraints on possible explanations of how subjects go about determining identity of shape of differently oriented objects. They are, however, consistent with an explanation suggested by the subjects themselves. Although introspective reports must be interpreted with caution, all subjects claimed (i) that to make the required comparison they first had to imagine one object as rotated into the same orientation as the other and that they could carry out this "mental rotation" at no greater than a certain limiting rate; and (ii) that, since they perceived the two-dimensional pictures as objects in a three-dimensional space, they could imagine the rotation around whichever axis was required with equal ease.

In the experiment each of eight adult subjects was presented with 1600 pairs of perspective line drawings. For each pair the subject was asked to pull a right-hand lever as soon as he determined that the two drawings portrayed objects that were congruent with respect to three-dimensional shape and to pull a left-hand lever as soon as he determined that the two drawings depicted objects of different three-dimensional shapes. According to a random sequence, in half of the pairs (the "same" pairs) the two objects could be rotated into congruence with each other (as in Fig. 19.1, A and B), and in the other half (the "different" pairs) the two objects differed by a reflection as well as a rotation and could not be rotated into congruence (as in Fig. 19.1C).

The choice of objects that were mirror images or "isomers" of each other for the "different" pairs was intended to prevent subjects from discovering some distinctive feature possessed by only one of the two objects and thereby reaching a decision

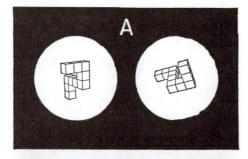

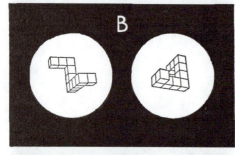

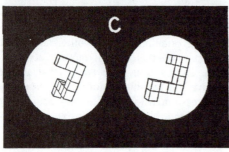

FIGURE 19.1 ■ Examples of Pairs of Perspective Line Drawings Presented to the Subjects. (A) A "same" pair, which differs by an 80° rotation in the picture plane; (B) a "same" pair, which differs by an 80° rotation in depth; and (C) a "different" pair, which cannot be brought into congruence by *any* rotation.

of noncongruence without actually having to carry out any mental rotation. As a further precaution, the ten different three-dimensional objects depicted in the various perspective drawings were chosen to be relatively unfamiliar and meaningless in overall three-dimensional shape.

Each object consisted of ten solid cubes attached face-to-face to form a rigid armlike structure with exactly three right-angled "elbows" (see Fig. 19.1). The set of all ten shapes included two subsets of five: within either subset, no shape could be transformed into itself or any other by any reflection or rotation (short of 360°). However, each shape in

either subset was the mirror image of one shape in the other subset, as required for the construction of the "different" pairs.

For each of the ten objects, 18 different perspective projections—corresponding to one complete turn around the vertical axis by 20° steps—were generated by digital computer and associated graphical output (*1*). Seven of the 18 perspective views of each object were then selected so as (i) to avoid any views in which some part of the object was wholly occluded by another part and yet (ii) to permit the construction of two pairs that differed in orientation by each possible angle, in 20° steps, from 0° to 180°. These 70 line drawings were then reproduced by photo-offset process and were attached to cards in pairs for presentation to the subjects.

Half of the "same" pairs (the "depth" pairs) represented two objects that differed by some multiple of a 20° rotation about a vertical axis (Fig. 19.1B). For each of these pairs, copies of two appropriately different perspective views were simply attached to the cards in the orientation in which they were originally generated. The other half of the "same" pairs (the "picture-plane" pairs) represented two objects that differed by some multiple of a 20° rotation in the plane of the drawings themselves (Fig. 19.1A). For each of these, one of the seven perspective views was selected for each object and two copies of this picture were attached to the card in appropriately different orientations. Altogether, the 1600 pairs presented to each subject included 800 "same" pairs, which consisted of 400 unique pairs (20 "depth" and 20 "picture-plane" pairs at each of the ten angular differences from 0° to 180°), each of which was presented twice. The remaining 800 pairs, randomly intermixed with these, consisted of 400 unique "different" pairs, each of which (again) was presented twice. Each of these "different" pairs corresponded to one "same" pair (of either the "depth" or "picture-plane" variety) in which, however, one of the three-dimensional objects had been reflected about some plane in three-dimensional space. Thus the two objects in each "different" pair differed, in general, by both a reflection and a rotation.

The 1600 pairs were grouped into blocks of not more than 200 and presented over eight to ten 1-hour sessions (depending upon the subject). Also, although it is only of incidental interest here, each such block of presentations was either "pure," in that all pairs involved rotations of the same type ("depth" or "picture-plane"), or "mixed," in that the two types of rotation were randomly intermixed within the same block.

Each trial began with a warning tone, which was followed half a second later by the presentation of a stimulus pair and the simultaneous onset of a timer. The lever-pulling response stopped the timer, recorded the subject's reaction time and terminated the visual display. The line drawings, which averaged between 4 and 5 cm in maximum linear extent, appeared at a viewing distance of about 60 cm. They were positioned, with a center-to-center spacing that subtended a visual angle of 9°, in two circular apertures in a vertical black surface (see Fig. 19.1, A to C).

The subjects were instructed to respond as quickly as possible while keeping errors to a minimum. On the average only 3.2 percent of the responses were incorrect (ranging from 0.6 to 5.7 percent for individual subjects). The reaction-time data presented below include only the 96.8 percent correct responses. However, the data for the incorrect responses exhibit a similar pattern.

In Fig. 19.2, the overall means of the reaction times as a function of angular difference in orientation for all correct (right-hand) responses to "same" pairs are plotted separately for the pairs differing by a rotation in the picture plane (Fig. 19.2A) and for the pairs differing by a rotation in depth (Fig. 19.2B). In both cases, reaction time is a strikingly linear function of the angular difference between the two three-dimensional objects portrayed. The mean reaction times for individual subjects increased from a value of about 1 second at 0° of rotation for all subjects to values ranging from 4 to 6 seconds at 180° of rotation, depending upon the particular individual. Moreover, despite such variations in slope, the *linearity* of the function is clearly evident when the data are plotted separately for individual three-dimensional objects or for individual subjects. Polynomial regression lines were computed separately for each subject under each type of rotation. In all 16 cases the functions were found to have a highly significant linear component ($P < .001$) when tested against deviations from linearity. No significant quadratic or higher-order effects were found ($P > .05$, in all cases).

The angle through which different three-dimensional shapes must be rotated to achieve congruence is not, of course, defined. Therefore, a function like those plotted in Fig. 19.2 cannot be

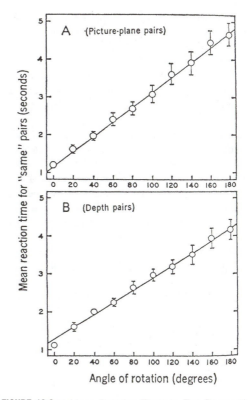

FIGURE 18.2 ■ Mean Reaction Times to Two Perspective Line Drawings Portraying Objects of the Same Three-dimensional Shape. Times are plotted as a function of angular difference in portrayed orientation: (A) for pairs differing by a rotation in the picture plane only; and (B) for pairs differing by a rotation in depth. (The centers of the circles indicate the means and, when they extend far enough to show outside these circles, the vertical bars around each circle indicate a conservative estimate of the standard error of that mean based on the distribution of the eight component means contributed by the individual subjects.)

constructed in any straightforward manner for the "different" pairs. The *overall* mean reaction time for these pairs was found, however, to be 3.8 seconds—nearly a second longer than the corresponding overall means for the "same" pairs. (In the postexperimental interview, the subjects typically reported that they attempted to rotate one end of one object into congruence with the corresponding end of the other object; they discovered that the two objects were *different* when, after this "rotation," the two free ends still remained noncongruent.)

Not only are the two functions shown in Fig. 19.2 both linear but they are very similar to each other with respect to intercept and slope. Indeed, for the larger angular differences the reaction times were, if anything, somewhat shorter for rotation in depth than for rotation in the picture plane. However, since this small difference is either absent or reversed in four of the eight subjects, it is of doubtful significance. The determination of identity of shape may therefore be based, in both cases, upon a process of the same general kind. If we can describe this process as some sort of "mental rotation in three-dimensional space," then the slope of the obtained functions indicates that the average rate at which these particular objects can be thus "rotated" is roughly 60° per second.

Of course the plotted reaction times necessarily include any times taken by the subjects to decide how to process the pictures in each presented pair as well as the time taken actually to carry out the process, once it was chosen. However, even for these highly practiced subjects, the reaction times were still linear and were no more than 20 percent lower in the "pure" blocks of presentations (in which the subjects knew both the axis and the direction of the required rotation in advance of each presentation) than in the "mixed" blocks (in which the axis of rotation was unpredictable). Tentatively, this suggests that 80 percent of a typical one of these reaction times may represent some such process as "mental rotation" itself, rather than a preliminary process of preparation or search. Nevertheless, in further research now underway, we are seeking clarification of this point and others.

NOTES

1. Mrs. Jih-Jie Chang of the Bell Telephone Laboratories generated the 180 perspective projections for us by means of the Bell Laboratories' Stromberg-Carlson 4020 microfilm recorder and the computer program for constructing such projections developed there by A. M. Noll. See, for example, A. M. Noll, *Computers Automation,* **14**, 20 (1965).

Introduction to Reading 20

Among the most important and most complex functions of vision is object recognition. It is easy to justify the importance of this function: one could argue that the central purpose of vision is to allow organisms to categorize objects so as to behave appropriately in their presence (e.g., to reach for or run away from or converse with them). The difficulty in explaining how object recognition is accomplished, especially given the apparent effortlessness with which we actually do it, is reflected in the fact that psychologists, physiologists, and computer scientists have been trying hard for several decades to solve this problem, and so far they have met with only limited success.

The reading reprinted here by Irving Biederman is one well-developed theory of object recognition that illustrates some of this work. Biederman's theory is an instance of one class of competing theories for object recognition. Debate about which theories best explain object recognition (and even which types of evidence are relevant) is vigorous. In the following paragraphs, the outlines of this debate are briefly sketched.

Biederman's Recognition-by-Components (RBC) theory belongs to a class called *structural description theories*; the theory of Marr and Nishihara (1978) is another member of this class. These theories hold that the stored representations of objects to which an encountered object is compared is a list of parts and the structural relations among the parts. The representation is an abstraction, and does not "look like" the thing represented. In the case of RBC, the parts are called *geons*, or geometrical ions, the building blocks of all visual object representations. They are selected from a palette of about 36 volumetric primitives (cones, cylinders, bricks, etc.) and the relationship between the parts (e.g., their relative locations and sizes) are specified to form potentially very complex objects (e.g., to represent a table lamp, one might specify a truncated cone that is on top of and has a larger base diameter than a cylinder).

The theory must do more than specify the nature of the representation, of course. It must also explain how this representation is extracted from an image. According to RBC, object recognition requires several steps. These include parsing a viewed object at regions of deep concavity (these are likely to be where parts are joined together), while simultaneously seeking nonaccidental prop-erties (see below) that constrain the set of geons thus discovered, and specifying the structural relations among the geons. The structural description thus extracted can be compared to stored structural descrip-tions in memory, and when a match is found, the object is recognized.

Among the most important properties of this sort of, mechanism is that its representations are viewpoint invariant. That is, one can recognize a familiar object from almost any viewpoint (except for some very odd ones, e.g., from directly above). This is desirable because viewpoint invariant representations are inherently more efficient than viewpoint-dependent ones (e.g., one is required to represent an item only once in abstract form, and not separately for every possible view), and because humans appear to exhibit viewpoint invariance under some conditions (although there is debate even about this empirical point, as discussed below). Many other theories do not produce viewpoint invariance without costs. The reason RBC is viewpoint invariant is because it assumes that geons can be recognized from almost any viewpoint by virtue of the presence of certain invariant "nonaccidental properties" that are used to detect them. For example, a cylinder has parallel contours along its major axis, no matter what the viewpoint, and parallel contours are unlikely to occur by chance if they are *not* the boundaries of a common object part.

A second major class of theories, termed *image-based theories*, make very different assumptions about how object recognition occurs. According to these theories (e.g., Tarr & Pinker, 1989; Ullman, 1989), object represen-tations are similar to templates that correspond to one or a small number of views of the object in question. When an object enters the field of view, the "closest" representa-tions are transformed so as to match as closely as possible the currently viewed object. This transformation might be a rotation in three dimensions (see Reading 19 by Shepard and Metzler), or it might entail some form of normalization to account for differences in size. The possibility of generalization over viewpoints is what makes image-based theories viable, because it avoids the problem of requiring a separate representation for every possible view.

The most direct evidence for this class of theories comes from experiments showing that object recognition efficiency is sometimes view-dependent. For example, Tarr and Pinker (1989) trained observers to recognize a set of novel letter-like forms that were viewed in only a small number of orientations during training. Once the objects could be named reliably in their familiar orientations, the observers were tested on the same objects when viewed in novel orientations. Response time to name the object depended on the angle of rotation between the nearest familiar orientation and the tested orientation: that is, responses were fastest when the tested orientation was one of the familiar ones, and slowest when the tested orientation was distant from any familiar one. This sort of result suggests that the observers mentally rotated an internal representation of familiar objects so as to match them with the currently viewed item. Logothetis, Pauls, & Poggio (1995) provide supporting evidence for this conclusion from measurements of single cell responses in monkey temporal cortex. Tarr and Bültoff (1998) provide a compendium of recent work in this area.

Despite the strengths of image-based models of object recognition, they face certain challenges. Because they are based on representations of specific items, they raise questions about the efficiency with which they can provide categorizations of novel items that are visually similar but not identical to any given stored exemplar. Furthermore, robust mechanisms for normalizing and matching stored representations with viewed items have not been specified in detail.

Both classes of theories, then, have significant strengths and limitations, and this has led to a continuing debate about how best to characterize visual object recognition. This is currently an intensively investigated area, and new empirical and theoretical results are likely to yield more definitive answers in the years ahead, answers that may well include some hybrid combination of the two approaches.

REFERENCES

Logothetis, N. K., Pauls, J., & Poggio, T. (1995). Shape representation in the inferior temporal cortex of monkeys. *Current Biology, 5*, 551–563.

Marr, D., & Nishihara, H. K. (1978). Representation and recognition of the spatial organization of three-dimensional shapes. *Proceedings of the Royal Society of London B, 200*, 269–294.

Tarr, M. J., & Bültoff, H. H. (Eds.) (1998). Object recognition in man, monkey, and machine. Cambridge, MA: MIT Press.

Tarr, M. J., & Pinker, S. (1989). Mental rotation and orientation-dependence in shape recognition. *Cognitive Psychology, 21*, 233–282.

Ullman, S. (1989). Aligning pictorial descriptions: An approach to object recognition. *Cognition, 32*, 193–254.

Recognition-by-Components: A Theory of Human Image Understanding

I. Biederman • State University of New York at Buffalo

The perceptual recognition of objects is conceptualized to be a process in which the image of the input is segmented at regions of deep concavity into an arrangement of simple geometric components, such as blocks, cylinders, wedges, and cones. The fundamental assumption of the proposed theory, recognition-by-components (RBC), is that a modest set of generalized-cone components, called geons ($N \leq 36$), can be derived from contrasts of five readily detectable properties of edges in a two-dimensional image: curvature, collinearity, symmetry, parallelism, and cotermination. The detection of these properties is generally invariant over viewing position and image quality and consequently allows robust object perception when the image is projected from a novel viewpoint or is degraded. RBC thus provides a principled account of the heretofore undecided relation between the classic principles of perceptual organization and pattern recognition: The constraints toward regularization (Pragnanz) characterize not the complete object but the object's components. Representational power derives from an allowance of free combinations of the geons. A Principle of Componential Recovery can account for the major phenomena of object recognition: if an arrangement of two or three geons can be recovered from the input, objects can be quickly recognized even when they are occluded, novel, rotated in depth, or extensively degraded. The results from experiments on the perception of briefly presented pictures by human observers provide empirical support for the theory.

Any single object can project an infinity of image configurations to the retina. The orientation of the object to the viewer can vary continuously, each giving rise to a different two-dimensional projection. The object can be occluded by other objects or texture fields, as when viewed behind foliage. The object need not be presented as a full-colored textured image but instead can be a simplified line drawing. Moreover, the object can even be missing some of its parts or be a novel exemplar of its particular category. But it is only with rare exceptions that an image fails to be rapidly and readily classified, either as an instance of a familiar object category or as an instance that cannot be so classified (itself a form of classification).

A Do-It-Yourself Example

Consider the object shown in Figure 20.1. We readily recognize it as one of those objects that cannot be classified into a familiar category. Despite its overall unfamiliarity, there is near unanimity in its descriptions. We parse—or segment—its parts at regions of deep concavity and describe those parts with common, simple volumetric terms, such as "a block," "a cylinder," "a funnel or truncated cone." We can look at the zig-zag horizontal brace as a texture region or zoom in and interpret it as a series of connected blocks. The same is true of the mass at the lower left: we can see it as a texture area or zoom in and parse it into its various bumps.

Although we know that it is not a familiar object, after a while we can say what it resembles: "A New York City hot dog cart, with the large block being the central food storage and cooking area, the rounded part underneath as a wheel, the large arc on the right as a handle, the funnel as an orange juice squeezer and the various vertical pipes as vents or umbrella supports." It is not a good cart, but we can see how it might be related to one. It is like a 10-letter word with 4 wrong letters.

We readily conduct the same process for any object, familiar or unfamiliar, in our foveal field of view. The manner of segmentation and analysis into components does not appear to depend on our familiarity with the particular object being identified.

The naive realism that emerges in descriptions of nonsense objects may be reflecting the workings of a representational system by which objects are identified.

An Analogy Between Speech and Object Perception

As will be argued in a later section, the number of categories into which we can classify objects rivals the number of words that can be readily identified when listening to speech. Lexical access during speech perception can be successfully modeled as a process mediated by the identification of individual primitive elements, the phonemes, from a relatively small set of primitives (Marslen-Wilson, 1980). We only need about 44 phonemes to code all the words in English, 15 in Hawaiian, 55 to represent virtually all the words in all the languages spoken around the world. Because the set of primitives is so small and each phoneme specifiable by dichotomous (or trichotomous) contrasts (e.g., voiced vs. unvoiced, nasal vs. oral) on a handful of attributes, one need not make particularly fine discriminations in the speech stream. The representational power of the system derives from its permissiveness in allowing relatively free combinations of its primitives.

FIGURE 20.1 ■ A Do-it-yourself Object. (There is strong consensus in the segmentation loci of this configuration and in the description of its parts.)

The hypothesis explored here is that a roughly analogous system may account for our capacities for object recognition. In the visual domain, however, the primitive elements would not be phonemes but a modest number of simple geometric components—generally convex and volumetric—of such as cylinders, blocks, wedges, and cones. Objects are segmented, typically at regions of sharp concavity, and the resultant parts matched against the best fitting primitive. The set of primitives derives from combinations of contrasting characteristics of the edges in a two-dimensional image (e.g., straight vs. curved, symmetrical vs. asymmetrical) that define differences among a set of simple volumes (viz., those that tend to be symmetrical and lack sharp concavities). As in speech perception, these contrasts need only be dichotomous or trichotomous rather than quantitative, so that the human's limited capacities for absolute judgment are not taxed. The particular properties of edges that are postulated to be relevant to the generation of the volumetric primitives have the desirable properties that they are invariant over changes in orientation and can be determined from just a few points on each edge. Consequently, they allow a primitive to be extracted with great tolerance for variations of viewpoint, occlusion, and noise.

Just as the relations among the phonemes are critical in lexical access—"fur" and "rough" have the same phonemes but are not the same words—the relations among the volumes are critical for object recognition: Two different arrangements of the same components could produce different objects. In both cases, the representational power derives from the enormous number of combinations that can arise from a modest number of primitives. The relations in speech are limited to left-to-right (sequential) orderings; in the visual domain a richer set of possible relations allows a far greater representational capacity from a comparable number of primitives. The matching of objects in recognition is hypothesized to be a process in which the perceptual input is matched against a representation that can be described by a few simple categorized volumes in specified relations to each other.

Theoretical Domain: Primal Access to Contour-Based Perceptual Categories

Our theoretical goal is to account for the initial categorization of isolated objects. Often, but not always, this categorization will be at a basic level, for example, when we know that a given object is a typewriter, a banana, or a giraffe (Rosch et al., 1976). Much of our knowledge about objects is organized at this level of categorization: the level at which there is typically some readily available name to describe that category (Rosch et al., 1976). The hypothesis explored here predicts that when the componential description of a particular subordinate differs substantially from a basic-level prototype, that is, when a subordinate is perceptually nonprototypical, categorizations will initially be made at the subordinate level. Thus, we might know that a given object is a floor lamp, a penguin, a sports car, or a dachshund more rapidly than we know that it is a lamp, a bird, a car, or a dog (e.g., Jolicoeur, Gluck, & Kosslyn, 1984). (For both theoretical and expository purposes, these readily identifiable nonprototypical members [subordinates] of basic level categories will also be considered basic level in this article.)

Count Versus Mass Noun Entities: The Role of Surface Characteristics

There is a restriction on the scope of this approach of volumetric modeling that should be noted. The modeling has been limited to concrete entities with specified boundaries. In English, such objects are typically designated by count nouns. These are concrete objects that have specified boundaries and

to which we can apply the indefinite article and number. For example, for a count noun such as "chair" we can say "a chair" or "three chairs." By contrast, mass nouns are concrete entities to which the indefinite article or number cannot be applied, such as water, sand, or snow. So we cannot say "a water" or "three sands" unless we refer to a count noun shape, as in "a drop of water" "a bucket of water," "a grain of sand," or "a snowball," each of which does have a simple volumetric description. We conjecture that mass nouns are identified primarily through surface characteristics such as texture and color, rather than through volumetric primitives.

Primal Access

Under restricted viewing and uncertain conditions, as when an object is partially occluded, texture, color, and other cues (such as position in the scene and labels) may constitute part or all of the information determining memory access, as for example when we identify a particular shirt in the laundry pile from seeing just a bit of fabric. Such identifications are indirect, typically the result of inference over a limited set of possible objects. (Additional analyses of the role of surface features is presented later in the discussion of the experimental comparison of the perceptibility of color photography and line drawings.) The goal of the present effort is to account for what can be called *primal access*: the first contact of a perceptual input from an isolated, unanticipated object to a representation in memory.

Basic Phenomena of Object Recognition

Independent of laboratory research, the phenomena of everyday object identification provide strong constraints on possible models of recognition. In addition to the fundamental phenomenon that objects can be recognized at all (not an altogether obvious conclusion), at least five facts are evident. Typically, an object can be recognized rapidly, when viewed most from novel orientations, under moderate levels of visual noise, when partially occluded, and when it is a new exemplar of a category.

The preceding five phenomena constrain theorizing about object interpretation in the following ways:

1. Access to the mental representation of an object should not be dependent on absolute judgments of quantitative detail, because such judgments are slow and error prone (Garner, 1962; Miller, 1956). For example, distinguishing among just several levels of the degree of curvature or length of an object typically requires more time than that required for the identification of the object itself. Consequently, such quantitative processing cannot be the controlling factor by which recognition is achieved.

2. The information that is the basis of recognition should be relatively invariant with respect to orientation and modest degradation.

3. Partial matches should be computable. A theory of object interpretation should have some principled means for computing a match for occluded, partial, or new exemplars of a given category. We should be able to account for the human's ability to identify, for example, a chair when it is partially occluded by other furniture, or when it is missing a leg, or when it is a new model.

Recognition-by-Components: An Overview

Our hypothesis, recognition-by-components (RBC), bears some relation to several prior conjectures for representing objects by parts or modules (e.g., Binford, 1971; Brooks, 1981; Guzman, 1971; Marr, 1977; Marr & Nishihara, 1978; Tversky & Hemenway, 1984). RBC's contribution lies in its proposal for a particular vocabulary of components derived from perceptual mechanisms and its account of how an arrangement of these components can access a representation of an object in memory.

Stages of Processing

Figure 20.2 presents a schematic of the presumed subprocesses by which an object is recognized. These stages are assumed to be arranged in cascade. An early edge extraction stage, responsive to differences in surface characteristics namely, luminance, texture, or color, provides a line drawing description of the object. From this description, nonaccidental properties of image edges (e.g., collinearity, symmetry) are detected. Parsing is performed, primarily at concave regions, simultaneously with a detection of nonaccidental properties. The nonaccidental properties of the parsed

regions provide critical constraints on the identity of the components. Within the temporal and contextual constraints of primal access, the stages up to and including the identification of components are assumed to be bottom-up.[1] A delay in the determination of an object's components should have a direct effect on the identification latency of the object.

The arrangement of the components is then matched against a representation in memory. It is assumed that the matching of the components occurs in parallel, with unlimited capacity. Partial matches are possible with the degree of match assumed to be proportional to the similarity in the components between the image and the representation.[2] This stage model is presented to provide an overall theoretical context. The focus of this

---

[1]The only top-down route shown in Figure 2 is an effect of the nonaccidental properties on edge extraction. Even this route (aside from collinearity and smooth curvature) would run counter to the desires of many in computational vision (e.g., Marr, 1982) to build a completely bottom-up system for edge extraction. This assumption was developed in the belief that edge extraction does not depend on prior familiarity with the object. However, as with the nonaccidental properties a top-down route from the component determination stage to edge extraction could precede independent of familiarity with the object itself. It is possible that an edge extraction system with a competence equivalent to that of a human—an as yet unrealized accomplishment—will require the inclusion of such top-down influences. It is also likely that other top-down routes, such as those from expectancy, object familiarity, or scene constraints (e.g., Biederman, 1981; Biederman, Mazanotte, & Rabinowitz, 1982), will be observed at a number of the stages, for example, at segmentation, component definition, or matching, especially if edges are degraded. These have been omitted from Figure 2 in the interests of simplicity and because their actual paths of influence are as yet undetermined. By proposing a general account of object recognition, it is hoped that the proposed theory will provide a framework for a principled analysis of top-down effects in this domain.

[2]Modeling the matching of an object image to a mental representation is a rich, relatively neglected problem area. Tversky's (1977) contrast model provides a useful framework with which to consider this similarity problem in that it readily allows distinctive features (components) of the image to be considered separately from the distinctive components of the representation. This allows principled assessments of similarity for partial objects (components in the representation but not in the image) and novel objects (containing components in the image that are not in the representation). It may be possible to construct a dynamic model based on a parallel distributed process as a modification of the kind proposed by McClelland and Rumelhart (1981) for word perception, with components playing the role of letters. One difficulty of such an effort is that the set of neighbors for a given word is well specified and readily available from a dictionary; the set of neighbors for a given object is not.

Stages in Object Perception

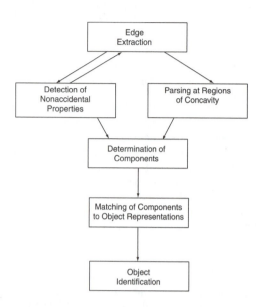

FIGURE 20.2 ■ Presumed Processing Stages in Object Recognition.

article is on the nature of the units of the representation.

When an image of an object is painted on the retina, RBC assumes that a representation of the image is segmented—or parsed—into separate regions at points of deep concavity, particularly at cusps where there are discontinuities in curvature (Marr & Nishihara, 1978). In general, paired concavities will arise whenever convex volumes are joined, a principle that Hoffman and Richards (1985) term *transversality*. Such segmentation conforms well with human intuitions about the boundaries of object parts and does not depend on familiarity with the object, as was demonstrated with the nonsense object in Figure 20.1.

Each segmented region is then approximated by

one of a possible set of simple components, called *geons* (for "geometrical ions"), that can be modeled by generalized cones (Binford, 1971; Marr, 1977, 1982). A generalized cone is the volume swept out by a cross section moving along an axis (as illustrated in Figure 20.5). (Marr [1977, 1982] showed that the contours generated by any smooth surface could be modeled by a generalized cone with a convex cross section.) The cross section is typically hypothesized to be at right angles to the axis. Secondary segmentation criteria (and criteria for determining the axis of a component) are those that afford descriptions of volumes that maximize symmetry, axis length, and constancy of the size and curvature of the cross section of the component. Of these, symmetry often provides the most compelling subjective basis for selecting subparts (Brady & Asada, 1984; Connell, 1985). These secondary bases for segmentation and component identification are discussed below.

The primitive components are hypothesized to be simple, typically symmetrical volumes lacking sharp concavities, such as blocks, cylinders, spheres, and wedges. The fundamental perceptual assumption of RBC is that the components can be differentiated on the basis of perceptual properties in the two-dimensional image that are readily detectable and relatively independent of viewing position and degradation. These perceptual properties include several that traditionally have been thought of as principles of perceptual organization, such as good continuation, symmetry, and Pragnanz. RBC thus provides a principled account of the relation between the classic phenomena of perceptual organization and pattern recognition: Although objects can be highly complex and irregular, the units by which objects are identified are simple and regular. The constraints toward regularization (Pragnanz) are thus assumed to characterize not the complete object but the object's components.

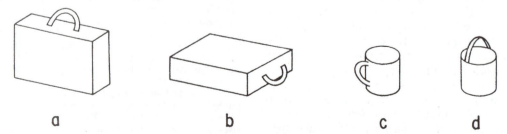

a   b   c   d

FIGURE 20.3 ■ Different Arrangements of the Same Components can Produce Different Objects.

Color and Texture

The preceding account is clearly edge-based. Surface characteristics such as color, brightness, and texture will typically have only secondary roles in primal access. This should not be interpreted as suggesting that the perception of surface characteristics per se is delayed relative to the perception of the components (but see Barrow & Tenenbaum, 1981), but merely that in most cases the surface characteristics are generally less efficient routes for accessing the classification of a count object. That is, we may know that a chair has a particular color and texture simultaneously with its componential description, but it is only the volumetric description that provides efficient access to the mental representation of "chair."[3]

Relations Among the Components

Although the components themselves are the focus of this article, as noted previously the arrangement of primitives is necessary for representing a particular object. Thus, an arc side-connected to a cylinder can yield a cup, as shown in Figure 20.3C. Different arrangements of the same components can readily lead to different objects, as when an arc is connected to the top of the cylinder to produce a pail (Figure 203D). Whether a component is attached to a long or short surface can also affect classification, as with the are producing either an attaché case (Figure 20.3A) or a strongbox (Figure 20.3B).

The identical situation between primitives and their arrangement exists in the phonemic representation of words, where a given subset of phonemes can be rearranged to produce different words.

---

[3]There are, however objects that would seem to require both a volumetric description and a texture region for an adequate representation, such as hairbrushes, typewriter keyboards, and corkscrews. It is unlikely that many of the individual bristles, keys, or coils are parsed and identified prior to the identification of the object. Instead those regions are represented through the statistical processing that characterizes their texture (for example, Beck, Prazdny, & Rosenfeld, 1983; Julesz, 1981), although we retain a capacity to zoom down and attend to the volumetric nature of the individual elements. The structural description that would serve as a representation of such objects would include a statistical specification of the texture field along with a specification of the larger volumetric components. These compound texture–componential objects have not been studied, but it is possible that the characteristics of their identification would differ from objects that are readily defined solely by their arrangement of volumetric components.

The representation of an object would thus be a structural description that expressed the relations among the components (Ballard & Brown, 1982; Winston, 1975). A suggested (minimal) set of relations will be described later (see Table 1). These relations include specification of the relative sizes of the components, their orientation and the locus of their attachment.

Nonaccidental Properties: A Perceptual Basis for a Componential Representation

Recent theoretical analyses of perceptual organization (Binford, 1981; Lowe, 1984; Rock, 1983; Witkin & Tenenbaum, 1983) provide a perceptual basis for generating a set of geons. The central organizational principle is that certain properties of edges in a two-dimensional image are taken by the visual system as strong evidence that the edges in the three-dimensional world contain those same properties. For example, if there is a straight line in the image (*collinearity*), the visual system infers that the edge producing that line in the three-dimensional world is also straight. The visual system ignores the possibility that the property in the image might be a result of a (highly unlikely) accidental alignment of eye and curved edge. Smoothly curved elements in the image (*curvilinearity*) are similarly inferred to arise from smoothly curved features in the three-dimensional world. These properties, and the others described later, have been termed *nonaccidental* (Witkin & Tenenbaum, 1983) in that they would only rarely be produced by accidental alignments of viewpoint and object features and consequently are generally unaffected by slight variations in viewpoint.

If the image is symmetrical (*symmetry*) we assume that the object projecting that image is also symmetrical. The order of symmetry is also preserved: Images that are symmetrical under both reflection and 90° increments of rotation, such as a square or circle, are interpreted as arising from objects (or surfaces) that are symmetrical under both rotation and reflection. Although skew symmetry is often readily perceived as arising from a tilted symmetrical object or surface (Palmer, 1980) there are cases where skew symmetry is not readily detected (Attneave, 1982). When edges in the image are parallel or coterminate we assume that the real-world edges also are parallel or coterminate, respectively.

These five nonaccidental properties and the associated three-dimensional inferences are described in Figure 20.4 (adapted from Lowe, 1984). Witkin and Tenenbaum (1983; see also Lowe, 1984) argue that the leverage provided by the nonaccidental relations for inferring a three-dimensional structure from a two-dimensional image edges is so great as to pose a challenge to the effort in computational vision and perceptual psychology that assigned central importance to variation in local surface characteristics, such as luminance gradients, from which surface curvature could be determined (as in Besl & Jain, 1986). Although a surface property derived from such gradients will be invariant over some transformations, Witkin and Tenenbaum (1983) demonstrate that the suggestion of a volumetric component through the shape of the surface's silhouette can readily override the perceptual interpretation of the luminance gradient. The psychological literature, summarized in the next section, provides considerable evidence supporting the assumption that these nonaccidental properties can serve as primary organizational constraints in human image interpretation.

Psychological Evidence for the Rapid Use of Nonaccidental Relations

There can be little doubt that images are interpreted in a manner consistent with the nonaccidental principles. But are these relations used quickly enough to provide a perceptual basis for the components that allow primal access? Although all the principles have not received experimental verification, the available evidence strongly suggests an affirmative answer to the preceding question. There is strong evidence that the visual system quickly assumes and uses collinearity, curvature, symmetry, and cotermination. This evidence is of two sorts: (a) demonstrations, often compelling, showing that when a given two-dimensional relation is produced by an accidental alignment of object and image, the visual system accepts the relation as existing in the three-dimensional world; and (b) search tasks showing that when a target differs from distracters in a nonaccidental property, as when one is searching for a curved arc among straight segments, the detection of that target is facilitated compared to conditions where targets and background do not differ in such properties.

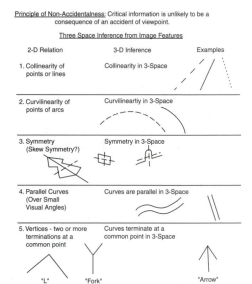

FIGURE 20.4 ■ FIve Nonaccidental Relations. (From Figure 5.2, *Perceptual organization and visual recognition* [p. 77] by David Lowe. Unpublished doctoral dissertation, Stanford University. Adapted by permission.)

Collinearity versus curvature. The demonstration of the collinearity or curvature relations is too obvious to be performed as an experiment. When looking at a straight segment, no observer would assume that it is an accidental image of a curve. That the contrast between straight and curved edges is readily available for perception was shown by Neisser (1963). He found that a search for a letter composed only of straight segments, such as a Z, could be performed faster when in a field of curved distracters, such as C, G, O, and Q, then when among other letters composed of straight segments such as N, W, V, and M.

Symmetry and parallelism. Many of the Ames demonstrations (Ittleson, 1952), such as the trapezoidal window and Ames room, derive from an assumption of symmetry that includes parallelism. Palmer (1980) showed that the subjective directionality of arrangements of equilateral triangles was based on the derivation of an axis of symmetry for the arrangement. King, Meyer, Tangney, and Biederman (1976) demonstrated that a perceptual bias toward symmetry contributed to apparent shape constancy effects. Garner (1974), Checkosky and Whitlock (1973), and Pomerantz (1978) provided ample evidence that not only can symmetrical shapes be quickly discriminated from asymmetrical stimuli, but that the degree of symmetry was also a readily available perceptual distinction. Thus, stimuli that were invariant under both reflection and 90° increments in rotation could be rapidly discriminated from those that were only invariant under reflection (Checkosky & Whitlock, 1973).

Cotermination. The "peephole perception" demonstrations, such as the Ames chair (Ittleson, 1952) or the physical realization of the "impossible" triangle (Penrose & Penrose, 1958), are produced by accidental alignment of the ends of noncoterminous segments to produce—from one viewpoint only—L, Y and arrow vertices. More recently, Kanade (l981) has presented a detailed analysis of an "accidental" chair of his own construction. The success of these demonstrations document the immediate and compelling impact of cotermination.

The registration of cotermination is important for determining vertices, which provide information that can serve to distinguish the components. In fact, one theorist (Binford, 1981) has suggested that the major function of eye movements is to determine coincidence of segments. "Coincidence" would include not only cotermination of edges but the termination of one edge on another, as with a T vertex. With polyhedra (volumes produced by planar surfaces), the Y, arrow, and L vertices allow inference as to the identity of the volume in the image. For example, the silhouette of a brick contains a series of six vertices, which alternate between Ls and arrows, and an internal Y vertex, as illustrated in Figure 20.5. The Y vertex is produced by the cotermination of three segments, with none of the angles greater than 180°. (An arrow vertex, also formed from the cotermination of three segments, contains an angle that exceeds 180°; an L vertex is formed by the cotermination of two segments.) As shown in Figure 20.5, this vertex is not present in components that have curved cross sections, such as cylinders, and thus can provide a distinctive cue for the cross-section edge. (The curved Y vertex present in a cylinder can be distinguished from the Y or arrow vertices in that the termination of one segment in the curved Y is tangent to the other segment [Chakravarty, 1979].)

Perkins (1983) has described a perceptual bias toward parallelism in the interpretation of this vertex.[4] Whether the presence of this particular internal vertex can facilitate the identification of a brick versus a cylinder is not yet known, but a recent study by Biederman and Blickle (1985), described below, demonstrated that deletion of vertices adversely affected object recognition more than deletion of the same amount of contour at midsegment.

The T vertex represents a special case in that it is not a locus of cotermination (of two or more segments) but only the termination of one segment on another. Such vertices are important for determining occlusion and thus segmentation (along with concavities), in that the edge forming the (normally) vertical segment of the T cannot be closer to the viewer than the segment forming the top of the T (Binford, 1981). By this account, the T vertex might have a somewhat different status than the Y, arrow, and L vertices, in that the T's primary role would be in segmentation, rather than in establishing the identity of the volume.[5]

Vertices composed of three segments, such as the Y and arrow, and their curved counterparts, are important determinants as to whether a given component is volumetric or planar. Planar components (to be discussed later) lack three-pronged vertices.

The high speed and accuracy of determining a

---

[4]When such vertices formed the central angle in a polyhedron, Perkins (1983) reported that the surfaces would almost always be interpreted as meeting at right angles, as long as none of the three angles was less than 90°. Indeed such vertices cannot be projections of acute angles (Kanade, 1981) but the human appears insensitive to the possibility that the vertices could have arisen from obtuse angles. If one of the angles in the central Y vertex was acute, then the polyhedra would be interpreted as irregular. Perkins found that subjects from rural areas of Botswana, where there was a lower incidence of exposure to carpentered (right-angled) environments, had an even stronger bias toward rectilinear interpretations than did Westerners (Perkins & Deregowski, 1982).

[5]The arrangement of vertices, particularly for polyhedra, offers constraints on "possible" interpretations of lines as convex, concave, or occluding (e.g., Sugihara, 1984). In general, the constraints take the form that a segment cannot change its interpretation, for example, from concave to convex, unless it passes through a vertex. "Impossible" objects can be constructed from violations of this constraint (Waltz, 1975) as well as from more general considerations (Sugihara, 1982, 1984). It is tempting to consider that the visual system captures these constraints in the way in which edges are grouped into objects, but the evidence would seem to argue against such an interpretation. The impossibility of most impossible objects is not immediately registered, but requires scrutiny and thought before the inconsistency is detected. What this means in the present context is that the visual system has a capacity for classifying vertices locally, but no perceptual routines for determining the global consistency of a set of vertices.

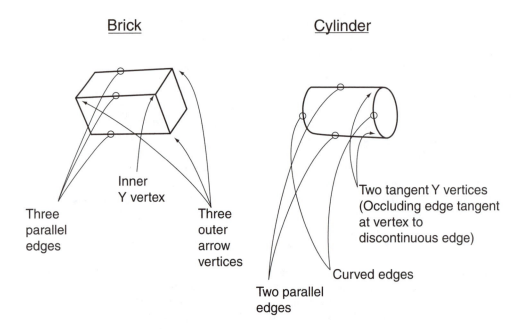

Brick

Cylinder

Inner
Y vertex

Three
parallel
edges

Three
outer
arrow
vertices

Two tangent Y vertices
(Occluding edge tangent
at vertex to
discontinuous edge)

Curved edges

Two parallel
edges

FIGURE 20.5 ■ Some Differences in Nonaccidental Properties Between a Cylinder and a Brick.

given nonaccidental relation (e.g., whether some pattern is symmetrical) should be contrasted with performance in making absolute quantitative judgments of variations in a single physical attribute, such as length of a segment or degree of tilt or curvature. For example, the judgment as to whether the length of a given segment is 10, 12, 14, 16, or 18 cm is notoriously slow and error prone (Beck, Prazdny, & Rosenfeld, 1983; Fildes & Triggs, 1985; Garner, 1962; Miller, 1956; Virsu, 1971a, 1971b). Even these modest performance levels are challenged when the judgments have to be executed over the brief 100-ms intervals (Egeth & Pachella, 1969) that are sufficient for accurate object identification. Perhaps even more telling against a view of object recognition that postulates the making of absolute judgments of fine quantitative detail is that the speed and accuracy of such judgments decline dramatically when they have to be made for multiple attributes (Egeth & Pachella, 1969; Garner, 1962; Miller, 1956). In contrast, object recognition latencies for complex objects are reduced by the presence of additional (redundant) components (Biederman, Ju, & Clapper, 1985, described below).

Geons Generated From Differences in Nonaccidental Properties Among Generalized Cones

I have emphasized the particular set of nonaccidental properties shown in Figure 20.4 because they may constitute a perceptual basis for the generation of the set of components. Any primitive that is hypothesized to be the basis of object recognition should be rapidly identifiable and invariant over viewpoint and noise. These characteristics would be attainable if differences among components were based on differences in nonaccidental properties. Although additional nonaccidental properties exist, there is empirical support for rapid perceptual access to the five described in Figure 20.4. In addition, these five relations reflect intuitions about significant perceptual and cognitive differences among objects.

From variation over only two or three levels in the nonaccidental relations of four attributes of generalized cylinders, a set of 36 geons can be generated. A subset is illustrated in Figure 20.6.

Six of the generated geons (and their attribute

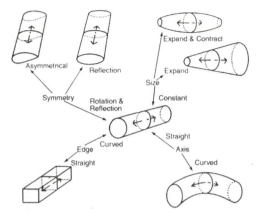

FIGURE 20.6 ■ An Illustration of how Variations in Three Attributes of a Cross Section (curved vs. straight edges; constant vs. expanded vs. expanded and contracted size; mirror and rotational symmetry vs. mirror symmetry vs. asymmetrical) and One of the Shape of the Axis (straight vs. curved) can Generate a set of Generalized Cones Differing in Nonaccidental Relations. (Constant-sized cross sections have parallel sides; expanded or expanded and contracted cross sections have sides that are not parallel. Curved versus straight cross sections and axes are detectable through collinearity or curvature. The three values of cross-section symmetry [symmetrical under reflection & 90° rotation, reflection only, or asymmetrical] are detectable through the symmetry relation. Neighbors of a cylinder are shown here. The full family of geons has 36 members.)

values) are shown in Figure 20.7. Three of the attributes describe characteristics of the cross section: its shape, symmetry, and constancy of size as it is swept along the axis. The fourth attribute describes the shape of the axis. Additional volumes are shown in Figures 20.8 and 20.9.

Nonaccidental Two-Dimensional Contrasts Among the Geons

As indicated in the above outline, the values of the four generalized cone attributes can be directly detected as contrastive differences in nonaccidental properties: straight versus curved, symmetrical versus asymmetrical, parallel versus nonparallel (and if nonparallel, whether there is a point of maximal convexity). Cross-section edges and curvature of the axis are distinguishable by collinearity or curvilinearity. The constant versus expanded size of the cross section would be detectable through parallelism; a constant cross section would produce a generalized cone with parallel sides (as with a cyl-

inder or brick); an expanded cross section would produce edges that were not parallel (as with a cone or wedge). A cross section that expanded and then contracted would produce an ellipsoid with nonparallel sides and extrema of positive curvature (as with a lemon). Such extrema are invariant with viewpoint (e.g., Hoffman & Richards, 1985) and actually constitute a sixth nonaccidental relation. The three levels of cross-section symmetry are equivalent to Garner's (1974) distinction as to the number of different stimuli produced by increments of 90´° rotations and reflections of a stimulus. Thus, a square or circle would be invariant under 90° rotation and reflection, but a rectangle or ellipse would be invariant only under reflection, as 90° rotations would produce another figure in each case. Asymmetrical figures would produce eight different figures under 90° rotation and reflection.

Specification of the nonaccidental properties of the three attributes of the cross section and one of the axis, as described in the previous paragraph, is sufficient to uniquely classify a given arrangement of edges as one of the 36 geons. These would be matched against a structural description for each geon that specified the values of these four nonaccidental image properties. But there are actually more distinctive nonaccidental image features for each geon than the four described in the previous paragraph (or indicated in Figures 20.7, 20.8, and 20.9). In particular, the arrangement of vertices, both of the silhouette and the presence of an interior Y vertex, and the presence of a discontinuous (third) edge along the axis (which produces the interior Y vertex) provide a richer description for each component than do the four properties of the generating function. This point can be readily appreciated by considering as an example, some of the additional nonaccidental properties differentiating the brick from the cylinder in Figure 20.5. Each geon's structural description would thus include a larger number of contrastive image properties than the four that were directly related to the generating function.

Consideration of the featural basis for the structural descriptions for each geon suggests that a similarity measure can be defined on the basis of the common versus distinctive image features for any pair of components. The similarity measure would permit the promotion of alternative geons under conditions of ambiguity, as when one or several of the image features were undecidable.

Partial Tentative Geon Set Based on Nonaccidentalness Relations

CROSS SECTION

Geon	Edge Straight S Curved C	Symmetry Rot & Ref ++ Ref+ Asymm -	Size Constant ++ Expanded - Exp & Cont--	Axis Straight + Curved -
	S	+ +	+ +	+
	C	+ +	+ +	+
	S	+	-	+
	S	+ +	+	-
	C	+ +	-	+
	S	+	+	+

FIGURE 20.7 ■ Proposed Partial Set of Volumetric Primitives (geons) Derived from Differences in Nonaccidental Properties.

Is geon identification two-dimensional or three-dimensional? Although the 36 geons have a clear subjective volumetric interpretation, it must be emphasized they can be uniquely specified from their two-dimensional image properties. Consequently, recognition need not follow the construction of an "object centered" (Marr, 1982) three-dimensional interpretation of each volume. It is also possible that, despite the subjective componential interpretation given to the arrangement of image features as simple volumes, it is the image features themselves, in specified relationships, that mediate perception. These alternatives remain to be evaluated.

Additional Sources of Contour and Recognition Variation

RBC seeks to account for the recognition of an infinitely varied perceptual input with a modest set of idealized primitives. A number of subordinate and related issues are raised by this attempt, some of which will be addressed in this section. This section need not be covered by a reader concerned primarily with the overall gist of RBC.

Asymmetrical cross sections. There are an infinity of possible cross sections that could be asymmetrical. How does RBC represent this variation? RBC assumes that the differences in the departures from symmetry are not readily available and thus do not affect primal access. For example, the difference in the shape of the cross section for the two straight-edged volumes in Figure 20.10 might not be apparent quickly enough to affect object recognition. This does not mean that an individual could not store the details of the volume produced by an asymmetrical cross section. But the presumption is that the access for this detail would be too slow to mediate primal access. I do not know of any case where primal access depends on discrimination among asymmetrical cross sections within a given component type, for example, among curved-edged cross sections of constant size, straight axes, and a specified aspect ratio. For instance, the curved cross section for the component that can model an airplane wing or car door is asymmetrical. Different wing designs might have different shaped cross sections. It is likely that most people, including wing designers, will know that the object is an airplane, or even an airplane wing, before they know the subclassifica-

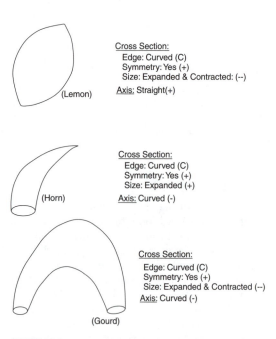

Cross Section:
Edge: Curved (C)
Symmetry: Yes (+)
Size: Expanded & Contracted: (--)
Axis: Straight(+)

(Lemon)

Cross Section:
Edge: Curved (C)
Symmetry: Yes (+)
Size: Expanded (+)
Axis: Curved (-)

(Horn)

Cross Section:
Edge: Curved (C)
Symmetry: Yes (+)
Size: Expanded & Contracted (--)
Axis: Curved (-)

(Gourd)

FIGURE 20.8 ■ Three Curved Geons with Curved Axes or Expanded and/or Contracted Cross Sections. (These tend to resemble biological forms.)

CROSS SECTION

Geon	Edge Straight S Curved C	Symmetry Rot & Ref ++ Ref + Asymm-	Size Constant ++ Expanded – Exp & Cont --	Axis Straight + Curved -
	S	+	+ +	–
	C	+	+ +	–
	S	+ +	–	–
	C	+ +	–	–
	S	+	–	–
	C	+	–	–

FIGURE 20.9 ■ Geons with Curved Axis and Straight or Curved Cross Sections. (Determining the shape of the cross section, particularly if straight, might require attention.)

tion of the wing on the basis of the asymmetry of its cross section.

A second way in which asymmetrical cross sections need not be individually represented is that they often produce volumes that resemble symmetrical, but truncated, wedges or cones. This latter form of representing asymmetrical cross sections would be analogous to the schema-plus-correction phenomenon noted by Bartlett (1932). The implication of a schema-plus-correction representation would be that a single primitive category for asymmetrical cross sections and wedges might be sufficient. For both kinds of volumes, their similarity may be a function of the detection of a lack of parallelism in the volume. One would have to exert scrutiny to determine whether a lack of parallelism had originated in the cross section or in a size change of a symmetrical cross section. In this case, as with the components with curved axes described in the preceding section, a single primitive category for both wedges and asymmetrical straight-edged volumes could be postulated that would allow a reduction in the number of primitive components. There is considerable evidence that asymmetrical patterns require more time for their identification than symmetrical patterns (Checkosky & Whitlock, 1973; Pomerantz, 1978).

Whether these effects have consequences for the time required for object identification is not yet known.

One other departure from regular components might also be noted. A volume can have a cross section with edges that are both curved and straight, as would result when a cylinder is sectioned in half along its length, producing a semicircular cross section. The conjecture is that in such cases the default cross section is the curved one, with the straight edges interpreted as slices off the curve, in schema-plus-correction representation (Bartlett, 1932).

Component terminations. When a cross section varies in size, as with a cone, it can converge to a point, as with the horn in Figure 20.8, or appear truncated, as with the cone in Figure 20.7. Such termination differences could be represented as independently specified characteristics of the structural description for the geon, determinable in the

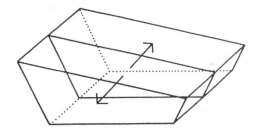

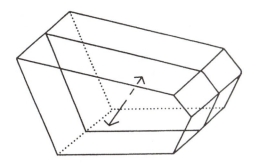

FIGURE 20.10 ■ Volumes with an Asymmetrical, Straight-edged, Cross Section. (Detection of differences between such volumes might require attention.)

image by whether the termination was a single L vertex (with a point) or two tangent Y vertices (with a truncated cone).

Another case arises when a cylinder has a cross section that remains constant for part of its length but then tapers to produce a point, as with a sharpened pencil. Such objects could be modeled by joining a cylinder to a cone, with the size of the cross sections matched so that no concavity is produced. The parsing point in this case would be the join where different nonaccidental properties were required to fit the volumes, namely, the shift from parallel edges with the cylinder to converging edges with the cone. Such joins provide a decidedly weaker basis—subjectively—for segmentation than joins producing cusps. The perceptual consequences of such variation have not been studied.

Metric variation. For any given geon type, there can be continuous metric variation in aspect ratio, degree of curvature (for curved components), and departure from parallelism (for nonparallel components). How should this quantitative variation be conceptualized? The discussion will concentrate on aspect ratio, probably the most important of the variations. But the issues will be generally applicable to the other metric variations as well.[6]

One possibility is to include specification of a range of aspect ratios in the structural description of the geons of an object as well as the object itself. It seems plausible to assume that recognition can be indexed, in part, by aspect ratio in addition to a componential description. An object's aspect ratio would thus play a role similar to that played by word length in the tachistoscopic identification of words, where long words are rarely proffered when a short word is hashed. Consider an elongated object, such as a baseball bat, with an aspect ratio of 15:1. When the orientation of the object is orthogonal to the viewpoint, so that the aspect ratio of its image is also 15:1, recognition might be faster than when presented at an orientation where the aspect ratio of its image differed greatly from that value, say 2:1. One need not have a particularly fine-tuned function for aspect ratio as large differences in aspect ratio between two components would, like parallelism, be preserved over a large proportion of arbitrary viewing angles.

Another way to incorporate variations in the aspect ratio of an object's image is to represent only qualitative differences, so that variations in aspect ratios exert an effect only when the relative

size of the longest dimensions undergo reversal. Specifically, for each component and the complete object, three variations could be defined depending on whether the axis was much smaller, approximately equal to, or much longer than the longest dimension of the cross section. For example, for a geon whose axis was longer than the diameter of the cross section (which would be true in most cases), only when the projection of the cross section became longer than the axis would there be an effect of the object's orientation, as when the bat was viewed almost from on end so that the diameter of the handle was greater than the projection of its length.

A close dependence of object recognition performance on the preservation of the aspect ratio of a geon in the image would challenge RBC's emphasis on dichotomous contrasts of nonaccidental relations. Fortunately, these issues on the role of aspect ratio are readily testable. Bartram's (1976) experiments, described later in the section on orientation variability, suggest that sensitivity to variations in aspect ratio need not be given heavy weight: Recognition speed is unaffected by variation in aspect ratio across different views of the same object.

Planar geons. When a three-pronged vertex (viz., Y, tangent Y, or arrow) is not present in a parsed region, the resultant region appears planar; as with the flipper of an penguin or the eye of an elephant. Such shapes can be conceptualized in two ways. The first (and less favored) is to assume that these are just quantitative variations of the volumetric components, but with an axis length of zero. They would then have default values of a straight axis (+) and a constant cross section (+). Only the edge of the cross section and its symmetry could vary.

Alternatively, it might be that a planar region is not related perceptually to the foreshortened projection of the geon that could have produced it. Using the same variation in cross-section edge and symmetry as with the volumetric components, seven planar geons could be defined. For ++symmetry there would be the square and circle (with

---

[6]Aspect ratio is a measure of the elongation of a component. For constant-sized cross sections and straight axes, it can be expressed as the width-to-height ratio of the smallest bounding rectangle that would just enclose the component. More complex functions are needed expressing the change in aspect ratio as a function of axis position when the cross section varies in size or the axis is curved.

straight and curved edges, respectively) and for +symmetry the rectangle, triangle, and ellipse. Asymmetrical (–) planar geons would include trapezoids (straight edges), and drop shapes (curved edges). The addition of these seven planar geons to the 36 volumetric geons yields 43 components (a number close to the number of phonemes required to represent English words). The triangle is here assumed to define a separate geon, although a triangular cross section was not assumed to define a separate volume under the intuition that a prism (produced by a triangular cross section) is not quickly distinguishable from a wedge. My preference for assuming that planar geons are not perceptually related to their foreshortened volumes is based on the extraordinary difficulty of recognizing objects from views that are parallel to the axis of the major components so that foreshortening projects only the planar cross section. The presence of three-pronged vertices thus provides strong evidence that the image is generated from a volumetric rather than a planar component.

Selection of axis. Given that a volume is segmented from the object, how is an axis selected? Subjectively, it appears that an axis is selected that would maximize the axis's length, the symmetry of the cross section, and the constancy of the size of the cross section. By maximizing the length of the axis, bilateral symmetry can be more readily detected because the sides would be closer to the axis. Often a single axis satisfies all three criteria, but sometimes these criteria are in opposition and two (or more) axes (and component types) are plausible (Brady, 1983). Under such conditions, axes will often be aligned to an external frame, such as the vertical (Humphreys, 1983).

Negative values. The plus values in Figures 20.7, 20.8, and 20.9 are those favored by perceptual biases and memory errors. No bias is assumed for straight and curved edges of the cross section. For symmetry, clear biases have been documented. For example, if an image could have arisen from a symmetrical object, then it is interpreted as symmetrical (King et al., 1976). The same is apparently true of parallelism. If edges could be parallel, then they are typically interpreted as such, as with the trapezoidal room or window.

Curved axes. Figure 20.8 shows three of the most negatively marked primitives with curved crossed sections. Such geons often resemble biological entities. An expansion and contraction of a rounded cross section with a straight axis produces an ellipsoid (lemon), an expanded cross section with a curved axis produces a horn, and an expanded and contracted cross section with a rounded cross section produces a banana slug or gourd.

In contrast to the natural forms generated when both cross section and axis are curved, the geons swept by a straight-edged cross section traveling along a curved axis (e.g., the components on the first, third, and fifth rows of Figure 20.9) appear somewhat less familiar and more difficult to apprehend than their curved counterparts. It is possible that this difficulty may merely be a consequence of unfamiliarity. Alternatively, the subjective difficulty might be produced by a conjunction–attention effect (CAE) of the kind discussed by Treisman (e.g., Treisman & Gelade, 1980). (CAEs are described later in the section on attentional effects.) In the present case, given the presence in the image of curves and straight edges (for the rectilinear cross sections with curved axis), attention (or scrutiny) may be required to determine which kind of segment to assign to the axis and which to assign to the cross section. Curiously, the problem does not present itself when a curved cross section is run along a straight axis to produce a cylinder or cone. The issue as to the role of attention in determining geons would appear to be empirically tractable using the paradigms created by Treisman and her colleagues (Treisman, 1982; Treisman & Gelade, 1980).

Conjunction–attentional effects. The time required to detect a single feature is often independent of the number of distracting items in the visual field. For example, the time it takes to detect a blue shape (a square or a circle) among a field of green distracter shapes is unaffected by the number of green shapes. However, if the target is defined by a conjunction of features, for example, a blue square among distracters consisting of green squares and blue circles, so that both the color and the shape of each item must be determined to know if it is or is not the target, then target detection time increases linearly with the number of distracters (Treisman & Gelade, 1980). These results have led to a theory of visual attention that assumes that humans can monitor all potential display positions simultaneously and with unlimited capacity for a single feature (e.g., something blue or something curved). But when a target is defined by a conjunction of features, then a limited capacity attentional system that can only examine one display position at a time must be deployed (Treisman & Gelade, 1980).

The extent to which Treisman and Gelade's (1980) demonstration of conjunction–attention effects may be applicable to the perception of volumes and objects has yet to be evaluated. In the extreme, in a given moment of attention, it may be the case that the values of the four attributes of the components are detected as independent features. In cases where the attributes, taken independently, can define different volumes, as with the shape of cross sections and axes, an act of attention might be required to determine the specific component generating those attributes: Am I looking at a component with a curved cross section and a straight axis or is it a straight cross section and a curved axis? At the other extreme, it may be that an object recognition system has evolved to allow automatic determination of the geons.

The more general issue is whether relational structures for the primitive components are defined automatically or whether a limited attentional capacity is required to build them from their individual-edge attributes. It could be the case that some of the most positively marked geons are detected automatically, but that the volumes with negatively marked attributes might require attention. That some limited capacity is involved in the perception of objects (but not necessarily their components) is documented by an effect of the number of distracting objects on perceptual search (Biederman, Blickle, Teitelbaum, Klatsky, & Mezzgnotte, 1998. In their experiment, reaction times and errors for detecting an object such as a chair increased linearly as a function of the number of nontarget objects in a 100-ms presentation of nonscene arrangements of objects. Whether this effect arises from the necessity to use a limited capacity to construct a geon from its attributes or whether the effect arises from the matching of an arrangement of geons to a representation is not yet known.

Relations of RBC to Principles of Perceptual Organization

Textbook presentations of perception typically include a section of Gestalt organizational principles. This section is almost never linked to any other function of perception. RBC posits a specific role for these organizational phenomena in pattern recognition. As suggested by the section on generating geons through nonaccidental properties, the Gestalt principles, particularly those promoting Pragnanz (Good Figure), serve to determine the individual geons, rather than the complete object. A complete object, such as a chair, can be highly complex and asymmetrical, but the components will be simple volumes. A consequence of this interpretation is that it is the components that will be stable under noise or perturbation. If the components can be recovered and object perception is based on the components, then the object will be recognizable.

This may be the reason why it is difficult to camouflage objects by moderate doses of random occluding noise, as when a car is viewed behind foliage. According to RBC, the geons accessing the representation of an object can readily be recovered through routines of collinearity or curvature that restore contours (Lowe, 1984). These mechanisms for contour restoration will not bridge cusps (e.g., Kanizsa, 1979). For visual noise to be effective, by these considerations, it must obliterate the concavity and interrupt the contours from one geon at the precise point where they can be joined, through collinearity or constant curvature, with the contours of another geon. The likelihood of this occurring by moderate random noise is, of course, extraordinarily low, and it is a major reason why, according to RBC, objects are rarely rendered unidentifiable by noise. The consistency of RBC with this interpretation of perceptual organization should be noted. RBC holds that the (strong) loci of parsing is at cusps; the geons are organized from the contours between cusps. In classical Gestalt demonstrations, good figures are organized from the contours between cusps. Experiments subjecting these conjectures to test are described in a later section.

A Limited Number of Components?

According to the prior arguments, only 36 volumetric components can be readily discriminated on the basis of differences in nonaccidental properties among generalized cones. In addition, there are empirical and computational considerations that are compatible with a such a limit.

Empirically, people are not sensitive to continuous metric variations as evidenced by severe limitations in humans' capacity for making rapid and accurate absolute judgments of quantitative shape variations.[7] The errors made in the memory for shapes also document an insensitivity to metric variations. Computationally, a limit is suggested by estimates of the number of objects we might know and the capacity for RBC to readily represent a far greater number with a limited number of primitives.

Empirical Support for a Limit

Although the visual system is capable of discriminating extremely fine detail, I have been arguing that the number of volumetric primitives sufficient to model rapid human object recognition may be limited. It should be noted, however, that the number of proposed primitives is greater than the three—cylinder, sphere, and cone—advocated by some "How-to-Draw" books. Although these three may be sufficient for determining relative proportions of the parts of a figure and can aid perspective, they are not sufficient for the rapid identification of objects.[8] Similarly, Marr and Nishihara's (1978) pipe-cleaner (viz., cylinder) representations of animals (their Figure 20.17) would also appear to posit an insufficient number of primitives. On the page, in the context of other labeled pipe-cleaner animals, it is certainly possible to arrive at an identification of a particular (labeled) animal, for example, a giraffe. But the thesis proposed here would hold that the identifications of objects that were distinguished only by the aspect ratios of a single component type would require more time than if the representation of the object preserved its componential identity. In modeling only animals, it is likely that Marr and Nishihara capitalized on the possibility that appendages (such as legs and some necks) can often be modeled by the cylindrical forms of a pipe cleaner. By contrast, it is unlikely that a pipe-cleaner representation of a desk would have had any success. The lesson from Marr and Nishihara's demonstration, even when limited to animals, may be that an image that conveys only the axis structure and axes length is insufficient for primal access.

As noted earlier, one reason not to posit a representation system based on fine quantitative detail, for example, many variations in degree of curvature, is that such absolute judgments are notoriously slow and error prone unless limited to the 7 ± 2 values argued by Miller (1956). Even this modest limit is challenged when the judgments

have to be executed over a brief 100-ms interval (Egeth & Pachella, 1969) that is sufficient for accurate object identification. A further reduction in the capacity for absolute judgments of quantitative variations of a simple shape would derive from the necessity, for most objects, to make simultaneous absolute judgments for the several shapes that constitute the object's parts (Egeth & Pachella, 1969; Miller, 1956). This limitation on our capacities for making absolute judgments of physical variation, when combined with the dependence of such variation on orientation and noise, makes quantitative shape judgments a most implausible basis for object recognition. RBC's alternative is that the perceptual discriminations required to determine the primitive components can be made categorically, requiring the discrimination of only two or three viewpoint-independent levels of variation.[9]

Our memory for irregular shapes shows clear biases toward "regularization" (e.g., Woodworth, 1938). Amply documented in the classical shape memory literature was the tendency for errors in

---

[7]Absolute judgments are judgments made against a standard in memory, for example, that Shape A is 14 cm. in length. Such judgments are to be distinguished from comparative judgments in which both stimuli are available for simultaneous comparison, for example, that Shape A, lying alongside Shape B, is longer than B. Comparative judgments appear limited only by the resolving power of the sensory system. Absolute judgments are limited, in addition, by memory for physical variation. That the memory limitations are severe is evidenced by the finding that comparative judgments can be made quickly and accurately for differences so fine that thousands of levels can be discriminated. But accurate absolute judgments rarely exceed 7 ± 2 categories (Miller, 1956).

[8]Paul Cezanne is often incorrectly cited on this point. "Treat nature by the cylinder, the sphere, the cone, *everything in proper perspective so that each side of an object or plane is directed towards a central point.*" (Cezanne, 1904/1941, p. 234, italics mine). Cezanne was referring to perspective, not the veridical representation of objects.

[9]This limitation on our capacities for absolute judgments also occurs in the auditory domain in speech perception, in which the modest number of phonemes can be interpreted as arising from dichotomous or trichotomous contrasts among a few invariant dimensions of speech production (Miller, 1956). Examples of invariant categorized speech features would be whether transitions are "feathered" (a cue for voicing) or the formants "murmured" (a cue for nasality). That these features are dichotomous allows the recognition system to avoid the limitations of absolute judgment in the auditory domain. It is possible that the limited number of phonemes derives more from this limitation for accessing memory for fine quantitative variation than it does from limits on the fineness of the commands to the speech musculature.

the reproduction and recognition of irregular shapes to be in a direction of regularization, in which slight deviations from symmetrical or regular figures were omitted in attempts at reproduction. Alternatively, some irregularities were emphasized ("accentuation"), typically by the addition of a regular subpart. What is the significance of these memory biases? By the RBC hypothesis, these errors may have their origin in the mapping of the perceptual input onto a representational system based on regular primitives. The memory of a slight irregular form would be coded as the closest regularized neighbor of that form. If the irregularity was to be represented as well, an act that would presumably require additional time and capacity, then an additional code (sometimes a component) would be added, as with Bartlett's (1932) "schema with correction."

Computational Considerations: Are 36 Geons Sufficient?

Is there sufficient representational power in a set of 36 geons to express the human's capacity for basic-level visual categorizations? Two estimates are needed to provide a response to this question: (a) the number of readily available perceptual categories, and (b) the number of possible objects that could be represented by 36 geons. The number of possible objects that could be represented by 36 geons will depend on the allowable relations among the geons. Obviously, the value for (b) would have to be greater than the value for (a) if 36 geons are to prove sufficient.

How many readily distinguishable objects do people know? How might one arrive at a liberal estimate for this value? One estimate can be obtained from the lexicon. There are less than 1,500 relatively common basic-level object categories, such as chairs and elephants.[10] If we assume that this estimate is too small by a factor of 2, allowing for idiosyncratic categories and errors in the estimate, then we can assume potential classification into approximately 3,000 basic-level categories. RBC assumes that perception is based on a particular componential configuration rather than the basic-level category, so we need to estimate the mean number of readily distinguishable componential configurations per basic-level category. Almost all natural categories, such as elephants or giraffes, have one or only a few instances with differing componential descriptions. Dogs represent a rare exception for natural categories in that they have been bred to have considerable variation in their descriptions. Categories created by people vary in the number of allowable types, but this number often tends to be greater than the natural categories. Cups, typewriters, and lamps have just a few (in the case of cups) to perhaps 15 or more (in the case of lamps) readily discernible exemplars.[11] Let us assume (liberally) that the mean number of types is 10. This would yield an esti-

[10]This estimate was obtained from three sources: (a) several linguists and cognitive psychologists, who provided guesses of 300 to 1,000 concrete noun object categories; (b) the average 6-year-old child, who can name most of the objects seen in his or her world and on television and has a vocabulary of less than 10,000 words, about 10% of which are concrete count nouns; and (c) a 30-page sample from Webster's Seventh New Collegiate Dictionary, which provided perhaps the most defensible estimate; I counted the number of readily identifiable, unique concrete nouns that would not be subordinate to other nouns. Thus, "wood thrush" was not included because it could not be readily discriminated from "sparrow," but "penguin" and "ostrich" were counted as separate noun categories, as were borderline cases. The mean number of such nouns per page was 1.4, so given a 1,200 page dictionary, this is equivalent to 1,600 noun categories.

[11]It might be thought that faces constitute an obvious exception to the estimate of a ratio of ten exemplars per category presented here, in that we can obviously recognize thousands of faces. But can we recognize individual faces as rapidly as we recognize differences among basic level categories? I suspect not. That is, we may know that it is a face and not a chair in less time than that required for the identification of any particular face. Whatever the ultimate

data on face recognition, there is evidence that the routines for processing faces have evolved to differentially respond to cuteness (Hildebrandt, 1982; Hildebrandt & Fitzgerald, 1983), age (e.g., Mark & Todd, 1985), and emotion and threats (e.g., Coss, 1979; Trivers, 1985). Faces may thus constitute a special stimulus case in that specific mechanisms have evolved to respond to biologically relevant quantitative variations and caution may be in order before results with face stimuli are considered characteristic of perception in general. Another possible exception to the exemplar/category ratio presented here occurs with categories such as lamps, which could have an arbitrarily large number of possible bases, shade types, and so on. But these variations may actually serve to hinder recognition. In a number of experiments in our laboratory, we have noted that highly stylized or unusual exemplars of a category are extremely difficult to identify under brief exposures (and out of context). The elements producing the variation in these cases may thus be acting as noise (or irrelevant components) in the sense that they are present in the image but not present in the mental representation for that category. These potential difficulties in the identification of faces or objects may not be subjectively apparent from the casual perusal of objects on a page, particularly when they are in a context that facilitates their classification.

mate of 30,000 readily discriminable objects (3,000 categories × 10 types/category).

A second source for the estimate derives from considering plausible rates for learning new objects. Thirty thousand objects would require learning an average of 4.5 objects per day, every day for 18 years, the modal age of the subjects in the experiments described below.

Although the value of 4.5 objects learned per day seems reasonable for a child in that it approximates the maximum rates of word acquisition during the ages of 2–6 years (Carey, 1978), it certainly overestimates the rate at which adults develop new object categories. The impressive visual recognition competence of a 6-year-old child, if based on 30,000 visual categories, would require the learning of 13.5 objects per day, or about one per waking hour. By the criterion of learning rate, 30,000 categories would appear to be a liberal estimate.

TABLE 20.1. Generative Power of 36 Geons

Value	Component
36	First component (G_1)
×	×
36	Second component (G_2)
×	×
3	Size ($G_1 \gg G_2$, $G_1 \ll G_2$, $G_1 = G_2$)
×	×
2.4	G_1 top or bottom or side (represented for 80% of the objects)
×	×
2	Nature of join (end-to-end [off center] or end-to-side [centered])
×	×
2	Join at long or short surface of G_1
×	×
2	Join at long or short surface of G_2
	Total: 74,649 possible two-geon objects

Note. With three geons, 74,649 × 36 × 57.6 = 154 million possible objects. Equivalent to learning 23,439 new objects every day (approximately 1465/waking hr or 24/min) for 18 years.

Componential Relations: The Representational Capacity of 36 Geons

How many objects could be represented by 36 geons? This calculation is dependent upon two assumptions: (a) the number of geons needed, on average, to uniquely specify each object; and (b) the number of readily discriminable relations among the geons. We will start with (b) and see if it will lead to an empirically plausible value for (a). A possible set of relations is presented in Table 20.1. Like the components, the properties of the relations noted in Table 2-.1 are nonaccidental in that they can be determined from virtually any viewpoint, are preserved in the two-dimensional image, and are categorical, requiring the discrimination of only two or three levels. The specification of these five relations is likely conservative because (a) it is certainly a nonexhaustive set in that other relations can be defined; and (b) the relations are only specified for a pair rather than triples, of geons. Let us consider these relations in order of their appearance in Table 20.1.

1. Relative size. For any pair of geons, G_1 and G_2, G_1 could be much greater than, smaller than, or approximately equal to G_2.
2. Verticality. G_1 can be above or below or to the side of G_2, a relation, by the author's estimate, that is defined for at least 80% of the objects. Thus giraffes, chairs, and typewriters have a

top-down specification of their components, but forks and knives do not. The handle of a cup is side-connected to the cylinder.
3. Centering. The connection between any pair of joined geons can be end-to-end (and of equal-sized cross section at the join), as the upper and lower arms of a person, or end-to-side, producing one or two concavities, respectively(Marr, 1977). Two-concavity joins are far more common in that it is rare that two arbitrarily joined end-to-end components will have equal-sized cross sections. A more general distinction might be whether the end of one geon in an end-to-side join is centered or off centered at the side of the other component. The end-to-end join might represent only the limiting, albeit special, case of off-centered joins. In general, the join of any two arbitrary volumes (or shapes) will produce two concavities, unless an edge from one volume is made to be joined and collinear with an edge from the other volume.
4. Relative size of surfaces at join. Other than the special cases of a sphere and a cube, all primitives will have at least a long and a short surface. The join can be on either surface. The attaché case in Figure 20.3A and the strongbox in Figure 20.3B differ by the relative lengths of the surfaces of the brick that are connected to the arch (handle). The handle on the shortest

surface produces the strongbox; on a longer surface, the attaché case. Similarly, the cup and the pail in Figures 20.3C and 20.3D, respectively, differ as to whether the handle is connected to the long surface of the cylinder (to produce a cup) or the short surface (to produce a pail). In considering only two values for the relative size of the surface at the join, I am conservatively estimating the relational possibilities. Some volumes such as the wedge have as many as five surfaces, all of which can differ in size.

Representational Calculations

The 1,296 different pairs of the 36 geons (i.e., 36^2), when multiplied by the number of relational combinations, 57.6 (the product of the various values of the five relations), gives us 74,649 possible two-geon objects. If a third geon is added to the two, then this value has to be multiplied by 2,073 (36 geons × 57.6 ways in which the third geon can be related to one of the two geons), to yield 154 million possible three-component objects. This value, of course, readily accommodates the liberal estimate of 30,000 objects actually known.

The extraordinary disparity between the representational power of two or three geons and the number of objects in an individual's object vocabulary means that there is an extremely high degree of redundancy in the filling of the 154 million cell geon-relation space. Even with three times the number of objects estimated to be known by an individual (i.e., 90,000 objects), we would still have less than $\frac{1}{10}$ of 1% of the possible combinations of three geons actually used (i.e., over 99.9% redundancy).

There is a remarkable consequence of this redundancy if we assume that objects are distributed randomly throughout the object space. (Any function that yielded a relatively homogeneous distribution would serve as well.) The sparse, homogeneous occupation of the space means that, on average, it will be rare for an object to have a neighbor that differs only by one geon or relation.[12] Because the space was generated by considering only the number of possible two or three component objects, a constraint on the estimate of the average number of components per object that are sufficient for unambiguous identification is implicated. If objects were distributed relatively homogeneously among combinations of relations and

geons, then only two or three geons would be sufficient to unambiguously represent most objects [. . .]

Conclusion

To return to the analogy with speech perception, the characterization of object perception provided by RBC bears a close resemblance to some current views as to how speech is perceived. In both cases, the ease with which we are able to code tens of thousands of words or objects is solved by mapping that input onto a modest number of primitives—55 phonemes or 36 components—and then using a representational system that can code and access free combinations of these primitives. In both cases, the specific set of primitives is derived from dichotomous (or trichotomous) contrasts of a small number (less than ten) of independent characteristics of the input. The ease with which we are able to code so many words or objects may thus derive less from a capacity for coding continuous physical variation than it does from a perceptual system designed to represent the free combination of a modest number of categorized primitives based on simple perceptual contrasts.

In object perception, the primitive components may have their origins in the fundamental principles by which inferences about a three-dimensional world can be made from the edges in a two-dimensional image. These principles constitute a significant portion of the corpus of Gestalt organizational constraints. Given that the primitives are fitting simple parsed parts of an object, the constraints toward regularization characterize not the complete object but the object's components. RBC thus provides, for the first time, an account of the heretofore undecided relation between these principles of perceptual organization and human pattern recognition.

REFERENCES

Attneave, F. (1982). Pragnanz and soap bubble systems. In J. Beck (Ed.), *Organization and representation in visual perception* (pp. 11–29). Hillsdale, NJ: Erlbaum.

Ballard, D., & Brown, C. M. (1982). *Computer vision.* Englewood Cliffs, NJ: Prentice-Hall.

Barrow, H. G., & Tenenbaum, J. M. (1981). Interpreting line-drawings as three-dimensional surfaces. *Artificial Intelligence, 17,* 75–116.

Bartlett, F. C. (1932). *Remembering: a study in experimental and social psychology.* New York: Cambridge University Press.

Bartram, D. (1976). Levels of coding in picture-picture comparison tasks. *Memory & Cognition, 4,* 593–602.

Beck, J., Prazdny, K., & Rosenfeld, A. (1983). A theory of textural segmentation. In J. Beck, B. Hope, & A. Rosenfeld (Eds.), *Human and machine vision* (pp. 1–38). New York: Academic Press.

Besl, P. J., & Jain, R. C. (1986). Invariant surface characteristics for 3D object recognition in range images. *Computer Vision, Graphics, and Image Processing 33,* 33–80.

Biederman, I. (1981). On the semantics of a glance at a scene. In M. Kubovy & J. R. Pomerantz (Eds.), *Perceptual organization* (pp. 213–253). Hillsdale, NJ: Erlbaum.

Biederman, I., & Blickle, T. (1985). T*he perception of objects with deleted contours.* Unpublished manuscript, State University of New York at Buffalo.

Biederman, I., Blickle, T. W., Teitelbaum, R. C., Klatsky, G. J., & Mezzanotte, R. J. (1998). Object search in non-scene displays. *Journal of Experimental Psychology: Learning Memory, and Cognition, 14,* 456–467.

Biederman, I., Ju, G., & Clapper, J. (1985). *The perception of partial objects.* Unpublished manuscript, State University of New York at Buffalo.

Biederman, I., Mezzanotte, R. J., & Rabinowitz, J. C. (1982). Scene perception: Detecting and judging objects undergoing relational violations. *Cognitive Psychology, 14,* 143–177.

Binford, T. O. (1971, December). *Visual perception by computer.* Paper presented at the IEEE Systems Science and Cybernetics Conference, Miami, FL.

Binford, T. O. (1981). Inferring surfaces from images. *Artificial Intelligence, 17,* 205–244.

Brady, M. (1983). Criteria for the representations of shape. In J. Beck, B. Hope, & A. Rosenfeld (Eds.), *Human and machine vision* (pp. 39–84). New York: Academic Press.

Brady, M., & Asada, H. (1984). Smoothed local symmetries and their implementation. *International Journal of Robotics Research, 3,* 3.

Brooks, R. A. (1981). Symbolic reasoning among 3-D models and 2-D images. *Artificial Intelligence, 17,* 205–244.

Carey, S. (1978). The child as word learner. In M. Halle, J. Bresnan, & G. A. Miller (Eds.), *Linguistic theory and psychological reality* (pp. 264–293). Cambridge, MA: MIT Press.

Cezanne, P. (1941). Letter to Emile Bernard. In J. Rewald (Ed.), *Paul Cezanne's letters* (translated by M. Kay, pp. 233–234). London: B. Cassirrer. (Original work published 1904)

Chakravarty, I. (1979). A generalized line and junction labeling scheme with applications to scene analysis. *IEEE Transactions PAMI,* April, 202–205.

Checkosky, S. F., & Whitlock, D. (1973). Effects of pattern goodness on recognition time in a memory search task. *Journal of Experimental Psychology, 100,* 341–348.

Connell, J. H. (1985). *Learning shape descriptions: Generating and generalizing models of visual objects.* Unpublished master's thesis, Massachusetts Institute of Technology, Cambridge.

Coss, R. G. (1979). Delayed plasticity of an instinct: Recognition and avoidance of 2 facing eyes by the jewel fish. *Developmental Psychobiology, 12,* 335–345.

Egeth, H., & Pachella, R. (1969). Multidimensional stimulus identification. *Perception & Psychophysics, 5,* 341–346.

Fildes, B. N., & Triggs, T. J. (1985). The effect of changes in curve geometry on magnitude estimates of road-like perspective curvature. *Perception & Psychophysics, 37,* 218–224.

Garner, W. R. (1962). *Uncertainty and structure as psychological concepts.* New York: Wiley.

Garner, W. R. (1974). *The processing of information and structure.* New York: Wiley.

Guzman, A. (1971). Analysis of curved line-drawings using context and global information. *Machine intelligence 6* (pp. 325–375). Edinburgh: Edinburgh University Press.

Hildebrandt, K. A. (1982). The role of physical appearance in infant and child development. In H. E. Fitzgerald, E. Lester, & M. Youngman (Eds.), *Theory and research in behavioral pediatrics* (Vol. 1, pp.181–219). New York: Plenum.

Hildebrandt, K. A., & Fitzgerald, H. E. (1983). The infant's physical attractiveness: Its effect on bonding and attachment. *Infant Mental Health Journal. 4,* 3–12.

Hoffman, D. D., & Richards, W. (1985). Parts of recognition. *Cognition, 18,* 65–96.

Humphreys, G. W. (1983). Reference frames and shape perception. *Cognitive Psyhology, 15,* 151–196.

Ittleson, W. H. (1952). *The Ames demonstrations in perception.* New York: Hafner.

Jolicoeur, P., Gluck, M. A., & Kosslyn, S. M. (1984). Picture and names: Making the connection. *Cognitive Psychology, 16,* 243–275.

Kanade, T. (1981). Recovery of the three-dimensional shape of an object from a single view. *Artificial Intelligence, 17,* 409–460.

King, M., Meyer, G. E., Tangney, J., & Biederman, I. (1976). Shape constancy and a perceptual bias towards symmetry. *Perception & Psychophysics, 19,* 129–136.

Lowe, D. (1984). *Perceptual organization and visual recognition.* Unpublished doctoral dissertation, Stanford University, Stanford, CA.

Mark, L. S., & Todd, J. T. (1985). Describing perception information about human growth in terms of geometric invariants. *Perception & Psychophysics, 37,* 249–256.

Marr, D. (1977). Analysis of occluding contour. *Proceedings of the Royal Society of London, Series B, 197,* 441–475.

Marr, D. (1982). *Vision.* San Francisco: Freeman.

Marr, D., & Nishihara, H. K. (1978). Representation and recognition of three dimensional shapes. *Proceedings of the Royal Society of London, Series B, 200,* 269–294.

Marslen-Wilson, W. (1980). *Optimal efficiency in human speech processing.* Unpublished manuscript, Max-Planck-Institut für Psychoinguistik, Nijmegen, The Netherlands.

McClelland, J. L., & Rumelhart, D. E. (1981). An interactive activation model of context effects in letter perception, Part I: An account of basic findings. *Psychological Review, 88,* 375–407.

Miller, G. A. (1956). The magical number seven, plus or minus two: Some limits on our capacity for processing information. *Psychological Review, 63,* 81–97.

Neisser, U. (1963). Decision time without reaction time: Experiments in visual scanning. *American Journal of Psychology, 76,* 376–385.

Palmer, S. E. (1980). What makes triangles point: Local and global effects in configurations of ambiguous triangles. *Cognitive Psychology, 12,* 285–305.

Penrose, L. S., & Penrose, R. (1958). Impossible objects: A special type of illusion. *British Journal of Psychology, 49,* 31–33.

Perkins, D. N. (1983). Why the human perceiver is a bad machine. In J. Beck, B. Hope, & A. Rosenfeld, (Eds.), *Human and machine vision* (pp. 341–364). New York: Academic Press.

Perkins, D. N., & Deregowski, J. (1982). A cross-cultural comparison of the use of a Gestalt perceptual strategy. *Perception, 11,* 279–286.

Pomerantz, J. R. (1978). Pattern and speed of encoding. *Memory & Cognition, 5,* 235–241.

Rock, I. (1983). *The logic of perception.* Cambridge, MA: MIT Press.

Rock, I. (1984). *Perception.* New York: W. H. Freeman.

Rosch, E., Mervis, C. B., Gray, W., Johnson, D., & Boyes-Braem, P. (1976). Basic objects in natural categories. *Cognitive Psychology, 8,* 382–439.

Sugihara, K. (1982). Classification of impossible objects. *Perception, 11,* 65–74.

Sugihara, K. (1984). An algebraic approach to shape-from-image problems. *Artificial Intelligence, 23,* 59–95.

Treisman, A. (1982). Perceptual grouping and attention in visual search for objects. *Journal of Experimental Psychology: Human Perception and Performance, 8,* 194–214.

Treisman, A., & Gelade, G. (1980). A feature integration theory of attention. *Cognitive Psychology, 12,* 97–136.

Trivers, R. (1985). *Social evolution.* Menlo Park, CA: Benjamin/Cummings.

Tversky, A. (1977). Features of similarity. *Psychological Review, 84,* 327–352.

Tversky, B., & Hemenway, K. (1984). Objects, parts, and categories. *Journal of Experimental Psychology: General, 113,* 169–193.

Virsu, V. (1971a). Tendencies to eye movement, and misperception of curvature, direction, and length. *Perception & Psychophysics, 9,* 65–72.

Virsu, V.(1971b). Underestimation of curvature and task dependence in visual perception of form. *Perception & Psychophysics, 9,* 339–342.

Waltz, D. (1975). Generating semantic descriptions from drawings of scenes with shadows. In P. Winston (Ed.), *The psychology of computer vision* (pp. 19–91). New York: McGraw-Hill.

Witkin, A. P., & Tenenbaum, J. M. (1983). On the role of structure in vision. In J. Beck, B. Hope, & A. Rosenfeld (Eds.), *Human and machine vision* (pp. 481–543). New York: Academic Pres.

Woodworth, R. S. (1938). *Experimental psychology.* New York: Holt.

PART 4

Object and Spatial Vision

Discussion Questions

1. Mishkin et al. propose that there are two fairly independent pathways for perceiving objects and locations, respectively. At the same time, objects have spatial extent and their parts have specific spatial relations with one another (e.g., above, to the right). To what extent can the representation of objects and of space really be independent? If they are not truly independent, then is the distinction between "what and where" useful? Why or why not?

2. Biederman's Recognition by Components theory of object recognition is designed to assign basic-level category labels (e.g., "chair" or "face," not "furniture" or "my neighbor Harry") to monochrome line drawings in an otherwise empty visual field. This was admittedly a first step, but an impressive one that has not been completely displaced an alternative theory in the last 20 years, despite its limitations. In your opinion, is this a good starting place for a theory of object recognition? Can you see how one might modify it (or other structural description theories) to deal with scenes that include color, depth, and clutter and to discriminate between instances of a basic level category (e.g., two different types of chairs)?

3. How might constraints such as those discussed by Adelson and Movshon in the case of motion be used to help explain observers' ability to correctly identify ambiguous perceptual shapes in object recognition?

4. Lissauer's patient exhibited a profound inability to recognize familiar objects. Would he have been able to perform well in Shepard and Metzler's mental rotation task?

Suggested Readings

Julesz, B. (1961). Binocular depth perception of computer-generated patterns. *Bell System Technical Journal, 39*, 1125–1162.

Wheatstone C. (1838). Contributions to the physiology of vision. Part I: On some remarkable, and hitherto unobserved, phenomena of binocular vision. *Philosophical Transactions of the Royal Society of London, 128*, 371–394. Wheatstone provided a very early and surprisingly modern analysis of stereoscopic vision that led to the invention of the first stereoscope. The principles articulated by Wheatstone inspired Julesz over a century later to investigate the possibility that the correspondence problem in stereopsis is solved in early vision with much less interpretation than had been assumed.

Wallach, H., & O'Connell, D. N. (1953). The kinetic depth effect. *Journal of Experimental Psychology, 45,* 205–217.

Johansson, G. (1973). Visual perception of biological motion and a model for its analysis. *Perception & Psychophysics, 14,* 201–211. Two famous examples of perceptual organization and constancy that characterize the extraction of 3-D structure from 2-D motion. Wallach and O'Connell showed observers the shadow of a bent coat hanger on a back projection screen. Twenty years later, Johansson produced movies of people walking or dancing in the dark with small lights attached to their joints ("point-light walkers"). While static snapshots of the scene looked like random dots, the dynamic structure of the moving points permitted observers to identify them effortlessly.

Biederman, I., Glass, A. L., & Stacy, E. W. (1973). Searching for objects in real-world scenes. *Journal of Experimental Psychology, 97,* 22–27.

Palmer, S. E. (1975). The effects of contextual scenes on the identification of objects. *Memory & Cognition, 3,* 519–526. These two papers show that the context in which an object is viewed can significantly alter the speed and accuracy with which that object is identified.

Palmer, S. E., Rosch, E., & Chase, P. (1981). Canonical perspective and the perception of objects. In J. Long and A. Baddeley (Eds.), *Attention and Performance IX* (pp. 135–151). Hillsdale, NJ: Erlbaum. The authors show that for most objects there exist canonical views from which that object can be most efficiently recognized, and that other noncanonical views (e.g., seeing a horse from directly above) can seriously slow object recognition. This finding provides the empirical foothold for viewpoint-specific theories of object recognition.

Tarr, M. J., & Pinker, S. (1989). Mental rotation and orientation-dependence in shape recognition. *Cognitive Psychology, 21,* 233–282. An example of a viewpoint-dependent theory of object representation.

Bisiach, E., & Luzzatti, C. (1978). Unilateral neglect of representational space. *Cortex, 14,* 129–133. A brain-damaged patient in Milan could imagine standing on the Cathedral steps looking out over the Piazza del Duomo and recall the shops and cafés to the right but not to the left; however, if he imagined standing *facing* the Cathedral, he could recall the shops that before he did not remember and vice-versa. The authors conclude that the stroke damaged an internal representational space used for performing judgments requiring mental imagery.

Visual Attention and Awareness

Introduction to Reading 21

In a passage describing an experiment on stereoscopic depth perception, Helmholtz (1925, p. 455) noted that an observer can focus attention on a particular location in the scene without eye movements, and commented that an explanation of this phenomenon would constitute an important first step in developing a theory of attention. However, as he was concerned with other matters at that time, he did not pursue this issue himself any further. It took many decades for experimental psychologists to return in force to the problem of selective attention, although the early part of the century saw several important treatments of the subject, including most notably those of James (1890) and Tichener (1908). During the behaviorist period of the first half of 20th century, attention was virtually ignored as a "mentalist" concept that was unworthy of scientific study.

With the rise of cognitivism in the 1950s, the study of attention moved to center stage. Initial psychophysical studies suggested that attention affected only the decision-making criterion adopted by an observer, but by the early 1980s it had been established that the deployment of attention could affect perceptual performance by improving the observer's sensitivity.

Attention is at the heart of cognitive control: an observer with a behavioral goal can modulate sensory input so that only relevant or highly salient objects and events in the scene are perceived. Studies in the 1960s and 1970s established the temporal and spatial constraints on deployments of selective attention. For example, Posner, Snyder, and Davidson (1980) showed that the time required to detect the appearance of a target dot was speeded significantly when the dot appeared at a location to which the observer was attending; this finding held even when eye movements were controlled.

Although by 1980 a great deal was known about how attention could affect performance, and that attentional limitations certainly existed, there was no clear consensus about just what attention was *for*. With the publication of this article by Treisman and Gelade, an answer was offered: the purpose of attention is to solve the binding problem (although at the time, the problem was not generally known by this name; see Roskies et al., 1999).

The binding problem is a reflection of the fact that the human visual system represents visual objects and events in a modular, distributed fashion (see, e.g., Reading 9 by Zeki et al.). A vast array of studies has shown that the brain consists of a large number of functionally specialized modules. For example, most neurons in primate area MT are selective for the direction and speed of moving stimuli, but few are selective for color; the reverse is true of area V4. These functional specializations create a puzzle: how is it that we perceive objects as unitary and coherent despite the fact that the attributes of an object are represented in a distributed network across many brain areas? In other words, how does the brain bind together the attributes of objects?

Treisman and Gelade suggested a simple solution.

When binding is required, the observer can direct attention to objects one at a time (and suppress the representation of all other objects). When an object is selected, only its properties will be actively represented. Thus the momentary assembly of activated properties (color, shape, motion, orientation, etc.) all belong to the attended object. The details of this idea constitute Feature Integration Theory, and Triesman and her colleagues, in this and subsequent articles, provided significant empirical corroboration for the theory.

This paper inspired an avalanche of work throughout the 1980s and well into the 90s that sought to further examine the implications of the theory. It was learned that some of the theory's specific details were not quite right, but the foundational idea has continued to serve as the basis for ongoing theoretical developments. Wolfe and colleagues (e.g., Wolfe, Cave, and Franzell, 1989; Wolfe, 1994) developed a modified version of Feature Integration Theory that is called Guided Search. It differs from FIT in that it asserts that the deployment of attention is not random, but is influenced by the distribution of features in the scene. However, this is an advancement of rather than a replacement for, the earlier theory.

REFERENCES

Helmholtz, H. von (1925). *Treatise on physiological optics* (Vol. III). Translated and Edited by J. P. C. Southall. New York: Optical Society of America. (original work published 1910)

James, W. (1890). *Principles of Psychology.* New York: Holt.

Roskies, A. L., et al. (1999) The binding problem. *Neuron, 24,* 7–125.

Titchener (1908). *Lectures on the elementary psychology of feeling and attention.* New York: The Macmillan Company.

Wolfe, J. (1994). Guided search 2.0: A revised model of visual search. *Psychonomic Bulletin & Review, 1,* 202–238.

Wolfe, J. M., Cave, K. R., & Franzell, S. L. (1989). Guided search: An alternative to the feature integration model for visual search. *Journal of Experimental Psychology: Human Perception and Performance, 15,* 419–433.

A Feature-Integration Theory of Attention

A. M. Treisman • University of British Columbia
G. Gelade • Oxford University

A new hypothesis about the role of focused attention is proposed. The feature-integration theory of attention suggests that attention must be directed serially to each stimulus in a display whenever conjunctions of more than one separable feature are needed to characterize or distinguish the possible objects presented. A number of predictions were tested in a variety of paradigms including visual search, texture segregation, identification and localization, and using both separable dimensions (shape and color) and local elements or parts of figures (lines, curves, etc. in letters) as the features to be integrated into complex wholes. The results were in general consistent with the hypothesis. They offer a new set of criteria for distinguishing separable from integral features and a new rationale for predicting which tasks will show attention limits and which will not.

When we open our eyes on a familiar scene, we form an immediate impression of recognizable objects, organized coherently in a spatial framework. Analysis of our experience into more elementary sensations is difficult, and appears subjectively to require an unusual type of perceptual activity. In contrast, the physiological evidence suggests that the visual scene is analyzed at an early stage by specialized populations of receptors that respond selectively to such properties as orientation, color, spatial frequency, or movement, and map these properties in different areas of the brain (Zeki, 1976). The controversy between analytic and synthetic theories of perception goes back many years: the Associationists asserted that the experience of complex wholes is built by combining more elementary sensations, while the Gestalt psychologists claimed that the whole precedes its parts, that we initially register unitary objects and relationships, and only later, if necessary, analyze these objects into their component parts or properties. This view is still active now (e.g., Monahan & Lockhead, 1977; Neisser, 1967).

The Gestalt belief surely conforms to the normal subjective experience of perception. However the immediacy and directness of an impression are no guarantee that it reflects an early stage of information processing in the nervous system. It is logically possible that we become aware only of the final outcome of a complicated sequence of prior operations. "Top-down" processing may describe what we consciously experience; as a theory about perceptual coding it needs more objective support (Treisman, 1979).

We have recently proposed a new account of attention which assumes that features come first in perception (Treisman, Sykes, & Gelade, 1977). In our model, which we call the feature-integration theory of attention, features are registered early, automatically, and in parallel across the visual field, while objects are identified separately and only at a later stage, which requires focused attention. We assume that the visual scene is initially coded along a number of separable dimensions, such as color, orientation, spatial frequency, brightness, direction of movement. In order to recombine these separate representations and to ensure the correct synthesis of features for each object in a complex display, stimulus locations are processed serially with focal attention. Any features which are present in the same central "fixation" of attention are combined to form a single object. Thus focal attention provides the "glue" which integrates the initially separable features into unitary objects. Once they have been correctly registered, the compound objects continue to be perceived and stored as such. However with memory decay or interference, the features may disintegrate and "float free" once more, or perhaps recombine to form "illusory conjunctions" (Treisman, 1977).

We claim that, without focused attention, features cannot be related to each other. This poses a problem in explaining phenomenal experience. There seems to be no way we can consciously "perceive" an unattached shape without also giving it a color, size, brightness, and location. Yet unattended areas are not perceived as empty space. The integration theory therefore needs some clarification. Our claim is that attention is necessary for the *correct* perception of conjunctions, although unattended features are also conjoined prior to conscious perception. The top-down processing of unattended features is capable of utilizing past experience and contextual information. Even when attention is directed elsewhere, we are unlikely to see a blue sun in a yellow sky. However, in the absence of focused attention and of effective constraints on top-down processing, conjunctions of features could be formed on a random basis. These unattended couplings will give rise to "illusory conjunctions."

There is both behavioral and physiological evidence for the idea that stimuli are initially analyzed along functionally separable dimensions, although not necessarily by physically distinct channels (Shepard, 1964; Garner, 1974; De Valois & De Valois, 1975). We will use the term "dimension" to refer to the complete range of variation which is separately analyzed by some functionally independent perceptual subsystem, and "feature" to refer to a particular value on a dimension. Thus color and orientation are dimensions; red and vertical are features on those dimensions. Percep-

tual dimensions do not correspond uniquely to distinct physical dimensions. Some relational aspects of physical attributes may be registered as basic features; for example we code intensity contrast rather than absolute intensity, and we may even directly sense such higher-order properties as symmetry or homogeneity. We cannot predict a priori what the elementary words of the perceptual language may be. The existence of particular perceptual dimensions should be inferred from empirical criteria, such as those proposed by Shepard and by Garner. This paper will suggest several new diagnostics for the separability of dimensions, which derive from the feature-integration theory of attention. In this theory, we assume that integral features are conjoined automatically, while separable features require attention for their integration. Consequently, we can infer separability from a particular pattern of results in the preattentive and divided attention tasks to be described in this paper.

We have stated the feature-integration hypothesis in an extreme form, which seemed to us initially quite implausible. It was important, therefore, to vary the paradigms and the predictions as widely as possible, in order to maximize the gain from converging operations. We developed a number of different paradigms testing different predictions from the theory. Each experiment on its own might allow other interpretations, but the fact that all were derived as independent predictions from the same theory should allow them, if confirmed, to strengthen it more than any could individually.

(1) Visual search. The visual search paradigm allows us to define a target either by its separate features or by their conjunction. If, as we assume, simple features can be detected in parallel with no attention limits, the search for targets defined by such features (e.g., red, or vertical) should be little affected by variations in the number of distracters in the display. Lateral interference and acuity limits should be the only factors tending to increase search times as display size is increased, perhaps by forcing serial eye fixations. In contrast, we assume that focal attention is necessary for the detection of targets that are defined by a conjunction of properties (e.g., a vertical red line in a background of horizontal red and vertical green lines). Such targets should therefore be found only after a serial scan of varying numbers of distractors.

(2) Texture segregation. It seems likely that tex-

ture segregation and figure-ground grouping are preattentive, parallel processes. If so, they should be determined only by spatial discontinuities between groups of stimuli differing in separable features and not by discontinuities defined by conjunctions of features.

(3) Illusory conjunctions. If focused attention to particular objects is prevented, either because time is too short or because attention is directed to other objects, the features of the unattended objects are "free floating" with respect to one another. This allows the possibility of incorrect combinations of features when more than one unattended object is presented. Such "illusory conjunctions" have been reported. For example, the pitch and the loudness of dichotic tones are sometimes heard in the wrong combinations (Efron & Yund, 1974), and so are the distinctive features of dichotic syllables (Cutting, 1976). In vision, subjects sometimes wrongly recombine the case and the content of visual words presented successively in the same location (Lawrence, 1971). Treisman (1977) obtained a large number of false-positive errors in a successive same–different matching task when the shapes and colors of two target items were interchanged in the two test stimuli. Each such interchange also added a constant to the correct response times, suggesting that the conjunction of features was checked separately from the presence of those features.

(4) Identity and location. Again, if focused attention is prevented, the features of unattended objects may be free floating spatially, as well as unrelated to one another. Thus we may detect the presence of critical features without knowing exactly where they are located, although we can certainly home in on them rapidly. Locating a feature would, on this hypothesis, be a separate operation from identifying it, and could logically follow instead of preceding identification. However, the theory predicts that this could not occur with conjunctions of features. If we have correctly detected or identified a particular conjunction, we must first have located it in order to focus attention on it and integrate its features. Thus location must precede identification for conjunctions, but the two could be independent for features.

(5) Interference from unattended stimuli. Unattended stimuli should be registered only at the feature level. The amount of interference or facilitation with an attended task that such stimuli can generate should therefore depend only on the fea-

tures they comprise and should not be affected by the particular conjunctions in which those features occur.

There is considerable evidence in speech perception that the meaning of unattended words can sometimes be registered without reaching conscious awareness (e.g., Corteen & Wood, 1972; Lewis, 1970; MacKay, 1973; Treisman, Squire, & Green, 1974). Since words are surely defined by conjunctions, the evidence of word-recognition without attention appears to contradict our hypothesis. However, the data of these studies indicate that responses to primed and relevant words on the unattended channel occurred only on 5–30% of trials. It may be possible for a response occasionally to be triggered by one or more features of an expected word, without requiring exact specification of how these features are combined. One study has looked at false-positive responses to relevant words on an unattended channel (Forster & Govier, 1978). They found far more GSRs to words which sounded similar to the shock-associated word when these were presented on the unattended than on the attended channel. This suggests either incomplete analysis of unattended items or incomplete sensory data.

These predictions identify two clusters of results, corresponding to the perception of separable features and of conjunctions. Separable features should be detectable by parallel search; they are expected to give rise to illusory conjunctions in the absence of attention; they can be identified without necessarily being located, and should mediate easy texture segregation; they can have behavioral effects even when unattended. Conjunctions, on the other hand, are expected to require serial search; they should have no effect on performance unless focally attended; they should yield highly correlated performance in the tasks of identification and location; they should prove quite ineffective in mediating texture segregation. Our aim was to test these predictions using two dimensions, form and color, which are likely, both on physiological and on behavioral grounds, to be separable. If the predictions are confirmed, we may be able to add our tests to Garner's criteria, to form a more complete behavioral syndrome diagnostic of separable or integral dimensions. Thus, if two physical properties are integral, they should function as a single feature in our paradigms, allowing parallel search, texture segregation, and detection without localization. If on the other hand, they are separable, their conjunctions will require focused attention for accurate perception, and its absence should result in illusory conjunctions. We may then use these paradigms to diagnose less clear-cut candidates for separability, such as the components of letters or schematic faces.

The first three experiments are concerned with visual search; they compare color–shape conjunctions with disjunctive color and shape features as targets; they investigate the effects of practice and the role of feature discriminability in conjunction search, and test an alternative account in terms of similarity relations. Experiment IV explores the possibility that local elements of compound shapes (e.g., letters) also function as separable features, requiring serial search when incorrect conjunctions could be formed. Experiments V, VI, and VII are concerned with texture segregation, using colored shapes and letters as texture elements. Experiments VIII and IX explore the relation between identification and spatial localization, for targets defined by a single feature or by a conjunction.

Experiment I

In an experiment reported earlier, Treisman et al. (1977) compared search for targets specified by a single feature ("pink" in "brown" and "purple" distracters in one condition, "O" in "N" and "T" distracters in another) and for targets specified by a conjunction of features, a "pink O" (O_{pink}, in distracters O_{green}, and N_{pink}). The function relating search times to display size was flat or nonmonotonic when a single feature was sufficient to define the target, but increased linearly when a conjunction of features was required. Experiment I replicates this study with some changes in the design, to confirm and generalize the conclusions. The most important change was in the feature search condition: subjects were now asked to search concurrently for two targets, each defined by a different single feature: a color (blue) and a shape (S). Thus they were forced to attend to both dimensions in the feature condition as well as in the conjunction condition, although they had to check how the features were combined only when the target was a conjunction (T_{green}). The distractors were identical in the two conditions (X_{green} and T_{brown}), to ensure that differences between feature and conjunction search could not result from greater heterogeneity of the distracters in the con-

junction condition. (This had been a possibility in the previous experiment.)

Another question which has become important in evaluating information-processing hypotheses is how stably they apply across different stages of practice. Neisser, Novick, and Lazar (1963), Rabbitt (1967), and Shiffrin and Schneider (1977) have all shown qualitative changes in performance as subjects repeatedly perform a particular task. Search appears to change from conscious, limited capacity, serial decision making to automatic, fast, and parallel detection. LaBerge (1973) studied the effects of practice on priming in a visual successive matching task. He found that familiarity with the stimuli eventually made matching independent of expectancy, and suggested that this was due to unitization of the features of highly familiar stimuli. We propose that feature unitization may account also for the change with practice from serial to parallel processing in a display, in conditions in which such a change occurs. Thus the development of new unitary detectors for what were previously conjunctions of features would free us from the constraints of focal attention to these features both in memory and in a physically present display. Experiment I explored the possibility that extended practice on a particular shape–color conjunction (T_{green}) could lead to a change from serial to parallel detection, which would suggest the possible emergence of a unitary "green T" detector.

Method

STIMULI

The stimulus displays were made by hand, using letter stencils and colored inks on white cards. The distracters were scattered over the card in positions which appeared random, although no systematic randomization procedure was used. Four different display sizes, consisting of 1, 5, 15, and 30 items were used in each condition. An area subtending $14 \times 8°$ was used for all display sizes, so that the displays with fewer items were less densely packed, but the average distance from the fovea was kept approximately constant. Each letter subtended $0.8 \times 0.6°$. To ensure that the target locations did not vary systematically across conditions, the area of each card was divided into eight sections. This was done by superimposing a tracing of the two diagonals and an inner elliptical boundary, which subtended $8.5° \times 5.5°$. For each condition and each display size, eight cards were made, one with a target randomly placed in each of the resulting eight areas (top outer, top inner, left outer, left inner, right outer, etc.). Another eight cards in each condition and display size contained no target.

The distracters in both conditions were T_{brown} and X_{green} in as near equal numbers on each card as possible. The target in the conjunction condition was T_{green}; in the feature condition, it was either a blue letter or an S. The blue letter (T_{blue} or X_{green}) matched half the distracters in shape, and the S (S_{brown} or S_{green}) matched half the distracters in color. The fact that there were four possible disjunctive targets in the feature condition (although the definition specified only "blue or S"), should, if anything, impair performance relative to the conjunction condition.

PROCEDURE

The stimulus cards were presented in an Electronics Development three-field tachistoscope and RT was recorded as described below.

At the beginning of each trial, subjects viewed a plain white card in the tachistoscope, and each of their index fingers rested on a response key. The experimenter gave a verbal "Ready" signal and pressed a button to display a second white card bearing a central fixation spot, which remained in view for 1 sec and was then immediately replaced in the field of view by a card bearing a search array. Subjects were instructed to make a key press with the dominant hand if they detected a target and with the nondominant hand otherwise, and to respond as quickly as possible without making any errors. RT was recorded to the nearest millisecond on a digital timer [Advance Electronics, TC11], which was triggered by the onset of the search array and stopped when a response key was pressed. Trials on which an error was made were repeated later in the testing session, and following each error a dummy trial was given, the results of which were not recorded. Subjects were told their RT and whether or not they were correct after each trial; they were not however informed of the dummy trials procedure, the purpose of which was to exclude slow posterror responses from the data.

Each subject was tested both on conjunctions and on features in separate sessions following an ABBAAB order. Half the subjects began with the feature targets and half with the conjunction tar-

gets. Six subjects did 3 blocks of 128 trials each in each condition, then two of these subjects volunteered to continue for another 4 blocks in the conjunction condition and two for another 10 blocks, making 13 altogether (a total of 1664 trials). The mean RTs for these two subjects on the first 3 blocks closely approximated the group means.

Within each block the presentation order of positive and negative trials and of different display sizes was randomized; thus in each block the subject knew what the target or the two alternative targets were, but did not know what the array size would be on any given trial. Each block contained 16 positive and 16 negative trials for each display size.

SUBJECTS

The six subjects, four men and two women, were members of the Oxford Subject Panel, ages between 24 and 29. Three of them had previously taken part in the search experiment described in Treisman et al. (1977).

Results

Figure 21.1 shows the mean search times for the six subjects over the second and third blocks in each condition; the first block was treated as practice. Table 1 gives the details of linear regression analyses on these data. The results show that search time increased linearly with display size in the conjunction condition, the linear component accounting for more than 99% of the variance due to display size. The ratio of the positive to the negative slopes in the conjunction condition was 0.43, which is quite close to half. These results suggest that search is serial and self-terminating with a scanning rate of about 60 msec per item. The variances increased more steeply for positive than for negative trials, and for positives the root mean square of the RTs increased linearly with display size as predicted for serial self-terminating search.

With the feature targets, the results were very different. For the positive displays, search times were hardly affected by the number of distracters, the slopes averaging only 3.1 msec. Deviations from linearity were significant, and the linear component accounted for only 68% of the variance due to display size. For the negatives, the linear component accounted for 96% of the variance due to

SEARCH FOR COLORED SHAPES

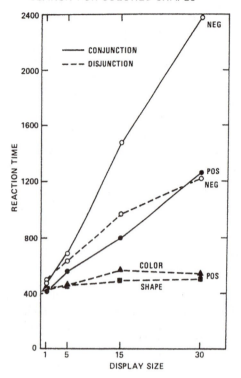

FIGURE 21.1 ■ Search Times in Experiment I.

display size, and departures from linearity did not reach significance. The slope was, however, less than half the slope for conjunction negatives. The ratio of positive to negative slopes with feature targets was only 0.12. In both conditions, all subjects showed the same pattern of results, with individuals varying mainly in the absolute values of slopes and intercepts.

Errors in the feature condition averaged 2.2% false positives and 2.1% false negatives; for the conjunction condition there were 0.8% false positives and 4.9% false negatives. There were no systematic effects of display size on errors, except that false negatives in the conjunction condition were higher for display size 30 than for 15, 5, or 1 (8.2% compared to 3.8%). The highest mean error rate for an individual subject was 5.5% in the conjunction condition and 3.5% in the feature condition.

It is important to the theory that the difference between conjunction and feature conditions is present only when more than one stimulus is presented. The mean positive RT for display size 1 was 422 msec for the conjunction targets, compared to 426 msec for shape and 446 msec for color in the feature condition. The negatives with display size 1 were also faster in the conjunction than in the feature conditions, 473 msec compared to 500 msec. Thus the difficulty of search for conjunctions arises only when more than one stimulus is presented.

The effects of practice on conjunction search are shown in Fig. 21.2. The positive slopes and intercepts decrease over the first 7 blocks and change little for the remaining 6 blocks. The negative slopes fluctuate across the first 9 blocks and stabilize at block 10. Both positive and negative slopes remained linear throughout: the proportion of the variance with display size that was due to linearity was above 0.99 in every block except

TABLE 21.1. Linear Regressions of Reaction Times on Display Size in Experiment I

		Slope	Intercept	Percentage variance with display size which is due to linearity
Conjunction	Positives	28.7	398	99.7
	Negatives	67.1	397	99.6
Feature mean	Positives	3.1	448	67.9[a]
	Negatives	25.1	514	96.6
Feature color	Positive	3.8	455	61.0[a]
Feature shape	Positive	2.5	441	78.5

[a]Cases where deviations from linearity are significant at $p < .01$. The positive shape feature also deviates considerably from linearity, but the significance level here is only .08.

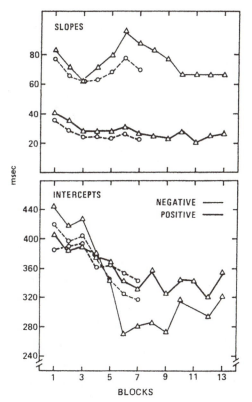

FIGURE 21.2 ■ The effects of practice on the slope and intercept of the function relating search time to display size. (The dotted lines are the data for the four subjects who did 7 sessions and the solid lines for the two subjects who continued for 13 sessions.)

positive blocks 3 and 12, when it was 0.98 and 0.97, respectively. Thus there is little indication of any change in the pattern of results and no sign of a switch from serial to parallel search over the 13 blocks of practice. The mean results for the two subjects who volunteered for this extensive practice were typical of the group as a whole on blocks 2 and 3 (negative and positive slopes of 67 and 31, respectively, compared to the group means of 67 and 29; intercepts 423 and 389 compared to 397 and 398).

Discussion

We suggested that focal attention, scanning successive locations serially, is the means by which the correct integration of features into multidimensional percepts is ensured. When this integration is not required by the task, parallel detection of features should be possible. The results, especially on positive trials, fit these predictions well. Despite the major changes in the feature search condition between this experiment and the earlier one (Treisman et al., 1977), the results are almost identical. The requirement to search for values on two different dimensions instead of one on each trial produced no qualitative and almost no quantitative change in performance; neither did the greater heterogeneity of the distractors. In both experiments the display was apparently searched spatially in parallel whenever targets could be detected on the basis of a single feature, either color or shape. Another important difference between the conjunction and the feature conditions is the difference in the relation between positive and negative displays. The slope for conjunction positives is about half the slope for the negatives, suggesting a serial self-terminating search. In the feature condition, however, the slope ratio is only 1/8, and the function is linear only for the negatives. This suggests that with single feature targets, a qualitatively different process may mediate the responses to positive and to negative displays. If the target is present, it is detected automatically; if it is not, subjects tend to scan the display, although they may not check item by item in the strictly serial way they do in conjunction search.

Practice for up to 13 sessions on the same target and distracters produced no qualitative changes in performance in conjunction search, no decrease in linearity, and no systematic decrease in either slope or intercept after about the seventh session. We had been interested in seeing whether practice could lead to unitization, in the sense of developing a special detector for the conjunction of green and "T," which could allow a change to parallel search. It is of course possible that longer practice, different stimuli, or a different training method could result in a change to parallel search. The present experiment, however suggests that unitization of color and shape is difficult and may be impossible to achieve. There may be built-in neural constraints on which dimensions can be unitized in this way.

Experiment II

The next experiment explores the relation between the discriminability of the features which define a conjunction and the speed of detecting that conjunction as a target in a display. If each item must be scanned serially in order to determine how its features are conjoined, it should be possible to change the slope relating search time to display size, by slowing the decision about the features composing each item. Thus by making the two shapes and the two colors in a conjunction search easier or harder to distinguish, we should be able to change the rate of scanning while retaining the characteristic serial search pattern of linear slopes and the 2/1 ratio of negative to positive slopes. We compared search for a conjunction target in distracters which were similar to each other (T_{green} in X_{green} and T_{blue}) and in distracters which differed maximally from each other (O_{red} in O_{green} and N_{red}). The decisions whether each item had the target color and the target shape should be easier for O versus N and red versus green than for T versus X and green versus blue. (We chose green and blue inks which were very similar to each other.)

A second question we investigated in this experiment was whether the previous results depended on the haphazard spatial arrangement of the items in the display. In this experiment, the letters were arranged in regular matrices of 2×2, 4×4, and 6×6. The mean distance of the letters from the fixation point was equated, so that density again covaried with display size, but acuity was again approximately matched for each condition.

Method

SUBJECTS

Six subjects (three females and three males) volunteered for the experiment which involved a test and re-test session. They were students and employees of the University of British Columbia ages between 16 and 45. They were paid $3.00 a session for their participation.

APPARATUS

A two-field Cambridge tachistoscope connected to a millisecond timer was used. The stimuli consisted, as before, of white cards with colored letters. Displays contained 1, 4, 16, or 36 items. The letters were arranged in matrices of 2×2, 4×4, or 6×6 positions. For the displays of 1 item each of the positions in the 2×2 matrix was used equally often. The 6×6 display subtended $12.3 \times 9.7°$;

the 4×4 matrix subtended $9.7 \times 9.7°$ and the 2×2 matrix subtended $7 \times 7°$. The mean distance of items from the fixation point was about $4.3°$ for all displays. Sixteen different cards, of which 8 contained a target, were made for each display size in each condition. In the easy condition, the distracters were O_{green} and N_{red} and the target was O_{red}. In the difficult condition, the distracters were T_{blue} and X_{green} and the target was T_{green}. The target was presented twice in each display position for the displays of 1 and 4, in half the display positions for displays of 16 (twice in each row and twice in each column), and twice in each 3×3 quadrant for the displays of 36.

Results

Figure 21.3 shows the mean RTs in each condition. The details of the linear regressions are given in Table 2. None of the slopes deviates significantly from linearity, which accounts for more than 99.8% of the variance due to display size in every case. The ratio of positive to negative slopes is 0.52 for the easy stimuli and 0.60 for the difficult ones. The slopes in the difficult discrimination are nearly three times larger than those in the easy discrimination, but the linearity and the 2/1 slope ratio is preserved across these large differences. The intercepts do not differ significantly across conditions.

Error rates were higher in the difficult discrimination condition. Two subjects were dropped from the experiment because they were unable to keep their false-negative errors in the large positive displays in this condition below 30%. For the remaining subjects, errors averaged 5.3% for the difficult discrimination and 2.5% for the easy discrimination. They were not systematically related to display size except that the difficult positive displays of 16 and 36 averaged 5.9 and 20.7% false-negative errors, respectively, compared to a mean of 2.2% errors for all other displays.

Discussion

In both conditions we have evidence supporting serial, self-terminating search through the display for the conjunction targets. The slopes are linear and the positives give approximately half the slope of the negatives. However, the rates vary dramatically: The more distinctive colors and shapes allow search to proceed nearly three times as fast as

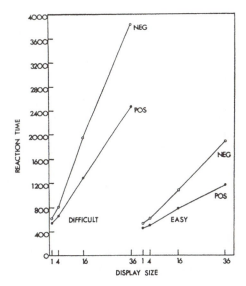

FIGURE 21.3 ■ Search Times in Experiment II.

the less distinctive. The mean scanning rate of 62 msec per item obtained in the conjunction condition of Experiment I lies between the rates obtained here with the confusable stimuli and with the highly discriminable stimuli. This wide variation in slopes, combined with maintained linearity and 2/1 slope ratios, is consistent with the theory, and puts constraints on alternative explanations. For example, we can no longer suppose that search becomes serial only when it is difficult. The need for focused attention to each item in turn must be induced by something other than overall load. The fact that the intercepts were the same for the easy and the difficult conditions is also consistent with the theory.

Experiment I used pseudo-random locations for the targets and distractors. The present experiment extends the conclusions to displays in which the stimuli are arranged in a regular matrix. The se-

rial scan is therefore not induced by any artifact of the locations selected or by their haphazard arrangement [. . .]

General Conclusions

The experiments have tested most of the predictions we made and their results offer converging evidence for the feature-integration theory of attention. While any one set of data, taken alone, could no doubt be explained in other ways, the fact that all were derived from one theory and tested in a number of different paradigms should lend them more weight when taken together than any individual finding would have on its own.

To summarize the conclusions: it seems that we can detect and identify separable features in parallel across a display (within the limits set by acuity, discriminability, and lateral interference); that this early, parallel, process of feature registration mediates texture segregation and figure-ground grouping; that locating any individual feature requires an additional operation; that if attention is diverted or overloaded, illusory conjunctions may occur (Treisman et al., 1977). Conjunctions, on the other hand, require focal attention to be directed serially to each relevant location; they do not mediate texture segregation, and they cannot be identified without also being spatially localized. The results offer a new set of criteria for determining which features are perceptually "separable," which may be added to the criteria listed by Garner. It will be important to see whether they converge on the same candidates for unitary features, the basic elements of the perceptual language.

The findings also suggest a convergence between two perceptual phenomena—parallel detection of visual targets and perceptual grouping or

TABLE 21.2. Linear Regressions of Search Times against Display Size in Experiment II

		Slope	Intercept	Percentage variance with display size which is due to linearity
Difficult discrimination	Positives	55.1	453	99.8
	Negatives	92.4	472	99.9
Easy discrimination	Positives	20.5	437	99.8
	Negatives	39.5	489	99.9

segregation. Both appear to depend on a distinction at the level of separable features. Neither requires focal attention, so both may precede its operation. This means that both could be involved in the control of attention. The number of items receiving focal attention at any moment of time can vary. Visual attention, like a spotlight or zoom lens, can be used over a small area with high resolution or spread over a wider area with some loss of detail (Eriksen & Hoffman, 1972). We can extend the analogy in the present context to suggest that attention can either be narrowed to focus on a single feature, when we need to see what other features are present and form an object, or distributed over a whole group of items which share a relevant feature. Our hypothesis is that illusory conjunctions occur either outside the spotlight of focal attention, or within it, if the spotlight happens to contain interchangeable features (e.g., more than one color and more than one shape), but they will not occur across its boundary. It follows that search for a conjunction target could be mediated by a serial scan of *groups* of items rather than individual items, whenever the display contains groups of items among which no illusory conjunctions can form. In a display divided into 15 red Os on the left and 15 blue Xs on the right, we are very unlikely to scan serially through each of the 30 items to find a blue O, even though it is a conjunction target. We may need to focus attention only twice in order to exclude the risk of illusory conjunctions. By treating each half of the display separately, we can convert the task into two successive feature search tasks, for blue on the left and for O on the right. The time taken should therefore be no longer than the time taken to search through just two items.

This discussion, however, raises a further question, since in a sense the conjunction results are paradoxical. The problem they pose is that any conjunction search could, in principle, be achieved by two parallel feature checks, one selecting, for example, all the green items and the second checking these for the presence of a T. Results with the disjunctive feature targets suggest that either of these operations should be possible without serial processing or focal attention. We have to explain, therefore, why the two operations cannot be applied to all relevant items in parallel when combined. Presumably the reason is that attention cannot be focused simultaneously on a number of different locations, when these are interleaved with

other locations to be excluded. Kahneman and Henik (1977) showed that subjects were much worse at reporting the red letters in a mixed display of red and blue letters when these were alternated in a checkerboard arrangement then when they were spatially separated into homogeneous groups. This suggests that selective attention to particular sets of items (e.g., all red items) must be mediated by attention to their spatial locations and cannot be directly controlled by their color. Moreover, there must be limits to the number and perhaps the complexity of the spatial areas on which the "spotlight" of attention can be simultaneously focused. The nature of these limits needs clarification; they could be set by simple parameters such as a requirement that the area be bounded by convex or straight edges, or by more complex Gestalt properties, such as symmetry or good continuation.

What problems does the integration model raise for our everyday perception of objects, complex scenes, words, and sentences in reading? Can we reconcile our theory with the apparent speed and richness of information processing that we constantly experience? Perhaps this richness at the level of objects or scenes is largely an informed hallucination. We can certainly register a rich array of features in parallel, and probably do this along a number of dimensions at once. But if we apply more stringent tests to see how accurate and detailed we are in putting features together without prior knowledge or redundancy in the scene, the results are much less impressive (e.g. Biederman, Glass, & Stacy, 1973; Rock, Halper, & Clayton, 1972).

It is of interest to note that some patients with visual agnosia appear to have difficulties specifically in assembling the different components or properties of objects. For example, one patient (Critchley, 1964) described his difficulty as follows: "At first I saw the front part—it looked like a fountain pen. Then it looked like a knife because it was so sharp, but I thought it could not be a knife because it was green. Then I saw the spokes . . . " etc. Another patient commented "Previously I'd have said 'well, of course that's a carnation—no doubt about it—it's quite evident. Now I recognize it in a more scientific fashion. To get it right I've got to assemble it.'" Gardner (1975) proposes an account of one type of agnosia, which seems closely related to the feature integration hypothesis: he says "if we assume that the ability to recognize configurations such as faces and objects requires the integration over a brief interval of a number of visual elements, then an impairment in simultaneous synthesis—in the capacity to pull the relevant elements together into a coherent unity—would be sufficient to explain the disorder." The suggestion in fact goes back to Liepmann's "disjunctive agnosia" (1908), which he believed resulted from the "fractionation of representations into primary elements" (Hecaen & Albert, 1978). Finally, Luria's account (1972) of "the man with the shattered mind" suggests a defect in retaining conjunctions in memory as well as in perception. His patient says "I'm in a kind of fog all the time, like a heavy half-sleep. Whatever I do remember is scattered, broken down into disconnected bits and pieces."

To conclude: the feature-integration theory suggests that we become aware of unitary objects, in two different ways—through focal attention, or through top-down processing. We may not know on any particular occasion which has occurred, or which has contributed most to what we see. In normal conditions, the two routes operate together, but in extreme conditions we may be able to show either of the two operating almost independently of the other. The first route to object identification depends on focal attention, directed serially to different locations, to integrate the features registered within the same spatio-temporal "spotlight" into a unitary percept. This statement is of course highly oversimplified; it begs many questions, such as how we deal with spatially overlapping objects and how we register the relationships between features which distinguish many otherwise identical objects. These problems belong to a theory of object recognition and are beyond the scope of this paper.

The second way in which we may "identify" objects, when focused attention is prevented by brief exposure or overloading, is through top-down processing. In a familiar context, likely objects can be predicted. Their presence can then be checked by matching their disjunctive features to those in the display, without also checking how they are spatially conjoined. If the context is misleading, this route to object recognition should give rise to errors; but in the highly redundant and familiar environments in which we normally operate, it should seldom lead us astray. When the environment is less predictable or the task requires conjunctions to be specified, we are in fact typically much less efficient. Searching for a face, even as familiar as one's own child in a school photograph, can be a painstakingly serial process and focused attention is certainly recommended in proof reading and instrument monitoring.

REFERENCES

Biederman, I., Glass, A. L., & Stacy, E. W. (1973). Searching for objects in real-world scenes. *Journal of Experimental Psychology, 97,* 22–27.

Corteen, R. S., & Wood, B. (1972). Autonomic responses to shock-associated words in an unattended channel. *Journal of Experimental Psychology, 94,* 308–313.

Critchley, M. (1964). The problem of visual agnosia. *Journal of Neurological Sciences, 1,* 274–290.

Cutting, J. E. (1976). Auditory and linguistic processes in speech perception: Inferences from six fusions in dichotic listening. *Psychological Review, 83,* 114–140.

De Valois, R. L., & De Valois, K. K. (1975). Neural coding of color. In E. C. Carterette & M. P. Friedman (Eds.), *Handbook of perception* (Vol. V.pp. 117–166). New York: Academic Press.

Efron, R., & Yund, E. W. (1974). Dichotic competition of simultaneous tone bursts of different frequency. I. Dissociation of pitch from lateralization and loudness. *Neuropsychologia, 12,* 149–156.

Eriksen, C. W. W., & Hoffman, J. E. (1972). Temporal and spatial characteristics of selective encoding from visual displays. *Perception and Psychophysics, 12,* 201–204.

Forster, P. M., & Govier, E. (1978). Discrimination without awareness. *Quarterly Journal of Experimental Psychology, 30,* 289–296.

Gardner, H. (1975). *The shattered mind.* New York: Alfred A. Knopf.

Garner, W. R. (1974). *The processing of information and structure.* Potomac, MD: Lawrence Erlbaum.

Hacean, H., & Albert, M. L. (1978). *Human neuropsychology.* New York: Wiley.

Kahneman, D., & Henik, A. (1977). Effects of visual grouping on immediate recall and selective attention. In S. Dornic (Ed.), *Attention and performance VI,* pp. 307–332. Hillsdale, NJ: Lawrence Erlbaum.

LaBerge, D. (1973). Attention and the measurement of perceptual learning. *Memory and Cognition, 1,* 268–276.

Lawrence, D. H. (1971). Two studies of visual search for word targets with controlled rates of presentation. *Perception and Psychophysics, 10,* 85–89.

Lewis, J. L. (1970). Semantic processing of unattended messages using dichotic listening. *Journal of Experimental Psychology, 85,* 225–228.

Liepmann, H. (1908). Uber die agnostischen Storungen. *Neurologisches Zentralblat, 27,* 609–617.

Luria, A. R. (1972). *The man with a shattered world.* New York: Basic Books.

MacKay, D. G. (1973). Aspects of the theory of comprehension, memory and attention. *Quarterly Journal of Experimental Psychology, 25,* 22–40.

Monahan, J. S., & Lockhead, G. R. (1977). Identification of integral stimuli. *Journal of Experimental Psychology: General, 106,* 94–110.

Neisser, U., Novick, R., & Lazar, R. (1963). Searching for

ten targets simultaneously. *Perceptual and Motor Skills, 17,* 955–961.

Rabbitt, P. M. A. (1967). Learning to ignore irrelevant information. *British Journal of Psychology, 55,* 403–414.

Rock. I., Halper, F., & Clayton, R. (1972). The perception and recognition of complex figures. *Cognitive Psychology, 3,* 655–673.

Shepard, R. N. (1964). Attention and the metric structure of the stimulus space. *Journal of Mathematical Psychology, 1,* 54–87.

Shiffrin, R. M., & Schneider, W. C. (1977). Controlled and automatic human information processing. II. Perceptual learning, automatic attending and a general theory. *Psychological Review, 84,* 127–190.

Treisman, A. (1977). Focused attention in the perception and retrieval of multidimensional stimuli. *Perception and Psychophysics, 22,* 1–11.

Treisman, A. (1979). The psychological reality of levels of processing. In L. S. Cermak & F. I. M. Craik (Eds.), *Levels of processing and human memory*. Hillsdale, NJ: Lawrence Erlbaum.

Treisman, A., Squire, E., & Green, J. (1974). Semantic processing in dichotic listening? A replication. *Memory and Cognition, 2,* 641–646.

Treisman, A., Sykes, M., & Gelade, G. (1977). Selective attention and stimulus integration. In S. Dornic (Ed.), *Attention and performance VI,* pp. 333–361. Hillsdale, NJ: Lawrence Erlbaum.

Zeki, S. M. (1976). The functional organization of projections from striate to prestriate visual cortex in the rhesus monkey. *Cold Spring Harbor Symposia on Quantitative Biology, 15,* 591–600.

Introduction to Readings 22 and 23

The account of attention offered by Treisman and Gelade (Reading 21) was based on the notion that somewhere in the visual system is a mechanism that is capable of selecting one object and ignoring all others so that the object features could be correctly integrated. This idea had been inspired in part by the studies of Hubel and Wiesel (Reading 7) and others that provided evidence for separate "feature maps" in visual cortex that each represented a different perceptual dimension such as color, orientation, and motion; such a visual system requires a mechanism for solving the binding problem. However, by the mid-1980s, the neural basis of this selective mechanism was unclear. There had been a few early studies revealing something of the neural basis of selection (e.g., Hernandez-Peon et al., 1955, in the auditory system; Lynch et al., 1977, in vision). However, little was known about just how attentional modulation of the sensory input took place.

Among the most persistent of these unanswered questions was *where* in the stream of visual information processing selection occurs. According to the early-selection account of Donald Broadbent (1958), there is an early "filter" that selects objects on the basis of simple visual features such as location or color. Attended items are permitted to pass through the filter to be identified and categorized, and everything else is rejected. Late-selection accounts (e.g., Deutsch & Deutsch, 1963) held instead that most sensory input reaches a quite high level of perceptual analysis (including identification), and that it is not until some action must be made (e.g., reaching for or naming an object) that attentional selection takes place. This debate raged for at least 25 years (and some would say it has not yet been fully resolved).

The experiment of Moran & Desimone provides strong neurophysiological evidence, however, for early selection. The attentional modulation of the neural response in area V4 reported in their article is clear. This may not be the opaque filter envisioned by Broadbent, but it bears a strong similarity to the attenuation mechanism proposed by Treisman (1969).

Many subsequent experiments have confirmed that other cortical regions are subject to atten-tional modulations (e.g., Motter, 1993; Treue & Maunsell, 1996). The view of attention that is emerging from results like these is one of "biased competition" (Desimone & Duncan, 1995). When a cell's receptive field contains both an effective or preferred stimulus and another, nonprefer-red stimulus, the response of the cell is suppressed to some extent compared to its response when the effective stimulus is presented alone. This suppression is a result of competi-tion between neural representations that is mediated by inhibitory connections between cells within a visual area. By directing attention to the relevant stimulus (which is implemented via a feedback signal from "higher" brain areas such as the prefrontal cortex), the strength of the cell's response can be returned to the level it achieved when there was only a single stimulus in the receptive field (Reynolds, Chelazzi, & Desimone, 1999).

The experiments reported by O'Craven and colleagues provide further evidence for attentional modulation of an early sensory area, but now in humans. In the dozen years that elapsed between the studies of Moran and Desimone and O'Craven et al., new neuroimaging technologies emerged that greatly accelerated the growth of the emerging discipline of cognitive neuroscience. Functional magnetic resonance imaging (fMRI) is a close cousin to the more established technique of positron emission tomography (see Reading 9 by Zeki et al.). fMRI provides spatially detailed images of brain activity during the performance of cognitive and perceptual tasks by imaging blood oxygenation level dependent (or BOLD) MRI contrast. That the BOLD signal is available to localize neural activity is an accident of nature: deoxygenated hemoglobin happens to have paramagnetic properties that can be measured using MRI. It offers two advantages over PET: first, fMRI does not require the use of a radioactive contrast agent, and so it is safer to use than PET; second, fMRI offers better temporal and spatial resolution than does PET.

O'Craven and colleagues applied this technology to investigate the deployment of attention in vision. The study exploited the modularity of the visual brain. Area MT can easily and selectively be activated by a stimulus containing motion. The question was whether the magnitude of the response in MT depended on the observer's attentive state. The very clear answer was that it does, a finding that extended to humans the related observation by Treue and Maunsell (1996) using single-cell recording in monkey. This study is important not only in revealing functional specialization in the human brain, but also for showing that even when no overt response is made, changes in brain state can be measured to reveal something of its function. Several more studies are reviewed by Kastner and Ungerlieder (2000).

REFERENCES

Broadbent, D. E. (1958). *Perception and communication*. New York: Pergamon Press.

Moran, R., & Duncan, J. (1995). Neural mechanisms of se-lective visual attention. *Annual Review of Neuroscience, 18,* 193–222.

Deutsch, J. A., & Deutsch, D. (1963). Attention: Some theo-retical considerations. *Psychological Review, 70,* 80–90.

Hernandez-Peon, R., Scherrer, H., & Jouvet, M. (1955). Modi-fication of electric activity in cochlear nucleus during "At-tention" in unanesthetized cats. *Science, 123,* 331–332.

Kastner, S., & Ungerleider, L. G. (2000). Mechanisms of vi-sual attention in the human cortex. *Annual Review of Neu-roscience, 23,* 315–341.

Lynch, J. C., Mountcastle, V. B., Talbot, W. H., & Yin, T. C. T. (1977). Parietal lobe mechanisms for directed visual atten-tion. *Journal of Neurophysiology, 40,* 362–389.

Motter, B. C. (1993). Focal attention produces spatially se-lective processing in visual cortical areas V1, V2, and V4 in the presence of competing stimuli. *Journal of Neuro-physiology, 70,* 909–919.

Reynolds, J. H., Chelazzi, L., Desimone, R. (1999). Com-petitive mechanisms subserve attention in macaque areas V2 and V4. *Journal of Neuroscience, 19,* 1736–1753.

Treue, S., & Maunsell, J. H. R. (1996). Attentional modula-tion of visual motion processing in cortical areas MT and MST. *Nature, 382,* 539–541.

Triesman, A. (1969). Strategies and models of selective at-tention. *Psychological Review, 76,* 282–299.

Selective Attention Gates Visual Processing in the Extrastriate Cortex

J. Moran and R. Desimone • National Institute of Mental Health

Single cells were recorded in the visual cortex of monkeys trained to attend to stimuli at one location in the visual field and ignore stimuli at another. When both locations were within the receptive field of a cell in prestriate area V4 or the inferior temporal cortex, the response to the unattended stimulus was dramatically reduced. Cells in the striate cortex were unaffected by attention. The filtering of irrelevant information from the receptive fields of extrastriate neurons may underlie the ability to identify and remember the properties of a particular object out of the many that may be represented on the retina.

Our retinas are constantly stimulated by a welter of shapes, colors, and textures. Since we are aware of only a small amount of this information at any one moment, most of it must be filtered out centrally. This filtering cannot easily be explained by the known properties of the visual system. In primates, the visual recognition of objects depends on the transmission of information from the striate cortex (V1) through prestriate areas into the inferior temporal (IT) cortex (1). At each successive stage along this pathway there is an increase in the size of the receptive fields; that is, neurons respond to stimuli throughout an increasingly large portion of the visual field. Within these large receptive fields will typically fall several different stimuli. Thus, paradoxically, more rather than less information appears to be processed by single neurons at each successive stage. How, then, does the visual system limit processing of unwanted stimuli? The results of our recording experiments on single neurons in the visual cortex of trained monkeys indicate that unwanted information is filtered from the receptive fields of neurons in the extrastriate cortex as a result of selective attention.

The general strategy of the experiment was as follows. After isolating a cell, we first determined its receptive field while the monkey fixated on a small target. On the basis of the cell's response to bars of various colors, orientations, and sizes, we determined which stimuli were effective in driving the cell and which were ineffective. Effective stimuli were then presented at one location in the receptive field concurrently with ineffective stimuli at a second location. The monkey was trained on a task that required it to attend to the stimuli at one location but ignore the stimuli at the other. After a block of 8 or 16 trials, the monkey was cued to switch its attention to the other location. Although the stimuli at the two locations remained the same, the locus of the animal's attention was repeatedly switched between the two locations. Since the identical sensory conditions were maintained in the two types of blocks, any difference in the response of the cell could be attributed to the effects of attention.

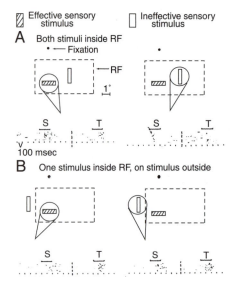

A Both stimuli inside RF

B One stimulus inside RF, on stimulus outside

FIGURE 22.1 ■ Effect of Selective Attention on the Responses of a Neuron in Prestriate Area V4. (A) Responses when the monkey attended to one location inside the receptive field (RF) and ignored another. At the attended location (circled), two stimuli (sample and test) were presented sequentially and the monkey responded differently depending on whether they were the same or different. Irrelevant stimuli were presented simultaneously with the sample and test but in a separate location in the receptive field. In the initial mapping of the receptive field, the cell responded well to horizontal and vertical red bars placed anywhere in the receptive field but not all to green bars of any orientation. Horizontal or vertical red bars (effective sensory stimuli) were then placed at one location in the field and horizontal or vertical green bars (ineffective stimuli) at another. The responses shown are to horizontal red and vertical bars but are not representative of the responses to the other stimulus pairings. When the animal attended to the location of the effective stimulus at the time of presentation of either the sample (S) or the test (T), the cell gave a good response (left), but when the animal attended to the location of the ineffective stimulus, the cell gave almost no response (right), even though the effective stimulus was present in its receptive field. Thus the responses of the cell were determined by the attended stimulus. Because of the random delay between the sample and test stimulus presentations, the rasters were synchronized separately at the onsets of the sample and test stimuli (indicated by the vertical dashed lines). (B) Same stimuli as in (A), but the ineffective stimulus was placed outside the receptive field. The neuron responded similarly to the effective sensory stimulus, regardless of which location was attended.

The task used to focus the animal's attention on a particular location was a modified version of a "match-to-sample" task. While the monkey held a bar and gazed at the fixation spot, a sample stimulus appeared briefly at one location followed about 500 msec later by a brief test stimulus at the same location. When the test stimulus was identical to the preceding sample, the animal was rewarded with a drop of water if it released the bar immediately, whereas when the test stimulus differed from the sample the animal was rewarded only if it delayed release for 700 msec. Stimuli were presented at the unattended location at the times of presentation of the sample and test stimuli, affording two opportunities to observe the effects of attention on each trial (2).

We recorded from 74 visually responsive cells in prestriate area V4 of two rhesus monkeys and found that the locus of the animal's attention in a cell's receptive field had a dramatic effect on the cell's response (Fig. 22.1A). When an effective and an ineffective sensory stimulus were present in a cell's receptive field, and the animal attended to the effective stimulus, the cell responded well. When the animal attended to the ineffective stimulus, however, the response was greatly attenuated, even though the effective (but ignored) sensory stimulus was simultaneously present in the receptive field. Thus when there were two stimuli in the receptive field the response of the cell was determined by the properties of the attended stimulus.

To characterize the magnitude of the attenuation, an attenuation index (AI) was derived for each cell by dividing the response (minus baseline) to an effective stimulus when it was being ignored by the response to the same stimulus when it was being attended. For the large majority of cells in V4, the outcome of ignoring an effective sensory stimulus in the receptive field was to reduce the response by more than half (median AI, 0.36 for the sample stimulus and 0.33 for the test) (Fig. 22.2A).

In the design described, the effective stimuli at one location in the receptive field always differed in some sensory quality, such as color, from the ineffective stimuli at the other location. Thus attenuation of the response to an ignored stimulus could have been based on either its location or its sensory qualities. For example, for the cell described in the legend to Fig. 22.1, effective horizontal or vertical red bars were presented at one location while ineffective horizontal or vertical

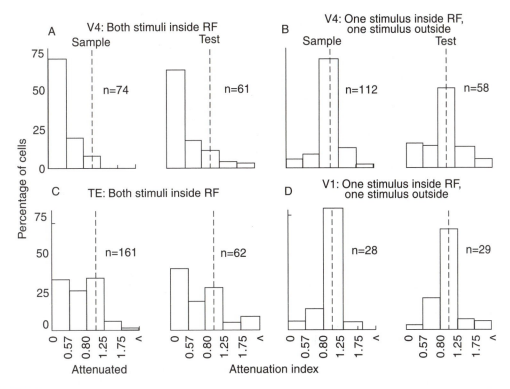

FIGURE 22.2 ■ Comparison of Effect of Attention in Area V4 (A and B), the IT Cortex (C), and the Striate Cortex (V1) (D). An attenuation index (AI) for each cell was calculated by first subtracting its baseline firing rate from the responses to the sample and test stimuli. The response to stimuli when ignored were then divided by responses to the same stimuli when attended. AI values less than 1 (dashed line) indicate that responses were reduced when a stimulus was ignored. The number of cells is indicated by *n*. For a few cells, irrelevant stimuli were paired only with the sample stimuli.

green bars were presented at the other. When the monkey attended to the green bars, the cell's response to the irrelevant red bars might have been attenuated because they were red or because they were at the wrong location. To test whether attenuation could be based on spatial location alone, for some cells we randomly intermixed the stimuli at the two locations so that, for example, red or green could appear at either spatial location on any trial.

When the locations of the effective and ineffective sensory stimuli were switched randomly, the responses of cells were still determined by the stimulus at the attended location. Cells responded well when the effective sensory stimulus appeared at the attended location and poorly when it appeared at the ignored location (median AI, 0.57 for the sample and test stimuli). Thus attenuation of irrelevant information can be based purely on spatial location.

When attention is directed to one of two stimuli

in the receptive field of a V4 cell, the effect of the unattended stimulus is attenuated, almost as if the receptive field has contracted around the attended stimulus. What, then, would be the effect on the receptive field if attention were directed outside it? To answer this, for 112 visually responsive cells (including 51 in the original sample) we placed an effective sensory stimulus inside the receptive-field and an ineffective stimulus outside (Fig. 22.1B). The cells gave a good response regardless of which stimulus was attended (Fig. 22.2B). Thus, when attention is directed outside a receptive field, the receptive field appears to be unaffected. Furthermore, since the firing rates of cells were the same regardless of whether attention was directed inside or outside the receptive field, we can conclude that attention does not serve to enhance responses to attended stimuli.

To test whether the attenuation of irrelevant information also occurs at the next stage of processing after V4, we recorded from 161 visually responsive neurons in the IT cortex. As in V4, when the animal attended to one stimulus inside the receptive field and ignored another, the response to the ignored stimulus was reduced. Unlike receptive fields in V4, which were typically 2° to 4° wide in the central visual field, those in the IT cortex were so large that the responses of cells could be influenced by attention to stimuli throughout at least the central 12° of both the contralateral and ipsilateral visual fields (the maximum distance that could be tested). The magnitude of the effect was somewhat smaller than in V4 (Fig. 22.2C), possibly because IT neurons generally gave weaker, more variable responses than neurons in V4.

The results from area V4 and the IT cortex indicate that the filtering of irrelevant information is at least a two-stage process. In V4 only those cells whose receptive fields encompass both attended and unattended stimuli will fail to respond to unattended stimuli. In the IT cortex, where receptive fields may encompass the entire visual field, virtually no cells will respond well to unattended stimuli.

In contrast to area V4 and the IT cortex, there was no effect of attention in V1. When relevant and irrelevant stimuli were in a receptive field (typically 0.5° to 0.9° wide), the animal could not perform the task. When one stimulus was located inside the field and one just outside, the monkey was able to perform the task, but, as in V4 under this condition, attention had little or no effect on the cells (Fig. 22.2D).

Our results indicate that attention gates visual processing by filtering out irrelevant information from within the receptive fields of single extrastriate neurons. This role of attention is different from that demonstrated previously in the posterior parietal cortex (3), to our knowledge the only other cortical area in which spatially directed attention has been found to influence neural responses. In the posterior parietal cortex, some neurons show enhanced responses when an animal attends to a stimulus inside the neuron's receptive field compared to when the animal attends to a stimulus outside the field.

Since parietal neurons have large receptive fields with little or no selectivity for stimulus quality, these cells may play a role in directing attention to a spatial location (4), but by themselves do not provide information about the qualities of attended stimuli. By contrast, in area V4 and the IT cortex selective attention may allow the animal to identify and remember the properties of a particular stimulus out of the many that may be acting on the retina at any given moment. If so, then the attenuation of response to irrelevant stimuli found in V4 and the IT cortex may underlie the attenuated processing of irrelevant stimuli shown psychophysically in humans (5).

NOTES

1. Gross, C. G (1973). Central Processing of Visual Information. In R. Jung (ed.), *Handbook of Sensory Physiology*, vol. 7, part 3, (pp. 451–482). Berlin: Springer. Ungerleider, L. G., & Mishkin, M. (1984). In D. J. Ingle, M. A. Goodale, & J. W. Mansfield, (eds.), *Analysis of Visual Behavior*, (pp. 549–586). Cambridge: MIT Press. Desimone, R., Schein, S. J., Moran, J., & Ungerleider, L. G. (1985). *Vision Res. 25*, 441.

2. Both sample and test stimuli were presented for 200 msec, with a delay between them of 400 to 600 msec. The sample and test were randomly chosen on each trial from a set of two stimuli, and the irrelevant stimuli were chosen from a different set of two. If the animal attempted to perform the task on the basis of the irrelevant stimuli, its performance would be governed by chance. The performance of the animals was 94 percent correct. The cue to the animal to switch the locus of its attention was to delete the test–time stimulus from the previously relevant location for two trials. On the first of these trials, the animals' performance dropped to 65 percent correct and their reaction time increased by 90 msec, indicating that they had been ignoring the irrelevant stimulus. The neural responses on the two cue trials were not counted. The locus of attention was switched frequently enough to achieve a minimum of ten trials per stimulus configuration. Fixation was monitored by a magnetic search coil, and trials were aborted if the eyes deviated from the fixation target by more than 0.5°.

3. Lynch, J. C., Mountcastle, V. B., Talbot, W. H, & Yin, T. C. T. (1977). *J. Neurophysiol., 40*, 362. Bushnell, M. C. et al. (1981). *J. Neurophysiol., 46*, 755.

4. Posner, M. I., Walker, J. A., Friedrich, F. J., Jr., & Rafal, D. (1984). *J. Neurosci., 4*, 1863

5. Broadbent, D. E. (1982). *Acta Psychol., 50*, 253. Kahneman, D. & Treisman, A. (1984). In R. Parasuraman and D. R. Davies (eds.), *Varieties of Attention*. New York: Academic Press.

Voluntary Attention Modulates fMRI Activity in Human MT-MST

K. M. O'Craven, B. R. Rosen, K. K. Kwong, and R. L. Savoy
• The Rowland Institute for Science and MGH–NMR Center
A. Treisman • Princeton University

How does voluntary attention to one attribute of a visual stimulus affect the neural processing of that stimulus? We used functional magnetic resonance imaging to examine the attentional modulation of neural activity in the human homolog of the MT–MST complex, which is known to be involved in the processing of visual motion. Using a visual stimulus containing both moving and stationary dots, we found significantly more MT–MST activation when subjects attended to the moving dots than when they attended to the stationary dots, even though the visual stimulus was identical during the two conditions.

Introduction

The visual system receives vast quantities of information. Attention allows the visual system to select a subset of that information for further processing, based either on properties of the stimulus (bottom up) or on a voluntary choice by the subject (top down). The present paper reports the results of experiments that demonstrate the influence of voluntary attention on the neural activity of the MT–MST complex, a region of human visual cortex that is specialized for the processing of visual motion.

Microelectrode recordings from neurons in monkey cortex have shown that attention can modulate the responses of individual neurons in visual cortex (Moran and Desimone, 1985; Spitzer et al., 1988; Motter, 1993; Maunsell and Ferrera, 1993; Treue and Maunsell, 1996; Conner et al., 1996; reviewed by Maunsell, 1995). Attention has

been shown to cause changes in receptive field size and in the tuning curves for color, orientation, and direction selectivity. Neuroimaging techniques such as positron emission tomography and functional magnetic resonance imaging (fMRI) now allow the examination of cortical function in humans. While these techniques cannot resolve neural activity at the spatial resolution of single neurons, they can detect the consequences of neural activity over a small region of cortex.

The present study asks whether voluntary attention can modulate neural activity in the human cortical areas responsible for processing simple visual motion information. If the visual stimulus remains unchanged, can we nonetheless detect differences in neural activity of visual areas based solely on the subset of the stimulus to which a subject attends? Specifically, given a visual stimulus containing both moving and stationary dots, will motion-processing areas of the human brain be more active if the subject attends to the moving dots than if the subject attends to the stationary dots? We have employed the technique of fMRI in two complementary experimental paradigms to answer these questions in the affirmative. The first experiment uses a fixed stimulus and demonstrates modulation of activity based solely on attentional changes. The second experiment uses a more complex stimulus paradigm to objectively define the regions under scrutiny and, simultaneously, to enable quantitative comparisons between stimulus-driven and attention-driven modulations of activity.

The experiments described here focus on the human homolog of the monkey motion-processing area MT–MST (also called V5), where most individual neurons are tuned to direction of motion. Neurons throughout this area are active when a large visual scene contains motion and inactive when it does not, thus differentially exciting a large enough region of cortex to be imaged easily using fMRI. In addition, the response properties of MT and MST have been well studied in monkeys. Finally, recent anatomical (Tootell and Taylor, 1995) and functional neuroimaging studies (Zeki et al., 1991; Watson et al., 1993; Tootell et al., 1995) have provided strong evidence that a human cortical area, in the ascending limb of the inferior temporal sulcus, corresponds well to the monkey area. This location probably corresponds to a small part of Brodmann's area 37 and is largely coincident with Flechsig's field 16, an area that is myelinated at birth (Zeki, 1993).

The critical visual stimulus for these experiments (Color Plate 23.5A) was a region containing both moving and stationary dots. All motion was radial, with all dots moving toward the central fixation cross, to make it easy for the subject to maintain fixation. (We also describe a control experiment in which eye movements were measured directly during scanning to confirm that subjects accurately maintained central fixation.)

In Experiment l, the visual stimulus, with moving white dots and stationary black dots, remained unchanged throughout the entire fMRI scan (Color Plate 23.5B). A verbal cue alerted the subject to attend first to the white dots, then to the black dots, alternating every 20 s for the 220 s duration of the scan. The consequence was that subjects attended alternately to the moving dots and then the stationary dots, although this motion distinction was never explicitly mentioned to the subjects.

A second experiment was run to 1) verify that the observed locus of the attentional effect is indeed the MT–MST complex by obtaining an objective functional localization of that region and to 2) allow a direct comparison of the magnitude of the attentional effect to the stimulus effect produced by manipulating the actual presence of motion in the stimulus. Experiment 2 addresses both the quantitative question and the localization question, using a single experimental paradigm called the "Castle" paradigm (O'Craven, unpublished data) because of the shape of the schematic diagram. The same critical visual stimulus (Color Plate 23.5A) containing both moving and stationary dots was embedded in the paradigm illustrated in Color Plate 23.6A.

The moving and stationary dot stimulus alternated every 20 s with a display that contained only stationary black dots. Subjects were instructed to attend to the black dots throughout the entire scan. Of the four critical epochs containing both moving and stationary dots, the first and third had moving black dots and stationary white dots, while the second and fourth had moving white dots and stationary black dots. As an additional baseline, each run began and ended with a 20 s period during which only the fixation cross appeared, with no dots.

Each subject participated in six runs of Experiment 2, three attending to black dots as just described, counterbalanced with three runs with complementary stimuli during which the subject attended to the white dots. In all six runs, the stimuli and instructions combined to require the subject to attend to the moving dots in the first and third epochs and the stationary dots in the second and fourth epochs.

Results

We imaged brain activity in five contiguous 7 mm slices parallel to the calcarine fissure. The MT–MST complex is located at the temporal–parietal–occipital juncture, which is typically in the slice below the calcarine fissure. Color Plate 23.5C is a statistical map for that slice in one subject, showing the results of a Kolmogorov–Smirnov (KS) test for Experiment 1, comparing, at each location, the magnitude of the MR signal during the time points when the subject was attending to the white (moving) dots with the magnitude of the signal during the time points when the subject was attending to the black (stationary) dots. Because the visual stimulus was identical during every time point, the difference in activation is a purely attentional effect. The location of the activated area is consistent with the location of human MT in other studies (Zeki et al., 1991; Watson et al., 1993; Tootell et al., 1995), implying that under these experimental conditions, attention modulates activation in the MT–MST complex.

For each subject, the region of interest was designated by selecting the voxels that met a threshold of $P < .0001$. The time course data for each subject was then normalized by converting to percent signal change from baseline, and the three subjects' data were averaged together. Color Plate 23.5D shows the average time course of the fMRI activation for the three subjects. The MR signal in the MT–MST complex was significantly greater while the subjects attended to the moving dots (closed pink bars) than when they attended to stationary dots and ignored the moving ones (hatched blue bars).

The inclusion of the "stationary dots alone" condition in Experiment 2 allowed the effects of the stimulus changes and the attentional changes to be observed separately and compared. The data from this experiment were therefore subjected to a two-stage analysis. First, the MT–MST complex was functionally localized for each individual subject by finding the voxels that were significantly more active when the visual stimulus included motion than when it contained stationary dots alone. Thus, the region was selected based on changes caused by the stimulus, independent of attention.

Color Plate 23.6B shows the KS statistical map for one subject in Experiment 2, comparing the MR signal during time points when the stimulus contained motion to time points when there was no motion. Based on neuroimaging and anatomical studies (Zeki et al., 1991; Watson et al., 1993; Tootell and Taylor, 1995; Tootell et al., 1995), we identified the strong activation seen laterally near the temporal–parietal–occipital juncture as area MT–MST and identified the dorsomedial activation as areas V1 and V2. For each subject, the MT–MST region of interest was defined as the lateral clusters containing voxels that met a threshold of $P < 10^{-10}$ ($P < 10^{-6}$ with Bonferroni correction) for the comparison of motion to no motion on the average data from six runs.

Once the voxels representing the MT–MST complex were specified for each subject, the time course of activation for that region was examined for attentional effects. The MT–MST time course (Color Plate 23.6C) was averaged across five subjects with six runs per subject. The MR signal in the MT–MST complex increased dramatically when a stimulus containing only stationary dots was replaced by one including moving dots. Additionally, the activation during the "attend moving" condition (closed pink bars) is consistently higher than activation during the "attend stationary" condition (hatched blue bars). Thus, for a region independently identified as the MT–MST complex, attention to the moving dots clearly increased the activation elicited by the mixed moving and stationary display. Note that although the attentional effect was only 29% as large as the sensory effect, for each subject, it was significant at the $P < .001$ level in a Student's t test, which compared the MR signals for the two conditions in the a priori region of interest. Figure 23.1 shows the time course data for each subject to illustrate the consistency of the result across subjects.

No attentional modulation was observed in V1–V2 (Figure 23.2). This region responded more when the stimulus contained motion than when it did not, perhaps due in part to the fact that dot density was greater when the moving dots were added to the stationary dot stimulus. However, there were no differences associated with the attention task ($P > .5$). This is not a claim that attention cannot affect activity in V1 or V2. It simply was not observed for this particular task comparing attention to motion with attention to stationary stimuli. Most microelectrode studies with monkeys have failed to find any effect of attention on V1 (Haenny and Schiller, 1988; Maunsell and Ferrera, 1993), but at least one investigator, who used a more demanding orientation discrimination task instead of an orienting task, reported effects of attention on V1 neuron responses (Motter, 1993). Some neuroimaging studies suggest that V1 may be attentionally modulated under certain task conditions, particularly when an attentional condition is compared to a passive viewing condition (Schmit et al., 1995; Simpson et al., 1995; Woodruff et al., 1996; Worden et al., 1996).

Eye Movements

Activity in MT and MST is known to be influenced by eye movements (Komatsu and Wurtz, 1988; Reppas, 1995). If subjects made different

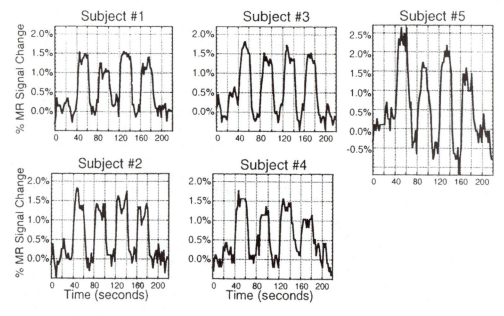

FIGURE 23.1 ■ The Time Course of Activation for Each of the Five Subjects. Each plot is the average of date from six functional scans, each lasting 220 s.

eye movements during the two attentional conditions, interpretation of our results would be problematic. Therefore, it is important to rule out the possibility that eye movements might play a role in producing the results. The stimuli were designed with this concern in mind. The radial motion of the dots, combined with the fact that the fixation point was at the center of both sets of dots, was intended to eliminate optokinetic nystagmus and to make accurate fixation easy. However, to definitively rule out an eye movement account, Experiments 1 and 2 were repeated with two subjects while their eye movements were monitored. We used an Ober2 infrared eye movement registration system modified to function safely and effectively in the magnet environment (Aisenberg, 1996). The horizontal and vertical positions of both eyes were sampled at 120 Hz. The functional data collected while eye movements were monitored produced results comparable to those already described. Eye movement traces obtained under five conditions are shown in Figure 23.3. Despite broadband noise in the eye movement data introduced by the RF pulses generated by the MR scanner, it is very clear that fixation was steady in both the "attend stationary" and the "attend moving"

conditions, and there were no noticeable differences between them and the "stationary dots alone" condition.

In a separate scan, the subject was instructed to track a single dot moving on a short diagonal path (~1°) near the fixation cross, while viewing the same stimuli used in Experiment 2. The clear eye movement responses in that record demonstrate that the system is sensitive to eye movements of the magnitude that might be expected if the subject had failed to fixate during the attention task. For calibration, the final trace shows a record of eye position when the subject made saccades to a target that alternated every 500 ms between two locations separated horizontally by ~2°.

Eye-blink frequency was also examined to determine whether blinks were more frequent during some conditions that others. One subject produced almost no blinks during the attention conditions, combining across the relevant epochs from both Experiments 1 and 2 (two blinks in 300 s of "attend stationary;" zero blinks in 320 s of "attend moving." The other subject showed an insignificant trend toward blinking more during "attend stationary" (23 blinks during 400 s) than "attend moving" (21 blinks in 440 s).

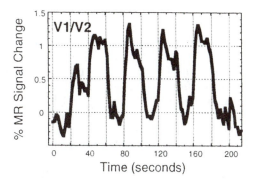

FIGURE 23.2 ■ Earlier Visual Areas (V1–V2) Were Also More Active in Response to a Stimulus Containing Moving and Stationary Dots than to Stationary Dots Alone. The time course of activation for the V1–V2 region of interest, averaged across six runs from each of five subjects, shows no effect of the attentional condition on activity in these areas of visual cortex ($P > .5$).

Discussion

These experiments taken together provide strong evidence that voluntary attention to different elements in a single visual display can affect neural activity in areas of visual cortex responsible for basic sensory processing of visual information. Specifically, the MT–MST complex is more ac-

tive when a subject attends to moving objects than when a subject viewing exactly the same stimulus attends to stationary objects in the stimulus.

Relationship to Electrophysiology Data

A very recent study of attentional influences on single unit responses in macaque monkeys (Treue and Maunsell, 1996) has shown results consistent with those described here for humans. They recorded from MT and MST neurons under three conditions. In each case, the cell's receptive field contained a dot moving in that cell's preferred direction. They found that neurons responded more strongly when the attended target was that dot than when the attended target was a different dot moving in the opposite direction (either inside or outside the receptive field). These attentional effects were present in both MT and MST neurons but were more pronounced in the MST neurons, perhaps indicating greater effects of extraretinal signals at more advanced stages of cortical processing. Because much of what we know about brain function comes from the monkey neurophysiology literature, it remains very important to test the underlying assumption that the two systems are similar. The comparison is particularly critical for experiments that explore higher level function, where the two systems are most likely to diverge.

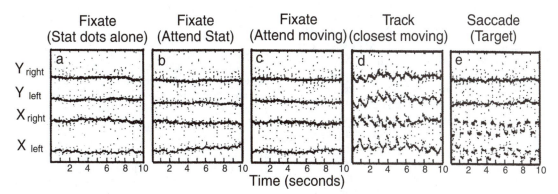

FIGURE 23.3 ■ Eye Movements
Eye movement traces obtained during fMRI scanning verify that subjects could fixate reliably while viewing stationary dots alone (a), as well as while performing the two attention tasks while viewing the visual stimulus containing moving and stationary dots ([b] and [c]). For comparison, also shown are the results of intentionally tracking the dot moving nearest to the fixation point ($1°$ path, repeating every second) (d) and of saccading at a stimulus-cued rate of 1 Hz between two targets separated by $2°$ horizontally (e). The scattered points are noise introduced by the simultaneous acquisition of MR images. The small oscillations in the X^{left} traces under the fixation conditions are similar in frequency to those expected if stimulus-induced eye movements were present, but they are instead also due to RF interference; they are equally prominent when the stimulus contains no motion (a).

Theoretical Implications

The results of the present experiments are relevant to a long-standing controversy in the field of cognitive psychology concerning the stage of processing at which attention operates. The "late selection" view of attention is that all sensory information is fully processed to the level of semantic meaning, but that attention then acts to select which information will reach consciousness, be stored in long-term memory, or be used as the basis for a behavioral response (Deutsch and Deutsch, 1963). In contrast, the foundation of the "early selection" view is that the "bottleneck" sometimes occurs much earlier in processing (Broadbent, 1958; Treisman, 1964) and that, in situations where the perceptual load is high (Lavie and Tsal, 1994; Lavie, 1995), full perceptual processing occurs only for information that is attended. Over the decades, evidence from experiments using priming, interference measures, and many other behavioral tasks has shown that the level at which attention operates depends on the task and the load. Evidence has also accumulated for the pervasiveness of feedback throughout the brain (Felleman and Van Essen, 1991), requiring some revision to models that assumed strictly sequential information processing. While there have been changes in the way that we think about early and late selection, it is still meaningful to ask at what level in the system the effects of attention can be detected. The fact that voluntary attention to a subset of objects in a visual stimulus can modulate neural activity as early as the MT–MST complex, even in the absence of stimulus or task differences, offers a clear example of early selection by top-down control of sensory processing.

Our experiments differ from other recent studies of attentional modulation in human visual cortex in that neither the stimulus nor the nature of the task changes between the two attentional conditions. In each condition, the subject is voluntarily attending to a subset of the dots in the display. The attended dots are specified by color but incidentally also differ from the other dots in terms of motion. In contrast, in the elegant positron emission tomography experiments of Corbetta et al. (1990, 1991), subjects viewed the same stimuli but performed different tasks in the different conditions (evaluating either the speed, shape, or color of the stimuli). This raises the possibility that the differences in activity that they observed reflect not attention to visual features but the use of that information to make an explicit decision (e.g., speed discrimination). The motion in the stimulus in our experiments was not explicitly a part of the task. While our subjects were certainly aware that various groups of colored dots moved differently, they neither needed nor were asked to use this information to perform the attentional task. Despite these differences, however, the present study agrees with the Corbetta experiments and others (Beauchamp and DeYoe, 1996) in concluding that neural activity in human MT can be modulated by attention.

The design of the present experiment intentionally did not have an explicit overt behavioral task. Subjects' attention was manipulated solely through the use of verbal instructions in order to measure the effects of attending to different subsets of the stimulus rather than the effects of performing different tasks. Imposing a behavioral task can be extremely useful in neuroimaging studies (such as in the Corbetta study), but it is by no means necessary, and the absence of an artificial task sometimes allows a more direct interpretation of the data (Pinker, 1994). As in any experiment, it is still necessary to have a manipulated variable and a dependent variable. With neuroimaging, however, the dependent variable need not require performance of an artificial task; it can instead be a direct neurophysiological measure. Covert tasks have been utilized with great success in a number of influential neuroimaging studies (Fiez et al., 1996).

In the present experimental paradigm, attending to one set of dots defined by their color elicited an increase in the processing of their motion, as indicated by increased activity in MT–MST. Such a finding is reminiscent of the "object-based" accounts of attention (Duncan, 1984; Kanwisher and Driver, 1992; Baylis and Driver, 1993; Treisman et al., 1993), which predict that when an object is attended, all aspects of the attended object are more fully processed, including features that are not specifically designated for attention. Although the motion of the attended group of colored dots was not an explicit aspect of the subjects' instructions, attentional modulation of the MT complex was nevertheless present. While the results of the present experiment by themselves cannot be taken as conclusive evidence regarding object-based attention (since it is possible that subjects used the motion cue as well as the instructed color cue to select the target dots), it is nonetheless suggestive.

This type of paradigm, either with or without a concurrent behavioral task, shows great promise for examining the extent to which attention can affect cortical processing throughout the human brain. The strategy of functionally localizing a brain region by using changes in stimulus or task, and then simultaneously presenting both stimulus types while the subject attends to one at a time, can be generalized to many situations. We believe that future experiments using this approach will broaden the current understanding of the roles that attention and consciousness play in influencing neural activity.

Experimental Procedures

Visual Stimulus

The critical visual stimulus was a field of 87 dots, each ~.15° in diameter, covering a 10° × 8° region. Black and white dots were of similar contrast relative to the intermediate gray background. Moving dots moved radially toward the central fixation point at 3°– 5.5°/s. Dot speed varied with eccentricity, with the more peripheral dots moving faster. Each moving dot had a lifetime of ~1 s, and initial positions of dots were sufficiently far from fixation that they expired before reaching the center. When a dot disappeared, it was immediately replaced with another dot having the same initial eccentricity as its predecessor, thus maintaining an approximately constant dot density in time and space.

The stimuli were controlled by a Macintosh IIvx computer running MacStim (written by D. Darby). Video output from the Macintosh was sent to an S-VHS projector (Sharp 2000), which projected the stimulus through a magnetically screened window into the magnet room. The image was focused by a large Buhl optical lens onto a rear-projection screen constructed of Dalite material (DaPlex Corp.), which was mounted directly inside the bore of the magnet with Velcro strips. Subjects lay supine inside the magnet, looking up at a mirror angled at ~45° to allow them to see the rear-projection screen.

Subjects

Five normal volunteers (ages 25–45) with normal or connected-to-normal vision participated in Experiment 2. Three of these subjects also participated in Experiment 1. All subjects gave their informed consent.

fMRI Scanning

A 1.5 Tesla General Electric Signa Scanner (modified by Advanced NMR to perform echo planar imaging) was used to image cortical activity while subjects fixated the center of the visual stimulus and performed the attention tasks. An asymmetric spin echo pulse sequence was used for functional imaging to minimize the contribution of large vessels. A surface coil (General Electric 5 inch) over the occipital pole was used to maximize the signal-to-noise ratio in visual areas. Five oblique slices parallel to the calcarine fissure were imaged (TR = 2000 ms; TE = 70 ms). Each slice was 7 mm thick (no gap) and contained an array of 128 × 64 voxels, each with an in-plane resolution of 3.125 mm × 3.125 mm.

Stimulus presentation was triggered by the MR scanner to allow precise synchronization of the stimuli with the MR images collected. This temporal coregistration made it possible to repeat an experiment several times and average the results. Subjects used a bite bar to reduce head motion during and between scans.

Anatomical scans were obtained prior to the functional scans. The sagittal series was used to identify the calcarine fissure for each subject, and oblique slices parallel to the calcarine were chosen and used for all subsequent scans. To obtain the best quality images possible, the magnet was then shimmed to modify the magnetic gradients to neutralize inhomogeneities in the magnetic field that were introduced by inserting a human body into the magnet bore. A flow series, which emphasized major blood vessels, was obtained in the oblique planes selected for functional scanning, followed by a high resolution T1 or T2 weighted Instascan series. The high resolution Instascan images are collected using the same gradients as in the functional images, so very little warping occurs between them, allowing functional activation to be overlaid directly on the high resolution anatomical images.

Data Analysis

Experiment 2

For each of the five subjects, the data from six runs were corrected for motion using a modified three-dimensional automated image registration algorithm (Woods et al., 1992; Jiang et al., 1995). The initial analysis was conducted separately for each subject. The strategy was to first localize MT–MST and V1–V2 and then to look at the magnitude of the MR signal in those specified regions of interest to determine whether activity there is modulated by differences in attentional instructions.

To get the best estimate of the location of the MT–MST complex for each subject, the data from all six runs were averaged. This was accomplished by taking the value of the MR signal in each voxel of each slice at each time point and calculating the mean across the six separate scans. In addition to improving the signal-to-noise ratio, this procedure eliminated the effects of color, since color was counterbalanced across runs. The resulting averaged data kept the effects of attentional instructions intact (the first and third epoch of Moving and Stationary Dots were always "attend moving," and the second and fourth were always "attend stationary"), but the stimulus differences for the two color variations canceled out.

We used a signed KS test to compare, for each voxel, the amount of activity during the images collected while the subject viewed "moving and stationary" dots (40 time points) versus the amount of activity in the images during which the subject viewed "stationary only" dots (50 time points). A 2 s delay was included to account for hemodynamic lag. The MT–MST complex and (to a lesser degree) primary visual cortex are known to be stimulated by visual motion. For each subject, the voxels that showed significantly greater activation ($P < 10^{-10}$; $P < 10^{-6}$ with Bonferroni connection) during the "moving and stationary" condition, and which were in the predicted vicinity of the MT–MST complex as localized in other experiments (Zeki et al., 1991; Watson at al., 1993; Tootell et al., 1995), were designated as MT–MST. From the same statistical comparison, the medial cluster of voxels was designated as V1–V2. The locations were consistent with those found by Sereno at al. (1995) in subjects whose visual cortices were extensively mapped with retinotopic procedures.

The KS statistic is a nonparametric test, which evaluates the probability that two sets of data points come from the same underlying distribution by comparing not just the means of the two samples (as many statistical tests do) but the entire distributions of the samples (Press et al., 1992). This statistic is often used in fMRI as a conservative way to evaluate how well the pattern of activation observed corresponds to the pattern predicted and thus to localize voxels that show changes in activation that are temporally locked with changes in the stimulus or task. The advantage of this statistic for fMRI data is that it relies on very few assumptions about the underlying distribution of the data.

Once the relevant regions of interest were defined for a subject, the magnitude of the activation in the region of interest at each time point was examined.

Experiment 1

For each subject, the average data from all runs (two for two subjects; four for the third subject) were subjected to a KS test that compared time points when subjects attended to the white (moving) dots with time points when the subjects attended to the black (stationary) dots. A 2 s delay was included to account for hemodynamic lag. The bilateral cluster of voxels that showed significant change ($P < .0001$) for this comparison was selected separately for each subject, and a time course of activation for that region was extracted. The raw values for signal strength were converted to percent change in MR signal, and the resulting time courses were averaged across the three subjects.

REFERENCES

Aisenberg, S. (1996). Measurement and analysis of binocular rapid eye movement, including saccades, saccadic prediction, fixations, nystagmus, and smooth pursuit. *Invest. Ophthalmol. Vis. Sci. Suppl. 37,* S274.

Baylis, G. C., & Driver, J. (1993). Visual attention and objects: evidence for hierarchical coding of location. *J. Exp. Psychol. [Hum. Percept.] 19,* 451–470.

Beauchamp, M., & DeYoe, E. (1996). Brain areas for processing motion and their modulation by selective attention. *Neuroimage 3,* 245.

Broadbent, D. E. (1958). *Perception and Communication.* (London: Pergamon Press).

Conner, C. E., Gallant, J. L., Preddie, D. C., & Van Essen, D. C. (1996). Responses in area V4 depend on the spatial relationship between stimulus and attention. *J. Neurophysiol.,* 75, 1306–1308.

Corbetta, M., Miezin, F. M., Dobmeyer, S., Shulman, G. L., & Petersen, S. E. (1990). Attentional modulation of neural processing of shape, color, and velocity in humans. *Science, 248,* 1556–1559.

Corbetta, M., Miezin, F. M., Dobmeyer, S., Shulman, G. L., & Petersen, S. E. (1991). Selective and divided attention during visual discriminations of shape, color, and speed: functional anatomy by positron emission tomography. *J. Neurosci., 11,* 2383–2402.

Deutsch, J. A., & Deutsch, D. (1963). Attention: some theoretical considerations. *Psychol. Rev., 70,* 80–90.

Duncan, J. (1984). Selective attention and the organization of visual information. *J. Exp. Psychol. [Gen.], 113,* 501–517.

Felleman, D. J., & Van Essen, D. C. (1991). Distributed heirarchical processing in the primate cerebral cortex. *Cerebral Cortex 1,* 1–47.

Fiez, J., Raichle, M., Balota, D., Tallal, P., & Petersen, S. (l996). PET activation of posterior temporal regions during auditory word presentation and verb generation. *Cerebral Cortex, 6,* 1–10.

Haenny, P. E., & Schiller, P. H. (1988). State dependent activity in monkey visual cortex: 1. Single cell activity in V1 and V4 on visual tasks. *Exp. Brain Res., 69,* 225–244.

Jiang, A., Kennedy, D. N., Baker, J. R., Weisskoff, R. M., Tootell, R. B. H., Woods, R. P., Benson, R. R., Kwong, K. K., Brady, T. J., Rosen, B. R., & Belliveau, J. W. (1995). Motion detection and correction in functional MR imaging. *Hum. Brain Mapping, 3,* 224–235.

Kanwisher, N., & Driver, J. (1992). Objects, attributes and visual attention: which, what and where. *Curr. Direct. Psychol. Sci., 1,* 26–31.

Komatsu, H., & Wurtz, R. H. (1988). Relation of cortical area MT and MST in pursuit eye movements. 1. Localization and visual properties of neurons. *J. Neurophysiol., 60,* 580–603.

Lavie, N. (1995). Perceptual load as a necessary condition for selective attention. *J. Exp. Psychol. [Hum. Percept.], 21,* 451–468.

Lavie, N., & Tsal, Y. (1994). Perceptual load as a major determinant of the locus of selection in visual attention. *Perception Psychophysics, 56,* 183–197.

Maunsell, J. H. R. (1995). The brain's visual world: Representation of visual targets in cerebral cortex. *Science, 270,* 764–769.

Maunsell, J. H. R., & Ferrera, V. P. (1990). Attention mechanisms in visual cortex. In *The Cognitive Neurosciences,* M.S. Gazzaniga, ed. (Cambridge, Massachusetts: MIT Press).

Moran, J., & Desimone, R. (1985). Selective attention gates visual processing in the extrastriate cortex. *Science, 229,* 782–784.

Motter, B. C. (1993). Focal attention produces spatially selective processing in visual cortical areas V1, V2, and V4 in the presence of competing stimuli. *J. Neurophysiol., 70,* 909–919.

Pinker. (1994). On language. *J. Cog. Neurosci., 6,* 92–97.

Press, W. H., Teukolsky, S. A., Vetterling, W. T., & Flannery, B. T. (1992). *Numerical Recipes in C. The Art of Scientific Computing,* ed. 2. (Cambridge: Cambridge University Press), pp. 623–626.

Reppas, J. (1995). Cortical contributions to the interpretation of visual image motion and the execution of pursuit eye movements. *Invest. Ophthalmol. Vis. Sci., 36,* S205.

Schmit, P. W., Neitz, J., Miller, D., & DeYoe, E. A. (1995). Differences in cortical activation during active versus passive viewing. *Invest. Ophthalmol. Vis. Sci., 36,* S374.

Sereno, M., Dale, A., Reppas, J., Kwong, K., Belliveau, J., Brady. T., Rosen, B., & Tootell, R. (1995). Borders of multiple visual areas in humans revealed by functional magnetic resonance imaging. *Science, 268,* 889–893.

Simpson, G. V., Belliveau, J. W., Ilmoniemi, R. J., Ahlfors, S. P., Baker, J. R., & Fore, J. J. (1995). Dynamic mapping of cortical activity during visual spatial attention. Presented at the Second Annual Meeting of the Cognitive Neuroscience Society, San Francisco, California.

Spitzer, H., Desimone, R., & Moran, J. (1988). Increased attention enhances both behavioral and neuronal performance. *Science, 240,* 338–340.

Tootell, R. B. H., & Taylor, J. B. (1995). Anatomical evidence for MT and additional cortical visual areas in humans. *Cerebral Cortex, 1,* 39–55.

Tootell, R. B. H., Reppas, J. B., Kwong, K. K., Malach, R., R. T., Brady, T. J., Rosen, B. R., & Belliveau, J. W. (1995). Functional analysis of human MT and related visual cortical areas using magnetic resonance imaging. *J. Neurosci., 15,* 3215–3230.

Treisman, A. M. (1964). Selective attention in man. *Br. Med. Bull., 20,* 12–16.

Treisman, A. M., Kahneman, D., & Burkell, J. (1993). Perceptual objects and the cost of filtering. *Perception Psychophysics, 33,* 527–532.

Treue, S., & Maunsell, J. H. R. (1996). Attentional modulation of visual motion processing in cortical areas MT and MST. *Nature, 382,* 539–541.

Watson, J. D., Myers, R., Frackowiak, R. S., Hajnal, J. V., Woods, R. P., Mazziotta, J. C., Shipp, S., & Zeki, S. (1993). Area V5 of the human brain: Evidence from a combined study using positron emission tomography and magnetic resonance imaging. *Cerebral Cortex, 3,* 79–94.

Woodruff, P. W. R., Benson, R. R., Bandettini, P. A., Kwong, K. K., Howard, R. J., Talavage, T., Belliveau, J., & Rosen, B. R. (1996). Modulation of auditory and visual cortex by selective attention is modality-dependent. *Neuroreport, 7,* 1909–1913.

Woods, R. P., Cherry, S. R., & Mazziotta, J. C. (1992). Rapid automated algorithm for aligning and reslicing PET images. *J. Comput. Assist. Tomogr., 16,* 620–633.

Worden, M., Schneider, W., & Wellington, R. (1996). Determining the locus of attentional selection with fMRI. Presented at the Third Annual Meeting of the Cognitive Neuroscience Society, San Francisco, California.

Zeki, S. (1993). *A Vision of the Brain.* (Oxford: Blackwell Scientific Publications).

Zeki, S., Watson, J. D. G., Lueck, C. J., Friston, K. J., Kennard, C., & Frackowiak, R. S. J. (1991). A direct demonstration of functional specialization in human visual cortex. *J. Neurosci., 11,* 641–649.

Introduction to Readings 24 and 25

There has been a surge of interest recently among neuroscientists and philosophers in coming to grips with the neural basis of consciousness. Crick and Koch (1998, p. 97) put the question as follows: "It is probable that at any given moment some active neuronal processes in your head correlate with consciousness, while others do not: *what is the difference between them?*" (italics in original).

One source of evidence about this question comes from the investigation of spared visual capabilities observed in persons who have lost portions of visual cortex, a phenomenon Weiskrantz and colleagues call "blindsight." Among the most well known of these cases is that of D.B., a man whose primary visual cortex (area V1) in the right hemisphere was surgically removed to relieve intractable headaches that appeared to be caused by a circulatory malformation in that area of his brain. The surgery left him with an intact V1 in the left hemisphere (sparing his vision of the right visual field), but a large region of cortical blindness in the left visual field, opposite the missing cortical area.[1]

In the article reprinted here, Weiskrantz and colleagues found that D.B. retained an ability to respond correctly to events in his "blind" field, despite a reported absence of conscious visual awareness there. This ability can be explained in part by the anatomical fact that there exists in humans a second visual pathway, an alternative to the familiar pathway from the eyes to the lateral geniculate nucleus in the thalamus and then to primary visual cortex. This second pathway sends axons from the eyes to the superior colliculus in the midbrain. The superior colliculus is strongly involved in the control of eye movements, and it has been suggested that this second pathway, which is evolutionarily more primitive than the pathway

---

[1]Note that the blindness was not associated with the right or left *eye*, but with the left half of the visual field in both eyes.

through the geniculate, subserves an orienting function, allowing for automatic and efficient eye movements to salient visual events (Schneider, 1969). The pattern of results reported here strongly suggests that there are aspects of visual functioning (that is, functioning of the second, collicular visual pathway) to which we do not have conscious access. A similar point has been made by Milner and Goodale (1995) in their analysis of patient D.F. (see the introduction to Reading 17 by Mishkin et al.). These observations also suggest that an intact pathway from the LGN to V1 and then to higher visual centers is crucial to visual awareness.

Other examples of neural activity to which we do not have conscious access have been reported. For example, He et al. (1996) exploited orientation-specific adaptation to investigate the locus of awareness. They knew that if an observer is shown a display containing vertically-oriented black and white bars for perhaps half a minute, then they will subsequently be impaired in detecting very dim bars of that orientation (specifically, the contrast of the bars must be increased in order for them to see the bars at threshold compared to bars of some other orientation). This phenomenon is thought to reflect neural fatigue following adaptation of cells in area V1. He et al. first verified the magnitude of the adaptation effect by presenting a patch of oriented bars in the visual periphery and then measuring the magnitude of the contrast increment required at threshold following adaptation. They then repeated the experiment, but this time they flanked the patch of oriented bars with additional distractor patches during adaptation. These flanking patches caused what He et al. call "attentional crowding," and prevented the observers from correctly reporting the orientation of the target patch of bars; they reported that they could see something in the target location, but it was indistinct. However, when He et al. once more measured the

adaptation-induced contrast increment at threshold, they found that it was as great as when the oriented patch was presented by itself. This latter result suggests that the cells in area V1 were responding to the oriented target patch just as strongly when it was flanked as when it was presented alone, because they became as fatigued (as measured by the adaptation effect). In contrast, the observers' perceptual experience was of an indistinct, fuzzy patch. This dissociation between what is consciously perceived and neural activity suggests that we do not have direct conscious access to the activity of neurons in V1. This conclusion is not inconsistent with the observations of D.F. reported by Weiskrantz et al., where damage to V1 caused a loss of conscious vision. The latter finding simply means that if the pathway through V1 is disrupted, visual awareness is lost; it could be that awareness arises in, say, V4, but because V4 did not have normal inputs via V1, it was not providing normal conscious experience.

The reading by Scheinberg and Logothetis reveals a part of the brain to which monkeys *do* appear to have conscious access. They investigated the behavior of single cells during binocular rivalry. Binocular rivalry is produced when an observer views two different visual scenes, one with each eye. Under these conditions, the observer typically sees only one of the two images at a time, as if it is the only one present at the moment, but the percept spontaneously dissolves to the scene in the other eye every few seconds. Scheinberg and Logothetis report that most cells in the inferior teporal (IT) cortex, which is known to represent visual objects, vary their firing rate in a manner that mirrors the monkey's report of his perceptual experience during rivalry.

The logic of this experiment is similar to that of Reading 10 by Newsome et al. It differs in one important respect, however: changes in the neural activity that were seen here were not responses to stimulus changes as in Newsome et al., but to an internal subjective change to which the monkey had direct access.

Tong et al. (1998) have reported similar results in humans using fMRI. They took advantage of the fact that there are two brain areas that appear to be specialized for representing faces (the fusiform face area or FFA) and places (the parahippocampal place area or PPA). They constructed binocular rivalry stimuli consisting of faces presented to one eye and places (e.g., scenes from a college campus) to the other eye, and first verified that binocular rivalry occurs with these stimuli. They then recorded neural activity in the FFA and PPA while observers reported with button presses which percepts

they were experiencing. They found that the activity in these two specialized brain regions closely followed the reported perceptual experiences of the observers.

These kinds of experiments have the potential to provide an answer to the question posed by Crick and Koch (1998). In just what ways do neurons whose responses are correlated with conscious experience differ from those that are not? Do they have consistently different location within the layers of the cortex? Do they have predictable patterns of axonal projections (e.g., long vs. short)? Do they exhibit a particular sort of discharge pattern that makes them special? Answers to these and related questions will provide some initial steps toward revealing the neural basis of consciousness.

REFERENCES

Crick, F., & Koch, C. (1998). Consciousness and neuroscience. *Cerebral Cortex, 8,* 97–107.

He, S., Cavanagh, P., & Intrilligator, J. (1996). Attentional resolution and the locus of visual awareness. *Nature, 383,* 334–337.

Milner, D., & Goodale, M. (1995). *The visual brain in action.* Oxford: Oxford University Press.

Schneider, G. E. (1969). Two visual systems. *Science, 163,* 895–902.

Tong, F., Nakayama, K., Vaughan, J. T., & Kanwisher, N. (1998). Binocular rivalry and visual awareness in human extrastriate cortex. *Neuron, 21,* 753–759.

Weiskrantz, L. (1997). *Consciousness lost and found: A neuropsychological exploration.* Oxford: Oxford University Press.

Visual Capacity in the Hemianopic Field Following a Restricted Occipital Ablation

L. Weiskrantz, E. K. Warrington, M. D. Sanders and J. Marshall
• The National Hospital, London

Damage to striate cortex and neighbouring regions in man is well known to produce severe loss of visual capacity in correlated regions of the visual field (Holmes, 1918; Teuber, Battersby and Bender, 1960). Depending on the duration, nature and extent of the damage, and the method of measurement, the resultant blindness may be more or less absolute. In the most extreme examples, a patient may acknowledge no visual information or only the onset or offset of a light in the scotoma. In less extreme cases vigorously moving or flickering stimuli may be seen (Riddoch, 1917). It is generally held, however, that man is more severely impaired by damage to the visual cortex than the monkey, even though the anatomical organizations of the visual pathways and cortex are closely similar. Indeed, the more thoroughly the monkey has been studied, the more remarkable has been the extent of residual visual capacity found: for example, the ability to discriminate two-dimensional patterns even when the whole of the striate cortex has been removed, with complete retrograde degeneration of the dorsal lateral geniculate nuclei (Pasik and Pasik, 1971). It has even been suggested that the monkey without striate cortex may be capable of qualitatively normal pattern vision but with reduced visual acuity (Weiskrantz, 1972; cf. Ward and Masterton, 1970). Recent animal results, however, also suggest strongly that a severe penalty is inflicted when damage to neighbouring posterior cortical areas is added to that of the stri-

ate cortex (Pasik and Pasik, 1971). For this reason, human cases in which damage is relatively restricted to area 17 (the only known cortical projection from the dorsal lateral geniculate nucleus), with only minimal damage to surrounding tissue, have a renewed interest.

There also have been suggestions, based on animal research, that the type of visual information processed by the direct pathway from the retina to the mid-brain is qualitatively different from that by the geniculo-cortical route (the "two visual system" hypothesis: Schneider, 1969; Trevarthen, 1968; Ingle, 1967). The former, it has been claimed, is primarily concerned with the detection of "salient" visual events in space and the control of ocular fixation, and the latter with the identification of such events once detected. Thus stated, the distinction is undoubtedly an oversimplification, and the hypothesis (of which there are a number of variants) is not free from controversy, but it does focus attention on the possibility that visual stimuli may be detected and located in the absence of striate cortex in man. Recently, Pöppel, Held and Frost (1973) have claimed that voluntary ocular fixation responses can be controlled (although rather weakly) by visual stimuli placed in regions of blindness caused by cortical damage, even though the patients deny seeing the stimuli. To the extent that such an ability (if confirmed) depends on the direct input to the midbrain from the retina, it would be important to examine this and other visual abilities in patients with striate cortex damage but with only minimal damage to the posterior association cortex, as the latter receives a projection (via the posterior thalamus) from the superior colliculus. Cases of relatively restricted visual cortex damage therefore assume special importance, and we here report our observations on one such patient, whose results have already been briefly communicated (Sanders, Warrington, Marshall and Weiskrantz, 1974).

Case History

The patient, D.B., a man of 34 years, began to experience headaches at the age of 14. The headaches were always preceded by a flashing light which appeared in an oval-shaped area immediately to the left of the fixation point and straddling the horizontal meridian. Over the course of a few minutes the oval enlarged, mainly by extension downwards. About fifteen minutes from the onset the flashing lights were replaced by a white scotoma covering the oval area with a crescent of coloured lights around its lateral and lower margins. At this stage headache appeared on the right side followed by vomiting some fifteen minutes later, by which time the scotoma had extended to include the crescent of coloured lights. The headache would persist for up to forty-eight hours but usually the patient slept and upon waking would find his vision normal and his headache gone.

The attacks occurred at intervals of six weeks until his twenties when the frequency increased to about once every three weeks. Following one attack at the age of 25 he noticed a persistent field defect, smaller than the scotoma of his attacks, appearing more as a blank than as the white area, and situated to the left of fixation more below than above the horizontal. In some recent attacks there was a sensory disturbance down the left side of his body.

An angiogram performed when he was 26 years old showed an arteriovenous malformation at the right occipital pole. Drugs for the treatment of migraine, including methysergide, gave no relief nor did a right cervical sympathectomy performed in 1970. As the attacks were posing a severe threat to his employment and his family and social life, professor Valentine Logue removed the malformation in June 1973. The excision extended approximately 6 cm anterior to the occipital pole and included the major portion of the calcarine cortex on the medial surface of the hemisphere. After operation he had a homonymous hemianopia which split the macula with a crescent of preserved vision at the periphery of the upper quadrant (Fig. 24.1). In addition he experienced flashing lights and well-formed visual hallucinations in the left half-fields but these gradually subsided over the course of the next five weeks and then disappeared. He has had no headaches since the operation.

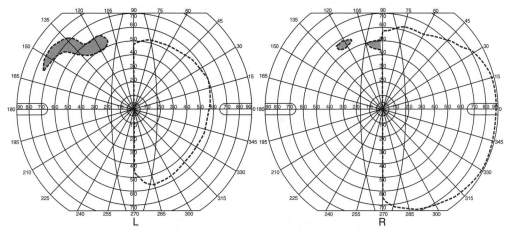

FIGURE 24.1 ■ Visual Fields as Plotted on Goldmann Perimeter Eight Months Post-Operatively, 1° Diameter Spot, Maximum Brightness. Broken lines show boundaries of intact normal visual fields. Hatched areas indicate intact but amblyopic regions.

Methods and Results

The experimental procedures were carried out over two five-day periods, two to eight months post-operatively, when clinical examinations were also conducted. D.B. was never given knowledge of results during the course of any experiment. With the exception of the eye fixation experiment, which was carried out in a windowless room, all experiments were carried out in an office or a corridor in which it was not possible to control the level of background lighting completely. But in these cases the conditions were as dim as venetian blinds made possible, and generally were only just bright enough for the testers to record the results. All tests were done binocularly. Experiment 1 was conducted two months post-operatively, and all other experiments eight months post-operatively.

Experiment 1. Locating by Eye Fixation

Method.—The subject was seated in the standard position for the Goldmann perimeter, using the chin rest. He was told that a spot of light would be flashed in his blind field and, on a verbal sig-

nal, he was to shift his eyes from the standard fixation point to the position where he "guessed" the spot had been projected. The largest stimulus size (2°) was used, with the brightest setting. On each trial the subject was asked to fixate the standard position; the stimulus was then turned on for 3 seconds at a horizontal eccentricity of 5°, 10°, 15°, 20°, 25°, 30° or 35° in random order. The spot was oscillated up and down by manual control over an are of approximately 4° during each presentation. After every 7 or 14 trials the calibration of the recording system was checked and adjusted if necessary. The subject was asked to move his eyes only after the stimulus was extinguished, but not to move his head. On some series of trials half of the presentations were "blanks," which were identical in all respects to the test trials except that the light was not turned on. For the present analysis a total of 35 light trials and 21 "blank" trials were used.

Eye position was measured binocularly by silver chloride electrodes placed at the medial and lateral canthi, and recorded using a DC system (Hood, 1968) located in an adjacent room. The subject did not always move his eyes to the "steady

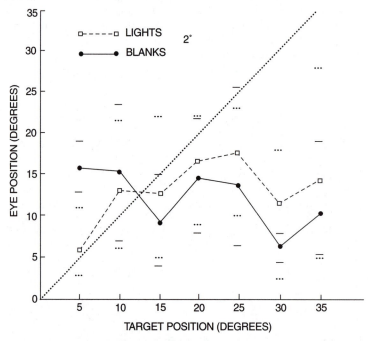

FIGURE 24.2 ■ Mean Eye Positions for Target Positions of Given Eccentricity (see text). For each target position, n = 5 for stimulus trials, and n = 3 for blanks. Bars above and below points indicate range of obtained eye position values. Dotted bars: stimulus trials. Solid bars: blank control trials.

state" position in one operation, but progressed to it after two or three intermediary saccades (occasionally the intermediary position was more eccentric than the final position). For the present analysis only the "steady state" position was used, that is, the position that the eyes finally adopted and maintained for at least two or three seconds.

Results.—As can be seen in Fig. 24.2, there was a weak correspondence between target position and eye position for stimuli placed between 5° and 25°, but not beyond. Each point represents the mean eye position (of 5 trials for lights and 3 trials for blanks) for a given target position. Also shown are the ranges. Despite the large amount of overlap and variability, the linear regression coefficient for eye position on target position, for values between 5° and 25°, is significant from zero (t-test, (P < ·01) although the difference between the regression coefficients for the lights and the blanks is only weakly significant (P < ·05). When all stimulus positions from 5° to 35° were included in the analysis, the regression coefficient for responses to the lights was no longer significantly different from zero (·05 < P < ·1) nor from the coefficient for the blanks (P > ·4). It should be noted that only those runs were included in which there was no drift in the records which would have required recalibration, but the subject's fixation and the electrodes were unusually stable and most runs could be included.

Experiment 2. Locating by Reaching with Finger

Method.—The subject was seated in the standard position for the Aimark perimeter, using the chin rest. He was asked to maintain constant fixation within each trial on the fixation mark, and never to move his head. He was told that a spot of light would be flashed in the blind field for three seconds and afterwards, on a verbal signal he was to reach with his forefinger to the guessed location of the spot without shifting his fixation. The spot was varied in size from 4° 15' to 23', and in some cases (Fig. 24.3, *a* to *e*) was projected on to the perimeter arm from behind the subject with a Keeler projector, and in others the Aimark projector itself was used (Fig. 24.4). In all cases the spot was as bright as the apparatus would permit. All stimuli were presented along the horizontal meridian. For any one test the size of the stimulus was held constant, and its position randomly placed

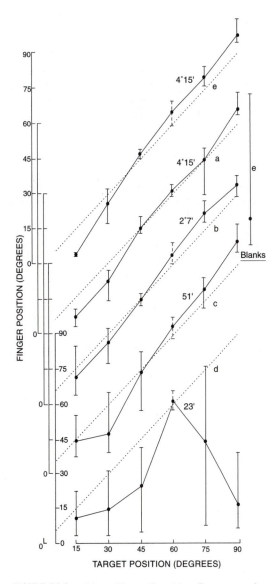

FIGURE 24.3 ■ Mean Finger Reaching Responses for Targets of Given Eccentricity (see text). Series was conducted in order a through e. Vertical bars refer to ranges of obtained values. For each point in a to d, n = 6; in e, n = 3. In condition e blank trials (n = 18) were randomly interspersed between stimulus trials, and mean response position and range for blanks are shown to right of experimental results.

at each of six eccentricities from 15° to 90° (in 15° intervals). Three such tests of 12 trials each were given for each stimulus size, using a different random order in each test. The series was presented in the order of descending size, as indicated in Fig. 24.3, *a* to *d*. Then the largest size was given again (Fig. 24.3, *e*), but with half the trials randomly presented as "blanks."

Also, the subject's reaching for stimuli in his intact right half-field was measured and compared with reaching in his "blind" field for a stimulus spot of 1° 40'. This was done by randomly intermixing the presentations in the right and left half-fields in two tests of 24 trials each, yielding 4 trials for each of the 6 positions in each half-field.

Accuracy of reaching in all cases was determined by using the smallest spot of the Aimark projector and quickly directing it to the position of the finger, and then reading the eccentricity of the spot off the Aimark scale to the nearest 0·5°. The subject was not instructed with which hand to reach, but the perimeter made it difficult to use the hand contralateral to the half-field tested, and the subject never did so.

Results.—The correspondence between target position and finger position was striking for stimuli larger than 23' in diameter and requires no statistical demonstration or justification. The points in Fig. 24.3 show the means (*n* = 6 for each point in

sections a through d and n = 3 for section e) and the ranges for all positions. As the stimuli decreased in size, there was a tendency for the range to increase, until with the smallest size the correlation broke down. The breakdown was not simply the result of the subject's fatigue because when the large size was repeated (section e) the results were very close to those obtained previously with that size. The re-run with the large size also contained "blanks" on half the trials, and the mean value and range are shown in the panel to the right of section e (*n* = 18). D.B.'s responses to "blanks" were highly variable, with a range of 65°, which was larger by a factor of 7 than the mean range (9·75°) of responses to all light positions. It will be noted that with all stimuli except the smallest there was a tendency to err towards the fixation point for stimuli placed less than 45° eccentrically and away from the fixation point for stimuli beyond 45°. The 60° point showed the greatest stability of response, and even with the smallest stimulus size the response to stimuli at this position was accurate. This was not the result of a response bias because, as can be seen in Fig. 24.3 *e*, the mean response to the "blanks" fell at 19·67°.

The results (means and ranges of 4 trials per point) of reaching to stimuli in the good and "blind" fields are shown in Fig. 24.4. In the good half-field the accuracy was high, and for three of the positions no error (to the nearest 0·5°) could be measured. The average deviation over all positions in the good half-field was ±038°. The results for the left half-field were similar to the family of curves obtained in the earlier series (Fig. 24.3, *a, b, c, e*), with an average deviation of ±3·8° (compared with an average deviation of ±4·9° for the earlier series).

Experiment 3. Horizontal vs. Vertical Lines, Diagonal vs. Vertical Lines and X vs. O.

Method.—The subject was seated from 119 to 168 cm in front of a white projection screen. The stimuli were projected on to the screen by a pair of projectors (Leitz Type 31 044 000, 150 watts, Elmaron lens, 1:2·8/85 mm) placed behind the subject. The size of the stimuli were varied either by changing the stimulus slides or, when necessary, the distance of the projectors from the screen. On some tests both projectors were used, one for each stimulus, and on others a single projector, with two slides placed in its carrier. The projec-

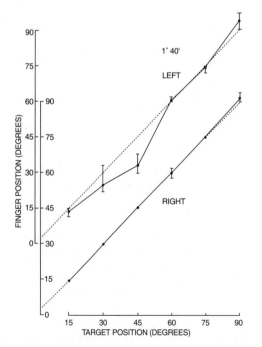

FIGURE 24.4 ■ Mean Finger Reaching Responses for Targets of Given Eccentricity. Stimuli in right and left halffields were randomly interspersed. Vertical bars refer to ranges, n = 4 for each point.

tors were always kept switched on, and the duration of the stimulus controlled by silently masking the front of the lens. For tachistoscopic presentations an electronically controlled shutter (Compur Electronics) was placed in front of the lens. The shutter was calibrated to within ±0·5 per cent.

A number of tests, as shown in Tables 24.1 and 24.2, were conducted over several days, in which the size, contrast (black on white or white on black), duration, and type of stimuli were varied. The testing was adapted as testing proceeded and the limits of the subject's capacity became clear; in general tests in which there was no time limit on the stimulus duration preceded those with tachistoscopic presentation, and the horizontal vs. vertical series came early and the diagonal vs. vertical series late in the experiments. For any particular test, the pair of stimuli was kept constant in size, contrast, position, and duration. For each type of differentiation the stimuli were positioned in most of the tests so that they fell in equally sensitive and acute regions of the retina; vertical and diagonal lines were usually placed below the fixation mark, so that they did not encroach upon the areas adjacent to the amblyopic remnant. The diagonal line was rotated 27° 33' from the vertical.

Each test consisted of 30 trials, 15 trials of one of the pair of stimuli and 15 trials of the other, presented singly in random order. A different random order was used in every test. Before any series the subject was first shown the pair of stimuli in his good half-field and was told that they would be projected in his "blind" field and he would be asked to guess which of the pair it was on each occasion. Fixation was maintained on a small marker on the screen throughout each test. Before the test proper the stimuli were projected into the "blind" field and adjusted in position and size so that the subject consistently denied seeing them. During each test this was repeatedly confirmed by asking the subject whether he had seen the stimulus. The stability of the boundaries of the "seeing" field was very impressive during such preliminary tests, as was the steadiness of fixation maintained by the subject throughout the entire series of experiments. After each stimulus presentation he was asked to guess and report verbally which of the pair had been presented, for example, "X" or "O".

Although no knowledge of results was given until the end of an entire series of tests, the subject was frequently questioned not only as to whether he "saw" the stimuli but for introspective content or "feelings" he might have had about them.

Results.—The results of all 18 tests are shown in Tables 24.1 and 24.2. It is quite evident that D.B. was able to guess at well above chance levels which of the pair of stimuli was presented, provided that (with horizontal vs. vertical lines and X vs. O) the stimuli were larger than a critical size. In the case of diagonal vs. vertical lines, his performance was perfect for the one size used and with unlimited duration. Nor, apparently, in the case of horizontal vs. vertical lines, did it matter whether the stimuli were white upon black background or black upon white background; the latter condition also effectively rules out a possible artifact based on diffusion of light into intact regions of the visual fields. (A similar check was also carried out for X vs. O, with comparable results, but is not reported here.) The effect of size on performance is shown in Fig. 24.5, for those stimuli in which contrast, approximate position, and duration were held constant. If threshold is arbitrarily defined as the 75 per cent performance level, then the threshold for horizontal vs. vertical at 62·5 msec is approximately equal to X. vs. O at 250 msec, and is approximately 12°.

As size decreased, the effect of duration may have become more critical (Fig. 24.6). Thus, with a large size horizontal vs. vertical task (Table 24.1, *b*), performance was 29/30 even at 62·5 msec duration, but for the smallest size performance was only 19/30 at this duration (Table 24.1, *f*). Both of the other tasks also were sensitive to decreasing duration, but in neither case was a very large size stimulus used. The results also demonstrate that performance could be well above chance even with the durations shorter than the latency for the initiation of a saccade, and hence it was not likely to have been dependent upon a fixation shift.

Not only was there internal consistency in the results for size and duration within each type of differentiation, but the three tasks could be roughly ordered in difficulty according to a priori expectations. Thus, at 62·5 msec performance on X vs. O (Table 24.2, *a*) was poorer than on diagonal vs. vertical (Table 24.1, *g*), which was in turn poorer than on horizontal vs. vertical (Table 24.1, *e*), with the size of all three types of stimuli in the same intermediate range of 13°–18°. Similarly, performance on diagonal vs. vertical with unlimited exposure and 125 msec (Table 24.1, *g*) was superior

TABLE 24.1. Stimulus Dimensions, Durations and Performance. In all Cases Uppermost Part of Stimulus Fell Below Horizontal Meridian Except Where Indicated "Above"

Test		Length	Thickness	Right edge to vertical meridan	Top to horizontal meridan	Contrast	Duration	Result
				Horizontal vs. Vertical				
(a)	Hor.	32° 23′	36′	9° 4′	0	W on B	UNL	30/30
	Vert.	39° 46′	36′	5° 28′	19° 53′ above			
(b)	Hor.	33° 39′	36′	4° 5′	4° 5′	W on B	UNL	30/30
							250 msec	30/30
	Vert.	33° 39′	36′	4° 5′	4° 5′		62·5 msec	29/30
(c)	Hor.	12° 20′	37′	4° 15′	4° 52′	W on B	UNL	25/30
	Vert.	12° 43′	37′	4° 52′	3° 3′ above			
(d)	Hor.	12° 26′	26′	2° 8′	1° 47′	B on W	62·5 msec	28/30
	Vert.	24° 30′	26′	2° 8′	1° 47′			
(e)	Hor.	12° 53′	26′	2° 25′	2° 25′	B on W	62·5 msec	25/30
	Vert.	12° 54′		2° 26′	2° 16′			
(f)	Hor.	8° 1′	26′	1° 43′	2° 27′	B on W	62·5 msec	19/30
	Vert.	8° 1′	26′	2° 34′	2° 16′			
				Diagonal vs. Vertical				
(g)	Diag.	16° 56′	35′	7° 21′	1° 7′	W on B	UNL	30/30
							125 msec	29/30
	Vert.	17° 15′	35′	7° 21′	1° 7′		62·5 msec	24/30

to X vs. O with unlimited exposure and 250 msec (Table 24.2, *a*). No effort was made, of course, to make a direct experimental comparison among the tasks, but the consistency is noteworthy considering their separation over several days and the lack of rigid control over background conditions such as lighting levels.

Experiment 4. "Minimal Separable Acuity"

Method.—The subject was seated 53 cm in front of the apparatus that contained diffraction gratings that could produce moiré fringes of varying width and separation. (The apparatus was the same as that used in monkey experiments by Weiskrantz

TABLE 24.2. Stimulus Dimensions, Durations and Performance

Test		Height	Width	Thickness	Right nearpoint to vertical meridian	Top to horizontal meridian	Contrast	Duration	Result
(a)	X	16° 48′	12° 12′	2° 58′	7° 31′	3° 47′ above	B on W	UNL	27/30
								250 msec	26/30
	O	18° 38′	15° 59′	3° 30′	5° 31′	4° 51′ above		62·5 msec	13/30
(b)	X	10° 59′	7° 55′	1° 53′	4° 35′	1° 53′ above	B on W	UNL	27/30
								250 msec	22/30
	O	11° 49′	10° 32′	2° 10′	3° 15′	3° 14′ above			
(c)	X	4° 48′	3° 9′	50′	3° 2′	1° 23′ above	B on W	UNL	19/30
								250 msec	17/30
	O	5° 50′	4° 38′	58′	3° 10′	1° 6′ above			

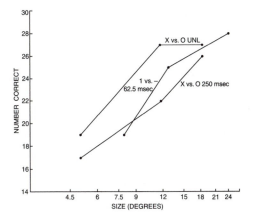

FIGURE 24.5 ■ The Effect of Size of Stimulus on Performance. Size scale logarithmic. Maximum score in all cases is 30; chance performance is 15.

and Cowey (1963), who describe it in detail.) In the normal field one could see a circular aperture (6° 39' in diameter) containing a variable number of vertical dark and light bars depending on their width. The design of apparatus ensured that the flux remained constant independently of the spatial frequency of the bars. A fixation point was placed 8° 48' to the left or the right of the centre of the stimulus field, according to which half-field was being tested. Every test consisted of 30 trials in which the narrowest grating (which appeared homogeneous in the good half-field) was paired with a particular larger bar width. These were presented singly in random order, and the subject asked to report verbally whether there were lines or no lines. In his "blind" half-field, of course, the subject did not "see" any lines, nor indeed even the entire stimulus field, and he was simply asked to guess. Testing was first carried out in the left half-field, starting with the largest bar width possible (25·6') and proceeding progressively to narrower bar widths (7·5', 2·24', 1·85', 1·63'). Then two more tests were given to check the reliability of the results for bar widths of 7·5' and 1·63'. Finally a control test was given in which both stimuli were set equally at the narrowest possible bar width (1·28'). Testing in the good half-field was done in the order 2·24', 1·63', and 1·36'. Also a rough test of acuity in the amblyopic remnant in the upper left half-field was carried out with a suitable fixation point by varying the bar width to wider and narrower values and determining the value at which the subject reported just seeing the lines.

Results.—The results are shown in Fig. 24.7. (The scale 0–180 on the abscissa refers to the calibration curve for this apparatus, cf. Weiskrantz and Cowey, 1963.) For the sake of simplicity the graph shows only the points as measured in directly descending order, and not the two replication checks for bar widths 7·5' and 1·63'. (The results for these two points were 26/30 and 21/30 respectively, as compared with 29/30 and 18/30 in the original series.) Taking the 75 per cent performance level as threshold, the "blind" half-field has an acuity of 1·9' and the right half-field an acuity of 1·5'. There was some slight evidence for a practice effect in this task, in that in the first test with the widest bars, in which the score was 27/30, the 3 errors occurred within the first 7 trials. If all the results are plotted in terms of per cent correct of the final 20 trials in all tests, the threshold in the "blind" half-field is marginally improved to 1·8'. On the control run in which both stimuli were set at the narrowest bar width, a chance score was obtained.

The threshold in the amblyopic remnant in the upper half-field was approximately 8·2'. Even though this is considerably worse than in the acuity for the region of the "blind" field that was measured, the subject always reported "seeing" the bars in the remnant when they were above threshold (and "seeing" the illuminated homogeneous aperture when they were below threshold), whereas he consistently reported seeing nothing, not even the aperture, in the "blind" region under any conditions of this test.

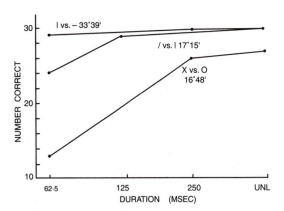

FIGURE 24.6 ■ The Effect of Stimulus Duration on Performance. Maximum score is 30; chance score is 15. UNL: unlimited duration, i.e. stimulus not extinguished until subject responded.

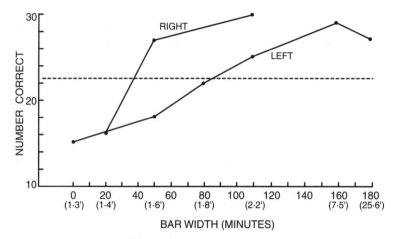

FIGURE 24.7 ■ "Minimal Separable Acuity" in Right and Left Half-fields. Upper numbers on abscissa refer to calibration curve for apparatus in Weiskrantz and Cowey (1963), lower numbers to width of bar (or space). Each point shows performance (maximum = 30) for given stimulus vs. narrowest bar width. Chance = 15. Dotted line shows 75 per cent correct level.

Experiment 5. Red vs. Green

Method.—This experiment must be considered as preliminary because of shortage of time and of a limited range of filters. Five tests of 30 trials each were given under the following conditions: (*a*) the subject was seated in the standard position for the Aimark perimeter. The stimulus was a 4° 15' red or green spot projected on to the perimeter arm from behind the subject to a position 15° to the left of fixation. The Keeler projector was used, with Wratten filters 29 and 61, which have peak transmission at 700 and 530 nanometers respectively. (*b*) The Aimark projector itself was used to produce a red or green spot 1° 40' in diameter, 10° horizontally to the left of the fixation point. The filters had maxima at 700 and 510 nanometers. (*c*) To control for differential sensitivity to the two coloured lights, condition (*a*) was repeated with the brightness level alternated between maximum brightness and a distinctly dimmer setting throughout the 30 trials. It was not possible to calibrate the dimmer setting. The order of red and green continued to be random. (*d*) Similarly condition (*b*) was repeated except that maximum brightness and a dimmer brightness alternated throughout the 30 trials. In this condition, D.B.'s head was positioned 7·6 cm nearer to the fixation point, and hence the effective angular size and the angular separation of the spot from the fixation point were slightly larger than in condition (*b*). (*e*) This was identical to condition (*d*) except that the two bright-

ness levels varied randomly from trial to trial instead of in alternation, and the dim level was made weaker so that it appeared as a faint coloured spot.

Results.—In the first condition (*a*), with a large stimulus size and no brightness variation, D.B. achieved a score of 29/30. With the smaller stimulus (*b*), his score was 21/30. With brightness levels alternated in conditions (*c*) and (*d*), his scores were 22/30 and 24/30. Finally, with the brightness level randomized, the score was 19/30. When questioned about the task, he denied that he saw anything when the stimulus was presented, let alone colour, but after persistent probing he said that he reported "green" when he had a "stronger feeling of something being there," and said "red" when he "felt there was nothing there." This is borne out to a certain extent by the data, which showed that he responded "green" to 28 out of the 45 bright stimuli in the last three tests, and "red" to 24 out of the 45 dim stimuli. In fact, he correctly identified every bright stimulus that actually was green (23/23) and only failed on 7 occasions to correctly identify every dim stimulus that actually was red (16/23). On the other hand, even when the physical brightness was in the opposite direction to his reported criterion (i.e. dim greens and bright reds) his performance did not drop below chance (26/44), and his over-all level of success in the last three control trials was 65/90. While these scores are in the direction of indicating at least some residual capacity to differentiate red vs. green, in the absence of more systematic and better stimulus control they cannot be taken as being more than suggestive.

Discussion

Properties of residual vision.—On the basis of the results thus far it would appear that in his defective field D.B. can locate stimuli in the frontal plane, can differentiate orientation of lines and at least one pair of shapes. All of these differentiations, however, require moderately large stimuli. The evidence also suggests that a slightly longer duration of exposure may be required, at least for a difficult discrimination such as vertical v. oblique lines, than is adequate for discrimination in the good field. (But to establish definitively whether duration per se is a more critical variable in the "blind" half-field than in the good half-field it would be necessary to test the good half-field with even smaller stimuli so that the two half-fields were matched with respect to their size thresholds.) This functionally "amblyopic" aspect of the defective field is combined with a lack of acknowledged awareness of vision even for those stimuli that field consistently near perfect performance. One can dismiss the suggestion that the "amblyopia" itself is sufficient to account for the unawareness, because the subject will always report actually "seeing" stimuli when they fall in the amblyopic remnant in the upper left far peripheral held, even though its minimal separable acuity is in fact poorer than that of the "blind" field in which the grating can be differentiated but not "seen."

Many other aspects of "blind-sight" remain to be determined, but those aspects which are already revealed are quite remarkable, given the dense scotoma yielded by conventional perimetry or by other methods that depend on asking the subject whether or not he "sees" something. The possibility that the subject perhaps inadvertently may have moved his good field on to the stimulus cannot be entirely ruled out, but it seems extremely unlikely that this occurred or could account for the results. Eye fixation was monitored visually by the investigators in all experiments, and in one experiment eye position was continuously monitored electrographically. Moreover, the subject could perform well above chance even with brief exposures below the latency for the initiation of a saccade. D.B.'s performance was also highly systematically related to parameters of the stimuli, such

as size, duration, and angular separation. As he was never given knowledge of results until the completion of an entire group of experiments (which sometimes lasted a number of days), including replication runs and "blank" trials, it would have required an extraordinary degree of skill on the part of the subject to have generated the results by some stratagem. Finally, D.B. throughout convinced us of his reliability. If the projected stimulus happened to fall on to the edge of the intact remnant of his left field he reported this promptly. When he was shown his results he expressed surprise and insisted several times that he thought he was just "guessing." When he was shown a video film of his reaching and judging orientation of lines, he was openly astonished. In an interview just afterwards he commented that he could see none of the stimuli and that he would have told us if he could have seen any, "because otherwise he would have been cheating himself."

Needless to say, he was questioned repeatedly about his vision in his left half-field, and his most common response was that he saw nothing at all. If pressed, he might say that he perhaps had a "feeling" that the stimulus was either pointing this or that way, or was "smooth" (the O) or "jagged" (the X). On one occasion in which "blanks" were randomly inserted in a series of stimuli in a reaching experiment, he afterwards spontaneously commented he had a feeling that maybe there was no stimulus present on some trials. But always he was at a loss for words to describe any conscious perception, and repeatedly stressed that he saw nothing at all in the sense of "seeing," and that he was merely guessing.

D.B. was able to reach with impressive accuracy using his arm and forefinger, whereas he was able to shift his eye fixation to the locus of the stimulus only slightly better than would be expected by chance, and then only if the stimulus required a shift of less than 30° from the initial fixation position. The eye fixation results are in accord with the findings of Pöppel, Held and Frost (1973). It is possible that if he had been able to move his head freely, his fixation performance might have been much better. It is, in general, rare to find saccadic shifts of more than 30° in free observation situations; more commonly, one uses the head to effect a gross movement, with the eyes "homing in" with saccades somewhat less than 30° in extent. The head was also not moved in the finger-pointing experiment, but under these conditions it may be easier to "reach" accurately with the arm and finger than with the eyes.

Before operation D.B. had a very small left homonymous paracentral scotoma no doubt caused by tissue destruction by the angioma, and so postoperatively he had a large "fresh" left field defect in combination with a much older one. It remains to be determined whether with more sensitive measures, for example brightness incremental thresholds using the "guessing" technique, one could differentiate the old and the new scotomatous regions. Whether or not this proves possible, one must leave open the question as to whether D.B.'s "blind-sight" will change with time and knowledge of results, as is true of the monkey (cf. Weiskrantz and Cowey, 1970). A whole host of questions about the possible properties of "blindsight" remain to be explored in detail, among them colour, depth, acuity as a function of retinal locus, adaptation, number of stimulus alternatives available, the perceptual constancies—in short, all of the attributes of normal "seeing" itself. The fundamental question, of course, is whether D.B.'s "blind-sight" is merely degraded normal vision or whether it represents a qualitatively distinctive visual capacity.

Relation to animal lesion studies.—Total removal of striate cortex in the monkey, with consequential total degeneration of cells in the dorsal lateral geniculate nucleus, does not abolish pattern discrimination altogether, although such animals are slower to learn such discriminations (Pasik and Pasik, 1971). They can also be trained to reach for a visual stimulus, such as a flash of light, placed randomly in the field, and can do this successfully even when the flash is very brief and below the saccade latency (Weiskrantz, Cowey and Darlington, in preparation, but in this study there is not yet histological confirmation). But the monkey's reaching behaviour is not absolutely precise and if two stimuli a few inches apart are presented the animal may reach in between them; with a single stimulus it tends to reach to a region in which the stimulus falls rather than to hit it precisely and reliably. On the basis of results of animal research, it has been speculated that the residual vision of a monkey lacking striate cortex is essentially normal qualitatively but is amblyopic, lacking capacity to discriminate fine detail (Weiskrantz, 1972).

In these respects, D.B.'s capacity is quite similar. His ability to differentiate failed when the

stimuli were smaller than a critical size (roughly 10° in length for orientation and X vs. 0), and his reaching also failed with a small stimulus (the critical size being somewhere between 50' and 23'). His "minimal separable acuity" was also lower than that of a corresponding portion of his good field. His reaching behaviour was less accurate for a stimulus in the bad field than in the good, with a mean deviation of approximately ±5°. and he showed a reliable tendency to mis-reach towards the fixation point for stimuli with an eccentricity of less than 45° and to mis-reach away from fixation point for more eccentric stimuli. Whether or not the monkey without striate cortex can discriminate colour is still unsettled, there being both positive and negative reports (Pasik and Pasik, 1971; Humphrey, 1970). The evidence for D.B. is no more than marginally positive for a discrimination between red and green (with intensity difference randomly varied), and more work remains to be done. A monkey with total unilateral striate removal or partial bilateral striate removal shows a raising of the incremental threshold for a 1° light flash, but there is a gradual improvement with postoperative training (Cowey and Weiskrantz, 1963; Cowey, 1967). This threshold was not measured in D.B.'s defective field.

The capacity of the destriated mammal has also been interpreted in the light of distinctions made under the rubric of "two visual system" theories between recognizing, identifying, or examining, on the one hand, and detecting or orienting on the other. Perhaps the best-known subject is "Helen," a monkey with a large bilateral striate cortex lesion who was studied by Humphrey over several years (Humphrey and Weiskrantz, 1967; Humphrey, 1970, 1972). He described her as being "unable to identify even those things most familiar to her. After six years she still does not know a carrot when she sees one, nor apparently can she recognize my face," despite an excellent ability to locate and detect visual events in her environment and to avoid obstacles in a free field. "In one sense she sees everything, in another sense, nothing" (Humphrey, 1972, p. 684). In one sense D.B. also fails to recognize familiar objects, but he also is unaware that he can detect. In behavioural terms he can both "detect" *and* "identify," at least under our conditions of testing, but he admits to no awareness of either capacity. It is possible that his ability to "identify" might derive from a capacity that is primarily attentional in character, in that the sharp onset or offset of different patterned stimuli might generate different degrees of "saliency" (Humphrey, 1970) and elicit directional orienting responses. It remains to be determined whether D.B.'s ability to differentiate orientation or pattern would diminish when the stimuli are presented for long durations.

In all of our testing to date with D.B. we had the advantage of being able to instruct him both by telling him what the range of possible stimuli were to be in any series and also by showing him examples in his good half-field. To train the destriated monkey to reach accurately or to discriminate requires long and patient training. Whether D.B. would be able to guess the identity or orientation of stimuli without previous instruction is an open question, but certainly it would make his task very much harder.

The doctrine of "encephalization of visual function" postulated that visual capacity becomes increasingly dependent on cortical structures with ascending phylogenetic status. The evidence for the doctrine was always far from adequate (cf. Weiskrantz, 1961), and the present results are a distinct embarrassment to it. In one important respect, however, it is difficult to make direct comparisons between D.B.'s capacity and that of lesioned animals. In terms of behavioural measures, as we have seen, they are not dissimilar, but D.B. is unaware of "seeing" the stimuli he differentiates. We do not know whether the lesioned animal similarly might be said to have "blind-sight." Operational purists might argue that such a question directed at the animal research is meaningless. It seems arbitrary to deny the monkey states of awareness or unawareness, but the design of a programme for studying such states in an animal presents something of a methodological and philosophical challenge.

Neural basis of residual vision.—D.B.'s left half-field can be divided into two regions, the larger portion in which the location, orientation, and distribution of stimuli can be differentiated within certain limits but in which the subject has no acknowledged awareness of those stimuli, and a smaller remnant in the upper peripheral region which definitely has reduced acuity (compared with a symmetrical region in the right half-field) but otherwise seems to be normal and in which awareness of stimuli is readily acknowledged. Two views can be offered for the anatomical dispositions of his right hemisphere lesion, depending upon whether it is assumed that a striate cortex lesion alone is sufficient to produce a scotoma with "blind-sight." It has been commonly assumed, following Gordon Holmes (1918), that a striate cortex lesion is sufficient to produce a scotoma and that the amblyopic fringes of such a scotoma are due to partial and perhaps patchy interruption of radiations or surrounding cortical tissue. On this basis, it would be inferred that there is still some intact and functional striate cortex in the anterior portion of the inferior bank of the calcarine fissure on the right side. An alternative suggestion (Weiskrantz, 1972) is that isolated striate cortex damage causes amblyopia, but that the greater the additional damage to prestriate and posterior association cortex the more severe is the deficit and the more it tends towards a capacity limited to total luminous flux discrimination. (The animal research does not allow us yet to say just which nonstriate cortical regions are critical.) On this view, D.B. would have little if any functional striate cortex in the right hemisphere, but the lesion would be expected to be smaller and more nearly restricted to area 17 in the far anterior lower bank of the calcarine fissure, and more posteriorly to involve area 17 together with the surrounding prestriate and additional association cortex.

The same issue is involved in understanding whether "blind-sight" depends upon there being a region of intact vision in a half-field. The control of eye fixation by stimuli in a scotoma reported by Pöppel, Held and Frost (1973) has not been found by them in either of their two cases with a complete homonymous hemianopia (personal communication). Because striate cortex is largely buried in the medial region of the human brain (Weiskrantz, 1972), any lesion leading to its complete destruction ipso facto would be highly likely to cause considerable damage to extrastriate tissue in addition, thereby removing the areas critical for "blind-sight."

In the absence of striate cortex in the primate, visual information can still reach the mid-brain and also other regions of the brain by parallel pathways. From the superior collicular there is a projection to the several areas of posterior association cortex through the posterior thalamus, and many of these same areas probably also normally receive direct projections from the intact striate cortex. Whether there are any regions of posterior association cortex which are critical for any of the capacities displayed by D.B., and whether it is the convergence of information from more than one route which is necessary for "seeing" cannot be answered as yet. But in evaluating D.B.'s capacities, attention naturally focuses on the tuning properties of superior colliculus cells and the retinotopic map found there. Collicular cells which respond selectively to orientation of lines in the cat or monkey are very uncommon if indeed they exist at all. Nevertheless, the organization of the relay pathways to the cortex may allow a sensitivity to orientation to emerge, just as orientation sensitivity is seen in area 17 but not in the lateral geniculate nucleus; there is a danger of evaluating the properties and capacities of the "second visual system" merely in terms of the responses of single units at one way-station, the superior colliculus.

The retinotopic map found in the superior colliculus of primates, especially in the upper layers in which the input arrives, may provide the basis for the adequate reaching responses shown by D.B. There has as yet been no anatomical demonstration in the monkey of a direct pathway from the foveal and parafoveal regions of the retina to the colliculus, perhaps because the fibres may be of small diameter (Wilson and Toyne, 1970), although an indirect pathway by way of the striate cortex certainly exists. On the other hand, electrophysiological responses in the colliculus to foveal and parafoveal stimulation of the retina are still preserved after striate cortex removal in the monkey (Schiller, Stryber, Cynader and Berman, 1974). It would be interesting to determine D.B.'s accuracy of reaching within the parafoveal region, but this remains to be done. Information regarding the "magnification factor" of the superior colliculus is also too imprecise to allow one to estimate effective resolving power in different regions of the field, but it is not surprising, given a much smaller population of cells in the colliculus for the visual field as a whole than in striate cortex, and also given the larger optimal stimulus size to which Y-cells are tuned (see below), that D.B.'s differentiations of location and orientation break down with smaller stimuli.

It is of interest to consider whether the "blindsight" of D.B. may be similar to the impairment of vision by split-brain patients for certain types of stimuli in their left half-fields (Gazzaniga, 1970; Trevarthen and Sperry, 1973), but there are also apparent differences; for example D.B. cannot "see" even those stimuli which the commissurotomy cases admit seeing in their left half-fields, and D.B.'s difficulty does not lie with access to verbal labels. There is no reason to believe that D.B. has an interruption to callosal fibres as such, but without further research using common testing methods it is premature to comment in detail on the similarities and differences between him and the split-brain patients. But quite independently of the resemblance, superficial (as we suspect it is) or otherwise, between split-brain phenomena and D.B.'s "blind-sight," it would be of considerable interest to compare the possible differences in the various components of "blindsight" in cases of right vs. left hemisphere occipital damage. It should be noted that Pöppel, Held and Frost's (1973) study of the control of voluntary eye fixation shifts included cases both of right and left half-field scotomata. It would also prove interesting to examine separately the two eyes and the four eye-hand combinations of D.B. and any other comparable patients.

Within recent years there has been increasing evidence in the cat for at least two classes, X and Y, of retinal ganglion cells and optic nerve fibres, with different tuning characteristics and partly different target regions in the brain (cf. Wright and Ikeda, 1974). The Y cells are larger and have larger axons, respond to transient rather than sustained retinal stimulation, are optimally tuned to larger stimuli than X cells, and project both to cortex (through the lateral geniculate nucleus) and to the colliculus. The projections of the X cells appear to be confined to the geniculostriate pathways (although it may be too soon to conclude that there are absolutely no X-type responses in the colliculus, especially in its most rostral portion). D.B.'s "minimal separable acuity" may reflect the operation of the Y system in the absence of the cortical target region of the X system. If this is so, the variation of his acuity as a function of retinal locus might be expected to be different from the well-known normal function relating acuity to retinal eccentricity. For this reason it is especially important to study his acuity at different retinal loci. It is even possible that this function would predict in detail the density distribution of Y cells in the retina, which in turn might be revealed independently by studying the retinae of monkeys deprived of striate cortex for several years (Cowey and Humphrey, in preparation) as well as by direct measure of normal retina. It is claimed, but not in detail, that there are differences between the distributions of X and Y cells in the cat's retina.

Future practical implications. The remarkable visual capacities of D.B. to differentiate stimuli within his "blind" field, displayed without acknowledged awareness, would appear to demand the re-examination of the whole range of field defects associated with retro-chiasmal damage. Any method that depends upon asking a patient whether or not he "sees" may seriously underestimate his residual visual capacity. We might expect, from the animal research, that the more extensive the posterior cortical damage the more restricted will be the capacity of the residual "blind-sight." The medial and buried disposition of striate cortex in man makes it extremely likely that when it is damaged surrounding association cortex also suffers damage, and this almost certainly applied to the two cases described by Brindley, Gautier-Smith and Lewin (1969) of virtually complete "cortical blindness." With further study, it might also emerge that damage to specific cortical regions might affect specific sub-categories of residual vision, including the acknowledgment of awareness itself. Therefore from future studies results might emerge allowing greater diagnostic power than is possible with the plotting of field defects by conventional perimetry or confrontation methods.

It has become clear that monkeys with bilateral striate cortex removal, if given the benefit of protracted and specific post-operative training regimes, can display much greater visual skill than would have been accepted traditionally. The improvement that the animals show is neither spontaneous nor inevitable without such training. The critical features of such therapy remain to be determined, but one important aspect appears to be the arranging of visual events in the animal's space in such a way that he can at first relate them to distinctive features of a tactile-kinaesthetic space and obtain rapid and reliable feed-back from those features. At the outset of such training, it looks to the human observer very much like an act of "discovery" by the animal that he possesses a viable visual space, and after the initial discovery performance can improve rather rapidly (Humphrey and Weiskrantz, 1967). Whether patients with "blind-sight" can be taught to exploit this capacity remains to be determined. The possible benefits to patients with cortical damage described clinically as "blind" in all or part of their visual fields obviously makes it important to explore the therapeutic potentialities of "blind-sight" intensively.

Summary

A patient with a restricted lesion of the right occipital lobe was investigated to assess the possibility of some visual capacity in his hemianopic field which was blind on conventional perimetric testing. Even though the patient had no awareness of "seeing" in his blind field, evidence was obtained that (*a*) he could reach for visual stimuli with considerable accuracy; (*b*) could differentiate the orientation of a vertical line from a horizontal or a diagonal line; (*c*) could differentiate the letters "X" and "O". These tasks could be performed accurately only if the stimuli were larger than a critical size, but good performance was still possible even with brief stimulus durations below the latency for the initiation of a saccadic eye movement. In addition, (*d*) the results of Pöppel, Held and Frost (1973) were confirmed in that there was a weak but significant correlation between target position and eye fixation for loci out to 30° eccentricity in the "blind" field, but not beyond. (*e*) The subject could differentiate a grating of vertical bars from a homogeneous field when the bars were sufficiently wide, and this provided a measure of "minimal separable acuity," which was only slightly poorer than the acuity of the symmetrical region in the good half-field. (*f*) Suggestive but inconclusive evidence was obtained for an ability to differentiate between red and green projected stimuli.

The observations suggest that the visual capacity remaining after damage to striate cortex may be much greater than is commonly accepted. The properties of the residual vision are compared with the behavioural capacities of monkeys with striate cortex damage. The possible neural basis of "blind-sight" is discussed, together with some implications for diagnosis and therapy.

REFERENCES

Brindley, G. S., Gautier-Smith, P. C., & Lewin, W. (1969). Cortical blindness and the functions of the non-geniculate fibres of the optic tracts. *J. Neurol. Neurosurg. Psychiat.*, *32*, 259–264.

Cowey, A. (1967). Perimetric study of field defects in monkeys after cortical and retinal ablations. *Q. Jl exp. Psychol.*, *19*, 232–245.

___, & Weiskrantz, L. (1963). A perimetric study of visual field defects in monkeys. *Q. Jl exp. Psychol.*, *15*, 91–115.

Gazzaniga, M. S. (1970). *The Bisected Brain*. New York: Appteton-Century-Crofts.

Holmes, G. (1918). Disturbances of vision by cerebral lesions.

Brit. J. Ophthal., 2, 353–384.

Hood, J. D. (1968). Electro-nystagmography. *J. Laryng., 82,* 167–183.

Humphrey, N. K. (1970). What the frog's eye tells the monkey's brain. *Brain, Behav. Evol., 3,* 324–337.

___ (1972) Seeing and nothingness. *New Scientist,* March 30, 682–684.

___, & Weiskrantz, L. (1967). Vision in monkeys after removal of the striate cortex. *Nature, Lond., 215,* 595–597.

Ingle, D. (1967). Two visual mechanisms underlying the behaviour of fish. *Psychol. Forsch., 31,* 44–51.

Pasik, K, T., & Pasik, P. (1971). The visual world of monkeys deprived of striate cortex: effective stimulus parameters and the importance of the accessory optic system. *Vision Research Supplement, No. 3,* 419–435.

Pöppel, E., Held, R., and Frost, D. (1973) Residual visual function after brain wounds involving the central visual pathways in man. *Nature, Lond., 243,* 295–296.

Riddoch, G. (1917) Dissociation of visual perceptions due to occipital injuries, with especial reference to appreciation of movement. *Brain, 40,* 15–57.

Sanders, M. D., Warrington, E. K., Marshall, J., & Weiskrantz, L. (1974). "Blindsight": Vision in a field defect. *Lancet,* April 20, 707–708.

Schiller, P. H., Stryber, M., Cynader, M., & Berman, N. (1974). Response characteristics of single cells in the monkey superior colliculus following ablation or cooling of visual cortex. *J. Neurophysiol., 37,* 181–194.

Schneider, G. E. (1969). Two visual systems. *Science, 163,* 895–902.

Teuber, H.-L., Battersby, W. S., & Bender, M. B. (1960). *Visual Field Defects after Penetratinig Missile Wounds of the Brain.* Cambridge, Massachusetts: Harvard University Press.

Trevarthen, C. B. (1968). Two mechanisms of vision in primates. *Psychol. Forsch., 31,* 299–337.

___, & Sperry, R. W. (1973). Perceptual unity of the ambient visual field in human commissurotomy patients. *Brain, 96,* 547–570.

Ward, J. P., & Masterton, B. (1970). Encephalization and visual cortex in the Tree Shrew (*Tupaio glis*). *Brain, Behav. Evol., 3,* 421–469.

Weiskrantz, L. (1961). Encephalization and the scotoma. In W. H. Thorpe & O. L. Zangwill (eds.), *Current Problems in Animal Behaviour* (pp. 30–58). London and New York: Cambridge University Press.

___ (1972). Behavioural analysis of the monkey's visual nervous system. *Proc. R. Sec. Lond. B., 182,* 427–455.

___, & Cowey, A. (1963). Striate cortex lesions and visual acuity of the rhesus monkey. *J. comp. Physiol. Psychol., 56,* 225–231.

___, ___ (1970). Filling in the scotoma: A study of residual vision after striate cortex lesions in monkeys. In E. Stellar & J. M. Sprague (eds.), *Progress in Physiological Psychology,* Vol. 3, pp. 237–260. New York and London: Academic Press Inc.

Wilson, M. E., & Toyne, M. J. (1970). Retino-tectal and cortico-tectal projections in *Macaca mulatta. Brain Res., 24,* 395–406.

Wilson, M. J., & Ikeda, H. (1974). Processing of spatial and temporal information in the nervous system: In F. O. Schmitt & F. G. Wordea (eds.), *The Neurosciences: Third Study Program,* pp. 115–122. Cambridge, Massachusetts, and London: The MIT Press.

READING 25

The Role of Temporal Cortical Areas in Perceptual Organization

D. L. Sheinberg and N. K. Logothetis
• Baylor College of Medicine

The visual areas of the temporal lobe of the primate are thought to be essential for the representation of visual objects. To examine the role of these areas in the visual awareness of a stimulus, we recorded the activity of single neurons in monkeys trained to report their percepts when viewing ambiguous stimuli. Visual ambiguity was induced by presenting incongruent images to the two eyes, a stimulation condition known to instigate binocular rivalry, during which one image is seen at a given time while the other is perceptually suppressed. Previous recordings in areas V1, V2, V4, and MT of monkeys experiencing binocular rivalry showed that only a small proportion of striate and early extrastriate neurons discharge exclusively when the driving stimulus is seen. In contrast, the activity of almost all neurons in the inferior temporal cortex and the visual areas of the cortex of superior temporal sulcus was found to be contingent upon the perceptual dominance of an effective visual stimulus. These areas thus appear to represent a stage of processing beyond the resolution of ambiguities—and thus beyond the processes of perceptual grouping and image segmentation—where neural activity reflects the brain's internal view of objects, rather than the effects of the retinal stimulus on cells encoding simple visual features or shape primitives.

Neurons in the visual areas of the anterior temporal lobe of monkeys exhibit pattern-selective responses that are modulated by visual attention and are affected by the stimulus in memory, suggesting that these areas play an important role in the perception of visual patterns and the recognition of objects (1, 2). To understand the role of these areas in perception and object vision, we conducted combined psychophysical and electrophysiological experiments in monkeys experiencing binocular rivalry. Binocular rivalry refers to the stochastic changes of perception when one is viewing two different patterns dichoptically. We have recently shown that the perceived image during

rivalry is independent of which eye it is seen through (3), a finding that suggests that binocular rivalry may be the result of competition between different stimulus representations throughout the visual cortex, rather than between the two monocular channels early in striate cortex (for review see ref. 4). The study of cell activity during binocular rivalry may therefore provide us with significant insights regarding the neural sites and mechanisms underlying the perceptual multistability experienced when one is viewing any ambiguous fig-

Abbreviations: STS, superior temporal sulcus; IT, inferior temporal cortex; SDF, spike density function.

ures, such as the well studied figure-ground reversals, and may lead to a better understanding of the principles of perceptual organization.

Methods

Two animals (*Macaca mulatta*) participated in the experiments reported in this paper. After the monkeys were familiarized with the laboratory environment and the experimenter, they underwent an aseptic surgery (5, 6). After recovery, the monkeys were trained to fixate a light spot and to perform a categorization task by pulling one of two levers attached to the front of their primate chair. They were taught to pull and hold the left lever whenever a sunburst-like pattern (left-object) was displayed and to pull and hold the right lever upon presentation of other figures, including images of humans, monkeys, apes, wild animals, butterflies, reptiles, and various manmade objects (right-objects). In addition, they were trained not to respond or to release an already pulled lever upon presentation of a physical blend of different stimuli (mixed-objects).

Example stimuli are shown in Fig. 25.1. The patterns were generated using a graphics computer (Indigo2, Silicon Graphics) and were presented on a display monitor placed 97 cm away from the animal. Stereoscopic presentations were accomplished using a liquid crystal polarizer (NuVision SGS19S) that allowed alternate transmission of images with circularly opposite polarization at the rate of 120 frames per sec (60 frames per sec for each eye). Polarized glasses were worn to allow the passage of only every other image to each eye.

During the behavioral task, individual observation periods consisted of random transitions between presentations of left-, right-, and mixed-objects. Juice reward was delivered only after the successful completion of an entire observation period. However, negative feedback was always given to the monkeys in the form of aborting an observation period following an incorrect response. Once the animals had learned to classify the different object types rapidly and accurately, periods of rivalrous stimulation (7–20 sec) were introduced in observation periods lasting 15–30 sec. During rivalrous periods, no feedback was given to the monkeys. Eye position was constantly monitored and stored. Excursions of the eyes outside of a $\pm 0.75°$ window surrounding the fixation spot automatically aborted the observation period.

Single-cell activity was recorded in both monkeys in the upper and lower banks of superior temporal sulcus (STS) and the inferior temporal cortex (IT) using of a chamber consisting of a ball-and-socket joint with a 18-gauge stainless steel tube passing through its center (7). The base of the well was secured to the skull using small skull-screws and bone cement. The position of the guide-tube could be varied before each experimental session in any direction using a calibration device, attachable to the outer part of the ball-and-socket joint. The placement of the chambers was aided by a set of x-ray images combined with a set of magnetic resonance images (2.4-Tesla Magnet; Bruker, Billerica, MA) acquired before the head-post surgery of each monkey. We recorded from three hemispheres in two monkeys with the chambers placed at AP = 20, L = 20; AP = 19, L = 20; and AP = 19, L = 19, respectively. By swiveling the guide tube, different sites could be accessed within an ≈8 × 8 mm^2 cortical region. Since both monkeys are still alive and participating in similar experiments, the recording areas were estimated from the stereotaxic coordinates of the guide tube and the white-to-gray matter transitions expected from magnetic resonance images. According to these estimates, the recording sites were probably in areas TPO1, TPO2, and TEa and in the gyral portion of IT, most likely areas TEm, TE1, and TE2.

"Left" Objects   "Mixed" Objects   "Right" Objects

FIGURE 25.1 ■ Example Stimuli Used During the Experiments. Stimuli consisted of geometrical sunburst patterns (left-objects), images of animate objects (right-objects), and physical blends of images that were used to mimic piecemeal rivalry (mixed-objects). The monkeys were trained to pull the left lever whenever the left-objects were visible, the right-lever whenever the right-objects were visible, and neither when mixed-objects were visible.

Results

Because the interpretation of the neurophysiological data of this study strongly depended on the reliability of the animals' behavioral responses, special care was taken to ensure that the monkeys were reporting their perceptions accurately, rather than alternately pulling the levers in a random fashion. To encourage reliable performance, each observation period consisted of randomly intermixed periods of rivalrous and nonrivalrous stimulation, during which left-objects and right-objects were displayed monocularly. The slightly lustrous appearance of a monocularly viewed image served to maximize the similarity of percepts elicited by nonrivalrous and rivalrous stimulation and to reduce the chances of the monkey adopting different behavioral strategies in the two different stimulation conditions. Moreover, to train the monkey to report only exclusive visibility of a figure, mixed-objects, mimicking piecemeal rivalry, were randomly intermixed within each observation period. The monkeys reliably withheld response during these mixed periods, even when such periods constituted an entire observation period.

Finally, we systematically compared the monkeys' psychophysical performance with that of humans in the same tasks. During binocular rivalry, the time for which different stimuli are perceived depends strongly on the images' relative stimulus strength, a term specifying the combined effect of such stimulus parameters as luminance, contrast, spatiotemporal frequency, and amount of contour per stimulus area (8). For our task, we varied stimulus strength by changing the spatial frequency content of one image in the stimulus pair by lowpass filtering it. In humans, limiting the spatial frequency content of an image has been shown to decrease the stimulus' predominance (9), where predominance of a stimulus is typically defined as the percentage of the total viewing time during which this stimulus is perceived (8). Since our stimuli were large enough (2.5 × 2.5°) to often instigate piecemeal rivalry, predominance of the stimulus was defined to be the ratio of the time for which one stimulus was exclusively visible to the total time for which either stimulus was exclusively visible.

Fig. 25.2 shows the remarkable similarity in the dependency of predominance of a visual pattern on its spatial frequency content in both monkeys and humans. We take the consistency in both sets

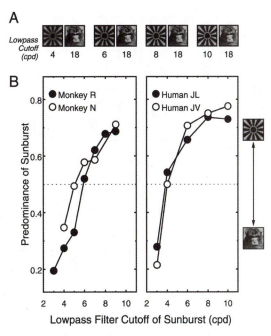

FIGURE 25.2 ■ Behavioral Verification of Monkey's Performance During Rivalry. (*A*) Each pair of images depicts a stimulus condition, wherein the image of the face remained unchanged while that of the sunburst was blurred, to various degrees, by lowpass filtering. Filtering was achieved by multiplying the amplitudes of forward Fourier transformed images by an exponential gain and then converting back to the space domain. The lowpass cutoffs shown below each image refer to the frequency at which the exponential filter was equal to l/e. (*B*) Predominance of a stimulus as function of spatial frequency bandwidth. Predominance is defined here as $T_{sunburst}/(T_{sunburst} + T_{face})$, where $T_{sunburst}$ and T_{face} are the time durations for which the sunburst and the face were exclusively visible. (*Left*) Data from monkeys and (*Right*) data from experimentally naive human subjects. Note that predominance is systematically related to the spatial frequency content of the sunburst pattern for both monkeys and humans; as the sunburst is blurred to greater extents, it is perceived dominant for a decreasing proportion of time.

of data as strong evidence for the reliability of the monkeys' behavior.

Following the initial behavioral training, we began the combined psychophysical-physiological experiments. We isolated 159 visually responsive single units. Responsiveness was determined by presenting stimuli from a battery of hundreds of visual images. The selectivity of these cells was tested by repeatedly presenting a subset of the available visual stimuli in pseudorandom order in

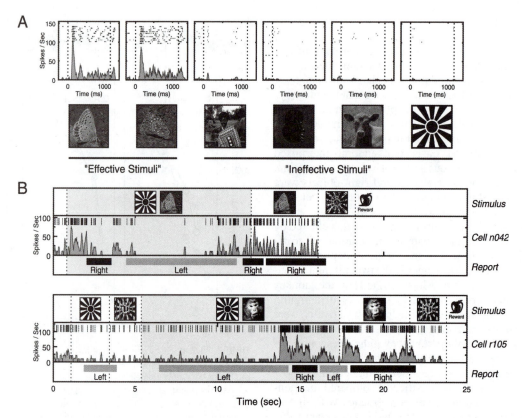

FIGURE 25.3 ■ Neural Responses During Passive Viewing and During the Behavioral Task. (*A*) Response selectivity of an IT neuron. Effective stimuli were the two butterfly images, while almost all other tested images (30 tested, 4 shown) elicited little or no response from the cell. Each plot shows aligned rasters of spikes collected just before, during, and after the presentation of the image depicted below the graph. The smooth filled lines in each plot are the mean SDFs for all trials. The dotted vertical lines mark stimulus onset and stimulus removal. (*B*) Example observation periods taken from the behavioral task for individual cells from monkey *N* (*Upper*) and monkey R (*Lower*). Observation periods during behavioral testing consisted of random combinations of nonrivalrous stimuli and rivalrous periods. Dotted vertical lines mark transitions between stimulus conditions. Rivalry periods, which could occur at any time during an observation period, are shown by the filled gray background. The horizontal light and dark bars show the time periods for which the monkey reported exclusive visibility of the left-lever (sunburst) and right-lever (e.g., butterfly or monkey face) objects. Note that during rivalry the monkey reports changes in the perceived stimulus with no concomitant changes of the displayed images. Such perceptual alternations regularly followed a significant change in the neurons' activity, as shown by the individual spikes in the middle of each plot and by the SDFs below the spikes. Note the similarity of the responses elicited by the unambiguous presentation of the effective and ineffective stimuli (white regions) with those responses elicited before either stimulus becomes perceptually salient during rivalrous stimulation (gray region).

search of one or more effective stimuli, while the monkey fixated a central light spot.

Example responses of an IT neuron are shown in Fig. 25.3*A*. The cell discharges action potentials upon presentation of the effective stimuli, here images of particular butterflies, and responds minimally to all other tested stimuli (including the sunburst pattern). Of the visually responsive neurons, 50 were found to be selective enough to be tested

during the object classification task under both nonrivalrous and rivalrous conditions. The rivalry stimuli were created by presenting the effective stimulus to one eye and the ineffective stimulus (i.e., the sunburst) to the other. Fig. 25.3*B* shows two observation periods during this task, one from each monkey. Each plot illustrates the stimulus configuration, the neuron's activity, and the monkey's reported percept throughout the entire observation period. In both cases, the neuron discharged only before and during the periods in which the monkey reported seeing the effective stimulus. During rivalrous stimulation, the stimulus configuration remained constant, but significant changes in cell activity were accompanied by subsequent changes in the monkeys' perceptual report.

The neural activity was further analyzed by constructing average spike density functions (SDFs), sorted by the monkey's perceptual reports. Fig. 25.4A shows these data for the same cell depicted in the Fig. 25.3B Upper. Fig. 4A Upper and Lower show responses in nonrivalrous and rivalrous conditions, respectively. As shown in Fig. 25.3A, this neuron fired vigorously when the monkey reported seeing the cell's preferred pattern in both the nonrivalrous and rivalrous conditions. However, when the monkey reported seeing the ineffective stimulus, the cell response was almost eliminated, even when the effective stimulus was physically present during rivalry.

To increase the instances of exclusive visibility of one stimulus, and to further ensure that the monkey's report accurately reflected which stimulus he perceived at any given time, we also tested the psychophysical performance of the monkeys and the neural responses of STS and IT cells using the flash suppression paradigm (10). In this condition, one of the two stimuli used to instigate rivalry is first viewed monocularly for 1–2 sec. Following the monocular preview, rivalry is induced by presenting the second image to the contralateral eye. Under these conditions, human subjects invariably perceive only the newly presented image and the previewed stimulus is rendered invisible. Previous studies have shown that the suppression of the previewed stimulus is not due to forward masking or light adaptation (10) and that instead it shares much in common with the perceptual suppression experienced during binocular rivalry (11). In our experiments, the monkeys, just like the human subjects, consistently reported seeing the stimulus presented to the eye contralateral to the previewing eye during the flash suppression trials.

To confirm that the animals responded only when a flashed stimulus was exclusively dominant, catch trials were introduced in which mixed stimuli were flashed, after which the monkey was required to release both levers. Performance for both animals was consistently >95% for this task. Fig. 25.4B shows the activity of an STS neuron in the flash suppression condition. Fig. 25.4B Upper

shows the cell responses for monocular presentations, and the Fig. 25.4B Lower shows the neuron's activity at the end of the monocular preview (to the left of the dotted vertical line) and when perceptual dominance is exogenously reversed as the rival stimulus is presented to the other eye (to the right of dotted vertical line). The cell fires vigorously when the effective stimulus dominates perception and ceases firing entirely when the ineffective stimulus is made dominant. To better understand the differences between the temporal areas and the prestriate areas, recordings were also performed in area V4 using the flash suppression paradigm (D. Leopold and N.K.L., unpublished observations). V4 neurons were largely unaffected by the perceptual changes during flash suppression. Presenting the ineffective stimulus after priming with the effective one caused no alteration in the firing rate of any of the cells; presenting the effective stimulus after priming with the other had an weak effect on a small percentage of V4 neurons.

Across the population of cells from which we recorded, we found significant differences in the temporal structure of individual neural responses. Some neurons responded in a sustained fashion, while others exhibited a periodic burst or very transient response (Fig. 25.5A). We were concerned that typical methods of characterizing cell response, such as counting the number of spikes occurring within a fixed time window, would ignore these potentially informative variations. We thus characterized the entire spike waveforms for each trial using a well established method of dimensionality reduction and then applied multivariate statistical tests on the data to test for differences in cell response between the ineffective and effective trials (13). A detailed description of the analysis methods is given elsewhere (14). Briefly, the spike train for each trial was defined as a discrete function over the interval $[0, N-1]$, where N was the number of points in the peristimulus time window (for population analysis, 800 points spaced 1 msec apart). The spike function takes the value 1 if a spike occurs at point t, with $t \in [0, N-1]$, and zero otherwise. Each trial's SDF was computed using the adaptive-kernel estimation process (15). These SDFs were subjected to principal components analysis (16), which is an orthogonal transform that typically results in a description of the data in a response space with strongly reduced dimensionality, and whose basis vectors, called the principal components, are uncorrelated (and can

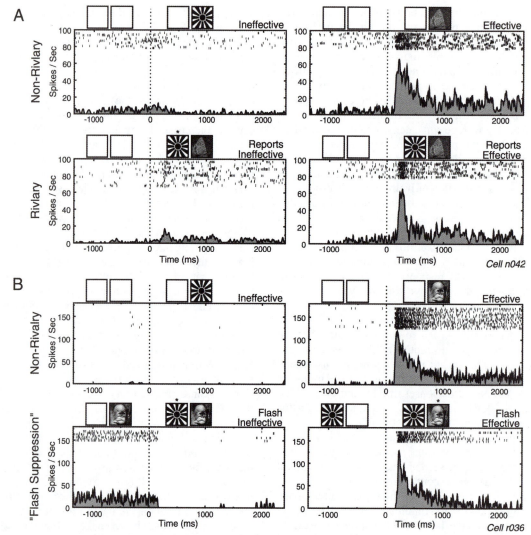

FIGURE 25.4 ■ Cell Activity Sorted by the Dominant Percept During Nonrivalrous and Rivalrous Conditions. (*A Upper*) Averaged responses to the monocularly presented ineffective and effective stimuli. Above each graph is a pictorial representation of the visual stimuli presented. At time zero, depicted by the dotted line, the stimulus changed from either a blank screen or a mixed-object (data not shown) to the ineffective (*Left*) or effective (*Right*) stimulus. The cell fired only in response to the butterfly pattern. Presentation of the sunburst had little or no effect on the neuron's activity. (*Lower*) Response of the cell just before and after the onset of rivalrous stimulation, with the effective stimulus presented to one eye and the ineffective to the other. The data are sorted based on the monkey's perceptual report: trials in which the monkey first reported seeing the ineffective stimulus (*Left*) and those for which the monkey first reported seeing the effective stimulus (*Right*) In these conditions, the stimuli presented are identical, but the recorded cell response correlates well with the monkey's reported percept. (*B*) Data collected using the suppression paradigm. The nonrivalrous trials (*Upper*) show that this cell consistently responded to the effective stimulus and not at all to the ineffective stimulus. The flash suppression trials are similar to the rivalry trials shown in *A* except that preceding the rivalrous stimulation, either the effective stimulus (*Lower Left*) or ineffective stimulus (*Lower Right*) was previously presented monocularly. Rivalry onset, marked by the dotted vertical line, thus consisted of adding either the ineffective or effective stimulus to the rivalrous pair. Following rivalry onset, the monkey's reported percept consistently switched to the newly presented stimulus, and the previewed stimulus was perceptually suppressed. Using this paradigm, phenomenal suppression was especially effective, and cell activity during the onset of rivalrous stimulation closely mirrored that during the nonrivalrous controls.

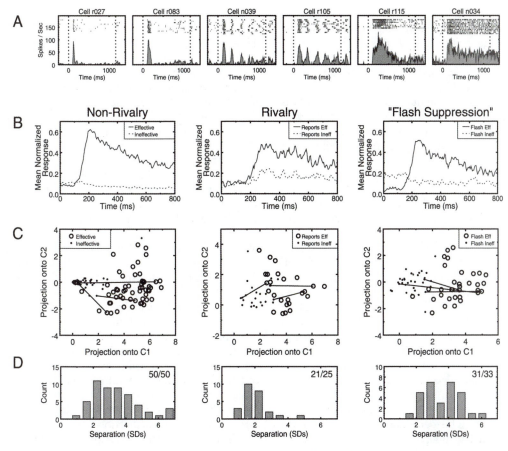

FIGURE 25.5 ■ (A) Examples of different response types of neurons in STS and IT. While some cells elicited relatively sustained responses to visual stimuli (e.g., cells r115 and n034), others exhibited a periodic bursting behavior (e.g., n039 and r105), or a highly transient response (e.g., r027 and r083). (B) Mean normalized cell responses in the nonrivalrous (50 cells), rivalrous (24 cells), and flash suppression (33 cells) conditions, for the effective (solid line) and ineffective (dotted line) trials. In all conditions, average cell response in the effective trials was elevated over response during the ineffective trials. (C) Scatter diagram of average cell responses for all tested neurons. For visualization purposes, only projections of the response vectors onto the two first components, C1 and C2, are presented. Each marker represents the mean of all ineffective (·) and effective (O) trials for a given cell. The distance (exemplified by the solid lines for three of the cells) between almost all pairs of responses are statistically significant (see below). (D) Separation of mean responses to the perceived effective and ineffective stimuli for the three stimulation conditions. Each individual response is represented by an eight-element vector. Separation is given by the Mahalanobis distance simulation conditions. (12), $D = \sqrt{(\mu_1 - \mu_2)\, '\Sigma^{-1}\, (\mu_1 - \mu_2)}$, where u_1 and u_2 are the mean response vectors for the effective and ineffective trials, respectively, and Σ is the covariance matrix of the eight-dimensional response vectors. Because the two response types usually had different variances, Σ was replaced by its unbiased estimate, $S_u = (n_1 S_1 + n_2 S_2)/(n - 2)$, where $S1$ and $S2$ are the covariance matrices for responses to the effective and ineffective stimulus, respectively, n_1 and n_2 are the number of presentations of each stimulus type, and $n = n_1 + n_2$. The significance of this variance-weighted distance was assessed by means of the Hotelling T^2 statistic (13) given by $(n_1 n_2/n)D^2 = (n_1 n_2/n)(\mu_1 - \mu_2)\,'\Sigma^{-1}(\mu_1 - \mu_2)$, which relates to the F distribution by $[n_1 n_2 (n - p - 1)/n(n - 2)\ p]D^2 \sim F_{p,n-p-1}$, where p stands for the dimensionality of the response space. The numbers in the top right of each plot show the proportion of cells for which the response in the ineffective and effective trials was significantly different at the $\alpha = 0.05$ level. It should be noted that the high percentages of modulating neurons reported here was not due to the specific multivariate analysis. Similar results, in terms of proportions of significantly modulating cells, were obtained by the more traditional analysis of counting the number of spikes occurring in individual trials. Computing mean rates, however, requires arbitrary decisions pertaining the time window over which these rates must be computed when neurons show highly variable temporal modulations.

thus be studied independent of one another) and ordered to represent decreasing proportions of the total variance of the data. In this study, the principal components of cell responses were extracted using the variances and covariances of subsampled (every 5 msec) SDFs, after centering the data (the mean SDF for a stimulus or report condition was subtracted from individual SDFs). Response vectors for individual trials were calculated by projecting a given SDF onto each of the leading principal components. For these data, a maximum of eight components was required to explain at least 75% of the cumulative response variance, and thus an eight-dimensional space was used to represent each cell's response to the two different perceptual conditions.

Fig. 25.5B shows that, on average, cell response was consistently higher for those trials in which the effective stimulus dominated perception compared with trials in which the ineffective stimulus dominated. Fig. 25.5C depicts each cell's mean response for the ineffective and effective trials, as projected into the first two dimensions of the eight-dimensional space used to analyze the data. In these graphs, each cell is represented twice, once for effective trials and once for ineffective trials. The separation of these populations at the individual cell level is further quantified in Fig. 25.5D, which shows a histogram of separations, in units of standard deviation, of each cell's ineffective and effective response vectors. Overall, ≈90% of the recorded cells in STS and IT were found to reliably predict the perceptual state of the animal. The proportion of cells showing statistically significant separations between the effective and ineffective conditions are shown in the top right of each plot in Fig. 25.5D.

The reliability of a given response pattern in predicting the animal's perceived stimulus was also tested by comparing the performance of a statistical pattern classifier with that of the monkey. Two eight-dimensional subspaces were generated by extracting the principal components of the responses to the effective and ineffective stimulus in the nonrivalrous trials. Individual responses in the rivalry trials were then assigned to one or the other subspace by using a minimum-distance statistical pattern classifier. On average, 78.5% (range = 66–91%) of the monkey's reported percept was predicted by this trial by trial classification method.

Discussion

These results show that the activity of the vast majority of studied temporal cortex neurons is contingent upon the perceptual dominance of an effective visual stimulus. Neural representations in these cortical areas appear, therefore, to be very different from those in striate and early extrastriate cortex. Only 18% of the sample in striate cortex (5) and ≈20% and 25% of the cells in areas MT and V4, respectively (5, 6), were found to increase their firing rate significantly when their preferred stimulus was perceived. Moreover, one-fifth of the studied MT neurons and 13% of V4 neurons responded only when the effective stimulus was phenomenally suppressed, while other cells showed response selectivity only during perceptual rivalry and not while the animal was involved in passive fixation. The different response types in these areas may be the result of the feedforward and feedback cortical activity that underlies the processes of grouping and segmentation—processes that are probably perturbed when ambiguous figures are viewed. If so, the areas reported here may represent a stage of processing beyond the resolution of ambiguities, where neural activity reflects the integration of constructed visual percepts into those subsystems responsible for object recognition and visually guided action.

It is worth considering how the present data can be interpreted in light of the growing body of literature concerning so-called attentional modulation of cortical activity (1, 17, 18). Indeed, paradigms employed in studies of visual selective attention bear great similarity to the rivalry paradigm, in that more than one competing stimuli is generally presented to the subject and the effects of this competition are closely monitored. These experiments have often found that the activity of cells in visual cortex is both a function of the visual stimulus and of the animal's set or state, indicating that other neural processes—generally referred to as attention—can influence cell activity above and beyond that which can be explained by the visual stimulus alone. Our view is that the phenomenon of binocular rivalry is also a form of visual selection, but that this selection occurs between competing visual patterns even in the absence of explicit instructions to attend to one stimulus or the other. Decades of research have failed to reliably demonstrate that the perceptual alternations experienced during rivalry are under the direct control of voluntary attention. As such, we believe that rivalry accentuates the selective processing that underlies basic perceptual processes including image segmentation, perceptual grouping, and surface completion. In this view, the modulation of cortical activity reported here may be of distinct origin from the modulatory effects reported for tasks in which attention is overtly directed to one stimulus or another. Nonetheless, it is striking that both the effects of modulation due to rivalry and to attention have been reported in many of the same visual cortical areas. It will be of great interest to see if and how the same neurons participate in both phenomena.

NOTES

1. Desimone, R., & Duncan, J. (1995). *Annu. Rev. Neurosci., 18,* 193–222.
2. Logothetis, N. K., & Sheinberg, D. L. (1996). *Annu. Rev. Neurosci., 19,* 577–621.
3. Logothetis, N. K., Leopold, D. A., & Sheinberg, D. L. (1996). *Nature (London), 380,* 621–624.
4. Blake, R. R. (1989). *Psychol. Rev., 96,* 145–167.
5. Leopold, D. A., & Logothetis, N. K. (1996). *Nature (London), 379,* 549–553.
6. Logothetis, N. K., & Schall, J. D. (1989). *Science, 245,* 761–763.
7. Schiller, P. H., & Koerner, F. (1971). *J. Neurophysiol., 34,* 920–936.
8. Levelt, W. J. M. (1965). *On Binocular Rivalry.* Assen, The Netherlands: Royal VanGorcum.
9. Fahle, M. (1982). *Vision Res., 22,* 787–800.
10. Wolfe, J. (1984). *Vision Res., 24,* 471–478.
11. Baldwin, J. B., Loop, M. S., & Edwards, D. J. (1996) *Invest. Ophthalmol. Visual Sci. 37,* Suppl., 3016.
12. Mahalanobis, P. C. (1936). *Proc. Natl. Inst. Sci. India, 12,* 49–55.
13. Mardia, K. V. (1972). *Statistics of Directional Data.* New York: Academic.
14. Richmond, B. J., Optican, L. M., Podell, M., & Spitzer, H. (1987). *J. Neurophysiol., 57,* 132–146.
15. Richmond, B. J., Optican, L. M., & Spitzer, H. (1990). *J. Neurophysiol., 64,* 351–369.
16. Jolliffe, I. T. (1986). *Principal Component Analysis.* New York: Springer.
17. Colby, C. L. (1991). *Child Neurol., 6,* S90–S118.
18. Maunsell, J. H. R. (1995). *Science, 270,* 764–769.

Visual Attention and Awareness

Discussion Questions

1. What is attention? What is awareness? Is attention a necessary condition for awareness, or are these just two words for the same thing? Some would argue that awareness by definition requires one to consider the role of memory. Do you agree?

2. The Feature Integration Theory proposed by Treisman and Gelade asserts that the purpose of attention is to bind visual features together into perceptual object representations. O'Craven et al. argued that the sensory modulations they observed in human MT are manifestations of attention, yet this task did not require one to integrate features. Are these two papers talking about different types of attention? Can they be reconciled?

3. Moran and Desimone liken the deployment of attention to "shrinking" a cell's receptive field to include only the attended object and to exclude the ignored object. Yet the objects to be attended in the O'Craven et al. experiments occupied interleaved spatial locations. Are different mechanisms required for these two attentional phenomena?

4. Blindsight as discussed by Weizkrantz et al. has obvious implications for our understanding of awareness. But given the apparently close association between awareness and attention, what are the implications of the existence of blindsight for our understanding of *attention*?

5. What should be our criteria for measuring visual awareness? Is this a purely philosophical question, or can it be approached scientifically?

Suggested Readings

Broadbent, D. E. (1958). *Perception and communication*. London: Pergamon. The classic work that brought the concept of attention, which had long been dormant in psychology, back to the forefront of perceptual research.

Corbetta, M., Miezin, F. M., Shulman, G. L., & Peterson, S. E. (1993). A PET study of visuospatial attention. *Journal of Neuroscience, 13,* 1202–1226. Before 1990, evidence for the neural mechanisms of attentional control in humans came almost exclusively from analyzing patterns of hemispatial neglect in brain-damaged patients. This paper reports PET evidence from neurologically intact subjects about the role of the parietal lobe in controlling shifts of attention between spatial locations.

Mountcastle, V. B. Brain mechanisms for directed attention. *Journal of the Royal Society of Medicine, 71,* 14–28. A scholarly review of the neurophysiological evidence collected by Mountcastle and others for neural basis of attention in primates.

Posner, M. I., Snyder, C. R. R., & Davidson, B. J. (1980). Attention and the detection of signals. *Journal of Experimental Psychology: General, 109*, 160–174. A landmark series of experiments that reveal how people can direct their attention in space based on instructional "cues."

Sperling, G. (1960). The information available in brief visual presentations. *Psychological Monographs, 74* (whole no. 498), 1–29. These experiments were designed to investigate the properties of visual sensory memory, but the innovative and elegant experimental task provided direct empirical evidence for an ability to attend to a location without moving one's eyes, something about which Helmholtz had speculated a century earlier.

Stroop, J. R. (1938). Studies of interference in serial verbal reactions. *Journal of Experimental Psychology, 18*, 643–662. The initial report of the so-called "Stroop effect" which reveals a fundamental limitation in our ability to selectively attend. When observers are shown a list of colors words printed in conflicting ink colors (e.g., "red" printed in yellow ink; "blue" printed in green ink, etc.), they exhibit a striking asymmetry in reading the words and ignoring the ink color (good performance) vs. naming the ink color and ignoring the words (slow and error-prone performance).

Appendix: Reading Journal Articles in Cognitive Psychology

H. L. Roediger, III and D. A. Gallo
- Washington University in St. Louis

Research in cognitive psychology and cognitive neuroscience is aimed at understanding the workings of the mind/brain. Cognitive processes are those involved in knowing the world, and cognitive scientists are interested in all facets—from sensing and perceiving, to attending and remembering, and on to thinking, reasoning and solving problems. Language processes are often a central part of the study of cognition, as language is regarded as "the light of the mind." Therefore, processes involved in listening to speech and in reading are frequently studied.

The study of cognition can proceed through use of purely behavioral methods or by methods from cognitive neuroscience. In the first approach, researchers control and manipulate stimulation to the senses and measure behavioral responses, often focusing on the speed of responses or the patterns of errors generated on a task. From these data, they make inferences about the mental processes involved in a task. The cognitive neuroscience approach involves the study of cognitive processes through use of neuroimaging techniques or from studying patients who have suffered various types of brain damage. The patients and people whose brains are scanned are usually given tests much like those in purely behavioral experiments, but interest centers on specifying neural correlates of performance.

As in all sciences, the journal article is the dominant form of communication among researchers in cognitive psychology. Many journals exist to report findings in the fields of cognitive psychology and cognitive neuroscience, and most subscribe to a similar format. The form of scientific journal articles is unlike that of forms of literature you have already experienced as students; journal articles are not like magazine articles, expository essays, short stories, or novels. The one feature in common is that the journal article, like these other forms, is intended to communicate information and tell a story about the research that was conducted.

The purpose of this appendix is to give you advice on how to approach the journal article. We assume that most readers will have had little more than a first course in psychology. Entering the world of scientific literature is, in our experience, rather like embarking on a journey in a foreign country where the language and customs are strange. To be sure, the words in these journal articles may be English, but often the terms (even ones that seem familiar, like *perceiving* or *paying attention*) are used in ways that take on technical meanings. Scientists, like members of all subcultures, have their own private languages to discuss the phenomena of their fields. You must learn their language for them to communicate with you, or vice versa. The jargon and format of the writing can be daunting.

Journal articles serve many functions and come in many forms. Some journals specialize in papers that review the literature or present theories. Other journals present findings in brief form and are intended for a wider audience than specialists. However, the standard article in most journals is written for specialists. This means that the authors assume quite a bit of knowledge and they will not bother to explain some terms that "everybody" in the field is supposed to know (e.g., between-subjects design, analysis of variance, or double-blind experiment). If some of the articles you read seem hard to follow or assume too much knowledge, it is probably because they were written for another specialist and not for a novice to the field. Most of the articles in the book you are holding were carefully selected by the editors to be appropriate for undergraduate students without much background in the topic. Nonetheless, some terms will be unfamiliar. If the article you are reading has terms that you do not understand, our advice is to look them up or to ask your professor or a graduate student in the field. However, as noted below, you will not necessarily be able to understand every aspect of each paper perfectly if you are just starting out in the field. Concentrate on the main points.

Scientific articles in psychology come in distinct parts, which usually appear in a systematic order. The main purpose of this chapter is to acquaint you with these sections and to let you know what to expect. These parts include the title and authors, the abstract, the introduction, the method, the results, the discussion, and the references. We cover these in the order they appear in a paper, but as you gain experience in the field, you may elect to read the parts of articles in a different order from their arrangement in the paper. For example, if you just want to know the main conclusions, you can usually get these by reading the discussion.

If you are unfamiliar with journal articles, it is important to avoid getting bogged down by details that are difficult for you to understand. Often you do not need to know these details (e.g., the details of some complicated statistical test) in order to understand the main points of the article. Concentrating on the complex details may only interfere with your grasp of the main points in the article (and you probably won't remember the details, anyway). So, keep your eyes on the forest (what are the important points to be gleaned from this article?) and do not let some scraggly trees (what is multiple regression, anyway?) interfere with your overall comprehension of the main thrust of the article.

Title and Authors

A good title should give you an accurate idea as to an article's content. The author who made the most significant contribution (i.e., to the research and writing) is typically listed first, and in a footnote, you can find out where the research was performed.

Abstract

The abstract represents a brief summary of the article. It usually tells what the research was about, what methods were used to study the issue under investigation, and what results were obtained. Finally, the abstract provides a brief assessment of either the practical value or theoretical importance of the findings. If properly written, the abstract entices you into the paper and gives you a framework for understanding it.

Introduction

The introduction specifies the problem to be studied and tells why it is important. A good introduction will have you involved in a fascinating scientific journey, so that by the end you will know the theory guiding the research and the hypotheses that were tested. In addition, the author also reviews the relevant research literature on the topic in the introduction. In citing relevant literature, psychologists put the name of the prior author doing the work right in the text (e.g., Jacoby, 1991) rather than in a footnote.[1] (The reference can be found at the end of the paper). Depending on how much prior work has been done (and how extensively the authors report it), the introduction may vary in length. By the end of a good introduction, you should be ready (even eager) to learn about the methods, results and conclusions that will be delivered in the remaining sections.

Method

The *method* section describes exactly how the experimenter conducted the study, and it should contain enough information so that another researcher could replicate the work. Although it is sometimes printed in smaller type to conserve space, it is still a critical part of the article, because it tells how the researchers approached the problem and what they did. Knowing the method is essential if you want to completely understand results of an experiment and form yous own interpretation of them.

The method section is usually divided into subsections that cover the participants (or subjects), the design of the experiment, the apparatus or materials, and the procedure that the participants experienced. The *participant* or *subject* section tells how many people (or animals) were studied, how they were selected and assigned to conditions (at random or by specified criteria) and who they were (college undergraduates taking introductory psychology, paid volunteers obtained by a newspaper ad, patients undergoing a certain medical procedure, etc.). Depending on the nature of the study, more or less detail may be provided. For example, in studies of aging it is typical to give quite a bit of detail about ages, education and other characteristics of the group of people being tested.

The *design* section provides a crisp description of the conditions that will be involved. For example, in an experiment on remembering, it might be that old, middle-aged and young subjects were asked to study pictures, words (i.e. the names of the pictures) or both types of material simultaneously. Thus, the design would be described as a 3 (age: young, middle, or old) × 3 (materials: pictures, words, or pictures + words) design. The dependent variable would be the number of items recalled on the memory test. The idea for the design section is to present the logic of the experiment concisely. The design just described has two independent variables or "factors" (age and type of material) with three levels of each factor. Recall that independent variables in experiments are those that the experimenters manipulate and dependent variables are the measures of behavior that are taken. The design section typically specifies the independent and dependent variables used.

The *apparatus* subsection of the method section describes any equipment used to test the subjects. This section might include such details as the model number of a computer or the resolution of a viewing apparatus. This section is referred to as the *materials* section when questionnaires, written or videotaped sketches, and similar means are used to test subjects. If they are long, lists of special materials may be placed in an appendix section, usually set

---

[1] Footnotes are used for asides, like this one, or to qualify the point under discussion with new information. However, in psychology (unlike some fields) they are not used for primary references. Footnotes are generally discouraged, but some authors cannot live without them.

in smaller type, or placed on the Internet with an address provided. (The difficulty with this last practice is that the website may become unavailable as technologies change).

The *procedure* section explains what happened to subjects in relatively great detail, so that the experimental techniques could be replicated. Therefore, the critical features must be clearly enumerated. Many "failures to replicate" past work often hinge on factors that were not well specified in the original procedure but that are discovered, after much later work, to have been critical. The procedure section should include instructions subjects received, the timing of events, the responses participants were required to make, the number of trials or events experienced, and so on. When reading the procedure, it is often helpful to imagine being a subject in the experiment to form an intuitive understanding of the task and the demands that were placed upon the participant.

Results

The results section tells the outcome obtained in the research. It is unusual to find raw data or individual subjects' scores reported in a journal article; instead, descriptive statistics are presented that summarize the data. Typical descriptive statistics are the mean of a distribution of scores, reflecting a central tendency or "average" score, and some measure of variance (the standard deviation or standard error of the mean) about the mean value. Inferential statistics provide the probability that the observed differences between the various experimental conditions could have been produced by random, or chance, factors. Statistically significant results are those that are judged unlikely to have occurred by chance; they are said to be reliable, which means that they can probably be replicated. This information helps both the researcher and the reader determine how confident to be that the independent variable(s) produced a change in the dependant variable. Both kinds of statistics are important to help psychologists understand the outcome of an experiment.

Either *tables* or *graphs* may be used to describe and summarize data. In the typical *table*, such as Table 1, data appear under various headings. The experiment required students to answer one of three types of questions about words they saw one at a time. Questions given before each word directed attention to simple perceptual features (Is the word in upper case letters?), to what it sounded like (Does the word rhyme with *chair*?), or to its meaning (Does the word refer to a type of animal?). If the word to be judged were *BEAR*, then the answer to any of the questions would have been *yes*. In actuality, half the time the presented word required a *yes* response and half the time it required a *no* response. After subjects had answered a question for each of the words, they were given a recognition memory test.

Before you look at the data, you should first read the title of the table. The title should be explicit enough to tell you what type of data appears in the table. The title of Table 1 tells you that it contains information about recognition of the words as a function of the questions that people were asked about the words. Sometimes you will also find a note at the bottom of the table, which is used to give more specific information about the data than is

TABLE 1. Mean Proportion of Words Recognized, as a Function of Question Type at Study (case, rhyme, or semantic) and Response Type ("yes" or "no").

Response Type	Question Type		
	Case	Rhyme	Category
Yes	.42	.65	.90
No	.37	.50	.65

Note. Adapted from Craik and Tulving (1975, Experiment 9).

provided in the title. Next, you should examine the headings and subheadings carefully. These will tell you about the conditions or variables that are relevant to the data in the table. Across the top of Table 1 is the Question Type, with three subheadings and columns representing the three types (Case, Rhyme, and Category). On the side are the responses people made to each question (*Yes* or *No*).

The data in the table show that the type of question asked had a powerful effect on probability of recognition, with category questions leading to better retention of words than the rhyme questions, which in turn produced better recognition than the case questions. This main effect is a replication of a result that has been well documented in the memory literature: items encoded with respect to meaning were better remembered than those encoded with respect to their surface features (the levels of processing effect; Craik & Tulving, 1975). Further, although the effect of type of question occurred with both responses, this effect was larger when the answer was *yes* than when it was *no*. This pattern represents an interaction between the two variables. That is, the effect of one independent variable (question type) on the dependent variable (recognition performance) depended on the other independent variable (response type). In these data, the levels of processing effect was greater for *yes* than for *no* responses.

Tables are useful to present numerous data points from various conditions. *Graphs* or *figures* are very effective ways of highlighting important aspects of the data and of showing trends. In Figure 1, we have graphed the data from Table 1 that we just discussed. The mean

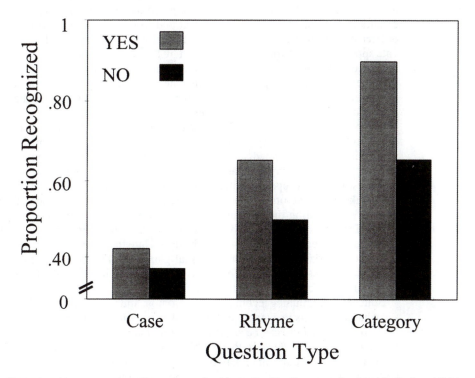

Figure 1 ■ Mean proportion of items recognized for each of the three question types in Craik and Tulving (1975, Experiment 9). The dependent variable (mean proportion of recognized items) is on the ordinate, or vertical axis, and one independent variable (question type) is on the abscissa, or horizontal axis. The other independent variable (response type) is represented by the different colored bars, as specified in the upper-left hand key. Note how the main effect of each independent variable, and their interaction, can be seen from the figure.

proportion of recognized items is represented on the vertical axis, or *ordinate*. On the horizontal axis, also called the *x-axis* or the *abscissa*, are the six question/answer conditions (that is, three questions to which there could be two answers). On the vertical axis (the *y-axis* or the ordinate), the proportion of items recognized is represented. Nearly all figures from any type of psychological research have a scale of the dependent variable (what is measured) on the ordinate. In figures from experiments, the independent variable (what is manipulated) is on the abscissa. In correlational research, where an independent variable is not manipulated, there is a dependent variable on both the ordinate and the abscissa. (If you have trouble remembering which axis is the ordinate and which is the abscissa, a good mnemonic or memory aid is that your mouth moves in the appropriate direction when you say the words: it widens side to side when you say *abscissa* and lengthens up and down when you say *ordinate*).

Be sure to examine the labels on the ordinate and the abscissa so you know what data are plotted in the figure. In Figure 1, the heights of the bars tell you the proportion of items recognized in each condition. The main effect of question type is represented by the fact that the bars increase from left to right, as the question was varied. Also, there is an effect of response type, so that words that required a *yes* response are generally better recognized than are those that required a *no* response. The interaction between these two independent variables can be seen by the fact that the difference between the *yes* and *no* bars varies from one question type to the next.

Figure 1 is a bar graph, and the data from an experiment are plotted as bars when the levels of the independent variable are not given in a measurable dimension. That is, the conditions here are qualitatively different and have different names, but they cannot be ordered on a quantitative dimension. A different way to plot data is shown in Figure 2. The data appear as points (triangles) connected by lines. A function like this is drawn when the independent variable is on a measurable dimension, so that an ordering of the measures is possible. In Figure 2, the graph represents the effect of study time (shown on the abscissa) on correct recall of words from a list (measured on the ordinate). Greater time to study each item (i.e. slower presentation rates) results in greater recall.

When you are trying to understand the data in a figure, be sure that you pay close attention to the scale of the dependant variable on the ordinate. Sometimes the scale can be misleading: An exaggerated scale with widely spaced numbers will tend to make differences appear more impressive, and a scale with numbers jammed close together will tend to make differences appear smaller. To see how this works, look back to Figure 2. Here we put breaks along the ordinate so that the scale could be widely spaced from .60 to .80, thereby exaggerating the differences in the data to highlight the effect of study time on recall. However, if we had simply allowed the scale to range from 0 to 1, as in Figure 3, one gets a much different impression from the data. Here the differences among the conditions are not emphasized as much, and a casual glance might lead to the conclusion that the manipulation was not nearly as effective as it appeared in Figure 2. However, exactly the same data are accurately plotted in both figures.

Both of these graphing techniques are common, and you should always look carefully to see what the scale is in a graph. But which way of graphing the results is right? In a sense, both are, because both can be argued to portray matters accurately. However, if statistical tests have shown a difference to exist between the three conditions, then Figure 2 would more accurately capture the relation between measures and show up the differences obtained. With experimental data, it is more important to determine whether a difference is statistically reliable than to determine whether the difference appears large when graphed, because whether a result appears large or small depends on the scale of the dependent variable on the ordinate.

Inferential statistics permit the assessment of whether differences that appear between

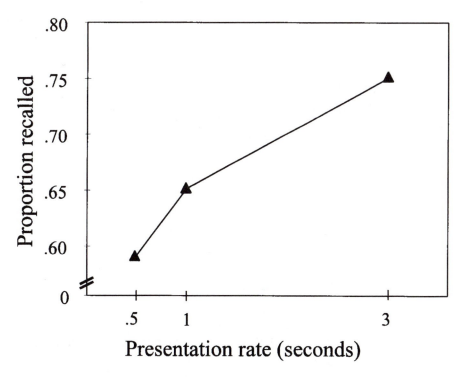

Figure 2 ■ Mean proportion of items recalled at each of the three presentation rates in Gallo and Roediger (2000, Experiment 2). Slowing presentation rate appears to result in a dramatic increase in recall.

conditions are the result of the experimental manipulations as opposed to unknown or chance factors. Inferential statistics about the data appear in such statements as "F (4, 60) = 2.03, MSe = 3.40, $p < .05$." This means that the odds for obtaining by chance an F-statistic at least as large as 2.03 would be less than 5% if the experiments were repeated (that's the $p < .05$ part of the reporting of the statistical test). That is, if the experiment were conducted 100 times, the direction of difference in the results should be the same in at least 95 out of the 100 repetitions. You do not necessarily need to know a lot about the statistical tests to survive as a consumer of the research being reported. By convention, results that meet the .05 level of confidence are deemed statistically significant; if you see $p < .05$ that means there is less than a 1 in 20 probability that these results occurred by chance, a good indicator that they are reliable.

Discussion

The discussion section is often the most creative part of an article. At the beginning of the section, the author will typically provide a concise statement of the outcome of the experiment, summarizing the results. Then the author will go on to draw theoretical or practical implications from the results and to relate them to the rest of the literature on this topic. How do these results change what we know about the topic at hand? How do these results fit in with past results? Besides answering these sorts of questions, the author may go on to describe future research that might be useful in answering questions that are left unresolved by the current research.

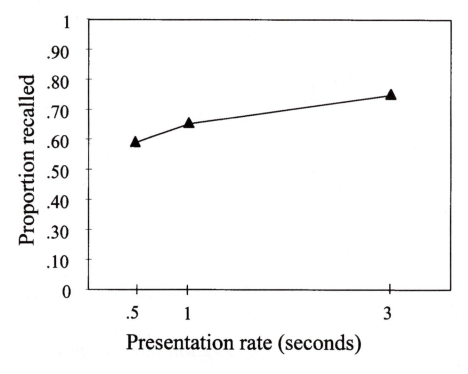

Figure 3 ■ Data from Figure 2 that have been plotted using the full range (from 0 to 1) of the dependent variable. Note that, although the data are the same as in Figure 2, the effects of presentation rate on recall do not appear to be as "dramatic" in this figure due to the change of scale.

References

References are found at the end of the article, and include only those articles that are cited in the text. This is different from a bibliography, which includes as many relevant citations as feasible. In contrast to journals in other disciplines, psychology journals list full titles of referenced articles. This practice helps to tell the reader what the article is about, making this section a valuable guide for related information. Furthermore, the references in an article can also be used as a good starting place to find out more about the topic. The cited articles usually refer to the most recently published works in the area before the current one you are reading, as well as including the most important previous publications.

Checklist for the Critical Reader

In this section, we offer some hints that have helped us to become better consumers of the information presented in psychological journals. Keep this checklist handy as you read through the journal articles included in this book. Although many of the points should seem redundant to you by now, going through them will help you identify which sections you may not be reading as effectively as possible, and will sharpen your skills at extracting the critical pieces of information from these sections.

Introduction

1. *What is the author's goal?* The introduction explains the reasons behind the research and reviews the earlier literature on the phenomena of interest. If one or more theories are related to the research, the introduction gives the predictions the theories make. As with scientists in other areas, psychologists do not necessarily agree as to the underlying mechanisms and theoretical interpretations of behavior. The author may present a particular theory that he or she thinks provides a useful explanation of behavior. Although the author may present more than one theory in the introduction, he or she will proceed later on to demonstrate that they do not all help equally to predict and explain the obtained results. Try to figure out which of the several theories the author believes and which are slated for subsequent rejection.
2. *What hypothesis will be tested in the experiment?* The answer to this should be obvious and stated directly within the introduction section.
3. *If I had to design an experiment to test this hypothesis, what would I do?* This is the key question for the introduction. You must try to answer this *before* continuing on the method section of the article. Many experiments are done within the context of a systematic investigation of behavior to test and support a particular theoretical framework developed by the author. If the author has any skill as a wordsmith, once you have finished the method section, you are likely to agree with the method that the author has advocated in the article. A clever author will plant the seeds to this answer in the introduction itself; this practice makes it harder for you to state a method independently. Write down your ideas for testing the hypothesis.

Method

Compare your answer to question 3 with the method used by the author. They probably will differ, if you have not peeked. Now answer questions 4a-c.

4a. *Is my proposed method better than the author's?* Regardless of who has the better method, you or the author, this forced comparison will make you think about the method section critically, instead of passively accepting it.
4b. *Does the author's method actually test the hypothesis?* The hypothesis is sometimes an early casualty, disappearing between the introduction and the methods sections. Always check that the method used is adequate and relevant to the hypothesis at hand.
4c. *What are the independent, dependent, and control variables?* This is an obvious question and can be answered quickly. Listing the variables helps you avoid passive reading of the methods section. After you have resolved differences between your proposed method and the author's, answer the next question.
5. *Using the participants, apparatus, materials, and procedures described by the author, what results would I predict for this experiment?* You must answer this on your own before reading the results section. Think about the procedure of the experiment, and how the different processes involved in the task would have influenced your performance had you been a participant. State your prediction in terms of the hypothesis and the independent and dependent variables. You may find it impossible to predict a single outcome. This is not really a problem, because the author probably also had more than one prediction originally. He or she may have done some preliminary investigations to narrow down possible outcomes; alternatively, he or she may have been surprised by the results and had to rethink the introduction once the results were in. Draw a rough sketch illustrating the most likely outcomes you have predicted.

Table 2. Questions for Critical Readers.

Introduction
1. What is the author's goal?
2. What hypothesis will be tested in the experiment?
3. If I had to design an experiment to test this hypothesis, what would I do?

Method
4a. Is my proposed method better than the authors?
4b. Does the author's method actually test the hypothesis?
4c. What are the independent, dependent, and control variables?
5. Using the participants, apparatus, materials, and procedures described by the author, what results would I predict for this experiment?

Results
6. How did the author analyze the data?
7. Did I expect the obtained results?
8a. How would I interpret these results?
8b. What applications and implications would I draw from my interpretation of the results?

Discussion
9a. Does my interpretation, or the author's, best represent the data?
9b. Do I or does the author offer the most cogent discussion of the applications and implications of the results?
10. Am I being too critical?

Results

6. *How did the author analyze the data?* Although you may not be totally comfortable with statistics yet, a good exercise is to note how the author presented and analyzed the data. Note *which* conditions are being compared and *why*. Data from experiments never come out exactly as anticipated, and authors will often focus on presenting data that they feel are important to convey their main point, while downplaying other data. Do try to understand the author's point of view, but also try to form your own impression about the data as a whole. Are there some unexplained puzzles in the results that the author overlooks?

7. *Did I expect the obtained results?* If not, then you will reach one of two conclusions: either your prediction was wrong, or the results are hard to believe. Perhaps the method the author selected was inappropriate and did not adequately test the stated hypotheses or introduced sources of uncontrolled variance. Or perhaps these results would not be obtained again if the experiment were repeated. Still, even if you did not expect the results, the author obtained them and clearly believes them. Also, if the editors selected the paper for this book of readings, the results are probably considered important to the field.

8a. *How would I interpret these results?*

8b. *What applications and implications would I draw from my interpretation of the results?* Try to answer these questions on your own, before reading the discussion.

Discussion

The discussion section includes the author's interpretation of the data in the form of conclusions. A good discussion section brings the reader full circle in that it provides a narrative response to the questions posed in the introduction. In addition, the author expands on his or her conclusions by offering insight regarding the applications and implications of the experimental results.

As a critical reader, you have constructed your own interpretation of the results. Compare the merits of your interpretation with the merits of the author's. Which one do you prefer? Answer questions 9a and 9b to help you critically assess yours and the author's interpretation of the results.

9a. *Does my interpretation or the author's best represent the data?* Because authors are allowed more latitude in the discussion section than in other sections, it is conceivable that an author has drawn conclusions that may not be warranted by the data. In other cases, authors draw conclusions that are largely appropriate but may proceed to extend these conclusions beyond what the data can support. The latter situation typically occurs when a researcher fails to recognize the limitations of the dependent variable. Still, the author has doubtless thought longer and harder than you have about the problem. Think critically about issues, but don't become nihilistic and believe nothing from what you read.

9b. *Do I or does the author offer the most cogent discussion of the applications and implications of the results?* This question is secondary to the question posed in 9a. Nonetheless, a researcher's responsibilities extend beyond that of conducting a tightly controlled experiment. He or she must also consider the rationale and theory that underlie the research. The extent to which an author identifies applications and implications of the results contributes to the overall integrity of the research process.

10. *Am I being too critical?* Although critical evaluation of a particular set of findings is an important element of science, it is equally important to be willing to accept new ideas and discoveries. Keep in mind that, with practice, anyone should be able to find problems or limitations of a particular piece of research. Only the best scientists are capable of acknowledging these limitations while, at the same time, recognizing the novel contributions an article may offer. The research glass may be mostly full, so you shouldn't necessarily see it as partly empty.

Authors' Note

Portions of this chapter have been adapted from D.G. Elmes, B.H. Kantowitz and H.L. Roediger, *Research methods in psychology*, 6e. Belmont, CA: Wadsworth. We thank the authors and Wadsworth Publishing Co. for permission to adapt pages 159–171 of the text.

REFERENCES

Craik, F. I. M., & Tulving, E. (1975). Depth of processing and the recognition of words in episodic memory. *Journal of Expermental Psychology: General, 104,* 268–294.

Gallo, D. A., & Roediger, H. L., III. (2000). *Variability among word lists in eliciting false memories: The roles of associa-*tive activation and decision processes. Manuscript in preparation.

Jacoby, L. L. (1991). A process dissociation framework: Separating automatic from intentional uses of memory. *Journal of Memory & Language, 30,* 513–541.

Author Index

Subject Index